TIME MACHINES

Time Travel in Physics, Metaphysics, and Science Fiction

Rod Taylor as the "Time Traveler" in the 1960 MGM film *The Time Machine*, about to depart for A.D. 802,701 in his beautiful Victorian gadget.

Photograph courtesy of the Academy of Motion Picture Arts and Sciences, Beverly Hills, CA.

TIME MACHINES

Time Travel in Physics, Metaphysics, and Science Fiction

Paul J. Nahin

Springer

Library of Congress Cataloging-in-Publication Data
Nahin, Paul J.
   Time machines: time travel in physics, metaphysics, and
   science fiction / Paul J. Nahin.
     p. cm.
   Includes bibliographical references and index.
   ISBN 1-56396-371-X
   1. Science fiction, American—History and criticism. 2. Science
fiction, English—History and criticism. 3. Time travel in literature.
4. Metaphysics in literature. 5. Physics in literature. I. Title.
PS374.S35N34   1994   92-75255
813´.0876209—dc20   CIP

Printed on acid-free paper.

Printed and bound by United Book Press, Inc., Baltimore, MD.
Printed in the United States of America.

9 8 7 6 5

ISBN 1-56396-371-X Springer-Verlag New York Berlin Heidelberg SPIN 10648583

For my loving wife, Patricia Ann, whose journey through spacetime has not often wandered far from my own—and who has for decades quietly tolerated huge, teetering piles of books and papers in her otherwise immaculate home—

and

for my splendid cat, Heaviside, who kept me company on many a quiet night as I struggled to understand time travel, and who, like Fritz Leiber's supercat Gummitch—IQ of 160 and planning to write a book on Space-Time—often gets a look in her eyes that says she knows more about it than I ever will.

A SAMPLE OF THINGS TO COME

There is only one kind of Science Fiction story that I dislike, and that is the so-called time-traveling. It doesn't seem logical to me. For example: supposing a man had a grudge against his grandfather, who is now dead. He could hop in his machine and go back to the year that his grandfather was a young man and murder him. And if he did this how could the revenger be born? I think the whole thing is the "bunk."

> —Letter-to-the-Editor from a seventeen-year-old
> reader of *Astounding Stories (Dec. 1931)*

"I'm not kidding you at all Phil," Barney insisted. "I *have* produced a workable Time Machine, and I am going to use it to go back and kill my grandfather."

> —opening line from "A Gun for Grandfather"
> by F. M. Busby [Busby, 1987]

"The past—it's pretty damn solid, Phil. It's a little like a compost pile—fairly soft near the surface but packed hard further down, with all that Time piled on top of it."

> —Barney tells Phil about his astonishingly unique
> insight concerning the organic nature of
> space-time

Calvin and Hobbes by Bill Watterson

CONTENTS

Prologue

Time travel is the thinking person's UFO, an improbability that nevertheless resonates with mysterious and sometimes marvelous possibilities.

—Richard Schickel, from his review in *Time* (4 Dec. 1989) of *Back to the Future, Part II*

As a youngster, at about age ten, I discovered science fiction stories. I read them, *devoured* them (to the great distress of my teachers), because the mind-expanding ideas of that tiny, often unfairly maligned corner of literature excited my imagination. The stories of alien intelligences, parallel Universes, voyages to other worlds, robots, the fourth dimension, paranormal powers, intergalactic wars, and of course *all the gadgets* were wonderful. BEMs (bug-eyed monsters) and telepathic mutants, beings often occurring in the same story (particularly those about radiation-blasted, post-nuclear-war societies), were fun, too. Still, it was the gadgetry of science fiction that mostly fascinated my preteenage mind. I loved reading about faster-than-light hyperspace rocket ships, invisibility and tractor beams, supercomputer brains, Dirac radios, matter transmitters, instantaneous language translators, disintegrator ray guns, and time machines. Ah, those time machines. God, how I loved time-travel stories!

I read comic books a lot then, too. When Superman solved a problem by traveling into the past by flying faster than light or when Walt Disney's nutty inventor Gyro Gearloose invented a time machine to deliver a letter that just had to get there yesterday—well, that was pretty neat. I was a science-fiction-contraption junky. There was a special thrill to time machines that made them king of all the gadgets, however, and any story with a time machine had me hooked. And if an author made brain-boggling logical paradoxes a critical part of his tale, then my happiness on Earth was complete. If there were causal loops, and characters running into themselves, and poor unfortunates unwittingly changing the past (or even killing their youthful grandfathers so that they caused themselves never to have existed)—for that I'd risk even the terrible wrath of my parents, who wanted me asleep in bed by ten, not reading a book by flashlight under the covers.

Mom and Dad subscribed to the view expressed by Vladimir Voinovich's time traveler in the 1986 novel *Moscow 2042*, who declared, "Science fiction ... is not literature, but tomfoolery like the electronic games that induce mass idiocy." And there *is* a lot of nonsense in science fiction, sure, but there's a lot of nonsense in every genre—the point is to be discriminating. Even in those long-ago days of the early 1950s, I sensed that there was much that is very good, indeed, in science fiction.

So science fiction was what I liked, but I also liked science and mathematics, and unlike some of my high-school friends who also read science fiction but who liked football and cars better than algebra, I went to college and majored in electrical engineering. And now I teach electrical engineering and rarely read science fiction for recreation. Still, even as I prepare my lectures, sit in department meetings, and sleep through faculty-senate debates on how outrageous is the new university parking fee, I find that my mind is still in love with time travel and time machines. I am now forty years and three engineering degrees removed from that technically naive teenage boy of the early 1950s, but the fascination with time travel (or "chronomotion") is as strong as ever. What I wouldn't give to be a chronoviator!

I still remember the surprise and joy I felt when I first learned that Kurt Gödel, among the twentieth-century's greatest mathematicians, had in 1949 actually published solutions to Einstein's general relativity gravitational field equations, solutions that appear to suggest the possibility of time travel to the past. It has been known since 1905 that Einstein's special theory of relativity allows travel into the future, but to return had been thought impossible—impossible both physically and philosophically. After all, what sense could there be to the classic paradox of a time traveler going back in time to kill his grandfather as a baby? How then could the time traveler come to be born? But Gödel's mathematics seemed to be saying that time travel to the past does make some sort of sense! Could it be, I recall wondering in amazement, that what I had reluctantly come to admit could only be just a fantastic dream *might really be possible*?

Today there are individual scientists all over the world seriously studying the physics and the philosophical implications of time travel. The two principal players, however, are Kip Thorne at the California Institute of Technology and Igor Novikov, a Russian, at the Academy of Sciences Astro Space Centre of the P. N. Lebedev Physical Institute in Moscow. These two men have also developed groups of advanced graduate students who work on various aspects of time machines and time-travel physics for their dissertation topics. It is to be expected that as these students receive their degrees and move on to their own teaching and research positions, that the level of scientific activity in this exciting new area of physics will continue to grow worldwide.

Realistically, however, no matter Gödel's astonishing theoretical discovery and the subsequent work of Thorne and Novikov, I suspect many physicists would still agree with words published over fifty years ago in the British magazine *Tales of Wonder* (I. O. Evans, "Can We Conquer Time?," Summer 1940): "Of all the fantastic ideas that belong to science fiction, the most remarkable—and, perhaps, the most fascinating—is that of time travel ... . Indeed, so fantastic a notion does it seem, and so many apparently obvious absurdities and bewildering paradoxes does it present, that some of the most imaginative students of science refuse to consider it as a practicable proposition." Still, not all physicists view the time-travel-paradox arguments as convincing. Provocative, yes, of course, but many are not yet prepared to write "signed, sealed and delivered" at the end.

The theological side of this book may strike some readers as a bit odd for a topic usually treated with heavy doses of thick mathematics, but I have learned that theology is a necessary dimension to any informed discussion on time travel. A literary linkage between time travel and theology has, in fact, existed for a long time. As pointed out in Paul Alkon's *Origins of Futuristic Fiction* [Alkon, 1987], "The first time-traveler in English literature is a guardian angel who returns with state documents from 1998 to the year 1728 in Samuel Madden's *Memoirs of the Twentieth Century*" (published in 1733, more than two-and-a-half centuries ago). Madden was an Irish-Anglican clergyman whose book was satire rather than science fiction, but its time-traveling aspect was a first. As Alkon also points out, "Madden [was] the first to write a narrative that purports to *be* a document from the future. He deserves recognition as the first to toy with the rich idea of time-travel in the form of an artifact sent backward from the future to be discovered in the present."

Much has happened in the area of time-travel studies since Madden's time. I therefore set myself two goals as I wrote this book. First, I attempted to find and read every time-travel story ever anthologized in the English language [and many others in their original (and only) magazine appearances]. I have also examined the popular-culture treatments of time travel in the comics and in the movies. From these sources I extracted the central fictional speculations on what time travel might be like and how the logical time-travel paradoxes were treated. This book demonstrates that the fascination with rational time travel is not a modern idea, but rather one that can be traced back to the mid-eighteenth century. One conclusion that is evident from this book is that even the very early science fiction writers tackled conceptual issues now taken quite seriously by philosophers and physicists. Science fiction writers have been enormously inventive with the concept of time travel (some of the ideas appearing now in the philosophical literature appeared decades ago in science fiction), and I have attempted to weave their more startling ideas into the text. As Robert Silverberg wrote in the "Introduction" to his 1977 anthology *Trips in Time* [Silverberg, TIT], "The only workable time machine ever invented is the science-fiction story." And where else but in a time-travel story would Einstein's gravitational field equations appear as the playtime chant of a bright child of the future (in Fritz Leiber's "Nice Girl with 5 Husbands" [Leiber, TC])?

As for my second goal, I have discussed, using prose only, the physical theory of time travel, including Einstein's special and general theories of relativity. For those who also appreciate a more mathematical approach, however, nine Tech Notes, appear as appendices, but I strongly emphasize that it is *not* necessary to understand calculus (or even algebra) to read this book. Even the Tech Notes themselves, which contain all the mathematics in this book, can be usefully read simply for their historical content.

What all this means is that one does not have to be either a science fiction fan or a mathematical whiz to read this book. The only requirement is to have enough curiosity and imagination to be fascinated by one of the oldest of fantasies— a fantasy that at least some of the best physicists in the world are now coming to think may not be so fantastic as to be impossible. This book does not advocate one view or another on time travel, although I do of course have my personal opinions that I am not shy in expressing. However, when I do offer a personal opinion, I have tried to be careful to state it as such.

The book contains a selection of illustrations concerned with time travel and the fourth dimension from early science fiction magazines and contemporary pop-culture art, and also a number of line illustrations in support of the technical discussions. The published literature cited includes over 1500 science fiction stories and papers from the professional journals in physics, mathematics, electrical engineering, philosophy, and theology. I believe this careful citation of sources and the extensive bibliography will make the book of interest and value to scholars as well as to science fiction fans (and other fiction fans who enjoy stories with intellectual content that are "good reads").

The book is structured with seven major components, as follows:

(1) Chapter 1, an overview of the entire book, touches on a wide assortment of topics, including the history of time travel in fiction, philosophical skepticism, the nature of time, black holes, the time-travel paradoxes and their historical development, Gödel's time travel Universe, and Frank Tipler's astonishing discovery of "how to make" a time machine;

(2) Chapter 2 introduces the fundamental concept of four-dimensional space-time, hyperspaces, the connection of each to time travel, and the uses (good *and* bad) by science fiction writers of these concepts in time-travel stories;

(3) Chapter 3 addresses in depth the nature of time, the distinction between past and future, and the uses of time, reverse time, and multiple-time dimensions, in works of science fiction;

(4) Chapter 4, which in my opinion is the most important chapter in the book, is devoted entirely to the time-travel paradoxes and how they have long been discussed in science fiction and are now also beginning to be considered in prominent physics journals;

(5) an Epilogue, a somewhat poetic wrap-up of the book;

(6) nine technical appendices, using no mathematics beyond differential and integral calculus, explain the relativity of simultaneity, motion-induced time dilation, four-dimensional spacetime, the Lorentz transformations, Minkowski diagrams, light cones, metrics, intervals, faster-than-light speeds, time travel in Gödel's and Tipler's works, and the wormhole time-machine analyses in the work of Thorne and Novikov;

(7) and finally, a Bibliography, representing the most extensive citation guide published to date on the fictional and scientific literature of time travel.

The Bibliography, in particular, plays such a central role in this book that some elaboration on it is appropriate. The references, in chronological order for each author (starting with the most recent publications), are from the vast time-travel literature in the fields of mathematics, physics, metaphysics, philosophy, theology, and very importantly, science fiction.

The early science fiction time-travel stories almost always first appeared in paperback monthly magazines that are now almost impossible to find. These "pulps," printed on inexpensive wood-pulp acid-based paper, are literally burning up, slowly but relentlessly, as they oxidize, turn yellow, and crumble in library archives. As Raymond Chandler once wrote, "Pulp paper never dreamed of posterity." I therefore decided to reference the stories, whenever possible, through the anthology collections that have reprinted and preserved the classics of this subgenre. As a last resort, I have cited the magazines themselves if they are available on microfilm. I make no claims for an exhaustive bibliography. The stories, books, and papers listed are the ones I found particularly useful, but if I have overlooked an item you feel should have been included, I would very much appreciate hearing about it.

The bibliography is strictly alphabetical; thus De Camp is in the *d*'s and Von Hoerner is in the *v*'s. In the text, when referring to an item in the bibliography, I have used the form of [author, year], as in [Busby, 1987]. If the same author has multiple items in the same year, the year is followed by lower-case letters, as for example [Weingard, 1979b]. Stories in anthologies that include multiple works referenced in this book are cited in the form [author, anthology code], as in [Padgett, SFAD]. The anthology codes are listed at the start of the bibliography. There are two exceptions to this. One is the multivolume anthology *The Great Science Fiction Stories*, currently being published by DAW Books. This excellent series is appearing at the rate of two volumes each year, each volume treating just one year (beginning with Volume 1 issued in 1979 with stories from 1939). Stories appearing in the DAW series are listed, along with the appropriate volume number, in the bibliography proper rather than with the anthologies. (In several cases a story can be found in more than one anthology, but I have listed only the one I happened to use first.) The other exception occurs for single-author anthologies; here I just list all the story titles, one after the other, in the book's entry in the bibliography proper under the author's name.

Now and then I refer to adventures in time and space experienced by various superheroes of the comics. My source for most of these bits of nearly lost popular-culture history is the marvelous multivolume, scholarly work-of-love by Michael L. Fleisher, *The Encyclopedia of Comic Book Heroes* [Fleisher, 1978]. A research bibliography that I found particularly detailed and useful (available in the Reference Department of most university libraries), even if a bit dated now, is *Index to Science Fiction Anthologies and Collections* [Contento, 1978]. Invaluable for any student of time travel in science fiction is Donald B. Day's *Index to the Science-Fiction Magazines 1926–1950* [Day, 1952]. More recent citations can be found in *The MIT Science Fiction Society's Index to the S–F Magazines, 1951–1965* [Strauss, undated]. For access to the novel-length literature from all over the world and all time periods, no serious student of fictional time travel could begin without reading the encyclopedic *Anatomy of Wonder: A Critical Guide to Science Fiction* [Barron, 1987]. The most recent source, with three *thousand* (!) synopses of stories from the early pulps, is the extraordinarily useful *Science-Fiction: the early years* [Bleiler, 1990].

This book is for all those who agree, as I do, with Professor David Park, who wrote in his book *The Image of Eternity* [Park, 1980]: "Is time travel in principle (never mind the difficulties) a possibility? It has received some thought in the past and deserves some more." As my book shows, it is such thought by *physicists* that will lead to a better understanding of time travel and to discovering if time travel is consistent with the known laws of physics. Readers of this book will, I believe, find that this process of discovery is no mere boring, scholarly drudgery, but rather an exciting, ongoing adventure. As Professor Adolph Baker wrote in his book *Modern Physics and Antiphysics* [Baker, 1970]: "Physics is engaged neither in the development of time machines nor in the fabrication of bombs. But it is the business of physicists to take flights of fancy which carry them far beyond the boundaries imposed by current technology." Even the most conservative critics of time machines and time travel will surely admit the truth of this, and I have worked hard to make this book a flight *well* beyond known boundaries. This is, I believe, a book for the adventurous in spirit.

Acknowledgements—A number of individuals helped me during the seven years I worked on this book. John Pokoski, Chair of the Electrical and Computer Engineering Department at the University of New Hampshire (UNH), was always supportive of what must have seemed to be a project very much unlike what my colleagues were doing. The UNH Library makes up for its occasionally incomplete holdings with some superb staff; in particular Karen Fagerberg and Susanne Gerred Seymour of Inter-library Loan, who almost never failed me in my quest for obscure books and microfilm reels of ancient science fiction magazines. I am particularly indebted to Texas A & M, Dartmouth College, the University of California at Riverside, the Claremont Colleges, the California State Universities at Northridge and Fullerton, Mount Holyoke College, the New York City Public Library, and the University of Delaware (with special thanks to Tom Muth of that institution's microfilm unit) for giving me access to their archives. David Deutsch of the Oxford University Mathematical Institute kindly provided me with a draft preprint of his research into the quantum mechanics of time travel. John Archibald Wheeler, Professor Emeritus of Physics at Princeton University, wrote me a long and friendly letter on his memory of Gödel's views on time travel to the past (and he included his own opinion of the concept as well). Matt Visser at Washington University, and Frank Tipler at Tulane, replied to my questions about time travel with thoughtful answers. Kip Thorne, Professor of Physics at Caltech, graciously sent me several preprints of the work he and his students had completed on closed timelike curves, as did Igor Novikov of the Nordisk Institut for Teoretisk Fysik/Copenhagen, and the P. N. Lebedev Physical Institute in Moscow. (Igor and Kip showed far more decency and manners in their prompt replies to my endless electronic and postal mail queries, than I did in literally deluging them with questions.) Hans Moravec, of the Robotic Institute at Carnegie Mellon University, took time from his sabbatical at Thinking Machines Corporation to send me a copy of his unpublished research on the computational implications of backward time travel. Edwin Taylor, Past Editor of *The American Journal of Physics*, and Gregory Benford, Professor of Physics at the University of California at Irvine, who is well-known to science fiction readers around the world, have been supportive of my efforts since they first read the entire book in typescript. Nan Collins and Alice Greenleaf of the UNH College of Engineering and Physical Sciences Word Processing Center typed all the mathematics in the Technical Notes as well as the seemingly endless revisions of the Bibliography. The final editing and writing for this book were done while I was on sabbatical leave at Harvey Mudd College in Claremont, California, during the Fall semester of 1991, and I gratefully thank the College for giving me the financial and administrative support required for that work. Special thanks, in particular, to Professor John Molinder, Chairman of the Engineering Department at Harvey Mudd, who originally suggested that a semester in Southern California was just what I needed after two winters in Virginia and fifteen more in New Hampshire. He was right. To teach again at Harvey Mudd, where I began my teaching career more than twenty years ago, was like a wonderful trip back in time. My debts to John Zumerchik, former Book Acquisition Editor at the American Institute of Physics, who started the book on its way, and to Jessica Bender, my copy editor who helped unwind most of my now-and-then convoluted prose, are hardly paid with a simple thank you. Still, to both of them: *thank you*.

As a final comment, I would like to say to all readers that while I have done my best to write a scholarly book, I really do not know if I have succeeded. I hope, of course, that everything I have had to say on the pages that follow is clear, correct, and if not always brilliantly witty then at least minimally interesting—but self-doubts do remain. This book was very difficult for me to write; it was not easy for me to hold in my mind all the seemingly countless and conflicting opinions, theories, and philosophical speculations concerning time travel. There were more than a few times when I dispaired, and wondered if I had gotten myself into a job simply too big for me. The experience was a bit like walking from Boston to Los Angeles, backward on my knees. As a Harvard professor stated many years ago, upon his retirement: "Is scholarship pleasure or pain? If someone cuts your leg off, you know it's pain, but with scholarship you never know." When I read that, I knew exactly what he meant!

Durham, NH
October 1992

Note added in proof (late November): As an example of what I implied earlier, that no bibliography in a book such as this one could possibly be complete, I offer the following. Before me as I write is an anthology of Rudyard Kipling's short tales, one I started to read as a treat to celebrate my liberation (at least for a while) from time-travel stories. And what did I find? The very first story I read was "Wireless," published in 1902, which tells of the wave transmission of the poetry of Keats not only across space but through time, as well. What else may I have missed? Please let me know! For readers with access to e-mail, I can be reached through Internet at paul.nahin@unh.edu.

CHAPTER ONE
An Overview of Time Travel

Woodn't it be grate to go bacc in tyme and korrect your mistakes? Wouldn't it be great to go back in time and correct your mistakes?

—motto of *Time Twisters* comics

What if you knew the course of history ... before it happens? Like Kennedy's assassination ... the World Series ... the stock market? Most of us would die for a chance to replay.

—from the paperback cover blurb of Ken Grimwood's novel *Replay*

Take me back—up the hill—to my grave. But first: Wait! One more look. Good-by, world. Good-by, Grover's Corners ... Mama and Papa. Good-by to clocks ticking ...

> —the despairing words of Emily Webb, after she returns from the dead to relive her twelfth birthday, but finds only unhappiness from knowing the future (from Thornton Wilder's *Our Town*)

The Mystery of Time Travel

To travel in time.

Could there possibly be a more exciting, more romantic, more wonderful adventure than that? I am willing to wager that given a random collection of middle-aged adults, an enthusiastic response about time travel would come from at least three-quarters of them. Make that a group of children over the age of five and the vote would be unanimous, as shown by the popularity of the juvenile novels of Madeleine L'Engle [L'Engle, 1976, 1978], of the 1960s television cartoon series "Mr. Peabody's Improbable History,"[1] and the 1981 film-fantasy romp through history, *Time Bandits*. For youngsters who are very young, even of pre-kindergarten age, there is *Professor Noah's Spaceship* [Wildsmith, 1980], in which Professor Noah takes endangered animals through a time warp back into the past (to just after the Flood), where they can once again lead happy lives. Nicely done versions of the time-travel tales "The Biography Project" [Gold, MT] and "Over the River & Through the Woods" [Simak, TC] are part of *The Bank Street Book of Science Fiction* [BSBSF] targeted for preteenagers. One of the more interesting Danny Dunn gadget stories uses a time machine [Williams and Abrashkin, 1963], as does *The Trolley to Yesterday* [Bellairs, 1989], and for older, more sophisticated children there are such books as *The Green Futures of Tycho* [Slea-tor, 1981] and *Alistair's Time Machine* [Sadler, 1986].

And, of course, for children of all ages (including the author), there is "Doctor Who" and his time-traveling police telephone booth [Haining, 1987]. This British TV series, still seen on both sides of the Atlantic to this day, had a somewhat less campy American counterpart in the 1966–1967 series "Time Tunnel." This show, about two time travelers caught in a secret government time-machine experiment gone wrong, took itself far more seriously than does "Doctor Who." Other than the quality of the special effects, however, there was nothing new in these shows—as a youngster in the early 1950s I recall watching time-travel episodes on the television pioneers "Space Patrol" and "Captain Z-Ro."

This fascination with time travel has actually been "scientifically" documented. In an intriguing study [Cottle, 1976], several hundred men and women were asked to consider the possibility of spending an hour, a day, and a year back in both their personal past (since their birth) and their historical past (before their birth). They were further told that it would cost them $10,000 to purchase such time-travel services. The responses indicating a willingness to spend this much money for a trip into the historical past were hour (10%), day (10%), and year (16%). For a trip to the personal past, the numbers increased: hour (18%), day (22%), and year (36%). As might be expected, as the cost dropped, the numbers rose even more, and if such trips were free, the interest levels were nearly unanimous.

Rod Serling used his fascination with time as the inspiration for many of the episodes on the enormously popular television series "The Twilight Zone." During its five years (1959–1964) it often presented stories that dealt in some manner with time, and specifically with time travel [Serling, TZ]. Several of the most popular episodes on the popular "Star Trek" series involved time travel. Such interest is easy to understand. To travel in time, as William Blake wrote in "Auguries of Innocence," would be to

> Hold infinity in the palm of your hand
> And eternity in an hour.

Or consider the opening lines from Elizabeth Allen's 1860 poem "Rock Me to Sleep," less majestic than Blake, perhaps, but still very much from the heart:

> Backward, turn backward, O time in your flight;
> Make me a child again, just for tonight.

As a modern writer [Paul, 1983] expressed it, "Time travel [is] the ultimate fantasy, the scientific addition to the human quest for immortality."

Some writers have recognized that time-travel fantasy has a strong appeal for adults as well as for children. There is an old saying, "Time is money," and wouldn't it be wonderful if we could save time just like money? This fantasy idea has been used many times, as in *Tourmalin's Time Cheques* [Anstey, 1891] and in

"Time Bank" [Bilenkin, 1978]. The German writer Wolfgang Jeschke's best-known book, for another example, is *Der Zeiter* (*The Time Person*), a collection of time-travel stories; the central story, which can be found in an English translation [Jeschke, BRW], is strongly flavored with the texture of a fairy tale. In this story two princes of the far future build a time machine and then the younger one sends his brother, who is heir to the throne, 11,000 years into the past to A.D. 1619, and thereafter he fears his brother's return. (The Brothers Grimm would have written a similiar tale if the time-machine concept had been popular in the early nineteenth century.) And the means of time travel in the Norwegian Johan Wessel's 1781 comedy-fantasy *Anno 7603* actually *is* a fairy.

Some of the best modern science fiction stories have played with the fantasy appeal of time travel by having gifts arrive by accident from the future, as in "Of Time and Third Avenue" [Bester, 1981], "Mimsy Were the Borogoves" [Padgett, 1981], "Something for Nothing" [Sheckley, 1955], "Thing of Beauty" [Knight, 1961], "The Little Black Bag" [Kornbluth, 1984], and "Child's Play" [Tenn, TSF]. More often than not, the fairy-tale moral of these stories is that such unearned gifts generally bring grief. The common fairy-tale theme of "The Three Wishes," in which the recipient ends up using the final wish to undo the unforeseen consequences of the first two, is in fact the precursor to all modern change-the-past stories. The editor's introduction to [Harness, FCW] expands on this idea, telling us with reference to another age-old form of adult fantasy that "time-travel stories about the Civil War have one thing in common with pornography; they serve to titilate an impulse [that is, in the case of time-travel stories to change history] and then to frustrate it."

A character in *The Bird of Time* [Effinger, 1986] captured the fantasy appeal of time travel with the simple statement: "The past ... is the home of romance." More scholarly is [Wachhorst, 1984]: "The time-travel [film] romance is an attempt to reenchant the world, to regain a sense of belongingness, to reinstate the magical, autocentric Universe of the child and the primitive." On a less poetic level, time travel and the stories about it fascinate us because they turn our everyday world-view upside down and inside out. They make us *think*. It is not surprising that the top film of 1985 in terms of both excellence and popularity, as determined in a *Boxoffice* magazine poll, was *Back To The Future*. And for sheer excitement, it is impossible to outdo the two time travelers in "The World of the Red Sun" [Simak, BGA1]; as they activate their time machine, one yells to the other, "Kiss 1935 good-bye!"

Still, perhaps not everybody is interested in time travel, as one adventurer from A.D. 2156, stranded 79,062,156 years in the past, learns to his shock and horror in "When Time Was New" [Young, SFD]. Offering to trade his knowledge for rescue by aliens who happen to be visiting the Earth at the time, he is told: "Mr. Carpenter, if we had wanted time travel, we would have devised it long ago. Time travel is the pursuit of fools. The pattern of the past is set, and cannot be changed ... And as for the future, who but an imbecile would want to know what tomorrow will bring?" Also, in "Out of the Past" [Eshbach, 1938] one scientist chastises a colleague with the words "If you don't stop this senseless theorizing upon something that's an obvious impossibility, you'll find yourself working alone! Your ridiculous ideas sound like the ravings of a madman. Anyone with average intelligence realizes that the mere thought of traveling through time is absurd." I will, of course, not follow this line of argument any further in this book nor will this book be sympathetic with the attitude of the writer in [Koestler, 1971] who, finding much of science fiction boring, declared (somewhat irrelevantly), "Time machines are no escape from the human condition."

To go forward in time would be to discover what wonders the future will bring or perhaps to witness, as did H. G. Wells' time traveler, the final stages of the decay of the human race. That might be quite an unpleasant sight, too. "The Choice" [Hilton-Young, SSFT], for example, tells the story of a time traveler who is given the choice of whether or not to remember the future after returning home—once back all he can recall is that he decided to forget. John W. Campbell's classic "Twilight" [Campbell, 1948] has a similiar theme, but in this tale we are told the grim details of the fate that waits for humanity. (A time traveler from A.D. 3059 goes seven million years into the future to find that machines, not men, rule the world.) In "An Adventure in Time" [Flagg, 1930] a man from 1950 travels over a thousand years into the future to find that the world is run by "mechanicals" (i.e., robots) and women (who keep men around mostly for breeding purposes). In the story "The Machine Man of Ardathia" [Flagg, 1927] this same author reverses the process by having a time traveler from 28,000 years in the future appear in the present with a report on the fate of humankind. In "John Sze's Future" [Pierce, GSFS1] a nuclear physicist is temporally displaced by accident to A.D. 2178 to find that the very name of his profession has become an obscenity in a world run by psychologists since the atomic blowup of 1987. Time travelers to the war-torn future in "Judson's Annihilator" [Wyndham, 1939] find that it is disease bombs and airborne bacilli that will do the world in. A twist on all this is found in "Now and Then" [Rosenbaum, 1957]. In this story a time traveler thinks, based on the primitive men he encounters, that he has gone back to 100,000 B.C. On his return he learns that he was actually just fourteen years in the *future*.

A future world of post-nuclear ruin is also the dramatic setting for the 1964 movie *The Time Travellers*, and the 1968 film *Planet Of The Apes* has an astronaut plunge through a time warp into a distant future in which English-speaking apes are the dominant species. An interesting variation on "travel to the future" is seen in the plot of the 1989 film *The Navigator*, in which individuals of fourteenth-century England, who are on a religious quest to save their village from the Black Death, are temporally displaced through a time warp in a cave into our world of the twentieth century. The resulting culture shock when 1348 meets 1988 is profound. These examples would seem to cast doubt on the words of one writer who rashly declared [Godfrey-Smith, 1980] that "forward [time] travel may be dismissed as boring."

The use of time machines to see the end of the world or at least the end of humankind is a common theme in science fiction; see, for example, "Alas, All Thinking!" [Bates, SFT], "Terror Out of Time" [Williams, TC], "Twilight" [Campbell, 1948], "Wanderers of Time" [Wyndham, 1933], and "When We Went to See the End of the World" [Silverberg, 1986]. So seductive is this theme that Edmond Hamilton in "The Man Who Evolved" [Hamilton, 1974] once even made do without a time machine, using instead cosmic rays to speed up evolution, to see what lies at the end of the road for humankind. In a twist on the seeing-the-end-of-the-world theme this same author did invoke a time machine in "In the World at Dusk" [Hamilton, LME], in an attempt by an end-of-the-world scientist to use the past to repopulate the dead Earth of the future. A similiar idea was used in the 1958 film *Terror from the Year 5000*, in which a female time traveler arrives in the present on a search for a healthy man to rejuvinate the battered genes of a radioactive future. The same idea was repeated yet again in the novel *Millenium* [Varley, 1983], and in "The Comedian" [Sullivan, TT].

A sobering variation on the "future-getting-something-from-the-past" approach occurs in "The Figure" [Grendon, TSF]. Appearing in 1947, this story reflects the concern, even in those early days, about the possible long-range implications of radioactive contamination from nuclear weapons. After being told of massive insect invasions after the atomic bomb blasts at New Mexico, Hiroshima, and Nagasaki (all hushed-up, of course), a government research team reaches an unknown time in the future by using a "grab," a gadget that can "warp space-time curvature so that anything 'Here-Then' would be something 'Here-Now.' " The object they retrieve is a three-foot-high silver statue, done in great detail and with impressive skill. It is an obviously intelligent and majestic figure—the figure of a beetle!

As long ago as 1856 (considerably before the fundamental idea of a "time machine" in the spirit of H. G. Wells was conceived), people were fascinated by the idea of seeing the future. In that year an article appeared in *Harper's* [Anonymous, 1856] that speculated on what A.D. 3000 might be like. (It wasn't very good prophecy, falling far short even of 1920.) The description of this far future is given by an anonymous narrator whose presence out of his own time is never explained. If we look at languages other than English, we can find even earlier tales that at least weakly attempt to give some sort of physical explanation or mechanism for time travel (although not for such travel by machine). In [Bulgarin, RRSF], for example, written in 1824, the Russian hero is swept overboard while sailing, and he awakens, wrapped in the preserving herb Radix Vitalis ("Root of Life"), a thousand years later in the year A.D. 2824—not terribly convincing, but still better than having it all turn out to be a dream à la Dickens' *Christmas Carol*, with its trips to Christmas Past and Future. However, Odoevski, a fellow countryman of Bulgarin's, regressed a decade later from even this limp attempt at explaining physical movement in time; instead he used hypnotic trances to transport his narrator to any country and period of time [Odoevski, RRSF]. In this way the author speculated about the forty-fourth century, but not through true time travel as we think of it today, or at least as I do in this book.

Time travel by dreaming (e.g., [Wells, 1924]) was at one time commonly used as a literary device in stories whose real purpose was social commentary. The use of a similar idea, "sleeping into the future," can be found in *Looking Backward* [Bellamy, 1983], *When the Sleeper Awakes* [Wells, 1899] and "Pausodyne" [Allen, BTS], all first published before the turn of the century. This is, indeed, a literary technique of ancient origin. As we learn in [Stern, 1936]; "About 600 A.D. Gregory of Tours told the story of the Seven Sleepers of Ephesus who slept for three hundred and seventy-two years ... And it was Frederick II's Boniface who in one day lived forty years ... Let us not forget, too, that Mohammed had 90,000 conversations with God while he washed his hands. So the mind vanquishes time." And, of course, Sleeping Beauty was comatose for a hundred years in her ancient fairy tale. Harry Geduld points out in his Introduction to [Wells, 1987] that this popular idea can also be found in more modern "olden" times, such as in L. S. Mercier's *L'An Deux Mille Quatre Cent Quarante* (1771), in which an eighteenth-century sleeper wakes up in the twenty-fifth century. The sleeping-to-the-future device was later resurrected in the famous "Rip Van Winkle" tale by Washington Irving in 1819 and again in 1836 in Mary Griffith's "Three Hundred Years Hence," and these were followed in 1887 by W. H. Hudson's *A Crystal Age*, in which a botany explorer falls off the edge of a ravine, knocks himself out, and wakes up an undisclosed but very long time later.

This hoary device has been used in modern times too to explain how Buck Rogers, born in the last days of the nineteenth century, could be around in the year A.D. 2432. (He was buried in a mine cave-in, but was kept alive in suspended animation for 500 years by the release of a mysterious radioactive gas.) In "The Man Who Awoke" [Manning, BGA2] we have a sleeper who snoozes 3000 years into the future—presumably measured from 1933, the year this tale appeared in *Wonder Stories*. Four years later, the even more outrageous story of an ancient Greek warrior-sailor stranded in Central America, was told in "Past, Present, and Future" [Schachner, BGA3]. This warrior used volcanic gases as a drug to sleep thousands of years; while he sleeps, he was worshipped as the Mayan god Quetzal. And in "The Fourth Dynasty" [Winterbotham, 1936] we have an embalmer(!) who perfects a fluid that gives a human body "a hardness of diamond, which could withstand even the erosive action of wind and water." This stuff allows the embalmer to be resurrected in the 1500th millenium.

By 1940 the sleeping-into-the-future technique was so well-known that lazy authors hardly bothered to explain it to their readers. In that year's January issue of *Fantastic Adventures*, for example, Don Wilcox's story "The Robot Peril" tells of characters who arrive in the year 2089. The how of how they do that is quick and to the point: "All three had emerged from a century and a half of temporary death from a pit of absolute zero, into which they had been hurled by a mad experimenter." The far superior 1958 story "Two Dooms" [Kornbluth, HV] has a physicist working on the Manhattan Project fall asleep and wake up 150 years later—to find the Germans and the Japanese in America as occupying forces. He returns to the present in an equally mysterious fashion. Woody Allen used this same idea in his 1973 comedy film *Sleeper*. Victor Rousseau's dystopian novel, *The Messiah of the Cylinder* [Rousseau, 1917], in which the hero travels a century into the future via suspended animation through freezing (using a vacuum cylinder equipped with a hundred-year clock) is just a bit more sophisticated than Allen's film. Leo Szilard, one-time collaborator with Einstein, used the freezing idea of Rousseau to let his hero travel ninety years into the future, where all sorts of odd developments have taken hold [Szilard, ED]. (Note, however, that the novel *10,000 Years in a Block of Ice* [Boussenard, 1898] had already used freezing to span a period more than a hundred-fold longer; also see the "corpsicles" in Larry Niven's 1976 *A World Out of Time*.) None of these characters is really a time traveler, of course, but rather each is a person "out of time." And finally, in his classic 1956 novel *The Door Into Summer* [Heinlein, 1986], Robert Heinlein, the master of science fiction time travel, even combined the cold-storage method of travel to the future with a time machine that allowed his hero to return to the present.

Professor H. B. Franklin [1966] has stated that "when one says time travel what one really means is an extraordinary dislocation of someone's consciousness in time." By this criterion, for example, it might be reasonably argued that the doomed Peyton Farquhar, captured Confederate sympathizer, time traveled because in the brief moments it took for him to drop with a noose around his neck in "An Occurrence at Owl Creek Bridge" [Bierce, 1964], he lived (in his mind) through a day. His "trip" through time ended, however, with a broken neck beneath the bridge. It seems to me that Franklin's definition is far too broad, and I will take a narrower position on what time travel is in this book. Besides excluding hanging, I will also take the position that smoking marijuana or taking amphetamines and/or LSD to achieve a nonlinear, hallucinogenic experience of time will not count as time travel in this book, even though some distinguished writers have used such approaches.

In his 1822 *Confessions of an English Opium-Eater*, for example, Thomas De Quincey wrote of his experience with a drug-induced altered time sense: "I sometimes seemed to have lived for 70 to 100 years in a night." Soon after this, Tennyson used drugs to freeze time in his "The Lotus Eaters," written over the period 1833–1842. The setting in this work is a place "in which it seemed always afternoon," similiar to the land where Odysseus nearly lost his crew to the same narcotic plant. H. G. Wells, himself, was not above using such a method, as shown by his tale "The New Accelerator" [Wells, 1966]. In this story we learn of Professor Gibberne's discovery of a drug that makes the personal time of its taker run thousands of times faster than usual; the whole world appears to be a frozen instant to anyone who drinks the "New Accelerator." (The frozen-instant type of theme was also used in "The Einstein Slugger" [Wellman, 1939] to speed up a boxer without drugs, and more recently it appeared in "The Six Fingers of Time" [Lafferty, 1970].) There is also mention by Wells of a "Retarder," a drug for achieving the opposite kind of result. An example from the horror story genre of the use of drugs to time travel is "The Ancestor" [Lovecraft and Derleth, 1957], in which a medical doctor states that "I have found that a combination of drugs and music, taken at a time when the body is half-starved ... makes it possible to cast back in time," but his experiments go terribly wrong. The same idea, with a slightly less ghastly ending, is in *The House on the Strand* [du Maurier, 1969].

In *An Age* [Aldiss, 1967] we find such drug-induced time travel aptly renamed as *mind travel*; Aldiss requires his travelers to leave a jar of blood behind in the present as a homing signal for a successful mental return. This sounds just like "time travel for drugged vampires." Although there is still talk of drugs, mind travel is somewhat less outrageous in *The Gap in the Curtain* [Buchan, 1932], in which several characters are able to read a newspaper a year in the future.

The appearance in 1927 of *An Experiment with Time* [Dunne, 1958], on mind travel via dreaming, attracted a fair amount of attention (see [Besterman, 1933]). John William Dunne (1875–1949) was a military man, not a mystic, and he attempted a rational explanation for his experiences of dreaming his way through time. (J. B. Priestley described Dunne as an "old regular-officer type crossed with a mathematician and engineer" [Priestley, 1964], and H. G. Wells thought highly of Dunne's ideas on time.) Dunne's explanation of mind travel involves an infinite regress of times, however, a philosophical horror, and his "time travel by dreams" is of no interest for us.

Machineless Time Travel Without Dreams or Drugs

In "The Hero Equation" [Arthur, 1959] we find mind travel without drugs or dreams; rather, a college professor discovers an equation that if you just *think*(!) about it, results in sending your personality back in time. The same idea received a powerful, more serious treatment in "The Primal Solution" [Norden, 1977], describing a Jewish survivor of Nazi Germany who mind travels back to the Vienna of 1913 to kill the then twenty-four-year-old Adolf Hitler. Grimwood [1976] described a woman who has her epileptic seizures controlled via electrodes implanted in her brain; when one particular electrode is energized, she mind travels into the body of a woman in Victorian London. In a popular series by Kelvin Kent (one of many pen names for Henry Kuttner), which appeared in *Thrilling Wonder Stories* during the late 1930s and 1940s, the central character also visits the past with the aid of similiar gadgetry, but its inventor is careful to explain [Kent, 1939] that "it isn't a time machine. There's no such thing ... You didn't travel in time. Your mind merely took possession of the brain and body [of a person in that time]." Most recently this technique can be found in Robert Silverberg's *Letters from Atlantis* [Silverberg, 1990]. Perhaps it is all merely a matter of personal taste when reading fiction, but mind travel is not what *I* mean by time travel. And beyond the pale is the Shirley MacLaine method of time traveling, i.e., the "channeling" offered by the New Age Time Travel Agency in Gore Vidal's irreverent spoof of the gospel stories, in *Live from Golgotha* [Vidal, 1992].

We will also be uninterested in this book in such stories as *Monsters From Out of Time* [Long, 1970], which talks of "time shifts" caused by "prehistoric monsters still surviving deep within the Earth, changed through long ages of evolutionary adaptation into animals with the ability to generate billions of electron volts." Why such creatures would disturb "the very keystone of matter itself" and the "space-time continuum as well" is never explained. Marginally better is the mention in "Flight Through Super-Time" [Smith, 1932] that "movement in the Time dimension could be controlled, accelerated or reversed, by the action of some special force," but the story is reduced to babble-talk in the very next sentence with the admission that the genius-hero "succeeded in isolating the theoretic Time force, though without learning its ultimate nature and origin." The reader begins to suspect a joke when he learns that the heart of the time device resembles a large hourglass!

Transporting one's self into the past by means of sheer willpower, as in *The Time Stream* [Bell, 1931], *Time and Again* [Finney, 1970], "The Ambiquities of Yesterday" [Eklund, FST], and *Bid Time Return* [Matheson, 1975], is also out. This approach is quite often found in time-travel stories written for young women. As observed in [Friend, 1982], "the heroines are abruptly shot into the past through their own personal upheaval during a time of extreme emotional pain and embarrassment." Such stories, such as "The Earlier Service" [Irwin, BFSF2], which tells of a sensitive young girl who suddenly finds herself about to be sacrificed during a Black Mass nearly six hundred years in the past, depend far more on romanticism than on rationality, but this does not mean they are not capable of tremendous emotional appeal. (In particular, Matheson's novel was made, with great affect, into the beautiful 1980 film *Somewhere in Time*.) In a similiar fashion, *A Traveler in Time* [Uttley, 1964] tells us of a young girl who finds herself slipping back and forth across more than three centuries, usually while daydreaming, but in one instance after falling down a flight of stairs; and in *The Victorian Chaise Longue* [Laski, 1954] all it takes for one young woman to travel back to the Victorian England of 1864 is to fall asleep on an antique couch.

This sort of machineless time travel is not used only by young women—when the undeniably macho Batman and Robin made their first trip through time, a 1944 visit to ancient Rome, it was via hypnosis. (Only in later adventures did they make use of the "time-box" invented by Professor Carter Nichols, the Gotham City scientist regarded as "the world's foremost authority on time travel.") In *The Devil on the Road* [Westall, 1978], a tough-talking English biker visits the world of witch-burning England of three hundred years ago—with the aid of his "time-cat"! And *The Devil in Crystal* [Marlow, 1944] gives us the fifty-year-old Mr. James Tidburnholme, who suddenly finds himself transported from the war-torn London of 1943 to the self-satisfied London of 1922. What it doesn't give us is any explanation of *how* this happened (except for a few references to the devil).

Also eliminated are such literary devices as a knock on the head by a crowbar à la Mark Twain's *A Connecticut Yankee in King Arthur's Court*. (This same idea was used by Chauncey Thomas, for travel to the year 4872, in his 1891 novel *The*

Crystal Button.) As old and now somewhat stale as this idea is, it still reappears from time to time; e.g., in "The Bones of Charlemagne" [Pei, GSF] (in which a linguistics professor travels back to ninth-century France after receiving a bump on the head in an auto accident), "Odd" [Wyndam, 1961] (in which a man in 1906 is knocked into 1958 by being run over by a tram), and *The Christ Commission* [Mandino, 1980] (in which a best-selling author is sent back to the time of Christ by being punched in a bar by a drunk). Public Television used this device in the 1990 movie *Brother Future,* in which a streetwise black Detroit teenager is hit by a car—and learns about slavery when he wakes up in 1822.

More interesting (i.e., more rational) is the approach used in L. Sprague de Camp's classic science fiction novel *Lest Darkness Fall* [de Camp, 1941], written by his own admission as a modern *Connecticut Yankee*. In Sprague's book the "granddaddy of all lightning flashes" hurls the archaeologist hero back to the Rome of A.D. 535. The how of it is unexplained, but at least the implied mechanism avoids the supernatural and the fantastic. (A similiar idea was used in the 1980 movie *The Final Countdown,* in which a fully armed nuclear aircraft carrier is sent back through a violent electrical storm to the time just before the Japanese attack on Pearl Harbor.)

Finally, it should go almost without saying that time travel by the trivial means of moving across time zones is totally without interest in this book. This is a common experience today (you can leave London on the Concorde and arrive in New York before you left), and one can actually trace this idea as far back as 1841, to Poe's short story "Three Sundays in a Week." A long expansion of Poe's idea was printed in one of the early science fiction magazines [Verrill, 1927], but the readers' response to it was uniformly negative. And correctly so—it simply isn't *time travel*.

A story that illustrates my view of machineless time travel by counter-example is the novel *Mastodonia* [Simak, 1978], which uses a godlike creature marooned on Earth (because of a spaceship crash centuries earlier) to make "time tunnels." Even as he wrote this mystical hocus-pocus, Simak seems to have had the feeling that perhaps it was all pretty weak stuff, and he tried to explain his ideas through words spoken by one of his characters. Finding disbelief in those told about his machineless method of time traveling, the character complains: "The whole trouble was that I couldn't tell them about some machine—a time-travel machine. If I could have told them we'd developed a machine, they'd have been more able to believe me. We place so much trust in machines; they are magic to us. If I could have outlined some ridiculous theory and spouted some equations at them, they would have been impressed." I believe Simak has this all wrong. We trust in machines not because they are magic, but for precisely the opposite reason. They are not magic, but rather *rational*. And to dismiss mathematics so brusquely is to admit that some nonnatural, some supernatural influence is at work. The supernatural is precisely what this book is *not* about.

Time Travel by Machine

We, instead, are interested here in physical time travel *by machine*. In addition, the machine must have a *rational explanation*. (For example, like the aircraft carrier in *The Final Countdown* film, a Navy vessel in *The Ship that Sailed the Time Stream* [Edmondson, 1965b] travels into the past. But unlike the movie, the novel offers a rational explanation; the ship's still, made from an oddly shaped copper coil in a vacuum jar, proves to be a time machine when powered by lightning bolts during storms!) For this book, such a rational basis is found in Einstein's general theory of relativity, his theory of gravity. (His *special* theory of relativity is for those situations where there is no gravity.) Until Einstein, the theory of gravity used by scientists was Newton's, a theory that while amazingly accurate under most situations, does have observable errors in certain astronomical applications. In addition, Newton's theory is a descriptive one, allowing the calculation of gravity effects without offering any explanation for gravity. Not only does Einstein's theory give the right answers even in those cases where Newton's doesn't, but it also explains gravity. It does this by treating the world as a four-dimensional one in which all four dimensions (three space and one time) are in a certain sense on equal footing. The resulting Einsteinian description of the world is that of a unified *spacetime*, while Newton's theory keeps space and time separate and distinct.

From the first (1905) it has been known that Einstein's special theory allows travel into the future. To return, however, to travel into the past, had been thought to be impossible. Yet, since 1949 it has been known that the general theory, which so far has passed every experimental test it has been subjected to, does allow time travel to the past under certain conditions. This is not a widely known fact, even among some science fiction writers and many technically trained people. It is the availability of a theory that separates time-travel speculations from the fantasy speculations with which it is often unjustly lumped and which are in the province of quacks (e.g., ESP, astrology, and mind-over-matter, i.e., "spoon bending").

In his general theory Einstein showed how spacetime can be either flat (in the no gravity, special-relativity case), or curved (with gravity), and he did this not by verbal, philosophical handwaving, but by writing mathematical equations—the famous gravitational tensor field equations. These equations are quite complicated and are very difficult to solve in most cases, but in certain special cases they have been solved. Those solutions show how matter and spacetime interact. As the popular shorthand phrase puts it, "curved spacetime tells matter how to move, and matter tells spacetime how to curve."

Astonishingly, in 1949 the mathematician Kurt Gödel (1906–1978) found one such solution to the field equations that describes the movement of matter not only through space but also *backward in time* along what are called *closed timelike world lines* in spacetime (see Tech Note 4). These world lines are such that if a human traveled on one (at less than the speed of light), he would see everything around him happening in normal casual order from moment to moment (e.g., the second hand on his watch would tick clockwise into the future), but eventually the world line would close back on itself and the traveler would find himself in his past! That is what the physics and the mathematics in Gödel's solution imply. That is what I mean by saying there is a rational basis for discussing time travel. It is important to note that travel along one of the closed timelike world lines discovered by Gödel requires a *machine*; that is, some kind of accelerating rocket ship.

The dual requirement of a machine with a rational explanation eliminates the previously discussed time-travel stories, as well as stories like Manly Wade Wellman's 1940 classic novella *Twice in Time* [Wellman, 1988]. In this story a time projector throws the time traveler to his destination in spacetime and does not itself go with him. To return, a second projector is needed. Its gruesome feature is the need to have a good supply of organic material at the destination, out of which to reassemble the traveler's tissues. As the hero (about to be tossed back from 1938 to the Florence, Italy, of 1470, during the days of the Medici) instructs a friend: "Tomorrow, at this time, have a fresh veal carcass, or a fat pig, brought here. That's for me to materialize myself back." This is more a ghoul's view of time travel than a physicist's! For the purposes of this book Wellman's machine is less interesting (although it is described in some detail) than is the time machine in *The World Below* [Wright, 1930] because Wright attempts to explain his machine rationally by making a fleeting reference to Einstein's curved space.

Years later, Brian Aldiss' timeslip novel *Frankenstein Unbound* [Aldiss, 1973] (which is a historical fantasy in which the hero travels back from the year 2020 to 1816, where he meets Mary Wollstoncraft Godwin and Frankenstein's monster) at least attempts to give a rational (though machineless) explanation for it all; that is, a nuclear war has supposedly unhinged spacetime. (The novel was made into an interesting 1990 movie.) Aldiss has repeated the same kind of idea in *Dracula Unbound* [Aldiss, 1991], except that there is a time machine in this novel.

It is interesting to note that even at the early date of 1930, Wright was not the only writer of fiction to understand that rational backward time travel would somehow be intimately linked to Einstein's work. In this same year, for example, Edmond Hamilton, one of the pioneering writers in science fiction magazines, published a quite sophisticated story, "The Man Who Saw the Future" [Hamilton, 1930], in which Einstein and other scholars of relativity are repeatedly mentioned. In this story a young man is hauled before the Inquisitor Extraordinary of the King of France to explain his mysterious disappearance from and subsequent reappearance in an open field, amid thunderclaps and in plain sight of many onlookers. As the story unfolds, we learn that the young man was transported five centuries into the future, from A.D. 1444 to 1944, by scientists working in twentieth-century Paris. The thunderclaps were produced by spacetime "rotations," as the air of 1944 and 1444 was reversed. The Inquisition finds the story preposterous, of course, and the first time traveler is burned at the stake as a sorcerer.

Early science fiction writer Philip F. Nolan (whose 1928 tale "Armageddon 2419 A.D." in *Amazing Stories* inspired the Buck Rogers character) used the idea of spacetime as well in "The Time Jumpers" [Nolan, 1965]. In this story, the then standard fiction character of the brilliant, lone inventor has cornered the world market in something called "dobinium." He did this because dobinium was the power source of his time-car and as he explained, "when induced to activity through the bombardment of rays from the cosmic generator, its [the dobinium] emanations formed the basis of the complex reactions of pure and corpuscular energy by which I was able to cut the *curvature of space-time* [my emphasis] and hurl a material object backward along the time coordinates."

Even as early as 1937 the New York stage was sufficiently sophisticated so that its time-travel play, *The Star-Wagon* [Anderson, 1937] used a machine based on the fourth dimension, not on fantasy. Indeed, the *New York Times* actually found time travel by machine all rather old hat, writing in a review of the play (30 Sept. 1937) about "the hackneyed theme of the time machine." Some days later (10 Oct.) the paper gave the play an even unhappier assessment, saying that "the theories of time, which seem to be breaking out like a rash in many quarters today, are worth more searching study than the *Star-Wagon* discloses." The word rash apparently referred to the time play *Time and the Conways* [Priestley, 1937] by J. B. Priestley, then getting a more appreciative reception on the London stage. Well, no matter the sophisticated sniffing of the *New York Times*—the romantic plays of Priestley and Anderson are interesting ones for us because they are rational.

And finally, a recent story written for youngsters(!), "The Little Monster" [Anderson, 1973], hints at a rational explanation for time travel. When a young boy asks his uncle-physicist how his time machine works, he is told "Come back when you know tensor calculus and I'll explain to you about *n*-dimensional forces and the warping of world lines."

H. G. Wells—Why His Time Machine Won't Work

It was H. G. Wells who in 1895 introduced the first time machine in the modern sense in his story about a Victorian scientist who masters the fourth dimension and makes a gadget that takes him to the end of the world. There were many imitators in the years that followed. In *The Time Journey of Dr. Barton* [Hodgson, 1929], for example, we have a scientist who moves through spacetime, 2000 years into the future, in a Wellsian-type machine. But such early machine stories always had a limited readership.

The first significant use of machine time travel in popular culture was in the comic strip "Alley Oop." (The earlier strip "Brick Bradford" had used a time machine, too—the "Time-Top"—but it's influence fell far short of that of "Oop." When "Brick Bradford" appeared in movie theaters in 1947 as a Saturday-afternoon serial, the "Time-Top" was there for a trip back to the eighteenth century, but it had already lost its chance to be the first movie time machine. That distinction belongs to the "Time-Ball" in the 1944 British film *Time Flies*.)

However, it was Oop who really brought time travel by machine into the public consciousness. Oop was an ape-man (with a Brooklyn accent and a pet dinosaur named Dinny) who originally lived in the very ancient past and at first all the action took place there. The strip first appeared in 1934 and, while popular for several years, by 1939 it was losing its readership. That's when its creator, V. T. Hamlin, got the idea of freeing Oop from his own remote time and letting him roam through all the ages. To this end, enter the Wellsian-type time machine invented by Dr. Wonmug (who, of course, is actually Einstein: *Ein stein = One mug!*).

After Oop, other time machines began to appear regularly in the comics. Wonder Woman, for example, often traveled in time. Wonder Woman's trips in time were not accomplished by wishing or dreaming or drugs but rather by machine, the wonderful "space transformation machine." Superman, too, has often journeyed in time, both forward and backward. Not infrequently he uses machines, or something called "time rays" but, unlike Wonder Woman or Batman, Superman also has the ability to make himself into a time machine. He does this by virtue of his superpower to move faster than light. In 1949, for example, Superman returned to his destroyed home-planet of Krypton *before* its destruction. An explanatory text tells us: "Time seems to stand still as Superman races at cosmic velocity, passing the speed of light ... faster ... faster ... until Superman breaks through the time barrier." Some of the science here is correct, as moving at a speed greater than that of light automatically allows backward time travel (see Tech Note 7).

Wells *almost* had time travel by machine right. But not quite right. As Tech Note 4 explains, a real time machine must move in space (like Superman!) as well as in time. All the theoretical models for time travel discussed in this book (Tipler cylinders, black holes, Gödel rockets, cosmic strings, and spacetime wormholes) require spatial displacement. Wells' machine, however, did not move; it always remained in the Time Traveller's laboratory (or on the spot that was the laboratory) unless he pushed it about after a trip. Such Wellsian-type time machines are common in science fiction. I even used one in "Newton's Gift" [Nahin, 1979b], but in fact they really just won't do. They have several troublesome problems, at least one of which is fatal. Such a machine would, for example, to take the worst first, run into itself!

Consider: There sits my time machine as I prepare for the first time journey ever, a trip back to the late-Mesozoic era to hunt dinosaur. I load my Continental .600 with Nitro Express cartridges the size of bananas, make sure my blood-proof boots are laced-up tight, kiss my wife good-by, and climb in. I pull the lever. Now, Wellsian-type time machines don't jump over time, but rather travel through time. (See the Time Traveller's own description of how things looked to him, a description faithfully and spectacularly reproduced in the 1960 movie.) Therefore, the time machine will instantly collide with itself at the micromoment before I pull the lever! The resulting destruction obviously introduces a nice paradox—since this happens before I pull the lever, then how did I manage to pull it? (Many of the early science fiction writers were not totally oblivious to collision problems, e.g., to avoid materializing inside of an object in the distant past or future, it was common to combine the time machine with an airplane, as in "The Time Valve" [Breuer, 1930a], "Via the Time Accelerator" [Bridge, 1931], and "The Time Cheaters" [Binder, 1940], although why this avoids the problem of colliding with the atmosphere is never explained. Wells' own Time Traveller worried about the collision problem, too.) Of course, one might argue that even Wells' machine does actually move, as it is attached to the Earth, which is moving, but why this should result in the time machine arriving in the temporal past of the Earth, rather than in some past region of space (almost surely a vacuum) is not clear.

The general problem of where things are for time travelers has been nicely illustrated by the physicist Gregory Benford in his novel *Timescape* [Benford, 1980]. In this story the world of 1998 is on the verge of total ecological collapse, and an attempt is made to change the past by aiming a backward-in-time message via faster-than-light tachyons (see Tech Note 7) at the pivotal year 1963. When the principal scientist involved in this effort is explaining the process to a potential financial backer, he is asked, "Hold on. Aim for *what*? Where *is* 1963?" The scientist replies, "Quite far away, as it works out. Since 1963, the Earth's been going round the Sun, while the Sun itself is revolving around the hub of the galaxy, and so on. Add that up and you find 1963 is pretty distant." An understanding of the question "where is everything?" actually goes quite a bit further back in fiction. For example, when after looking through a TV-like gadget to view the past one character in "Dead End" [Jameson, 1941] complains, "You said you'd find Captain Kidd's treasure, but all I can see is fog and static," he is told, "It's too far back—1698 or thereabouts. The Earth was billions of miles from here then, and there are too many cosmic rays between." (The cosmic rays are presumably the cause of the interference.)

But let's suppose we ignore this concern about where things are for a time traveler, as do most science fiction stories. Still another problem with a true Wellsian-type time machine is that since it travels *through* time, the machine must always appear to be located in the same place. For example, to travel from Ford's Theatre today to Ford's Theatre on the evening of Good Friday April 14, 1865, in a misguided attempt to save Lincoln from Booth's bullet (see Chapter Four for an explanation of why it would be futile to try this), a Wellsian-type time machine would have to occupy every instant of the intervening century and more. For observers outside the machine, the machine would appear to have been sitting in the same place all those years. (One modern story that gets this point right is "The Very Slow Time Machine" [Watson, 1979].) Wells, himself, was aware of the loss of story-telling credibility such immobility entails and he tried to explain the problem away. (For details on his attempt, see Note 1 of Chapter Four.) An immediate implication of this immobility is that if you are being chased by an angry mob somewhere in time (perhaps you unwittingly violated a sensitive social taboo), hopping into your Wellsian-type time machine isn't going to help because the machine just sits there. The mob could take its deliberate time in first building a roaring fire and then pushing the machine (and you) into it. As [Cook, 1982] so nicely put it, "You might as well try to escape danger by taking a nap." To argue about time travel in terms of a Wellsian-type time machine is to build your house of cards in the middle of a storm, with as much meaning as discussing evolution in terms of unicorns, but one still runs across such analyses in the philosophical literature (e.g., [Dummett, NOT]).

Traveling to the Future

In fact, it *is* theoretically possible to travel by machine as far as you wish into the future and to see the future for yourself, a conclusion solidly endorsed by the solidly accepted special theory of relativity. By traveling in a rocket ship fast enough (but never, unlike Superman, faster than the speed of light) and far enough, one could leave the Earth, loop out on a vast journey perhaps halfway across the Universe, and then return hundreds, thousands, even millions of years in the future. You could do this, in fact, with the apparent passage of "personal time" (as measured by your wrist watch or the beating of your heart) as short as you'd like. (Physicists call this "proper time.") This astonishing statement (see Tech Notes 2, 5, and 6) quite literally put a lot of Victorian-era trained scientists into shock.

However, it did not take long for the early science fiction magazine writers to pick up on the concept of time distortion via high speed; it appeared as early as 1930 in "The FitzGerald Contraction" [Breuer, 1930b]. "The Time Express" [Schachner, 1932] used the so-called time-dilation effect to travel into the future without a rocket ship, using instead mysterious rays that vibrated a time traveler's body at nearly the speed of light! We are not told, however, how the time travelers managed to return to their own time. This story is particularly interesting, as it was a pioneer at using the idea of time travel for touring purposes. The story opens with an ad for a time-machine company, displayed on red neon lights twenty-feet high:

> HOOK'S TOURS THROUGH TIME. PERSONALLY CONDUCTED, ALL-EXPENSE TOURS INTO THE FUTURE. VISIT YOUR GREAT GRANDCHILDREN IN THE TRADITIONAL HOOK COMFORT. THE LAST WORD IN TOURS.

Far more sophisticated is "Out Around Rigel" [Wilson, SFT], with a space traveler returning from a high-speed trip out to the blue supergiant Rigel in the constellation Orion. The 900 or so light-years of the round-trip had taken just six months of ship or personal time, but a thousand years of back-home time. The traveler returns to find all he had left behind long dead and reduced to dust: "Sometimes I waken from a dream in which they are all so near ... all my old companions ... and for a moment I cannot realize how far away they are. Beyond years and years." Another tale that achieves a similiar emotional effect, this time via a Wellsian-type time machine rather than by Wilson's spaceship, is *The Year of the Quiet Sun* [Tucker, 1979]. Here a time traveler is trapped in post-nuclear-war times, where there is no energy to power his machine. As the story ends, he finds the girl he had loved and left behind in the past; she is now the elderly widow of another man, having married his rival because the traveler had never returned.

A trip into the future does not have to be serious or sad. For example, "Far Centaurus" [Van Vogt, SS] tells the story of a spaceship crew that sets off for Alpha Centauri, over four light-years distant. They will survive the trip, which requires 500 years of personal time, with the aid of a preserving drug (shades of Radix Vitalis!). Long before they arrive, however, the secret of faster-than-light travel is discovered and they arrive at their destination to find a human reception committee. As shown in Tech Note 7, knowledge of such speedy travel would be equivalent to knowing the secret of time travel, and the shocked crew is sent back in time, to Earth, to just one year after they left (and they even listen to their own early radio reports arriving from deep space).

Lester del Rey explored the idea of time travel to the future for military gain, to get advanced weaponry, in "Unto Him That Hath" [del Rey, TC]; the humiliating, ironic result is that the gadgets brought back are so advanced that nobody can figure out how they work. A chilling version of this idea appeared more recently in the undated Number 17 issue of *Time Twisters* comics. A medieval sorcerer, forced to fight a knight, reaches into the future for the ultimate weapon. (It isn't clear why with such an ability that the sorcerer really needs any help!) He obtains a Second World War submachine gun, but unfortunately sights along the barrel in the wrong direction as he pushes the trigger. "Quit Zoomin' Those Hands Through the Air" [Finney, FCW] describes the failed use of the Wright brothers' first airplane to win the Civil War. (It was temporarily borrowed from the Smithsonian Institution by a time-traveling Union major-cum-Harvard College professor from 1864!) In what may be the most cynical (but perhaps most realistic) use of time travel to the future, *The Year of the Quiet Sun* [Tucker, 1979] has the first time machine restricted so that it only serves the tawdry political needs of a failed President. Three time travelers are sent on various forward penetrations in time to see who opposes him, what their tactics are, if he is reelected, and so on.

Traveling to the Past

The real adventure in time travel would be to go backward in time, to visit the past. I believe this longing for the past (even if only subconscious, as used in Jack Finney's "I'm Scared" [Finney, 1986] to explain sudden, mysterious disappearances) accounts for the sweet pleasure most people get from experiencing almost any recreation of times gone-by, as shown by the steady market in old-time radio tapes, or the popularity of nostalgia movies like Woody Allen's *Radio Days*,[2] or that of weekly television shows about a romanticized past, such as "Happy Days," "The Waltons," and "The Little House on the Prairie." The weekly theme of the 1979 TV show "Time Express" involved going back in time to "do things right."

Nostalgia for the past is nothing new. The Victorians were nostalgic, too, as witnessed for example in the writings of William Morris. His 1890 *News from Nowhere* was a mirror of socialist utopian perfection (as viewed in a dream set sometime in the twenty-first century), which reflected Morris' idealized image of the past. Even though all the events described occur in the future, there is much talk of the past and his descriptions of places are generally as he remembered them from his childhood. Morris' idea of the perfect future found its inspiration in nostalgia, not in wonder-gadgets-to-come. Indeed, he wrote *News* as a rebuttal to Bellamy's *Looking Backward* (published two years earlier), which found its salvation-to-come in a highly regimented, machine-oriented society. Morris' was a popular view but, perhaps ominously, it is Bellamy's work that is the better known today. When *News from Nowhere* first appeared in serial form in *The Common-weal*, it enjoyed the same sort of enthusiastic reception that Garrison Keillor's nostalgic "News from Lake Wobegon" did on the 1980s radio show, "The Prairie Home Companion." *News from Nowhere* was not Morris' first excursion into literary longing for the past. In his earlier *The Earthly Paradise* (1868) he wrote:

> "Come again,
>
> Come back, past years! Why will ye pass in vain?"

As the promotional text on the videotape package of the 1986 movie *Peggy Sue Got Married* says, "to do it again" is "the golden opportunity almost everyone has longed for at least once." Writing less romantically, one philosopher [Sorensen, 1987] declared that a "major source of interest in the time travel question is our general fascination with the exotic and the child-like frustration we sometimes feel at being confined to the present. We wish that the benefits of moving through space could be supplemented with the benefits which would accrue from movements through time."

Less happy with time travel to the past was Jack Feathersmith in "Blind Alley" [Jameson, GSSF], who made a pact with the Devil in order to be sent back a half-century to the "good old days" of 1902. As have many others who have made such arrangements, Mr. Feathersmith overlooked a few subtle loopholes in the contract.[3] Much less enthusiastic is the character in "Hobson's Choice" [Bester, 1986], who delights in pointing out all the bad points of living in the past. Tell him when, and he ticks off the disadvantages. To live in ancient Greece would let you rub shoulders with Aristotle, sure, but you already know what he said and you'd pretty soon regret the lack of modern plumbing. The years of the American Revolution might let you exchange greetings with George Washington, but you'd also have to put up with cholera in Philadelphia, malaria in New York, and the fact that if you need an operation there is anesthesia nowhere. The Victorian Age appeals to twentieth-century romantics, but before you go you'd better have your eyes and teeth checked, make sure you're not poor, and you absolutely had better not be the member of a religious minority (or of any minority at all). The time traveling historian in *Doomsday Book* [Willis, 1992] has her appendix prophylactically removed, and is also advised to have her nose cauterized against all the awful stinks of her destination, the fourteenth century. The medical concern, in particular, serves as a dramatic source of conflict in [Laski, 1954], as the time traveler, who suffers from tuberculosis, falls asleep in the present and wakes up in

1864—where she finds her illness is untreatable. Similiar medical concerns are pondered by a character in [Grimwood, 1976], and in "The Hertford Manuscript" [Cowper, 1977] we learn the fate of Wells' Time Traveller—he journeys back to the seventeenth century, where his time machine malfunctions. Trapped in the year 1665, he perishes in the Great Bubonic Plague then sweeping London.

On the other hand, the time traveler from the future in "Time Track" [Sprague, 1951] makes a very good living in the past by winning bets on yet-to-happen events whose outcomes he knows. And the failed professor in "April in Paris" [Le Guin, 1975] finds the Paris of 1482 infinitely better than the Paris of 1961. Moving in the backward direction, too, is the time-traveling anthropologist in the novel *Mists of Dawn* [Oliver, 1952], who solves the mystery of why the museum skeletons of ancient man, dug up in the nineteenth century, are not there in any past more remote than 25,000 B.C. (See also "Transfusion" [Oliver, GSF].) Traveling back even further is the high-school history teacher in a Jack Williamson 1932 novella *The Moon Era* [Williamson, BGA1]. In this story an antigravity spaceship that "moves along the fourth dimension" turns out also to be a time machine. The hero visits the Moon of the ancient past, where he has many fantastic adventures.

Robert Silverberg, a science fiction writer who has used the time-travel theme often and effectively, expressed Sorensen's wish clearly when he wrote "Ms. Found in an Abandoned Time Machine" [Silverberg, 1986]: "Suppose you had a machine that would enable you to fix everything that's wrong in the world ... The machine can do anything ... it gives you a way of slipping backward and forward in time ... Call this machine whatever you want. Call it Everybody's Fantasy Actualizer. Call it a Time Machine Mark Nine." Silverberg gives a masterful demonstration of what he means in "Many Mansions" [Silverberg, BSZ], a tale of the year 2006 when time machines actually exist. Even so, the characters use their imaginations to explore their fantasy worlds and wishes, wishes that could (if they really wanted them) be realized with a real time machine.

Perhaps Silverberg had Clifford Simak's story "Project Mastodon" [Simak, 1962] in mind when he wrote of his "Fantasy Actualizer." Simak visualized the past as a sanctuary for those wishing to escape from the war worries of modern times. (See also "Over the River & Through the Woods" [Simak, TC] and *Mastodonia* [Simak, 1978].) Silverberg, himself, devoted an entire novel, *The Time Hoppers* [Silverberg, 1967], to this theme. In this work a woman who has just lost her husband to this form of escape comes to realize that "her husband had put thumb to nose and disappeared on a one-way journey to the past. 'Good-by, Beth, good-by, kids, good-by, lousy twenty-fifth century', he might have said, as he vanished down the time tunnel. The coward couldn't face responsibility."

A Beatles' song expresses the lure of the past, "I need a place to hide, that's why I believe in yesterday," and in the words of the involuntary time traveler in *The Devil in Crystal* [Marlow, 1944], "Put back the Universe and give me yesterday!" Ray Bradbury's sad story "The Fox and the Forest" [Bradbury, 1980] also makes effective use of such an idea, with a bomb designer and his wife fleeing from the evils of 2155 back to the Mexico of 1938. Jack Finney was influenced by this story to write the similar "Such Interesting Neighbors" [Finney, 1986], and he even has one of his characters allude to Bradbury's story. J. B. Priestley repeated the theme by having a time traveler flee from an alien invasion of the far-future in "Mr. Strenberry's Tale" [Priestley, 1953], as does the entire population of Earth in *Our Children's Children* [Simak, 1974b]. And the occasionally incoherent 1989 film *The Time Guardian* has humanity fleeing the forty-first century to the twentieth, in an attempt to evade an army of killer robots.

One author, however, has written a cautionary tale about the error of believing in the past as a retreat. In "Hobson's Choice" [Bester, 1986] we learn that time travel is used mostly as therapy for the discontented of the future; one can pick any point in the past to visit, and if that doesn't work out then you can try another. As it turns out, hardly anyone seems to get much benefit from time travel. When one character asks another about where people like to go, he gets a cynical reply: "Any place but where they belong. They keep looking for the Golden Age. Tramps! Time-stiffs. Never satisfied. Always searching, shifting ... bumming through the centuries ... Half the panhandlers you meet are probably time-bums stuck in the wrong century."

In addition to using time traveling to find peace, Simak also expounded on an opposite theme in "Project Mastodon;" that of time travel to the past for military purposes; that is, one could move troops into the past while on home ground, then travel in ordinary fashion to the proto-territory of the enemy, and finally return to the present to appear in dramatic and astonishing fashion in the surprised foe's midst (an idea briefly mentioned again in his later novel *Mastodonia* [Simak, 1978]). Simak offered up, therefore, the ultimate fantasy for both doves and hawks in a single story. More conventional are two "what-if" Civil War stories, [Turtledove, FCW] and [Byram, FCW]. In Turtledove's story twenty-first-century assault rifles end up in the hands of Confederate troops, and in Byram's work a World War II regimental combat team is transported 80 years backward in time. More gruesome is the idea in "Brooklyn Project" [Tenn, 1983], which posits that Newton's third law of motion (which states that for every action there is an equal but opposite reaction) holds for time travel. This "time recoil" is said to be so violent that no human could survive. As an enthusiastic government hack explains to reporters at a press conference: "Do you realize what we could do to an enemy by virtue of that property alone? Sending an adequate mass ... into the past while it is adjacent to a hostile nation would force that nation into the future—all of it simultaneously—a future from which it would return populated only with corpses!"

An indirect military application of backward time travel is mentioned in Simak's "Project Mastodon"—the mining of early uranium deposits before they have had time to reduce themselves to lead via radioactive decay. In "The Wings of a Bat" [Ash, SFD] the main character is employed as a time traveler for the "Mining and Processing Branch of Cretaceous Minerals, Inc.," and "Wildcat" [Anderson, SFD] has an oil-drilling crew in the Jurassic period. This idea of using the perishable resources of the past has been pursued by others, too; e.g., *The Last Day of*

Creation [Jeschke, 1982], which details a diabolical military plot to extract Middle Eastern oil five million years in the past, and "Death of a Dinosaur" [Moskowitz, TC], which has a food distributor selling frozen dinosaur steaks. (See also "A Statue for Father" [Asimov, SFD].)

The most direct use of the past's unique resource, *itself*, is seen in "History in Reverse" [Laurence, 1939]. After purchasing the motion picture rights to H. G. Wells' *Outline of History*, the head of a movie studio uses a time machine to send his ace cameraman into the past to get live action footage. Prehistoric animals, the last ice age, Cheops building his pyramid, the destruction of Pompeii by the eruption of Vesuvius, the Battle of Hastings, Columbus, all the originals appear in the film. A more sophisticated treatment of this same idea appeared in the 1947 short story "E for Effort" [Sherred, 1983]. Years later this idea was further developed in novel length in the very funny *The Technicolor Time Machine* [Harrison, 1967], in which a movie director uses the distant past of the eleventh century as a realistic setting for a picture.

Who Else Might Be Interested in Time Travel

You do not have to be a dinosaur-steak fan or a movie producer to have a special fascination for time machines; criminals and lovers probably would, too. As one science fiction writer [Niven, 1971] put it: "If one could travel in time, what wish could not be answered? All the treasures of the past would fall to one man with a submachine gun. Cleopatra and Helen of Troy might share his bed, if bribed with a trunkful of modern cosmetics." Or as the tragically flawed inventor in Anthony Boucher's "Elsewhen" [Boucher, 1953] dreamed before using time travel to commit the perfect murder: "The Great Harrison Partridge would have untold wealth. He could pension off his sister Agatha and never have to see her again. He would have untold prestige and glamor, despite his fat and baldness, and the beautiful and aloof Faith Preston would fall into his arms like a ripe plum." (Partridge's dreams are shattered because he overlooks a detail about time travel.)

Instead of viewing the past as an aid to crime, some authors have seen it as a possible dumping ground for criminals, as a convenient place to get them out of the way, as in "My Object All Sublime" [Anderson, SFS] and "Hawksbill Station" [Silverberg, CJSF]. There can be no breakout from the prison of the past. On the other side of the law-and-justice coin, a police officer in "The Future is Ours" [Dentinger, 1969] travels to the future to learn new crime-fighting techniques— only to find that in the thirtieth century it is socially acceptable to be a crook, and so there are no police. And in "The Face in the Photo" [Finney, 1986] criminals escape into the past with the help of a physics professor.

Museum curators would seem obvious clients for time-machine companies. Indeed, we find such a business, "Time Researchers," in *The Lincoln Hunters* [Tucker, 1958]. T-R, whose corporate motto is "We Sift the Sands of Time," hires itself out as a futuristic version of Indiana Jones, recovering lost historical artifacts (e.g., original sound recordings of one of Lincoln's unreported speeches) for customers who can pay the substantial charges. In "Man of Distinction" [Shaara, SFS] Genealogy, Inc. uses its "time scanner" to provide its clients with a list of distinguished predecessors—its corporate motto is "An Ancestor for Everybody." And in *The Cross-Time Engineer* [Frankowski, 1986] we read of the Historical Corps, whose time travel agents are "writing the definitive history of mankind." Another historical use for time travel to the past, one of the most unusual I have come across, was suggested in the philosophical article [Graves and Roper, 1965], which considers a hoary question: "If everything in the Universe doubled in size overnight while we slept, could we tell what had happened when we woke up next morning?" The usual answer to this puzzle, called by philosophers the "Universal nocturnal expansion," is *no* (but see [Nerlich, 1991] for why this is so only in Euclidean space, which is not our kind of space). Graves and Roper suggest that even in Euclidean space all we need do is take a yardstick back to yesterday and compare it with itself! As so often happens, however, this scholarly idea was introduced even earlier by a science fiction writer [Sycamore, 1959].

Several other uses for the past are discussed in *Mastodonia* [Simak, 1978]. After going into the time-travel business, for example, *Time Associates* finds itself receiving a request from a United States senator, who wants to send the disadvantaged of today back into the remote past, where they could have a fresh start with a virgin Earth. Another potential client is a religious fringe group that wants to purchase exclusive rights to the time of Jesus—not to visit, but to forbid anyone from visiting. The group fears that such visitors would "learn the truth," which might contradict the very legends that form the heritage of Christianity. (The same concern is expressed in *The Fury Out of Time* [Biggle, 1965].) In what may be the most ingenious idea of all, *Time Associates* itself does not directly do business in the present, but rather 150,000 years in the past in a "new" country called Mastodonia. The corporate lawyer, you see, has determined that legally this means that the company is thus a foreign company doing business outside the United States, and so therefore it would not be liable for taxes to the IRS!

The tourist trade, in general, is a booming business in science fiction time travel, with dinosaur hunting at the top of the list; e.g., "Poor Little Warrior!" [Aldiss, SFD], "A Sound of Thunder" [Bradbury, 1980], and *Mastodonia* [Simak, 1978]. Historical tours to great events of the past are described in *Up the Line* [Silverberg, 1969], "When We Went to See the End of the World" [Silverberg, 1986], "Vintage Season" [Kuttner and Moore, T3], and "Let's Go to Golgotha!" [Kilworth, 1985]).

As a symbol of the prehistoric past, perhaps nothing equals the dinosaur in power and vulnerability. After ruling Earth for hundreds of millions of years, about sixty-five million years ago they simply vanished. Did they die out because they were hunted to extinction? Asimov's "Day of the Hunters" [Asimov, SFD], an expansion of "Big Game" [Asimov, BGA3], has a twist on who the hunters were (as does "The King and the Dollmaker" [Jeschke, BRW]). In "The Twentieth Voyage of Ijon Tichy" [Lem, 1976] there is an ingenious time-travel explanation for the death of the dinosaurs that has nothing to do with hunting. Rather, the first experiments in time travel run amoke and inadvertently terrorize the far past—besides creating Meteor Crater in Arizona and causing the Ice Ages (to say nothing of the canals of Mars), the dinosaurs are also all killed off by a tremendous burst of "time-machine radiation." In "Dinosaurs" [Landis, D] the dinosaurs are wiped out when a Soviet missile attack is diverted into the past! Even more gradiose than killing dinosaurs, however, is the concept in "T" [Aldiss, 1966], in which an entire planet is destroyed by a time machine miscalculation in the past (thus creating the asteroid belt between Mars and Jupiter).

The obvious advantages to be gained by knowing the future, of knowing the history of things to come, receive an interesting presentation in "What We Learned from This Morning's Newspaper" [Silverberg, 1986]. An entire block of homeowners wakes up on Monday, November 22, to find the New York Times on the doorsteps—for Wednesday, December 1. No explanation for this is given, except that perhaps it is some sort of fluke of the fourth dimension. The happy suburbanites do the obvious, and use the week's advance notice to make money on the stock market. On the other hand, "Snulbug" [Boucher, 1980b] takes the view that knowing the future provides no advantage at all; e.g., if you try to change the future, you will get stuck in a temporal loop until you decide to give up the attempt. (As we will see in Chapter Four, this idea of repeating closed time loops is not correct.) The developers of a time machine in "History in Reverse" [Laurence, 1939] use their knowledge of the stock market's past behavior and a small test model to go back a few days into the past to make enough money to complete a bigger machine.

In "Forever Is Not So Long" [Reeds, 1942] knowledge of the future proves to be a curse. On the night of the first human trip in time, the traveler says good-by to his fiance and departs ten years into the future. It is England 1931 that night, and the future looks bright and inviting. When he steps out into 1941, however, he of course finds devastation and death. Indeed, he learns that he was (will be) blown to bits at Dunkirk and that his wife, "now" a widow, lost an arm in a German air attack. So back he goes to 1931, where the words of greeting from his wife-to-be are hollow with irony: "We'll be the happiest people in the world, Steve. The happiest, gayest, most in love people in the world. And we'll go on being that, Steve—forever." Agreeing with Reeds is the Russian writer Dmitri Bilenkin. In "The Ban" [Bilenkin, 1978] a physicist tries to discourage research into "left-spiraling photons," particles that can carry information into the past. He does this because he is convinced knowledge of the future will cause only unhappiness. And in another story, "The Inexorable Finger of Fate" [Bilenkin, 1978], a man tunes-in a news broadcast from tomorrow; the result is only grief.

Egomaniacs would find time machines useful, too. In "Ghost Lecturer" [Watson, TT], for example, the inventor of the "Roseberry Field" uses it to "yank past geniuses out of time, supposedly to honor them so they would know their lives had been worthwhile in the eyes of the future. But then he would go on to tell them—oh so kindly—where they had gone wrong or fallen short of the mark. And how much more we know nowadays. 'You almost got it right, boy! You were on the

right track, and no mistake. Bravo! *But ... .'* " Watson makes the interesting observation that one can easily imagine playing this pathetic game of Whig history
with scientists, but what could even the most talented modern do to upstage a
Mozart or a Shakespeare?

Some Problems

The seductiveness of the past has never been written about better than by Jack
Finney, who has practically made writing fiction on this theme his speciality; see
in particular his "The Third Level" [Finney, 1986]. The past isn't necessarily any
better than the present, however, as is made clear in the humorous story "Status
Quondam" (with the perfect generic Latin title suitable for any story about time
travel to the past) by P. Schuyler Miller [Miller, 1951]. Tired of the mid-twentieth
century, the hero travels to Greece in the fifth century B.C., only to be grateful in
the end to escape literally with just his skin. (His initial attempt to return to the
present falls a bit short, with his appearance in the nude in 1895 in the midst of a
group of Victorians touring "modern" Athens.)

Boucher [1980a], however, has made the interesting observation that in the
nude may actually be the most reasonable way for a time traveler to appear. As we
are told in "Barrier," nakedness is the one costume common to all ages, and we
are asked, "which would astonish you more, a naked man, or an Elizabethan
courtier in full apparel?" Consider, for example, the time traveler from A.D. 5050
in "Time Tourist" [Murphy, 1951] who journeyed back to the twentieth century
wearing historically authenticated clothing—a blue serge Hoover coat, a Sinatra
silk butterfly tie, shiny red and yellow marching band pants, an opera hat, and
ballet shoes. As we learn to no surprise, he created quite a stir. The time travelers
in the 1984 movie *The Terminator* and in its 1991 sequel, *Terminator 2,* however,
arrive from the future naked. And in *The Year of the Quiet Sun* [Tucker, 1979], it
is said to be very expensive to transport weight through time—this novel's time
travelers travel nude to save money.

Less amusing was the visit to the past experienced by the protagonist of J. B.
Priestley's story "Look After the Strange Girl" [Priestley, 1953], who suddenly and
without explanation finds himself a half-century in the past, at a 1902 English
upper-crust party. It is the year after Queen Victoria's death, and the merrymakers
still have their nineteenth-century conviction that God smiles with particular
brightness on England. Our time hopper, however, knows of the approaching
horrors of the Great War and even the dates of the deaths of some of the people
present. In lonely words (similar to those of the space traveler in "Out Around
Rigel" [Wilson, SFT]) he realizes that "distance in time [is] apparently harder to
bear than distance in space ... back in his own time he would have felt less
desolate, he was certain, if he had suddenly found himself wandering on South
Cape, Tasmania, half the globe away from home. Was home, then, more in time
than in space?"

The unstated horror of a trip backward in time is, of course, that it would bring the dead past, filled with all its dead occupants, alive again, literally resurrected from dank and moldering graves. And could anything be more remote, more inaccessible, more dead and gone, than the past? The top of Mount Everest, the bottom of the Marianas Trench, the sands of Mars—none of these exotic places can even be mentioned in the same breath with *the past*. I recall, with a shiver, the opening words to a story that perfectly captures the mystery, fascination, the horror the past holds for us. See if you react as I do to Reginald Bretnor's first line in "The Past and Its Dead People" [Bretnor, 1956]: "When Dr. Flitter came into the room, it seemed as though the past and its dead people came in with him, clinging to him like stale surgery smells, like the cold sweat of ancient autopsies."

Emily Webb's words in the last quote that opens this chapter are perhaps a warning that we should not ignore. In *The Devil in Crystal* [Marlow, 1944] the time traveler anticipates a meeting with a long-dead lover as he "shivered with a renewal of horror ... She ought to be grateful to him for having raised her from the dead, even briefly." The horror of the "dead alive again" is graphically detailed in *The Victorian Chaise Longue* [Laski, 1954]. Once the central character realizes that her mind has traveled back in time, almost a century, to the body of another, the terror begins: "This body I am in, it must have rotted filthily, this pillowcase must be a tatter of rag, the coverlet corrupt with moth, crisp and sticky with matted moths' eggs, falling away into dirty crumbling scraps. It's all dead and rotten—these hands, all this body stinking, rotten, dead. She shuddered, and knew she was shuddering in a body long ago dead. Her flesh crawled away, and it was flesh that had turned green and liquescent and at last become damp dust with the damp crumbling coffin wood."

Certainly no one better captured the horror of a similiar communication across time with the past than did Ambrose Bierce [Bierce, 1964] and H. P. Lovecraft [Lovecraft, 1982]. Bierce's "John Bartine's Watch" is the story of a Tory traitor who was executed by the American rebels, only to reappear in a ghastly manner, across a hundred years, in the body of his great-grandson. Lovecraft's weird, macabre tale "The Shadow Out of Time" tells about Professor N. Wingate Peaslee of Miskatonic University and about his astonishing discovery that his mind has been among grotesque creatures that inhabited Earth 150 million years ago. (Mental time travel still appears now and then in fiction, as in H. Beam Piper's "Time and Time Again" [Piper, 1983].) The stories by Bierce and Lovecraft are time-travel horrors in the marvelously disgusting (I say this in admiration, by the way) tradition of Poe. Indeed, Poe himself experimented with time travel via exchanges of personal identity (see his 1844 "A Tale of the Ragged Mountains" [Franklin, 1966]), but as I have already explained, this is not a time-travel mechanism of interest in this book.

The potential for horror almost certainly explains why Jack the Ripper, whose identity is still unknown, has been speculated to have been a time traveler (see "A Toy for Juliette" [Bloch, DV] and "The Prowler in the City at the Edge of the World" [Ellison, DV]). A time traveler, by definition, can strike literally at any time, and to imagine Jack suddenly materializing behind you while walking on a dark, foggy London street is a bit unnerving.[4] The 1979 movie *Time After Time* played on this idea, with Jack fleeing to modern-day San Francisco after stealing a time machine, with H. G. Wells himself in hot pursuit. When Wells' brilliant work *The Time Machine* appeared in serial form in 1895 in the *New Review*, the *Review of Reviews* called the author "a man of genius" but then ended its notice with "he has an imagination as gruesome as that of Poe" [Parrinder, 1972].

A trip into the past would require careful planning and not just a little crafty caution. As the opening line to L. P. Hartley's 1954 novel *The Go-Between* says, "The past is a foreign country: they do things differently there." To be different may possibly invite unpleasant attention, as the time traveler in *Berkeley Square* [Balderston, 1941] learns to his unhappy surprise. By revealing the knowledge of a 1928 man to people he meets in 1784, he first arouses nervous glances and then outright hostility and fear. The time traveler in *The Devil in Crystal* [Marlow, 1944] knows the danger he runs from the start. As he thinks to himself while in the midst of friends: "Will they notice anything funny about me? They'd tear me to pieces if they found out! Alien, as no one else could be alien. They couldn't stand it if they knew! The only thing would be to kill me."

I know of no stories, however, that better capture the pathos a trip back in time might have or the plight of being trapped out of one's normal time in the foreign land of yesterday than "The Man Who Came Early" [Anderson, 1988a], "The Doctor" [Thomas, AO] and "The Ugly Little Boy" [Asimov, T3]. Anderson's sad tale is of a modern soldier suddenly hurled a thousand years into the past (as was the archaeologist in *Lest Darkness Fall* [de Camp, 1941]) by a powerful electrical storm. Even his high-technology weapons cannot save the solider from a brutal end in the violent tenth-century world of warrior Iceland. Thomas tells of the tragic fate of a medical doctor, the lone survivor of the first time-travel expedition gone terribly wrong. Trapped half-a-million years in the past, he is doomed to live out his life among primitive cave dwellers. And Asimov's novella, perhaps one of the most moving of all time-travel stories, tells us of a nurse who refuses to let a little Neanderthal boy be sent back to the past alone. She has come to love him as her own, and when the scientists who plucked him out of time grow weary of him, she goes back with him—to unknowable, almost surely fatal dangers.

Backward in Time—Can It Really Be Done?

The question we must address before going one step further is the obvious one—is *physical* time travel to the past possible? It is one thing to say special relativity permits us to travel to the future, but quite another to ask if we can come back (and our present is, of course, the future's past). As we study this question throughout the rest of this book we will find, as Professor Monte Cook [Cook, 1982] put it, that "travel through time is an odd business" and, in particular, that "travel to the past" is when "time travel is at its oddest."

Science fiction writers, ironically, are generally not enthusiastic boosters of what Polish writer Stanislaw Lem calls "chronomotion" (or alternatively "chronokinesis," a word invented by science fiction writer and editor Anthony Boucher). Isaac Asimov unequivocally rejected backward time travel. (A glance at the Bibliography, however, shows that he loved to write stories using the idea.) For example, he wrote in [Asimov, 1984b] that "The dead giveaway that true time travel is flatly impossible arises from the well-known 'paradoxes' it entails ... So complex and hopeless are the paradoxes ... so wholesale is the annihilation of any reasonable concept of causality, that the easiest way out of the irrational chaos that results is to suppose that true time travel [Asimov's term for travel at will via a machine under human control both forward and backward in time] is, and forever will be, impossible." Asimov was never inconsistent in his views, and more recently in an essay prompted by the *Peggy Sue* movie he wrote [Asimov, 1986a]: "In many science-fiction stories, the trip into the past is by way of some futuristic machine that can take you through time at will ... That, however, is totally impossible on theoretical grounds. It can't and won't be done." And later, in the Introduction to Damon Knight's time-travel story "Anachron," Asimov stated [Knight, 1987]: "To my way of thinking it is precisely because time travel involves such fascinating paradoxes that we can conclude, even in the absence of other evidence, that time travel is impossible."

Asimov's fellow science fiction writer, Arthur C. Clarke, however, hedges a tiny bit, first declaring [Clarke, 1972] that "I feel certain (well, practically certain!) that time travel is impossible," and later [Clarke, 1985] that "I do not take time travel very seriously; nor, I think does anyone else." Certainly Basil Davenport didn't; writing in his Introduction to Olaf Stapledon's impressively massive (if often ponderous) "history of the Universe" [Stapledon, 1953], Davenport observed, "There appears to be more objective evidence for apparitions of the dead—ghosts— ... than for the possibility of time travel."

Some early science fiction fans shared this particular view; in the January 1933 issue of *Astounding Stories*, one Letter-to-the-Editor declared, "No one can travel forward or backward in time ... I believe that it will be possible, mechanically at some time, to communicate with the spirits of the departed, but this other—I can't see it!" And if a believer did surface, others were quick to pounce. For example, when P. Schuyler Miller (an early fan who later authored at least two time-travel classics [Miller, FSFS]) wrote a Letter-to-the-Editor at *Astounding Stories* (June 1931) stating that "there is nothing in physics ... to prevent you from going into the past ... and shaking hands with yourself or killing yourself," he got this in reply (*Astounding Stories*, Dec. 1933): "P. S. Miller once wrote that time traveling is not incompatible with any laws of physics ... 'he don't know from nothin.' " This intemperate letter did offer up an interesting technical objection: "Time traveling is impossible because it is contrary to the laws of conservation of mass and energy." (I will pursue this concern and its answer in Chapters Two and Four.)

Taking the contrary position and arguing for the rationality of time travel is the eminent philosopher David Lewis, who began a famous essay [Lewis, 1976] with the lines "Time travel, I maintain, is possible. The paradoxes of time travel are oddities, not impossibilities. They prove only this much, which few would have doubted: that a possible world where time travel took place would be a most strange world, different in fundamental ways from the world we think is ours."

Robert Forward, until 1987 a senior scientist on the Director's staff at the Hughes Research Laboratories, thinks similarly. Writing as a long-time researcher in experimental general relativity, he declares [Forward, 1988] with admirable optimism: "Some of us now living may ... wonder [after time machines have been invented] about those ancient philosophers of the twentieth century who worried so much about those 'time machine paradoxes.' "

There are many besides Asimov and Clarke, however, who think Lewis and Forward are wrong. The "hard science" science fiction writer Larry Niven, for example, is so convinced of the impossibility of time travel that he has elevated its denial to a metaphysical law [Niven, 1971]:

NIVEN'S LAW: IF THE UNIVERSE OF DISCOURSE PERMITS THE POSSIBIL-ITY OF TIME TRAVEL AND OF CHANGING THE PAST, THEN NO TIME MACHINE WILL BE INVENTED IN THAT UNIVERSE.

A weakened form of Niven's law is the idea that if a Universe does allow the creation of a time machine, then its use will change the past to undo the invention. As I write, for example, the wormhole time machine (see Tech Note 9) is the one being talked about most, and one commentator has invoked a sort of Niven-type argument against it [Clarke, 1990]. After conceding the remote possibility that a stable wormhole might somehow be formed, Clarke asks what might happen if one really tried to use it as a time machine. His answer: "The most likely outcome [is] that the back-reaction of the physical fields on the space-time would destroy the time machine." Clarke's view was actually anticipated in fiction ("Time Bomb" [Zahn, 1988]) with vivid descriptions of quantum field back reactions on all attempts to build a theoretically possible time machine. But Niven would prob-ably not accept even a slight possibility of time travel. He simply says "No time machines! Ever! Period!" (As with Asimov, however, the Bibliography shows Niv-en's fascination with the concept.) David Gerrold dedicated his now classic time-travel novel, *The Man Who Folded Himself* [Gerrold, 1973], to Niven: "A good friend who believes that time travel is impossible. He's probably right." Just as blunt as Niven is the physicist Milton Rothman, who flatly declares [Rothman, 1988] that "no one will ever build a time-travel machine."

Murray Leinster had one of his characters in "Interference" [Leinster, BML] actually offer up an impossibility proof: "There was a guy proved that if you could travel in time you'd have to pass through all the time in between where you started from and where you went, and passing through means being there, so you'd have to spread out through all the time in between. And if you were spread out over a coupla hundred years it would be the same thing as being spread out over a coupla hundred miles ... Not healthy." One well-known philosopher has offered an even more succint impossibility proof [Smart, 1963]: "Motion is rate of change of *space* [my emphasis] with respect to time, and so we cannot have motion through time." (I find this proof-by-grammar to be completely unconvincing.) An interesting variation on Niven's law is an anthropic one that says time-travel paradoxes are actually acceptable as long as there are no conscious, intelligent entities in the Universe to be aware of them [Gribbin and Rees, 1989]; that is, a paradox isn't really a paradox unless there is somebody around to be bothered by it! This strikes me as being a conceited and completely unacceptable argument.

Smart, however, speaks for many. One author, to demonstrate how utterly implausible was Ernest Lawrence's plan to build a one-hundred-million-volt cyclotron just before the start of the Second World War, wrote that "Lawrence's project for a hundred million volts was no more practicable than a time machine."[5] For Professor Smart and those of his persuasion, time traveling is even more unlikely than is the impossibility (as declared by Robert Louis Stevenson) of "welding ice and iron."

The Problem of Paradoxes

The change-the-past paradox was well established even in early science fiction. In a story originally published in 1936, "Tryst in Time" [Moore, 1975], we find the paradox explicitly stated, along with a possible solution that is similar to the kind of explanations that have appeared more recently in the philosophical literature (e.g., [Fulmer, 1980]):

> "Suppose you landed in your own past?," queried Eric.
>
> Dow smiled.
>
> "The eternal question," he said. "The inevitable objection to the very idea of time travel. Well, you never did, did you? You know it never happened!"

A few years later in 1944, during his first comic-strip trip in time back to ancient Rome, Batman reveals his secret identity without concern because, as he correctly explains, history shows that his identity is not known to the present as knowledge from the past, so revealing it cannot possibly pose a danger.

Martin Gardner, however, who for years wrote the acclaimed "Mathematical Games" column in *Scientific American*, thinks that time travel will be, at best, enormously difficult precisely because of the paradoxes that philosopher David Lewis so boldly accepted in the previous section [Gardner, 1974]. The classic change-the-past paradox is, of course, the so-called grandfather paradox, which poses the question of what happens if an assassin goes back in time and murders his grandfather before his (the murderer's) own father is born? If his father is never born, then neither is the assassin and so how can he go back to murder his grandfather...!? (In an amusing observation [Hollinger, 1987] notes that "this is never posed as a 'Father Paradox.' It is as if [science fiction] is evading the Oedipal aspects implicit in its favorite model of temporal paradox." Soon afterward, however, Cal Tech physicist Kip Thorne began to refer to the paradox of a time traveler killing his own mother, so time travel *is* sexually unbiased when it comes to backward murder.)

One story, "Status Quondam" [Miller, 1951], pushes the grandfather paradox to its logical limit to show the dangers for a time traveler of combat in the past. Having traveled to Greece in the fifth century B.C., the protagonist suddenly realizes (with just a little exaggeration): "Ninety-five generations back you'd have more grandfathers than there are people on Earth, or stars in the Galaxy! You're kin to everyone ... You as much as take a poke at anyone, and the odds are you won't even get to be a twinkle in your daddy's eye." An earlier story, "Ancestral Voices" [Schachner, 1933], illustrated this point in a graphic way—in A.D. 452 a time traveler shoots and kills one of Attila's Huns (who would have been his many-times-removed great-grandfather!); the result is that 50,000 of the Hun's descendents vanish. In "The Time Imposter" [Schachner, 1934] Schachner repeated his idea, so dramatic was it for his readers. (In Chapter Four we will see why this particular view, while entertainingly provocative, is illogical.)

The idea of killing ancestors in the past is used to great effect in the 1984 film *The Terminator*. In this film a time-traveling robot-killer from the future of 2029 appears in the Los Angeles of the present to murder the woman who will (already has?) give(n) birth to a son who has (will have?) enemies in the future. In the 1985 movie *Back to the Future*, a comedy spoof of this potential sexual paradox, Marty McFly uses the plutonium-powered "flux-capacitor" to travel back to the 1955 high-school days of his parents. When he accidently almost prevents his parents from marrying (the reason, of course, for his own existence), Marty is horrified to see himself fading out of an old picture of the family that he carries in his wallet.

As one philosopher [Horwich, 1987] has observed, it is, of course, not necessary to kill your grandfather, or even more remote ancestors as in Schachner's stories, to cause a paradox. Using the Marty McFly approach you could commit or *try* to commit what Horwich calls "autofanticide," the killing of yourself as an infant. This idea was anticipated by the Russian writer Grigoriev, who presented it clearly in "Vanya" [Grigoriev, LDA], a story in which the time machine itself is the direct instrument of "not-being." An earlier version of this same idea is in "Perfect Murder" [Gold, SFAD]. One science fiction solution to the "killing your ancestors or your younger self" paradoxes is that somehow the murder fails to take place; e.g., the gun jams, the knife blade snaps, a wind gust blows the poison dart off target, the murderer faints just before he can do the foul deed, etc., etc. No matter how many times the murderer tries and no matter how clever his scheme, he fails. Such an explanation was offered by C. L. Moore in her 1936 story "Tryst in Time."

This particular problem of the unchangeability of past events is of particular interest to theologians, because it is directly related to the question of free will versus fatalism; i.e., are humans the creators of the future or are they mere fated puppets of destiny? Is a time traveler to the past unable to alter events because that was the only way they could happen? The Bible offers no definitive help on this issue. In his *Guidance to the Duties of the Heart*, the eleventh-century Jewish philosopher Bahya ibn Paquda lists several scriptural texts in support of predestination and yet another list in support of free will; e.g., compare Psalm 127 with Job 34:11. Bahya aptly presents his lists in the form of a dialogue between the (rational) mind and the (emotional) soul; in the dialogue the mind attempts to ease the soul of its concern with the "ills of the body," one of which is the conflict between free will and predestination.

That same ill is in "Typewriter from the Future" [Worth, 1950], which offers a solution: "The answer is quite simple. When the man goes back in time and kills his grandfather, and returns to his own time again, he finds to his surprise that he made a mistake. It was not his grandfather at all! And no matter how many times he goes back and kills his grandfather ... he always finds he made a mistake." A twist on this idea is that a recurrent, psychological failure of will is the critical factor, as in [Knight, 1961]. This moving story, "Time Enough," has a thirty-year-old man continually trying to relive and reshape the painful boyhood incident that warped his emotional development. He fails again and again, but of course there is always "time enough" to try one more time.

Or perhaps the time traveler never gets a second chance. In one of Robert Silverberg's stories, "The Assassin" [Silverberg, SFS], for example, the doomed hero journeys back to 1865 to save Lincoln from Booth—but his "time-distorter" is quickly taken from him by suspicious guards. Its internal workings tick and they think he is an assassin with a bomb. They destroy it, haul him away to his fate, and Lincoln goes on to meet his.

L. Sprague de Camp's story "A Gun for Dinosaur" [de Camp, 1978] puts forth the terrifying idea that nature itself will take any corrective action required to avoid paradoxes (or "chronoclasms," as Wyndham called them in "The Chronoclasm" [Wyndham, 1956]). de Camp's story has two big-game hunter-guides using "Professor Prochuska's time machine at Washington University" (built with the aid of a "cool thirty million" dollar grant from the Rockefeller Foundation) run a safari-for-hire business taking hunters back to the late-Mesozoic era. When a disgruntled client tries to go back to the day before a previous trip (to shoot the guides, who had, or rather would, displease him the following day), we learn just how nasty de Camp thinks Mother Nature might be in order to avoid a paradox. (The guides had, of course, *not been* shot on the original safari, and so they *could not be* shot): "The instant James started [to ambush the guides] the space-time forces snapped him forward to the present to prevent a paradox. And the violence of the passage practically tore him to bits [making his body look] as if every bone in it had been pulverized and every blood vessel burst, so it was hardly more than a slimy mass of pink protoplasm."

Ray Bradbury's classic "A Sound of Thunder" [Bradbury, 1980] also uses the dinosaur-hunting idea, but it does allow for changing the past. On one such trip a client fails to follow instructions, accidently kills a butterfly, and so causes enormous changes in history, as indicated by the "before" and "after" versions of the time-machine company's ad:

before

TIME SAFARI, INC.
SAFARIS TO ANY YEAR IN THE PAST.
YOU NAME THE ANIMAL.
WE TAKE YOU THERE.
YOU SHOOT IT.

after

TYME SEFARI INC.
SEFARIS TU ANY YEER EN THE PAST.
YU NAIM THE ANIMALL.
WEE TAEK YU THAIR.
YU SHOOT ITT.

Bradbury describes the death of the butterfly as having started the knocking "down [of] a line of small dominoes and then big dominoes and then gigantic dominoes, all down the years across Time." This is, of course, a somewhat unconvincing argument. After all, previous dinosaurs, when shot, must have fallen to the ground and destroyed a lot of butterflies! With such threats for every decision, no matter how seemingly innocent, hanging over the head of a time traveler, it would take a brave soul to do much more than to stand still and just breathe while in the past. Indeed, a recent novel, *Krono* [Harness, 1988], introduces the curious idea of prospective time travelers to the past being required first to file Historical Impact Statements with the proper authorities.

Not all would receive permission. In "The Rescuer" [Porges, SFS], for example, we have the story of a time traveler who takes a rifle and five thousand rounds of explosive bullets back to Golgotha. His intention—to be history's first Rambo by picking off any Roman soldier who gets within a hundred yards of Jesus! Even as outrageous as this concept is (but who among those now reading this won't admit to at least a momentary thrill at the idea, and perhaps even a secret willingness to do it yourself, if you could), it isn't the story's peak. That comes when the reader is reminded that it was Christ's desire to die on the Cross, that he had to die for our sins; to prevent that from happening would change all of history. So what should the time-traveler's colleagues do when they discover his plan? Should they stop him or not? What might happen if they do interfere? A twist on the idea of a time traveler saving Jesus is in "Un Brilliant Sujet" [Rigaut, 1970], in which the time traveler commits many disturbed acts in the past, including murdering the infant Jesus with an injection of potassium cyanide. Similarly, David Gerrold has used changing-the-past with an equally chilling effect in *The Man Who Folded Himself*

[Gerrold, 1973]. A time traveler experiments with "making things different"—in his words (and the last word is particularly horrible): "Once I created a world where Jesus Christ never existed. He went out into the desert to fast and never came back. The twentieth century I returned to was—different. Alien."

This is an old idea, of course. Mark Twain had Satan give a good lecture on it in an early draft (written before the turn of the century) of his last novel, *No. 44, The Mysterious Stranger*: "If at any time—say in boyhood—Columbus had skipped the triflingest little link in the chain of acts projected and made inevitable by his first childish act, it would have changed his whole subsequent life, and he would have become a priest and died obscure in an Italian village, and America would not have been discovered for two centuries afterward. I know this. To skip any one of the billion acts in Columbus' chain would have wholly changed his life. I have examined his billion of possible careers, and in only one of them occurs the discovery of America."

Less well known than these tales is the far more horrifying one, "Brooklyn Project," [Tenn, 1983] by Penn State English professor Philip Klass, who writes under the pen-name of William Tenn. In this story the first major experiment in time travel results in horrendous changes, with humans as observers at the start, but at the end altered into things with "purple blobs" on "slime-washed forms." The irony of this story comes from the reader's knowledge of what has happened, all the while the once-human characters "see" nothing happen.

Taking the opposite approach in tampering with the past is "Thus We Frustrate Charlemagne" [Lafferty, AO]. Here the tampering is intentional, done for the specific purpose of observing the changes in the present caused by a single, precise alteration centuries in the past. In this story the past is treated something like a lump of Play-Doh. A similar approach to time travel is in *Lord Kelvin's Machine* [Blaylock, 1992]. As [Herbert, 1988] poetically declares: "Disembarking in the past without warning, uninvited guests from the future would be free to change crucial events, the effect of these changes rippling through time to modify the present drastically. The ability to willfully change the past amounts to a virtual omnipotence over human history. No mere temporal tourists, these doughty travelers in time. Omniscience, omnipresence, and omnipotence are the traditional attributes of divinity. The power to execute U-turns on time's one-way street would make time travelers nothing less than gods." (Note that this is not the prevailing philosophical position.)

The idea that the past might be changed and then consciously changed back again if things don't improve is, interestingly, *not* a common one in fiction. The earliest example of it that I know of is in the stage play *The Star-Wagon* [Anderson, 1937] by Maxwell Anderson. Here a proverbial self-taught inventor, when told by his wife of thirty-five years that perhaps their marriage has been a mistake, travels back to 1902 to give them both a chance to make a new future. When once again we see them in 1937, matters are much worse with their new mates. So, back again goes the time traveler to 1902 to put things back the way they were. More recently, the "change-the-past-until-you-get-it-right" idea has appeared in the novel *Changing the Past* [Berger, 1989]—the dust jacket of this novel cleverly shows an eraser against a blank background.

The Fictional Origins of "Change the Past"

In a January 1963 personal letter to the editor of *The Magazine of Fantasy and Science Fiction*, Robert Heinlein wrote [GG]: "Mark Twain invented the time-travel story; six years later H. G. Wells perfected it *and its paradoxes* [my emphasis]. Between them they left little for latecomers to do." How a man as widely read as Heinlein, who was the author of two of the best time-travel short stories ever written [Heinlein AHT, MI], could write such an erroneous statement is a mystery to me: *A Connecticut Yankee in King Arthur's Court* and *The Time Machine*, while works of genius, are *not* pioneers in paradox. And Heinlein's own stories are proof enough that there was a lot left to do with time travel well after 1900.

The very first story to be written that even hints at the particular time-travel paradox of changing-the-past seems to be by the Unitarian minister Edward Everett Hale (1822–1909), best known now as the author of the 1863 story "The Man Without a Country." Hale wrote "Hands Off" in 1881 (and published it anonymously in *Harper's New Monthly Magazine* [Hale, 1986]) with the expressed purpose of stirring up some theological debate (which it didn't), and he had no idea he would come to be recognized by scholars as a pioneer in the yet-to-be-invented genre of science fiction.

The story opens with the mysterious words "I was in another stage of existence. I was free from the limits of Time, and in new relations to space." These words were written by an unnamed narrator who seems just to have died and who finds himself in his new form observing "some twenty or thirty thousand solar systems" while in the company of "a Mentor so loving and so patient." Under the guidance of this Mentor, the narrator alters the Biblical account of Joseph and his imprisonment in Egypt. At first subsequent history is better, but then humanity sinks into irreversible depravity. In the end the narrator watches the last handful of humans kill each other at that most symbolic place for all the Christian world: "The last of these human brutes all lay stark dead on the one side and on the other side of the grim rock of Calvary!" There would be no Crucifixion and Resurrection for the salvation of humankind, which naturally greatly disturbs the narrator. But the Mentor calms him, saying "Do not be disturbed, you have done nothing." It has, after all, been just an experimental world, an alternate Universe, and the narrator has learned his lesson of "Hands Off."

Hale's story, of course, is a better Sunday sermon than it is a change-the-past time-travel story, and the device of experimenting on a not really real Earth is disappointing from a modern science fiction point of view. But Hale's story almost certainly did have an immediate impact. There is no proof, but with its appearance in a national magazine it seems likely that it was read by Edward Page Mitchell (1852–1927), an editor on the daily New York newspaper the *Sun*. Just six months after Hale's story appeared, the *Sun*, in its issue of 18 September 1881 printed

Mitchell's "The Clock That Went Backward." This story, published anonymously, was both the first to use a machine for time travel *and* the first to incorporate a time-travel paradox as its central idea. The story predates Wells' *Time Machine* by fourteen years, and Wells' novel did not even include a paradoxical element.

The mechanism of Mitchell's time machine, an eight-foot-high, sixteenth-century Dutch clock, is quite simplistic, even bordering on fantasy. It is simply stated that if the clock runs backward, then it travels backward in time—a rather disappointing explanation. The same idea was used eight years later (still six years before Wells) by Lewis Carroll in his *Sylvie and Bruno*, which featured the "Out-landish Watch." This marvelous timepiece "has the peculiar property that, instead of *its* going with the *time*, the *time* goes with *it*." That is, the time its hands are set to *is* the time. So attractive is this idea that it is still occasionally used; e.g., [Wilhelm, 1975]. Like Carroll, Mitchell did not provide a scientifically plausible reason for the remarkable property of his clock. (The story is, of course, typical Carroll nonsense and, indeed, since his story was for children, Carroll wanted to avoid anything plausible.)

It was Wells who took the last, crucial step of presenting a science-based rationale for the workings of a time machine. This is the original contribution that Wells introduced in his *The Time Machine*. Ever since these stories of Hale, Mitchell, and Wells, then, the question of changing, or trying to change, the past has been one of the fundamental puzzles of time travel via a scientifically explained machine. The fascination of this puzzle is difficult to exaggerate.

An old 1960s television science fiction program, "The Outer Limits," for example, did an interesting production of a story about changing the past (and the future) called "The Man Who Was Never Born" (available today on videotape). A horribly deformed man from two hundred years in the future travels backward in time to kill the scientist whose research will lead to the medical disaster that mutilates humankind (hence the time traveler's terrible physical appearance). He arrives rather too far back in time, however, and finds his target has not yet been born. He locates the mother-to-be, though, and prevents her marriage by the simple act of bringing her back with him to his world of the future. Thus is the birth of her baby prevented and this does indeed change history. But there is an unexpected twist—the title refers not only to the unborn scientist but to the time traveler himself, as he was never born in the new future, either. He vanishes, leaving a very confused young lady to try and sort things out.

Another author [Locke, PSF] made the point that perhaps the past might be changed, but what happens after the change may be rather unpredictable. As his cleverly titled story "Demotion" opens, Mars has been settled for a century and a half, since five years after the end of the six-month World War III in 1960. (World War II had ended shortly after a Lieutenant Charles Leslie had bombed Berchtes-gaden and killed Hitler in 1943—this clearly is not "our history.") Faced with an apparently unresolvable military crisis with the settlers on Mars, the "Temporal Lab" concludes that the planet was opened up for colonization too soon. The initial rocket landing on Mars was headed by the then General Charles Leslie, and so they reach back in time, disable his rocket, and thus abort the landing.

Alas, the crisis is not undone. Things are a bit different back in the Temporal Lab now, but nobody notices since history after 1965 and memories have been revised. The problem with Mars is now thought to be solvable by not letting World War III end so quickly. This will be accomplished by canceling the event that resulted in the war's termination—the use of the first atomic bomb by none other than Colonel Charles Leslie. Once again Leslie will be denied. This is done, but still the Mars crisis persists.

Additional changes in the Temporal Lab have occurred, of course, but of course nobody notices. The new fix is to let World War II go on for a while more, and so the Berchtesgaden bombing is undone. Hitler lives and the Mars crisis at last ends. The story closes with Charles Leslie (who has had the high points of his entire military career blotted out, although of course nobody knows this since they didn't happen) leaving the Air Force after World War II, getting a Ph.D. in mathematics, and becoming a professor. (Presumably this is yet another demotion.) Professor Leslie's area of research is on how to change the past, and so the end result has been a future (with a history different from ours) changing the past to end up with our history via the manipulation of the life of a single individual who turns out to be the inventor of the theory that allows such changes to be made. The next time you have trouble getting to sleep, try mulling that over for a while!

Ways to Avoid Paradoxes

The various forms of changing-the-past paradoxes and of what seems to be a lack of free will are, of course, among the reasons why philosophers and theologians have been so attracted to the time-travel question. If a time traveler can visit the past and is able to change events, then paradoxes like killing your grandfather result. If the time traveler cannot change events, then *why* not? Is free will simply an illusion? And what if we could see the future? Could we then change it? Does it mean anything to talk about changing events that have not happened yet?

Interesting variations on *physical* backward time travel in science fiction, which neatly avoid the paradoxes caused by interacting with and affecting the past, use gadgets that let story characters hear or see the remote past without introducing paradox-producing changes (a concern specifically mentioned in the mind-transference story "Balsamo's Mirror" [de Camp, 1979]). This is, in fact, such an extraordinarily popular idea among science fiction writers that it has actually been mentioned in the technical literature. A recent example can be found in "Time Shards" [Benford, 1986]; Benford (who is a physicist) writes in an afterword that his story about what we might hear in a sound recording accidently made on a clay pot in the year A.D. 1280 was motivated by an actual letter to the world's preeminent electrical engineering journal [Woodbridge, 1969].

In fact, both Benford's and Woodbridge's ideas were preceded by years by the story of "The Sound-Sweep" (a play on the more familiar chimney sweep)

FIGURE 3. This illustration from "The Time Eliminator" (*Amazing Stories*, Dec. 1926) shows the inventor demonstrating his gadget to his future wife and father-in-law. Able to look back in time, the gadget's screen is displaying scenes from the older man's courtship, decades in the past.

Illustration for "The Time Eliminator" by Frank R. Paul, ©1926 by Experimenter Publishing Co.; reprinted by permission of the Ackerman Science Fiction Agency, 2495 Glendower Ave., Hollywood, CA 90027 for the Estate.

[Ballard, 1971].[6] Using a gadget called the sonovac, the sound-sweep removes extraneous and discordent noises such as coughing, crying, and the mumbling of prayer that have recorded themselves in the walls of churches. The residues of previous performances and of shuffling crowds in theaters get similiar treatment. This story, in turn, was preceded by decades by Gardner Hunting's novel *The Vicarion* [Hunting, 1926], which has a gadget called the Vicarion that reproduces scenes and sounds from the past from impressions indelibly imprinted on the ether (this device "makes vicarious experiences easy"). Hunting tried to show how such an instrument would violently disrupt society, an idea repeated in "The Dead Past" [Asimov, AHT].

Science fiction is simply bursting with gadgets for seeing the past that avoid the paradoxes of changing the past. For example, the "Palaeoscope" in "The Time Valve" [Breuer, 1932a], which was more constrained than was the Vicarion, had to be in actual physical contact with the object whose history was to be viewed. Eric Temple Bell [Bell, 1934] created "television in time" in his novel *Before the Dawn*; with this gadget one could see all the history of any object that had ever been exposed to light, no matter how long ago. The descriptions of ancient flash floods a thousand feet high and of the death agonies of decapitated dinosaurs still make absolutely horrifying reading. A similiar gadget called Tempevision is in *Traveller in Time* [Mitchell, 1936]; in "Through the Time-Radio" [Coblentz, 1938] Eskimos of the forty-first century use a time radio (which is similiar to Hunting's gadget, as is the obscurascope in "Matter is Conserved" [Palmer, 1938]) to watch the destruction of New York City in the twentieth century. The posthumously published, incomplete story "The Dark Tower" [Lewis, 1977] by C. S. Lewis, written before 1940, tells the story of the mysterious chronoscope that could see through time. And there is a gadget for filming the past in "E for Effort" [Sherred, 1983].

Some stories, however, have gadgets that can do much more than just see the past. In "Private Eye" [Padgett, 1984], for example, there is a device that can both hear and see the past and in "Brooklyn Project" [Tenn, 1983], there is the chronar for filming the past, which was able, in fact, to do much more. And Horace Gold, the editor of *Galaxy Science Fiction* magazine, invented in "The Biography Project" [Gold, MT] a Biotime Camera that can film the past. (This gadget was preceded by the similar "history-scanning machine" in "Forgotten Past" [Morrison, 1943]). John Wyndham conceived of the ultimate in voyeuristic time-peeking in "Operation Peep" [Wyndham, TC]. The gadgets in all these clever stories allow for *affecting* the past, not just for looking at it.

Reversing the time direction from the past and toward the future was John W. Campbell's probability wave tube in "Elimination" [Campbell, 1948] (also called, à la Lewis, the "chronoscope"); not only could it see all of the past, but in addition Campbell's gadget could display all possible futures. Eric Frank Russell's psychophone in "Mechanical Mice" [Russell, 1980], looking something like an old crystal radio set, let its inventor copy inventions from the future. Similiar to this was the scanner in "What You Need" [Padgett, OSF], which provided its

inventor with a livelihood selling people what they will need to survive an immi-
nent crisis; e.g., a pair of scissors to cut away a scarf suddenly caught in a printing
press. More utilitarian is the chrono-camera, an investigative tool used by the
police in *Time Bomb* [Tucker, 1955] to film what happened (will happen) at a
crime scene *before* the crime occurs. More ambitious is "The Evil Eye" [Gillespie,
NWF] and its camera that produces instant pictures of how whatever it photographs will appear twenty years *in the future.* "Johnny Cartwright's Camera"
[Bond, 1946] does the same thing, but it only has a reach of one day into the
future, while "A Most Unusual Camera" [Serling, TZ] can peek just five minutes
ahead. Lloyd Biggle, Jr.'s Chronus is a TV-Display gadget that shows the unalterable future to police detectives assigned to the "Department of Future Crime"
[Biggle, 1967]. In "Guilty As Charged" [Porges, CJSF] an unnamed gadget that can
look into the future reveals what a criminal trial of A.D. 2183 will be like. A
character in "Controlled Experiment," a 1963 episode of "The Outer Limits," uses
a Martian temporal condenser to watch a murder that will occur. In a spooky
analysis that treats the effect such future-looking gadgets as these would have on
society if in general use, Damon Knight's story of the Ozo [Knight, 1980] is a
cautionary tale in the best tradition of "Be careful of what you wish for—you might
get it."

Perhaps if she had read any of these gadget stories, Virginia Woolf would have
reconsidered her wishful words [Woolf, 1976] written shortly before her death in
1941: "Is it not possible—I often wonder—that things we have felt with great
intensity have an existence independent of our minds; are in fact still in existence?
And if so, will it not be possible, in time, that some device will be invented by
which we can tap them? ... Instead of remembering here a scene and there a
sound, I shall fit a plug into the wall; and listen in to the past. I shall turn up August
1890."

A second fictional way to squirm out of the change-the-past/free-will problem
was conceived by John R. Pierce, who wrote in "Mr. Kinkaid's Pasts" [Pierce,
1954]: "There is no unique past! The uncertainty principle of Heisenberg, which
philosophers use to assure us that the world is not a predestined machine, without
room for free will, leading to one unique future, just as decisively contradicts the
idea of a unique past ... there is an infinity of pasts which are consistent with all the
evidences in our present Universe, and any of these pasts is as much the real past
as any other." In other words, the state of the world now neither determines the
state tomorrow nor was the state today determined by the state yesterday. Thus,
no paradox can result from tampering with the past since the state of the past does
not matter anyway! (This is the fictional echo of the words of the Russian religious
philosopher Nikolai Berdyaev (1874–1948), who wrote:[7] "The past which we so
much admire has never really existed—it is but a creation of our own imagination
which cleanses it from all evil and ugliness. The past we so love belongs to eternity
and never existed in bygone ages: it is merely a composite part of our present;
there was another present in the past as it actually was, a present with all its own
evils and shadows.")

Unlike Pierce's character, who argues that one can tweak the past without limit and without paradox, the approach of Fritz Leiber is probably the classic of those stories that assert it is very difficult to change the past. In "Try and Change the Past," [Leiber, SFS] a sequel to his 1958 novel *The Big Time* [Leiber, 1976] about the Change War (a war fought by time travelers who attempt to change the past), Leiber wrote: "Change one event in the past and you get a brand new future? Erase the conquests of Alexander by nudging a Neolithic pebble? Extirpate America by pulling up a shoot of Sumerian grain? Brother, that isn't the way it works at all! The space-time continuum's built of stubborn stuff and change is anything but a chain-reaction. Change the past and you start a wave of changes moving futureward, but it damps out mighty fast. Haven't you ever heard of temporal reluctance, or the Law of the Conservation of Reality?" Or, as he wrote in the original novel itself, which told about the Change Winds, the ripple effect of a change in the past that blows into the future "thousands of times faster than time moves:" "Most of us [begin as participants in the Change War] with the false metaphysic that the slightest change in the past—a grain of dust misplaced—will transform the whole future. It is a long time before we accept with our minds as well as our intellects the law of the Conservation of Reality: that when the past is changed, the future changes barely enough to adjust, barely enough to admit the new data. The Change Winds meet maximum resistance always." L. Sprague de Camp put forth this same philosophy in *Lest Darkness Fall* [de Camp, 1941]: "History is a four-dimensional web. It is a tough web ... . If a man did slip back [in time], it would take a terrible lot of work to distort it. Like a fly in a spider web that fills a room."

Much later Aldiss in the novel *An Age* [Aldiss, 1967] went beyond Leiber and de Camp and denied that any change could occur at all from the actions of time travelers: "They were walled off completely from the reality all round them. They were spectres, unable to alter by the slightest degree the humblest appurtenances of this world [of the past]—unable to kick the smallest pebble out of the way—unless it was by haunting it they altered the charisma of the place."

The immutability of the past, and its consequent immunity to paradox, is not a new idea or even one unique to science fiction. We find it, for example, in "Roads of Destiny," one of O. Henry's most celebrated stories from the turn-of-the-century. In this story a young poet is faced with a decision with three possible choices. We follow him down all three, and find that ultimately it makes no difference—each results in his death by a single shot from the same pistol. This fatalistic philosophy is also stated in "When the Bough Breaks" [Padgett, BTS]. When time travelers from the future inform a man in the present that they are going to make some changes but nothing serious will happen in response, he asks, "The past, you mean it's plastic?" They reply, "Well, it affects the future. You can't alter the past without altering the future, too. But things tend to drift back. There is a temporal norm, a general level. In the original time sector [we were not here]. Now that's changed. So the future will be changed. But not tremendously." An eerie Russian novel, *The Strange Life of Ivan Osokin* [Ouspensky, 1948], about a young man sent (by a magician) back twelve years in time expresses a harder version of this same view. As the magician explains to his client: "If you go back ... you will do the same things again and a repetition of all that happened before is inevitable. You will not escape from the wheel; everything will go on as before."

More successful at changing the past than was Ivan Osokin, although he comes to regret it, is the time traveler in "The Histronaunt" [Seabury, 1961]. Seabury, a professor of political science, wrote his tale as a parody (and a splendid one it is) of the arms race between the Soviet Union and the United States—only now the ultimate weapon is not the Bomb, but the (time) Machine. As Seabury tells us, the secret of time travel may be discovered by physicists, but its use as a weapon will be decided by historians. (Physicists, however, might take consolation in the thoughts of the time traveling historian in *Bring the Jubilee* [Moore, 1953] when he meets the inventor of the time machine: "I looked at her with respect. Anyone, I thought, can read a few books and set himself up as a historian: to be a physicist means genuine learning.") Seabury tells us that "at the Desert Springs Conference of Historiographical Manipulation, attended by a carefully selected group of Harvard and Berkeley historians, the matter was broached as calmly and fully as men can broach the fantastic. The selective manipulation of history dwarfed even the decision to use nuclear weapons in the Second World War: tampering with history was dangerous precisely because of the inability ... to judge the infinite ramifications of even the slightest change." Despite this inability, the histronaunt is given an assignment involving somewhat more than just a slight change—he travels back to 1917 and assassinates Lenin! When he returns, he finds 1968 Washington under curfew—by order of the German Gouverneur-General.

Equally successful in changing the world is a researcher in time travel in the 1956 tale "Aristotle and the Gun" [de Camp, 1972]. Deciding that what is wrong with the world can be traced to the scientific method getting off to a late start, he thinks he can correct matters by traveling back to 340 B.C. and educating Aristotle on the proper scientific attitude. (Aristotle, you see, believed that observing the real world was inferior to pure thinking about how things ought to work.) This the traveler does, with utterly disastrous consequences. He returns to the present to find a scientifically retarded world that makes him a slave. In his cell he writes on a wall the lesson he has learned too late—"Leave Well Enough Alone."

de Camp may well have written his story as a twist on Asimov's classic 1949 story "The Red Queen's Race" [Asimov, 1972], which puts forth a position now found in many modern philosophical papers. An idealistic physics professor, convinced that the world's political problems are the result of the comparative newness of scientific thought and tradition, tries to change the past (and thus the present) by sending a Greek translation of a modern chemistry text back 2000 years to the Hellenic days of Leucippus, Lucretius, and Democritus. He dies in the attempt, but succeeds in the transmission. When a government investigator (called in because the professor drained an entire nuclear reactor to power his time machine!) discovers that the transmission takes a day to travel back a hundred years, he fears "our" world will vanish in twenty days and be replaced by a "new" one. In the end, however, he learns you can't change the past that way. As one of the late professor's colleagues tells him: "While you are right that any change in the course of past events, however triffling, would have incalculable consequences ... I must point out that you are nevertheless wrong in your final conclusions. *Because THIS is the world in which the Greek chemistry text WAS sent back.*" (This story's conception of a time machine appeared a few years later in the philosophical literature [Gale, 1964]. The author called it "fantastic, yet nevertheless logically conceivable," but still could not bring himself to call it a time machine; his name for a device that runs backward a hundred years per minute was the "History of Philosophy Machine!")

In their stories Leiber, Asimov, and O. Henry have free will falling to defeat in the face of the overpowering dominance of predestination. There are, however, far more subtle problems with time travel than the question of free will versus predestination. Most physicists who have not thought very hard about time travel just ignore the paradoxes of time travel except to invoke them to "prove" time travel is impossible, much as Zeno's paradox was once used to prove motion is impossible, a proof shown to be false by the very act of moving one's hand to write the paradox down. The paradox, of course, as was well known from the very beginning, involves the puzzle of how apparently logical reasoning could result in such an obviously incorrect conclusion. (Zeno's argument is used in a fictional time-travel setting in "Dark Interlude" [Reynolds and Brown, GRSF1].) To prove by paradox is a risky business, as all such a line of reasoning may show is a lack of imagination and insight.

Physicist/philosopher David Malament of the University of Chicago forcefully rebutted the illogic of arguing-by-paradox when he wrote in [Malament, 1984] that one "view is that time travel ... is simply absurd and leads to logical contradictions. You know how the argument goes. If time travel were possible, one could go backward in time and undue the past. One could bring it about that both conditions P and not-P obtain at some point in spacetime. For example, I could go back and kill my earlier infant self making it impossible for that earlier self ever to grow up to be me. *I simply want to remark that arguments of this type have never seemed convincing to me ... The problem with these arguments is that they simply do not establish what they are supposed to* [my emphasis]. To be sure, if I could go back and kill my infant self, some sort of contradiction would arise. But the only conclusion to draw from this is that if I tried to go back and kill my infant self then, for some reason, I would fail. Perhaps I would trip at the last minute. The usual arguments do not establish that time travel is impossible, but only that if it *were* possible, certain actions could not be performed." This last point still bothers, of course, as it pulls in the issue of free will versus determinism.

Still, the grandfather paradox is commonly put forth by those who deny the rationality of even thinking about time travel, but who are seemingly unaware of the fatal logical flaw in their position. For example, in [Rothman, 1988] we find this statement: "the time-travel paradox, a classic in science fiction, forces us to consider what would happen if you could travel back in time so as to prevent the mating between your father and your mother. In that event you could not be born.

But if you were not born you could not travel back in time to prevent that fateful meeting. But then you would be born, etc., etc. Do you exist, or don't you. The paradox can not be untangled." There are other, far more subtle time-travel paradoxes than the now moot one put forth by Professor Rothman. (Modern philosophers mention grandfather-type paradoxes only to refute them à la Malament, and even the generally low-level and humorous [Blumenthal *et al.*, 1988] is correct in its treatment of the grandfather paradox.) These more interesting paradoxes will be discussed in Chapter Four.

The grandfather paradox is, as Rothman states, a classic. We find a version of it, for example, in the 1930 novel *The World Below* [Wright, 1930], in which the Professor tells us: "It is obviously impossible to project anything into the past, which is fixed irrevocably. Otherwise there would be no finality, and the confusion would be intolerable ... for instance, upon reading of a long-past murder, I could project myself into the past, and intervene to save the victim. In such event the murder would both have occurred, and been prevented: which is absurd." But of course Malament's argument and similiar arguments found in [Lewis, 1976] and [Horwich, 1987] (contrary to Rothman's assertion) *do* untangle the illogic of the Professor's paradox.

Where Are All the Time Travelers?

Arthur C. Clarke discusses a much more interesting objection to time travel than the "kill yourself" or other grandfather-type paradoxes. He writes [Clarke, 1985]: "The most convincing argument against time travel is the remarkable scarcity of time travelers. However unpleasant our age may appear to the future, surely one would expect scholars and students to visit us, if such a thing were possible at all. Though they might try to disguise themselves, accidents would be bound to happen—just as they would if we went back to Imperial Rome with cameras and tape-recorders concealed under our nylon togas. Time traveling could never be kept secret for very long." As a skeptic in "Time's Arrow" [McDevitt, FCW] explains Clarke's problem to a would-be time-machine inventor: "If it [time travel] *could* be done, someone will eventually learn how. If that happens, history would be littered with tourists. They'd be *everywhere*. They'd be on the *Santa Maria*, they'd be at Appomattox with Polaroids, they'd be waiting outside the tomb, for God's sake, on Easter morning." From the moment after the first time machine is constructed, through all the rest of civilization, there would be numerous historians (to say nothing of weekend sightseers) who would want to visit every important historical event in recorded history. They might each come from a different time in the future, but all would arrive at destinations crowded with temporal colleagues—crowds for which there is no historical evidence!

Philosophers are well aware of Clarke's objection; indeed, the objection considerably predates Clarke, being mentioned in [Farley, 1950]. For example, Fulmer [1980] writes: "Actually I know of only one argument against the possibility of time travel that seems to carry any weight at all. This is the fact that it does not appear ever to have happened. That is, it might be argued that there will be no time trips from 1985 to 1975, since we were here in 1975 and saw no time travelers. But this argument is far from conclusive." Professor Fulmer then mentions some possible explanations, but it is his last one that, contrary to his position, I find to be the most technically interesting: "Finally, and even less interesting to philosophers, there might be some pettifogging physical limitation on time travel: perhaps the energy expenditure varies as the fourth power of the time traversed, making only very short trips feasible, and its discovery lies too far in the future for its effects to have yet been felt."

Isaac Asimov used a variation of Fulmer's energy-limitation idea in "Button, Button" [Asimov, 1975], the story of Otto Schlemmelmayer's machine that can retrieve objects from the past—but only if they don't weigh too much. The problem is one of energy, with the relationship being an inverse exponential; all the power in the Universe could bring back maybe two grams. Robert Heinlein uses a similiar idea in *The Door Into Summer* [Heinlein, 1986]. As one character explains: "Now if there was some way to photograph the Crucifixion ... but there isn't. Not possible ... there isn't that much power on the globe. There's an inverse-square law tied up in [time travel]."

Clarke, always intellectually honest and with no ideaological position to defend, presents some other possible rebuttals from science fiction to his own objection. As Clarke writes: "Some science-fiction writers have tried to get round this difficulty [about where all the time travelers are] by suggesting that Time is a spiral; though we may not be able to move along it, we can perhaps hop from coil to coil, visiting so many millions of years apart that there is no danger of embarrassing collisions between cultures. Big game hunters from the future may have wiped out the dinosaurs, but the age of *Homo sapiens* may lie in a blind region which they cannot reach."

This particular idea of time as a spiral was popular in early science fiction; e.g., typical was "A Flight Into Time" [Wilson, 1931], in which the time traveler suddenly finds himself not in 1933 but in 2189. His situation is explained to him thus: " [the] time stream is curved helically in some higher dimension. In your case, a still further distortion brought two points of the coil into contact, and a sort of short circuit threw you into the higher curve." In "The Sands of Time" [Miller, FSFS], published in 1937, we find the same spiral-time concept; with a 60-million-year pitch to the time helix, there is no danger of a grandfather paradox. Spiral time is also the central scientific theme in the play *I Have Been Here Before* [Priestley, 1939] by J. B. Priestley.

The spiral time mentioned by Clarke, Wilson, and Miller is a close cousin to a circular-time concept. Circular time is the theme in "Wanderer of Time" [Fearn, MBSFS], in which the final thoughts of the time traveler (who has just been executed in an electric chair) are "They had done all this before somewhere—would do it again—endlessly, so long as Time itself should exist. Death—transition—rebirth—evolution—back again to the age of the amoeba—upward to man—the laboratory—the electric chair—Eternal. Immutable!"

More successful in his experiments with circular time than is Fearn's character is the time traveler in "Flight to Forever" [Anderson, LME], who finds after a trip one hundred years into the future that he can't get all the way back because the required energy rises exponentially with increasing time travel into the past (recall Professor Fulmer's suggestion). Still, it is very cheap in energy to go forward, and so he does that, in search of help from the future's advanced technology. He never finds what he needs, however, and so goes forward right into the collapse of the Universe and through a new Big Crunch/Big Bang that forms an identical new cycle of time. He thereby returns home just before he left. Again we have, as in Fearn's story, an eternal recycling of identical, circular time.[8] The experience is so terrifying that our hero decides to suppress what he has learned, and maybe that is why there are no apparent time travelers! There are, in fact, theoretical models of spacetime that lead to time travel to the past by traveling into the future, as, for example, in [Weingard, 1979b], but as Professor Weingard writes, this "is not quite what we are after. True, one can travel back in time *in the sense* of being able to travel to one's past. But this is done, not by really traveling back in time but by traversing the whole history of the Universe."

Stephen Hawking has recently invoked the "missing time travelers" argument as experimental evidence for his theoretical arguments in his "Chronology Protection Conjecture" [Hawking, 1992], in which he denies the possibility of time travel to the past because "we have not been invaded by hordes of tourists from the future." Not everybody finds the lack (so far) of such mass visitations from the future to be as compelling as Hawking does in denying time travel (see Thorne's rebuttal in Note 21 for this chapter). For example, in [Kriele, 1990b] we read: "The assumption of chronology is a serious drawback because chronology violation can not be ruled out by physical reasoning. We are only able to conduct local [i.e., small-scale] experiments, but causality violation in general relativity is a global [i.e., large-scale] effect, and so the lack of experience cannot give evidence of its absence. So chronology violation can only be discussed on philosophical grounds, grounds which have often enough turned out to be nothing but prejudice." Then, after observing that all such philosophical arguments, if nontrivial, are based on the free-will issue, Professor Kriele goes on to suggest that Einstein's general relativity will eventually prove to be the limiting case of a more general (no pun intended) theory of gravity, in which " 'free will' is something like a second order effect and therefore it is possible that the classical limit space-time of our world contains closed timelike curves [implying the possibility of time travel to the past] though we enjoy the comfort of free will."

Still, Hawking's question about the missing time travelers *is* a puzzle, no doubt about it, one that echoes Enrico Fermi's nearly half-century-old question about alien intelligent life in the Universe—if "they" exist, *where are they?* The common point to "Absolutely No Paradox" [del Rey, 1951b] and "Invasion" [Podolny, 1970], which attempt to answer the question of "where are they?" is that time travel is possible only into the future. There are no time travelers from the future in the present, because they can travel only in the other time direction. A "proof" of the impossibility of backward time travel has even been offered by an economist(!), who claims [Reinganum, 1986] that the fact we observe positive interest rates "is proof that time travelers do not and can not exist." That is, time travelers from the future if actually in the past could by virtue of their advanced knowledge of things to come make financial killings so numerous and extensive as to drive interest rates to zero. Interest rates are not zero, however, and so time travelers are not among us, concludes this proof. Other even less serious economic arguments for why there are no time travelers among us are in [Queenan, 1990].

More interesting than greedy time travelers is the speculation that backward time travel is possible, but extraordinarily dangerous. If so, it seems reasonable that it would be difficult to get anyone to willingly do it. In *Hot Wireless Sets* [Compton, 1971], for example, we learn of volunteer Roses Varco, the local village fool, who time travels because he does not really understand what is about to happen. Another disturbing idea was put forth in "The Man from When" [Plachta, SFSSS]; There will be only *one* time traveler to the past whose first and last experiment will destroy the Earth—and he will be from eighteen minutes in the future. This suggestion of the potential danger of time travel is actually an old concern. In "The Time Ray of Jandra" [Palmer, 1930], for example, in what was probably intended to be a horrifying scene (but which reads today more like a stupendous and silly joke), a time traveler moves into the future by means of a "time-ray"; unfortunately, the ray works differently on the various chemical elements, and not at all on either hydrogen or oxygen. Thus, the time traveler (or at least most of him) and his machine do vanish into the future, but left behind are "several gallons of water spilled on the floor"!

The most imaginative and disturbing answer to the "where are all the time travelers?" question that I have come across in fiction is in "Time Payment" [Shaara, 1954]. In this story backward time travel is possible, and in fact one of the inventors of the first time machine has just returned from 1938. Still, the inventors are puzzled about "The Problem:" "But if *we* have time traveled, then obviously men in the future have time traveled. They will be able—*are* able to come back. [So] where are they?" They finally conclude that there can only be two possible answers. Either there is nobody in future, or time travel is so dangerous (is that why the future might be empty?) that all who invent it suppress it. And that is what they decide they must do.

Yarov, a Russian writer, answered Clarke's puzzle by hypothesizing in "The Founding of Civilization" [Yarov, 1968] that "a cardinal rule of [time travel] categorically forbids [time travelers] to stop at any point in time." One might wonder what the point of time travel would then be, but Yarov's story introduces the wonderful sport of "TM racing;" i.e., seeing who can go back in time the farthest in the least time. Imagining time machines to be something like sports cars ("Once the machines were warmed up it was difficult to idle them, to restrain them from bucking backward into time before the race began"), Yarov talks about these ghostly apparitions whisking across the ages causing various reactions in those who happen to see the passage of a chronoviator: the superstitious shrink back in horror, while courageous philosophers write of atmospheric effects! But under no circumstances does a time traveler stop (until one does, briefly, after suffering an accident in 33,000 B.C., with astonishing repercussions).

An interesting answer to the question "Where are all the time travelers?" is that they *are* here, but for some reason (contrary to Clarke) they manage to avoid giving themselves away. In "The Fox and the Forest" [Bradbury, 1980], the idea for avoiding the difficulty of a too-talkative visitor from the future was to imagine that time travelers would have a psychological bloc installed to prevent any knowledge of the future or of the mechanism of time travel from being revealed to the past. The same idea was also used by Lester del Rey in his spooky 1942 time-machine story, "My Name is Legion" [del Rey, SFF], which is about the ideal fate for the then still alive Adolf Hitler. The private investigator in "Unborn Tomorrow" [Reynolds, 1959], hired to find a time traveler, somewhere, anywhere, finds hundreds of them—at the annual *Oktoberfest* in Munich, a beer celebration that "makes the New Orleans Mardi Gras look like a quilting party." Time travelers like to go there, you see, because everybody gets so drunk there is no danger of giving yourself away! The psychologists of 3046 in "Unthinking Cap" [Pierce, 1943], going far beyond mere alcohol, have a particularly diabolical means for ensuring the silence of those time travelers they return to the past. And Norman Knight's "Short-Circuited Probabilty" [Knight, BSF] reverses the process described in Bradbury's tale; the time traveler uses hypnotic deception on those around him.

Of course, one shouldn't overlook the possibility that a time traveler might find the judgments of his audience of little matter. Consider, for example, the visitor from the year 2999 in Robert Silverberg's brilliant 1970 novel *Vornan-19* (more recently reprinted as *The Masks of Time*). When the time traveler arrives in the world of 1999 he is initially greeted with some skepticism. When asked why anyone should believe his claim to be from the future, he replies "Why, feel free to believe none of it. I'm sure it makes no difference to me."

Skepticism and Time Travelers

A thought-provoking possibility for explaining the discouraging scarcity of certified time travelers is the central thesis for a fascinating paper in the philosophical literature [Sorensen, 1987]. Sorensen argues that nobody would believe a time traveler even if he willingly confessed and revealed his knowledge of the future or even the details of his time machine! Indeed, Sorensen makes the rather astonishing assertion that even the time traveler himself would have doubts! This is a fairly shocking suggestion, and deserves some elaboration, especially as Sorensen invokes a philosophical authority, the Scottish philosopher David Hume (1711–1776), the patron saint of skeptics, to buttress his position. An important caveat, explicitly stated in Sorensen's paper, is crucial to keep in mind: "The key question will not be 'Is time travel possible?' We shall instead ask whether it is possible to justify a belief in a report of time travel." This gets to the real heart of Clarke's puzzle.

Much of the resistance to the idea of time travel lies in sheer skepticism. For many, time travel (to the past, in particular) is simply too much out of the ordinary to be taken seriously. For many, time travel would literally be miraculous. Hume's great work, *An Enquiry Concerning Human Understanding*,[9] contains a section on how a rational person should react to a claim that a miracle has occurred. Hume proclaimed that a miracle *by definition* violates scientific law and that since such scientific laws are rooted in "firm and unalterable experience," any violation of one or more of these scientific laws immediately provides a refutation for the report of a miracle. In Hume's own words: "Nothing is esteemed a miracle, if it ever happened in the common course of nature. It is no miracle that a man, seemingly in good health, should die on a sudden; because such a kind of death, though more unusual than any other, has yet been frequently observed to happen. But it is a miracle, that a dead man should come to life; because that has never been observed in any age or country... When anyone tells me, that he saw a dead man restored to life, I immediately consider with myself, whether it be more probable, that this person should either deceive or be deceived, or that the fact, which he relates, should really have happened. I weigh the one miracle against the other; and according to the superiority, which I discover, I pronounce my decision, *and always reject the greater miracle* [my emphasis]."

It is a strict interpretation of Hume that Sorensen adopts in claiming that a time traveler would have no success (among rational persons, anyway) with tall tales of "different places." As Sorensen explains, "Clearly, the time traveler cannot persuade a reasonable person by baldly asserting 'I am a time traveler.' The improbability of his claim places a heavy burden of proof on him. But perhaps he could shoulder the burden by means of artifacts, predictions, and demonstrations." Sorensen dismisses all of these possibilities, however, by reminding us of the slightly sleazy history of parapsychology and ESP, which run counter to known scientific laws, but which still have duped "many a respected scientist." Any artifact, prediction, or demonstration of time travel, argues Sorensen, is more likely the result of deception and fraud than of actual time travel: "Should the time traveler take observers for a spin in his time machine, the skeptics will have us compare their adventures with seances." The rational reaction to such a spin around the centuries, according to Sorensen's presentation, would be like that of a magician who can not figure out how a colleague has just done his newest act: "Nice trick! How did you do it?"

For many, such skeptical reactions to time travelers seem dogmatic in the extreme, the response of one with no imagination, no spirit, and a head full of cement. Humean skepticism requires, it seems, the rejection of anything and everything that is profoundly surprising, leaving the world a place of utter predictability and boredom. As Robert Sheckley put it in "Something for Nothing" [Sheckley, 1955], "When the miraculous occurs, only dull, workaway mentalities are unable to accept it." Sorensen answers this harsh criticism as follows: "Humeans respond by distinguishing between surprises. Most surprises in science do not violate accepted scientific laws. The strange wildlife of Australia was not excluded by biology. X-rays were not precluded by physics." Sorensen does well, however, to avoid mentioning such profound surprises as, for example, the spectrum of black-body radiation and, later, the photoelectric effect, which were not in the domain of known classical science. Those puzzling, surprising, *totally mystifying* effects required new science—the discovery of the quantum concept by Max Planck. A strict Victorian-age Humean, as described by Sorensen, would have wrongly rejected the experimental reports of all quantum phenomena and would (perhaps just as wrongly) have rejected all reports of time travel.

Not all modern philosophers subscribe to the strict Humean definition (as described by Sorensen) that a miracle requires a violation of one or more of the scientific laws of nature. In [Ahern, 1977], for example, the definition of a miracle is any event that "can be explained *only* [my emphasis] by reference to the intervention of a supernatural force." Time travel, by this interpretation, is not a miracle since general relativity and not God is all that is required. Professor Ahern asserts that his definition was actually Hume's position.

C. S. Lewis, late professor of Medieval and Renaissance Literature at Cambridge University, absolutely rejected Hume's position on how a rational person should react to certain surprising events. Lewis, one of the most thoughtful modern writers on Christian theology, had no patience with skeptics (or, as Lewis called them, "materialists"), such as those Sorensen describes. Professor Lewis graphically illustrates the dug-in position of such skeptics [Lewis, 1986]: "If the end of the world appeared in all the literal trappings of the Apocalypse; if the modern materialist saw with his own eyes the heavens rolled up and the great white throne appearing, if he had the sensation of being himself hurled into the Lake of Fire, he would continue forever, in that lake itself, to regard his experience as an illusion and to find the explanation of it in psychoanalysis, or cerebral pathology." If the end of the world would receive such a skeptical response, then a mere time traveler would surely have no hope at all of being believed.

Lewis would certainly have rejected Sorensen's most astonishing assertion which stated: "So far I have concentrated on the time travel question from the perspective of the time traveler's audience. What about the time traveler himself? Can he at least know he is a time traveler?" Sorensen argues that a time traveler, if authentic, should be able to convince us, and that if he can't (and he cannot if we are Humean skeptics), then the traveler must entertain doubts, too! No matter, says Sorensen, that the time traveler has memories of his adventures and no matter that he knows in his heart that he speaks the truth. Using words that echo Lewis' sarcasm, Sorensen quickly dismisses the importance of the time traveler's self-knowledge, declaring such memories to be merely the symptoms of some deep psychosis and the traveler's introspective sincerity to be a product of gross self-deception.

In Hume's defense, it should be clearly understood that he was not arguing for disbelief in absolutely anything surprising, but rather for rational analysis. Historically, the context of Hume's times was that of what he took to be nonrational arguments for a belief in God, i.e., as Professor Peter Heath put it in a wonderfully entertaining as well as scholarly essay,[10] Hume was "an exposer of bad arguments in rational theology." For Hume, second-hand (or even more remote) tales of the return of a man from the dead (the claim that literally kept Christianity alive after Christ's execution) were suspect. As Heath explained: "Hume ... makes no attempt to deny the supposed facts; he simply argues that they are consistent with other explanations and other analogies of a less ambitious kind. There is no right to attribute to the causes of such phenomena abilities more extensive than are needed to produce the observed effects."

Sorensen specifically mentions the traditional Humean response to astonishing reports when he cites earlier writers on time travel from the philosophical literature. One of those analyses [Putnam, 1962], for example, argued for the reasonability of a rational belief in time travel using the statement that "I have been amused and irritated by the spate of articles proving that time travel is a 'conceptual impossibility' " along with the argument that there is a *mathematically consistent* explanation for such belief (see the discussion of Minkowski spacetime diagrams in Tech Note 4). Ten years after Putnam wrote, however, came Weingard's Humean-style rebuttal to Putnam [Weingard, 1972a]. Weingard showed how to explain all of the time-travel phenomenon that Putnam describes without invoking time travel. (This isn't to say that Weingard didn't require some pretty astonishing gadgets and other things himself, such as matter transmitters and antimatter humans, but he didn't need a time machine.) A resurrected Hume would surely applaud Weingard's analysis (although he would probably doubt his own fresh existence).

Not everybody would be happy with Weingard's gadgets for avoiding time travel, however. They are, like a time machine, incredible, and as Professor Challenger said in Arthur Conan Doyle's "The Disintegration Machine," "You cannot explain one incredible thing by quoting another incredible thing." An interesting science fiction exposition of Professor Challenger's Humean philosophy occurs when an issue of the *New York Times* shows up a week early in "What We Learned from This Morning's Newspaper" [Silverberg, 1986]. It seems the explanation is either that the paper really is from the future or that it is a hoax. The first-person narrator of the tale provides us with his reason for believing the former: "I don't find either notion easy to believe but I can accept fourth-dimensional hocus-pocus more readily than I can the idea of a hoax. For one thing unless you've had a team the size of the *Times'* own staff working on [a hoax] it would take months to prepare it." For those who prefer classical authority, I like Aristotle's observation that "Plausible impossibilities should be preferred to unconvincing possibilities." We have, at least, a theory for time travel (that is, general relativity), but nothing at all to support Weingard's matter transmitters and antimatter people.

What would Arthur Clarke think of skepticism toward those who claim to have a time machine? It was, after all, his thoughts about the difficulty time travelers would have in maintaining low profiles that began the previous section, and so we might wonder what Clarke would think of Humean skepticism as it relates to time travel. It would be best to ask Clarke personally, of course, but I would guess that he would have little patience for such incredulity. The surprise of being confronted by a time traveler would soon turn to awe and pleasure IF—and I emphasize the IF—Clarke were taken for a spin in the stranger's machine; he would surely quote his own famous "Clarke's Third Law" [Clarke, 1972] to explain the wonder of it all: "Any sufficiently advanced technology is indistinguishable from magic." Or perhaps he would recall the opening line to S. Fowler Wright's novel *The World Below* [Wright, 1930]: "Applied science is always incredible to the vulgar mind." In a similiar vein, Robert Heinlein's character Lazarus Long once asserted: "One man's 'magic' is another man's engineering. 'Supernatural' is a null word." Or as a comparatively ancient science fiction story, "The Four-Dimensional Roller-Press" [Olsen, 1951] put it in 1927, "These things [fourth dimensional objects] sound like miracles; but, after all, what are miracles but phenomena which, on account of our ignorance, we cannot explain?"

As a matter of fact, even Hume could be convinced of quite strange matters, and I think Sorensen does interpret the late philosopher a little too narrowly. In his essay concerning Hume's position on believing in God,[10] Professor Heath wonders if there is "empirical evidence [imaginable] which would persuade any reasonable mind of the real existence of an infinite God." Heath answers his own question as follows: "If the stars and galaxies were to shift overnight in the firmament, rearranging themselves so as to spell out, in various languages, such slogans as I AM THAT I AM, or GOD IS LOVE—well, the fastidious might consider that it was all very vulgar, but would anyone lose much time in admitting that this settled the matter ... . Confronted with such a demonstration, the hard-line Humean [but not Hume, himself, I think] could continue, of course, to argue that, for all its colossal scale, the performance is still finite, and so cannot be evidence of more than the finite, though immense power that is needed to achieve it."

Heath concludes with what I think is the perfect rebuttal to anyone who would refuse to admit to time travel, even after taking a quick trip backward a few tens of millions of years to the late-Mesozoic era to hunt *Tyrannosaurus rex* and even after seeing the instant photographs of the dead monster with the skeptic's own foot on its head or of his boots dripping a bloody puddle of unholy size on the floor of the time machine. Writing about the Humean unconvinced, even when faced with a rearranged firmament, Professor Heath notes: "But this now seems a cavil, designed only to prove that even omnipotence is powerless against the extremer forms of skeptical intransigence." Where God would fail to convince, a simple time traveler could hardly hope to do better!

In fiction from long ago it is easy to find examples of how out-of-the-ordinary, or even unthinkable, time travel was viewed or not viewed by most people. The puzzling story in "Who Is Russell?" [Eggleston, 1875b], for example, tells of a man who suddenly, without explanation, appears in the midst of a Union military camp during the American Civil War. This man quickly displays strange lapses in his background as well as the knowledge of many different things well beyond anything that could be called common. The details of the story are not important here, but if published in a modern science fiction magazine, the stranger would almost surely quickly be identified in most readers' minds as a time traveler. In 1875, however, the author's narrator found his punch line in "his firm conviction that the quiet, gentle, well-behaved, modest gentleman, so singularly gifted ... is, in plain terms, the devil!" Time travel certainly never entered the author's thoughts; or if it did, he lost his nerve at the idea of using it in his pre-Wells story.

Modern science fiction writers have often used skepticism as a means of building conflict and tension in time-travel stories. The skeptical reception, for example, is extreme for the time traveler in "The Oldest Soldier" [Leiber, 1961]. In this story a soldier-in-time, who has fought in wars from the ancient past to a billion years in the future, finds that nobody believes him when he openly speaks of his temporal adventures during a visit to a bar in the present. Everybody merely thinks it is all a hilarious gag. Often the skeptical reaction is less benign. As the inventor of the time viewer explains in "E for Effort" [Sherred, 1983]: "I've watched scribes indite the books that burnt at Alexandria; who would buy, or who would believe me, if I copied one? What would happen if I went over to the Library and told them to rewrite their histories? How many would fight to tie a rope around my neck if they knew I'd watched them steal and murder and take a bath? What sort of a padded cell would I get if I showed up with a photograph of Washington, or Caesar? Or Christ?" The padded cell was indeed the fate of the time traveler in "The Ambassador from the 21st Century" [Shay, 1953], who journeyed from A.D. 2007 back to 1952 to warn of a future war—he was committed to a mental institution to receive help for his "illusion."

If his reception committee is a crowd of conservative, cautious Humeans, a time traveler is doomed. In "Spectator Sport" [MacDonald, SSFT], for example, we learn of the awful fate of a time traveler who, on arriving in the future, falls into the hands of skeptics. The science fiction writer Manly Wade Wellman attempted to avoid the problem of a time traveler needing to convince strangers of his identity by using the interesting idea of the time traveler convincing his earlier self. In a story with the appropriate title "Who Else Could I Count On?" [Wellman, MT], John (the older) travels back forty years to John (the younger) to enlist his aid in alerting the world to the coming war. He succeeds in convincing his younger version of who he is, but the closing words "Lord have Mercy!" of John (the younger) do have the ring of a residual shock. This story is a greatly condensed short-short version of "... backward, O Time!" [Wellman, 1949], in which the final words of shock, after the younger version realizes that he is talking to himself, are "Good grief!" Indeed. It is amusing to note that in C. S. Lewis' eerie, unfinished story "The Dark Tower" [Lewis, 1977], which tells the tale of the chronoscope, an invention that "does to time what the telescope does to space," the persistent skeptic in the story is a Scot, surely created by Professor Lewis in the image of Hume.

Einstein, Gödel, and The Past

The eleventh-century Persian poet-philosopher Omar Khayyam was blunt in his evaluation of the likelihood of reliving the past; as he so beautifully wrote in one of the quatrains of the *Rubaiyat*:

> The Moving Finger writes; and, having writ,
> Moves on: nor all your Piety nor Wit
> Shall lure it back to cancel half a Line,
> Nor all your Tears wash out a Word of it.

Quite a bit later the English poet Thomas Heywood in his 1607 play *A Woman Killed with Kindness* had one of his characters express a similiar thought:

> O God, O God, that it were possible
> To undo things done, to call back yesterday;
> That Time could turn up his swift sandy glass
> To untell the days, and to redeem these hours.
> Or that the Sun
> Could, rising from the west, draw his coach backward,
> Take from the account of Time so many minutes,
> Till he had all these seasons called again,
> ...
> But O! I talk of things impossible,
> And cast beyond the moon ...

Wyn Wachhorst, a scholar of popular culture, has an odd way of rejecting time travel. Transporting Wells' Victorian time traveler to the wrong century and invoking Einstein, he writes [Wachhorst, 1984]: "We are indebted to H. G. Wells not only for the notion of voluntary time travel but also for the image by which we conceive it: a sunny, Edwardian [sic] gentleman perched on an ornate steam-age contraption that moves through time in much the same manner that a streetcar moves across town. This spatialized view of time, along with its Newtonian catechism, has increasingly gone the way of bowler hats and high button shoes in the new world of Einstein and quantum mechanics." Wachhorst's final comment is ironic because it is Einstein's field equations that provide the basis for the modern theory of time travel.

Well, you might say, these deniers of time travel are just storytellers, philosophers, poets, and magazine essayists—what do they know about the possibility of time travel? It is what physicists and mathematicians think that is important because, after all, if a time machine is ever built, it will be as a result of new understandings at a profoundly deeper level of mathematical physics than we have today. And curiously enough, there are physicists and mathematicians who do think things may not be so gloomy about the possibilities of time travel. For example, Kurt Gödel, described in an obituary notice as one of the greatest mathematical logicians of all time,[11] published [Gödel, 1949b] (for a model of a rotating

Universe composed of a perfect fluid at constant pressure) a solution to Einstein's field equations for general relativity that, as he put it, implies it is "theoretically possible in these worlds to travel into the past, or otherwise influence the past." That is, in Gödel's model of a Universe there exist closed timelike world lines in spacetime.[12] These world lines are the possible paths of space travelers, who always move into the local future but who nevertheless eventually arrive back in their own past. Such rotating-Universe models had been studied as early as 1924 by the Hungarian physicist Cornelius Lanczos, but it was Gödel who discovered their potential for backward time travel. (In Tech Note 8 I give an elementary exposition on how time travel occurs in Gödel's Universe.)

It is an astonishing fact that one of the great twentieth-century physicists, Hermann Weyl (a colleague of both Einstein and Gödel at the Institute for Advanced Study in Princeton), wrote the following anticipatory passage *three decades before* Gödel [Weyl, 1952]: "It is possible to experience events now that will in part be an effect of my future resolves and actions. Moreover, it is not impossible for a world-line (in particular, that of my body), although it has a time-like direction at every point, to return to the neighborhood of a point which it has already once passed through. The result would be a spectral image of the world more fearful than anything the weird fantasy of E. T. A. Hoffmann [an early nineteenth-century German writer of the eccentric] has ever conjured up. In actual fact the very considerable fluctuations of the [components of the metric tensor—see Note 2 of Tech Note 4] that would be necessary to produce this effect do not occur in the region of the world in which we live. ... *Although paradoxes of this kind appear, nowhere do we find any real contradiction to the facts directly presented to us in experience* [my emphasis]." It would be thirty years after Weyl wrote these amazing words before Gödel finally presented his rotating Universe that showed just how those considerable fluctuations might actually occur.

In the pivotal year 1949 in an invited essay [Gödel, 1949a], Gödel specifically mentioned the paradoxical aspect of his time-travel result: "By making a round trip on a rocket ship in a sufficiently wide course, it is possible in these worlds to travel into any region of the past, present, and future, and back again, exactly as it is possible in other worlds to travel to distant parts of space. This state of affairs *seems* [my emphasis] to imply an absurdity. For it enables one e.g., to travel into the near past of those places where he has himself lived. There he would find a person who would be himself at some earlier period of his life. Now he could do something to this person which, by his memory, he knows has not happened to him." Gödel defended his statements about the paradoxes of a time traveler meeting himself with what I think is an astonishingly unconvincing argument (particularly so for a logician), based primarily on *engineering* limitations: "This and similiar contradictions, however, in order to prove the impossibility of the worlds under consideration, presuppose the actual feasibility of the journey into one's own past. But the velocities which would be necessary in order to complete the voyage in a reasonable time are far beyond everything that can be expected ever to become a practical possibility.[13] Therefore it cannot be excluded *a priori*, on the

"Miss! Oh, Miss! For God's sake, stop!"

Drawing by Whitney Darrow, Jr.; ©1957, 1985 The New Yorker Magazine, Inc.

FIGURE 4. In a chapter on time travel in [Watzlawick, 1976], the author says this 1957 *New Yorker* cartoon combines time and space travel. This would be remarkable (if true), as it had been only eight years since Gödel showed how backward time travel might be done via rocket ship. But could even readers of *The New Yorker* be that sophisticated as to chuckle over a joke based on a paper in *Reviews of Modern Physics*? At first glance it does seem to be a visit to the Garden of Eden, in an attempt to change the past. But of course it isn't since the creatures aren't human (look closely at their heads). Time travel was surely not the artist's intention.

YOUNG SELF: "Did you ever manage to articulate the bones of that
    microglamaphoid lizard?"
OLD SELF: "I'm not sure. But I've articulated the whole past of mankind
    on this planet—and the whole future too. I don't think you know
    very much about the past, do you? It's all perfectly beastly, believe
    me. But the future's going to be all perfectly splendid . . . after a bit.
    And I must say I find the present very jolly."

FIGURE 5. Sir Max Beerbohm (1872–1956), drama critic of *The Saturday Review* from 1898 to 1910, was the friend of many of the literary giants of his time, including H. G. Wells. To be rendered in caricature by Beerbohm was to be noticed by someone who mattered. Here we see one of his "The Old and the Young Self" drawings, and who but the author of *The Time Machine* could be a more fitting subject for what seems to be a time traveler going back to meet himself? In fact, Beerbohm did nearly two dozen such drawings with the same title, featuring various personalities, such as Rudyard Kipling, George Bernard Shaw, and Joseph Conrad; time travel was no doubt the furthest thing imaginable from Beerbohm's mind as he sketched this meeting of the old and the young Wells.

Reproduced by permission of Octopus Publishing Group Library, from Max Beerbohm's *Observations,* William Heinemann Ltd., 1925.

ground of the argument given, that the space-time structure of the real world is of the type described." That is, Gödel was trying to head off critics of his rotating-Universe model, critics who might point to the time-travel result as proof the model was flawed.

In reply to Gödel, Einstein wrote [Einstein, 1949] "Kurt Gödel's essay constitutes, in my opinion, an important contribution to the general theory of relativity, especially to the analysis of the concept of time. The problem here involved disturbed me already at the time of the building up of the general theory of relativity, without my having succeeded in clarifying it ... the distinction "earlier-later" is abandoned for world-points which lie far apart in a cosmological sense, and those paradoxes, regarding the *direction* of the causal connection, arise, of which Mr. Gödel has spoken ... . It will be interesting to weigh whether these are not to be excluded on physical grounds."

Gödel's analysis was later attacked (and also defended), but always on the basis of how to interpret his bizarre solution, not on whether he had made a mathematical error. For example, [North, 1965] writes of Gödel's solution: "This property [of time travel] must be judged an absurdity by anyone committed to the ordinary modes of speech." In [Chari, 1960] we read that Gödel's solution is a "bizarre conception" and a "mere mathematical curiosity," and the previously cited obituary notice states that a "novel feature of the Gödel Universe is that it contains closed timelike world-lines ... . The unpalatable consequences [of time travel to the past] represents not so much time travel as a breakdown of causality. For this reason Gödel's solution cannot be taken too seriously as a model for the real Universe."

Other physicists have criticized the critics, however, as in [Pfarr, 1981]: "What strikes us as rather precarious is the exclusion of Gödel's space-time ... only because of closed timelike world lines ... . Rather than rule out such solutions by means of reference to logical paradoxes ... it should be investigated whether physical reasons can be presented which require an exclusion. [Note that this was Einstein's position.] During the last 30 years [now, as I write, more than 40] since Gödel's discovery his solution could not be excluded by cosmological arguments alone. It seems that the 'physical grounds' for excluding this solution which Einstein mentioned in his reply to Gödel have to be looked for beyond the theory of gravity."

Ozsvath and Schucking thought that one possible explanation for excluding the time travel in Gödel's solution, based on "physical grounds," could be developed using the observation that Gödel's Universe is infinite. Perhaps, they argued, a rotating, *finite* Universe would exclude time travel [Ozsvath and Schucking, 1962]. The primary concern of these authors was that Gödel's rotating Universe fails to incorporate Mach's principle (which states that the inertia of any object is determined by the distribution of all the rest of the mass in the Universe). Einstein himself originally believed that the general theory satisfied this principle, and until Gödel's counterexample in 1949 all known solutions to the gravitational field equations were, in fact, in agreement with the principle. Ozsvath and Schucking, speculating that Mach's principle might perhaps be retained in a finite rotating Universe, thus decided to search for a new counterexample; i.e., for a rotating solution that is finite and does not allow time travel to the past and yet still violates Mach's principle. In this quest, they succeeded. Their desire to find such a solution was particularly understandable, as Gödel had tantalizingly claimed that in 1950 that he had already found such models himself [Gödel, 1952]. (Unfortunately, he had given no details.) In fact, in their 1962 paper Ozsvath and Schucking actually mention in passing that they had received a personal communication from Gödel indicating that one of the temporally benign models he had had in mind was, in fact, theirs. In their 1962 paper Ozsvath and Schucking sketch the outline of their solution, and they later published a much more detailed analysis of it in [Ozsvath and Schucking, 1969]. And thus was Mach's principle finally banished from the general theory.

Theoretical time travel could not so easily be dismissed, however, as some years later other time-travel solutions were discovered; e.g., [Som and Raychaudhuri, 1968], [Banerjee and Baneji, 1968], and [De, 1969], with the general conclusion in the last paper being that a general relativistic situation violating causality could be formulated; that is, time travel was found to be no mere anomaly of Gödel's particular analysis, but rather was built into the basic gravitational field equations of general relativity.

Quantum Mechanics, Black Holes, Singularities, and Time Travel

A fundamental objection based on general relativity to Gödel's ideas (and to the possibility of time travel) is that in a very deep sense general relativity itself is known to be incomplete. That is, it is incompatible with quantum mechanics, which is the physics of the very, *very* tiny, of objects smaller than a single atom. In quantum mechanics the discrete nature of the atomic world appears in such phenomena as the photoelectric effect in which light acts like individual particles rather than as continuous waves. General relativity works beautifully on a cosmological scale, but like Maxwell's theory of electromagnetism it fails utterly when applied deep in the interior of the atom. Quantum theory, on the other hand, seems to work *everywhere*. As physicist Nick Herbert writes in his excellent book *Faster Than Light* [Herbert, 1987]: "As far as we can tell, there is no experiment that quantum theory does not explain, at least in principle ... . Though physicists have steered quantum theory into regions far distant from the atomic realm where it was born, there is no sign on the horizon that it is ever going to break down."[14]

As mentioned earlier in this chapter, one of the central concepts in relativity is the *world line*, which is the complete story of a particle in spacetime. A world line assigns a definite position to the particle at each instant of time. This is a classical, prequantum concept, however, and today we use the probabilistic ideas of quantum mechanics to describe the position and momentum of a particle once we get down to the atomic level. Quantum theories are discrete theories in which the values of physical entities vary discontinuously (in "quantum jumps"), while in classical theories the values of physical entities are continuous. The difference between the two types of theories is something like the difference between sand and water. Just one of the more curious results of the fusing of quantum mechanics with general relativity may be *quantum time*. In such theories the smallest increment of time that has physical meaning (this is sometimes called the *chronon*) may have a nonzero value. But this is all very speculative. To paraphrase Caltech's Kip Thorne, what you get when you mix sand and water is quicksand, which pretty much describes the fate, so far, of all quantum theories of gravity. The search for connections between general relativity and quantum mechanics continues, however, and how all this relates to time travel is via a fantastic sequence of recent discoveries in relativistic physics.

General relativity predicts that a sufficiently massive star (greater than about four times the mass of the Sun) will, when its fuel is nearly gone and its nuclear fires are beginning to fade, experience a truly spectacular death called total gravitational collapse. When its fuel-exhausted, weakened radiation pressure is no longer able to keep an aged star inflated against the collapsing force of its own gravity, the star will literally implode and crush itself into what is called a *black hole* (a term coined in 1967 by the Princeton physicist John Wheeler in an address before the American Association for the Advancement of Science). This is an object with a gravitational field so enormous that even light cannot escape (hence the term "black") and whose center is a singularity in spacetime; this center would be a place where it seems spacetime is either terribly weird or perhaps no longer even exists. As theoretical physicist Paul Davies has dramatically written [Davies, 1981], "once gravity runs out of control, spacetime smashes itself out of existence at a singularity," or to quote Stephen Hawking [Hawking, 1976], "A singularity is a place where the classical concepts of space and time break down as do all the known laws of physics."

A singularity, according to general relativity, is infinitely dense and has a gravity field infinitely strong.[15] The curvature of spacetime at a singularity is infinite. The "gravity graveyard" infinity of a black hole is both exciting and suspicious, however. The infinity seems to be intertwined with time travel, but historically when such infinities have occured in physical theories, it has meant that the theories have been extended too far. The infinity may just mean that once the collapsing star has fallen into a region incredibly smaller than even an electron, then Einstein's general relativity is no longer valid (just as Newton's theory fails at speeds comparable to that of light) and most if not all of its predictions are then wrong.

If, however, during our mathematical analyses we stay away from a singularity, then general relativity is certainly correct. For example, around the singularity of a black hole, at a distance directly proportional to the mass of the collapsed object, the theory predicts the formation of a *spacetime horizon*, which is a surface in spacetime through which anything can fall into the hole, but through which nothing, not even photons, can escape; the singularity at the center of a collapsed star, therefore, is not visible (i.e., it is not 'naked') to a remote observer. For an observer beyond the horizon of any black hole, the only observable properties of a hole are its mass (via its gravitational effects), angular momentum, and electric charge.

There are, in fact, two fundamentally different types of black holes. If the collapsed star forms a nonrotating (i.e., zero angular momentum), spherically symmetric object, then the result is called a *Schwarzschild* black hole, after the German astronomer Karl Schwarzschild (1873–1916), who found the first exact solutions to Einstein's general relativity equations just months after Einstein published them. The radius of the spacetime horizon is called, in this case, the *Schwarzschild radius*.[16] Much more interesting, however, are the theoretical time-travel properties of *rotating* black holes.[17] (These are called *Kerr holes*, after the New Zealand mathematician Roy Kerr, who first solved the general relativity equations for the spacetime region exterior to a spinning hole [Kerr, 1963]). There are other solutions to the gravitational field equations that imply that the interiors of such rotating holes are portals into other spacetime regions that are otherwise inaccessible from our Universe and that some of these regions are past (or future) versions of "our" Universe. That is, such portals are the doors into time machines.

This is all very speculative, of course, and the eminent physicist John Wheeler for one is not convinced that there is any sense to the notion of black-hole time travel. As he related in a poignant story [Wheeler, 1981]: "I received one day a long distance telephone call from a distinguished Washington lawyer. "My wife and I have lost our only child, our twelve-year old son. Without him nothing has any meaning for us. We're willing to run any risk, pay any price, do whatever it takes to be transported back in time to his company. We have heard that black holes exist and that time goes backward in the neighborhood of a black hole. Is that true?' I had to tell him, 'I'm so sorry; no.' "

Wheeler's objection to black-hole time travel is based (ignoring the formidable engineering problems posed by the lawyer's request) on the quantum field *fluctuations* of gravity fields,[18] which are related to the uncertainties inherent in our knowledge of the values of physical entities. Such fluctuations, vanishingly small in systems of everyday size, increase dramatically at very tiny distances (such as twenty orders of magnitude smaller than the nucleus of an atom!) and may result in effects that preclude the formation of a singularity. There does seem to be some astronomical evidence for black holes, but the matter is not settled by any means and perhaps they do not actually exist; or even if black holes do exist, maybe they contain no singularities. When the theory of quantum gravity is at last developed then we will probably learn if black holes really are potential time machines (although at least one writer has already asserted that the coming of quantum gravity will not prevent the formation of singularities [Misner, 1969a]).[19]

One physicist [Soleng, 1989] takes a pessimistic position with regard to using singularities in general for time traveling. He begins by saying: "Einstein's theory ... runs repeatedly into singularity problems. These problems may, however, be swept under the rug by saying that the extreme conditions of the very early Universe or those inside black holes, are beyond the region of validity of the theory. In these cases quantum effects will dominate." But he remains highly skeptical of the correctness of trying to sweep time-travel problems under the rug: "The causality problems of the Gödel model ... cannot be avoided [by appealing to quantum effects]. Rather they point at a serious flaw in our understanding of space-time. Can we accept a theory that allows such paradoxical solutions, or is it possible [to eliminate] the bizarre possibility of closed timelike curves?"

Another physicist, Brandon Carter, has been equally skeptical of black-hole time travel. In [Carter, 1968] he concluded, in a discussion of the Kerr black hole solution, "When the charge or angular momentum [is sufficiently large] causality violation is of the most flagrant possible kind in that it is possible to connect any event to any other by a future-directed timelike line." That is, backward time travel is allowed, even though the traveler is always moving at less than the speed of light into his local future (see Tech Note 4). Carter did not like this conclusion at all, declaring such a result to be "pathological" and calling such a timelike path "vicious." So disturbed was Carter about the possibility of time travel that he felt "the breakdown in general relativity may be [so severe] the whole theory may have to be abandoned."

Very recently, however, other physicists have come to recognize the danger in drawing conclusions from what may only seem to be paradoxical. For example, after a brief description of how very *un*restrictive general relativity is in imposing constraints on the geometry of spacetime, Yurtsever [1990] observes: "it is neither suggested nor warranted by the theory to discard any entire class of space-times as 'unphysical,' regardless of how strange and counterintuitive their properties may be. Attitudes that led to such selective, ad hoc dismissals of space-time phenomena may be misleading and counterproductive." Yurtsever then goes on to remind his readers that it was not so long ago that physicists rejected the spacetime horizons of black holes as "unphysical," and yet today's physicists actively search for black holes and believe that they have good evidence that such things do indeed exist.

Similarly, the prediction by the general theory of gravitational radiation (literally ripples in spacetime) was once viewed with great skepticism. Today, however, most theoreticians believe such radiation exists and its detection from astronomical sources merely a matter of time and improved instrumentation. (Still, see the cautionary note [Xin, 1992].) Spacetime horizons and gravitational radiation as "crazy ideas" have now been replaced by spacetimes with acausal behavior. Perhaps, warns Yurtsever, present-day physicists might do well to remember the hasty judgments of the past. And it is a paradoxical fact that in 1970 Hawking and Roger Penrose published [Hawking and Penrose, 1970] what has since become a famous theorem. This theorem states singularities must occur if certain assumptions are made; one of which is that backward time travel is impossible. The singularities that so horrify Carter and Soleng, because they allow time travel, were declared to be inevitable if time travel could *not* occur! The assumption of global causality has, however, recently been weakened in the Hawking and Penrose theorem [Kriele, 1990a], and so it seems we *can* have both singularities and time travel.

The time-travel property of rotating black holes makes them a favorite of science fiction writers, of course, e.g., *Re-entry* [Preuss, 1981] and *The Forever War* [Haldeman, 1984]. There is talk of a "micro-black-hole cluster," too, in "Houston, Houston, Do You Read?" [Tiptree, 1978], in which a spaceship is sent three centuries into the future. For the present, however, we do seem to be left with the conclusion expressed in [Lightman, 1986]: "The catch is that it is impossible to find any concrete solutions of Einstein's equations that permit time travel and are at the same time well behaved in other respects. All such proposals either require some unattainable configuration of matter, or else have at least one particularly nasty point in space called a 'naked singularity' that lies outside the domain of validity of the theory. It is almost as if General Relativity, when pushed toward those circumstances in which all of physics is about to be done away with, digs in its heels and cries out for help."

Tipler's Time Machine

In 1974 a young physics graduate student at the University of Maryland, Frank Tipler, caused a bit of a stir when he published in [Tipler, 1974] what seemed to be the specific construction details for a time machine. Indeed, the final sentence in his paper says, "In short, general relativity suggests that if we construct a sufficiently large rotating cylinder, we create a time machine." Nobody had ever made such a statement before in a respectable physics journal,[20] and best of all there were no apparent singularities involved, as with black holes. However, a close look at Tipler's analysis does turn up some difficulties with his theory.

What Tipler had actually done was to show that if one had an *infinitely long*, *very dense* cylinder rotating with a surface speed of at least half the speed of light, so that the rotation speed is such that the centrifugal forces are balanced by gravitational attraction, then this allowed a closed timelike line to connect any two events in spacetime. This means that by moving around the surface of such a fantastic cylinder one could travel through time into the past—but not to earlier than the creation of the cylinder.[21] Tipler's cylinder would also allow the time traveler to return to his original time, to go "back to the future." Tech Note 8 shows a simple illustration (taken from Tipler's dissertation) that demonstrates how the cylinder works as a time machine. No one, in fact, disputes this. It *is* true. On paper.

But Tipler did *not* prove that this time-travel property holds for cylinders of long but finite length, which are the only kind we could actually build from a finite amount of matter; he merely suggested such might be the case. This suggestion *seems* reasonable because if our time traveler orbits at the midpoint of the cylinder, near the surface, then the gravitational end-effects of sufficiently remote ends of the cylinder should be negligible. Similiar mathematical approximations are routinely made, for example, when calculating the electrical effects of charged cylinders of finite length. But as Kip Thorne warned [Thorne, 1970], "Extrapolation from cylindrical symmetry to reality is very dangerous, since spacetime is not even asymptotically flat around an infinite cylinder." (In [Gribbin, 1983], however, we find the estimate that a 10-to-1 ratio of cylinder length to radius may be enough for Tipler's cylinder to be "infinite.") However, there is still a potential problem because there is a strong likelihood that a Tipler protocylinder would collapse under its own internal gravitational pressure before it could be made nearly long enough to be even approximately infinite. That is, such a finite-length cylinder might actually crush itself along its long axis into a pancake-shaped blob, something like what happens to a long cylinder of jello stood on-end. (An ordinary can of jellied cranberry sauce, so popular at Thanksgiving, will also sometimes display this curious behavior.)

The required rotational speed causes a problem, too. We are, you see, not talking about cylinders the diameter of a pencil or even that of a large water pipe (the larger the diameter, the less the centrifugal acceleration at the cylinder's surface). It is easy to calculate that even a huge cylinder ten kilometers in radius (and so at least 100 kilometers in length) would have, with a surface speed of half the speed of light, a centrifugal acceleration *two hundred billion* times the acceleration of the Earth's surface gravity. No known form of ordinary matter could spin this fast and not explosively disintegrate. But Tipler cylinders would not be ordinary in any sense of the word. Tipler has estimated that required density for a time-machine cylinder would be 40 to 80 orders of magnitude above that of nuclear matter.[22] Made from such superdense stuff, a cylinder would typically be as massive as the Sun but many trillions of times smaller. Showing no lack of imagination, Tipler has himself suggested [Tipler, 1977] the possibility of speeding up the rotation of an existing star as an alternative approach to that of actually trying to build a cylinder.[23] This is, of course, a project for a far-future society with a very advanced technology!

Science fiction writer Poul Anderson used Tipler cylinders (he called them "T-machines") in his novel *The Avatar* [Anderson, 1978]. He describes such cylinders as scattered about the Universe by ancient, altruistic aliens called "the Others," to be used by any with the wits to decipher how. Anderson recognized the obvious problems with Tipler cylinders and had one of his characters say of T-machines, "I have no doubt whatsoever that here is the product of a technology further advanced from ours than ours is from the Stone Age." Indeed, in his 1977 paper Tipler had written that whatever these cylinders might be made of, it could only be called "unknown material." This requirement for supermatter seems to be a feature of time machines in general; as discussed in Tech Note 9, the wormhole time machine invented by Kip Thorne and his colleagues at Cal Tech also requires what they call "exotic" conditions.

So, alas, Tipler cylinders are out, at least for a while, as practical time machines (but even "no time machine, ever" Larry Niven liked the idea well enough to lift Tipler's title for a short time-travel story, "Rotating Cylinders and the Possibility of Global Causality Violation" [Niven, 1979][24]). The significance of Tipler's result, and of Gödel's, too, is that they hold out at least a little hope for the physical possibility of time travel.[25] The fact that their particular mechanisms for achieving it are not possible (in the engineering sense) is irrelevant. Other, yet unthought-of methods, what one writer calls "future magic" [Forward, 1988], could perhaps be engineering possibilities.

There is, however, still the major objection to time travel to consider, the one that bothered Einstein about Gödel's solution, and it is the one that is the hardest to wave away. It is the problem of causality violation. This has already been briefly discussed in this chapter, but the problem warrants much more attention, and a chapter all its own. And that is Chapter Four. But first we need to take a closer look at Time itself, the "stuff" or "thing" or ...? we are interested in traveling "through" or "around" or "across" or ...?

Chapter Two
On The Nature of Time, Spacetime, and the Fourth Dimension

I do not believe that there are any longer any *philosophical* problems about Time; there is only the physical problem of determining the exact physical geometry of the four-dimensional continuum that we inhabit.

—Professor Hilary Putnam [Putnam, 1967]

What, then, is time? I know well enough what it is, provided that nobody asks me; but if I am asked what it is and try to explain, I am baffled.

—Saint Augustine, *Confessions*

The Fourth dimension is just a hypothetical math concept. Or else it's time, or something. Just a lot of sci-fi crud.

—Laura's reaction in *The Boy Who Reversed Himself* [Sleator, 1986] after an oddly behaving new boy in school says he has been in the fourth dimension

Science fantasy enthusiasts know that "time is the fourth dimension" and that Einstein's theories are the hopeful but as yet unrealized basis for all kinds of marvellous possibilities, from time machines to weird spacetime warps in the fabric of the Universe which enable the gifted to pass through discontinuities into the exotic world of the *n*th dimension. Einstein's theories do *not* in fact suggest these things.

—a more than slightly exasperated comment by two physicists in their book on relativity [Sears and Brehme, 1968]

What Is Time?

Christian clerics had identified time as something unusual long before science fiction writers and their time-travel stories. We can trace their interest back at least fifteen centuries to Saint Augustine. Certainly the seventeenth-century Spanish Jesuit Juan Eusebius Nieremberg caught the spirit of the wonder that time holds for the devout when he wrote in his *Of Temperance and Patience* that "*Time* is a sacred thing; it flows from Heaven ... It is an emanation from that place, where eternity springs ... It is a *clue* cast down from Heaven to guide us ... It hath some assimilation to Divinity." Going outside of Christianity, we can find equally strong reactions to the mystery of time. The *Laws of Manu* of Hinduism, the *Torah* of Judaism, the *Koran* of Islam, and the revealed truths of Gautama Buddha are all full of references to time. It is, in fact, to the pagan gods of Greek mythology that we owe our image of Chronos, or Father Time.

Not just the Greeks made time a god. In the *Bhagavad Gita (Song of the Lord)*, the central religious romantic-epic of Hinduism, which predates Christ by five centuries, one of the characters reveals his divine nature and declares his power thus: "Know I am Time, that makes the worlds to perish, when ripe, and bring on them destruction." And in the even older Egyptian *Book of the Dead,* dating back over three thousand years, the newly deceased was thought literally become as one with time itself. The merging of time and the resurrection of the body after death is shown in the line "I am Yesterday, Today and Tomorrow, and I have the power to be born a second time."

One anonymous wit pushed his brain to the limit and found the best he could come up with as an answer to the question "What is time?" is the definition "Time is just one damn thing after another." This may or may not have been the same person who declared, "Time is what keeps everything from happening at once." The introduction to [Farley, 1950] attributes this quote to the early science fiction writer Ray Cummings, and the words do in fact appear in his story "The Time Professor" [Cummings, 1921]. Later Cummings used them again in the opening to his novel *The Man Who Mastered Time* [Cummings, 1929]. Cummings certainly thought the phrase to be his, as in a Letter-to-the-Editor of *Astounding Stories* (April 1931) he repeated the words in such a way as to imply he was not quoting someone else. He again rephrased the same concept years later in *The Shadow Girl* [Cummings, 1946]: "This same Space; the spread of this lawn ... what would it be in another hundred years? Or a thousand? This little Space, from the Beginning to the End so crowded with events and only Time to hold them apart!"

Horwich, a modern philosopher, has expressed Cummings' sentiment in more scholarly fashion in words that echo Saint Augustine's [Horwich, 1987]: "Time is generally thought to be one of the more mysterious ingredients of the Universe." However, perhaps the most pragmatic approach to the meaning of time is the one expressed by English essayist Charles Lamb in a letter he wrote in 1810 [Mendilow, 1952]: "Nothing puzzles me more than time and space and yet nothing puzzles me less, for I never think about them."

Long before 1940 the science fiction connection between the fourth dimension and time was common (e.g., see "The Machine Man of Ardathia" [Flagg, 1927]). Indeed, by 1939 Robert Heinlein had the central character in his first published science fiction story "Life-Line" [Heinlein, 1979] assert that "you have been told that time is a fourth dimension ... It has been said so many times that it has ceased to have any meaning. It is simply a cliche that windbags use to impress fools." To illustrate Heinlein's point, a typical story of the pre-1940 period is "An Adventure in Futurity" [Smith, 1970] from a 1931 issue of *Wonder Stories*; it is the tale of a man from 1930 who befriends a visitor from A.D. 15,000 and so receives an invitation to visit the future. The machine that accomplishes this visit is briefly (and somewhat confusingly) described as making "possible a journey in that fourth-dimensional space known as time."

Despite the bold words of Hilary Putnam, a distinguished twentieth-century Harvard professor, in the first quote opening this chapter, I suspect most people would tend to agree with the distinguished late-fourth-century sinner (in the second opening quote) who became a distinguished early-fifth-century Christian theologian. The passage of fifteen hundred years has, in fact, done little to clarify the meaning of time, and most of us might actually agree mostly with Laura (in the third opening quote).

Ray Bradbury wrote a beautifully poetic passage about the mystery of time in "Night Meeting," one of the splendid substories in his episodic masterpiece *The Martian Chronicles* [Bradbury, 1950]. A modern man of A.D. 2002, who is one of the modern inhabitants of Mars, somehow meets the ghostly image of a long-dead Martian one cold August night. The conditions are just right for such a cross-time encounter. As the man thinks to himself: "There was a smell of Time in the air tonight. He smiled and turned the fancy in his mind. There was a thought. What did Time smell like? Like dust and clocks and people. And if you wondered what Time sounded like it sounded like water running in a dark cave and voices crying and dirt dropping down upon hollow box lids, and rain. And, going further, what did Time *look* like? Time looked like snow dropping silently into a black room or it looked like a silent film in an ancient theater, one hundred billion faces falling like those New Year balloons, down and down into nothing. That was how Time smelled and looked and sounded. And tonight ... tonight you could almost *touch* Time."

Lovely words, yes, but still they don't really tell us what time *is*. Perhaps Einstein can tell us. In the *New York Times* of 3 December 1919 we find him quoted as follows: "Till now it was believed that time and space existed by themselves, even if there was nothing—no Sun, no Earth, no stars—while now we know that time and space are not the vessel for the Universe, but could not exist at all if there were no contents, namely, no Sun, no Earth, and other celestial bodies." Less than two years later Einstein stated these beliefs again (the *New York Times*, 4 April 1921): "Up to this time the conceptions of time and space have been such that if everything in the Universe were taken away, if there were nothing left, there would still be left to man time and space." Einstein went on to deny this view of space and time, saying that according to his general theory of relativity time and space would *cease* to exist if the Universe was empty. This has the ring of one of Einstein's favorite philosophers, Spinoza, who declared in his *Principles of Cartesian Philosophy* that "there was no Time or Duration before Creation." In a correspondence with Samuel Clarke (Newton's friend who translated Newton's *Optiks* into Latin), Leibniz (who began the correspondence in late 1715) expressed similar ideas: "Instants, consider'd without the things, are nothing at all; ... they consist only in the successive order of things."

The pragmatic scientist would agree with Leibniz. After all, what does it mean to talk of time unless you can measure it. And what you use to measure time is a clock, some kind of a changing configuration of matter (such as spinning gears, ticking pendulums, and rotating dial pointers). Mere unchanging matter alone is not sufficient to measure time, as a still clock records nothing. Changing matter seems to be required. Yet not surprisingly, not everybody agrees. The counter view that time has nothing to do with change was expressed in an interesting manner by a science fiction fan in a Letter-to-the-Editor of *Wonder Stories* (January 1931): "Just one thing, you have these time-traveling yarns, good stuff to read all right, but bunk, you know; because if there's no such thing as time, which there isn't, only change, how can one travel in ... something that doesn't exist. To our planet which goes around the Sun there is simply a turning and warming of one side and then the other; time, i.e., years, days, hours, minutes, etc., is something purely artificial, invented by man to tell him when to do certain things, work and stop work ... ."

Going even beyond the ideas of Einstein, Spinoza, Leibniz, and our science fiction fan, at least one metaphysician feels that time would have no meaning, even in a massive Universe, without the additional presence of conscious, rational beings [Taylor, 1987]. A few years before this, however, a fellow philosopher [McCall, 1976] had argued for the opposite view that temporal passage is independent of the existence of conscious beings.

All this divergence of view perhaps explains why even a lightweight movie like Mel Brooks' 1987 *Spaceballs* can get a laugh from a time joke. Even kids know that the characters, when talking about time, do not know what they are talking about, and so the joke in the movie is actually not trivial at all. The movie, which is a spoof on such classics as *Star Wars, The Wizard of Oz,* and *Raiders of the Lost Ark,* quickly reaches a point of crisis. To find out what to do next, the evil Lord Helmet and his chief henchman decide on a novel approach—they will look at an instant videotape of their own movie. (Instant videos are available *before* the movie is finished!) Perplexed at watching on a television screen everything that he is doing as he does it (the screen correctly shows an infinite regression of television screens, each being watched by a Lord Helmet), Lord Helmet initiates the following rapid-fire exchange (which is, of course, a clever take-off on Abbott and Costello's "Who's on First?"):

> "What the hell am I looking at? When does this happen in the movie?"
>
> "Now! You're looking at now, sir. Everything that happens now, is happening, now."
>
> "What happened to then?"
>
> "We're past that."

"When?"

"Just now. We're at now, now."

"Go back to then."

"When?"

"Now."

"Now?"

"Now."

"I can't."

"Why?"

"We missed it."

"When?"

"Just now." [The henchman then sets the video to rewind.]

"When will then be now?"

"Soon."

We may laugh at this, even dismiss it as mere movie madness, but could any of us really do much better if like Saint Augustine we were backed into a corner and asked to explain time? Somehow, I think even Professor Putnam would find it difficult to know where to begin. He might even become as confused as the time traveler in the 1968 French film *Je t'aime, Je t'aime*, whose oscillations in time from present to past and back again leave him so befuddled that he decides he'd rather be dead!

Speculations on the Reality of Time

The mystery of time was well captured by R. H. Hutton, the literary editor of the *Spectator*, when he wrote in his 1895 review [Parrinder, 1972] of Wells' *Time Machine* that "the story is one based on that rather favourite speculation of modern metaphysicians which supposes *time* to be at once the most important of the conditions of organic evolution, and the most misleading of subjective illusions ... and yet Time is so purely subjective a mode of thought, that a man of searching intellect is supposed to be able to devise the means of traveling in time as well as in space, and visiting, so as to be contemporary with, any age of the world, past or future, so as to become as it were a true 'pilgrim of eternity.' "

Novelist Israel Zangwill (1864–1926) wrote a similiar but much more analytic review of Wells' novel for the *Pall Mall Magazine* [Parrinder, 1972]. Zangwill was the only Victorian reviewer to attempt a scientific analysis of time travel. While he thought Wells' effort was a "brilliant little romance," Zangwill also thought the time machine, "much like the magic carpet of *The Arabian Nights*," was "an amusing fantasy." Zangwill continued with what even then was a common idea about a way one might actually be able, at least in principle, to look backward in time; one could travel far out into space by going faster than light and then watch the light from the past as it catches up with you. (Note that this was in 1895, ten years before Einstein and special relativity.) In this way, Zangwill wrote, one could watch "the Whole Past of the Earth still playing itself out." Indeed, even before Zangwill the well-known French astronomer Camille Flammerion (1842–1925), had made this dramatic idea a centerpiece of his novel *Lumen* [Flammerion, 1897], first published in 1887. This book, a best-seller in Europe even before its English appearance, describes how a man just dead (in 1864) instantly finds his spirit on the star Capella, where he is able to watch the light then arriving from the Earth of 1793—he watches the French Revolution play itself out, and in fact sees himself as a child. (Flammerion may have been inspired to write his novel by an essay written several years earlier, in 1883, by the British physicist J. H. Poynting. Poynting's essay, which immediately states that it was in turn inspired by an anonymous pamphlet published "thirty or forty years ago" on the same issue, specifically mentions watching historical events from Capella [Poynting, 1920].)

Early magazine science fiction found the idea of looking backward in time with delayed light to be a romantic one; e.g., see the murder-romance "The Time Reflector" [England, 1905]. And in "Faster Than Light" [Sharp, 1939] a scientist loses his wife to a rival, who kidnaps her and escapes in a faster-than-light rocket ship headed for parts unknown. After years of searching for them with his own brilliant invention of the ampliscope (several quantum leaps beyond the telescope), the scientist finally locates the couple skipping from planet to planet light-years distant. His only pleasure, then, is to use his own faster-than-light craft to outrun the light-bearing images of his lost love and watch them over and over, but eventually he comes to realize the ultimate futility of it all. As the last line of the story says, "It would be senseless, I knew, chasing on and on after yesterdays." Weisinger's "Time On My Hands" [Weisinger, 1938] used the same idea in a very short story, which specifically cited Flammarion.

A different way to look backward in time is found in a curious idea; that of looking forward in time, an idea that assumes time is a closed loop. Plato (circa 400 B.C.), for example, thought of time as having a beginning, but his conception of time did not have it extending off into the indefinite future (which is essentially the modern, everyday view of time), but rather he visualized it as curving back on itself; that is, as *circular* time. This was a reasonable reflection of what Plato could see all about in nature, with the seemingly endless repetition of the seasons, the regular ebb and surge of the tides (the old English word *tid* was a unit of time), the unvarying alternation of night and day, and the rotation of the planets in the sky. Whatever might be observed today would, it seemed obvious, happen again in the future. Several fictional examples of circular time were discussed in Chapter One; another is "Night Broadcast" [Hobana, PWO], in which a television signal from the past is picked up by a gadget that probes the future—"by going far enough into the future one comes upon what we call the past." James Joyce's novel *Finnegans Wake*, which opens in mid-sentence and ends with the first part of the same sentence, is an exercise in cyclical time. This view of time has a powerful, ancient visual symbol, the Worm Ouroborous or World Snake that eats its own tail endlessly.

Plato's most famous student, Aristotle, was a keen observer of physical fact, and for him time was motion—in a world in which nothing moved, there would be no time (see Note 3 of Tech Note 1)—and he expressed this in his famous metaphor "Time is the moving image of eternity." For Aristotle, time and change were inseparately intertwined. For Aristotle the world had existed for eternity, and the circularity of time was still a central and powerful image; using his vivid illustration, we could claim with equal truth that we live prior to the Trojan War, as well as after it.

In the West it was the Christian theological doctrine of unique historical events that gave rise to linear time in the minds of the common folk. The creation of the world and of Adam and Eve, Noah and the cataclysmic Flood, the Resurrection: these were all events that occurred in sequence and each only once. None would happen again and thus, for Christianity, circular time just would not do. In addition, it has been argued that the major spiritual content of Christianity and a significant reason for its popular support in the face of brutally harsh Roman suppression is that it brought the *expectation of change* into the static world of ancient times. It is, in fact, a curious observation that it was in ancient religious teachings that our modern belief in linear time found its origin, a belief that most people today (including the most hardened agnostic physicist) find to be as natural as Plato and Aristotle found circular time. But just to show how one can find support for almost any view in the same religious dogma, Ecclesiastes 1:9 would seem to be a claim for circular time: "The thing that hath been, it is that which shall be; and that which is done is that which shall be done; and there is no new thing under the Sun."

Interestingly, the little-known American poet Joseph Stickney thought circular and linear time might possibly be one and the same. Because of his death from a brain tumor at the early age of thirty, little of his work has survived. In one fragment, however, called "The Soul of Time," Stickney used the mathematician's view of a straight line as the limiting case of the circumference of a circle with infinite radius:

Time's a circumference
Whereof the segment of our station seems
A long straight line from nothing into naught.

Circular time, with its closed topology, was favorably presented in Stephen Hawking's famous book *A Brief History of Time* [Hawking, 1988], in which he concludes that there is no need for God. Hawking arrived at this position because in circular time there is no first event and hence no need for a First Cause. Vigorous philosophical rebuttals to Hawking's analysis can be found in [Craig, 1990] and [Le Poidevin, 1991].

Even though linear time was the norm after Christ, there was still plenty enough about time to perplex thinkers, and the next two thousand years resulted in plenty of thinking. Discourses on time by philosophers like Descartes, Spinoza, Hobbes (who in the seventeenth century associated the points of a straight line with the instants of time), Kant, Nietzsche, and Hegel can be found on the spines of books by the yard in any decent university library. With Newton's discussion of *absolute time*, which is the belief that time is the same everywhere in the Universe (for more on this see Tech Note 1), there was, at last, a *physicist* writing about time, but in spite of Newton's genius, the mystery about time remained.

In 1905 Einstein's name appeared among the contributors to the study of time, and at last something besides metaphysical speculation was added to the body of human thought. Einstein's paper introduced the idea of *relative time*, which is the belief that the passage of time is not the same everywhere, but rather depends on local conditions. (For more on this see Tech Note 2.) In retrospect, Einstein's paper seems to be the perfect reply to the comment by Isaac Barrow (Newton's teacher and the first Lucasian professor of mathematics at Cambridge, the Chair held today by Stephen Hawking) that "because *Mathematicians* frequently make use of Time, they ought to have a distinct Idea of the meaning of the Word, otherwise they are Quacks."

Then just three years after Einstein, along came another astonishing paper [McTaggart, 1908] which claimed to prove that whatever time might be thought to be (even by Einstein), it really wasn't that because time wasn't even real! Written by Cambridge philosopher John Ellis McTaggart (1866–1925), this paper denied the reality of time via an infinite-regress argument that has been called by one modern writer [Mink, 1960] the *pons asinorum* (literally the "bridge of asses," in an allusion to the difficulty of the argument) of the riddle of time. As McTaggart's opening sentence freely admits, "It doubtless seems highly paradoxical to assert that Time is unreal, and that all statements which involve its reality are erroneous."

McTaggart began his argument by observing that there are two separate and distinct ways of talking about events in time. Following his symbolism, one can say that events are either future, present, or past (the so-called A-series), or one can say that events are temporally ordered by each being later than some events and earlier than others and simultaneous with still others (the B-series). He continued by asserting that time requires change, and followed this with the observation that the A-series (but not the B-series) incorporates such change. That is, if event X is earlier than event Y, then it is *always* earlier than event Y, and thus there is no change in this (or in any other) example of the B-series. (For example, let Y be the birth of a child, and X be the birth of its mother). In contrast, if event X is first in the future, then is in the present, and finally is in the past, then this example of an A-series represents change and hence *time*. (For example, let X be the next time you blink.)

With this rather pedestrian start, McTaggart then pulled the rabbit out of the hat. It makes no sense, he argued, to talk of the 'future', 'present', and 'past' for an event since they are mutually exclusive; i.e., no two of these predicates can apply at once and yet, paradoxically, every event possesses all three, and thus we have a contradiction, and so it makes no sense to talk of future, present, or past. And since it makes no sense to talk of them, then they do not exist, and there can be no A-series and hence no change and so there can be no time. McTaggart realized quite well how astounding all this would seem, and in fact he played devil's advocate (D.A.) in his paper by trying to anticipate the various objections people could raise. Of course he always managed to refute the D.A. at every turn.

The predicates of future, present, and past are really not incompatible for any event, he says some will claim, because the *real* predicates we should use are '*was* future', '*is* present', and '*will be* past', and these can be possessed all at once by any event. Ah, counters McTaggart, but this does not solve the problem. By allowing such modified predicates, we must allow for all nine possibilities, some of which are still incompatible. That is, the 'was', 'is', and 'will be' could each be potentially attached to 'future', 'present', and 'past'; and, for example, 'was past' is incompatible with 'will be future.'

Oh, counter-counters McTaggart (alias the D. A.), we can solve this by allowing even more complex modified predicates to arrive at the third level: 'is going to have been past' and 'was going to be future' and these *are* compatible. But then the real McTaggart pops up to bat this argument away, too, by displaying new incompatibilities as well as by showing that this process of ever increasing predicate complexity is a vicious infinite regress that drags the seeds of its own doom along at every step.[1] There is no escape, and hence we were fated to fail at the very first step, and so there is no time.

Well! What can one do when presented with such an argument, one that seems to claim philosophers can wrest free the secrets of nature by pondering the historical accidents of English syntax? As David Hume once said, "Nothing is more usual than for philosophers to encroach on the province of grammarians, and to engage in disputes of words, while they imagine they are handling controversies of the deepest importance and concern." At least one modern philosopher [Christensen, 1974] seems to agree, at least in the case of McTaggart's 'Proof', and he has been pretty blunt with his evaluation: "McTaggart's famous argument for the unreality of time is so completely outrageous that it should long ago have been interred in decent obscurity. And indeed it would have been, were it not for the fact that so many philosophers are not sure that it has ever really been given a proper burial, and so from time to time someone digs it up all over again in order to pronounce it *really* dead. These periodic autopsies reveal that something more remains to be said." This is certainly true, as McTaggart's disarmingly innocent argument has caused disagreement and furrowed brows among philosophers for decades.

In fact, it is easy to find examples of the continuing debate over McTaggart's analysis. At least one philosopher [Smith, 1986a] has actually argued that McTaggart did not really understand his own proof though his conclusions were correct anyway, but Smith was quickly refuted in turn [Oaklander, 1987]. My own reaction is that McTaggart's proof may mean something to grammarians, but it simply does not have any significance when it comes to the business of physics. But see [Currie, 1992] for how McTaggart's ideas have found their way into modern philosophical debates on the meaning of time in the cinema; particularly in analyzing the problems of *anachrony* (the telling of a story out of normal time sequence), such as occurs in time travel films.

Other sorts of metaphysical proofs for the unreality of time have been offered besides McTaggart's. For example, it has been argued that time is unreal, at least in a world empty of consciousness, because there could not possibly be any meaning to the concepts of past, present, and future unless events could be remembered, experienced, and anticipated. Or, for a second example, some have held time to be unreal, at least in a deterministic world (as some argue four-dimensional spacetime is), because any event whose occurrence follows from present conditions and physical laws would exist now. This argument, which seems to say that everything should happen at once, I fail to understand enough even to be bothered by it, but see [Gale, 1963] for what I think are good rebuttals of it and other such claims.

Debates between those who believe in the common-sense idea that present, past, and future are attributes of events (the 'tensers') and those who deny it (the four-dimensional spacetime, block-Universe 'detensers') continue to rage on across the pages of philosophy journals. In [Weingard, 1977] we even find one philosopher who sees merit to both positions. Less than a month before his death, Einstein revealed his feelings about the meaning of present, past, and future. In a letter written on 21 March 1955 to the children of his dearest friend, Michele Besso, who had just died, Einstein said (with full knowledge that his own illness would be his last):[2] "And now he has preceded me briefly in bidding farewell to this strange world. This signifies nothing. For us believing physicists, the distinction between past, present, and future is only an illusion, even if a stubborn one." Later in this chapter we will return to these curious words and speculate on what Einstein may have meant by them.

Has the Past Been for Ever?

Our modern concept of linear time as a straight line extending from the dim past through the present and disappearing into the misty future gives rise immediately to twin questions: "Did time have a beginning?" and "Will time ever end?" As one philosopher [Stearns, 1950] put it, "Endings and beginnings are rooted in the very conception of time itself." For now we will limit our concern to the question of whether the past is infinite or finite in duration and will take up the possibility of time having an ending later.

Early Biblical scholars, of course, believed that the answer was *finite* (the world came into being because of a First Cause, i.e., God's creation of everything) and, indeed, they expended vast quantities of energy (and, need I say it, time itself) on calculating the date of creation. Martin Luther, for example, argued for 4000 B.C. as roughly when everything, including time, began. Johannes Kepler adjusted this date by a notch, to 4004 B.C., and later the Calvinist James Ussher, Archbishop of Armagh and Primate of All Ireland, tweaked it again. His date is the most impressive of all, at least in detail: the first day of the world was 4003 years, seventy days, and six hours before the midnight that started the first day of the Christian era, and six days after that first day of the world, Adam was made—as a final dash of specificity, this last date was declared to be Friday, October 28! Ironically, while Christian theology may be given the credit for introducing linear time, it certainly did not provide very much of it; the Beginning of time was just six thousand years or so ago, and of course the End—in the form of the Battle of Armageddon—has been awaited (with varying degrees of eagerness) for the last one thousand years. (The famous, ancient question that this view of history prompts—"What was God doing before he created the world?"—has the equally famous, ancient answer "Creating Hell for those who ask that question." See, however, [Leftow, 1991] for how a modern philosopher has put a curious twist on that answer.)

The discovery in the seventeenth century of geological time cast a certain amount of skepticism on these early calculations. With the discovery that the very Earth itself could be decoded, the lure of trying to decode a book, admittedly of finite age, declined for most people, although it cannot be denied that modern Creationists still find such doings convincing. Geological time was discovered to be a chasm of time, extending backward for billions of years, a duration that is essentially incomprehensible. It has become fashionable for geologists to refer to these enormous time spans with the apt term of *deep time*, a subtle play on the metaphor of the "ocean of time." In his "The Future," the nineteenth-century English poet Matthew Arnold used a related watery image, the flow of time as a river, to express the brief duration of an individual life. For each of us, the past is simply myth and the future but speculation:

> Vainly does each, as he glides,
> Fable and dream
> Of the lands which the river of Time
> Had left ere he woke on its breast,
> Or shall reach when his eyes have been closed.
> ...
> Only the thoughts,
> Raised by the objects he passes, are his.

It is nothing less than humbling to historians who pause to think how little of the past is known, i.e., recorded. As the ever available anonymous wit put it, "History is a damn dim candle over a damn dark abyss." In his 1944 doctoral thesis to the University of London, H. G. Wells wrote,[3] "A thousand years is a huge succession of yesterdays beyond our clear apprehension." Yet, even as enormous as it is, the age of the Earth is not infinite. However, is ancient but finite geological time or even the cosmic time of the age of the very Universe itself (which appears to be many billions of years greater than the age of the Earth) the limit? Or is the past actually, really, *infinite*? An implicit assumption of the infinity of the past (and of the future[4]) can be found in Book Three of Lucretius' science poem *De Rerum Natura* (*On the Nature of Things*), where, just before the birth of Christ, Lucretius argues for the irrationality of fearing death: "The bygone antiquity of everlasting time before our birth was nothing to us. Nature holds this up to us as a mirror of the time yet to come after our death. Is there anything in this that looks appalling, anything that means an aspect of gloom? Is it not more untroubled than any sleep?"

Professor G. J. Whitrow [Whitrow, 1978] has traced the origins of the rational analysis of the duration of the past back as far as the sixth century A.D. The argument presented then by the Christian philosopher Joannes Philoponus of Alexandria (otherwise known as John the Grammarian) is simply that the world could *not* have been forever because that implies an infinity of successive acts could then have taken place, but that, according to Philoponus, is impossible. Infinity was just too big for the ancient mind. (Zeno's hoary pre-Christian paradoxes, as is well known today, are based on subtle nuances of infinity.) Even as late as the twelfth century the debate among Christian theologians was not about the possibility of an infinite past, but rather if the Biblical "six days of Creation" actually had taken place simultaneously or not [Gross, 1985]. For many in this debate, the past was definitely finite. Not all Christians accepted this, however, and the next century saw St. Thomas Aquinas, a follower of Aristotle, arguing the opposite persuasion for an infinite past.

Thomas' contemporary, St. Bonaventure, however, argued for a *finite* past, and it is with Bonaventure that we start to see some mathematical sophistication in the argument [Sweeney, 1974]. He argued that in a world infinitely old the Sun would have made an infinite number of its annual trips around the ecliptic. But for each such trip, the Moon will have made twelve (monthly) trips around the Earth; this second infinity would then be twelve times as great as the first one, and how could that be? Infinity is infinity and how can something be twelve times bigger than infinity?

Agonized, convoluted theological analyses of God, infinity, and eternity continued long after Aquinas and Bonaventure. One example should give the flavor of their nature; consider this one on the immortality of the soul: If $A = B$, then $2A = 2B$. Let $A =$ 'half alive' and $B =$ 'half dead' (where $A = B$ in the same sense that a glass half full is also half empty). Then, $2A =$ 'fully alive' and $2B =$ 'fully dead'. Thus, to be dead is to be alive, and so the soul is immortal. End of Proof!

The question of the duration of time is still the source of some lively philosophical debate. Consider, for example, Whitrow's proof [Whitrow, 1978] of the impossibility of an infinite past, an echo of Philoponos' disbelief in an infinite past because that implies that an actual infinity of events would already have happened (which of course is absurd). The only way out of this inconsistency, goes Whitrow's conclusion, is to deny the initial assumption of an infinite past. To add scientific support to this philosophical analysis, Professor Whitrow concluded by citing the prediction from general relativity of a singularity in spacetime at some finite past time; i.e., the prediction that time (and everything else) had its beginning in the now famous Big Bang.

There is, however, a philosopher for every point of view (or so it seems). Whitrow's analysis provoked a flurry of replies, with [Popper, 1978] and [Bell, 1979] disagreeing. Then [Craig, 1979] replied to support Whitrow and refute Popper, but Craig was to suffer a similiar fate himself, as he was refuted by [Small, 1986]. That didn't put an end to the debate, however. The following year saw another paper in support of the logical possibility of an infinite past [Smith, 1987], which was met by a mathematical rebuttal in [Eells, 1988]. And, indeed, this same year revealed that Smith only believed in the logical possibility of an infinite past, but that in fact he really believed that the Universe is of finite age and that it originated in an uncaused (i.e., no God required) Big Bang [Smith, 1988]. Most recently Smith has been rebutted on this latter position by [Smith and Weingard, 1990], which argues that Smith has overlooked the complications of quantum effects under nonsingularity conditions. Smith has, of course, replied [Smith, 1991]. An interesting parallel debate on the same issue took place during these same years between Craig and the Canadian philosopher Julian Wolfe; see [Wolfe, 1971], [Craig, 1978, 1980, 1981], and [Wolfe, 1985]. When will all these debates end? Not until the end of the (infinite?) future, I'd wager!

There was one reply to Whitrow, however, that addressed the scientific view of the beginning of time that Professor Whitrow had raised. This paper [Weingard, 1979c] pointed out that while general relativity and its predicted spacetime singularity in the distant past may indeed allow for a finite past, this still does not totally close the door to the possibility that the Big Bang was a continuation in time from a previous contraction phase of the Universe (and so on, ad infinitum). To quote T. S. Eliot ("Little Gidding"):

> What we call the beginning is often the end
> And to make an end is to make a beginning.
> The end is where we start from.

In an ingenious observation that seems to have been missed by most philosophers, E. A. Milne, a professor of mathematics at Oxford, suggested in his 1948 book *Kinematic Relativity* that with general relativity it is conceivable to have both a single Big Bang and an infinite past. More recently, Misner, a physicist, has made a similar observation [Misner, 1969b]. Pointing out that to talk meaningfully of time implies a clock to measure it by, Professors Milne and Misner looked for a Universal clock more enduring than our heartbeats, Big Ben, the rotation of the Earth about the Sun, the finest Timex, or anything else that exists only transiently. They suggested the expansion rate of the Universe itself as the ideal clock. As we go back in time toward the Big Bang, the expansion rate rises toward infinity and, as Misner puts it: "We see the Universe ticking away ... quite actively. *The Universe is meaningfully old because infinitely many things have happened since the beginning* [Misner's emphasis]." In this view cosmic time is taken as proportional to the negative of the logarithm of the normalized volume V of the Universe ($V = 1$ represents infinite volume). Thus, as V goes to zero as we go backward in time, time runs ever faster. Since this view puts the Big Bang (with $V = 0$) infinitely long ago, it has the virtue of sidestepping the issue of what happened before the creation of the Universe and of time. (See also [York, 1972].) Thus, the answer to the question that is this section's title is *yes*, the past is infinite when time is measured by the largest clock imaginable, the Universe itself.

Time and Clocks

Looking for clocks to measure time is clearly of fundamental importance. Going to the other extreme for the ultimate clock, from the Universe clock of Milne and Misner down to the microscopic, was one mathematician [Ellis, 1974] who, in his words, offered "a radical and far-reaching declaration: the variation of an elementary particles's time *is* the variation of its radius; time is size and size is time; old is big and young is small, or vice versa; time is but a grand illusion." No one, to my knowledge, has pursued this curious suggestion, one that sounds like something Humpty Dumpty might have said to Alice, but as with the Universe clock, it is *change* that is important in Ellis' particle clock. To quote the Elizabethan poet Edmund Spenser who wrote in his *Faerie Queene* of the end of time:

> ... when no more *Change* shall be,
> But stedfast rest of all things firmely stayd
> Upon the pillours of Eternity,
> That is contrayr to *Mutabilitie*.

These are odd clocks by ordinary standards; the Universe is not the usual sort of thing we associate with being a clock. Clocks are supposed to run at a fixed, uniform rate, while the Milne/Misner cosmic clock runs faster as we go backward in time and slower as we go forward. Of course, to say one clock is not running at a uniform rate implies that we have a second clock that *is* running at a uniform rate to use as a master for comparison. And how do we know the master is indeed running at a uniform rate? Do we need a third, super-master clock (and then a fourth, and ...)? Are we again facing a McTaggart-like infinite-regress horror of clocks? The answers to these questions are almost paradoxical. Special relativity tells us that time does *not* always pass at the same rate, and yet the same theory tells us that just one clock will do, as all clocks are related in their timekeeping.

No one would question that our lives are intimately entangled with time, and hence with the clocks we use to measure it by. As we read in [Mendilow, 1952], life in modern times is ruled by the clock: "Achievement is estimated in terms of the length of time taken to accomplish our purposes, for time is money, and in a changing Universe we have no time to waste or lose. While factories turn out thousands of new appliances to save time, the entertainment industry spends millions on amusements to kill time. Life seems to be resolving itself into a feverish scramble for the last drinks before the inexorable barmaid calls out her fatal 'Time, gentlemen, time' and shuts up shop for good." Or in the wonderfully morbid words of Philip Van Doren Stern in his editorial introduction to the fantasy anthology *Travelers in Time* (Doubleday 1947), "The clock is a dreadful instrument, the impartial ruler of the brief span of consciousness which lies between the warm darkness of the womb and the cold everlasting night of the grave."

We might think this slavery to clocks is a fairly new development, but consider the following passage from "The First Voyage" (to Lilliput) of Captain Lemuel Gulliver, written more than two hundred fifty years ago.[5] Upon searching the Captain the Lilliputians made an inventory of their findings, which included his watch or, as they called it, "a wonderful kind of Engine." As the inventory continues: "And we conjecture it is either some unknown Animal, or the God that he worships: But we are more inclined to the latter Opinion, because he assured us ... that he seldom did any Thing without consulting it. He called it his Oracle, and said it pointed out the Time for every Action of his life."

Gulliver's mechanical watch had an ancient ancestory. The very first clocks to measure the passage of time (as opposed to just counting off the days with the alternation of night and day, and the years by the cycling of the seasons) were the shadow clocks of Egypt, dating back at least to 1500–2000 B.C. and almost certainly much earlier than that. Progress was steady, if sporadic, and by Newton's time seagoing chronometers were precise enough to allow worldwide navigation. By the nineteenth century the balance spring and wheel clock proved to be astonishingly accurate (an error of one second per year was achievable), and futher significant advances had to wait until the twentieth-century technology of electric-quartz and atomic-gas clocks. The invention of the electric-quartz clock increased accuracy to one second of error in decades, and today's atomic-gas clocks have reached the nearly incomprehensible accuracy of one second of error in a hundred centuries.

For our purposes in this book, however, the clock of most interest is one that has never actually been built—the *photon clock*. To understand this clock imagine two parallel mirrors with a pendulum of light, a photon, reflecting endlessly back and forth where each pair of bounces is a single tick-tock of the clock. The idea of a photon clock has been around in physics for well over half a century. This clock is important because, as shown in Tech Note 2, it allows us to derive, with nothing more than simple algebra and elementary geometry, the central result of special relativity—the conclusion that time is not Newton's absolute (see Tech Note 1), but in fact is Einstein's relative time, which depends on the spatial state of the observer. This mixing together of space and time was one of the greatest intellectual insights in all of human history, but it is just one of a large number of astonishing ideas from relativity, as we will begin to discuss in the next two sections.

Hyperspace and Wormholes

The idea of a fourth dimension to space is viewed by many as simple-minded nonsense,[6] as Laura stated in the third quote that opened this chapter. And in his 1897 Presidential Address to the American Mathematical Society [Newcomb, 1898], Simon Newcomb declared, "The introduction of what is now very generally called hyper-space, especially space of more than three dimensions, into mathematics has proved a stumbling block to more than one able philosopher." Einstein later stated the issue somewhat more bluntly [Einstein, 1961]: "The non-mathematician is seized by a mysterious shuddering when he hears of 'four-dimensional' things, by a feeling not unlike that awakened by thoughts of the occult." Anybody can just see that there are exactly three dimensions, and that is that. For science fiction writers, however, the fourth dimension (and hyperspace, in general) is a major concept.

Writing in *Analog*, today's premier "hard science" science fiction magazine, the physicist John Cramer [Cramer, 1985b] has nicely summed up what is so fascinating about the idea of an extra dimension (or even more) from the fictional point of view: "Are there hidden dimensions not accessible to us, dimensions in which we could go adventuring, dimensions within which malevolent hyper-dimensional aliens may be lurking, ready to pierce our flimsy paper-thin three-space bodies with their terrible hyper-sharp claws?" The early science fiction magazines encouraged this image; e.g., the editorial blurb opening the other-dimensional monster story "Into Another Dimension" [Duclos, 1939] stated that "it was a strange world in which Lester and Florence found themselves. A world of sudden death and strange science, ruled by inhuman beasts."

And just what is *hyperspace*? It is a space of higher dimension than the one we obviously seem to live in. As we will see later in this chapter, our Universe appears to be a four-dimensional (three spatial and one temporal) world called *spacetime*. This four-dimensional world can, at least mathematically, be thought of as the boundary or surface of a five-dimensional hyperspace. In the remarkably sophisticated early story "The Gostak and the Doshes" [Breuer, GSFS] from a 1930 issue of *Amazing Stories*, an eccentric scientist exclaims, "A mathematical physicist lives in vast spaces ... where space unrolls along a fourth dimension on a surface distended from a fifth." This is analogous to the way the two-dimensional space of the surface of a sphere bounds the three-dimensional space of the sphere itself. For the inhabitants of *Sphereland* [Burger, 1983], their hyperspace is the interior of the sphere (excluding time) that the surface they live on bounds. For such beings, for example, there would be two ways to travel from one pole to the other—the usual way on the obvious world of the surface or the hyperspace way that takes them through the sphere along the polar diameter.

By thinking of the sphere as an apple and of the hyperspace path as a tunnel through the apple, it has become popular to call all such shortcuts through any hyperspace, what ever its dimension may be, *wormholes* (e.g., see [Morris and Thorne, 1988]). The general theory of relativity predicts the existence of such wormholes, and in fact they were first discovered theoretically in mathematics as early as 1916 by the Viennese physicist Ludwig Flamm. Later analyses were done by Einstein himself [Einstein, 1935a], while Cohen [Cohen, RAG] discusses another solution as a possible model for a pulsar (usually thought of as a rotating neutron star). Recently [Ori, 1991b] has presented theoretical analyses suggesting that the interior of a charged black hole may be the entrance to a wormhole. All these solutions are often generically called "Einstein-Rosen bridges." (Nathan Rosen was Einstein's co-author in the 1935 paper). The term *wormhole* was coined in the 1950s by John Wheeler. (Wheeler used them to show how electric charge could be thought of as lines of force trapped in the changing topology of a multiply-connected, empty space [Brill, MWM], [Wheeler, 1962a], [Misner and Wheeler, 1957]. Indeed, Wheeler has claimed that the observation of what we call electricity is experimental proof that space is not simply connected.) More poetically, I have even seen wormholes referred to as spacetime subways! (For more about wormholes and about how they are related to time travel see Tech Note 9.)

It is immediately obvious that in the case of sphereland the hyperspace or wormhole path is shorter than the surface path (but in "FTA" [Martin, SFSSS] we find a clever tale based on precisely the opposite idea). Getting around in hyperspace (assuming it is really there), however, may not be a trivial task. "The Mapmakers" [Pohl, 1956], for example, tells the story of how one of the first spaceships to explore hyperspace gets lost. As Pohl puts it, the trouble with hyperspace travel is that "You go in at one point, you rocket around until you think it's time to come out, and there you are. Where is 'there'? Why, that's the surprise that's in store for you, because you never know until you get there. And sometimes not even then." This idea plays a central role in *Tunnel in the Sky* [Heinlein, 1955], in which a "hyperspace gate" is discovered by accident during failed time-travel experiments.

Isaac Asimov's "Take a Match" [Asimov, 1975] asks a similiar question and arrives at the same answer: "When you took the Jump ... how sure were you *where* you would emerge? The timing and quantity of the energy input might be as tightly controlled as you liked ... but the uncertainty principle reigned supreme and there was always the chance, even the inevitability of a random miss ... a paper-thin miss might be a thousand light-years." And in "The Trouble with Hyperspace" [Sharkey, 1965], instantaneous travel through hyperspace is related to backward time travel and the serious causality problems thereby created.

A common way to comprehend hyperspace shortcuts is to imagine the beginning and end of a journey as points A and B in the two-dimensional surface of a

FIGURE 6. This illustration of a "super science" gadget accompanied a 1939 story by Maurice Duclos in *Fantastic Adventures*. The gadget operated by vibrating an object faster than light, whereupon the Lorentz-FitzGerald contraction predicts an *imaginary* size for the object—which really means (so we are told) that the object has entered "another plane of existence." The inventor (the one with the gun) is inviting his grim-faced assistant to give it a try. (The original caption reads "Get into that vibrator! Get in, I say!")

Illustration for "Into Another Dimension" by Kenneth J. Reeve, ©1939 by Ziff-Davis Publishing Co.; reprinted by arrangement with Forrest J. Ackerman, Holding Agent, 2495 Glendower Ave., Hollywood, CA 90027.

piece of paper. Then, imagine further that the paper is folded so as to position *A* over *B*, perhaps even with *A* almost touching *B*. The distance from *A* to *B* through hyperspace (the three-dimensional space in which the folding takes place) can be much less than the distance through normal space (the paper). This idea has broken free from science fiction, in fact, and can be found in modern stories in other genres, as well. For example, in the Stephen King story "Mrs. Todd's Short-cut" [King, 1985] a woman keeps finding ever shorter ways to drive from Castle Rock, Maine, to Bangor. As the crow flies it is 79 miles, but she gets the journey down to 67 and later to 31.6 miles. When doubted, she replies: "Fold the map and see how many miles it is then ... it can be a little less than a straight line if you fold it a little, or it can be a lot less if you fold it a lot." The doubter remains uncon-vinced: "You can fold a map on paper, but you can't fold *land*." For our purposes, of course, the creation of wormholes in spacetime, we have to imagine much more: the folding of four-dimensional spacetime through a five-dimensional hy-perspace.

Despite the final quote that opened this chapter, not just science fiction fans take this conception of hyperspace with some seriousness. For example, in [Whis-ton, 1974] we find a mathematician writing that "most science fiction addicts are familiar with the notion of 'hyperspace,' a higher dimensional space-time bounded by Space-Time through which, in the far distant future, interstellar voyages short-cut the (otherwise unsurmountable) distances between the stars. The purpose of this article is to demonstrate that any ... relativistic space-time model is the bound-ary of some ... five-dimensional hyperspace." This, of course, is just what Breuer's magazine character said—in 1930!

The idea of dimensional gateways between a plurality of worlds is an old one in science fiction. Jack Williamson, for example, used it in his 1931 story "Through the Purple Cloud" [Williamson, 1975], which somewhat implausibly imagines that the spacetime barrier might somehow be torn asunder by the puny energy of a mere chemical reaction. He repeated this idea in the story "In the Scarlet Star" [Williamson, 1933], which has a gadget that lets a man step through a dimensional portal into another world, which is hinted to be our world's ancient past. More recently, "Triple-Time Try" [Collins, 1959] has a geologist bouncing around in the remote past, from Silurian to Carboniferous to Cretaceous to Miocene times, be-cause a big meteor strike on the California coast had released "enough mass-conversion-energy to breach the space-time continuum;" somehow three alter-nate realities were temporarily linked by the breach. Unconstrained by any limits on his imagination, the great H. G. Wells himself used the portal idea in 1895 (the same year *The Time Machine* appeared in book form) in his *The Wonderful Visit* [Wells, 1895]. This novel, clearly not conventional science fiction by any stretch of meaning, concerns the strange adventures of an angel who in some unexplained manner literally flies into our world (where he is shot in the wing by a vicar's gun!). There is, however, a brief bit of speculation about the fourth dimension: "There may be any number of three dimensional Universes packed side by side." And Friedman, a physicist, [Friedman, 1988] even interpreted C. S. Lewis' wardrobe (in the children's book *The Lion, the Witch and the Wardrobe*) as a wormhole connecting our world and that of Narnia. *Stonewords* [Conrad, 1990] which is a change-the-past story, uses a similar idea (a wormhole staircase in an old house) to connect the world of 1870 to the present.

A different sort of discussion of hyperspace is given in "Avoidance Situation" [McConnell, 1983]. The author, who is an academic psychologist, has put himself into this story of a starship captain who explains to the crew psychologist how he feels about hyperspace: (or subspace, as McConnell called it): "God forsaken. That's just what it is. Completely black, completely empty. It frightens me every time we make the jump through it ... it frightens me because—well, because a man seems to get lost out there. In normal space there are always stars around, no matter how distant they may be, and you feel that you've got direction and location. In subspace, all you've got is nothing—and one hell of a lot of that. It's incredible when you stop to think about it. An area—an opening as big as the whole of our Universe, big enough to pack every galaxy we've ever seen in it ... and not a single atom of matter in it ... until we came barging in to use it as a shortcut across our own Universe."

The vastness of hyperspace got a more down-to-Earth treatment from the early science fiction author Bob Olsen, who wrote the following as the introduction to his "The Four Dimensional Auto-Parker" [Olsen, 1934]:

> I read a yarn the other day—
> A crazy concept, I must say.
> It states that objects have extension
> In what is called the 'Fourth Dimension'.
>
> In hyperspace one could, no doubt,
> Make tennis balls turn inside out;
> And from a nut remove the kernel
> And not disturb the shell external.
>
> A crook could pilfer bonds and stocks,
> Then laugh at prison bars and locks;
> One step in this direction queer,
> And presto! He would disappear!
>
> Let's hope, in planning new inventions,
> They'll give us cars with four dimensions.
> When searching for a parking place
> We sure could use some hyperspace!

The next two sections elaborate on the various properties of hyperspace mentioned in Olsen's amusing doggerel.

Monsters in Hyperspace

As Professor Cramer implies, speculation about aliens in hyperspace has long been popular. "The Einstein See-Saw" [Breuer, 1932b] limits itself to mere beasts with "rows of teeth that came together with a snap," ripping the hero's trousers. In "The 32nd of May" [Ernst, BSF], however, things are more serious. The narrator, while visiting his friends the Bartons, gets up to leave just as the clock is about to strike midnight. As the clock rings out with the eleventh note, he passes "between two mirrors, facing each other at an angle allowing both my face and my back to be seen by me," and then he stumbles. He stumbles, in fact, into a strange, alien place where he is confronted by a two-dimensional creature that "watched me with callous interest out of its inhuman eye." After observing a lengthy battle between this first creature and a second over which will have the right to kill him, the narrator manages in the nick of time to stumble back into his friends' living room. As he does so, he hears the clock strike the twelfth note of midnight as well as one of his hosts exclaiming, "How funny! You know, just for a fraction of a second after you tripped, I couldn't see you! I guess that means another trip to the oculist." But the narrator knows better—as he tells the reader, "I passed between the mirrors in the Bartons' oddly angled living room. I fell—into another world, or plane, or dimension, or whatever you wish to call it, where unimaginable creatures seemed to fight ... . It would seem that there are powers in untried combinations of angles undreamed of by man—and that perhaps geometry is a bridge between worlds. And it would seem that by chance the mirrors formed an angle that transported me instantly from one plane to another. But your guess is as good as mine."

The violence shown by these hyperspace creatures toward one another could also be directed against humans. As the editorial lead-in for "Hell's Dimension" [Curry, 1931] luridly announced, "Professor Lambert deliberately ventures into a Vibrational Dimension to join his fiancee in its magnetic torture-fields." (There is a hint at the possible distortion of time in hyperspace in this story, as well. When eventually rescued by a genius-colleague, the professor and his lady learn that they haven't been gone for just a few hours as they had thought, but rather for eight days.) A less violent but equally hectic story is "The Captured Cross-Section" [Breuer, FM], in which a mathematician loses his fiancee to a fourth-dimensional being.[7] After building a gadget that can rotate the fourth dimension into 3–space, he accidently traps one of the higher-dimensional beings in it. There is a brief struggle, the young lady screams, and then she vanishes. The mathematician is quick to understand what has happened: "There is only one possible conclusion — the struggles of the fourth-dimensional creature swept her out into hyperspace."

Aliens from the fourth dimension entering *our* world are even more threatening, as is demonstrated in "The Monster From Nowhere" [Bond, 1939a]. This is the tale of an explorer who manages to catch such a creature while on expedition to the Maratan Plateau in Upper Peru. The narrator (and we) soon learn more from the explorer who has brought the "thing" back to civilization when the fellow delivers a mini-tutorial on how all we can see in our world is a three-dimensional cross section of the higher-dimensional monster; at last it sinks into the narrator's head what he is looking at: "This time I got it. I gasped: 'Then you think that *thing* in the work-shed is a cross-section of a creature from the ... ' Yes, Len. From the Fourth Dimension!" The "thing" eventually escapes and returns to its world, but not before killing one man and taking another with it back into the fourth dimension.

Those early readers of magazine fiction who found the idea of hyperspace monsters intriguing, must have thought Clifford Simak's "Hellhounds of the Cosmos" [Simak, 1932] was the ultimate story. After first telling us of his theory of cosmic evolution, that it is downward rather than upward, the fictional professor in the tale reveals the precise nature of the strange creatures then attacking Earth — they are creatures whose ancestors were higher-dimensional beings who have since degenerated down to the mere fourth dimension. They view Earthlings, who are of course only three dimensional, as "fodder, something to be eaten as we eat vegetables and cereals." As the professor finally cries in dispair, "We are facing an invasion of fourth dimensional creatures ... We are being attacked by life which is one dimension above us in evolution. We are fighting, I tell you, a tribe of hellhounds out of the cosmos. They are unthinkably above us in the matter of intelligence. There is a chasm of knowledge between us so wide and so deep that it staggers the imaginaition." (As I typed Simak's hysterical prose I couldn't help but recall, from the Editor's Introduction to the anthology FSFS, that so much in early magazine fiction was "science that was claptrap and fiction that was graceless.")

Hollywood has not made much use of the idea of invasions from other dimensions, and then has used it only as a joke. The most recent example is the insipid 1984 film *The Adventures Of Buckaroo Bonzai,* in which the hero (so talented he moonlights both as a brain surgeon and as a rock-band singer) battles invaders from the eighth dimension. This is a hollow copy of the adventures in the comics of Wonder Woman, who was in the fourth dimension in 1944 (battling a villain with the curious name Anton Unreal), and in the X–dimension in 1958 (she got there with the aid of Professor Alpha's gadget called, appropriately enough, the "X-dimension machine"). The use of other dimensions is a popular idea for the comic writers—in 1940 Batman and Robin were in the fourth dimension (if only in a dream), and in 1965 Superman's Metropolis was invaded by "It," a "whirling behemoth" thrust out of its world by a vicious tornado that had torn a hole in something called the "dimensional barrier." Superman, of course, rose to the occasion and thrust "It" back where it belonged (wherever that was).

"Beings from other dimensions" is an idea that some believe had its genesis well before the science fiction writers got hold of it. One writer [Bailey, 1972] asserts that a visitor from some realm of non-Euclidean space-time is described in Guy de Maupassant's 'The Horla' (1887) [de Maupassant, 1955], but I fail to find de Maupassant's idea for the origin of his creature quite that specific. Bailey also claims that Ambrose Bierce's 1893 story "The Damned Thing" [Bierce, 1964]

FIGURE 7. This illusration from the original magazine appearance of Nelson Bond's "Monster From Nowhere" shows the monster. The three-dimensional cross section of the fourth-dimensional monster looks amazingly like an ordinary monster.

Illustration for "Monster from Nowhere" by Jay Jackson, ©1939 by Ziff-Davis Publishing Co.; reprinted by arrangement with Forrest J. Ackerman, Holding Agent, 2495 Glendower Ave., Hollywood, CA 90027.

presents another visitor from a dimension beyond the third, and again I don't see it. The story seems to me to be more a precursor to Wells' *Invisible Man*, although perhaps a reasonable case could be made for a being from other dimensions in Bierce's tale as he did express in other writings an interest in higher-dimensional spaces.

Predating both these stories is the tale "What Was It? A Mystery" [O'Brien, 1988] by Fitz-James O'Brien, a writer thought by some critics to be the equal of Poe and Lovecraft in the horror genre. This story by the Irish-born American who died in the Civil War (it first appeared in the March 1859 issue of *Harper's New Monthly Magazine*) is written as a first-person narrative of an incident "so awful and inexplicable in its character that my reason fairly reels at the bare memory of the occurrence." Retiring for the evening in a house reputed to be haunted, the narrator suddenly feels a "Thing" drop upon his chest from the dark. He is forced into a "struggle of awful intensity" for his very life. Overcoming it at last, he incapacitates the Thing and lights the gas-burner—only to find his attacker, like the Damned Thing, is invisible. Not to be stopped by this, the narrator then chloroforms the Thing and has a plaster cast of it made! The result shows a small, heavily muscled creature looking like a "ghoul, capable of feeding on human flesh." Unable to determine what else it might eat, the narrator watches the creature soon starve to death and then secretly buries it. A living, breathing Thing, with a beating heart, it was clearly not a ghost—was it perhaps from a dimension beyond ours? I think not.

The clear, common feature of these three particular nineteenth-century creatures is their malignancy, not their other-dimensionality. O'Brien's Thing eats human flesh, the Horla drives one man mad, and Bierce's Damned Thing kills in a most gruesome manner. In my opinion, commentators who see hyperspace in nineteenth-century tales of mysterious creatures are simply seeing too much.

As Simak's "hellhounds" demonstrates, the science fiction of the early twentieth century is different from earlier works when it comes to hyperspace monsters. Over time, however, writers have become more sophisticated, so hyperspace aliens don't *always* win,[8] or aren't always murderous (e.g., "The Captured Cross-Section" [Breuer, FM]), and in fact in many stories of the fourth dimension, there aren't any aliens at all. In "The Shape of Things" [Bradbury, TOT], for example, we have just the opposite, a fourth-dimension story based not on horror, hellhounds, or savage hyperbeasts, but rather on love and compassion. Despite, indeed because, of the latest in high-tech hospital gadgetry, a baby is born into hyperspace. As the doctor explains to the understandably stunned father (in a smooth bit of science fiction obfuscation): "The child was somehow affected by the birth pressure. There was a dimensional distructure caused by the simultaneous short-circuitings and malfunctionings of the new birth-mechs and the hypnosis machines. Well, anyway, your baby was born into ... another dimension." The baby, named Py, is healthy but odd-appearing to his 3–space parents; he looks like a small blue pyramid (hence his name) with three eyes and six appendages. Fearing for his emotional development and learning that the doctors cannot bring Py into 3-space, it is decided that the parents will join their child in 4–space. The romantic appeal of escape into the fourth dimension with the aid of helpful hyperspacians will probably never fade; the idea appeared as recently as in a 1985 story in the slick, mass-market magazine *Omni* ("Tangents" [Bear, MTMW]).

Not only writers for science fiction paperback magazines (the "pulps") were fascinated by other-dimensional worlds. In 1930, for example, *Amazing Detective Tales* published a short, still scary story of the perfect murder. In "Murder in the Fourth-Dimension" [Smith, 1964], written by fantasy and horror writer Clark Ashton Smith, the fourth dimension proves to be the perfect place for disposing of the body—until the murderer realizes he has made a fatal mistake, made all the more awful when it proves not to be quite so fatal after all. The physical conception of the fourth dimension is rather primitive in this tale, which speaks of "the theory that other worlds or dimensions may co-exist in the same space with ours by reason of a different molecular structure and vibrational rate, rendering them intangible for us." More modern, of course, is the view that our three dimensions are just three of the four (or five or more) dimensions that constitute hyperspace, just as Flatland's two dimensions are two of our three dimensions. (Molecular vibration rate has nothing to do with the issue.) And in the comics one of Superman's more interesting adversaries is Mr. Mxyzptlk (pronounced *mix-yez-pittle-ick*), a being with seemingly magical powers from the Land of Zrfff in the fifth dimension. It isn't really magic, however, but merely the result of his two extra dimensions.

Space as the Fourth Dimension

The idea in fiction of the fourth dimension as a space dimension, although possessing a history stretching well back into the nineteenth century, is itself pre-dated by academic speculation and commentary. Bork, a scholar on the history of the concept [Bork, 1964], has found that by 1911 there were at least 1800 papers on *n*-dimensional geometry, with three-fourths of them from before 1900. In 1873, for example, we find an essay in *Nature* that refers to well-known mathematicians who even earlier had shown they had an inner assurance of the reality of transendental space.[9] Just five years later, we find the eminent mathematical physicist Peter Tait, in a comment tossed out in casual passing, telling us that "Prof. Klein, of Munich, some time ago showed, *as is well known* [my emphasis], that knots cannot exist in space of four dimensions".[10] Tait goes on to indicate the basis, for some, for believing in a fourth spatial dimension; it offered one way to explain otherwise inexplicable occurrences, such as ghosts, the reading of sealed letters, and rope tricks: "It is some time since [a friend] told me *his* jocular mode of arguing from Klein's discovery—that all the secrets of the spiritualistic 'rope-trick' could be at once explained by supposing that *inside* the mysterious cabinet (in which the tambourines and the musical boxes fly about) space was of four dimensions—so that the well-corded performers were at once loosened from their bonds on entering it!"

But is it really plausible that there might be four spatial dimensions? After all, we experience only three independent directions. In [Ouspensky, 1981] we find, for example, "By an *independent direction* we mean ... a line lying at right angles to another line. Our geometry ... knows *only three* such lines which lie simultaneously at right angles to one another and are not parallel in relation to each other.

Why are there only three and not ten or fifteeen? This we do not know." Indeed, in an 1888 talk to the Philosophical Society of Washington, Simon Newcomb (see Note 21 for more on Newcomb) dismissed the view that space must necessarily be three dimensional as an "old metaphysical superstition" [Beichler, 1988].

Yet, despite Newcomb's open-mindedness, it has been shown that in the framework of classical physics there are powerful reasons for why there must be *exactly* three dimensions. A beginning of these arguments can be found in Kant, who believed that the three-dimensional nature of the world and Newton's inverse square law for gravity were intertwined, but he offered nothing beyond philosophical speculation. Using very fundamental physical arguments, however, it is not difficult to demonstrate that the Poisson-Laplace equation (a second-order partial differential equation that describes the potential functions for both Newtonian gravity and electrostatics) does not allow stable planetary or atomic orbits in any space with dimensionality greater than three. This idea can be traced back to Paul Ehrenfest's work in 1917. Further, the distortionless, reverberation-free propagation of waves (electromagnetic and sound) is possible only in spaces of dimensions one and three.

These conclusions have been shown to hold even when we go beyond classical physics to general relativity and quantum mechanics. On an even more abstract level, *if* we believe in the existence of a unified field theory of gravitation and electromagnetism (which was by 1924 shown to be contained in Einstein's general theory, even though Einstein seems never to have been aware of this; see [Misner and Wheeler, 1957] and [Wheeler, 1962]), and *if* we believe that the Maxwell and the Einstein equations correctly describe the electromagnetic field and spacetime, respectively, *then* only in a four-dimensional world do these field equations mathematically determine their fields with equal strength. Since time is one of these dimensions, we are again back to three dimensions for space. Mathematical proofs of all these statements can be found in the literature.[11]

Using a slightly different approach, a biological-topological argument has been advanced for why space could not have less than three dimensions. In all of our common experiences, complex intelligent life is always found to occur as an aggragate of a vast number of elementary cells interconnected via electrical nerve fibers. Each such cell is connected to several others, not all immediate neighbors, by these fibers. If space had only one or two dimensions, then such highly interconnected nets of cells would be impossible, as the overlapping nerve fibers would have to intersect, which would result in their mutually shorting one another.

Some nineteenth-century academics, either ignorant of or willing to ignore all the preceeding, associated the fourth dimension with the luminiferous ether. This mysterious stuff, in analogy with all known wave phenomena, was thought to be necessary to give light something in which to move (particularly in a vacuum). For example, Karl Pearson of London's University College attempted a typical Victorian explanation of various optical and chemical phenomena via a mechanical model of something he called an "ether squirt." This was motivated by Lord Kelvin's observation that under certain conditions two sources of incompressible liquid would attract each other with an inverse-square-law force. This seemed so suggestive of gravitational and electromagnetic behavior that it seemed such sources (and analogous sinks) might allow an explanation of these phenomena.

Pearson thought of the luminiferous ether as being Kelvin's liquid (pulsating atoms would be its sources and sinks), and he imagined the ether flowing into and out of our three-dimensional world. So—from where did the ether come and where does it go? Pearson cautiously hinted at the fourth dimension: "From whence the squirt comes into three-dimensional space it is impossible to say; the theory limits our possibility of knowledge of the physical Universe to the existence of the squirt. It may be an argument for the existence of a space of higher dimensions than our own, but of that we can know nothing." A few years later came a half-joking response,[12] which called the whole business of ether squirts "A Holiday Dream," and which said that it compels "us to the supposition of a fourth dimension, which belongs to the domain of nightmares, not of dreams, and we try to shake ourselves from the idea." Nightmarish or not, such scientific speculations on the nature of the ether, and its possible explanation in terms of a four-dimensional hyperspace, were not uncommon in the last two decades of the nineteenth century [Beichler, 1988].

There are, in fact, two particular nineteenth-century individuals who are most closely identified with bringing the fourth dimension out of academia and into public consciousness; Charles Howard Hinton (1853–1907) and Herbert George Wells (1866–1946). Hinton was no angle-trisecting crank, having earned an M.A. at Oxford, an appointment in the mathematics department at Princeton and then another at the University of Minnesota.[13] Later, with the help of the eminent astronomer Simon Newcomb, he obtained a position at the Naval Observatory in Washington, D.C., and was on the United States Patent Office staff at the time of his sudden death. Hinton was a man to be taken seriously.

Hinton's first published essay, "What is the Fourth Dimension?," appeared in 1880 and then in book form in 1884 as part of his *Scientific Romances*. This book received a generally favorable review in *Nature*.[14] The four-dimensional-space essay, itself, almost certainly had impact. At one point he wrote: "We might then suppose that the matter we know extending in three dimensions has also a small thickness in the fourth dimension," an idea that was used a few years later by the well-known mathematician W. W. Rouse Ball [Ball, 1891] in an attempt to explain gravity. Ball specifically cites Hinton as having priority, but he also claims that he was unaware of Hinton's work until after his own was completed. Hinton was extremely inventive, and he also put forth four-dimensional-space models for static electricity.

In Henderson's massive work [Henderson, 1983] on the influence of the idea of a fourth spatial dimension on art and literature, a very complete summary of its appearance in nineteenth-century literary works is given. H. G. Wells is, of course, the best known of the authors, but many other well-known non-science-fiction writers also used the concept, including Dostoevsky in *The Brothers Karamazov* (1880) and Oscar Wilde in "The Canterville Ghost," (1891). Wilde's use of the

fourth dimension in "The Canterville Ghost" is brief, but it does show the fascination this idea held for supernaturalists; the ghost, at one point, makes a quick
retreat by disappearing through the wainscoting, "hastily adopting the Fourth Dimension of Space as a means of escape." This identification of the fourth dimension with the spirit world can actually be traced as far back as the mid-seventeenth
century, to the philosopher-poet and Cambridge Platonist Henry More. Two centuries later the idea of two parallel worlds, ours and the other inhabited by the
spirits of the dead sharing a common temporal dimension with us but displaced in
space, was used to great effect by Elizabeth Phelps in her 1868 internationally
best-selling novel *The Gates Ajar*. Phelps wrote to offer ease from the terrible
emotional pain suffered by the legions who had lost loved ones in the Civil War
and who had received little comfort from traditional nineteenth-century religions.

Some years after Phelps, Scottish writer Robert Barr wrote a tale, "The Hour
Glass" [Barr, 1989], in which a ghost lays claim to his lost timepiece, an hourglass,
across nearly two centuries; there is the strong hint in this story of a connection
between the time dimension and the supernatural. The use of higher dimensions in
supernatural fiction has been continued by modern writer Algernon Blackwood,
who liked the concept enough to use it more than once. Some of his stories
explicitly mention nineteenth- and early twentieth-century mathematicians, such
as Gauss, Lobachevski, Einstein, Minkowski, Bolyai, and Hinton, who worked with
geometrical extensions both of Euclid's geometry and beyond the third dimension.
There are running through Blackwood's stories [Blackwood, 1949] repeated references to a new direction at right angles to the three known ones. Other writers
have also connected ghosts and the fourth dimension. For example, Ray Cummings explained ghosts in his "Into the Fourth Dimension," a 1926 story appearing in *Science & Invention* (Hugo Gernsback's magazine that was a precursor to
the science fiction pulps). Goulart [1975] wrote a modern story that has the
inventor of the first time machine as a "renowned ghost detective and occult
investigator," and [Cartur, SSFT] links ghosts with spatial dimensions beyond the
third.

All sorts of fourth-dimension tricks were part enough of common knowledge
even before the turn of the century that one can find them integrated into stories
appearing in popular, general readership magazines of the day. For example, "The
Conversion of the Professor" [Griffith, 1899] (with the subtitle "A Tale of the
Fourth Dimension") is essentially a love story in which a curmudgeonly math
professor is convinced by a meeting with a four-dimensional version of himself
that he should not block his daughter's marriage plans—the dramatic revelation
comes when he sees two rings interlocked without either being broken, a feat
impossible in the third dimension, but not in the fourth.

Popular fascination with space as the fourth dimension reached a peak with an
essay contest run by *Scientific American* in 1900. The top prize of $500 for the
best explanation of 4–space attracted 245 entries from all over the world, the very
best of which have been preserved in [Manning, 1960], first published in 1910. Of
course, it wasn't long before these ideas found their way into science fiction. "The

Fifth-Dimension Catapult" [Leinster, SFT] was typical of the early stories. As its title implies, the story is about the fifth dimension,[15] and its hero, Tommy Reames, is a playboy genius who in his spare time writes such papers as "On the Mass and Inertia of the Tesseract" and "Additions to Herglotz's Mechanics of Continua." The dialogue reads at times like Raymond Chandler; for example, informed that the inventor of the catapult is marooned in the fifth dimension, Tommy "pulled out a cigarette case and lighted a cigarette and said sardonically, 'The fifth dimension? That seems rather extreme. Most of us get along very well with three dimensions. Four seems luxurious. Why pick on the fifth?' " There is a beautiful girl, and gangsters, too (but no Philip Marlowe), in this potboiler.

Another early use of space as the fourth dimension is in "Four Dimensional Transit" [Olsen, 1928a]. An awkward rewrite of Verne's *Around the World in Eighty Days*, Olsen's work has a professor and his crew fly into hyperspace and around the world (and to the moon and back) in less than a day, using a plane equipped with a fourth-dimensional rudder. A more interesting illustration of the fourth dimension as a spatial dimension is given in "The Vanishing Man" [Hughes, MM], the tragic 1926 story of a math professor who actually learns how to move into hyperspace and back. A colleague catches him at it and, once over his astonishment, asks how it is done. The Professor replies: "My assumption is that the fourth dimension is just another dimension—no more different in kind from length, say, than length is from breadth and thickness, but perpendicular to all three. Now suppose that a being in two dimensions—a flat creature, like the moving shadows of a cinematagraph—were suddenly to grasp the concept of a third dimension [e.g., as in Edwin Abbott's 1880 classic fantasy *Flatland*] and so step out of the picture. He might move only an inch, but he would vanish completely from the sight of the world."

The Professor has, you see, learned how to step out of 3–space into 4–space, but when asked to explain how, all he can say is "How can I explain? It's just the *other* direction. It's *there*!" His colleague can't see it but is quick to grasp the practical implications: "This is power! Think of it! A step, and you are invisible! No prison cells can hold you,[16] for there is a side to you on which they are as open as a wedding ring! No ring is secure from you: you can put your hand *round the corner* and draw out what you like. And, of course, if you looked back on the Universe you had left, you would see us in sections, open to you! You could place a stone or a tablet of poison right in the very bowels of your enemies!"

Early science fiction, in fact, was literally overrun with nutty professors whose experiments with the fourth dimension went amiss. Some of these stories were interesting, even instructive, but often they were simply silly (e.g., "Scandal in the 4th Dimension" [Long, 1934]). In "Dr. Fuddles' Fingers" [Bond, 1946], however, we meet another, more interesting professor, whose right hand has been modified through an accident to exist in the fourth dimension. To finance his research, he uses this talent to become the perfect pickpocket, able to reach into any wallet no matter how well protected! He also can, indeed, reach right into the very bowels of his fellow man. And he *does*—when he demonstrates his hand to the policeman

FIGURE 8. An experiment in hyperspace goes astray in this illustration from "Four Dimensional Surgery" (*Amazing Stories*, Feb. 1928). The young man is pulling on "Hyper-
Forceps" in an attempt to retrieve a surgeon who has fallen out of 3-space (along with his
patient, a professor of non-Euclidean geometry, who suffers from gallstones)!

Illustration for 'Four Dimensional Surgery" by Frank R. Paul, ©1928 by Experimenter
Publishing Co.; reprinted by permission of the Ackerman Science Fiction Agency, 2495
Glendower Ave., Hollywood, CA 90027 for the Estate.

who has arrested him for being a thief, the astonished officer chokes on a lemon
drop. Dr. Fuddles, of course, removes the drop from the poor fellow's windpipe
with ease.

Some of the best science fiction stories are concerned simply with space itself as the fourth dimension rather than with any creatures, monsters, or ghosts that may exist there. A classic example is "No-Sided Professor" [Gardner, FM] which, in addition to teaching its readers that a *Möbius band* is a single-sided surface with a single edge,[17] comes complete with technical footnotes—just like a journal article. In Gardner's wonderfully imaginative story we learn of a fantastic discovery by Professor Stanislaw Slapenarski that goes beyond Möbius—Slapenarski has found a *no*-sided surface! When he demonstrates this by folding an oddly cut piece of paper (which promptly vanishes in "a loud pop"), he is openly challenged by an unconvinced colleague. Enraged, the Professor knocks his critic out and, powerful man that we are told he is ("He was built like a professional wrestler"), he folds the poor fellow up into a no-sided professor and the critic departs in an explosion. A stunned witness to all this asks: "Can he ... be brought back?" 'I do not know, I do not know,' Slapenarski wailed. 'I have only begun the study of the surfaces—only just begun. I have no way of knowing where he is. Undoubtedly it is one of the higher dimensions, probably one of the odd-numbered ones. God knows which one.' "

It is amusing to note that if Bond's Dr. Fuddles had turned his right hand over in the fourth dimension he would have then had two left hands (see Note 16 again). Curiosity about the relationship of space and handedness can be traced back at least to Kant, and for a technical spacetime discussion of Kant's views on this see [Earman, 1971]. Professor Earman points out, for example, that Kant erred in his claim that left-handed and right-handed objects cannot alternately occupy the same space. For Kant, it was obvious that there simply is no nondeforming, continuous transport that makes a left hand into a right hand. Kant was wrong, however, and the fact that such a transport does exist can be demonstrated (in two dimensions) by sliding a two-dimensional hand around a Möbius strip as described in Gardner's tale. (This, of course, effectively flips the hand over in three-dimensional space.) To flip a three-dimensional hand, we would have to do it in four-dimensional space, a trick Kant (understandably) missed. Hollywood, for some reason, seems not to have been much fascinated by these possibilities for strange fourth-dimension visual effects. The only film I know of with "space as the fourth dimension" as its central theme is the 1959 *4D Man*, in which a man is shown walking through walls. This effect, while dramatic, is as incorrect as it would be for a flatland filmmaker to make "3D Man" showing the hero moving through a closed curve, instead of suddenly vanishing on one side and then suddenly appearing on the other.

Two modern classics of the spatial fourth dimension are "—And He Built a Crooked House" [Heinlein, FM] and "A Subway Named Möbius" [Deutsch, OSF]. In Heinlein's story an architect learns the danger of building on top of an earthquake fault in Los Angeles. He builds a house that is a tesseract—a four-dimensional cube—or, at least, that looks the way such an object would appear in ordinary 3–space. *If* the house were actually in 4–space, it would have wonderful properties, as the architect explains to his initially somewhat reluctant clients:

"That's the grand feature about a tesseract house, complete outside exposure for every room, yet every wall serves two rooms and an eight-room house requires only a one-room foundation. It's revolutionary." It certainly is, especially when an earthquake pushes it over the edge of stability—with the architect and his clients inside. The architect finally figures out what has happened: "This house, while perfectly stable in three dimensions, was not stable in four dimensions. I had built a house in the shape of an unfolded tesseract; something happened to it, some jar or side thrust, and it collapsed into its normal shape—it folded up ... From a four-dimensional standpoint this house was like a plane balanced on an edge. One little push and it fell over, collapsed along its natural joints into a stable four-dimensional figure."

In Deutsch's story the Boston subway suddenly extends itself into hyperspace after its connectivity becomes so high (indeed, it becomes beyond calculation) that a train could travel from any one station to any other station in the whole system. Trains, in fact, can go to even more places than that and they suddenly start to disappear by wandering off into the fourth dimension. The management needs the services of a topologist, fast—fortunately "The best in the world is at Tech [presumably this is MIT]," but unfortunately he is also on a missing train.

Time as the Fourth Dimension

The idea of time as the fourth dimension, rather than space, is much more current these days. As with the spatial interpretation, the time interpretation is an old one; In fact, Professor A. M. Bork has traced the idea back to the late eighteenth century, as he found references to it in the works of the French mathematical physicists d'Alembert and Lagrange from before 1800 [Bork, 1964]. In fact, [Meyerson, 1985] even quotes from a 1751 passage written by d'Alembert, who indicated that it is some unknown person to whom the credit is really due: "I have said [that it is] not possible to imagine more than three dimensions. A clever acquaintance of mine believes, however, that duration could be regarded as a fourth dimension and that the product of time and solidity would be in some way a product of four dimensions; that idea can be contested, but it seems to me that it has some merit, if only that of novelty."

Yet, it wasn't until a curious letter appeared in *Nature* during 1885 that the concept of time as the fourth dimension was mentioned seriously in an English language scientific journal. The author, mysteriously signing himself only as "S.," began by writing "What is the fourth dimension? ... I [propose] to consider Time as a fourth dimension ... Since this fourth dimension cannot be introduced into space, as commonly understood, we require a new kind of space for its existence, which we may call time-space." Who was this prophetic writer? Nobody knows, but it is interesting to note that Professor Bork speculates that it was an acquaintance of H. G. Wells.[18]

The idea of time as the fourth dimension entered the popular mind around 1894–1895 with the first of H. G. Wells' so-called scientific romances, *The Time*

Machine. Then, after Wells' pioneering use of time as the fourth dimension, science fiction writers quickly took the idea as the basis for one of their most popular subgenres. For example, just as he had been one of the first with a four-dimensional-space story, Murray Leinster was just as quick to capitalize on time as the fourth dimension; his "The Fourth Dimension Demonstrator" is typical [Leinster, OW]. Leinster's very first published story, "The Runaway Skyscraper" [Leinster, 1967], in fact, interprets the fourth dimension as time. First appearing in 1919 in *Argosy* magazine, this is the incredible tale of a Manhattan skyscraper (and its 2000 occupants) sent back several thousand years in time when its foundation slips in an unexplained way along the fourth dimension. The scientific sophistication of the story is primitive, with just one of the logical flaws being a vivid description of the time travelers living normal, forward-in-time lives even as their wristwatches run backward. Indeed, when Hugo Gernsback reprinted the tale in one of the early issues of *Amazing Stories*, a reader complained about this very point. Gernsback felt compelled to defend the story in his November 1926 editorial "Plausibility in Scientifiction," but he could muster only a weak rebuttal based on an author's right to "poetic license."

Some stories have discussed both space and time as the fourth dimension. A major modern story in science fiction that straddles the distinct interpretations of the fourth dimension as spatial and, alternatively, as temporal is [Clifton, MM]. The enigmatic title "Star, Bright" is soon explained. Star is a little girl whose mental abilities are so far beyond those of a genius that she herself invents a new category — she is a "Bright." At age three she discovers the Möbius strip and astonishes her father (a mere genius or, as Star calls him, a "Tween"—for being in-between a "Bright" and the ordinary "Stupids") by using a crayon to show its one-sidedness (see Note 17). By age six Star has discovered how to use the Möbius strip to make a Klein bottle and then a "twisted cube," i.e., a tesseract à la Heinlein's earthquake house,[19] and then, as Star explains to her father, she manipulates "the twisted cube all together the same way you did Klein's bottle. Now if you do that big enough, all around you, so you're sort of half twisted in the middle, then you can [teleport] yourself anywhere you want to go." Star later discovers that spacetime is just a Möbius strip (an idea later played with in the technical literature, as in [Weingard, 1977]), and she learns how to time travel up and down the strip. The story ends with Star getting off the strip into a new present, and with her frantic father trying to catch up with his lost child.

Another story using a fourth dimension involving both space and time is "The Maladjusted Classroom" [Nearing, BFSF3]. Here we encounter what Professor Ransom (of the Mathematics Faculty at an unnamed University) calls "A three-dimensional Möbius strip that twists through the fourth-dimension—it's called a Klein bottle." Ransom, you see, has accidently made such a thing from a bicycle tire(!) and he ends up sending a colleague, an Army Colonel ROTC professor, on a wild ride through it. Indeed, when the Colonel finally emerges from hyperspace, he finds himself miles distant and an hour backward in time. This is explained, in a blink, with only the words "Fourth dimension. Time factor. *You* know ... " And in a subtle little joke, the young couple in "When the Bough Breaks" [Padgett, BTS], who were visited by time travelers from five hundred years in the future live in Apartment 4–D.

Much more serious in substance, and certainly in consequence, is "Technical Error" [Clarke, SFF]. Here an electrical engineer is caught in the middle of an enormous electromagnetic field surge produced by a short circuit in a power plant. As a physicist explains to the shocked board of directors of the utility: "It now appears that the unheard-of current, amounting to millions of amperes ... must have produced a certain extension into four dimensions ... I have been making some calculations and have been able to satisfy myself that a 'hyperspace' about ten feet on a side was, in fact, generated: a matter of some ten thousand quartic—not cubic!—feet. Nelson was occupying that space. The sudden collapse of the field [when the overload breakers finally cut the circuit] caused the rotation of the space." Being rotated through 4–space has inverted the unlucky Nelson (see Note 16) and to bring him back to normal he must be flipped again. The physicist brushes aside a question about the fourth dimension as time, asserting the whole issue is one of space. Poor Nelson is, therefore, again subjected to a stupendous power overload—only now he disappears! Too late, the physicist realizes that the fourth dimension is both space and time—Nelson has been spatially flipped once more, yes, but also temporally displaced into the future (to a particularly monstrous fate I'll not reveal here).

In a similiar fashion, when one of the characters in "Yesterday Was Monday" [Sturgeon, SFAD] becomes displaced in time, he asks for an explanation from a higher-dimensional being that appears on the scene: " 'Just where is Tuesday?' he asked. "Over there [and when the being extends its hand it disappears].' 'Do that again.' 'What? Oh—Point toward Tuesday? Certainly.' " The being explains what happened to the astonished, involuntary time traveler thus: "It is a direction like any other direction. You know yourself there are four directions—forward, sideward, upward, and—*that* way! ... It is the fourth dimension—it is duration." In the same way, in "The Middle of the Week After Next" [Leinster, SFAD] a mad inventor discovers how to make a substance whose atoms resist being pushed by "pushing back at right angles to all of the other directions;" i.e., to push on this stuff is to risk being pushed "off into the fourth dimension [which we are told is time] ... into the middle of the week after next."

H. G. Wells on Space and Time

It was H. G. Wells who pioneered time travel as we think of it in this book (but see the qualifying remarks about stationary versus moving time machines in Chapter One and Tech Note 4). It is of more than mere curious interest to look carefully at what this literary genius thought of space and time. His *The Time Machine* has never been out of print, something most books almost a century old cannot claim, and it is now recognized as one of the modern classics of the English language. The book opens with "The Time Traveller" expounding on a recondite matter to a group of his friends.[20] As he asserts, "There is no difference between Time and any of the three dimensions of Space except that our consciousness moves along it." When asked to say more about the fourth dimension, he replies: "It is simply this. That Space, as our mathematicians have it, is spoken of as having three dimensions, which one may call Length, Breadth, and Thickness, and is always definable by reference to three planes, each at right angles to the others. But some philosophical people have been asking why *three* dimensions particularly—why not another direction at right angles to the other three?—and have even tried to construct a Four-Dimensional geometry. Professor Simon Newcomb was expounding this to the New York Mathematical Society only a month or so ago."[21]

Wells, I think it interesting to realize, was not primarily motivated by an interest in either the fourth dimension or in time travel to write his *Time Machine*. Rather, he was attempting to refute the nearly suffocating, unjustified (in his mind) smug optimism of the Victorian age [Philmus, 1969]. (In fact, with the same goal in mind, novelist Grant Allen, a contemporary of Wells, wrote in *British Barbarians* [Allen, 1895] of a visitor from the twenty-fifth century who is appalled at the hypocrisy of Victorian customs and taboos.) And so, on his journey into the future to the year A.D. 802,701, the Time Traveller discovers the awful decay of humanity in the cannibalistic subjugation of the Eloi by the Morlocks. Wells' pessimistic attitude concerning the future is reflected in his nonfictional writings before 1895; e.g., in 1891 Wells wrote:[22] "There is a good deal to be found in the work of biologists quite inharmonious with such phrases as 'the progress of the ages', and the 'march of the mind' ... There is no ... guarantee in scientific knowledge of man's permanence or permanent ascendency ... so far as any scientist can tell us, it may be that ... Nature is, in unsuspected obscurity, equipping some now humble creature with wider possibilities of appetite, endurance, or destruction, to rise in the fullness of time and sweep *homo* away into the darkness from which his Universe arose. The Coming Beast must certainly be reckoned in any anticipatory calculations regarding the Coming Man."

Three years later, and while still polishing the prose of *The Time Machine*, Wells was even more depressing:[23] "The life that has schemed and struggled and committed itself, the life that has played and lost, comes at last to the pitiless judgement of time, and is slowly and remorselessly annihilated. This is the saddest chapter of biological science ... the tragedy of Extinction ... the most terrible thing that man can conceive as happening to man [is] the Earth desert through a pestilence, and two men, and then one man, looking extinction in the face."

Still, Wells was not always gloomy about the future. On 24 January 1902 he delivered an invited lecture to the Royal Institution[24] called "The Discovery of the Future," an invitation that demonstrates his highly visible and admired position in the elitist world of Victorian/Edwardian British science. He did, indeed, talk of such possible calamities as pestilence, cometary impact, atmospheric poisoning, and the extinction of the Sun, but his final sentence was prophetic as well as poetic: "All this world is heavy with the promise of greater things, and a day will come, one day in the unending succession of days, when beings, beings who are now latent in our thoughts and hidden in our loins, shall stand upon this Earth as one stands upon a footstool, and shall laugh and reach out their hands amidst the stars."

It was in this address that Wells made it clear what his answer would be to the question we briefly touched on in Chapter One—How sensitive is the future to events in the past?—an issue *not* treated in *The Time Machine*: "I must confess I believe that if by some juggling with space and time Julius Caesar, Napoleon, Edward IV, William the Conqueror, Lord Roebery and Robert Burns had all been changed at birth, it would not have produced any serious dislocation of the course of destiny. I believe that these great men of ours are no more than ... the pen-nibs Fate has used for her writing, the diamonds upon the drill that pierces through the rock." Wells in this same address came quite close to asserting that there will never be a real time machine: "The portion of the past that is brightest and most real to each of us is the individual past, the personal memory. The portion of the future that *must remain darkest and least accessible* [my emphasis] is the individual future."

What irony! The Father of the Time Machine seems to have had no faith in his own conception. But, no matter, *The Time Machine* was an enormous success, finding itself reviewed even in *Nature*,[25] a journal not usually given to commenting on works of fiction. The review read: "Ingeniously arguing that time may be regarded as the fourth dimension ... the author of this admirably-told story has conceived the idea of a machine which shall convey the traveler either backward or forward in time. Apart from its merits as a clever piece of imagination, the story is well worth the attention of the scientific reader ... from first to last the narrative never lapses into dullness."

Of course not everybody was taken by Wells' story. Such persons might agree with the Devil in "Enoch Soames" [Beerbohm, DD] who says (in reply to the question "*The Time Machine* is a delightful book, don't you think? So entirely original!"): "It is one thing to write about an impossible machine; it is a quite other thing to be a Supernatural Power." Agreeing with the Devil was the philosopher Lafleur, who wrote [Lafleur, 1940] that "the fallacies of Wells are obvious enough ... a man could go back into past time and change the course of history, even to the extent of bringing it about that he would never be born, and hence never take his backward trip into the past!"

More imaginative souls than the Devil and Lafleur were caught up by Wells, however. British motion picture pioneer Robert Paul read *The Time Machine* and was so swept up by its theatrical possibilities that he immediately wrote to Wells. The two men met, and a short time later Paul received a British patent on a mechanical gadget to simulate the sensation of an actual journey through time [Ramsaye, 1926].

It is a curious observation that after explicitly introducing time as the fourth dimension, Wells then returned in [Wells, 1966] to the alternative idea of the fourth dimension being spatial. For example, in "The Plattner Story" an incompetent chemistry teacher is literally blasted into hyperspace by an experiment gone wrong; in "Davidson's Eyes" a man can apparently see through a "kink in space" to the other side of the planet, an effect induced while "stooping between the poles" of a "big electro-magnet" which gave "some extraordinary twist to his retinal elements" (an idea that Wells then has his narrator amusingly dismiss with but that "seems mere nonsense to me"). In *The Invisible Man* Wells also hints at this same idea when he has the central character explain the secret of his discovery: "I found a general principle ... a formula, a geometrical expression involving four dimensions."

The supposed link between invisibility and time travel itself has been advanced more recently in [Coates, 1987]. Here we read that "the thinning out of matter at high speed (says Wells) renders the Time Traveller invisible and invulnerable [see Note 1 for Chapter Four] ... So long as he moves ... he can slip through matter with the ease of a ghost (ghosts being, after all, the prototypical time travelers): he is himself the laser-beam of time. Hence Wells' Time Traveller and his Invisible Man are related figures: for as long as he travels, the Time Traveler *is* the invisible man (for we cannot see time)." A film that connects the two ideas of time travel and invisibility is the 1984 movie *The Philadelphia Experiment*. This is the story of a 1943 Navy experiment that uses an electronic "invisibility cloak" (à la the Klingon gadget in "Star Trek"), but the experiment goes wrong and sends an entire destroyer forward in time into the 1980s.

Spacetime and the Fourth Dimension

The poet Henry Van Dyke wrote in his 1904 "The Sun-Dial at Wells College" that:

> The shadow by my finger cast
> Divides the future from the past:
> Before it, sleeps the unborn hour,
> In darkness, and beyond thy power:
> Behind its unreturning line,
> The vanished hour, no longer thine:
> One hour alone is in thy hands,—
> The NOW on which the shadow stands.

The very next year came Einstein's special relativity theory, and then three years after that Minkowski's spacetime interpretation of it. Van Dyke's poetry was given a mighty blow by these developments in mathematical physics. In the rest of this section, we will see how this happened.

The view of reality that the past and present and future are joined together into a four-dimensional entity called *spacetime* is due to the work of Hermann Minkowski (1864–1909), Einstein's mathematics professor when he was a student in Zurich. Minkowski gave spacetime to the world during a famous address to the 80th Assembly of German Natural Scientists and Physicians meeting in Cologne on

21 September 1908. Entitled "Space and Time" [Minkowski, BST], his words were electrifying then and still are today. He began dramatically:[26] "Gentlemen! The views of space and time which I wish to lay before you have sprung from the soil of experimental physics, and therein lies their strength. They are radical." Then came the famous line (quoted in so many freshman physics texts and philosophy papers) concerning spacetime: "Henceforth space by itself, and time by itself, are doomed to fade away into mere shadows, and only a kind of union of the two will preserve independence."

Minkowski explained what spacetime is in these words to his audience:

> A point of space at a point of time, ... I will call a *world-point*. The multiplicity of all thinkable *x, y, z, t* systems of values we will christen the *world*. With this most valiant piece of chalk I might project upon the blackboard four world axes ... Not to leave a yawning void anywhere, we will imagine that every-where and everywhen there is something perceptible. To avoid saying 'matter' or 'electricity' I will use for this something the word 'substance'. We fix our attention on the substantial point which is at the world-point *x, y, z, t,* and imagine that we are able to recognize this substantial point at any other time. Let the variations *dx, dy, dz,* of the space coordinates of this substantial point correspond to a time element *dt*. Then we obtain, as an image, so to speak, of the everlasting career of the substantial point, a curve in the world, a *world-line* ... The whole Universe is seen to resolve itself into similiar world lines, and I would fain anticipate myself by saying that in my opinion physical laws might find their most perfect expression as relations between these world lines ... *Thus also three-dimensional geometry becomes a chapter in four-dimensional physics* [my emphasis].

With these words Minkowski gave mathematical expression to the philosoph-ical exposition of Wells' Time Traveller. But not everybody understood Minkowski. In a little known, yet quite erudite, essay published just after the first experimental verification of general relativity (the bending of starlight by gravity), an anonymous author presented an optical analogy to help those who thought relativity "a mathematical joke." Signing himself only as "W. G.," he included the following passage:[27]

> "Some thirty or more years ago [it was forty] a little *jeu d'esprit* was written by Dr. Edwin Abbott entitled 'Flatland.' ... Dr. Abbott pictures intelligent beings whose whole experience is confined to a plane, or other space of two dimen-sions, who have no faculties by which they can become conscious of anything outside that space and no means of moving off the surface on which they live. He then asks the reader, who has consciousness of the third dimension, to imagine a sphere descending upon the plane of Flatland and passing through it. How will the inhabitants regard this phenomenon? They will not see the ap-

proaching sphere and will have no conception of its solidity. They will only be conscious of the circle in which it cuts their plane. This circle, at first a point, will gradually increase in diameter, driving the inhabitants of Flatland outward from its circumference, and this will go on until half the sphere has passed through the plane, when the circle will gradually contract to a point and then vanish, leaving the Flatlanders in undisturbed possession of their country ... Their experience will be that of a circular obstacle gradually expanding or growing, and then contracting, and they will attribute to *growth in time* what the external observer in three dimensions assigns to motion in the third dimension. Transfer this analogy to a movement of the fourth dimension through three-dimensional space. Assume the past and future of the Universe to be all depicted in four-dimensional space and visible to any being who has consciousness of the fourth dimension. If there is motion of our three-dimensional space relative to the fourth dimension, all the changes we experience and assign to the flow of time will be due simply to this movement, *the whole of the future as well as the past always existing in the fourth dimension* [my emphasis]."

W. G.'s words are a clear and unequivocal statement of the so-called *block-Universe* concept of four-dimensional spacetime, of reality as a once-and-forever entity. Of course, one can find the block-Universe concept in ancient philosophers, too. For example, Parmenides on reality, saying: "It is uncreated and indestructible; for it is complete, immovable, and without end. Nor was it ever, nor will it be; for now it *is*, all at once, a continuous *one*." And sometime later, in Thomas Aquinas' *Compendium Theologiae* written in the thirteenth century, we find: "We may fancy that God knows the flight of time in His eternity, in the way that a person standing on top of a watchtower embraces in a single glance a whole caravan of passing travelers." The difference is that while for Parmenides it was metaphysics and for Aquinas it was theology, for Einstein and Minkowski it was science that explained the block-Universe concept.

The block-Universe concept may explain the rather enigmatic statement made by Einstein at the death of Michele Besso (quoted near the beginning of this chapter). As Horwitz, Arshansky, and Elitzur [1988] so nicely put it: "It seems that Einstein's view of the life of an individual was as follows. If the difference between past, present, and future is an illusion, i.e., the four-dimensional spacetime is a 'block Universe' without motion or change, then each individual is a collection of a myriad of selves, distributed along his history, each occurrence *persisting on the world line, experiencing indefinitely the particular event of that moment* [my emphasis]. Each of these momentary persons, according to our experience, would possess memory of the previous ones, and would therefore believe himself identical with them; yet they would all exist separately, as single pictures in a film. Placing the past, present and future on the same footing this way, destroys the notion of the unity of the self, rendering it a mere illusion as well."

It appears that by his words Einstein was indeed in agreement with the block-Universe concept, and that he was attempting to give Besso's family some reason to believe that Michele still lives "somewhen." There is, however, the additional and to some minds, perhaps, the rather awful logical implication that if Michele is still living, then there are also other Micheles 'still' dying, a ghoulish sentiment Einstein surely did not mean to convey.

Not everybody believes that this view of spacetime was Einstein's position, however. Karl Popper, the Austrian philosopher of science wrote twenty-eight years after the scientist's death that "Einstein was a strict determinist when I first visited him in 1950: he believed in a 4-dimensional Block-Universe. But he gave this up."[28] Shortly before he wrote these words, however, Popper must have learned something new to convince himself of his final comment since just three years earlier he had declared that Einstein was a determinist (see his Forward to CPP). Popper, in fact, offers no evidence for his claim of Einstein's conversion, and it would seem that the Besso letter is still the best evidence of Einstein's actual view of spacetime just before his death.

The origin of the specific term *block Universe* is due to the Oxford philosopher Francis Herbert Bradley (1846–1924) who in his 1883 book *Principles of Logic* wrote: "We seem to think that we sit in a boat, and are carried down the stream of time, and that on the bank there is a row of houses with numbers on the doors. And we get out of the boat, and knock at the door of number 19, and, re-entering the boat, then suddenly find ourselves opposite 20, and, having then done the same, we go on to 21. And, all this while, the firm fixed row of the past and future stretches in a *block* [my emphasis] behind us, and before us." The house numbers would seem to be Bradley's way of referring to the centuries. Notice that this statement was written twelve years before *The Time Machine*, and it preceded Minkowski by a quarter-century.

The contribution of *mathematical* spacetime to physics, however, originated with Minkowski, not with Bradley or even with Einstein, who often gets credit for it even though he did not use the concept in his revolutionary presentation of special relativity three years before, in 1905. Eventually Einstein did come to appreciate the power and conceptual beauty of four-dimensional spacetime, and it quickly began to play a central role in his ideas about gravity (gravity for Einstein is curved spacetime).

Of course, Newtonian physics did talk about an analytical (as opposed to mere philosophical) space and time before Minkowski and Einstein, but Newtonian spacetime (see [Stein, 1967] and [Earman and Friedman, 1973]) was something very different from the new Minkowskian view. In the Newtonian view there is a Universal time, a *cosmic time*, which is the same time for everyone everywhere in the Universe. At every instant, a cosmic simultaneity exists (see [Hawking, 1968] for a precise definition of cosmic time, and how it requires that time travel to the past be impossible). Newton's space is Euclidean; e.g., parallel lines never meet, through any point exterior to a line exactly one parallel line can be constructed, and all triangles (no matter how large) have an interior angle sum of 180 degrees. For Newton, space and time were absolutely and uniquely separable. They were, as philosophers are prone to say, "distinct individuals." Minkowski changed all this. For Minkowski, space and time are only relatively separable, and the separation is different for observers in relative motion. For Newton, space and time are the *background* in which physical processes evolve. For Minkowski, spacetime *is* the world.

Taking the Minkowskian view of the primacy of spacetime as the ultimate building stuff of reality has been Princeton Professor of Physics John Wheeler, who wrote [Misner and Wheeler, 1957]: "There is nothing in the world except empty curved space. Matter, charge, electromagnetism ... are only manifestations of the bending of space. *Physics is Geometry*." Wheeler developed this theme (which many physicists find, to use Minkowski's word, "radical") in detail in his beautiful book *Geometrodynamics* [Wheeler, 1962a]; see also [Wheeler, 1962b]. The same year, 1962, saw a hint that even time itself might, like spacetime, find an explanation in geometry [Baierlein, Sharp and Wheeler, 1962]. Since then Wheeler's ideas have continued to evolve (more recently it is not geometry, but something called pregeometry, that to Wheeler is the basic building stuff of the world; see [Grunbaum, 1973] for an extended discussion of this evolution in Wheeler's ideas).

Wheeler's original idea of the fundamental nature of spacetime has not been forgotten, however. For example, the time traveler in *Moscow 2042* [Voinovich, 1987] sounds a lot like Wheeler when he says "Anyone with even a nodding acquaintance with the theory of relativity knows that nothing is a variety of something and so you can always make a little something out of nothing." The starting point for such ideas was in Minkowski's creation: as [Rindler, 1977] says, it is Minkowski who truly deserves the title of "father of the fourth dimension." The spacetime diagrams (see Tech Note 4) that are a basic conceptual tool for discussing time travel are often called *Minkowski diagrams*.

A famous philosophical paper [Williams, 1951b] by an advocate of the block-Universe interpretation, states: "I ... defend the view of the world ... which treats the totality of being, of facts, or of events as spread out eternally in the dimension of time as well as the dimensions of space. Future events and past events are by no means present events, but in a clear and important sense they do exist, now and forever, as rounded and definite articles of the world's furniture." In an even more famous paper published the same year [Williams, 1951a], Professor Williams makes clear his belief in the passage of time as a myth; he poetically declared "the total of world history is a spatio-temporal volume, of somewhat uncertain magnitude, chockablock with things and events." Williams did indeed embrace four-dimensional spacetime. He has become famous, in fact, for the following incredible passage: "It is then conceivable, though doubtless physically impossible, that one four-dimensional area of the time part of the manifold be slewed around at right angles to the rest, so that the time order of that area, as composed by its interior lines of strain and structure, runs parallel with a spatial order in its environment. It is conceivable, indeed, that a single whole human life should lie thwartise of the manifold, with its belly plump in time, its birth at the east and its death in the west, and its conscious stream running alongside somebody's garden path.''

Good Lord!

Now I am willing to admit that Professor Williams probably wrote this wonderful passage mostly for effect, but I ask—what, if anything, does it mean? It is, frankly, marvelous to read and yet it remains (for me) mysterious. It should come as no surprise that Professor Williams originally presented his paper to the Metaphysical Society of America, rather than to the American Physical Society. But it was not without impact in areas beyond metaphysics, as a few years later a science fiction story "The Rubber Bend" [Wolfe, 1974] appeared that read as if it had been inspired by Williams—a scientist discovers how to bend his perception of the four dimensions so as to view verticality as duration, and duration as verticality. Thus, while sitting down he is in October but when he stands up he is in November! (But, I must admit, this sort of coordinate interchange does occur in the theory of time machines, too; e.g., see Tech Note 8 on the operation of Tipler's cylinder.)

I must mention, however, that despite the enthusiastic embrace of the block Universe by Williams and others, there have been those who have been harsh in their criticism of Minkowski's spacetime. The major philosophical problem with the block-Universe interpretation of four-dimensional spacetime is that it appears to be fatalism disguised as physics. It seems to be a mathematician's proof of determinism and a denial of free will dressed up in geometry. For example, the block-Universe view is savaged in [Geach, 1968] for being fatalistic, but Geach's remarks provoked ridicule from Professor Smart [Smart, 1972], who feels that Geach's interpretation of free will as being an ability to change the future is either trivial or absurd. Indeed, Geach's argument *is* inconsistent. On the one hand, he does not like the block Universe because of its implication that the future already exists, but on the other hand if the future is not there, then what sense can be made of being able to change it? How do you change something that does not exist?

Hans Reichenbach [Reichenbach, 1956] has a charming little story that vividly demonstrates the compelling need in many humans to deny a fatalistic world: "In a moving picture version of *Romeo and Juliet*, the dramatic scene was shown in which Juliet, seemingly dead, is lying in the tomb, and Romeo, believing she is dead, raises a cup containing poison. At this moment an outcry from the audience was heard: 'Don't do it!' We laugh at the person who ... forgets that the time flow of a movie is unreal, is merely the unwinding of a pattern imprinted on a strip of film. Are we more intelligent than this man when we believe that the time flow of our actual life is different? Is the present more than our cognizance of a predetermined pattern of events unfolding itself like an unwinding film?" Most people in the Western world would answer *yes*. Most such people, for example, find

Khayyam's *Rubaiyat* to be a beautiful poem, but they reject its fatalistic message: "And the first Morning of Creation wrote, What the Last Dawn of Reckoning shall read".

Equally unhappy with the block Universe was Herbert Dingle, who declared in his last book before his death (see Tech Note 5 for more about Professor Dingle and his book) that "it is to Minkowski that we owe the idea of a 'space-time' as an objective reality—which is perhaps the chief agent in the transformation of the whole subject [of relativity] from the ground of intelligible physics into the heaven (or hell) of metaphysics, where it has become, instead of an object of intelligent inquiry, an idol to be blindly worshipped ... Reduced to its essence, Minkowski's [work] is a piece of pure mathematics—as such, extremely elegant and admirable, but, insofar as it purports to contribute to physics, as it does, calamitous." And in his 1965 British Academy lecture, P. T. Geach attacked the Minkowskian view [Geach, 1968] as "very popular with philosophers who try to understand physics and physicists who try to do philosophy." Geach clearly believes both groups have failed. P. F. Strawson, in an introduction to Geach's essay, put in his two cents by calling the four-dimensional, spacetime view of reality as nothing but "fanciful philosophical theorizing."

Besides fatalism, another reason for the stinging words of these critics is that in Minkowski's spacetime it seems that things don't happen—they just *are*; there seems to be no temporal process of *becoming* in Miskowski's spacetime. Everything is "already" there, and as what we perceive as the passing of time occurs, we become conscious of ever more of Minkowski's "world-points" or *events* that lie on our individual world lines. Hermann Weyl (1885–1955), a German mathematical physicist who in his last years was a colleague of Einstein and Gödel at the Institute for Advanced Study in Princeton, expressed this position in words that have since become famous,[29] words that sound very much like those of Wells' Time Traveller: "The objective world simply *is*, it does not *happen*. Only to the gaze of my consciousness, crawling upward along the life line of my body [Minkowski's world-line], does a section of the world [i.e., spacetime] come to life as a fleeting image in space which continuously changes in time [i.e., the now or present]."

Weyl was skillful at finding poetic ways to express the world-line view, and did so often. Not everybody liked this approach, of course, as this view is a denial of the idea of time flowing, and of temporal passage, and it effectively says that time is mind-dependent, a mere illusion. The philosophers J. J. C. Smart and Max Black had no sympathy with Weyl on this issue. Observing that four-dimensional spacetime is *timeless*, as indeed Weyl's own words indicate, Professor Smart wrote [Smart, 1955b]: "Within the Minkowski representation we must not talk of our four-dimensional entities changing or not changing. This sort of mistake is often made in expositions on relativity. We often read of light signals being transmitted from one point of Minkowski space to another. This is liable to lead to metaphysical error, such as that of consciousness crawling up world-lines."

Professor Black was even harsher in his objection to Weyl. As he wrote in no uncertain terms,[30] "this picture of a 'block Universe,' composed of a timeless web of 'world-lines' in a four-dimensional space, however strongly suggested by the theory of relativity, is a piece of gratuitous metaphysics." Another philosopher [Mundle, 1967] has gone beyond mere name-calling to suggest one fascinating speculation on what Weyl's four-dimensional spacetime might really imply. Written as a generally critical reply to Smart, Professor Mundle declares: "If the physical world is conceived as a 4–D manifold, it is, as Smart acknowledges, logically impossible for a physical thing, a 4–D solid, to move or otherwise change ... Since Smart is conceiving the physical world and its contents as changeless [it must be] our states of consciousness which change as we become successively aware of adjacent cross-sections of the 4–D manifold [Weyl's "crawling"]. But this makes sense only if we, the observers, are *not* in Space-Time."

That is, our conscious minds somehow must exist on a level beyond anything physics can tell us about. This is, of course, a radical view, one not enjoying much support among most scientists. Mundle makes it clear, in fact, that he is of a different mind from Smart when it comes to science, and he wrote that "Smart seems to have been influenced mainly by Physics ... we must not be blinded by science." As Sherlock Holmes would no doubt reply, "What a singular statement!" Still, no matter how odd an idea is Mundle's suggestion, a close variant of it was used in a science fiction story even as Mundle wrote. In *The Technicolor Time Machine* [Harrison, 1967], for example, time travel takes place in the "extratemporal continuum." And in Isaac Asimov's famous time-travel novel *The End of Eternity* [Asimov, 1986b], the time police (called Eternals) oversee the endless centuries from a place outside of time (called Eternity).

We can actually find the block-Universe idea in fiction before Minkowski. Consider "The True Story of Bernard Poland's Prophecy"[Eggleston, 1875a], for example, the tale of a man who sees his own death in the American Civil War, years in the future. As Bernard says to his unnamed friend (the narrator):

> "Do you know," said Bernard, presently, "I sometimes think prophecy isn't so strange a thing ... I really see no reason why any earnest man may not be able to foresee the future, now and then ... "
>
> "There is reason enough to my mind," I replied, "in the fact that future events do not exist, as yet, and we can not know that which is not, though we may shrewdly guess it sometimes ... "
>
> "Your argument is good, but your premises are bad, I think," replied my friend, ... his great, sad eyes looking solemnly into mine.
>
> "How so?" I asked.

"Why, I doubt the truth of your assumption, that future events do not exist as yet ... Past and Future are only divisions of time, and do not belong at all to eternity ... To us it must be past or future with reference to other occurrences. But is there, in reality, any such thing as a past or a future? If there is an eternity, it is and always has been and always must be. But time is a mere delusion ... To a being thus in eternity, all things are, and must be present. *All things that have been, or shall be, are* [my emphasis]."

Also, consider Wells' Time Traveler's speech to his friends: "There is no difference between Time and any of the three dimensions of Space except that our consciousness moves along it ... here is a portrait of a man at eight years old, another at fifteen, another at seventeen, another at twenty-three, and so on. All these are evidently sections, as it were, Three-Dimensional representations of his Four-Dimensional being, *which is a fixed and unalterable thing* [my emphasis]." All this, was written in 1895, thirteen years before Minkowski and his world lines, and of course decades before Weyl's famous quote. This passage made a considerable impression on at least one well-known physicist, who referenced it in his early book on relativity.[31] In another book on realitivity published the same year,[32] we again see the same interpretation of Minkowski's spacetime as a block Universe: "With Minkowski, space and time become particular aspects of a single four-dimensional continuum ... all motional phenomena ... become timeless phenomena in four-dimensional space. The whole history of a physical system is laid out as a changeless whole."

The block-Universe concept appeared very early in magazine science fiction stories. In "The Machine Man of Ardathia" [Flagg, 1927], for example, a time traveler from the future and a man in the present have the following exchange:

"I have just been five years into your future."

"My future!" I exclaimed. "How can that be when I have not lived it yet?"

"But of course you have lived it."
I stared, bewildered.
"Could I visit my past if you had not lived your future?"

And in *The Man Who Mastered Time* [Cummings, 1929], as a time traveler is about to set out on his first journey to the world 28,200 years in the future (where he has already observed a beautiful young girl via a mechanism that lets him see through time), he tells his friends: "You say that girl *will be* living in the future. I say she *is* living in the future. She is living just as you and I are living—right here in this exact spot we call New York—within a few hundred yards of this room. She is separated from us, not by space, but only by time."

"Life-Line" [Heinlein, 1979], published in 1939, uses world lines as its central scientific concept. The story makes an analogy comparing a world line with a telephone cable(!); the beginning and end points in spacetime for the world line (birth and death) are associated with breaks (faults) in the telephone cable. By sending a signal up and down the cable and measuring the time delay until the arrival of the echo produced by such discontinuties, a technician can both detect and locate the faults. In the same manner, Heinlein's story gadget sends a signal of unspecified nature up and down a world line and thus locates the birth and death points. Knowledge of this latter date, in particular, causes financial stress among life insurance companies, and an examination of this tension is the fictional point of the story. Less scientific and more mystical is "Damnation Morning" [Leiber, 1961], where we learn of an eternal time-war in which the soldiers are recruited from the newly dead; i.e., they are resurrected by being cut out of their lifeline [world line] and given the freedom of the fourth dimension.

The idea that past and present coexist got a dramatic treatment in "Temporary Warp" [Long, 1937], the story of a high-school teacher who invents a "spacetime warp" theory and who is deceived by an evil industrialist into implementing it in the form of a gun; the weapon produces incredible effects when it is tested. For example, an allosaurus appears, which we are told is "a carnivorous dinosaur of the Jurassic Age, the most frightful engine of destruction that ever walked the Earth!" By story's end the teacher explains things to a crowd of breathless newspaper reporters: "Spacetime was warped slightly ... The Einsteinian spacetime continuum buckled ... Because it was superficial, only a little of the past, a little of the future broke through. The folds of the warp distorted spacetime evanescently, erratically skirting the vast gulf where the past lies buried and lightly tapping the vast stores of the future. It is a truism of modern speculative physics that the past and the future exist simultaneously and coextensively in higher dimensions of space. De Sitter has speculated as to the possibility of seeing an event before it happens. It is quite possible, gentlemen. Events of the far future already exist in spacetime." That explains the dinosaur. In the teacher's words: "You tell me that two men saw an incredible beast ... They swear it looked like a dinosaur. I think it was a dinosaur, gentlemen. It broke through when the warp tapped the past."

In a modern story that copies Wells' title, "The Time Machine" [Jones, BO], but which has the human brain and memory as the time machine ("The time machine operates on an organic, electrochemical basis"), Weyl's view is adopted. After telling us that the Universe is a four-dimensional ring, the author then says, "Time is merely the attention [of an observer] constantly and involuntarily operating on a different part of the ring, giving the impression of movement and animation to what is in fact a static object."

The static concept of the block Universe was invoked by one science fiction fan who wrote in support of time travel after another fan had cited a resulting failure of mass/energy conservation in an attempt to disprove the notion. The exchange began with a Letter-to-the-Editor at *Astounding Stories* (Nov. 1937), written in response to the time-travel story "The Time Bender" [Saari, 1937]: "Let us say that there is, at a certain time, 'x' amount of matter in the Universe, and 'e' amount of energy. Then if a man of 'a' mass travels backward in time to this particular instant aforementioned, the total amount of matter is thus 'x' plus 'a' while, if no other such mass changing occurrences take place, the amount of matter in that future is 'x' minus 'a'. Only a corresponding loss and gain respectively in the amount of energy could explain this conservation of energy and matter, advocates [of time travel] say what they may. But you can't rob or add energy to a Universe nilly-willy! Or perhaps time doesn't enter in on the matter. Perhaps you can add matter in a Universe provided you take it away on some future date."

This fan's concern obviously made an impression on science fiction writers, as one finds the necessity for conservation of energy stated in many of the time-travel stories after that time; e.g., *Lest Darkness Fall* [de Camp, 1941], "Time Waits for Winthrop" [Tenn, 1962], and *The Time Hoppers* [Silverberg, 1967]. However, a reply was received by the magazine in a letter (Jan. 1938) from still another science fiction fan: " [A recent letter] implies that the idea of time travel is incompatible with the law of conservation of mass and energy. I believe [the] reasoning is wrong [and that the] difficulty lies primarily in the assumption that a body moved in time is transported into a different Universe. According to Einstein, time and the three normal dimensions are so related as to form a continuous, insepable medium we call the spacetime continuum. Time is in no way independent of the other components of our Universe. Hence a fixed mass [a time traveler and his machine] moved in time is by no means lost from the Universe, the action being analogous to a shift along any other dimension." The block, or frozen, Universe of Minkowski is clearly reflected in those words.[33]

The block-Universe concept made a quick impression on popular culture, as well. For example, in a 1928 New York stage play, "Berkeley Square" [Balderston, 1941], which the author said was suggested by Henry James' unfinished (and, in my opinion, unreadable) novel *The Sense of the Past* [James, 1917], the action alternately takes place in the years 1784 and 1928. To explain how this can be, the character who is doing the time traveling says to another: "Suppose you are in a boat, sailing down a winding stream. You watch the banks as they pass you. You went by a grove of maple trees, upstream. But you can't see them now, so you saw them in the *past*, didn't you? You're watching a field of clover now; it's before your eyes at this moment, in the *present*. But you don't know yet what's around the bend in the stream there ahead of you; there may be wonderful things, but you can't see them until you get around the bend, in the *future*, can you?" Then, after this prologue about the stream of time, comes the block-Universe idea: "Now remember, *you're* in the boat. But *I'm* up in the sky above you, in a plane. I'm looking down on it all. I can see *all at once* the trees you saw upstream, the field of clover that you see now, and what's waiting for you, around the bend ahead! *All at once!* So the past, present, and future of the man in the boat are all *one* to the man in the plane." And finally, the theological conclusion: "Doesn't that show how all Time must really be one? Real Time—real Time is nothing but an idea in the mind of God!" This powerful play was made into a 1933 movie of the same name, and it appeared again in 1951 as the movie *I'll Never Forget You*.

Decades later we find the same kind of idea used in *Doctor Brodie's Report* [Borges, 1972], which tells the strange story of the discovery of the long-lost, first-person manuscript of David Brodie, D.D. (found "among the pages of one of the volumes of Lane's *Arabian Night's Entertainments*, London, 1839"). This manuscript describes the strange ape-men discovered by Brodie, who calls them Yahoos. Among their many unusual characteristics is the ability of Yahoo witch doctors to see the future. As the Brodie manuscript puts it: "Hundreds of times I have borne witness to this curious gift, and I have also reflected upon it at length. Knowing the past, present, and future already exist, detail upon detail, in God's prophetic memory, in His Eternity, what baffles me is that men, while they can look indefinitely backward, are not allowed to look one whit forward."

Men may not be able to look forward in time, but in the comics there are no such restrictions. Mr. Mxyztplk, for example, in one of his misadventures with Superman in 1954, begins selling the *Daily Mpftrz* in competition with the *Daily Planet*. Unlike the traditional newspaper that reports what has happened, the *Daily Mpftrz* prints what will happen. As Mr. Mxyztplk explains, "You see, as a resident of the fifth dimension, I can get all the news I want from the *fourth* dimension!" The science editor at the *Daily Planet* explains the meaning of this to his boss, Perry White: "That's right, Mr. White, ... many physicists consider *time* the fourth dimension ... so if Mr. Mxyztplk can travel from the fifth dimension to our three-dimensional world, he most likely *is* able to see into the future!" Which leaves unanswered the question of why he continues to challenge Superman when he knows he will be defeated. (He *always* is!)

Spacetime, Omniscience, and Free Will

Some ancient theology on God's omniscience, as discussed in Aquinas' *Summa Theologiae*, is seemingly given support by Minkowski's spacetime: "Now although contingent events come into actual existence successively, God does not, as we do, know them in their actual existence successively, but all at once; because his knowledge is measured by eternity, as is also his existence; and eternity which exists as a simultaneous whole, takes in the whole of time ... Hence all that takes place in time is eternally present to God." Somewhat paradoxically, however, Aquinas did make a distinction between past and future. In this same work he declares that "God can cause an angel not to exist in the future, even if he cannot cause it not to exist while it exists, or not to have existed when it already has." For Aquinas the future is plastic while the past is rigid and unchangeable, which is not the block-Universe view of spacetime.

As pointed out in [Craig, 1985], this does not mean that Aquinas thought God viewed all events as simultaneous with one another. (The story "The Weed of Time" [Spinrad, 1980] graphically describes what a nightmare that might be.) Using an interesting analogy, Craig says that Aquinas could have thought of the relationship between God and events as being similiar to that between the center of a circle and all the points on the circumference. That is, each point on the circumference has its own identity, coming before and/or after any other, but the center is related to each and every point on the circumference in precisely the same way. The center, then, is "eternity," and the circumference is the temporal series of physical reality. Craig supports this view with Aquinas' words from *Summa contra Gentiles*: "The divine intellect, therefore, sees in the whole of its eternity, as being present to it, whatever takes place through the whole course of time. And yet what takes place in a certain part of time was not always existent. It remains, therefore, that God has a knowledge of these things that according to the march of time do not yet exist."

The issue of God's eternity and his relationship to spacetime is presently a hot topic among theologians with a scientific bent. Practically every issue of the learned journal *Religious Studies*, for example, carries an article on the subject, often invoking relativity theory to support some argument. The Bible, itself, is a confusing guide on this matter. For example, consider the Old Testament story of King Ahab (First Kings 21). Ahab, King of Sumeria, coveted Naboth's vineyard, but Naboth would not sell it. The King retreated, but his wife Jezebel arranged for Naboth's downfall and judicial murder, and thus the arrival of all his property into her husband's hands. This angered God, who commanded Elijah to prophesy disaster on Ahab's house. Ahab responded with sackcloth, and at that God shifted the disaster to the house of Ahab's son—which causes concerns about a benevolent God, but that's another story. The point here is that God, declared to be omniscient, seems to have been surprised at Ahab's penitance! God is still aware of everything, but only as it happens; i.e., God's knowledge is subject to growth. This Hebrew concept of God as a participant in history is at odds with the contemporary Christian conception of divine knowledge of all that has been, all that is, and all that will be.

In the *New Review* serialization of *The Time Machine* [Wells, 1975], in a passage not appearing in the now classic version of the story, the Time Traveller explains: "I'm sorry to drag in predestination and free-will, but I'm afraid those ideas will have to help ... Suppose you knew fully the position and properties of every particle of matter, of everything existing in the Universe at any particular moment of time: suppose, that is, that you were omniscient. Well, that knowledge would involve the knowledge of the condition of things at the previous moment, and at the moment before that, and so on. If you knew and perceived the present perfectly, you would perceive therein the whole of the past. If you understood all natural laws the present would be a complete and vivid record of the past. Similarly, if you grasped the whole of the present, knew all its tendencies and laws, you would see clearly all the future. To an omniscient observer there would be no forgotten past—no piece of time as it were that had dropped out of existence— and no blank future of things yet to be revealed ... present and past and future would be without meaning to such an observer ... He would see, as it were, a Rigid Universe filling space and time ... If 'past' meant anything, it would mean looking in a certain direction, while 'future' meant looking the opposite way." Wells' "rigid Universe" certainly sounds like the block Universe, and he seems to have believed that it held important implications for the concept of free will.

With Einstein's discovery of the relativity of simultaneity, however, there seems to be a problem with how there can be divine knowledge of any sort in a relativistic, four-dimensional spacetime. In some frames of reference, event A is observed before event B, while in other frames the temporal order is reversed (this point is discussed at the end of this section). If God is to be actively involved in human affairs, what is *his* frame of reference? Does God have a special frame in which he is immune to the relativity of simultaneity and in which he imposes an absolute order on the sequence of becoming? Does it make any sense to say God enjoys what might be called 'divine immediacy'? What should we think, in fact, of a God who follows rules different from those that govern all he is supposed to have made? Theologians have argued these questions for decades (e.g., [Wilcox, 1961], [Ford, 1968], and [Fitzgerald, 1972]), while physicists (including Einstein) have been either unaware or unimpressed by their arguments. However, one paper, [Bennett *et al.*, 1949], written by a philosopher and two mathematicians, describes a five-dimensional unified field theory in which the fifth dimension is initially given the provocative label of the "eternity" axis (but then the authors lost their nerve and quickly elected to rename it "anti-time"). A theological interpretation of this theory is in [Stromberg, 1961].

In theology the idea of supernatural beings existing outside of mortal time is an old one, and the idea would also be found in the secular literature long before science fiction appeared. For example, in the first act of Lord Byron's 1821 poem *Cain*, the fallen angel Lucifer tells Cain and his wife that:

> With us acts are exempt from time, and we
> Can crowd eternity into an hour,
> Or stretch an hour into eternity.
> We breathe not by a mortal measurement,
> But that's a myst'ry.

Professors Black and Smart would certainly be unhappy with Lucifer's claim, and Weyl himself might have been rather surprised at how far afield his views have been taken by others. In another rebuttal to Weyl's view, the philosopher Dobbs wrote [Dobbs, 1969]: "While philosophers may be forgiven intellectual extravagances of this kind, I think it is a pity when they receive encouragement from theoretical physicists, even if these share a common mystical experience." Physicists, no doubt, will be flattered to learn that they have such a profound influence on philosophers (excluding, of course, Professor Mundle from the previous section)!

The idea of tampering with the future (that "already exists") is given an interesting treatment in "What We Learned from This Morning's Newspaper" [Silverberg, 1986]. Here, an event in the present (warning a heart patient of her obituary notice in next week's *New York Times*) so upsets the future that spacetime is destroyed! This story takes the view that the future is delicate. As one character puts it to the sister of the lady-soon-to-die: "The future mustn't be changed ... For us the events of ... the future are as permanent as any event in the past. We don't dare play around with changing the future, not when it's already signed sealed and delivered in that newspaper. For all we know the future's like a house of cards. If we pull one card out, say your sister's life, we might bring the whole house tumbling down. You've got to accept the decree of fate ... You've got to." Disagreeing with this plea was the time traveler in "The Man Who Saw Through Time" [Raphael, 1941], who while visiting the future ten years hence learns he will be arrested, tried, and executed for the murder of a colleague and friend. To avoid this, to change the future, he returns and successfully arranges his own immediate death. The novel *The Gap in the Curtain* [Buchan, 1932], on the other hand, in agreement with the block-Universe concept, argues that the future is nothing less than petrified.

Before Minkowski, the debates over fatalism and free will had been the exclusive province of philosophers, theologians, and lawyers. (If someone has no control over his actions, then can we punish him if these actions happen to constitute a crime?) After Minkowski and his spacetime, the physicists joined the debates. The major motivation behind these debates is, according to Williams [Williams, 1951b], "the age-old dread that God's foreknowledge of our destiny can in itself impose the destiny upon us." The implication here, of course, is that God is 'outside of time' and so He can take in the entire Minkowski block Universe at a glance.

Indeed, the relativistic view of the Universe as a timeless four-dimensional spacetime seems to many to provide scientific, mathematical support for the conclusion that not only is the past fixed, but so is the future. Does this mean that the future is what it will be (and if so, then why bother agonizing over the many apparent decisions each of us faces every day)? If the answer is yes, and the future will be what it will be, then Christian theologians are left with the puzzling task of explaining what could possibly be meant by the Biblical exhortation (Deuteronomy 30:19): "I call Heaven and Earth to record this day against you, that I have set before you life and death, blessing and cursing: therefore choose life, that both thou and thy seed may live."

This puzzle is the central issue in Boethius' influential *De Consolatione Philosophiae* (circa A.D. 500), which was written during a year of imprisonment before his execution for treason; perhaps he wondered during this year if his fate could have been anything different. Certainly he might have found some consolation in determinism, but in fact he tried to argue that God's vision of *all* temporal reality does not limit the freedom to act. According to Boethius, "The expression 'God is ever' denotes a single Present, summing up His continual presence in all the past, in all the present ... and in all the future." That is, God sees in one timeless and eternal moment all that has and will be freely chosen. Kurt Vonnegut called this ability "chrono-synclastic infundibulated" vision, in *The Sirens of Titan* [Vonnegut, 1959], a novel that was meant to be a parody of God's omniscience. Boethius would not have appreciated Vonnegut's wit, and neither would have the British scientist Oliver Lodge (1850–1940), who in one of his innumerable popular essays, one on time and the fourth dimension [Lodge, 1920], wrote; "Is the future all settled beforehand, and only waiting to be 'pushed through' into our three-dimensional ken? Is there no element of contingency? No free will? I am talking geometry, not theology."

Chaucer made a translation of *Consolatione*, and was obviously inspired by it when he wrote his very long poem on the nature of love (*Troilus and Criseyde*) more than six hundred years ago (Book IV.140):

> Some say "If God sees everything before
> It happens—and deceived He cannot be—
> Then everything must happen, though you swore
> The contrary, for He has seen it, He."
> And so I say, if from eternity
> God has foreknowledge of our thought and deed,
> We've no free choice, whatever books we read.

Inspired prose, yes, but Chaucer's poetry misstates Boethius' philosophy, when Troilus declares that divine foreknowledge is incompatible with free will. A recent paper in the philosophical literature [Craig, 1988] makes the connection between spacetime physics and the free-will issue explicit. As Professor Craig writes, "For philosophers in either field, philosophy of science and philosophy of religion are too often viewed as mutually irrelevant ... . This is unfortunate, because sometimes the problems can be quite parallel and a consistent resolution is required. One especially intriguing case in point concerns, in philosophy of science, the possibility of ... time travel and, in philosophy of religion, the relationship between divine foreknowledge and human freedom."

The sardonic wit of Ambrose Bierce was irresistibly drawn to ridicule the hair-splitting distinctions made by Boethius. As he wrote in *The Devil's Dictionary* (1911), "Predestination, n. the doctrine that all things occur according to programme. This doctrine should not be confused with foreordination, which means that all things are programmed, but does not affirm their occurrence ... The difference is great enough to have deluged Christendom with ink, to say nothing of the gore."

Vonnegut tries to see a happy side to omniscience with his creation in *Slaughterhouse-Five* [Vonnegut, 1971] of the alien inhabitants of the planet Tralf-amadore. These beings can see in four dimensions: "When a Tralfamadorian sees a corpse, all he thinks is that the dead person is in bad condition at that particular moment, but that the same person is just fine in plenty of other moments." This sort of writing lacks Einstein's poetry, but it does seem to reflect Einstein's position in the Besso letter. Recently the English professor Blackford has called Vonnegut's expression of the block Universe "a variety of facile mysticism" [Blackford, 1985].

Science fiction writings have also addressed the free-will issue. In "Turn Backward, O Time" [Kubilius, 1951], for example, a man in the twenty-fifth century is about to travel back into the past to escape criminal prosecution. He is asked where he'd like to go, and he replies "I do not understand the paradoxes—what if I choose to build gravity-deflectors in Ancient Rome?" When he is told (correctly) that this can't happen because it didn't happen, he persists: "But if I can choose any period, it means that I can alter history at will—which presumes that the present can also be changed." Then, at last, we get the explicit answer that bothers nearly everyone: "The real answer is that in final analysis your decision to choose a certain time period is already made, and the things you will do [in the time traveler's proper time] are already determined. Free will is an illusion; it is synonymous with incomplete perception." The same idea appears in "Beep" [Blish, 1976]; when one character says "What you are saying is that the future is fixed, and that you can read it, in every essential detail," the response is "Quite right ... both those things are true."

Since 1951 philosophers have become steeped in relativity theory, and this increased sophistication has appeared in their more recent papers. For example, Capek gave a direct response [Capek, 1965] to Williams' myth-of-passage paper, calling it "an interesting piece of science fiction"; in his paper Capek likened the block-Universe interpretation of Minkowski spacetime to a "giant refrigerator." That is, in a play on Williams' title, Capek turned the tables and called the concept Williams professed the "myth of frozen passage." Capek is the first philosopher to have appreciated the fact that the temporal ordering of potentially causal events in both the future and past of one observer is invariant for any other observer, whatever that second observer's motion may be. It is only in *elsewhere*, the region of spacetime that is not causally linked to an observer's now, that temporal ordering can be reversed as seen by some other observer (assuming, as special relativity does, that speeds are limited by the speed of light). (For more information on this see Tech Note 4). Williams responded to Capek in a paper printed immediately after Capek's in the same book. William's work is a rather poetic essay, but it fails to address the substantive technical points raised by Capek. Certainly it failed to change Capek's mind as ten years later Capek wrote [Capek, 1975] that Donald Williams "is clearly unaware of the basic difference between classical and relativistic space-time." After Capek, the philosophers who wrote on spacetime did at least refer to this difference. For example, [Le Poidevin, 1990] makes the point that the proper task for philosophers is not to try to show that time has any particular topology by logical necessity, but rather to explore the consequences of its empirical, contingent properties.

Some years after Professor Williams' poetic essays, his type of style was harshly dismissed with these words from [Earman, 1970b] (they are the opening passage to a critical "guide to spacetime for philosophers"): "Space-time is the basic spatiotemporal entity. Many philosophers have mouthed this truth, but few have swallowed it, and very few have digested it ... an appreciation of this truth is crucial to what is commonly referred to as the philosophy of space and time ... in large measure the lack of progress in this area can be traced to the fact that philosophers have not taken seriously the corollary that talk about space and time is really talk about the spatial and temporal aspects of space-time." For more on this same theme, see also [Earman, 1970a].

What provoked Professor Earman to say this was his perception that philosophers were not talking science when they wrote of space and time, but rather were in the business of telling each other irrelevant stories and myths. This philosophical approach of "telling tales" reached its peak in the early and mid-1960s (prompting Earman's exasperated comments). The story of how this story telling came about is an interesting one. It all began with a paper by the Oxford philosopher Anthony Quinton [Quinton, 1962], who argued that while there can be multiple, disjointed spaces, there can only be a single time. The validity of this conclusion is not the issue here, but rather it is Quinton's technique for arriving at it; that is, myth construction. While popular among philosophers, myth construction usually strikes those trained in the technical sciences as being interesting, but certainly quaint and almost always totally beside the point.

In his paper Quinton tells a fairy tale, one about how he thinks someone can live continuously in time and yet via dreaming be in two different spatial worlds (when awake in one world, you are asleep in the other). He argues that this multispatial myth is plausible, but that a search for an analogous multitemporal myth is doomed from the start. In reply, Swinburne, another philosopher, rebutted Quinton [Swinburne, 1965b] by using a countermyth, this one about the "warring tribes of the Okku and Bokku." The details of this second story are unimportant for us except to note that the story started a vigorous debate in the literature; e.g., see [Skillen, 1965], [Swinburne, 1965a], [Hollis, 1967b], all of which presented even more stories.[34]

It was this continuous spinning of hypothetical tales that caused Earman to write in his 1970b paper that "the procedure for arriving at answers to these questions [about space and time] adopted by Quinton and most of the other authors is, to say the least, a curious one: a story is told about a mythical land—usually called something like the land of the Okkus-Bokkus—and then we are asked what we would say if confronted by experiences like those of the Okkus-Bokkusians. As often happens with such a question, people have said all sorts of things, not all of which are interesting or enlightening."

Smart [1967] was even harsher in his rejection of the philosphers' fairy-tale approach to spacetime physics: "Swinburne, Skillen, and Hollis follow Quinton in inviting us to say what we should think in certain strange circumstances which they describe within common-sense language [as opposed to scientific terminology]. I must say that if I found myself in the circumstances which they describe (for example Swinburne's savage tribe disappearing when a medicine man waves his magic wand [and so we see the 'land of Okkus-Bokkus' is an outrageous pun!]) I just would not know what to think. Probably I should simply conclude that I had gone mad, or at any rate madder than I normally am ... It looks as though these writers are inviting us to consider what we should say if we knew no science."

In fact, it is in Professor Smart's essay that we at last find the modern view of time and space, the issue originally raised by Quinton. Smart notes that the issue of space and time loses whatever philosophical mystery it may seem to have when one thinks in terms of relativistic spacetime. As Smart explains, "The reason why there could be two totally disparate space-times is simply the quite obvious one that two totally disparate four-dimensional spaces can exist within a suitable five-dimensional space. There is no difficulty in mathematical conceivability here. Now let one of these four-spaces be our own space-time world, and let the other four-space be more or less similiar, in accordance with whatever story you wish to tell about it."

At about the same time Smart's article appeared, one last apparent attempt at mythmaking was published [Hollis, 1967a], this time about two men (Peabody and Snooks) and also about a tribe of two-dimensional, live tiddly-winks! This would seem to be an example of the reprehensible sort of doings that so irritated Smart and Earman, but in fact what Hollis was doing was demonstrating the essential worthlessness of philosophical stories (and so Smart erred in lumping Hollis in with the fairy-tale philosophers): "Whenever a human being produces an argument which opens 'Suppose I had 23 senses ... '. 'Suppose I were God ... '. 'Suppose I experienced objects extended in four spatial dimensions ... ', we can protest that the argument is worthless. For in supposing that he has transcended our human point of view, he has also transcended the limits of our understanding." As Hollis amusingly concluded his paper, such opening sentences are the signatures of myths from "The Philosopher's Fairy Book." He is prepared to accept the failure of his message to convince, however, as he says he is waiting for the paper that begins "Twice upon a time in another space no distance in any direction from here ... "!

Despite this concern, there *were* others besides Hollis who had gotten the message that telling fairy tales just would not do. For example, the opening quote to this chapter comes from Professor Putnam's paper [Putnam, 1967] in which he, like Williams, argues for the block-Universe view of spacetime but unlike in Williams' paper, we see in Putnam's work not poetic prose, but Einstein. Putnam asks us to imagine two observers, one stationary (him) and the other moving at a very high speed (you). At some particular instant the moving observer (you) passes very close (arbitrarily close) by the stationary one (him). At this point of closeness, the two of you share a common event in spacetime, and so experience the same present or 'now'. But, argues Putnam, his future light cone and yours are tilted relative to each other (you *must* read Tech Note 4 to understand this!) Thus, says Putnam, "It is well known that, as a consequence of Special Relativity, there are events [in spacetime] which lie 'in the future' according to *my* coordinate system and which lie in the present of ... *your* coordinate system." Since all the events in the present of the moving observer (you) are clearly real, then the future of the stationary observer (according to Putnam) which contains at least some of those same events, is at least partially real, too. Putnam is, however, simply incorrect; in Tech Note 4 it is shown that if an event is in the future of one observer, then it is also in the future (not in the now) of the moving observer. (In an astonishing coincidence, another paper [Rietdijk, 1966] appeared just a few months before Putnam's and this was followed a decade later by [Rietdijk, 1976]. Rietdijk's works elaborated on the same theme and arrived at the identical conclusion as Putnam by making essentially the same arguments.)[35]

Putnam's argument was quickly refuted in [Harris, 1968]. Professor Harris demonstrated that Professor Putnam's reasoning is not in accord with special relativity; specifically, he showed that distant simultaneity can only be determined after the fact, perhaps long after, and that the moving observer will not know the reality of all the events simultaneous with the 'local now' he shares for an instant with the stationary observer until these events are in his (and the stationary observer's) past. Reitdijk apparently had anticipated this rejoinder (and perhaps that is why Harris fails to cite Reitdijk) when he wrote that "only an extreme positivism: 'that which can not yet be observed does not yet exist', can possibly withstand the conclusion" of a deterministic, block-Universe spacetime.

On this point, in fact, my personal sympathy lies with Rietdijk. Being unknown is not equivalent to being undetermined. On the other hand, [Capek, 1975] makes the cogent observation that if something is unobservable, then (as were the historical cases of the ether, caloric, and phlogiston) there is nothing to be gained by postulating their existence. On the other hand, [Sklar, 1974] has objected to Capek's position by claiming that to say an event does not exist because it is not happening at our time is as absurd as saying that an event does not exist because it is not happening at our location.

So Putnam felt a bullet whiz by, while Reitdijk escaped—but not for long. A second refutation [Stein, 1968] appeared that bounced a verbal cannon ball off Putnam's head, but this time there was one for Reitdijk, too. The rebuttal was along the same lines as Harris'. Stein stated that Putnam and Reitdijk had simply misapplied special relativity. Professor Stein, however, unlike Harris, was at times absolutely scathing: "Putnam ... has used ... a collection of principles of philosophical interpretation derived from dubious authority, subjected to no adequate critical examination, and in point of fact demonstrably inappropriate to the scientific context in which they are employed ... these defects seem to me to merit comment precisely as symptoms of a *prevalent* laxness in philosophical discussion, which is very much to be deprecated. Technical mistakes and errors of detail can be corrected ... but the lowering of critical standards in philosophical discourse itself precludes understanding and is the death of philosophy."

Well, that seems a pretty harsh dismissal of poor Professor Putnam! Would no one defend him? (Putnam himself seems never to have replied.) For a year there was silence, and then a paper appeared [Fitzgerald, 1969], written in a tutorial, nonconfrontational style (which must have elicited a sigh of relief from the beleaguered Putnam). In his paper, Professor Fitzgerald presents a summary of the "traditionally competing philosophical views about the ontological status of the future," and then follows this with analyses of how each such view appears after reformulation in relativistic terms. Both Putnam and Stein are cited, but no mention is made of the extreme disagreement between Putnam and his critics. Fitzgerald then adds a little mathematics by invoking the Lorentz time transformation (see Tech Note 3) but of the distant simultaneity objection *he does not say a word*.[36] The precise technical points central to the dispute between Putnam and his critics are ignored in Fitzgerald's paper.

A few years later a defense of substance [Weingard, 1972b] at last appeared—or at least it was sort of a defense. Weingard opened with "Hilary Putnam concludes that all events in special relativistic spacetime, whether past, present, or future, are equally real ... Although I believe this conclusion is correct, I think Putnam's argument is not." That is, Professor Weingard rejects Putnam's specific arguments (and thus avoids the power of Stein's specific rebuttals) and yet retains the view of spacetime as a block Universe in which everything already is, the view expressed by Weyl and that which Einstein appears also to have held when writing his letter to Besso's family. As have all critics before and since, Weingard faults Putnam for a failure to understand what distant simultaneity does and does not mean. He then uses the idea of arbitary conventionality about the two-way versus the one-way velocity of light to arrive at a conclusion in agreement with Putnam's.[37]

The debate over the reality of the future continues to this day. In [Zemach, 1979], for example, we see a failure to understand Capek, as we find the author concluding with "Hence, it is nonsense to say that 'the past' or 'the future' are not fully real; each point-event in the Universe is past with respect to some selves, and future with respect to others; all are equally real." In [Fitzgerald, 1985] we see that the idea that relative simultaneity of events for an observer exists only outside of the light cones of that observer, in *elsewhere*, has at last become part of the philosophical literature as written by philosophers. (Indeed, this was explicitly stated earlier in [Godfrey-Smith, 1979], which also mentions Reitdijk's error in reasoning.)

For the purposes of time travel, it is of course mandatory to accept the reality of past and future, an idea Capek emphatically denies when he writes that "fortunately, such fantasies have not the slightest basis in the physics of relativity" [Capek, 1983]. It is not clear why Capek used such a judgmental word as *fortunately*, as if something awful would otherwise occur, but in any case not all philosophers refuse to accept the equal reality of past and future. In [Smart, 1981] we find an author who does refuse, but who also says that "it is very hard to convince those who are not professional philosophers that the future is real." As an example of how absurd he finds this situation to be, Smart asks us to "conceive of a soldier in the twenty-first century ... cold, miserable and suffering from dysentery, and being told that some twentieth-century philosphers and non-philosophers had held that the future was unreal. He might have some choice things to say."

Putting aside the relevance (or the lack of it) of Smart's imaginary exercise, it is interesting to note that this very situation was used in science fiction more than thirty years ago in "Soldier" [Ellison, 1989]. In that story, originally published in 1957 (and available today on videotape as an episode from "The Twilight Zone"), a soldier from the far future is hurled back to our time by the beam energy flux of enemy weapons fire. The soldier tells tales of the utter horror of future warfare (and here Harlan Ellison unleashes a monstrous, graphic picture of horror in his description of telepathic "brain burners" and other terrors) and this generates a backlash to war. But even as peace engulfs the world, there are those who wonder if the future *can* be changed—perhaps it *is* rigidly frozen into a Minkowski/Capek refrigerator universe, into a Wellsian Rigid Universe. Perhaps today's peace movement, led by the soldier from tomorrow, is precisely what leads to the future at war.

Arguing the opposite view is "Nobody Here But Us Shadows" [Lundwall, BRW], a story in which one can go "Upside" (into the future) and examine alternatives ("probability lines"). One only looks, however, and never interacts. Indeed, the time machine is locked from the outside to prevent the traveler/observer from exiting. This is done because on one of the first trips the observer did take something back, a girl. Years later, when an observer journeys upside along that same probability line, he finds it utterly vanished. That once-possible future was destroyed by the removal of what was only a possibility (the girl) and by her entrance into the present as an out-of-time fact. (An eerie twist on this idea is in "A Few Minutes" [Janifer, 1973], which describes a machine that lets one explore what would have been the future if different choices had been made in the unchangeable past.)

As for the question of the persistence of the past, I find particularly evocative a passage from Grant Allen's Introduction to his sleeping-into-the-future novel *British Barbarians* [Allen, 1895]: "I am writing in my study on the heather-clad hilltop. When I raise my eye from my sheet of foolscap, it falls upon miles and miles of broad open moorland. My window looks out upon unsullied nature. Everything around is fresh and pure and wholesome ... But away below in the valley, as night draws on, a lurid glare reddens the north-eastern horizon. It marks the spot where the great wen of London heaves and festers." It *is* tempting to think of Allen somehow still there in his study in 1895 and of heaving and festering late-Victorian London, too, with H. G. Wells himself in the middle of it, still reading the first rave reviews of *The Time Machine*.

Even if events in all their infinitely infinite spatial and temporal web (what [Gold, MDT] calls the "world map") are really laid out in a four-dimensional universe, there still remains the great mystery of why we see them unfold in the particular sequence that we do. Why not in reverse order? Why, indeed, do we see what we call time run from what we call the past to what we call the future and, indeed, what do we mean by past and future? As we will see in the next chapter, these are not easy questions and the view of nearly everybody who has thought about them is that we are not even close to knowing the answers.

CHAPTER THREE
The Arrows of Time

On a microscopic level there is *no preferred* direction for time. The equations of motion don't give a damn whether time moves forward or backward.

—[Eisenberg, AO]

If space is 'looking-glassed' the world continues to make sense; but looking-glassed time has an inherent absurdity which turns the world-drama into the most nonsensical farce.

—[Eddington, 1929]

Now we are also in a position to shed some light on a problem being frequently discussed nowadays: the possibility that the direction of the flow of time is reversed. This subject used to be considered fit for science fiction only ...

—[Zwart, 1972]

Of all the problems which lie on the borderline of philosophy and science, perhaps none has caused more spilled ink, more controversy and more emotion than the problem of the direction of time ... the main problem with 'the problem of the direction of time' is to figure out exactly what the problem is or is supposed to be!

—[Earman, 1974]

Talk of the flow of time or the advance of consciousness is a dangerous metaphor that must not be taken literally.

—[Smart, 1954]

The Language of Time Travel

For the phrases "flow of time" and "direction of time" to have any objective meaning at all, it must be somehow possible to identify a difference between past events and future ones. The special moment at which this distinction occurs is known as the *now* or the *present*, and as events make the transition associated with this distinctive difference between past and future, the now moves, or flows. Philosophers (and physicists, too) call this common feeling that all humans have of the passage of time the *psychological arrow of time*.

In principle, so it would seem, we can have perfect knowledge of what has happened but only imperfect prediction of what might happen. Can we tell past from future? At first glance, the nature of this distinction seems obvious—we can remember past events, but not future ones. As philosophers have so nicely put it, events in the past have formed traces (such as a skull, a footprint in the sand, fossil bones, a surgical scar, photographs, tape recordings, a carved stone), while future events have not. Still, is this necessarily so? Is it impossible for future events to create traces? The common sense reaction to this is yes, certainly; there must be asymmetry in trace formation because of cause-and-effect; i.e., traces are the effects of prior causes. This line of reasoning leads us quickly to the issue of causation.

Part of the problem we have with backward time travel and cause-and-effect is our language. The distinct and separate concepts of the ordering of events in time and of causality have become merged in everyday thought. It is considered obvious that if event *A* causes event *B*, then *A* must happen first. It is virtually inconceivable in most minds that it could be otherwise. There is, however, at least one historical example of a similiar merging of concepts that is parallel to our modern mixing of order and causality; an example that shows how an issue could seem so obvious and natural to the minds of the period and yet today seem so confused, odd, peculiar, even laughable. I quote from [Csonka, 1969], which presented this example in a paper on advanced (i.e., inverted causality) effects: "Ancient Egypt was an essentially one-dimensional country strung out along the Nile, which flows from south to north. The winds were conveniently arranged to be predominantly northerly. To go north, a traveler could let his boat drift, while with a sail he could move south against the slow current. For this reason, in the writing of the ancient Egyptians, 'go downstream (north)' was represented by a boat without sails, and 'go upstream (south)' by a boat with sails. The words (and concepts) of north-south and up-downstream became merged. Since the Nile and its tributaries were the only rivers known to the ancient Egyptians, this caused no difficulties until they reached the Euphrates, which happened to flow from north to south. Their confusion is recorded in their reference to 'that inverted water which goes downstream (north) in going upstream (south)'."

An interesting example of how we practice a similiar confusion concerning time was commented on by Francis Bacon as long ago as 1605 in his *The Advancement of Learning*. He pointed out that while each generation thinks of itself as living through days of youth (and of the past as always the good old days), we are really the "ancients of the world" (to paraphrase Tennyson), the most distantly removed—from the start of the world—of all who have lived. We make the error of reckoning time *backward from our present*, rather than from the instant of the Beginning.

Often we can work our way free of the difficulties we create with language, but only by mutual agreement. For example, the Chairman of the Board calls a meeting to order with the mixed tenses, in "The meeting *will* take place *now*" and then says, at the end, "We will meet again *next* month, *same* time." We all know what these sentences mean, but only by our cultural heritage, and not by the process of applying a logical calculus! The language problem troubles both fictional time travelers and the physicists/philosophers who study time travel. Reader beware!

Does Time Have a Direction?

The answer seems obvious. *Of course* time has a direction; everybody knows it flows from past to future. There is a curious language problem here, however, because we also like to say that the present recedes into the past, which is consistent with a flow in the opposite direction, from future to past. Given this uncomfortable situation of snarled syntax, can we at least distinguish past from future, whichever way time might flow? That at least would be a start, but even this simplified question is not so simple to answer. The central debate here is between what is called *objective time* (the idea that time really does flow), and *mind-dependent time* (the belief that time flow is an illusion).

The idea of time flowing is a popular one, and it repeatedly appears in the time-travel literature as the "river of time" (or the "ocean of time"). The deep psychological appeal of this sort of language has, not surprisingly, attracted the attention of philosophers. We can find one of the earliest expressions of the concept in the *Meditations* of the second-century Roman emperor and Stoic philosopher Marcus Aurelius, who wrote, "Time is like a river made up of events which happen, and a violent stream; for as soon as a thing has been, it is carried away, and another comes in its place, and this will be carried away, too." A most interesting essay on why such metaphors often seem so intuitive is [Smart, 1949]; Professor Smart points out that their seductiveness is sufficiently great that we can often find them in the scientific literature, too. For example, even Newton wrote specifically of time flowing (see Tech Note 1). As for why such metaphors have a powerful grip on our imaginations, I think we need look no further back than Kant. As he wrote in *Critique of Pure Reason*, "Time is nothing but the form of inner sense, that is, of the intuition of ourselves and of our inner state ... because this inner intuition yields no shape, we endeavour to make up for this want by analogies."

Still, no matter how intuitive such metaphors may be, they can still easily befuddle us as well. To quote Professor Smart: "Time a river! A queer sort of river that. Of what sort of liquid does it consist? Is time a liquid? A very peculiar liquid indeed!" A classic paper by Donald Williams, which rejects the liquid view of time, addresses this issue of language [Williams, 1951a]. Professor Williams presents a truly staggering collection of entertaining examples, of which I repeat only a few. Time flies, goes, flows, marches, rolls. The evolution of our lives is like "a moving picture film, unwinding from the dark reel of the future, projected briefly on the screen of the present, and rewound into the dark can of the past." Time is a snowball with the past in the center while ever new presents accrete around it (presumably as the snowball rolls down the hill of history). A young person sees time as an ocean on which golden mornings arrive like waves from the future, while for an old person liquid time is a nightmare flood, a swollen black torrent sweeping him first into the yawning abyss of the past and, ultimately and finally, into the eternal silence of the dark grave.

Charles Nordmann opened and closed his 1925 book *The Tyranny of Time* with this gloomy but all too true summary of the overwhelming sense we all have of the inexorable, one-way flow of time (the ellipses denote over 200 pages!): "Nothing can equal the bitter sweetness of dreaming on the banks of Time, that impalpable and fatal river strewn with dead leaves, our wistful hours carried down stream like rudderless wrecks ... In the eternal wave which rocks us, carries us along and soon swallows us up there is no rock to which we can fasten our frail barques; the very bouys we put out to measure our course are only floating mirages; and on the mysterious foundation of things our anchors slide along and fail to bite."

The early science fiction magazine story "The Time Annihilator" [Manley and Thode, 1930] played with the erosive nature of time in a dramatic way. As two time travelers speed into the future to rescue a friend, one of them describes the scene for us: "We huddled together in the whirling time-girdling machine, cutting through the years as a ship's prow breasts surging waves. I could not help but think of the years as waves, beating in endless succession on the sands of eternity. They wore all away before them with pitiless attrition. Time seemed to eat all with dragon jaws." The same sentiment is captured in the famous opening words to the nineteenth-century English poet Austin Dobson's "The Paradox of Time." This poem grimly turns the metaphor of moving time upside down (Dobson freely admitted that his opening was inspired by a nearly identical couplet due to the sixteenth-century French poet Pierre de Ronsard):

> Time goes, you say? Ah, no!
> Alas, Time stays, *we* go.

Manley and Thode's watery image of time was taken a step further in "Wanderers of Time" [Wyndham, 1933], a story in which a large number of time travelers from all over time find themselves stranded at precisely the same place. One of them offers his theory of what has caused this remarkable coincidence; they all have faulty time machines, like faulty boats, and all have hit the same snag on the "river of time." As he explains, "You may turn boats adrift on a river at many points, and they will all collect together at the same serious obstacle whether they have traveled a hundred miles or two miles. We are now at some period where the straight flow of time has been checked—perhaps it is even turning back on itself ... we have struck some barrier and been thrown up like so much jetsam."

Max Black, a philosopher, argues [Black, 1959b] that questions about the direction of time are meaningless because there can be no direction to something that (he claims) does not flow. His reasoning is that if time did flow, then he ought to be entitled to ask how fast it flows. This requires, in turn, a metatime or supertime for measuring the flow rate of ordinary time. But since supertime flows, too, we would need a super-supertime, and off we trip into what would seem to be the black hole of a McTaggart-like infinite regress.[1] As mentioned in Chapter One, [Dunne, 1958] tried to explain precognition in terms of an infinite regress of times, an attempt that attracted nothing but polite rejection from philosophers (e.g., see [Broad, 1935]). A hierarchy of hypertimes has not bothered other analysts, however, and a whole subfield of speciality in time analysis is that of multidimensional time. Indeed, one such analyst [Webb, 1960] sarcastically rejected the infinite-regress objection as being "a crushing and unanswerable position," and he observed that it is not at all clear why supertime must flow. After all, Webb observed, we measure the flow of a river with respect to its banks without requiring that the banks also flow. (This strikes me as a rational position, but I have not been able to find any mention of it in the later philosophical literature. The idea of multiple-time dimensions is particularly attractive for a sort of time travel, and while it enjoys far more popularity among science fiction writers and philosophers than it does with physicists, we'll take it up at the end of this chapter.)

Black realized that there are uses of the word direction that are not directly tied to something flowing, such as in the statement "He is facing in the direction of north." Black argued that this is mere pointing, and not at all the same as moving north. He then dismissed the possibility of there being any meaning to the direction of time, writing that making an analogy of time "with a sign-post or an index finger is too farfetched to be worth considering." This is, of course, an affirmation of the myth-of-passage view (mentioned in Chapter Two) that was made famous in [Williams, 1951a]. In his novel *October the First Is Too Late*, which tells about a world in which different parts of the Earth experience widely different eras of the past [Hoyle, 1966], British cosmologist Fred Hoyle used far blunter language than did Williams, calling the river of time a "grotesque and absurd illusion," and a "bogus idea."

Cause and Effect

The central puzzle of time travel is its apparent denial of causality; the belief that we live in a world where every effect has a cause and that the cause always happens first. First we flip the switch and then the kitchen light comes on. Never the other way. So deeply embedded is the temporal ordering of cause and effect in our feelings about how the world (and all the rest of the cosmos) works that the philosopher J. L. Mackie calls it the "cement of the Universe." Without causality, says Mackie, everything comes unglued and falls apart. Electrical engineers, too, when designing electronic systems they actually plan to construct, always insist that the result be *causal*. By this they mean that the system must have no output before the input is applied and that the system must not be able to anticipate the application of an input. This may all seem self-evident, but there are subtle problems here.

For example, it has become almost a cliche to say that nothing can go faster than light; this is what physicists mean by *relativistic causality*. No cause can produce an effect at a distant location sooner than the time lapse required for a light pulse to make the trip. Classical mechanics, however, the science of Newton's laws, which engineers use all the time, is *not* relativistically causal. Push the left end of a rigid rod, for example, and the right end moves instantly. Most of the time the lack of this form of causality causes no problems, but the fact remains that the mechanics all engineers first learn in school is flawed on a fundamental level. A rigid rod is an impossibility in Einstein's mechanics.

Occasionally I daydream about how, after a discussion of causality, a traditional engineering professor would respond if challenged by a bright student. Causality might not look so obvious, after all. Suppose, for example, such a student stuck his hand up in class and said: "Professor, you've told us that everything that happens in nature is due to a cause. That what we see happening all around us, as the world unfolds, is the domino-process of ... cause-effect-cause-effect- ... , and so on into the future. But suppose, Professor, that at some instant, somehow, every particle in the world suddenly reverses its velocity vector. Wouldn't that mean, given the time-reversible nature of the classical equations of motion, that the world would then run backward along the same path it had followed up until the instant of reversal? Wouldn't that mean that what was 'effect' is now 'cause', and what was 'cause' is now 'effect'? And if cause and effect can change roles like that ... well, Professor, what does it *mean*?"

Let me immediately short-circuit one possible answer our beleaguered professor might give in his desperation: the idea that somehow the equations of physics may not be time reversible. Indeed, it was discovered more than a quarter-century ago that in certain very rare, fundamental particle decay processes (involving the neutral K mesons, or *kaons*), there is the hint that perhaps nature can distinguish between the two directions of time. In particular, kaons violate CP symmetry and so the TCP theorem says T symmetry must also fail (see Note 11 for Chapter Two). So important was this discovery [Christenson *et al.*, 1964] that the principal investigators, James Cronin and Val Fitch, received the 1980 Nobel Prize in physics for their work. Later, [Casella, 1968, 1969] reported on direct observations of the failure of T symmetry, thereby providing experimental confirmation of the TCP theorem. (In an astonishing example of prescience, the use of K mesons in a machine for affecting the past and thus the present is mentioned in "Target One" [Pohl, 1956], a story published in 1955, years before the peculiar decays were first observed!)

As [Hurley, 1986] put it so well, "The decay of the neutral K meson is not time-reversal invariant; perhaps it is this ubiquitous meson which is responsible for the cream diffusing uniformly throughout our coffee in the morning. Possibly, but again this conjecture cannot account for the computer models which have no neutral K mesons." This tiny chink in the rock of time-direction indistinguishability, if it is actually there, is however still an active area of research and speculation. In general, of course, even with such a chink the fact that the classical laws appear to be insensitive to a direction of time while the real world (which seems in no way dependent on kaons) seems distinctly asymmetric is a puzzle of the first-rank. As [Earman, 1969] expresses it, "The Universe seems asymmetric with respect to past and future in a very deep and non-accidental way, and yet all the laws of nature are purely time symmetric. So where can the asymmetry come from?" Lots has been written on this. As [Hurley, 1986] states, "There are few paradoxes which have been resolved so often as the time-asymmetry paradox," but the question continues to puzzle.

Yet, there is, in fact, powerful experimental evidence that with the rare exception of kaons the classical laws of physics are time reversible. Perhaps the most compelling such evidence comes from the *reciprocity theorem* that electrical engineers who design antennas use routinely. The theorem is easy to state. Suppose two electrical engineers, Bob in Boston and Lois in Los Angeles, send radio signals to each other. Bob sends his message by exciting his antenna with an electrical signal (a current), which thus launches electromagnetic radiation into space. Lois' distant antenna intercepts some of this radiation, which then creates a signal (a current) in it. The reciprocity theorem says that if she makes a tape recording of this signal and plays it back as the excitation signal to her antenna, then the signal created in Bob's antenna will be the original signal he sent. This result is completely independent of the two antennas (which can be totally different in design) and of the details of the propagation path between Boston and Los Angeles (as long as the details do not change with time). The reciprocity theorem is true (it can be *measured* to be true as accurately as one wishes to perform this procedure) because of the reversibility of physics right down to the electronic level. The answer to the professor's problem of explaining the reversal of causality to his student has not yet been found in the known laws of physics.

To make things even more interesting, what can we say about mutual or *simultaneous* causation? When a ball sits motionlessly in the depression on a pillow, is the ball motionless because it sits in the depression, or is there a depression because the ball sits motionless? When two leaning dominoes A and B hold each other up, is A upright because of B or is it B that is upright because of A? When two children bob up and down on a see-saw, whose motion is the cause and whose is the effect? Simultaneous causation leads us quickly to puzzling questions. For example, causation is generally thought of as being transitive; if A causes B, and B causes C, then A causes C. But if A and B are mutually causative, then A causes B coupled with B causes A leads to A causes A (and B causes B); i.e., mutual causation implies self-causation! Except for those theologians who like this kind of discussion (because it lets them answer the question 'Who made God?' with 'He made Himself'), hardly anyone likes mutual causation. But how do we avoid the conclusion that perhaps the mutual causation of two leaning dominoes represents an experimental proof that God could have made himself? This is certainly outrageous stuff, but don't you wonder how our poor professor would respond to all this? I do!

And, I wonder, for yet another example, what our professor would have to say about the debates caused(!) by Dirac's discovery in 1938 of an apparent violation of cause and effect in electrodynamics? (This will be discussed later in this section.) More recent still is the application of "time-reversed light" to undo the severe distortion that beams of light can suffer in atmospheric propagation. This technique, called optical phase conjugation [Giuliano, 1981], seems almost magical, but it is science. (This technique is, in fact, essentially the velocity vector reverser, in this case for photons, that was mentioned by the "student" earlier in this section, and it finds practical use in the removal of turbulence blurring in satellite imagery of the Earth's surface.) But these are actually far more complicated examples than are necessary to show how our ordinary, everyday ideas of cause-and-effect can be turned inside out.

Consider, for example, the problem of the signal processing of recorded time signals; e.g., information written onto magnetic tape. Typical examples include the strata-probing seismic echoes from dynamite explosions set off by oil exploration geologists; arms control compliance monitoring stations that listen for the acoustic rumbles of earthquakes and underground nuclear tests and try to distinguish one from the other; and the gathering by various military intelligence agencies of turbine shaft/propeller noise signatures emitted by different kinds of submarines.

In each of these situations the raw information is recorded and later processed with a certain degree of unhurried calm and leisure. That pool of oil, after all, has been down there for several hundred million years and waiting a few more days (or weeks) for a computer analysis of an explosion echo is not a big concern. Such processing of recorded data is said to be done off-line, in nonreal time. When we play the tape back, however, we can do all sorts of neat things, like speed the tape up (make time "run fast") or slow the tape down (make time "run slow") or even reverse the tape (make time "run backward"). For various technical reasons, generically called spectrum shifting, this is often very useful. The way we get the information off the tape, of course, is to run it through a playback machine with a read-head that senses the magnetic flux variations on the tape. The electrical signal produced by the read-head is just like the original signal, and in fact we can pretend we don't know it is really coming off a tape, but instead can imagine that it is the original signal. For the new high quality digitally recorded music tapes, in fact, it is virtually impossible to distinguish the original from the playback; and that, of course, is why we buy them.

But—suppose we make our playback machine with two read-heads, with the new head sensing the tape before the old head. The two heads produce the same electrical signal, but the signal from the new head is ahead in time of that from the old head. The new head is seeing the future of the old head! We can use these two signals, with the old one representing now time and the new one future time, to build real systems that are not causal. The causality violation occurs in nonreal time, of course, not *our* time, but no matter; some absolutely astonishing signal processing can be achieved. The Universe is about fifteen billion years old—pretending that time has shifted a few milliseconds or so doesn't seem like we're doing too much violence to reality.

This method is often used on call-in radio talk shows; to catch and prevent inappropriate remarks from intemperate callers being broadcast, a short time-delay is introduced by tape, and what is heard on the radio *now* is actually five seconds or so old. A caller can get terribly confused if he does not turn his radio off, as one ear hears the present on the telephone while the other hears the past. Two fictional attempts to show just how confusing such living out-of-sync might be are "Man in His Time" [Aldiss, TTT], the story of an astronaut who returns from a trip to Mars and finds he is 3.3077 minutes ahead of everybody else, and "The Man Who Saw Too Late" [Binder, 1939], which tells us what it might be like to have a three-minute delay in just our vision. The 1956 British film *Timeslip* develops the same idea, with an atomic scientist's perception advanced seven seconds into the future as the result of an accidental radiation exposure. These three characters each become terribly confused and disoriented.

The mixing of the ideas of temporal ordering (that is, of before and after) and that of causality is also a source of potential conceptual confusion. Despite my previous words, it is not necessarily obvious that it is proper to reason that if A causes B, then A happens first. This was Immanuel Kant's view, but David Hume thought the reasoning should go the other way: if A happens before B (and A and B are causally linked), then A is the cause and B is the effect. It is all too easy to fall into the trap of the Egyptian sailors and think that one concept implies the other. And, of course, two events may not have a causal connection at all even if one always follows the other. A little example may demonstrate this easy-to-make error—the cock always crows just before sunrise, but his crowing is not the cause of the sun rising.

All this has been the compost for growing countless arguments about what is called *backward* or *reverse* (or even *retro*) causation. What is generally meant by *forward* causation is, of course, that any event that occurs at time t is caused only by events that occurred at an earlier time. Backward causation says that at least one of the causing events occurs after time t. Backward causation is clearly a close relative to time travel. The topic, understandably, is the root of many hot philosophical debates, though not everybody thinks these debates are illuminating. For example, in [Earman, 1976] we read: "Causation as a topic of philosophical discussion refuses to die. Each year, books and articles on causation continue to pour forth. Of course, all this activity may simply be a symptom of the necrophilia that infects so much of philosophy."

Why does Professor Earman take this harsh position? He offers as one example the following common philosophical proof of the impossibility of backward causation—by definition a cause is always before its effect: Yes, that's the entire proof. One can, of course, win any argument by invoking 'by definition'; i.e., by defining the answer to be what it is you want to believe. More interesting, and very pertinent to time travel, is the argument that says that if backward causation were possible, then one could change the past, but this cannot be done because the past is dead and gone and thus unchangeable. This does seem to be a pretty solid argument, but Earman rebuts it by pointing out that the same logic could also be applied to the future, and thus the usual forward causation must then be denied, too. That is, whatever the future will be, *will be* (literally by definition), so one cannot change that either. A similar argument appeared earlier in [Smart, 1958], where we find the statement: "Suppose that someone says 'I can change the future. I can do *this* or I can do *that*'. Well, then, suppose that he does *that*. Has he changed the future? No, because doing *that* was the future."

Even our everyday uses of cause and effect are not nearly so straightforward as one might think, even when they are under far less stress than imposed by the issues of backward causation and time travel. Consider, for example, the endless problems that are easy to imagine in the legal world. If a man falls off the roof of a ten-story building and is electrocuted as he plunges through power lines twenty feet above ground, was it gravity or electricity that was the cause of death? Or was it both? If an athlete breaks a leg during a sporting event and later dies under anesthesia at the hospital, what was the cause of death—the accident on the playing field or the accident in the operating room? If a man with a paper-thin skull dies after being accidently struck on the head by another who in turn was bumped into him by a third individual, who (or what) was the cause of death? One does not even have to discuss time travel before getting into serious trouble about cause and effect e.g., see [Mackie, 1992], but *with* time travel things can be certainly quite perplexing; e.g., we normally think it foolish to prepare now for an event that has already happened, but the prudent time traveler about to visit the Ice Age would surely be wise to pack a fur coat before getting into his time machine.

Are there actual phenomena that justify a belief in the possibility of effect before cause in real time (not just tape recorder time)? The only example I know of, and a controversial one at that (but see also the series of papers [Rietdijk, 1978, 1981, 1987] for claimed retroactive effects in quantum mechanics), is a theoretical result of Dirac's formulation of electrodynamics [Dirac, 1938]. Classical theory models electrical charges as point objects of zero size, which causes problems when one tries to calculate certain details, such as the total field energy of a single electron — the answers come out as infinity. In an attempt to find more reasonable, i.e., finite, answers to such questions, Dirac returned to the idea (originally due to Lorentz) of viewing charges as being extended objects in space, while retaining the validity of Maxwell's equations right down to a point. To calculate how such objects will behave, however, one has to include what are called the self-interaction forces; e.g., the force that one side of an electron exerts on the other side. When it was all worked out, Dirac arrived at a third-order differential equation of motion that involves a force term proportional not to the first time derivative of the velocity (i.e., the acceleration), but rather to the second derivative (the rate of change of the acceleration, a quantity of direct interest mostly to the designers of automobile suspensions; their technical term for it is the *jerk*).

There is no other force in physics that shows this sort of dependency, at least not in Newtonian physics, and there are some curious consequences. One results from what is called the "runaway" solution, which says that an electron experiencing no external force can still continually accelerate. Dirac showed how this solution can be eliminated by picking a particular value for what until then was an arbitrary constant of integration, but this trick causes, in turn, a second result called "pre-acceleration." That is, if a charged particle is subjected to an external disturbance (Dirac considered a passing pulse of electromagnetic radiation), the charge will accelerate *before* the pulse reaches the electron's position. This seems to be an argument for backward causation. The time interval during which the pre-acceleration occurs is very brief, on the order of the time it takes light to travel across the width of the extended charge (about a millionth of a billionth of a billionth of a second for an electron), but no matter. The apparent crack in the door of causality may be slight, but that was enough for some philosophical analysts.

Not everybody likes this apparent failure of causality in Dirac's theory. Technical details can be found in [Plass, 1961] and [Davies, 1977] as well as in Dirac's beautifully written original paper, of course; Davies for one is clearly uneasy about it all, calling pre-acceleration "unpleasant" acausal behavior. On the other side, however, one can find believers; e.g., [Earman, 1974]. Earman's paper provoked a strong reply from Grünbaum who argued that the whole business is a nonproblem [Grünbaum, 1976]. Professor Grünbaum makes, in fact, a very interesting point. He argues that since Dirac's equation is non-Newtonian, we have no reason for coupling force and acceleration together as a cause-and-effect pair. In Newtonian mechanics we do use this particular coupling, yet we do not think of force and velocity as such a cause-and-effect pair because there is an integration operation involved in getting from one to the other. In Dirac's theory we have an integration operation separating force and acceleration.

The exchanges over these matters became quite heated, indeed personal. For example, in his argument for the seeming backward-causation result from Dirac's theory, Earman wrote, "I believe that backward causation is a conceptual possibility and that the question of whether backward causation exists in nature is a question which must be settled not by armchair philosophers but by natural philosophers." In his paper Earman had some critical words for Adolf Grünbaum who, it will be recalled, totally rejects pre-acceleration as a case for backward causation. Grünbaum struck back at Earman by ending his paper [Grünbaum, 1976] with "Earman's uncritical depiction of Dirac's preacceleration as an example of retrocausation is a case of an armchair philosopher misinterpreting what a natural philosopher has wrought." The battle continued with [Earman, 1976] and the reply [Grünbaum and Janis, 1977, 1978], and a new attack [Nissim-Sabat, 1979], which provoked a very long response that called Nissim-Sabat "incredibly undisciplined."

One curious aspect to this debate is that many of the modern commentators seem not to have paid much attention to what Dirac himself had to say about pre-acceleration. A Nobel laureate, it seems hardly likely he would let such a result pass unnoticed, and indeed his paper contains the following physical explanation: "It would appear here that we have a contradiction with elementary ideas of causality. The electron seems to know about the pulse before it arrives and to get up an acceleration ... The behavior of our electron can be interpreted in a natural way, however, if we suppose the electron to have a finite size. There is then no need for the pulse to reach the center of the electron before it starts to accelerate. It starts to accelerate ... as soon as the pulse meets its outside. Mathematically, the electron has no sharp boundary." I think Dirac explained it all pretty well, but some modern philosophers and physicists seem to have a problem in appreciating his explanation. One reason for their negative reaction may be that Dirac went on to show how this effect does in fact imply the possibility of building a device for sending a faster-than-light signal backward in time! Science fiction writers, of course, were quick to grab the idea (while most physicists and philosophers were nonplussed) and such gadgets were dubbed "Dirac radios," e.g., see "Beep" [Blish, 1976].

A recent paper [McKeon and Ord, 1992] hints at a fascinating connection between travel backwards in time and Dirac's relativistically correct, quantum mechanical description of the electron. It is shown by McKeon and Ord that, in flat two-dimensional spacetime (see Tech Note 4), the assumption of time travel to the past leads in a natural way to Dirac's equation. If, on the other hand, time travel into the future-only is assumed, then additional assumptions are also required to derive Dirac's equation.

One of the most disturbing aspects of backward causation is that it seems to allow for the possibility of *causal loops* and for the potential breaking of such loops, a prime ingredient in many of the very best time-travel stories. For example, suppose there were a gadget such that if I push its control button now, then today's lecture notes will have appeared in the gadget's output tray yesterday. Indeed, yesterday I found today's notes there, and in fact I am about to go to class to deliver that lecture (and a mighty good one it is, so good I think I will send it back to yesterday in just a few minutes). But I haven't yet pushed the button. What if I now decide to let the entire day pass without pushing the button? Why did the notes appear? Modern philosophers call this attempt at the breaking of a causal loop a *bilking paradox*. (See Chapter Four for information on how such paradoxes have appeared in the physics literature since the 1940s.)

In science fiction, however, such paradoxes were being discussed long before World War II. In a Letter-to-the-Editor in *Astounding Stories* (June 1932) a fan clearly stated his objection to time travel by using a bilking paradox. He suggested the following experiment: Immediately publish an open offer to the inventor of time travel (who will appear, presumably, at some future time) to travel back to one week before the offer is published; but of course (argued the fan) we'd have a pretty problem if we then decide not to publish the offer after the inventor shows up! As that fan wrote: "Paradoxical? I'll say so, if time-travel is possible." And in "The Time Cheaters" [Binder, 1940], for another example, we have the story of time travelers who just before they begin a trip into the future see the Earth invaded by Martians. (There is an amusing reference in this tale to Orson Welles' famous 1938 radio-drama hoax.) At first the invaders are unbeatable, but then the defending military forces of Earth suddenly and mysteriously acquire a fantastically powerful new weapon. It is not long before the time travelers realize where it came from—they themselves will go into the far future and will return with it to what is now their own past. But then they wonder what might happen if they don't go, if instead they "cheat time." After all, they reason, why bother now to hunt for the weapon—the invasion has already been defeated. We are told that this is a "sinister conception, crawling evilly within their brains, like an unanswerable enigma."

Some philosophers and practically all physicists agree with this last assessment and believe that there is simply nothing more to say; that puzzles like these show that causal loops (and backward causation) are thus impossible. They feel this way about time loops and backward causation because, as has been discussed, time travel to the past creates paradoxes. But such paradoxes are often offensive only to human, culturally biased intuitions about how things "ought to" work, since the classical physical laws are not offended by a reversal in the direction of time, which of course underlies what time travel is all about. As the chemist G. N. Lewis [Lewis, 1930] expressed it, "Our common idea of time is notably unidirectional, *but this is largely due to the phenomena of consciousness and memory* [my emphasis]."[2] Lewis' work caught the eye of the editor at *Astounding Stories*, who summed it up for his readers in a half-page essay ("Two-Way Time," Sept. 1931) that contained dramatic words hinting at backward causation: "A new theory of time ... reveals the possibility that events now occurring are among the factors that decided Caesar nearly 2,000 years ago to cross the Rubicon."

Lewis' willingness to accept causality violations is not a popular view today. For example, in [Visser, 1990] we read: "It is fair to say that most conservative physicists have very serious reservations about the admissibility and reality of causality-violating processes. Causality violation (i.e., the existence of a 'time machine') is such an extreme violation of our understanding of the cosmos that it behooves us to be as conservative as possible about introducing such unpleasant effects into our models." Visser then declares closed timelike loops to be verboten because "the existence of closed timelike loops leads to such unpleasant situations as meeting oneself five minutes ago." Visser sums up his philosophical position nicely with "any theory that is 'just a little bit causality violating' is 'just a little bit inconsistent'."

Agreeing with Visser is at least one philosopher [Dummett, 1964], who believes that the "association of causality with a particular temporal direction is not merely a matter of the way we speak of causes, but has a genuine basis in the way things happen," and that there is indeed an asymmetry with respect to past and future that is bound up with our concept of intentional action. But Dummett goes even further, stating that being an agent of cause is not a necessary condition for seeing the asymmetry; being an observer is enough; even an immobile yet intelligent tree(!) could detect the difference between past and future. Alas, there seems no immediate hope for putting this fascinating idea to an experimental test.

Others, however, are not so sure about these matters as are Visser and Dummett; e.g., see [Yurtsever, 1990] and also [Weir, 1988], which presents an explanation for causal loops in terms of an oscillating Universe (see [Schmidt, 1966]) and circular time. For our purposes here, it will be my approach to adopt the position of Australian philosopher Huw Price. Despite the present lack of experimental evidence for acausal phenomena, Price has convincingly argued [Price, 1984] that it is the job of philosophers to ensure that physicists do not ignore major and promising avenues in a mistaken belief that ideas concerning backward causation are nothing but philosophical traps for the foolish.

What Does "Now" Mean?

In [Gale, 1963] there is an overview analysis of various reality-of-time arguments other than McTaggart's (whose rejection of the reality of time was discussed in Chapter Two). Gale even presents an amusing gastronomical interpretation of time. As one of Gale's examples of the kinds of arguments that can be found in the philosophical literature, we read that "New slices of salami are continually being cut from a nonexistent chunk of salami called the future. *The* present is the slice on top of the pile. The past are the pieces beneath this, and even though they are not present they still continue to exist in the same way that the top slice of salami does. This is a version of the River-of-Time metaphor, since it treats becoming as a type of motion; and it faces humiliation before the embarrassing question of how fast the pile of salami slices grows." It also runs into trouble with the psychological aspect of time that makes the now seem not like a zero-duration instant, but rather as having, itself, some extent. For example, if we watch the second hand of a ticking clock, we see it move; and if we hear someone knock at the door, we hold each entire knock from start to finish in our *now*. These are phenomena that have led to the concept of the so-called *specious present* with non-zero-duration; i.e., the top slice of the salami pile is not infinitely thin at all, but rather has a thickness. (This concept was first clearly recognized by the American psychologist William James.) So, just how thick *is* the slice of time called the *now*?

Advocates of the doctrine of process theism, the concept that God is a temporal entity that participates in becoming, have actually tried to calculate the duration of the now for God. This might seem like a resurrection of the angels-on-the-head-of-a-pin debates of a thousand years ago, but the analysis does have a certain charm to it. The idea is that God, through his divine immediacy, his cosmic omniscience, is aware of what is happening with every mentality in the Universe. As [Baker, 1972] states, "God must be able to prehend the satisfaction of every actual entity of the temporal process. God's omniscience requires this." The theologian John Cobb has used this requirement for omniscience as the basis for calculating what is essentially the speed of thought in God's mind! As Cobb writes [Cobb, 1965]: "We may ask how many occasions of experience would occur for God in a second. The answer is that it must be a very large number, incredibly large to our limited imaginations. The number of successive electronic occasions in a second staggers the imagination. God's self-actualizations must be at least equally numerous if he is to function separately in relation to each individual in this series. Since electronic occasions are presumably not in phase with each other or with other types of actual occasions, still further complications are involved."

To demonstrate how to calculate what [Baker, 1972] calls the "temporal extension of the divine experience," God's now if you will, Baker provides several examples. I repeat one here that is particularly interesting. Suppose first, says Baker, that since every entity must be "creatively related to God," then we may conclude that "God's life must be synchronized with the lives of every actual entity." This assumption of divine synchronization avoids what Cobb described as further complications due to a lack of phasing. Next, suppose that the durations of the nows of whatever life-forms we find in the Universe may be different, but not very different, from our own of approximately one-tenth of a second (see Note 1 of Tech Note 1). For sake of calculation let us suppose that there are just twelve minds in the Universe, with twelve distinct but only slightly different rational durations:

$$1/9 \qquad 1/10 \qquad 1/11$$

$$2/19 \qquad 2/21 \qquad 2/23$$

$$3/28 \qquad 3/31 \qquad 3/34$$

$$4/37 \qquad 4/41 \qquad 4/45.$$

If we were to write these fractions with a common denominator, then we would find the least common denominator, easily calculated to be nearly five trillion; more precisely, each second God must experience 4,842,179,260,380 nows. Imagine now the trillions upon trillions of minds there may actually be in the Universe, utilizing a continuum of now-durations—the number of God experiences per second must be beyond finite expression.

Analyses like these make many think that the salami analogy, at least when applied to God, is actually baloney. And as for the concept of a duration to the present, the English mathematician A. A. Robb expressed a dissenting view of the specious present with non-zero-duration when he wrote the somewhat enigmatic "the present properly speaking does not extend beyond itself."

For physicists there is nothing in time that marks the present moment as unique, and therefore nothing that reflects a flow of time, nothing that models the events of now becoming part of the past and future events becoming now. For everyone (including physicists), however, there is the powerful psychological sense that time *does* flow. Despite this, the relativistic, four-dimensional block-Universe view of spacetime that many physicists so dearly love clearly seems to have no room for an objective theory of time flow. (Recall Weyl's views and Black's sharp response to them from the previous chapter.) All events simply have coordinates in spacetime, and there is nothing corresponding to 'have been' (past), 'are' (present), or 'will be' (future). There is no moving now except for its subjective presence in our conscious minds. All we can say from physics is that events are ordered in an earlier/later sequence, and even this relatively weak condition is true only for causally related events. As shown in Tech Note 4, non-causally-related events can have different temporal orderings for observers in different reference frames. For such observers, then, earlier/later has no more meaning than does past/future, and indeed both pairs of words become empty of physical meaning.

Science fiction has, not surprisingly, incorporated the relativity-of-language idea. In the 1958 story "Two Dooms" [Kornbluth, HV], for example, we learn why one character thinks there is some truth to the speculation that Hopi indian children of the American Southwest understand Einstein's relativity theory as soon as they can talk: "The Hopi language—and thought—had no tenses and therefore no concept of time-as-an-entity; it had nothing like the Indo-European speech's subjects and predicates, therefore no built-in metaphysics of cause and effect. In the Hopi language and mind all things were frozen together into one great relationship, a crystalline structure of space-time events that simply were because they were." Kornbluth was clearly influenced in writing this passage by the work of the amateur American ethnolinguist Benjamin Lee Whorf [Whorf, 1956]. A fascinating essay on the differences in time conceptions of between Indo-European languages and that of the Hopi Indians, based on the writings of Whorf, is [Cox, 1950]. In particular, Cox imagines how physics (and general relativity) might have developed in a society using a tenseless language. For example, Cox speculates that the lack of the concept of relative simultaneity might have resulted in the Lorentz spacetime transformation equations (see Tech Notes 1 and 3) as an automatic assumption of Hopian mathematics! A year after Kornbluth's story, however, at least one philosopher began to have his doubts about Whorf's claims [Black, 1959a] and more recent scholarship has conclusively shown that Whorf's assertion that the Hopi language is timeless is simply incorrect [Malotki, 1983]. So Cox's essay loses its power to convince us of its dramatic thesis.

Modern physics takes the view that time is simply a *parameter*, a *label*, just as the tick marks along the axes of a graph denote different values of a spatial parameter. When we draw an *x-y* graph, we do not think of either *x* or *y* as moving, and similarly a physicist would argue that when we draw a spacetime diagram we should not think of time as moving. As I mentioned before, physicists call our feeling of moving time *psychological time* because the equations of physics provide no physical interpretation for it. This is not to say that psychological time does not have great fascination and significance in human affairs, but just that the physicist's view is that physical time is the fundamental concept. Physical time can be imagined to have meaning in a Universe devoid of consciousness, but for psychological time this is clearly not possible (at least not in a Universe inhabited by beings that use physical processes to operate anything like a brain).

The philosopher Max Black has stated in no uncertain terms (see Note 30 for Chapter Two) how he feels about the profound difference between physical and psychological time: "So wide is the gap between the common-sense notion of time and the physicist's *t* that clarity would be fostered if physicists were to imitate the psychologist's practice of talking about *g* rather than about intelligence by referring to their own concept as *t* rather than as 'time'. It is not shocking to be told that *t* may have a unique origin like the absolute zero of the temperature scale, or may have several dimensions, or even that it may 'run backward'; it is only when such aphorisms are transformed into corresponding statements about time that paradox emerges and philosophical hackles rise.''

The one view of the block Universe that Black accepts, that there is no time flow except in the minds of conscious beings (including, I suppose, Dummett's tree), has received strong advocacy from the modern philosopher Adolf Grünbaum. Indeed, I'd hazard that most physicists and the majority of philosophers agree with Grünbaum, who declared [Grünbaum, 1963] ''I believe the issue of determinism vs. indeterminism is *totally irrelevant* to whether becoming is a significant attribute of the time of physical nature independently of human consciousness.''

But not everybody agrees with Black and Grünbaum. Indeed, Grünbaum himself quotes Hans Reichenbach, who took the opposite stance (saying that time *does* flow) with equal vigor. Writing in 1925, Reichenbach asked: ''What does 'now' mean? Plato lived before me, and Napoleon VII will live after me. But which one of these three lives *now*? I understandably have a clear feeling that *I* live now. But does this assertion have an objective significance beyond my subjective experience?'' Reichenbach goes on to answer this question in the affirmative and deduces that the block Universe is an incomplete representation of reality: ''In the condition of the world, a cross-section called the present is distinguished; the 'now' has objective significance. *Even when no human being is alive any longer, there is a 'now'* [my emphasis] ... In the four-dimensional picture of the world, such as used by the theory of relativity, there is no such distinguished cross-section. But this is due only to the fact that an essential content is omitted from this picture.'' And what is the missing essential content? Feeling that the block Universe is unacceptably deterministic (in his words of ridicule, ''The morrow has already occurred today in the same sense as yesterday''), he found his answer in the antithesis of determinism, the probabilistic theory of quantum mechanics.

Laplacian physics had argued that given total information about the state of the world *now*, one could calculate perfectly the future or the past (that is, one can predict and retrodict). In contrast, quantum mechanics distinguishes past from future in a fundamental way. Quantum mechanics does not deny that in principle we can know the past with exquisite precision since each and every event leaves traces; evidence for an event is available to all with the means to find and decode it. This is called the *archivalist* view of the past. But quantum mechanics also takes as a postulate that there is an irreducible uncertainty to the future. The instant that this uncertainty is crystallized into fact was taken by Reichenbach to be the very definition of what we mean by now. The ever-increasing record of the past, in turn, defines the movement of the now. Reichenbach believed that with these ideas he had at last found the moving now in mathematical theory, that he had elevated it from psychology to physics, and that it was independent of the presence of a conscious mind.

Grünbaum's associate, Lynne Rudder Baker, however, has since written [Baker, 1975] a powerful philosophical analysis of the time-flow issue that comes down solidly in support of the contrary position, that the moving now is only in our minds and is not an intrinsic attribute of reality. Her most interesting point is that a mind-independent flow of time is incompatible with the relativity of simultaneity because it implies a Universal now, which Einstein showed is an illusory concept. This objection also applies to the thesis of *probabilism*, which says that at any instant there are many alternative futures, but just one past. This instant is simply a synonym for the moving now, and so Maxwell, a supporter of probabilism, concludes [Maxwell, 1985] that special relativity must be deficient because of its denial of cosmic simultaniety! This is, of course, not the majority view among physicists (see [Dieks, 1988], [Maxwell, 1988], and [Stein, 1991]).

Science fiction stories are full of theories about the nature of now, the vast majority of which have no basis in scientific thought. Some of them are ingenious, however, and while they are mostly the pet ideas of their authors (and no one else's), perhaps they resulted in some of the young readers of the science-fiction magazines of the 1930s and 1940s thinking about more philosophical matters than "Buck Rogers," the "Lone Ranger," or "Terry and the Pirates." For example, according to "Today's Yesterday" [Ray, 1934] time is a wave, and the moving now we experience is carried on a crest of that wave, just as a piece of wood is carried along on the crest of a water wave. There are time waves both ahead and behind the crest we happen to be on, of course, and each such crest carries a different now for a different reality (so the story says)—hence the curious title.

More recently, in the story "The Trouble with the Past" [Eisenstein, 1971], about object duplication by time travel, nine(!) copies of the same person from the year 2314, James Thomas, meet in 1870 and try to figure out what is going on. Part of their debate is the following analysis of the 'present':

> "Gentlemen, I think I understand," said the first James Thomas.
>
> Eight faces turned toward him, and he felt as though he were looking into multiple mirrors.
>
> "We hold that time is a single instant—the Instant of the Present—which travels through Duration—do we not?"
>
> Eight heads nodded.
>
> "We assume that time passes in a manner analogous to the stringing of an infinite number of beads. Each bead is the instant of Now when it is last on the chain. Beads are continually being added, and each one is only the Now until another is placed after it."
>
> "Yes, that is my theory," said another James Thomas. "It can also be likened to the process of knitting. No matter how many stitches are knitted, there is only one last stitch, only one Now."

Einstein, too, was greatly bothered by the place of the 'now' in time, perhaps even more than was James Thomas and his friends. In an autobiographical essay, the philosopher Rudolf Carnap recalled one of his conversations with Einstein in the early 1950s at the Institute for Advanced Study in Princeton:[3] "Once Einstein said that the problem of the Now worried him seriously. He explained that the experience of the Now means something special for man, something essentially different from the past and the future, but that this important difference does not and cannot occur within physics. That this experience cannot be grasped by science seemed to him a matter of painful but inevitable resignation ... Einstein thought ... that there is something essential about the Now which is just outside of the realm of science." But see [Nor, 1992], that claims to have found a geometrical explanation for the flow of time, and which the author believes gives objective, mathematical reality to the moving present.

Irreversibility

Well, no matter if time doesn't actually flow or not, most of us still believe we have had a past and hope we will have a future. Each of us thinks we can easily tell one from the other, too. We have, in fact, many not so subtle indications of this obvious direction to time from our everyday lives. Nearly all of these indications have the common theme of *irreversible change*. As Sylvester, a great British mathematician, put it [Sylvester, 1869], "The whirligig of time brings about its revenges." Ovid, who died when Christ was a teenager, said the same in his *Metamorphoses* with his famous "Time, the devourer of all things." Yet, as grim as this sentiment is, people seem to want to keep expressing it in some way; in his infinitely sad time play *Time and the Conways* [Priestley, 1937], for example, J. B. Priestley wrote, "There's a great devil in the Universe, and we call it Time." It certainly appears to be true. No one yet, for example, has escaped the biological decay processes of time, whether it be the evolution of a loved pet from kitten to large window cat to death or the appearance of aches and pains in our own bodies that once seemed immune to them.

The image of time as devourer of all that is mortal was brilliantly presented by James Barrie in his *Peter Pan*, with the crocodile who had swallowed a ticking clock chasing Captain Hook all about Neverland. Inanimate objects are not immune to this aspect of time, either. Logs and cigarettes burn in the stove and ashtray, but never unburn. Our cars rust, but never derust. An explosion has never been seen to reverse itself, to form a dynamite stick or bomb casing out of a collapsing fireball.

Our world seems, indeed, literally to be built on an irreversible movement toward chaos, death, and decay. Rubens in the seventeenth century and Goya in the nineteenth painted well-known works showing this movement through the use of horrific symbolism. These paintings, both of which are known today as "Saturn Eating One of His Children," depict Saturn, who is the Roman planet god often associated with the Greek Chronos, or Father Time. The opening words to the best-known poem of the seventeenth-century Englishman Robert Herrick ("To the Virgins, to make much of Time") makes the same point, only slightly more subtly:

> Gather ye rosebuds while ye may,
> Old Time is still a-flying;
> And this same flower that smiles to-day,
> To-morrow will be dying.

This observation of time as destroyer, runs all through the works of Shakespeare, the consummate interpreter of human experience. One hardly knows where to begin to select a quote on time in his works. A particularly good example, perhaps, is from the poem *The Rape of Lucrece*, in which time is called the "eater of youth," and time's function is declared to be:

> To fill with worm-holes stately monuments,
> To feed oblivion with decay of things,
> To blot old books and alter their contents,
> . . . .
> And waste huge stones with little water-drops.

And time shows no favorites. In *Cymbeline* we are reminded that

> Golden lads and girls all must,
> As chimney-sweepers, come to dust.

Two centuries or so later, Lewis Carroll repeated the message. In *Through the Looking-Glass* Alice tells Humpty Dumpty "one can't help growing older." And speaking of Humpty Dumpty, his famous fall provides a dramatic example of a one-way evolution from past to future; he wasn't convinced that Alice was correct, but once he splattered,

> All the King's horses and all the King's men
> Couldn't put Humpty Dumpty together again.

While on the matter of Mr. Dumpty, it is also worthwhile to note that nobody has ever figured out how to unscramble an egg. Why is this? One philosopher has speculated that it is because of such "irreversible organic phenomena" (presumably taking place in our brains) that our flow of consciousness is always in the same direction [Margenau, 1954].

More subtle than the undignified undoing of a prideful egg is the phenomenon of memory, which seems trivial only because most people have not thought very carefully about it. We remember the past while we remember nothing about the future, which is not the case for a time traveler to the past, of course. We might be tempted to use the phenomenon of memory to give an answer to the question of how to tell past from future—anything you can remember is the past. The circularity of this argument was discussed in [Smart, 1954]; Smart pointed out that to ask why memory is always of the past "is as foolish as to ask why uncles are always male, never female." In *Through the Looking-Glass* the White Queen tells Alice that "it's a poor sort of memory that only works backward," but except for the claims of clairvoyants, it seems that is the only sort of memory any of us has. Why is this so?

For physicists, the question of the direction of time is one of profound mystery. There seems, in fact, to be no fundamental physical reason for why time should *not* be able to go from future to past (and then what would future and past *mean*?) even though no one has ever observed it to do so. All of the laws of classical mechanics (such as energy and momentum conservation), electrodynamics, gravity, and even quantum mechanics (except for kaons, of course) involve time in such a way that they ignore its sign, i.e., replacing t with $-t$ results in a perfectly good description of something that could actually happen. But not all such possibilities are observed to happen. Why not?

In an unpublished paper written in 1949, while doing the work that would bring him a share of the 1965 Nobel prize in physics, the young genius Richard Feynman wrote [Schweber, 1986]: "The relation of time in physics to that of gross experience has suffered many changes in the history of physics. The obvious difference of past and future does not appear in physical time for microscopic events ... Einstein discovered that the present is not the same for all people [see Tech Note 1 on the relativity of simultaneity] ... It may prove useful in physics to consider events in all of time at once and to imagine that we at each instant are only aware of those that lie behind us. The complete relation of this concept of physical time to the time of experience and causality is a physical problem which has not been worked out in detail. It may be that more problems and difficulties are produced than are solved by such a point of view."

Feynman did not elaborate on what he meant by the problems and difficulties with this point of view (i.e., the block Universe), but surely he had the logical paradoxes of time travel high on his list. Certainly time travel was on the minds of others. As Yale philosopher Henry Margenau wrote [Margenau, 1954] in a tutorial paper on Feynman's work, "The theory of quantum electrodynamics developed by Feynman incorporates reversals in the course of time and thereby cherishes, in the minds of many, an *age-old phantasy* [my emphasis] of more than scientific appeal."

Since the individual microscopic classical equations of physics are time-reversible, the distinction between past and future for individual particles disappears. The equations are said to be symmetrical with respect to time; the algebraic sign of t is irrelevant in the classical laws. There is, it must be understood, a crucial distinction to be made here. When a physicist says *time-reversal* he is talking about a system evolving *backward* in *forward* time; i.e., all the individual particle velocity vectors are reversed. This is distinct from the time-reversed worlds of philosophers (see the next section) in which time itself runs backward. The physicist's point of view is expressed clearly in [Lewis, 1930]: "Every equation and every explanation used in physics must be compatible with the symmetry of time. Thus we can no longer regard effect as subsequent to cause. If we think of the present as pushed into existence by the past, we must in precisely the same sense think of it as pulled into existence by the future." More than three decades later, two mathematicians presented similar ideas [Penrose and Percival, 1962]: "In classical dynamics, the past completely determines the present, and therefore, by symmetry, the future also completely determines the present."

There is an interesting theological connection to time reversal, too. As expressed in [Mehlberg, BIPT]: "If all natural laws are time reversal invariant and no irreversible processes occur in the physical Universe then there is no inherent, intrinsically meaningful difference between past and future ... If this is actually the case, then all mankind's major religions which preach a creation of the Universe (by a supernatural agency) and imply, accordingly, a differentiation between the past and the future ... would have to make appropriate readjustments."

There are dissenters to the idea that the classical laws of physics are time reversible. The great English physicist Paul Dirac, for example, wrote [Dirac, 1949] that "I do not believe there is any need for physical laws to be invariant under time and space reflections, although all the exact laws of nature so far known do have this invariance." Indeed, with the subsequent discovery of kaons, Dirac's position is seen to have been ahead of its time! Dirac did not, unfortunately, elaborate on just why he felt this way. And, in fact, the actual macroscopic world appears to be decidedly asymmetrical. The puzzle of why this is so has generated a vast scientific literature, including entire books on the physics of time-reversibility in physical systems (e.g., [Sachs, 1987], [Davies, 1977], and [Zeh, 1989]). Some philosophers, such as Grunbaum and Reichenbach, find an explanation for the asymmetry in the statistical irreversibility of complex processes. Others, like Earman, disagree since such asymmetry can also be found in at least one nonstatistical case, as commented on in [Finkelstein, 1958] and [Davies, ET] in their analyses of the one-way nature of the event horizon of a black hole.

Worlds in Reverse

Philosophers and writers of speculative fiction were the first to wonder what things might be like in a world where the asymmetry is reversed—where time runs backward. Indeed, there is a hint of this in the Old Testament! When afflicted by a fatal illness, King Hezekiah of Judah pleaded for his life, a request that God granted. When given his choice of having God move the shadow on a sundial either ten degrees forward or ten degrees backward as the sign of this gift, Hezekiah naturally enough elected to see time run backward. (This story is told both in Second Kings 20 and Isaiah 38).

The reversed-time world is an important philosophical concept. Before the turn of the century, Francis Bradley, the originator of the early version of the block Universe, thought about reversed-time worlds in which time itself runs backward and concluded that such places would be quite odd:[4] "Let us suppose ... that there are beings whose lives run opposite to our own ... *if* in any way *I* could experience *their* world, I should fail to understand it. Death would come before birth, the blow would follow the wound, and all must seem to be irrational." More sympathetic with the possibility of reversed-time worlds was W. R. Inge. In his November 1920 Presidential Address to the Aristotelian Society, in the scholarly Conference Hall of the University of London Club, he felt safe enough to make time-reversed existence his topic [Inge, 1921]. Still, even though he was more flexible on the possibility of a time-reversed world than was Bradley, Inge did feel it necessary to conclude with "I have not discovered Mr. Wells' Time Machine."

Thirty years later, the philosopher J. N. Findlay took Bradley's position supporting a skeptical attitude toward time-reversed worlds. Writing in a book review,[5] Findlay declared: "The reversed world in question wouldn't merely strike us as queer, but definitely crazy: it would be a world where what is wildly and intrinsically *improbable* was always occurring. It would, in fact, be much more startling than the original asymmetry that led us to think of it." The question of backward-running time so fascinated Findlay, in fact, that some years later he posed it as a problem for the readership of the journal *Analysis*. In [Findlay and McGechie, 1956], he presents both his own negative view of reversed worlds and that of the best response received, which was from McGechie. Findlay showed admirable open-mindedness by awarding the title of best to an argument that refutes his own position. Findlay, however, remained unconvinced about the concept of reversed-time worlds, stating that "I continue to feel that a total reversal of my experiences is a terrifying possibility."[6] Anybody who has watched a movie film or videotape played backward would certainly agree with Findlay. See "This Side Up" [Banks, 1961], for example, for a fictional treatment of the temporal confusion that can be caused by projecting a film in the wrong direction of time.

The fact is, however, that the prevailing position today is that to the inhabitants of such a counterclock world, the view of things would be the kind of view we have in our world of normal time. This is a fairly new approach however, and even the relatively recent philosophical literature occasionally shows a misunderstanding of how a reversed world would appear to its inhabitants (e.g., [Dummett, 1964]). The modern idea of a normal-appearing reversed-time world appears to have been first explicitly stated in [Smart, 1954], but I do not find Professor Smart's arguments persuasive. (In fact, [Whitrow, 1980] calls them "fallacious or, at best, trivial.") More compelling analyses than Smart's appear in [Narlikar, 1965] and in [Stannard, 1966]. Narlikar and Stannard introduce the concept of a Universe made of matter in which every particle interaction occurs with a reversed time sense. For example, a neutron does not decay into a proton, electron, and an antineutrino (see Note 11 of Chapter Two), but rather neutrons are created by the collision of these three particles. As Stannard points out, the spacetime diagrams (see Tech Note 4) of such interactions are merely those of our world with the time axis reversed; he calls such matter interactions *faustian* (from Goethe's play *Faust*, in which the normal flow of time is routinely violated) and hypothesizes that interactions between normal (our) and faustian matter cannot occur. Indeed, mat-

earlier		Jim (normal time)		later
t_0	t_1	t_2	t_3	t_4
T_4	T_3	T_2	T_1	T_0
LATER		Midge (reversed time)		EARLIER

FIGURE 9. Opposite time directions in reversed worlds.

ter with a reversed-time sense is thought by many to be antimatter for our world,[7] and such interactions would be spectacular! (This particular objection to time travel is raised several times in the novel *Vornan-19* [Silverberg, 1970].) Stannard's hypothesis is a sort of censorship principle, and if true, it eliminates Bradley's concern about our world experiencing a reversed world.

Even if beings from two such opposite worlds could meet, the philosopher J. R. Lucas has argued that they still could not communicate.[8] As he states: "If two beings are to regard each other as communicators, they must both have the same direction of time. It is a logical as well as a causal prerequisite." This matter is well worth our efforts to understand, as it is intimately tied to time travel. At first blush Lucas' words seem almost self-evident and, after a little thought, absolutely irrefutable. The philosopher Murray MacBeath, however, takes exception [MacBeath, 1983].

In his paper MacBeath opens with a story to demonstrate that the persuasive power of Lucas' position is only superficial. In this story of Jim and Midge, Jim is one of us, while Midge is a faustian time-antagonist (what [Rothman, 1987] calls a "retro-friend"). In his analyses, MacBeath uses capitalized words and symbols for the time-reversed Midge. As Professor MacBeath explains, "While Jim and Midge are together a face-to-face conversation is hardly likely to get off the ground. To make this clear let us say that they are together from t_0 until t_{10} on Jim's time-scale, and from T_0 until T_{10} on Midge's TIME-scale; t_0 is then the same temporal instant as T_{10} and, in general, $t_n = T_{10-n}$. If Jim at ... t_2 asks Midge a question, and Midge hears the question at T_8, she will answer at T_9, and Jim will hear his question answered at t_1, before he asked it. What is more, if Jim is inexpert at interpreting backward sounds, and at t_4 asks Midge to repeat her answer, Midge will hear this request at T_6, BEFORE she has heard the original question; and her puzzled reply at T_7 will again be heard by Jim at t_3, before he has uttered the request."

Certainly this is a mess in time, and Lucas seems to be on safe ground with his denial of the possibility of communication. MacBeath, however, shows how to refute all of Lucas' arguments if Midge and Jim are allowed to be clever about how they send messages back and forth; that is, if we give up our usual ideas of what a conversation is like. Professor MacBeath's analyses are far too lengthy and detailed to present here, but we can appreciate his approach with the following simplified example, a version of one he offers himself. To follow the logic, it will be helpful to look at Figure 9 for the time directions for Jim and Midge:

We imagine that Jim and Midge will not actually talk and thus have to decipher backward-spoken language. Rather, they will exchange messages via handwritten notes or computer-generated text displayed on monitor screens. We can, in fact, imagine that Jim and Midge are separated by a window that is proof against all penetration but light.[9] Now, at t_0 Jim brings a computer to the window. He programs it to wait for four days, until t_4, and then to display the following message on its screen: "This message is from Jim, who experiences time in the sense opposite to yours. Please study the following questions and display your answers on a computer screen three days from now."

Jim's message ends with the list of questions. Since this will all appear at t_4, Midge sees it at what we will now call T_0. As requested, she brings her computer to the window, enters the answers to Jim's questions, and programs the machine to display them (after a three-day delay) on its screen. Thus, at T_3, which is Jim's t_1, Jim sees Midge's computer screen light up with: "Hi, Jim. This is Midge. The answers to your questions are at the end of this message. Now, I've got some questions for *you*. Please display the answers two days from now." Midge's message ends with Jim's answers and her list of questions. Jim sees Midge's message at t_1, enters the answers to her questions and sets his machine to answer after a two-day delay. At t_3, which is Midge's T_1—and by now you see how the process goes. It's cumbersome, but it does work. Professor MacBeath provides other, increasingly more complicated analyses in his paper that treat some of the more subtle problems that can be imagined. I will mention just two that have direct analogs with what we normally think of as time travel.[10]

For the first problem, consider Jim's initial message, created at t_0 to be sent at t_4. He receives Midge's answer at t_1, *before* the message is displayed through the window. So, what happens if at t_2 Jim cancels the message and it is not displayed. He has already gotten the reply, but how can that be if he does not send the message? This is, of course, once again a bilking paradox, and my discussion of it will be deferred until Chapter Four when we look at paradoxes in general.

A second curious problem is the possibility of creating a causal message loop. For example, let's say that at t_0 Jim suddenly decides to send a message through the window. (His reason for this sudden urge will be explained soon.) He thinks all night about what to send and at t_1 finally settles on the following: "Greetings to the people on the other side of the window. This message comes from Jim, who hopes you will reply." Midge sees this through the window at T_3 and is suddenly caught up with the desire to respond. She thinks all night about what to send and, hoping to be thought witty, at T_4 she finally decides on the following: "Greetings to the people on the other side of the window. This message comes from Midge, who hopes you will reply."

Jim sees this through the window at t_0—and now we know why he decided to send his message. And he *will* send his message—*because* Midge replied to it! Causal loops are very strange things, with events happening in the present because of events in the future (which, in turn, are caused by those present events when they are 'later' in the past). Unlike the grandfather paradox, which most philosophers believe is now solved, causal loops have yet to be given a satisfactory explanation. MacBeath does not like causal loops at all, admitting that while he believes them to be conceptually possible, he finds causal loops to have "so queer a smell" that he prefers to avoid thinking about them. Later, in Chapter Four, we will think about them and, not surprisingly, we will find that some of the most puzzling (and entertaining) time-travel stories are based on causal loops.[11] In another of MacBeath's papers [MacBeath, 1982], these are called "loopy stories!"

It should now be clear that the faustian world of backward time would indeed seem quite strange since its inhabitants would remember what we call the future. But, of course, our world would seem just as strange to them because what we remember, our past, is their future! As Stannard points out, "This rather odd situation, it will be recalled, has a close parallel in the special theory of relativity where two observers in relative motion are equally convinced that it is the other's clock that is going slowly [see Tech Note 3]." When Merlyn the magician makes his first appearance in T. H. White's 1939 fantasy masterpiece *The Once and Future King*, he explains how he knows the future of others: "Ordinary people are born forward in Time, if you understand what I mean, and nearly everything in the world goes forward too. ... But I unfortunately was born at the wrong end of time, and I have to live backwards from its front, while surrounded by a lot of people living forwards from behind. Some people call it having second sight." More recently, alien beings that remember the future are described in "The Propitiation of Brullamagoo" [Laumer, 1991].

This is precisely what happens in "This Way to the Regress" [Knight, 1956], where everybody knows what will happen (as they live backward) by reading "prediction books." What distinguishes this story from many others on the same theme is the conversation a student has with a philosophy professor about how things would be if time went the other way:

> "How can we tell? The reverse sequence of causation may be just as valid as the one we are experiencing. Cause and effect are arbitrary, after all."
>
> "But it sounds pretty far-fetched."
>
> "It's hard for us to imagine, just because we're not used to it. It's only a matter of viewpoint. Water would run downhill and so on. Energy would flow the other way—from total concentration to total dispersion. Why not?"

The student is unconvinced, however, and when he tries to visualize such a peculiar world (our world!) it gives him a "half-pleasant shudder." Imagine, he wonders in horror, never knowing the date of your own death.

More recently, in a review of [Reichenbach, 1956],[12] Hilary Putnam restates the problems of time-reversed worlds in the form of a provocative question: "How do you know that one man's future isn't another man's past?" He begins by pointing out the interesting observation that for us even to be able to observe such a backward-running Universe, we would have to provide our own normal radiation source because the counterclock stars in it suck radiation in rather than

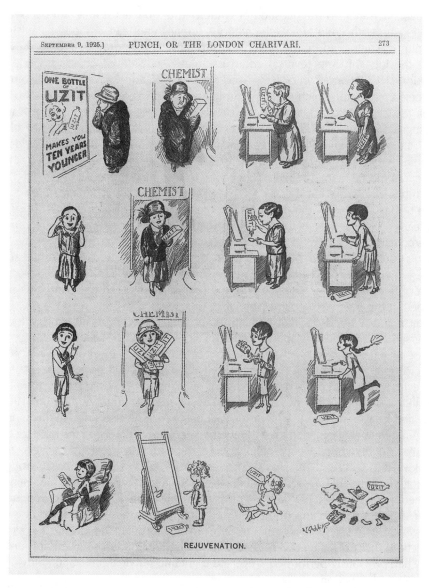

FIGURE 10. One way to reverse time! Reproduced by permission of *Punch*.

supplying it.[13] He concludes with a cautious warning: "It is difficult to talk about such extremely weird situations without deviating from ordinary idiomatic usage of English. But this difficulty should not be mistaken for a proof that these situations could not arise."

This challenge is no doubt why so many writers outside of science fiction and fantasy have tackled the question of what it would be like if time ran backward. For example, the mid-twentieth-century German-American composer Paul Hindemith was intrigued by the possibility of a musical palindrome, and he showed that the idea of time reversal could be treated outside of prose—his one-act musical skit *Hin und Zuruck* (*Here and Back*) has an angel appear at midpoint to reverse time, upon which the very music itself reverses. The fascination with this idea actually dates back through thousands of years, as it can be found in Plato's dialogue *Statesman*, written (most probably) fifteen years before Plato's death in 347 B.C. At one point Plato offers an extended description of the world suddenly running backward in time in the ancient past. After one character is told that at that time "all mortal beings halted on their way to assuming the looks of old age, and each began to grow backward ... ," he asks, "But how did living creatures come into being ... Sir? How did they produce their offspring?" The answer is shocking: "Clearly ... it was not of the order of nature in that era to begat children by intercourse ... It is only to be expected that along with the reversal of the old men's course of life and their return to childhood, a new race of men should arise, too—a new race formed from men dead and long laid in Earth ... Such resurrection of the dead was in keeping with the cosmic change, all creation being now turned in the reverse direction."

In fiction we find the first (though rather weak) attempt at an explanation of reversed time in the Outlandish Watch of Lewis Carroll's *Sylvie and Bruno*; because of a "reversal-peg" that does the job, some things in Carroll's story go in reverse (e.g., people walk backward), but other things still go forward (such as speech). Mark Twain, in a dramatic use of reversed time in Chapter 32 of his last, posthumously published novel *No. 44, The Mysterious Stranger* [Gibson, 1969], decided he would have to go outside rationality for reversed time. In this work a supernatural being called "No. 44" reverses the world's time, and the narrator tells us that "everywhere weary people were re-chattering previous conversations backward ... where there was war, yesterday's battles were being refought, wrong-end first; the previously killed were getting killed again ... we saw Henry I gathering together his split skull ... " This dramatic recital is logically flawed, however, as other descriptions of the reversed time have people "scared and praying- ... gazing in mute anguish" at the Sun moving through the sky in the wrong direction. In a truly time-reversed world, no one would perform such acts unless they had previously performed "reversed fright and praying" at the Sun moving in the forward direction.

Such mainstream writers of the first half of the twentieth century as F. Scott Fitzgerald and the Cuban writer Alejo Carpentier also applied their considerable imaginations to the idea of backward time. Fitzgerald's famous 1922 story "The Curious Case of Benjamin Button" [Fitzgerald, 1944] is a bit strange in its own unique way, with the backward-living adult-sized Benjamin Button appearing not from the grave, but from his mother's womb! How he fit seems such an obvious logical flaw. Carpentier's beautiful story "Journey to the Seed" [Carpentier, 1967], which tells of a dying man suddenly reversing his time sense, is not so blatantly erroneous as is Fitzgerald's, but it suffers from yet another logical flaw also present in the Fitzgerald story—why are these individuals who are living backward in a forward-running world the only ones doing so (and why can they understand and be understood by those around them)?

Science fiction writer Nelson Bond tried his hand at this sort of fantasy version of reversed time; his story "The Fountain" [Bond, 1941b], about an old man who finds Ponce de Leon's Fountain of Youth, explores the problems of a man who is continually forgetting as he lives backward in forward time; i.e., he is younger in year $X+1$ than he was in year X. (Many readers will recognize that this story was anticipated by Nathaniel Hawthorne's 1837 short story "Dr. Heidegger's Experiment," but the continual loss of memory is Bond's original touch.) Even more curious is *The Man Who Lived Backward* [Ross, 1950], the story of a man who lives backward in a different way. Born in 1940, the man wakes up each morning, lives a normal forward day, goes to bed at night, and wakes up in yesterday! This continues until he dies in 1865, in a futile attempt to save Lincoln (whose fate he has known since he could read history books). There is no explanation for this character's astonishing condition, but the obvious problems of such a life are cleverly worked out.

To find science fiction writers speculating on reversed time is really no surprise, of course. The early reversed-time story "The Man Who Lived Backwards" [Hall, 1938] gives an outstanding treatment of the logical nuances of reversed time. (People in the story talk backward, and there is a marvelous bathroom scene of a man un-washing his hands.) The tale tells about a young physics teacher who is "twisted into a reversed Time Stream" by an electrical discharge. As he lives backward in time, he observes everybody about him seeming to run in reverse, but even more puzzling is that they have developed a "dreadful, granite-like hardness." We soon learn why: "For a while he could not understand the impenetrable hardness of external objects which he had experienced; it seemed they ought rather to be of intangible transiency, much as a dream, since he was re-viewing the Past. But a moment's thought gave him the logical answer. The Past is definite, shaped, unalterable, as nothing else in Creation is. Therefore, to argue that he could move or alter any object here was to argue that he could change the whole history of the world or cosmos. Everything he saw about him had happened, and could not be changed in any way. On the other hand, he was fluid, movable, alterable, since *his* future still lay before him, even if it had been reversed; he was the intruder, the anomaly. In any clash between himself and the Past, the Past would prove irresistible every time." This is, I believe, a unique presentation of the unchangeability of the past. Why Hall's young teacher could displace the Past's air, however, is left unanswered.

In addition to Hall's logical tale and Knight's short story "This Way to the Regress" [Knight, 1956] on "prediction books," another early brush at the idea of time-reversed worlds is in the novel *Time Bomb* [Tucker, 1955]. Here we find the intriguing idea of political assassination by time bomb, where the bombs actually time travel to their targets. A policeman begins to suspect what is happening when it becomes evident that one of the explosions was actually an implosion: "The time bomb ... had been going in and had carried the force of the blast with it. Inward. Into the past. He frowned at that. A backward explosion? An explosion which ran counter to the normal flow of time, to the normal method of living-? ... How would an explosion appear to a man if the blast happened in the opposite manner? If it began exploding now, in this moment, but continued backward instead of forward? Would it be an implosion?"

The distinction of being the first in science fiction to treat time reversal in depth, however, goes to Philip K. Dick's aptly named 1967 novel *Counter-Clock World* [Dick, 1979]. It is also perhaps the definitive reversed-time horror treatment.[14] Dick's world was once our world, but then as in Plato's tale, time suddenly began to run backward. People still alive reverse their direction of aging (but still think, walk, and talk in forward time), and dead, buried people come alive again (as the "Sacrament of Miraculous Rebirth" is intoned by a priest) and emerge from graveyards; all live their way back to the womb, just as in Plato's tale 1600 years earlier.[15]

Such imagery is powerful, emotional stuff, but the novel is terribly flawed on a logical level. Dick says nothing, for example, about what happens in the case of cremated people whose ashes have been scattered or about missionaries who were devoured by cannibals, and he is not consistent in his presentation. He delights in describing characters disgorging food as they eat, but avoids obvious (if indelicate) speculation on what happens at the other end. (Knight called these processes "increting" and "exgesting" in "This Way to the Regress" [Knight, 1956].) Dick's caution is understandable and, indeed, perhaps we should be grateful to Dick for his restraint! The philosopher Hilary Putnam [Putnam, 1962], for example, described a human living backward in time as "not a *person* at all, but a human *body* going through a rather nauseating succession of physical states." However, to the logical mind Dick's avoidance of the issue is a disturbing omission.[16] Again, Dick has men paste whisker stubble on their faces each morning and then slowly absorb it, but I looked in vain for the obvious bathroom scene of someone unbrushing his teeth, with toothpaste appearing on the brush and then slipping smoothly back up into the tube. Apparently, although it is never explicitly stated, only biological processes are time reversed.

Dick also loves playing amusing word games, such as making "You're a horse's mouth" and "You're full of food" epithets of abuse. "Food!" is the new ubiquitous curse. This is fun for a while (and then it gets to be a bit of a bore), and it is amusing for a while to have people say hello as they part and good-by as they meet, but why characters who are living their ever younger lives in forward time would say such things does not make much sense. The same logical flaw appears in the de-aging, reversed-time stories "Victims of Time" [Rao, PWO] and "The Man Who Never Grew Old" [Leiber, 1987].

Much better with its logic than is Dick's novel is "The Chronokinesis of Jonathan Hull" [Boucher, GSSF]. Here we are given a rational explanation that involves the ill-fated experimenter Jonathan Hull, who develops a machine to achieve a reversal of the time sense. There are none of Dick's dead bodies coming alive and clawing free from dank graves here; and not only does the rest of the world walk backward to Hull's eyes, but also it talks backward. The story, in fact, is an ingenious examination of the real physical effects of reversed time, including the details of how to survive in a world that is going in the opposite direction to oneself.[17]

One thing Dick's often illogical novel does do, with great effect, is to discuss the theological side to reversed time. A once-dead, now resurrected character admits, for example, to having no memory of much of anything beyond the grave and is told, "I guess that disproves God and the Afterlife." The modern Lazarus replies, logically enough, "No more so than the absence of pre-uterine memories disproves Buddhism."

Another science fiction writer has also used reversed time to explore a religious theme. In [Watson, 1979] we learn of "The Very Slow Time Machine," or VSTM, which suddenly appears one day in the National Physical Laboratory to the understandable astonishment of all present. It soon becomes apparent that the VSTM is actually traveling backward through time, and its arrival was really its departure. This confusing state of affairs is gradually explained as the story unfolds. (As far as I can tell, all of Watson's description makes logical sense, too, if one accepts the possibility of time travel at all, admittedly a pretty big acceptance.) Some of Professor MacBeath's ideas on backward-in-time communication, in fact, can be found anticipated in Watson's story; the time traveler sealed inside the VSTM communicates with our world via appropriately timed handwritten messages displayed through a window, in the same way as described earlier for Jim and Midge. The idea is that a young man in the year 2020 wants to appear in the year 2055 as the Messiah. To go forward 35 years first requires (according to Watson's assumed "laws of time travel") a trip backward by the same amount. This initial part of the journey is like the slow arming of a crossbow, done in reverse at the rate of minus one second of external time per second of internal machine time (hence the name VSTM). The forward trip is done instantaneously, in the same way that the arrow from the crossbow is launched to its target. The lonely, backward trip, however, drives the would-be holy man crazy, in reverse fashion, so that at his first appearance in the laboratory he appears crazy to the external observers, who then see him slowly become less crazy. Remember, the man is traveling through time backward. As this amazing tale ends, the narrator wonders about the appearance of the VSTM in 2055: "What then, when God rises from the grave of time, *insane*?"

Reversed time appears to be simply too bizarre for the movies. The only example I know of in that medium is the Czechoslovakian film *Happy End* from twenty-five years ago. The movie opens with a close-up of a head in a coffin. As the camera pulls back, we see that there is no body. This is the end (or the beginning) of a man who has just been (or is about to be) guillotined, and the rest of the film shows us why in reverse. The makers of this picture certainly didn't take any of it very seriously, using Mack-Sennet-era music throughout as the score.

When *Time* (28 June 1968) took notice of the film a witty reviewer thought it all a bit too much: " ... the whole conceit might have made a delightful short. Much too hour an is it of minutes 73 but."

The Philosophy and Physics of Reversed Time

In support of the logical possibility of time travel to the past, [Putnam, 1962] asks us to imagine the spacetime diagram of one Oscar Smith, who in Figure 11 is at spatial position A next to his time machine. At time t_0 Oscar has not yet gotten into his time machine. A little later, at time t_1, we suddenly see Oscar not only at A, but *two more* Oscars have appeared (apparently out of thin air) moving away from spatial position B! Between t_1 and t_2 we see both the original Oscar at A and the two spontaneously created Oscars at B (a total of three Oscars, labeled in the figure as $Oscar_1$, $Oscar_2$, and $Oscar_3$) move forward in time, but one of the new Oscars ($Oscar_2$) lives a decidedly odd existence in that it seems to be in reverse! Eventually, at time t_2 the original Oscar ($Oscar_1$) and the weird, reverse Oscar merge—and seemingly annihilate one another, vanishing into thin air to leave only a single Oscar ($Oscar_3$) for all time after t_2. Professor Putnam argues that, although strange, this is still sensible and, indeed that this spacetime diagram itself, the very fact that one can draw it, supports the case for backward time travel. He claims this because while this spacetime diagram does show time increasing upward for all three Oscars (since that is the time direction for the external observer) it all is sensible if $Oscar_2$ is understood to be a time traveler into the past since then his time direction would be pointed the other way.

Weingard, however, takes exception to Putnam's presentation; and he offers in [Weingard, 1972a] an even less plausible mechanism for Putnam's kinked space-time diagram than time travel. Weingard advocates, instead, an explanation based on matter transmitters and antimatter, the latter an idea he credits to Feynman (who actually got it from John Wheeler). Indeed, in [Feynman, 1949a] we find the famous suggestion that a positron (appearing to us to be moving forward in time) is actually an electron traveling backward through time. Logically, of course, this greatly weakens Weingard's argument because he is using antimatter (which can be explained in terms of backward time travel) to argue against backward time travel! But let's ignore this, give Weingard the benefit of the doubt, and see how antimatter and backward time travel are connected.

Feynman asks us first to imagine the process shown in the spacetime diagram in Figure 12. Gamma ray A spontaneously creates an electron-positron pair, with $electron_2$ moving off to some distant region, while the positron soon meets with $electron_1$, resulting in mutual annihilation and the production of gamma ray B. This description involves three particles, and each segment of the kinked line is a distinct particle. Feynman said there is another way to look at this, however, and he gave a description using just *one* particle. According to Feynman, the kinked line on the figure is the world line of a single electron; the middle segment is the electron traveling backward in time, and so we must reverse the arrow on it.

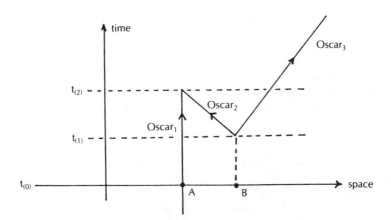

FIGURE 11. A time traveler and his world line.

There are two central questions at this point. First, why is a positron (with a positive electric charge) moving forward in time mathematically equivalent to an electron (with a negative charge) moving backward in time? The answer is that the reversal in charge sign, which results from the reversal of the electron's time direction, follows from the *TCP* theorem (see Note 11 for Chapter Two). And second, what causes our single electron suddenly to move backward in time? Picturesquely, it is recoiling from the emitted energy burst of gamma ray *B*. Just as momentum and space are complementary variables (momentum conservation is the consequence of space direction invariance in the laws of physics) and just as a particle can reverse its direction of motion in space if it loses enough momentum, so a particle can reverse its direction of motion in time if it loses enough energy. This follows because energy and time are another pair of complementary variables. (Conservation of energy is the consequence of time-direction invariance in the laws of physics.) Similarly, the absorption of the energy of gamma ray *A* by the electron recoiling backward in time causes a second recoil, giving the world line of what we originally called electron$_2$. This reinterpretation of a kinked spacetime diagram was described as follows in Feynman's famous words: "It is as though a bombardier flying low over a road suddenly sees three roads and it is only when two of them come together and disappear again that he realizes that he has simply passed over a long switchback in a single road.'"

Feynman's radical idea has, of course, many severe critics among philosophers. Professor Smart, who it will be recalled from the start of this chapter rejects as nonsense the ideas that time has a direction and is flowing, finds Feynman's interpretation equally hard to swallow. He writes [Smart, 1958]: "One at once smells a category mistake here. After all, does an electron normally move *forward* in time? Clearly not. (If it did, how fast would it move? How many seconds per second?) Both 'forward in time' and 'backward in time' are equally nonsense."

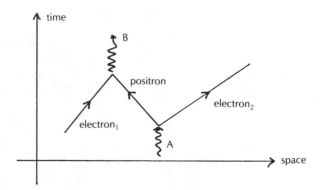

FIGURE 12. Antimatter through backward time travel.

(See Note 7 again.) Perhaps the most startling puzzle of Feynman's interpretation is that it seems to say that the same electron can be at two different places in space at the same time (a point also raised by Smart)—of this [Reichenbach, 1956] said, "The concept of physical identity is shaken to its very foundation."

Two physicists [Graves and Roper, 1965] answered Reichenbach's worry by arguing that the "same time" is that of some observer, but that for a clock traveling with the electron and recording the local or *proper* time (see Tech Note 5), time is always increasing; when the electron is in different places, proper time is also different. In a reply to Graves and Roper, [Earman, 1967a] pointedly rejected their point of view. (Note that Reichenbach in his original paper [Reichenbach, 1956], published years before Graves and Roper wrote, had already rejected an explanation based on the use of different clocks; he felt the confusion of temporal ordering of events along the kinked world line as a function of which clock you used, observer's or electron's, was "the most serious blow the concept of time has ever received in physics.") Earman particularly disliked Graves and Roper's attempt to argue about backward time travel in terms of bent-back world lines, which have to reverse direction sharply in order to stay within the requirements of special relativity that nothing of substance participating in a causal event chain can move faster than light (see Tech Note 4). The significance of special relativity to discussions of backward time travel is weak, however, and the thesis of this book is accurately contained in Earman's closing words, "General relativity seems to offer more hope than special relativity to the proponent of time travel." Indeed, in Tech Note 8 I show how the world line of a backward time traveler can always satisfy special relativity's causality constraint.

Entropy as Time's Arrow

While the reversed-time fictional worlds of Dick, Fitzgerald, and Carpentier are of course metaphors on the human condition,[18] Boucher in "The Chronokinesis of

Jonathan Hull" was clearly trying to appeal to the analytical, logical mind of the scientist. After a little mood-setting with some babble words on how the method involves the rotation of a temporomagnetic field against the natural time stream, Boucher has one of his characters face up to the real puzzle of it all: "How can a man live backward? You might as well ask the Universe to run in reverse entropy." This cogent question brings us, in fact, to the first scientific explanation developed to explain the observed asymmetric nature of time.

It was the Englishman A. S. Eddington who gave the picturesque name of the "arrow of time" to the observed asymmetric nature of time's direction from past to future. He was also one of the popularizers of an explanation for the arrow, using the famous second law of thermodynamics [Eddington, 1929]. The second law of thermodynamics states that a measure of the internal randomness or disorder, which is called the *entropy*, of any closed (that is, one free of external influences) system continually evolves toward that of maximum disorder, the condition called *thermodynamic equilibrium*. Indeed, so striking is this increase of entropy S with time in a macroscopically large system that the increase of entropy has come to be thought of as defining the direction of time, pointing to the future. Eddington, however, was not the originator of the entropy concept itself. The credit for this can be traced back before the turn of the century to the great Austrian scientist Ludwig Boltzmann (1844–1906) and to his famous H–theorem of 1872, in which the quantity H is directly related to the more familiar entropy.[19]

The steady increase in entropy is an often observed phenomena in the everyday world. A drop of ink in a glass of water, for example, spreads out in an expanding cloud, a cloud we never see collapse backward into a drop, and a long rod of metal, initially hotter at one end than the other, evolves toward a constant temperature along its entire length. We never see a uniformly warm rod spontaneously begin to cool at one end and grow hot at the other. A hot bath grows cool— nobody has ever seen a bath at room temperature suddenly begin to heat up and then boil. In all of these cases the end state (the future) represents greater internal randomness or disorder than does the beginning state (the past).

The first formal entropy model for the direction of time was put forth in a 1907 paper by the Austrian physicist Paul Ehrenfest (1880–1933), a friend of Einstein's, and his Russian-born wife Tatyana (1876–1964) who was a skilled mathematician and her husband's occasional collaborator. In their paper the Ehrenfest's developed the idea, one of the mainstays of physics, of the so-called *entropic gas clock*. This clock, a statistical model based on the then new mathematics of Markov chains [after the Russian mathematician A. A. Markov (1856–1922)], describes how gases diffuse, and it is both a simple and powerful concept. (A lovely mathematical description of the Ehrenfest model is in [Wheeler, 1979]).

Formally, as derived by Boltzmann in 1877, the entropy of a system in a given state is S, proportional to W, which is the number of different possible ways the state can occur due to variations of the system's internal, microscopic structure. The calculation of W in practical, everyday systems can be quite complicated, but in various ideal systems it is straightforward. Consider, for example, a vacuum cylinder with a thin membrane dividing the interior into halves. Then, in the left half we insert (to be specific) six molecules. If we define the microscopic state of the system to be the number of molecules in the left half, then initially $W=1$ as there is just one way to put all six molecules in the left half. This represents the state of *minimum* entropy, the state most distant from equilibrium. If we now puncture the membrane, the trapped molecules are free to move about the entire cylinder. At each instant of time we can count the number of molecules in the left half—suppose eventually this becomes five, with one molecule entering the right half. Then, $W=6$ (there are six ways to pick the molecule that leaves), and so the entropy of the system has obviously increased.

We think of the thermodynamic equilibrium state as being the state with equal numbers of molecules in both halves, and this gives the *maximum* entropy, which is associated with $W=20$. With such a small number of molecules, it is not clear that W (and thus S) will inexorably increase with time; perhaps, after one of the six molecules has gone to the right, it might return to the left before any of its companions have joined it on the right. Such an event is called a *reversal*, and it happens with some nonzero probability. But the more molecules in the cylinder (instead of six make the number a million million million, still a small amount of gas in our everyday world, hardly enough to fill a sewing thimble), the more likely it becomes that the value of S will monotonically increase with time.

That is, low entropy was in the past, high entropy will be in the future. The increase of entropy defines a direction to time, and so entropy has come to be called the *thermodynamic arrow of time*. More correctly, it should be called the probabilistic (or statistical) arrow of time. These statements are all accepted today as certainly being true as far as they go. But there is clearly a puzzle here, too. The puzzle is that the motion of each of the molecules individually is time reversible, while the statistical behavior of the many is not—and the use of averages over large collections implies the loss of detailed information about the individual molecules. How can it be that by reducing our knowledge of a system, we then find it displaying a new property (asymmetric time evolution) that we did not see before? And if this question isn't troublesome enough, we also have the two puzzles called the "reversibility" and the "recurrence" paradoxes.

The reversibility paradox is, of course, the issue raised earlier in this chapter—that the classical equations of physics work just as well with time running in either direction. So why don't things go backward? This question, originally raised by Lord Kelvin in 1874, was brought to Boltzmann's attention in 1876 by the German physical chemist Johann Loschmidt (1821–1895), one of Boltzmann's professors at the University of Vienna. Boltzmann's answer to this paradox was that it *is* imaginable that a world could run backward if initial conditions are suitable; e.g., if all the velocity vectors of every particle in an equilibrium state are reversed, the system will unwind backward in time toward its original nonequilibrium condition. That is, a system in thermodynamic equilibrium, the state of highest entropy, could evolve toward one of low entropy. Boltzmann even suggested that such might be the case for regions in our own Universe, i.e., there might be beings in a world somewhere out there who experience time running counter to our experience. (He said this in 1877, a remarkable statement for a conservative nineteenth-century professor, nearly a century before Dick!) But, argued Boltzmann, from most given states there are vastly more ways for entropy to increase than there are for it to decrease, and that is why we see what we see.[20]

The recurrence paradox is something entirely different; it is based on a result established by the great French mathematician Henri Poincaré (1854–1912) in 1890 in his paper "On the Three-Body Problem and the Equations of Dynamics." Motivated by the question of the stability of the motion of three masses governed by Newton's laws of mechanics, Poincaré showed that starting from almost any initial state, any fixed volume system with a finite amount of energy and a finite number of degrees of freedom will return infinitely often (and with arbitrarily little deviation) to almost every previous state. If you wait long enough, implies Poincaré's theorem, Pearl Harbor will happen again—and again, and again and ... . In 1896 the German mathematician Ernst Zermelo (1871–1953) used this result, which is called the 'eternal return' by philosophers, to claim that there could be no truly irreversible processes, and thus he cast doubt on the inexorable increase of entropy.

Even for very small systems, however, such as a mere handful of molecules, the recurrence time is extremely large (this was, in essence, Boltzmann's reply to Zermelo's concern). For example, if our gas-filled cylinder contains just 100 molecules and if transitions from one half of the cylinder to the other half take place at the rate of one million each second, then the recurrence time has been calculated to be 30 million billion years [Blatt, 1956]. And for the Universe, itself, the recurrence time is simply incomprehensible—mathematicians call one followed by a hundred zeros a *googol*, and the recurrence time for the Universe (in years) has been estimated to be one followed by a googol of zeros (a googolplex of years).[21]

An expanding Universe would also seem to violate the Poincaré condition of fixed volume. Eddington put this as follows in one of his 1934 Messenger Lectures at Cornell [Eddington, 1935]: "In an expanding space any particular congruence becomes more and more improbable. The expansion of the Universe creates new possibilities of distribution faster than the atoms can work through them, and there is no longer any likelihood of a particular distribution being repeated. If we continue shuffling a pack of cards we are bound sometime to bring them into their standard order—but not if the conditions are that every morning one more card is added to the pack." And [Tipler, 1980] shows that if one considers general relativity, then the recurrence theorem is not true. More specifically, Tipler assumes only that gravity is always attractive and that spacetime satisfies a special condition that avoids such bizarre situations as backward causation. (See Note 9 of Tech Note 9 for information about this so-called *Cauchy condition*, which is of particular interest in the theory of time machines.) Tipler concluded that "in general relativity, singularities intervene to prevent recurrence. General relativistic Universes are thought to begin and end in singularities of infinite spacetime curvature, and these singularities force time in general relativity to be linear rather than cyclic."

A connection between time-reversed worlds (using entropy as the arrow of time) and faster-than-light tachyons (see Chapter Four) is given in [Gott, 1974]. There it is shown how the assumption of a Big Bang Cosmology, in which a time singularity is prevented by quantum effects, leads to the conclusion that our observed Universe ('normal' time direction and matter) may be joined to both a Universe containing tachyons *and* to a time-reversed, antimatter Universe.

It did not take long for science fiction to incorporate entropy into time travel. In 1930, for example, there is a brief statement that entropy is behind the operation of "The Time Valve" [Breuer, 1930a]. In "Temporary Warp" [Long, 1937], as the inventor of a "warp gun" explains, "The stupendous distortion of the warp may actually bring about a sort of kink in spacetime, and result in a reversal of entropy" —and when the gun is fired, a woman who is hit by the warp ages seventy years in seconds (which is, of course, the wrong effect!)

Later, in 1938, *Amazing Stories* published "Time for Sale" [Farley, 1950], the story of a college student about to flunk his senior physics course. The final examination is scheduled for the following day, but he needs a week and a half of study time. To his rescue comes ENTROPY, INC., a company that sells time by placing clients inside a "time-cabinet" in which the increase of local entropy is greatly accelerated. To someone looking through a window at the interior of the time-cabinet, the occupants would appear as characters in a speeded-up movie. Referring to Eddington by name, the author tells us that "entropy is what makes time irreversible—is what gives us the feeling of the flow of time (in "Half-Past Eternity" [MacDonald, 1971] the factor is 36,000!)." This time-cabinet device is, of course, for travel into the near future only—to travel into the past is not possible as that would require the reversal and decrease of entropy for the entire external world (although this fantastic idea is used in "The Bacular Clock" [Bond, 1946] to run the entire world backward to undo a terrible train accident). It is a funny sort of time travel into the future, too. Too long a stay inside a time-cabinet would result in the occupant emerging as an old man, while his companions outside would still be young. More recently, "ARM" [Niven, E] has repeated this idea in the far more scientifically sophisticated story about a time compressor, in which time runs 500 times faster than normal time (in "Half-Past Eternity" [MacDonald, 1971] the factor is 36,000!). One could imagine a variation on this theme, of course, in which the increase in entropy is slowed relative to the outside world. And, indeed, Farley's story has this twist, too—the hero enters this modified time-cabinet and then, after just a few hours for him, emerges to find that years have gone by on the outside. This is just fine with him, as the daughter of the married woman he originally loved has now had time to grow up and ... surely you can finish the romantic story line yourself.

Poul Anderson used entropy in a fascinating way in his "Time Heals" [Anderson, 1949], describing how a scientist had discovered "a field in which entropy was held level." As Anderson explains, "An object in such a field could not experience any time flow—for it, time would not exist"; this is because time flow is a *change* in entropy, and the change of a constant is zero. Anderson speculates in this tale about how such a field could have fantastic home uses ("Imagine cooking a chicken dinner, putting it in the field, and taking it out piping hot whenever needed, maybe twenty years hence!"), but its real use in the story is as a stasis generator for preserving fatally ill people until medical science has learned how to cure their diseases. This is, then, a high-tech method of suspended animation, of time travel by sleeping into the future. The gadget that does this is called (somewhat sinisterly) the "Crypt." Anderson tells us that it also makes a great bomb shelter because "not even an atom bomb could penetrate a stasis field." The reason for this is intriguing: "The field requires a finite time in which to collapse—only there is no time in it." The interior of the Crypt is, literally, a frozen block of time.

Somewhat later came A. C. Clarke's story about the tragic end of a geologist, fifty million years in the past [Clarke, 1959a]. This aptly named tale ("Time's Arrow") uses the idea of entropy to justify a time machine. Entropy has clearly fascinated Robert Silverberg, too. For example, when a newspaper from the future appears on people's doorsteps in "What We Learned from This Morning's Newspaper" [Silverberg, 1986], the initial astonishment is replaced by puzzlement as the papers rapidly disintegrate. It is the result, we are told, of "entropic creep." The explanation continues, informing us that it is sort of like a strain in a geological fault (Silverberg lives in Oakland, California, now and then the site of large to huge earthquakes, and it isn't surprising that he uses this particular imagery): "Entropy you know is the natural tendency of everything in nature to come apart at the seams as time goes along. These newspapers must be subject to unusually strong entropic strains because of their anomalous position out of their proper place in time."

In his "In Entropy's Jaws" [Silverberg, 1986] we see the randomness that underlies entropy running through the entire story. Silverberg's central character is a telepathic "Communicator" who is burned out by an information overload while mentally linking two clients. He thus becomes "unstuck in time"—like Vonnegut's Billy Pilgrim in *Slaughter-House Five* [Vonnegut, 1971], the time traveler in *Je t'aime, Je t'aime*, and Van Vogt's Chris McAllister in *Weapons Shops of Isher* [van Vogt, 1954, 1980], he starts oscillating, wildly and uncontrollably, back and forth between past and future. He is literally masticated by the teeth of time. The play on entropy and the job of Communicator is clear (since entropy plays a central role in the mathematics of information theory),[22] and Silverberg's character is caught in entropy's jaws. Silverberg is fascinated by this idea of swinging forward and backward through time, and has repeated it in his appropriately titled novel *Project Pendulum* [Silverberg, 1987].

Other Arrows of Time

After all the previous discussion, it is still not clear if the evolution of a system from past to future is always accompanied by an irreversible increase in entropy, that is, by an inexorable increase in some measure of the system's disorder. This is an empirical observation, after all, one we can justify via statistical calculations as being very likely, but certainly not as certain. Eddington, therefore, was wrong when he dramatically stated [Eddington, 1929]: "The law that entropy always increases holds, I think, the supreme position among the laws of nature. If someone points out to you that your pet theory of the Universe is in disagreement with Maxwell's equations—then so much the worse for Maxwell's equations ... but if your theory is found to be against the second law of thermodynamics, I can give you no hope; there is nothing for it but to collapse in deepest humiliation."

Contrary to Eddington, the second law of thermodynamics is not on the same level with, for example, the fundamental conservation laws, which *never* fail in classical physics. And also contrary to Eddington, Maxwell's equations are on a higher, not lower, step of the ladder with respect to the second law. In classical physics Maxwell's equations *never* fail. The increase of entropy, on the other hand, *can* fail; there can be fluctuations in the evolution of a system so as to have, at least for a time, a decrease in entropy. All we can say is that for macroscopically sized systems even small fluctuations in entropy are most unlikely.

Yet, entropy is for most physicists still just too useful an idea to give up even though entropy does not always increase. One such interesting approach, for example, which argues for the irreversibility of a system whose basic microlaws are reversible, is in [Morrison, ET]. Professor Morrison finds the unavoidable perturbing effects of outside influences sufficient so that they always preclude the possibility of a real velocity-reversal of the parts of a system. He finds, in fact, that it takes literally almost nothing to disturb a system to the point where it will never unwind in reverse; as he explained, "One may estimate that a gravitational force exerted by a falling apple a kilometer away over an arc of ten centimeters is ample to mix up the trajectory of a mole of normal gas, in a time of milliseconds!" Because of this, he also concludes that the entropic arrow of time would be independent of the expansion/contraction state of the Universe. (See Note 15 and the next page on the cosmological arrow of time.) Morrison's logic merely begs the question, however, because his supposed explanation for time asymmetry has asymmetry built into it; i.e., he assumes such perturbing influences will always increase entropy (which is precisely what he is trying to explain) rather than reduce it.

Well, whatever you may think of Morrison's theoretical approach, there are also serious philosophical problems with entropy as the ultimate arrow of time. For example, events in the past leave traces, which are taken to be ordered states or at least more ordered than the general surroundings. The classic example is the footprint in the sand, a highly organized structure. This is the trace of a past event; such a trace was all the evidence Robinson Crusoe needed to know that another human had walked that way. But now consider Earman's famous counterexample, that of a bombed city [Earman, 1974]. Certainly there are traces aplenty of this, and in fact one has to be careful literally not to trip over or to fall into them! The puzzle, of course, is in trying to argue that random bomb craters, strewn rubble, and crushed buildings somehow constitute a more organized state than did the original city and the surrounding unbombed area.

And for a second example, consider the situation described in [Denbigh, 1989], of a cloud of noncolliding particles initially moving toward each other. At first, the radius of the smallest sphere that contains this cloud decreases, but eventually as the particles move past one another, the radius will grow without bound. Indeed, this inexorable increase could be taken as defining the direction of time pointing toward the future. But in what sense is the disorder of the particle cloud increasing? At all times as the cloud expands, it looks the same, with only its scale changing. One might reply that this is an example of an open or unbounded system, while the entropic gas clock is defined as a closed, bounded system. So, let's admit that—but the question still stands: What has entropy to do with our expanding-into-the-future cloud? Perhaps nothing.[23] Perhaps what is needed is a new arrow of time.

So far we have looked in some detail at two of the so-called arrows of time: the subjective, psychological feeling we have of time flowing (which has no counterpart in physics) and the thermodynamic, statistical quantity of entropy. A third arrow I have hinted at is the cosmological arrow, the expansion of the Universe. This is an arrow not nearly so obvious as the first two. It was only in modern times (since the 1920s as a result of the work of the American astronomer Edwin Hubble) that the expansion of the Universe was discovered.

An observation concerning the expanding Universe that has been made many times before (e.g., see [Gold, 1962]) is that if the thermodynamic arrow of time runs one way in an expanding Universe, then shouldn't it reverse direction if the Universe begins contracting? The usual objection to this suggestion is simple enough. If the direction of time did reverse, then we would see (so goes this argument) all sorts of odd events that would require enormously improbable physics; for example, a shattered glass mirror reassembling itself. The error in this objection is subtle, but equally simple. It *presupposes the retarded causality of our expanding Universe.* In a contracting Universe with a reversed thermodynamic arrow, however, there would be advanced causality and nothing at all improbable about such things as a self-assembling mirror. An interesting analysis of the relationship between the thermodynamic and the cosmological arrows, making this argument, is [Schulman, 1973].

Yet another arrow of time is the electromagnetic arrow, which refers to the observed nature of electromagnetic radiation always to propagate into the future, but never into the past. This is a mysterious fact because Maxwell's equations for the electromagnetic field, like the other laws of physics, have no intrinisic time sense. We will pursue this particular arrow in great detail in Chapter Four.

Multidimensional Time

Could there be such a thing as more than one direction to time's arrow at each instant? At first this seems to be an absurd idea, something akin to the man who jumped upon his horse and rode off in all directions at once. As with so many other of the radical concepts in time travel, however, science fiction writers were dealing with multidimensional time long before it became a respectable topic in learned philosophical journals. In "Elsewhen" [Heinlein, 1953], for example, a story originally published in the September 1941 issue of *Astounding Science Fiction*, we find a professor asking his redundantly named class in speculative metaphysics, "Why shouldn't time be a fifth, as well as a fourth, dimension?" In response to a generally skeptical reception to this, the professor goes on to say, "I believe in the existence of a two-dimensional time scheme ... Ordinarily, most people think of time as a track they run on from their births to their deaths ... Think of this time track we follow over the *surface of time* as a winding road [it is the idea of a surface that gives the professor two time dimensions] ... Once in a while another road crosses at right angles. Neither its past nor its future has any connection whatsoever with the world we know." (This story has an amusing scene, in which one of the professor's students accidently jumps time tracks and enters a new track with his time arrow pointing backward.)

The same magazine had also published another tale, "Bombardment in Reverse," that went well beyond a mere two time dimensions [Knight, 1940]. We are told in this story of two countries on an alien planet at war in the distant future. The war is a stalemate until one side begins to fire a gun at its foe from just two miles from its target in the heart of enemy territory—and from the middle of next week! The gun's shells are truly "time bombs." This is not mere ordinary time travel along one time track, however, but a multidimensional effect. Using a photograph of the gun in actual operation to support his astonishing discovery, an agent for the side being shelled reports to his superior that "the gun and its crew are existing along another time axis at right angles to the direction of our 'normal time', so that from our point of view they are existing perpetually in the same instant." This explains why the gun crew can (will) operate without interference in the future, as they are in their adversary's time only for the instant that the two time tracks intersect. The spy uses the same trick to obtain his undetected photograph, however—"I secured the photograph by orienting myself along still another time axis at right angles to that of the gun, and approached it as an instantaneous, invisible entity." By the story's end, both sides are using and counterusing this technique, evading each other "to and fro along an ever increasing complexity of mutually perpendicular time axes." Indeed, the final count exceeds 75(!) time axes, making two-dimensional time look rather skimpy by comparison.

Well, of course 75 time directions *is* science fiction, and physicists are not so enamored with multidimensional time as are science fiction writers.[24] For example, Eddington long ago wrote that he found the idea of any region of spacetime with two-dimensional time to "defy imagination."[25] More recently, [Dorling,

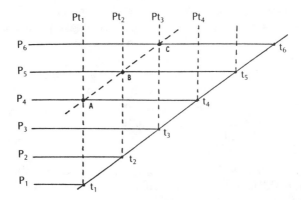

FIGURE 13. Multidimensional time.

1970] has looked at the idea more analytically. Dorling showed that the extremal property of timelike geodesics (see Tech Note 4) would fail for multidimensional time, which Dorling then associates with the stability of matter. In addition, he makes a connection between multidimensional time and a failure of causality.

Some philosophers, on the other hand, are fascinated by the idea of multidimensional time. Why their interest in something so different from anything we actually experience? Where does the motivation come from? Of what *use* is multidimensional time? I think the answer is that it offers a model that supports those philosophers who argue that it makes sense to say there is meaning to the idea that the past can change. In a trivial sense, of course, the past is always changing. For each of us the past is, after all, the set of all events that have happened, arranged in a before/after temporal order,[26] and this set is continually increasing; i.e., changing. This is not, however, what most people mean by a changeable past. What *is* meant is that there may be some kind of change in the temporal ordering of events or that an event that once was a member of the set of past events no longer is a member. Two-dimensional time offers a way to make sense of such things, which one-dimensional time cannot do. To see how this works, let's follow the presentation in [Meiland, 1974], a paper that forcefully argues that it does make sense to talk about alterations of the past.[27]

Professor Meiland is aware that some might find his model ad hoc, or even "incredibly weird" (in his own words), but he justifies his efforts by taking a refreshingly enlightened, non-Humean view of what he thinks is the proper response to meeting time travelers: "If strange machines containing people in futuristic garments and speaking strange tongues (or perhaps using ESP instead of speech) were to appear and were to claim to be from the future, we might very well begin to search for a theory of time that allows their claim to be true." In Figure 13, we see how Meiland has tried to do just that. The solid diagonal line, marked with the points $t_1, t_2, \ldots$, represents our usual one-dimensional image of time. The lines P_1t_1, P_2t_2, ... (which we can simply call P_1, P_2, ... , for short) are the pasts for the present instants t_1, t_2, ... That is, P_1 is the past with respect to the present t_1, P_2 is the past with respect to the present t_2, and so on. The dashed vertical lines allow us to locate any moment in any past; e.g., the intersection A of P_4 with Pt_1 is the location of t_1 in the past with respect to t_4.

With this model Meiland then analyzes in detail several interesting special cases. For example, suppose t_1 and t_2 are one year apart and that there are similar time separations between all adjacent, marked present moments on the solid diagonal. Let us further suppose that the time traveler at t_4 journeys backward three years to t_1; then he will arrive at point A in the diagram. Assume he stays in the past two years—then his temporal locations lie along the dashed diagonal ABC; i.e., at B he is three years in the past of t_5, and at C he is three years in the past of t_6. From the diagram, then, we can imagine the time traveler saying as he climbs into his time machine at t_4, "One year from now I'll be two years from now."

This rather astonishing statement makes sense when we take both uses of now to be t_4, and observe that B (one year from A) is two years in the past with respect to t_4. Williams, a critic of time travel, uses what he claims to be the absurdity of a statement like this one for one-dimensional time to support his rejection of time travel [Williams, 1951a]. One of Professor Meiland's stated reasons for developing his model was, in fact, to be able to reply to Williams' objection.

As a last example of his time model, Meiland briefly discusses how it does away with the grandfather paradox; i.e., he does not explain the paradox, but rather he argues that the paradox simply does not exist. Take the extreme case of time-travel suicide: at t_4 the time traveler journeys back three years to A, kills his younger self (and secretly takes the victim's place), stays a year until B, and then travels forward three years to t_5. On the solid diagonal the time traveler is seen to disappear at t_4 and then reappear at t_5. In the past a man vanishes at B. The one-dimensional time paradox is avoided, however, because the traveler did not visit t_1, but rather t_1's location at A in the past of t_4; i.e., the traveler's existence along the solid diagonal is uninterrupted except during his trip into the past.

Professor Meiland's model is undeniably fascinating, but in fact it has no theoretical justification at all (or experimental either as far as I know).[28] It is simply not necessary to assume two-dimensional time to explain Meiland's "strange machines containing people in futuristic garments" from the future; it is possible to do so with one-dimensional time in four-dimensional spacetime. The grandfather and suicide paradoxes, too, are understandable without two-dimensional time. In the next chapter I show how all this can be done.

CHAPTER FOUR
Time-Travel Paradoxes and (some of) Their Explanations

Time travel is so dangerous it makes H–bombs seem like perfectly safe gifts for children and imbeciles. I mean, what's the worst that can happen with a nuclear weapon? A few million people die: trivial. With time travel we can destroy the whole Universe, or so the theory goes.

> —*Millennium* [Varley, 1983]

He felt the intellectual desperation of any honest philosopher. He knew that he had about as much chance of understanding such problems as a collie has of understanding how dog food gets into cans.

> —a time traveler, perplexed by paradoxes in "By His Bootstraps" [Heinlein, AHT]

"There's a lot we don't know about time travel. How do you expect logic to hold when paradoxes hold, too." "Does that mean you don't know?" "Yes."

> —excerpt from a conversation between two paradox-puzzled time travelers in "Bird in the Hand" [Niven, 1973]

What *was* this time traveling? A man couldn't cover himself with dust by rolling in a paradox, could he?

> —the incredulous Editor, astonished at the disheveled appearance of Wells' Time Traveler upon his return from A.D. 802,701, and beyond

Paradoxes

The first opening quote, from John Varley's imaginative novel *Millennium* (which was made into a 1989 movie), is typical of one common reaction to the threat of time-travel paradoxes. This view assumes nature has no stomach for paradoxes, and if one should be forced upon her, then the Universe would be torn apart. Varley calls this the *cosmic disgust theory*, and expresses it in the form of a petulant note to the offending time traveler:

If you're going to play games like that, I'll take my marbles and go home.

Signed,

God.

"Rotating Cylinders and the Possibility of Global Causality Violation" [Niven, 1979], a story that adopts Varley's view, is about a paradox on the verge of occurring through the use of a Tipler-cylinder time machine. Rather than letting the paradox occur, the Universe decides to avoid the problem by eliminating the perpetrators of the attempted paradox via a local nova. In a weaker form we saw this same response, of nature protecting herself against time-travel paradoxes, in Chapter One in De Camp's "A Gun for Dinosaur." Varley's and Niven's extreme, catastrophic visions of nature preempting paradoxes can be found in other stories as well; e.g., those in [Brown, 1958]. On the other hand, time-travel paradoxes do not always have to be gloomy, as shown in the following (hypothetical?) exchange between father and son in the (perhaps?) not too distant future:

> "Hey, Dad. Can I borrow the time machine tonight?"
> "Sure, son. Just be sure you have it back before you leave."

Fredric Brown was a master of the special category of science fiction story called the "short-short," in which everything happens in 500 words (or less). The oddities of time travel were natural attractions for a quirky science fiction talent such as Brown's. For example, in "Experiment" the inventor of the first time machine demonstrates it and a famous paradox to two colleagues by sending a brass cube five minutes into the future. After placing the cube into the machine, the cube vanishes and then five minutes later reappears. No paradoxes here—it is the trip into the past that has the potential for deadly repercussions.[1] The inventor next declares that at three o'clock he will again place the cube into the time machine. Until then he will hold the cube in his hand. Thus, at five minutes before three the cube will vanish from his hand and simultaneously appear in the time machine (because five minutes after that, at three o'clock, he will send it back).[2] And, indeed, at five minutes before three, the cube does vanish from his hand and appear in the time machine!

Then, slightly before three, as the three men stand pondering what has happened, one of the observers asks what would happen if the inventor does not put the cube into the machine at three? "Wouldn't there be a paradox of some sort involved?" he wonders. The inventor, curious, tries it (this is a bilking paradox—recall the discussion of such paradoxes in Chapter Three), and the Universe vanishes in compliance with Varley's cosmic disgust theory.

Time travel, of course, is full of paradoxes. A paradox, according to the usual dictionary definition, is something that appears to contain contradictory or incompatible parts, thus reducing the whole to seeming nonsense. And yet there is also evident truth to the whole, too. The history of science and mathematics has left a long trail of paradoxes, with the time travel ones merely among the most recent. Not all the puzzles in time travel involve physics. For example, [Dwyer, 1978] observes: "Doubtless time travel will raise a host of legal difficulties, e.g., should the time traveler who punches his younger self (or vice versa) be charged with assault? Should the time traveler who murders someone and then flees to the past for sanctuary be tried in the past for his crime committed in the future? If he marries in the past can he be tried for bigamy even though his other wife will not be born for almost 5000 years? Etc., etc. I leave such questions for lawyers and writers of ethics textbooks to solve."

One way science fiction writers have of responding to the puzzles of time-travel paradoxes is just to give up and to concede that the logical paradoxes are over-whelming (but not all writers have given up; the answer to the last of Dwyer's questions can be found in "All in Good Time" [deFord, 1960]). In "Dead End" [Jameson, 1941], for example, the inventor of the Chronoscope (a gadget that can view the past) explains: "This is no time travel machine. Such a thing is a logical impossibility, treated seriously only by half-cracked writers of fantasy. Such a machine would lead at once into a hopeless paradox." Three decades later, in his introduction to [Vance, 1973], Robert Silverberg wrote, "We believe, of course, that time travel is a logical impossibility." Silverberg wrote this for the same reason that the history graduate student in *Time of the Fox* [Costello, 1990], when he learns that the Columbia University Physics Department is doing experiments in time travel, blurts out, "I'm no physicist, but even I know the logical difficulties with time travel. It's open season on coherent history, with goofy paradox-es ... Lots of fun for stories but absolutely crackers as a real possibility."

Paradoxes offend common sense. But are there really paradoxes at all? Or is it true, as the extraordinary boy prodigy in "Vanya" [Grigoriev, LDA] who invented a time machine exclaimed when his teacher asserted that some questions could never be answered because "Nature is full of paradoxes": "Ah, Professor, what nonsense! Nature is harmonious; it is we who bring the paradoxes into it." Saying the same, in a paper on the circular orbits of photons around black holes, are two physicists [Abramowicz and Lasota, 1986]: "There are no paradoxes in physics, but only in our attempts to understand physical ideas by using inadequate reason-ing or false intuition." As the time traveler in "Via the Time Accelerator" [Bridge, 1931] coolly declared to a friend after an astonishing adventure in the year A.D. 1,001,930: "Paradoxical? My dear fellow, the Einstein Theory is full of apparent paradoxes, yet to him who understands it there is no inconsistency whatever. Give me another cigarette, will you, Frank?" Equally unconcerned is the character in the very funny 1941 tale "The Best-Laid Scheme" [de Camp, 1970] who at the end tells his friend "My dear Collingwood, don't drive yourself crazy trying to resolve the paradoxes of time travel. The [time machines] are gone ... Have a drink." Somewhat more concerned about time-travel paradoxes, however, was the time traveler in "The Time Cheaters" [Binder, 1940], who told his partner just before their first trip into the future that "I'm not sure any more about getting back.

There're some unpredictable terms in the time-travel equation—paradoxes. Maybe we *won't* get back."

The concern expressed by this time traveler was not shared by *Rip Hunter— Time Master*, a comic book series published in the early 1960s. Rip Hunter, inventor of the "time sphere," was the leader of a "famous foursome" of time travelers who operated out of a secret mountain laboratory. *Rip Hunter* was unconcerned with the real puzzles of time travel, and paradoxes played no role in any of the stories. Time travel was simply a device to get the characters into a new story setting each issue. The formula for the stories was to send Rip and his pals into the past to film history for museums and photoarchives; there they would suffer some accident which would lead to a crisis. For example, in one 1964 tale, while Rip and his fellow travelers are filming the interior of Nazi Germany, the time sphere (which could fly) is shot down by antiaircraft fire. Before this particular story was through, the time travelers arranged a meeting between Hitler and Napoleon(!), with no one expressing the slightest concern over the paradoxes of disturbing history.

Early Science Fiction Speculations On Time-Travel Paradoxes

The late 1930s and 1940s are generally thought of as the "golden age" of the genre science fiction magazines. Before this (of course) came the pre-golden-age, the first decade of the "scientifiction pulps," which is generally dated from the appearance in April 1926 of Hugo Gernsback's *Amazing Stories*. Gernsback's earlier publications, *Science & Invention* and *Radio News*, had published science fiction from time to time, as had many of the "ten-cent family magazines" since the 1890s. Frank Munsey's *The Argosy*, which began in 1896, was the first all-fiction pulp, and his *The All-Story Magazine* was also an all-fiction adventure pulp since its beginning in 1905. Both magazines had often published the story form called the "scientific romance" (a term used as early as 1888 by C. A. Hinton for his fourth-dimension essays; recall the discussion of Hinton's work in Chapter Two), but they carried other sorts of stories, too. There were many other adventure and "weird story" pulps, such as *The Popular Magazine* (1903), *The Cavalier* (1908), and *The Thrill Book* (1919), but *Amazing Stories* was the first pulp to be devoted totally to science fiction. And with its motto of "Extravagant Fiction Today—Cold Fact Tomorrow," and the illustration on the contents page showing Jules Verne bursting free of his grave in a pose made famous by Superman years later, there could be no doubt as to what kind of fiction the reader would find under the dramatic, multicolored cover art.

It is in *Amazing Stories* that we find the first *non*-fictional speculations about time travel by machine in a pulp magazine. Gernsback started these speculations by reprinting Wells' *Time Machine*, which sparked a fair number of readers' letters that were published in the magazine's "Discussions" section. Typical is this comment from a letter in the July 1927 issue: "In the 'Time Machine' I found something amiss. How could one travel to the future in a machine when the beings of the future have not yet materialized?" (See Tech Note 6 for an answer to this reader's question.) More interesting was the letter from the reader who wrote in the same issue:

> How about this 'Time Machine?' Let's suppose our inventor starts a 'Time voyage' backward to about A.D. 1900, at which time he was a schoolboy ... his watch ticks forward although the clock on the laboratory wall goes backward. Now we are in June 1900, and he stops the machine, gets out and attends the graduating exercises of the class of 1900 of which he was a member. Will there be another 'he' on the stage? Of course, because he *did* graduate in 1900... Should he go up and shake hands with this 'alter ego'? Will there be two physically distinct but characteristically identical persons? Alas! No! He can't go up and shake hands with himself because ... this voyage back through time only duplicates actual past conditions and in 1900 this strange 'other he' did *not* appear suddenly in quaint ultra-new fashions and congratulate the graduate. How could they both be wearing the same watch they got from Aunt Lucy on their seventh birthday, the same watch in two different places at the same time. Boy! Page Einstein! No, he cannot be there because he wasn't there in 1900 (except in the person of the graduate) ... The journey backward must cease on the year of his birth. If he could pass *that* year it would certainly be an effect going before a cause ... Suppose for instance in the graduating exercise above, the inventor should decide to shoot his former self ... he couldn't do it because if he did the inventor would have been cut off before he began to invent and he would never have gotten around to making the voyage, thus rendering it impossible for him to be there taking a shot at himself, so that as a matter of fact he *would* be there and *could* take a shot—help, help, I'm on a vicious circle merry-go-round ... Now as to trips into the future, I could probably think up some humorous adventures wherein [the inventor] digs up his own skeleton and finds by the process of actual examination that he must expect to have his leg amputated because the skeleton presents positive proof that this was done.

All of the ingenious puzzles in this letter (signed only with the initials "T.J.D.") intrigued Gernsback, and no doubt it was no coincidence that that same issue featured the new, original time-machine story "The Lost Continent" [White, 1927]. This is the tale of a scientist who transports an entire ship at sea 14,000 years back in time and causes it to hover over lost Atlantis! This story provoked a sharp letter from a reader who claimed its logic had a fatal flaw—the story's author indicated the Atlantians observed the time travelers, when "of course" (asserted the reader) the time travelers must actually have been invisible. The reader explained his reasoning as follows, beginning by defining A as one of the Atlantians: "Now A lived his life, thousands of years ago, and died. All right, now let us pass on in time 14,000 years. Now, back we come in time when A is again living his life. Lo and behold, this time A sees before he dies a strange phenomenon in the sky! He sees the shipload of people observing him. And yet these people are necessarily observing him during his one and only lifetime, wherein he certainly did not, could not, have observed them." Gernsback printed this letter in his September 1927 editorial ("The Mystery of Time") and concluded by saying, "I do ... agree ... that the inhabitants of Atlantis would probably not have seen the ... travelers in time." Other readers felt this same way because after Gernsback published yet another time-machine story, "The Machine Man of Ardathia" [Flagg, 1927], the same "invisibility" argument again appeared in the "Discussions" column.

In the December 1929 issue of *Science Wonder Stories*, Gernsback published Henry F. Kirkham's story "The Time Oscillator." (By this time Gernsback had lost control of *Amazing*, and *Science Wonder* was part of his comeback as a publisher of pulp scientifiction.) This story plays with the question of the role of time travelers in the past—could they actually participate in events ("mix into the affairs of the period," in Gernsback's words) or would they just be unseen observers? This question, obviously inspired by the earlier discussion in *Amazing Stories*, intrigued Gernsback as much as it did his readers, and along with Kirkham's story he printed a challenge entitled "The Question of Time-Traveling":

> In presenting this story to our readers, we do so with an idea of bringing on a discussion as to time traveling in general. The question in brief is as follows: Can a time traveler, going back in time—whether ten years or ten million years—partake in the life of that time and mingle in with its people; or must he remain suspended in his own time-dimension, a spectator who merely looks on but is powerless to do more? Interesting problems would seem to arise, of which only one need be mentioned: Suppose I can travel back into time, let me say 200 years; and I visit the homestead of my great great great grandfather, and am able to take part in the life of his time. I am thus enabled to shoot him, while he is still a young man and as yet unmarried. From this it will be noted that I could have prevented my own birth; because the line of propagation would have ceased right there. Consequently, it would seem that the idea of time traveling into a past where the time traveler can freely participate in activities of a former age, becomes an absurdity. The editor wishes to receive letters from our readers on this point; the best of which will be published in a special section.

Gernsback's challenge did not pass unnoticed, and over the next year or so he published a large number of reader responses in the magazine's letters column "The Reader Speaks." Indeed, a few months later in his introduction to "An Adventure in Time" [Flagg, 1930], Gernsback wrote that ever since the publication of Kirkham's tale "there has been a great controversy among our readers as to the possibility of time flying and the conditions under which it may be done." Most of those letters, and the ones that followed, are interesting but not particularly profound—with one exception. Appearing in the February 1931 issue, this letter may well have served as inspiration for several of the classic time-travel tales published during the next twenty years:

Some time ago you asked us (the readers) what our opinions on time traveling were. Although a bit late, I am now going to voice four opinions ...

(1) Now, in the first place if time traveling were a possibility there would be no need for some scientist getting a headache trying to invent an instrument or 'Time-Machine' to 'go back and kill grandpa' (in answer to the age-old argument of preventing your birth by killing your grandparents I would say: 'who the heck would want to kill his grandpa or grandma!') I figure it out thusly: A man takes a time machine and travels into the future from where he sends it (under automatic control) to the past so that he may find it and travel into the future and send it back to himself again. Hence the time machine was never invented, but!—from whence did the time machine *come*?

(2) Another impossibility that might result could be: A man travels a few years into the future and sees himself killed in some unpleasant manner,—so—after returning to his correct time he commits suicide in order to avert death in the more terrible way which he was destined to. Therefore how could he have seen himself killed in an entirely different manner than really was the case?

(3) Another thing that might corrupt the laws of nature would be to: Travel into the future; find out how some ingenious invention of the time worked; return to your right time; build a machine, or what ever it may be, similiar to the one you had recently learned the workings of; and use it until the time that you saw it arrives, then if your past self saw it as you did, he would take it and claim it to be an invention of his (your) own, as you did. Then—who really *did* invent the consarn thing?

(4) Here's the last knock on time traveling: What if a man were to travel back a few years and marry his mother, there by resulting in his being his own 'father'? ...

Jim H. Nicholson
40 Lunado Way
San Francisco, Cal.

Gernsback's reply to this was favorable, opening with "Young Mr. Nicholson does present some of the more humorous [?] aspects of time traveling. Logically we are compelled to admit that he is right—that if people could go back into the past or into the future and partake of the life in those periods, they could disturb the normal course of events." Gernsback apparently still liked the "invisibility of time travelers" view, as he had only a few months earlier again published such a tale ("The Time Ray of Jandra" [Palmer, 1930]).

Nicholson's letter *is* ingenious, and it anticipated the central ideas of many science fiction tales. For example, his Item (2) is a precise plot outline of "The Man Who Saw Through Time" [Raphael, 1941], which was mentioned in Chapter Two; and a version of Item (4) was used, decades later, in Robert Heinlein's famous short story "All You Zombies—" [Heinlein, MI]. However, In the next several sections we will also see why, contrary to Gernsback's view, Nicholson's comments are *not* logical.

Two Basic Time-Travel Paradoxes

Professor Williams [1951a] makes the claim that a time traveler about to set out on a trip a century into the past is also about to utter a contradiction when he says "five minutes from now, I will be a hundred years from now"; i.e., how can he be *both* times from now? Professor Smart [Smart, 1963] calls this a "neat argument against the possibility of time travel," and even Professor Horwich [Horwich, 1987], who ultimately rejects Williams' paradox, begins his discussion of it with the title "Is 'time travel' an oxymoron?" In Chapter Three we saw how such Williams-type statements can make sense with multidimensional time—but what if we limit ourselves to the one temporal dimension we actually know?

Williams uses his paradox to deny the rationality, in particular, of the closing, haunting words to Wells' *Time Machine*, when the narrator speculates about the fate of the Time Traveler: "He may even now—if I may use the phrase—be wandering on some plesiosaurus-haunted Oolitic coral reef, or beside the lonely saline seas of the Triassic Age." Williams would have declared equally nonsensical the bold claim of the time traveler in "Time's Arrow" [McDevitt, FCW] who tells a friend that "it *is* possible to reverse the arrow of time in the macroworld. Tonight you and I will have dinner in the nineteenth century." Professor Horwich correctly rebuts Williams by observing that if the five minutes and the hundred years are measured in different reference systems, then the time traveler's assertion can make perfect sense. Indeed, Smart raises this possibility, too, in his paper. And, indeed, Professor Smart even admits that for travel into the future all that is needed is a high-speed rocket, and then it is possible to be a century from now in five years *if* the century is Earth time and the five years is rocket time. But as for trips to the past, Smart says not possible because "fast rockets will not enable us to experience past ages." Professor Smart's words lose much of their strength because of the time-travel-by-rocket results of Gödel, however (which Smart might assert to be inappropriate because our Universe seems not to be rotating) and from other more recent work (see Note 12 for Chapter One).

This kind of argument against time travel is tough in dying. Years later another version of it appeared once more in [Christensen, 1976], written by yet another philosopher who, like Williams and Smart, also rejects time travel: "Consider a sample statement asserting the occurrence of time travel: 'I stepped into the time machine *and then* I saw Caesar being stabbed'. We may re-word this to read 'My stepping into the time machine was earlier than Caesar's being stabbed'; but because it is also true that Caesar's stabbing was earlier than my time-machine entry, we have a flat contradiction—unless the first 'earlier than' involves something other than ordinary time." Christensen claims that only the equally flawed concept of meta-time ("whatever *that* might be") could possibly save the day, but the same reply can be given to him as to Smart. He has failed to distinguish between the proper time of the time traveler and the time of the non-time-travelers. Ijon Tichy's encounter with the doomed time traveler (he ages and dies as he travels into the future) in *Memoirs of a Space Traveler* [Lem, 1982] is based on this same error of confusing proper time and cosmic time. The reverse error occurs in "I Died Tomorrow" [Worth, 1949b], when a time traveler is killed in the year 4000 but returns to life when a colleague brings his body back to the present.

As for our second basic paradox, we find it in Professor Smart's paper, directly following his claim about rockets being unable to visit the past. He begins: "Suppose it is agreed that I did not exist a hundred years ago. It is a contradiction to suppose that I can make a machine that will take me to a hundred years ago. Quite clearly no time machine can make it be that I both did and not exist a hundred years ago." I wonder if Professor Smart wrote this outrageous argument in seriousness, as the first sentence is simply an initial hypothesis equivalent to a denial of backward time travel, and so it seems unnecessary for him to bother saying one word more. How does he know he didn't exist a hundred years ago? Why does he so quickly agree with this assertion? If time travel to the past of a hundred years ago is possible and his time trip to the past won't begin until next year, then Smart simply makes a mistake in so readily agreeing to his earlier nonexistence. If his argument proves anything, it is just that if a time machine can be made, then he well might have existed a hundred years ago! Even the nonenthusiastic analyst of time travel, the British philosopher Jonathan Harrison, has admitted the force of this position [Harrison, 1971].

A variant of Smart's example is found in the well-known college philosophy text by Hospers.[3] Hospers argued against the logical possibility of time travel, writing: "We can imagine ourselves as having been born in a different era and being with the Egyptians building the pyramids. But can we imagine ourselves, *now*, in the 20th century A.D., *being* (not merely in our imagination) in 3000 B.C.? How can we be in the 20th century A.D. and the 30th century B.C. *at the same time*?" This so misstates what is meant by time travel that I doubt Professor Hospers would find many who would agree that his statement is even superficially plausible. A Socratic dialogue is a fine teaching tool, yes, but there is a burden of creating at least a facade of reasonableness in setting up one's red-herrings.

Hospers next tries to play Devil's Advocate and presents the obvious rational rebuttal against this ridiculous straw-man position: " 'But', one may object, 'this is not the situation we are imagining. What we are imagining is being one day in the 20th century and then moving backward in time so that the next day we are in the year 3000 B.C.—and on that day we are no longer in the 20th century A.D.' " This is certainly true, but Professor Hospers then refutes his reasonable statement in a most astonishing manner. In essence, he says that if the first day of your trip is January 1, then the next day in your life has to be January 2, and certainly not some day in 3000 B.C.! Like Smart, Professor Hospers is begging the question because he is saying nothing more than time travel to the past is impossible because it's not possible. It is, so he claims, a contradiction in terms and hence logically impossible. With this we have a grammarian's disproof of time travel when what is really needed is mathematical physics.

Can the Present Change the Past? Can the Past Be Un-Done?

Professor Hospers unleashes what he thinks is the supreme argument against time travel, with an opening line equivalent to asserting the impossibility of time travel: "Many centuries B.C., the pyramids were built, and when all this happened you were not there—you weren't even born. It all happened long before you were born, and it all happened without your assistance or even your observation. This is an unchangeable fact: *you can't change the past*. That is the crucial point: the past is what has happened, and you can't make what has happened not have happened. Not all the king's horses or all the king's men could make what *has* happened *not* have happened, for this is a logical impossibility. When you say that it is logically possible for you (literally) to go back to 3000 B.C. and help build the pyramids, you are faced with the question: did you help them build the pyramids or did you not? The first time it happened, you did *not*: you weren't there, you weren't yet born, it was all over before you came on the scene. All you could say, then, would be that the *second* time it happened, you *were* there—and there was at least a difference between the first time and the second time: the first time you weren't there, and the second time you were."

One science fiction fan long-ago summed up Hospers' argument in a Letter-to-the-Editor to *Astounding Stories* (August 1931): "It is said that the past cannot be changed, and that any effort to do so would be useless. In my belief, no matter where or when a man goes into the past, if he appears in a year or day that has already gone by, *he is changing the past*. Then there should be no room for doubt: time traveling is impossible. It never will be done." Both Hospers and the science fiction fan claim that the past is unchangeable, a claim that is not in dispute. But it simply does not follow, as both assert, that backward time travel is therefore impossible.

Hospers' puzzle is, of course, the grandfather paradox in different clothes. Hospers' error in his argument against time travel, in particular, is precisely at the point where he states his belief that 3000 B.C. occurs twice. In fact, there is no reason for believing this—3000 B.C. (or any year!) happens just once. If you *will* go back to 3000 B.C., then you *were* there; and if you WEREN'T there then you *won't* go. You don't remember 3000 B.C. even if you were there (and even though that year is in the past) because your time trip is not in your past but rather in your (personal) future. This all seems odd, of course, but it is not illogical. Even as Hospers wrote his book, it was known that his reasoning is faulty; certainly, today, the philosophical consensus is that the idea of backward time travel is perfectly consistent with the four-dimensional block Universe as discussed in Chapter Two.

Hospers' error is repeated by a physicist in [Herbert, 1988], who claims that with the existence of a time machine "no longer would there have to be a 'road not taken'—we could simply travel back in time and make some other choice. And if that choice didn't work out, we could go back into the past and try again. In a

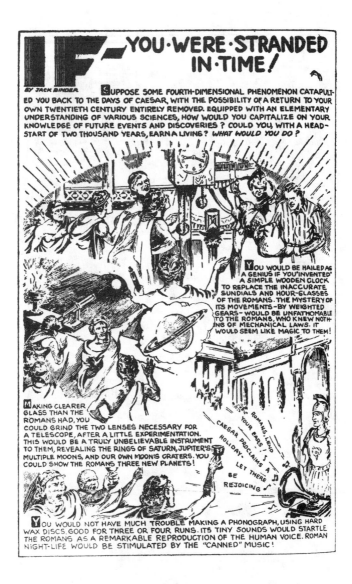

FIGURE 14. Illustrator Jack Binder was author of a continuing series called "IF ... " in *Thrilling Wonder Stories*. The dashed line would each issue be replaced with some phrase like "the Sun exploded," "there was another ice age" or "there was no friction." This installment appeared in December 1938 and asserted that the past could be changed by a time traveler. Binder was the brother of writers Earl and Otto, who under the fused pen-name "Eando" wrote some of the more literate time-travel stories of the 1930s and 1940s (e.g., [Binder, 1940]).

FIGURE 14. Continued.

time-traveling society, our actions would no longer be irreversible." In fact, none of these statements is true precisely because, as Hospers himself states, the past is unchangeable.

Early science fiction writers were just as puzzled by the grandfather paradox as were Hospers and many of his fellow philosophers, but sometimes the writers were more open in admitting so. For example, in "Dark Interlude" [Reynolds and Brown, GRSF1] we read the following from the inventor of the first time machine: "I have devised a method [for travel] into the distant past. The paradox is immediately pointed out—suppose [the time traveler] should kill an ancestor or otherwise change history? I do not claim to be able to explain how this apparent paradox is overcome in time travel; all I know is that time travel *is* possible. Undoubtably, better minds than mine will one day resolve the paradox, but until then we shall continue to utilize time travel, paradox or not." Admirable courage, yes, but certainly not as risky as it sounds now that we realize there is no paradox here at all. Less admirable is the way out used in "Time Dredge" [Arthur, 1942]— here the heroes simply decide not to think about the paradox anymore because it makes them dizzy!

Some medieval theologians argued passionately that the past could be changed, but only by God. The eleventh-century Italian cleric Peter Damian (who became a Christian saint) is a famous exponent of this radical view [McArthur and Slattery, 1974], [Remnant, 1978]. Writing in his *De Omnipotentia Dei* ("On the Divine Omnipotence in Remaking What Has Been Destroyed and in Undoing What Has Been Done"),[4] Damian made it clear he believed nothing could withstand the power of God, not even the past. Ralph Waldo Emerson's beautiful poem "The Past" ("All is now secure and fast, Not the gods can shake the Past") would have been blasphemy for Damian. The following famous words from Damian show the strength of his commitment to a belief in the possibility of changing the past:[5] "Just as we can duly say 'God was able to make it so that Rome, before it had been founded, should not have been founded', in the same way we can equally and suitably say, 'God can make it so that Rome, even after it was founded, should not have been founded'."

Two centuries after Damian, Aquinas argued the contrary view that changing the past is not in God's power to do. While Damian felt it impossible to deny any act to God, Aquinas took the far more moderate position that part of God's law is that there be no contradictions in the world, and that certainly God would be bound by his own law. As he wrote, "It is best to say that what involves contradiction cannot be done rather than that God cannot do it." In his *Paradise Lost*, John Milton's God is constrained even more; he is free to act or not, but if he does freely decide to act, it can only be to "do right." That might seem to preclude causing contradictions, e.g., changing the past, but perhaps not. Milton's contemporary, Thomas Hobbes, for example, declared that there is no *a priori* standard of goodness, and thus (for Hobbes) there are no constraints on God's powers. For Hobbes, therefore, it would seem that God could change the past.

Theological changing of the past leads, as might be expected, to all sorts of mindboggling, logical puzzles. Because of such puzzles, theology would certainly be influenced by time travel, but just as certainly theological reasoning will not answer the question of the possibility of time travel. Philosophers like Hospers who incorrectly argue that similiar change-the-past puzzles occur with backward time travel have simply failed to grasp that time travel is a question for mathematical physics, not for theology. Modern philosophers who understand relativistic physics admit that the past cannot be changed and, further, that backward time travel in no way implies that it could be changed. Yet perhaps one should not be too critical of philosophers like Hospers, as it will be recalled from Chapter One that even the man who started serious time-travel analyses (Kurt Gödel) erroneously believed that backward time travel would allow changing the past.[6]

One philosopher has advanced a nonrelativistic argument for why it is not possible to change the past [Anscombe, 1971]. The stage is set with the seemingly benign words "Things have taken a certain course, which perhaps can and perhaps cannot be reversed; some actions can be undone. But it makes sense to wish they had never been done, and when one says 'The past cannot change' one is stating that this is [impossible]." Anscombe then toughens her stance with "But 'a change in the past' is *nonsense*, as can be seen from the fact that if a change occurs we can ask for its date. If the idea of a change in the past made sense, we could ask the question 'When was the battle of Hastings in 1066?' and that not in the sense 'When in 1066 was the battle of Hastings'. *The idea of change in the past involves the idea of a date being dated* [my emphasis]." Finally, in case the point of her argument has been missed, she hammers her thesis home with "This consideration helps to remove the impression that when one says 'the past cannot change' one is saying of something *intelligible* that it is an impossibility." That is, the phrase 'changing the past' is not an issue that may or may not be possible, but rather it is simply a silly sequence of words devoid of meaning. For Anscombe, philosophers speaking of changing the past are equivalent to veterinarians debating how to best perform a medical procedure on a unicorn.

I happen to agree with Anscombe's conclusion, but as might be expected for an argument supported by the nuances of the meaning of words, there is always someone who interprets the words differently. For example, recall philosophy professor Jack Meiland, the advocate of multidimensional time as discussed in Chapter Three, who used that concept to argue for the logical possibility of changes in the past. Meiland tried to rebut Anscombe's argument. For Meiland, there is (he claims) a perfectly sensible, possible response to Anscombe's question about the date of a change in the past. To use Meiland's example: "Suppose a change occurs in the battle of Hastings after that battle is over. For example, suppose that Harold took part in the battle when it occurred, but after the change in the past battle he was no longer a participant in that battle. At some point in time Harold ceased to take (or to have taken) part in the battle of Hastings. This means that up to a certain point in time, say up to July 20, 1955, the proposition 'Harold participated in the battle of Hastings' is true and after that date that proposition is false. In this way we can date the change in the past battle of Hastings: the change occurred on July 20, 1955."

Curiously enough, Meiland goes on to present what he thinks Anscombe's reply to this might be, but Meiland then *fails to refute it*! That is, Meiland destroys his own position, and I might add that he does a rather thorough job of it. The problem with dating the change of a date is that, as he himself points out, "this method does not show that changes in past events can, even in principle, be dated, because this method is not a method that can in principle be used; we could never find out that the truth value of a proposition about a past event had changed; so we would never be able to assign dates to alleged changes in past events." That is, if an event in the past has changed, there could be no surviving evidence of its prior value—if there is, then the event did not change!

Meiland tried to offer an example of how such evidential issues might occur by using a philosopher's story attached to a version of Damian's thesis that God can change the past. Meiland asks us to consider the situation where a Roman ruin suddenly vanishes one day. With no other explanation available and assuming one believes in God, Meiland asserts that it is reasonable to conclude that God has changed the past so the ruin no longer plays the role in past events it once played. This story begs the question about evidence, however, because *if* we accept Meiland's story, *then* we remember the ruin, and that memory itself is all the evidence needed to assign a date to the change in the past. But why would our memories be unaltered? Of course, we might also wonder why they shouldn't remain unchanged.

The problem is that we are dealing in Meiland's example with a philosopher's fairy tale, not with physics, and there simply isn't anything logical that can be deduced from it about the possibility of changing the past. Anscombe's objection that changes in the past should be datable stands, and Meiland's example is an empty (if entertaining) one. Changing the past, whether by God or by mortal time traveler, is *logically* impossible. As a time traveler in "The Poundstone Paradox" [Dee, 1954] is told, "You can't possibly create a paradox in time, you see, because anything you do in the past must have been done already or you couldn't have been there to do it in the first place."

One philosophical writer [Fraser, 1978] has referred to "the vicious circle of time travel" and has explained why he has this negative reaction as follows, using the faulty argument (à la Hospers) that time travel implies changing the past: "Time travel into the past. (a) Misdirect your grandfather so that he will never meet your grandmother. You do not exist. (b) Find that it is impossible to intefere with the past. You are then a historian, not a time traveler." Fraser's points are not nearly as telling as he seems to think. His (a) is simply not accepted as logical by modern students of time travel because you *do* exist and so your grandfather *did* meet your grandmother. To claim otherwise is like claiming black is white, and if you are going to argue that, then there isn't much left to say. His (b) is somewhat more interesting, but it represents a common misunderstanding of what time travel would mean, a misunderstanding that should be cleared up by the end of this chapter.

Even though the consensus today is that the past cannot be changed, science fiction writers have used the idea of changing the past to good effect. Consider, for example, this passage from *The Fall of Chronopolis* [Bayley, 1974], which is a novel about a "time-war." Temporal invaders have just been detected: "They had come in from the future at high speed, too fast for defensive time-blocks to be set up, and had only been detected by ground-based stations deep in historical territory. If the target was to alter past events—the usual strategy in a time-war—then the empire's chronocontinuity would be significantly interfered with." In *Time of the Fox* [Costello, 1990], American physicists battle KGB physicists in a war of time travelers in the past, with each side attempting to change history to its advantage. In this story the history changers isolate themselves from all the alterations taking place outside their Time Lab, and compare their stored historical records with those of external libraries—this allows the staff historian to adjust for each new round of changes. As the historian explains, outside the Time Lab "History might change, but here [in the Time Lab] the past lives on." And in *Time and Again* [Simak, 1951], a novel of a galactic-wide confrontation between humans and androids, the time-travel idea is integral to "A war in time ... It would reach back to win its battles. It would strike at points in time and space which would not even know that there was a war. It could, logically, go back to the silver mines of Athens, to the horse and chariot of Thutmosis III, to the sailing of Columbus ... It would ... twist the fabric of the past ... " No, contrary to Simak, all those things would *not* be logical (and neither are Bayley's and Costello's novels).

The lesson of the unchangeability of the past is painfully learned by the history student in "Fire Watch" [Willis, 1985]. Sent back a hundred years to the London Blitz of 1940, he becomes part of the fire watch team that saves St. Paul's Cathedral from destruction. But just as the salvation of the church in that war could not be changed, he knows the later vaporization of the church in a nuclear war in the early twenty-first century also can not be avoided.

The movies have often illustrated the uses of time travel to change the past. In the 1960 film *Beyond the Time Barrier*, a test pilot cracks both the speed of sound and the "time barrier" and flies into the year 2024 to a post-nuclear-war world. He returns to the present in an effort to prevent the war from occurring. The 1987 *Timestalkers* gets changing-the-past terribly wrong, with the hero first seeing his family killed in an auto accident and then using a time machine to make that crash not have happened. In the original *Back to the Future* film there is a subtle change-the-past sequence that is easy to miss. When young Marty McFly returns to 1955, he leaves from the parking lot of the Twin Pines Mall, so-named because of the two pine trees that stand nearby. Marty arrives in the past with a bang, inadvertently destroying one of the (then) young pines. Near the end of the movie, when he returns to the future, he finds the mall is now the Lone Pine Mall. This is charming and fun, indeed clever, but modern scholars of time travel reject this, as well as any other claim of changing of the past, as not logically possible. What Marty's trip would explain is why the mall would have always had the name of the Lone Pine Mall. As Lady Macbeth coolly declares concerning the murder of Banquo, "What's done cannot be undone: to bed, to bed, to bed."

Changing vs. Affecting the Past

The fear of time travelers from the future attempting to alter the past has led some philosophers like Hospers and Fraser (and not just a few physicists, too) to assert that time travel is impossible because it would mean the impossible could happen; i.e., changing the past. One philosopher [Geach, 1968], who identified the error in this conclusion (but for the wrong reason, as his paper is a misguided attack on the Minkowskian view of spacetime) wrote: "Squandering vast sums on foolish enterprises is an everyday occurence. [For example,] will the U.S. time explorer get back and eliminate Lenin before his Russian rival gets back even earlier and eliminates George Washington? ... If such spectacular folly once gets under way because governments have been convinced of some nonsensical theory, a logician will not ... lose any sleep about who is going to succeed ... ."

In fact, Geach is correct; you could not travel anywhere into the past unless you've already been there, and when you do make the trip, you will do what you've already done. You could not, as did the time traveler in "Ben Franklin's Laser" [Beason, 1990], change the course of history by revealing twentieth-century physics in the eighteenth century. This does not mean you will necessarily be ineffectual during your stay in the past. Not being able to change the past is not equivalent to being unable to *influence* or *affect* the past. You cannot prevent either the Black Death in the London of 1665 or the Great Fire the following year, but it is logically possible that you—a careless time traveler—could be the cause of either or both. (This was the fate of the time-traveling historian from A.D. 2461 in "The Misfit" [Edmondson, 1965a], who was the cause of plague in Rome A.D. 562 as well as in England nearly 800 years later.) And the entire point, in fact, of the beautiful short story "The Day of the Green Velvet Cloak" [Clingerman, 1958] was how something the modern-day heroine did in the present affected events in 1877. In my own story "Newton's Gift" [Nahin, 1979b], it is the visit of a time traveler from the future that causes Newton's descent from first-rate physics to third-rate theology, about which the time traveler knew from historical records (although he did not know the reason for it).

The distinction between changing and affecting the past has been understood only in relatively recent times. Recall that even Gödel slipped on this point, when he wrote of a time traveler being able to visit himself in the past and then doing something he does not remember having done. To illustrate Gödel's view from a different angle, consider the story "Journey" [Hunter, 1951] in which we find a thirteen-year-old boy going forward in time from 1935 to 1950 to meet himself. It happens on a day he plays hookey, taking a streetcar into Los Angeles—suddenly he finds himself in the future. After seeing a movie, he finds his adult-self and discovers he will be (is) unhappily married with all his ambitions unfulfilled. It is then that the Gödelian objection occurs to him, and as he asks his older-self, "Wouldn't *you* remember [all this] happening to you when *you* were thirteen?" The answer comes back (one Gödel himself apparently never thought of): "One time when I was your age I can remember ditching school and hopping a streetcar to L.A. I know I went to a movie." Then we are told that on the way home that night he couldn't remember what had happened after the movie. In an attempt to change his life, the adult-self then puts his younger-self on a streetcar back home (and to the past) with the admonition "Damn you, *don't forget!*" And the happy (and illogical) ending is that he doesn't forget—and so presumably the future is changed. Isaac Asimov tripped over the mirror image of this error when he wrote [Asimov, 1984b] that "to go into the past and do *anything* would change a great deal of what followed, perhaps everything that followed." Not true.

In *Farnham's Freehold* [Heinlein, 1964], the story of a family that is literally blasted twenty-one centuries into the future when their bomb shelter receives a direct hit from a Soviet nuclear warhead, we find the following exchange as two of the characters are about to return via a time machine:

> "The way I see it, there are no paradoxes in time travel, there can't be. If we are going to make this time jump, then we already did; that's what happened. And if it doesn't work, then it's because it didn't happen."
>
> "But it hasn't happened yet. Therefore, you are saying that it didn't happen, so it can't happen. That's what I said."
>
> "No, no! We don't know whether it has already happened or not. If it did, it will. If it didn't, it won't."

Modern philosophers, and many physicists as well, who have examined the concept of time travel, agree with this explanation from Heinlein's character, and now use the so-called *principle of self-consistency* [Friedman et al., 1990]: "The only solutions to the laws of physics that can occur locally in the real Universe are those which are globally self-consistent." That is, strict causality is not invoked, but only a logical consistency between events at different times is required. Statements of the principle have, in fact, been around in the physics literature for decades. For example, [Driver, 1979] traces it back to 1903! The idea also appeared long ago in science fiction, e.g., in the time-travel story "Time Wants a Skeleton" [Rocklynne, 1980], originally published in 1941, one character, after puzzling over a paradox, realizes "Future and present demanded co-operation, if there was to be a logical future!" (This story was very possibly inspired by the last lines of T.J.D's 1927 letter to *Amazing Stories*, quoted at the beginning of this Chapter.) A hint at the principle is in "Hunters in the Forest" [Silverberg, 1991], made without elaborate explanation, perhaps because the principle is now part of the accepted background knowledge that writers of time-travel science fiction assume in their readers. A man from August 2281 meets in the past a woman from September 2281 while each is on a one-day dinosaur-watching vacation courtesy of "Cretaceous Tours." He thinks, "When we get back [to 2281] maybe I'll look her up.

The September tour, she said. So [I'll] have to wait a while after [my] own return." He concludes this because she does not know him in the past, and thus had not (won't) meet him before her departure. He *must* wait until her return to 2281 if the future and the past are to be consistent.

Recently one writer has turned the principle upside down and has used it to *deny* the possibility of time travel [Waelbroeck, 1991]: "A closed timelike curve is a time machine. A time traveler may follow this path in spacetime and, at the end of his trip, find himself ready to depart. The argument goes that he may then pull out a gun and shoot his younger image, forbidding himself to make the journey. The solution to this paradox is that the end of the time traveler's journey must be consistent with its start. Thus, a closed timelike curve introduces a periodicity condition on the time evolution. Considering the experimental evidence against such periodicity, we will take the conservative view that one should reject any initial data that leads to closed timelike curves." Professor Waelbroeck, however, tells us neither what this experimental evidence is nor how we would ever recognize it!

It is important to realize that there are ways to affect the past that avoid any sense of time travel, but in fact they are mere word games; "Affecting the Past" [Swinburne, 1966] describes several such cases. For example, the truth of the statement 'the atom bomb dropped on Hiroshima was the first of the only two such bombs to destroy populated cities' can be altered by the later actions of statesmen and soldiers. The truth of whether or not Father Jones baptized in 1990 the greatest pianist of the twenty-first century depends on the subsequent career of Baby John. These are trivial examples, of course, and they are not really what we mean by a claim that it is (or is not) possible to affect the past.

Swinburne says that what we really mean by talk of affecting the past is something like "Nothing anyone can do now can make it not to have rained yesterday if, in fact, it *did* rain yesterday." This statement is true, but this is not what is meant by affecting the past, either; rather, it is an example of the impossibility of changing the past. What Swinburne should have written (given the title of his paper and the position he takes in it) is "Nothing anyone can do now can be the *cause* of it not having rained yesterday." If it rained, it rained, and that's final. The philosophical issue still at hand is merely *when* did the cause of the rain occur—before or after the rain? Exploration of this question can be found in the science fiction from more than a half-century ago. In "The Time Bender" [Saari, 1937], for example, a time traveler leaves the Chicago of 1942 for the year 3000. Much later, in the year 2564, another time traveler interested in history journeys back to 2253 in an attempt to learn the cause of the great Chicago explosion of that year. The explosion was centered on the site of an ancient laboratory, once used by a scientist who mysteriously vanished in 1942. The second time traveler begins his journey on the same spot, and plans to go back to the day before the explosion. At the end we learn that disaster was the result of the two time travelers colliding. The backward-traveling historian, by pushing a button in 2564, is the cause of an event that happened 311 years earlier.

A special, historically interesting case of a belief in the possibility of affecting the past is the retroactive petitionary prayer. Examples of such prayers are the surgical patient who prays just before an exploratory operation that his tumor is not malignant, or the soldier's wife who prays that her husband is not among those killed in yesterday's battle. These prayers are for a happy outcome to an event that is over and done with at the time of the prayer. One might accept the rationality of praying about the future ("Please, God, let me survive tomorrow's battle and I'll be good for the rest of my life"), but are prayers about the past even sensible? In an appendix "On 'Special Providences' " in his book on miracles [Lewis, 1978], C. S. Lewis answers this question as follows: "When we are praying about the result, say, of a battle or a medical consultation, the thought will often cross our minds that (if only we knew it) the event is already decided one way or the other. I believe this to be no good reason for ceasing our prayers. The event certainly has been decided—in a sense it was decided 'before all worlds'. But one of the things taken into account in deciding it, and therefore one of the things that really causes it to happen, may be this very prayer that we are now offering. Thus, shocking as it may sound, I conclude that we can at noon become part causes of an event occurring at ten a.m. (Some scientists would find this easier than popular thought does.)"[7]

Here we see Lewis, a prominent lay theologian, arguing for the present influencing (but not changing) the past. What can we make of this? Was Lewis arguing for backward causation? I think perhaps so—the last sentence in the quote above makes it seem he at least might have had it in mind. That is a view, after all, that does find much support in the block-Universe interpretation of Minkowski spacetime. Lewis never mentions the block-Universe concept by name, but it is clear that he believed in the idea of God being able to see all of reality at once (recall the words of Aquinas and Boethius from Chapter Two). Lewis believed, therefore, that God knew of the petitionary prayer before it was made.

There have been all sorts of opinions expressed through the ages in reaction to the idea of affecting the past via the retroactive petitionary prayer, many of which centered on that old bug-a-boo of free will versus determinism that we wrestled with in Chapter Two. Brown [1985] gives a good summary of these opinions, and in particular he adds a clever twist to the free-will issue. Most theologians (as did Lewis) want to retain free will, and backward causation lets them do so, in addition to keeping divine omniscience. That is, it is not God's foreknowledge that causes our later actions, that forces our behavior and turns us into automatons, but rather it is our later actions that cause God's foreknowledge! The philosopher Michael Dummett discusses [Dummett, 1964] Lewis's retrospective-prayer concept with great sympathy.

We find the origin of the modern philosophical debate on the issue of affecting the past in the companion papers [Dummett and Flew, 1954]. Dummett, who believes in the logical possibility of backward causation, unfortunately presented his case in the form of philosopher's stories, an approach I dismissed in Chapter Two as one of questionable merit. Specifically, Dummett asks us to imagine a man who always wakes up in the morning three minutes before his alarm clock goes off (unless he forgot to wind it, and then he sleeps late); a magician who finds the weather is fine in Liverpool yesterday after he recites a spell today (assuming he does not know ahead of the recitation what the weather actually was); a man who finds that if he says "click" before opening an envelope, it never contains a bill. Dummett argues that by broadening our idea of cause we can retain such odd occurrences in a logical world. But since there is simply no evidence for these curious events (they are simply the offspring of Dummett's imaginative mind), why should we be willing to broaden what appears to be an already complete concept of causation? It is like an answer in search of a question that has not yet been asked. Dummett never offers us the slightest physical explanation or even hints of a mechanism for his tales. Whatever may be the truth of his conclusions, his method has no compelling power to persuade.[8]

In his reply rejecting Dummett, however, Antony Flew was no more successful in convincing the reader of the logic of his own argument. He would not even give Dummett the inch of being willing to entertain the logical possibility of backward causation (which is all Dummett was claiming). Flew declared "that the cause must be prior to ... the effect is not a matter of fact but a truth of logic." This sounds very much like Aristotle, who like Galileo could have simply dropped two unlike balls to see what would happen, but who instead preferred to argue "logically"—and falsely, and with such a declaration there is nothing left to say. Flew, of course, convinced few with such a begging of the question. Indeed, he had completely missed the point, as was pointed out some years later in [Brier, 1973], which correctly charged Flew with having confused changing and affecting the past. In a reply immediately following Professor Brier's paper, Professor Flew showed that the arrow had hit the mark, as Flew wrote that he found the distinction between the two concepts "quite breathtakingly perplexing." Compounding this admission of ignorance about the difference between changing and affecting the past, Flew went on to declare that the distinction Brier was attempting to make was "one with which any faithful reader of the philosophical journals is [not] acquainted."

This prompted a reply [Dwyer, 1977], which took as its goal the education of Professor Flew on this central issue. Referring to an earlier critique of Hospers [Dwyer, 1975], Dwyer wrote of a Gödelian time traveler visiting the past in a rocket: "Time travel, entailing as it does backward causation, does not involve changing the past. The time traveler does not undo what has been done or do what had not been done, since his visit to an earlier time does not change the truth values of any propositions concerning the events of that period. Thus even before the time traveler enters his rocket in 1978 to begin his successful mission to the year 3000 B.C., an accurate catalogue of all the events occurring in Ancient Egypt that year would include an account of his arrival from the sky, as well as an account of his various actions and reactions in that new environment. The contents of such a catalogue may never be revealed but that is beside the point. And yet, while the time traveler thus does not *change* the past when he goes back to it (for he cannot *do* anything in 3000 B.C. that was not *done* in that year) he does *affect* the past in that the arrival of his rocket, as well as his pyramid-building activities, etc., are members of the class of events that characterize the (unique) year 3000 B.C. It seems to me that there is a clear distinction to be made here, between the case where a person is presumed to change the past, which indeed involves a contradiction, and the latter case where a person is presumed to affect the past by dint of his very presence in that period."

Dwyer's paper concludes with the statement that "certain criticisms of backward causation theories, such as Flew's response to Brier, are ... easily seen, in the context of time travel, to be based on misunderstandings." Another philosopher Dwyer would surely accuse of misunderstanding time travel is J. R. Lucas, who in writing about time-machine stories says:[9] "Often we are invited to imagine ourselves witnessing past events. Provided we are inactive and invisible, no paradox need ensue. If we are merely passive spectators, we are not altering the unalterable past; and provided we cannot be seen, heard or felt by any of the actors of the events, our presence makes no difference, and the purity of the past is preserved untouched." As does Hospers, Lucas appears to think the past happens twice, once without the time traveler and then again with the traveler.

For Dwyer's presentation to have persuasive power we must, of course, be willing to accept at least the *possibility* of time travel; else we are reduced to the telling of a new philosopher's story that tries to explain one extraordinary idea (backward causation) in terms of another even more extraordinary one (time travel). For the thesis of this book, the importance of Dwyer's 1977 paper is that in it he explicitly gives us a rational mechanism: "One can provide an *explanation* for time travel in terms of the field equations of General Relativity, together with initial conditions of the distribution of mass-energy in a certain region of space-time."

I agree with Dwyer, but of course not everybody does. For example, in [Spellman, 1982] we find: "I do not intend to enter the debate over whether time travel is conceivable. What I do want to hold, however, is that there is no reason to call Dwyer's example *backward* causation. Dwyer describes pyramid building as in the [time traveler's] 'causal future' but part of his 'chronological past'. But if time travel is possible, what reason is there for saying that pyramid building *precedes* the rocket's firing? Rather, from the [time traveler's] point of view, what happens is perfectly ordinary causation—an earlier event (rocket firing) causes a *later* one (arrival at one's destination)." Spellman is certainly correct in his logic, as far as it goes, but what of the point of view of a non-time-traveling observer who watches the entire process linearly from 3000 B.C. to A.D. 1978? For him (and if such a lengthy life span is bothersome, just replace 3000 B.C. with A.D. 1950) the process certainly *does* involve backward causation.

As discussed in Chapter One, many science fiction stories have gone to great lengths to show how time travelers would have to be excruciatingly careful on a trip to the past, e.g., Ray Bradbury's "A Sound of Thunder." At the other extreme is "Over the River & Through the Woods" [Simak, TC], which intentionally tries to change the past. While modern philosophers may find such stories charming, they rightfully reject them as illogical. These stories are illogical because they erroneously make the analogy of time travel into the past with ordinary travel through space. With the latter you can indeed visit places you have never been to before, and once there you can do things you never did before.

Not so, however, with time travel. When the narrator in *A Time to Remember* [Shapiro, 1986], wondering if he can save Kennedy from Oswald, asks "Can I really go back to 1963 and stop the unspeakable crime, to unstitch historical fabric and resew the past?" the answer is no. You can't save Joan of Arc with a fire extinguisher either or Jesus with a rifle (see "The Rescuer" [Porges, SFS]) because either you weren't there then and so you can't *be* there then, or if you were (are going to be) there then, we already know you failed. Trying to intercept John Wilkes Booth outside of Ford's Theatre or warning the Nazis of D-Day are equally doomed. And as a special, personal case, if some day you come into possession of a time machine, it will be similarly futile to attempt to visit yourself at any time you know you were alone. Go back to a time when there were lots of people around, but don't try to talk to yourself (unless you recall a time when a mysterious yet somehow familiar stranger approached you with talk about traveling through time!) If you *weren't* then, you can't *be* then. As Shakespeare's Pericles observes, "Time's the king of men; He's both their parent, and he is their grave, And gives them what he will, not what they crave."

In Poul Anderson's "time war" novel *The Corridors of Time* [Anderson, 1966], a twentieth-century man recruited by a visitor from the future exclaims: " 'Huh? Wait! You mean you people *change* the past?' " The logical reply, from his visitor: " 'Oh, no. Never. That is inherently impossible. If one tried, he would find events always frustrated him. What has been, is. We time travelers are ourselves part of the fabric.' "

A failure to understand this time traveler's point is the rock on which "Sidetrack in Time" [McGivern, 1941] crashes. This is the story of the inventor of a time machine whose assistant plots to do away with him and steal his gadget. Emotionally unable simply to shoot the inventor, the assistant waits until their first test trip, a 5000-year forward journey. There he knocks the inventor down, leaps into the time machine, and returns alone. His victim is as good as dead, he thinks, stranded in the far future. The assistant's plan develops a fatal twist, however, as upon his return to the time machine laboratory he sees and hears the inventor—he has accidently returned to the day *before* the start of the test! His nerve breaks under the shock, and pulling a gun he shoots himself dead—"the blasting report reverberated through the lab." But this did not happen in the initial description of that day (and it would have been hard for the assistant to have overlooked his own death), and so it cannot happen.

The distinction between changing and affecting the past also provides an answer to the so-called "cumulative audience paradox" in the novel *Up the Line* [Silverberg, 1969]. This paradox claims that as time travelers to the past continue to visit certain historically interesting dates, there will be an ever-increasing number of people present. (Recall Stephen Hawking's *Chronology Protection Conjecture* from Chapter One, and Kip Thorne's response to it in that chapter's Note 21. As stated in the novel, "Taken to its ultimate, the cumulative audience paradox yields us the picture of an audience of billions of time-travelers piled up in the past to witness the Crucifixion, filling all the Holy Land and spreading out into Turkey, into Arabia, even to India and Iran ... Yet at the original occurrence of [that event], *no such hordes were present!*" And later, more poetically, "A time is coming [when we] will throng the past to the choking point. We will fill all our yesterdays with ourselves and crowd out our own ancestors." The proper conclusion to make from this is not that therefore there were no time travelers present at the Crucifixion, but rather that *all* the time travelers who are *ever* present at that event are in the "original" hordes. (Siverberg's use of the word *original* is also objectionable, as it is a repeat of Hospers' error in believing the past happens more than once.)

A quite clever story that has its subtle but quite fatal flaw in a failure to appreciate the difference between changing and affecting the past is "The Ring" [Hudec, PWO], which illustrates object duplication (which Silverberg calls a special case of the cumulative audience paradox). A time traveler makes a huge amount of money by selling the same diamond ring ninety-four times; that is, he sells ninety-four different rings, yet the rings are "identical, definitely and absolutely, down to the last atom." There is no crime involved here, no fraud, as the rings are each worth every penny charged. But a police inspector is intrigued and manages to get the story—the time traveler merely went back to seventeenth-century Amsterdam and bought the same ring over and over, each time one hour earlier than before, until the time when the jeweler had not yet himself acquired the ring! From the Minkowskian spacetime view, however, when he presented himself the first time (for him, but the last time for the jeweler) he would have been thought crazy—"But sir," the jeweler would cry, "you have already bought the ring of which you speak!" The ring would simply not be in the jeweler's shop after the purchase furthest back in time. The same idea (and flaw) can be found in the much earlier "The Fourth-Dimensional Demonstrator" [Leinster, OW].

Perhaps the classic of object-duplication stories is the enormously clever, diabolical "My Name is Legion" [del Rey, SFF]. In this story the object duplication is accomplished by "reaching into the *future*," not the past; the inventor of the gadget that does this (whose wife and children had been murdered by the Hitler Youth) explains, "I pull an object back from its future to stand beside its present. I multiply it in the present. As you might take a straight string and bend it into a series of waves or loops, so that it met itself repeatedly." The string is certainly Del Rey's metaphor for the world line of the object. What gives this story particular power is that the duplicated object is Adolf Hitler, duplicated 7000 times (one from each of the subsequent twenty-four hours for the next 20 years), with each increasingly older copy being slightly more decrepit than the last. (The story appeared in 1942, before Hitler's real fate was known). The mind of Hitler is thus forced to live through the next twenty-four hours 7000 times. (Del Rey avoids

Silverberg's error of repeating history 7000 times by having 7000 Hitlers present at once, instead of one additional Hitler for each repetition.)

Some writers of fiction find object duplication so objectionable that they simply deny it. In [Compton, 1971], for example, when Roses Varco (the mentally retarded time traveler we met in Chapter One) returns to the year he was (is) eighteen, he is "found [by the equivalent of Varley's cosmic disgust theory] to be philosophically impossible." He simply vanishes with "a roar like that of an express train," leaving behind no trace other than the strange odor of the novel's strange title; *Hot Wireless Sets, Aspirin Tablets, the Sandpaper Sides of Used Matchboxes, and Something that Might Have Been Castor Oil.*

An early, but scientifically sophisticated spacetime presentation of the basic idea behind all these stories, again in science fiction, is in "Forgotten Past" [Morrison, 1943]. One character explains it all to another: "Most of this talk of time travel is rot. Notice that I don't say all of it, but most of it. You can't travel into the past. The past is an infinite region in the four-dimensional space-time continuum whose nature has been completely determined. All the world-lines, as Minkowski put it, the world-surfaces, the world-volumes are completely known. Traveling in the past would change them. It can't be done." This argument loses its force, of course, given the position taken in this book; that is, if one accepts the idea that the world lines of the time traveler are bent back into the past; and so time travel does not change the past but rather is built into the past. The story "The Chronoclasm" [Wyndham, 1956] also fails to grasp this idea, and it is full of erroneous concerns by all the characters, concerns that time-traveling historians are changing the past, when in fact all the quirky historical happenings cited (e.g., Hero demonstrating a steam-turbine in B.C. Alexandria, Archimedes using napalm ["Greek fire"] at the siege of Syracuse, and Da Vinci's drawings of parachutes) *are* history. The leakage of information by loose-tongued time travelers is not changing the past, but rather is affecting it. It is, in fact, necessary for this leakage to occur to avoid altering the past as we know it.

Some stories, however, have correctly distinguished affecting the past from changing it. For example, in "The Time Cheaters" [Binder, 1940], a friend tries to talk two time travelers into having a little fun after their successful initial test trip and before they leave 1941 New York for the future: "Why not take in the World's Fair before you leave again? You won't have another chance. Or—uh—will you?" [This shows the risk of predicting the future—the story appeared March 1940, while the Fair was still open, but it closed just a few months later, in October, after declaring bankruptcy.] One of the chrononauts answers with a laugh, "We will. We'll have the distinction of going into the future, reading about the Fair being over, and then coming back to see it!" Replies the friend, "I don't believe it! You can't do that ... If the Fair is over without you two being in it, you never *were* in it."

Another such tale, one of the best, is "The Biography Project" [Gold, MT], about the Biotime Camera that can film the past (alas, no sound). Using this wonderful gadget, the Biofilm Institute funds teams of biographers to study the lives of past great leaders. In particular, the lives of those who developed neurotic psychoses are of great interest, including Robert Schumann, Marcel Proust, and Isaac Newton. And, indeed, the Biotime Camera does capture these individuals' images as they begin to display increasingly disturbed behavior. Newton, for example, is watched as he begins to peer into dark corners, looking for those he believes are spying on him. On his death bed the biography team assigned to him reads his lips and discovers that his final words are "My guardian angel. You've watched over me all my life. I am content to meet you now." It is then that the Biofilm Institute realizes what it's done. Newton *was* in fact being spied upon—by the Biotime Camera, which has not changed the past, but *has* affected it. (Present medical thought is that Newton's odd behavior was due to mercury poisoning from alchemy experiments, not from being time viewed!)

The idea of time-viewing has recently appeared again in the popular, nonfictional literature. John L. Cotter, curator emeritus of The University Museum of the University of Pennsylvania, was so inspired by his reading of the wormhole time machine report in [Morris, Thorne, and Yurtsever, 1988] that he responded as follows:[10] "Thorne and his colleagues ... say that if travel into the past is theoretically possible, this possibility would have 'profound philosophical consequences'. It sure would. It could put archaeologists out of business. It would also offer a dilemma for historians and theologians. Imagine reviewing the actual lifetimes of Moses, Jesus, Mohammed, or Gautama Buddha, to say nothing of Lucy, Neanderthal Man, the artists who painted Lascaux Cave, Ikhnaton, Sargon, and Julius Caesar." Cotter then offered up an unsettling new observation for most of his readers (but which we recognize as the Biotime Camera): "It must occur to us that *we* may be viewed by those living 2,000 or more years in the future." Ponder that the next time you *think* you're alone before you do anything you'd hate to see show up in a graduate student's doctoral thesis in the fortieth century!

The two *Terminator* movies incorporate both affecting and changing the past. The central idea common to these movies is that after a self-aware military computer intentionally starts the nuclear holocaust of 1997, killer-machines enter into a continuing conflict with the human survivors, who are inspired by a charismatic leader. In the original *Terminator*, the machines send a killer-colleague back to 1984 to change the past by terminating the mother-to-be of the leader-to-be before he is born. To counter this, the leader sends a friend back to warn his mother—and this friend becomes his father. That is, the leader exists in 2029 because in that year he does something that *affects* 1984; he arranges for his father to meet his mother! In the 1991 sequel, *Terminator* 2, we learn how the self-aware computer came into being. At the end of the original movie, the killer-robot is destroyed before it can complete its (impossible) task, but a single computer chip from its "brain" is salvaged—the high-tech innovations of that chip lead to the invention of the self-aware computer and, therefore, to the war of 1997. In the second movie, a second robot is sent back in time to kill the leader as a child (another impossible task), and again the killer is thwarted. Indeed, that machine fails precisely because the leader sends back another robot to protect himself (as a boy). In addition, that second "good robot" finds and destroys the advanced computer chip left in the past of 1984 before it can be deciphered; this prevents the construction of the self-aware computer.

These two movies send the message that by changing the past the future can be changed, an assertion that most physicists (and philosophers, too) would say has no meaning. The general conclusion, then, is that you cannot change the past, but you might well be able to affect it. This view rejects, for example, the position taken in "Pebble in Time" [Goldstone and Davidson, 1970], which relates how an elder of the Church of Latter-Day Saints invented a time machine so he could travel back to 1847 to watch Brigham Young declare "*This is the place!*" at what would become Salt Lake City. Inadvertently interferring with the past, however, the shocked time traveler hears instead "*This is not the place! Onward!*," and watches B.Y. continue on to San Francisco. As home of the Morman Church, of course, San Francisco becomes associated with the initials L.D.S. (which, recalling this story appeared in 1970, constitutes a period joke on the well-known initials associated with the drug culture of that time and place, L.S.D.) In contrast, when in Michael Moorcock's brilliant novel *Behold the Man* [Moorcock, 1969] a disturbed man journeys backward in time to ancient Galilee to meet Christ, he discovers that there is no such person and so he assumes the role and lives out the biblical accounts up to and including dying on the Cross. He has not changed the past, but he certainly plays (affects) an important role in it!

Physicists who worry about cosmic disaster if a time machine were actually built or who reject physical theories because they predict time travel are simply worrying about a nonproblem.[11] Even if time travel is possible, you cannot go back and kill your grandfather before your father is conceived (or even "better," you cannot kill yourself), but it *is* logically possible that you could be the one who introduces your grandfather to your grandmother.[12] Even the funny conversation two time travelers have with themselves in a time loop (we see it twice, once from each side of the exchange) in the 1989 movie *Bill & Ted's Excellent Adventure* is logical.

Why Can't a Time Traveler Kill His Grandfather?

When all is said about the impossibility of changing the past and when they are finally willing to concede this point, even then most people still cannot help wondering *why* the time traveler can't kill his grandfather? There the time traveler is, after all, just two feet away from the nasty young codger (I assume he is nasty to make the whole unpleasant business as palatable as possible); a perfectly functioning and well-oiled revolver is in his hand, cocked and loaded with powerful factory-fresh ammunition that even Dirty Harry would find excessive—what can possibly prevent the time traveler from simply raising his arm and doing the deed? Indeed, the opening illustration to "Thompson's Time Traveling Theory" [Weisinger, 1944] shows this act in detail, including the smoking gun in the hand of the time traveler who has just taken a shot at grandpop. And if that still leaves open the remote possibility of an aiming error through nervousness, then why can't a suicidal time traveler just wrap his entire body in factory-fresh dynamite and blow up granddad (as well as himself and everything else within a hundred feet)!?

As the rest of this section will demonstrate, killing your grandfather is *logically* impossible. No one will ever find a note in the empty laboratory of a missing time traveler who, skeptical of the grandfather paradox, has written: "To prove the falsity of the grandfather paradox, I will take my time machine back fifty years and kill my grandf ... ." Nor will the inventor of a time machine have to be concerned about the pretty little twist in Fredric Brown's "First Time Machine" [Brown, 1958]. The inventor of a time machine shows the gadget to three friends; one of them steals the machine to go back sixty years to kill his grandfather; the story closes with a repeat of the opening, with the inventor showing the gadget to *two* friends.

It is a shame that the classic time-travel paradox takes such a murderous form, but that is the historical origin of the idea. One Letter-to-the-Editor at *Astounding Stories* (January 1933) commented on this as follows: "Why pick on grandfather? It seems that the only way to prove that time travel is impossible is to cite a case of killing one's own grandfather. This incessant murdering of harmless ancestors must stop. Let's see some wide-awake fan make up some other method of disproving the theory." As we proceed, we will find how clever have been those who have answered that fan's plea; but even today, even as it stands revealed as a red-herring, it is the grandfather paradox that stands preeminent.

If an answer to the grandfather puzzle escaped early science fiction writers, they would just mysteriously refer to it and then quickly pass on to other matters. For example, in "The Time Mirror" [South, 1942] we have the following exchange between the stock pulp-fiction characters of a young hero and a brilliant old scientist:

> "You mean that time travel really is possible? That men can be transported into the future or the past—."
>
> The other held up a restraining hand. "Yes. Time travel *is* possible ... "
>
> "But professor! Think of what you're saying! You're telling me that I could go back and murder my own grandfather. That I could prevent myself from being born—."
>
> Again the elder man sighed. "I was afraid of this," he said. "I knew you could not understand." He hesitated. Then: "At any rate, take my word for it that time travel is possible. Also, I assure you that there are any number of perfectly sound theoretical and practical reasons why you never could hope to murder your grandparents."

We are, however, not told just what these reasons might be.

The earliest story that I've found in which a time traveler specifically kills his grandfather in the past is "The Time Tragedy" [Palmer, 1934], but the paradoxical aspects of the act are not developed. One year before, however, the far more sophisticated story "Ancestral Voices," based on the possibility of killing more

FIGURE 15. The inventor of a time machine demonstrates it by sending the family cat on a trip, in this illustration from Raymond A. Palmer's "The Time Tragedy" (*Wonder Stories*, Dec. 1934). The inventor travels back to 1901 where he accidently kills his grandfather in an early, nonparadoxical version of the famous riddle.

Illustration for "The Time Tragedy" by Frank R. Paul, ©1934 by Continent Publications Inc.; reprinted by permission of the Ackerman Science Fiction Agency, 2495 Glendower Ave., Hollywood, CA 90027 for the Estate.

ancient ancestors, caused a brief stir [Schachner, 1933]. In Schachner's tale people vanish by the tens of thousands because *one* man is killed fifteen centuries
earlier. Schachner himself seems to have believed this makes sense, as in a Letter-
to-the-Editor of *Astounding Stories* (December 1933) he wrote that " 'ancestral
Voices' attempts the logical unfolding" of the grandfather paradox. A subsequent
flurry of fan letters to the magazine, however, showed that many readers did not
find the story at all logical. But other writers found the grandfather paradox irresistible; twenty years later the time traveler in "Time Goes to Now" [Dye, 1953]
topped Schachner's story by accidentally killing the original "intelligent baboon" in
the ancient past, thereby wiping out the entire human race!

The grandfather paradox nags and pulls at all students of time travel. As a
character in "Typewriter From the Future" [Worth, 1950] says, "The resolution of
[the grandfather paradox] is the key to time." And it *is* troublesome (if not quite as
central to the core of time as Worth so melodramatically declared). As [Gorovitz,
1964] says, time travel and its concommitant backward causation (e.g., the apparent possibility of the time traveler to do away with both his grandfather and
himself) gives "rise to such puzzles that we are forced to question its intelligibility."
Gorovitz correctly believes that the past cannot be changed, and so these potential
acts of violence simply can't happen. But then he goes on to say that the inability
of the time traveler to kill either himself or his grandfather results in our being
"faced with the problem of explaining why it is [he] cannot fire the gun or, if [he]
can, why it is [he] can fire only in certain directions [i.e., the ones that miss]."
Gorovitz asserts that there can only be two possible answers: "Either the gun is not
behaving as the normal physical object we take it to be, or the notion of voluntary
action does not apply in the usual way." (Here, at last, we have explicit concern
over the issue of free will.) Herbert [1988], too, calls the grandfather paradox the
strongest argument he knows against time travel, and one of the characters in
"Thompson's Time Traveling Theory" [Weisinger, 1944] uses the grandfather paradox to conclude that "all time traveling stories are one hundred percent sheer oil
of over-ripe bananas!"

Gorovitz has gotten himself into his logical quagmire precisely because, like
Hospers, he is now thinking of the past as happening twice—once without the
time traveler and his gun, and again with him and it. With this second chance,
Gorovitz argues, the time traveler should have the ability to do something that
wasn't done on the first try. So why can't he? The puzzle is all of Gorovitz's own
making because he is violating his own fundamental belief in the unchangeable
nature of the past. Assuming that the time traveler did once confront his grandfather (or himself), then he *must* fail because he *did* fail. To demand an accounting
for the specific why of failure before accepting the failure is as misguided as a
stranded motorist refusing to believe his car won't start until he knows why.

Some science fiction stories have missed this point and have invoked forces
(mysterious and otherwise) to protect the fragile past from future tampering; e.g.,
the so-called "time police." These time commandos roam the corridors of time,
disrupting the plans of those who would change history to suit their personal

desires. Stories of temporal cops are simply westerns, or mysteries, or police procedurals, or some other similiar speciality story form wearing thin camouflage, and this story device can be, as [Lewis, 1976] calls it, "a boring invasion."[16] So why do we find it so often in fiction, as in Poul Anderson's many stories about the time patrol? As do the writers of such stories, many philosophers feel it is the only way to have both time travel and free will. Let me give two examples of this supposed conflict.

First, returning one last time to Professor Hospers, we find the following tale: "Our hero in 1900 pulls the lever [of his time machine] and finds himself in ... the future. There he meets a girl, marries her, and takes her back with him in the time machine to the year 1900. The girl wasn't born until A.D. 40,000, yet she gave birth to his child in 1900, long before she was born. One is tempted to speculate: What if he had decided, in the year 40,000, *not* to marry her and bring her back after all? Then her child (born in 1900 though the mother wasn't born until 40,000) wouldn't have been born either; and yet after 1900 he had already been born. Indeed, that child might have become the prime minister of Britain, and affected the course of the world in such a way that no human beings would have existed on the Earth in the year 40,000: What if there had been a nuclear explosion in 1990 that obliterated life forever from the Earth?"

All these questions tell us more about Hospers' badly mangled concept of what constitutes a paradox than they do of time travel. To complain about the girl giving birth before her own birth is to beg the question of time travel itself; this is simply backward causation, which is inherent with time travel. The free-will issue arises when Hospers wonders "what if" the hero does not bring the girl back to 1900— the answer is simply that then the time traveler's son won't have been born in 1900 and he would not have gone on to become the prime minister responsible for wiping all life out in A.D. 40,000. Indeed, if all life is so wiped out, it is Hospers' obligation to explain to us why the girl is alive then! On the other hand, if his son was born in 1900, then the hero *must* bring the girl back—it is the *must* that bothers Hospers. But Hospers has created these problems for himself by demanding to have matters both ways. If there was a nuclear explosion in 1990 that obliterated all life, then the hero simply would not find a girl in 40,000. Again, Hospers has manufactured his own puzzle by claiming both that the girl is there in A.D. 40,000 *and* that all life vanishes forever in 1990. There is no more of a paradox in this than in first declaring a gun is empty without any evidence for it and then being surprised when you shoot yourself in the foot.

Martin Gardner makes the same kind of argument [Gardner, 1982] and the same error in his tale of Professor Brown, who goes forward 30 years, carves his name on an oak tree, and then returns to the present—and then promptly cuts the tree down! How, asks Gardner, if Brown cuts the tree down now, can it be there 30 years in the future for him to carve his name into? The answer is simply that if the tree exists in the future, then the Professor simply didn't (won't) cut it down— or if he does cut it down, then it won't be there 30 years later. Gardner forces the paradox himself by demanding that the tree be there. What is really bothering

FIGURE 16. A time-machine inventor makes an experimental test of the grandfather paradox in this illustration from [Weisinger, 1944].

Illustration for "Thompson's Time Traveling Theory" by Malcolm Smith, ©1944 by Ziff-Davis Publishing Co.; reprinted by arrangement with Forrest J. Ackerman, Holding Agent, 2495 Glendower Ave., Hollywood, CA 90027.

Gardner is that if the Professor does find the tree in the future, then why can't he cut it down upon his return? This is the mirror image of the grandfather paradox, of course. The answer is the same—we don't know why; we just know that the Professor won't (perhaps his axe will break or he will be arrested for attempted vandalism, etc., etc.) And there is no second (or third or fourth) chance—the Professor's world line in spacetime brings him to the tree *once* and he fails (for some reason) to cut it down.

One science fiction story that does get the grandfather paradox right is the clever "Thompson's Time Traveling Theory" [Weisinger, 1944]. A time traveler journeys back from 1943 to 1870 and shoots his then fourteen-year old grandfather in the head. Leaving his victim lying on the ground with "blood oozing all over the youth's forehead," the would-be killer returns to 1943. Once back, however, he finds himself in a strange place where he learns from two men that the Germans destroyed New York in 1920 with poison gas! Suddenly realizing the death of his grandfather has apparently changed history (a curious oversight for anyone smart enough to invent a time machine), he decides he'd rather be dead than cutoff for all time from *his* world, and so he shoots himself. As he lies dead, we learn the two men are really inmates in an asylum who like to make up stories for unsuspecting strangers—and that the time-traveler's grandfather's photographs *always* did show him with a "white, furrowed-scar on his forehead that might have been caused by a glancing bullet."

In an attempt to analyse the free-will issue in time travel in the context of the grandfather-type of paradox, Paul Thom presents an interesting grammatical analysis [Thom, 1975]. Professor Thom asks us to imagine the usual situation: a time traveler as a mature man travels into the past and confronts himself as a boy. Can the time traveler kill the boy (himself)? As I have argued, the answer is yes, but also that he won't because he didn't. The fact that he won't (didn't) doesn't mean he can't (couldn't). But now Thom pursues this and says that if the time traveler *can*, then one would appear to be on safe ground in assuming that there is no logical inconsistency in imagining this "could happen" event actually occurring. But, of course, the time traveler killing his younger version would lead to a logical paradox, thus seeming to refute the possibility of a possible event actually occurring! If this is so, then what does (what could) *possible* mean?

Professor Jack Meiland has made a very pointed reply to this paradox in his [Meiland, 1974]. There he writes of time-travel suicide (a theme treated fictionally in "Mission" [Neville, 1953]): "If we assume that it is impossible for [a time traveler] to kill his younger self, some people are inclined to ask such questions as this: 'But how can the laws of logic prevent him from killing his younger self? Do they cause his finger to slip on the trigger or the bullet to fly apart in mid-air?' The implication of such questions is that the laws of logic cannot prevent such actions. But such questions are like asking: 'How do the laws of logic prevent the geometer from trisecting the angle or squaring the circle? Do they, for example, cause his ruler to slip at a crucial moment every time he tries it?' " A similiar point was made later, with a different example, in [Arntzenius, 1990]: "Surely it is not an impairment of 'freedom of action' ... that, e.g., you cannot push another person any harder than he/she pushes you. Just as one would explain this is the case by reference to Newton's third law, one could explain the impossibility of [causing a paradox] by reference to the laws which imply such an impossibility. If this explanation is taken to be unsatisfactory, it would seem that one is saddled with a general problem concerning the reconciliation of physics and 'freedom', and not with a specific argument against [paradoxes]."

The short (29-minute) 1963 French film *La Jette* accurately captures the concept of a time traveler moving on a closed timelike curve that brings him together fatally with a younger-self. After the Third World War has rendered the Earth's surface so radioactive that the survivors are driven underground, experiments in time travel are started in an attempt to escape the horrors of the present. The first trial uses a man obsessed with a childhood memory of seeing, while he is watching the planes at Orly airport, a running man shot dead on the runway. The initial test sends him into the past, where he falls in love with a beautiful woman. Then he is pulled back to the present to prepare for a second test, this one a trip to the future. That test succeeds, too, but while there he asks the denizens of the future to use their advanced knowledge to send him directly back to the past, to his love. This they do, and he arrives in the past at Orly airport. Seeing the woman, he runs toward her, but is shot by one of the time-travel experimenters from the "present" (who has followed him into the past to execute him for his attempt at personal escape). As he falls dead on the runway, his final thought is that "one cannot escape time," that he himself was the man he saw shot when he was a child; and, indeed, he realizes that his child-self is even then watching him as he dies.

A blatant, explicit rejection of free will combined with a passionate embrace of the block-Universe concept is in "Beep" [Blish, 1976]. Here one character tells another after discovering how to receive radio signals from the future: "I *was* going to do all those things. There were no alternatives, no fanciful 'branches in time', no decision-points that might be altered to make the future change. My future, like yours ... and everybody else's, was fixed. It didn't matter a snap whether or not I had a decent motive for what I was going to do; I was going to do it anyhow. Cause and effect ... just don't exist. One event follows another because events are just as indestructible in space-time as matter and energy are." Blish's tale is actually a sophisticated elaboration of the much earlier story "The Time Annihilator" [Manley and Thode, 1930]. In that story time travelers from 1945 see the destruction of humanity in 2250—and realize there is nothing they can do to avoid it. In his editorial introduction to Manley and Thode's tale, Hugo Gernsback wrote that "we cannot change the future by one iota. No matter how we strain against and battle against the events of some future era, we cannot alter them the least bit. They are written indelibly in the book of fate."

To many the philosophical view of the rejection of free will, as expressed by Gernsback and by the stories of Manley and Thode, and of Blish, may seem awful (and to others it might eliminate a lot of guilt for poor past decisions), but it contrasts greatly with the statements made at the conclusion of the 1990 film *Back to the Future III*, (obviously directed at the youngsters in the audience) that the future is theirs to make. This film takes the view expressed in Melville's *Mardi*: "The future is all hieroglyphics." This position is also taken in the 1991 movie *Terminator 2*, in which the past is changed to change the future—at one point, a character carves the words "No Fate" into a table top.

In an afterword to his story "Dead City" [Leinster, 1946], Murray Leinster observed: "You've heard the old argument that a man can't travel backward in time because he might kill his grandfather. I've wondered why nobody has argued that a man can't travel forward in time because he might be killed by his grandson." Perhaps nobody argued this because it isn't much of a puzzle. The answer to it is simply that if at the moment our forward-bound time traveler departs, he has not yet sired a child, then there simply won't be a murderous grandson waiting for him. Or if he has sired a child before his trip begins, then there could be an ungrateful descendent who, without paradox, could indeed kill him.

One writer who no doubt would disagree with nearly all I have written in this section is Martin Gardner, who wrote [Gardner, 1979] "In all time-travel stories where someone enters the past the past is necessarily altered. The only way the logical contradictions created by such a premise can be resolved is by positing a Universe that splits into separate branches the instant the past is entered."[13] As I have argued, I think Gardner is mistaken, with his confusion originating in a failure to distinguish properly between changing and affecting the past. But his last line *is* intriguing. Indeed, it leads us into the next section, where we find how some physicists have invoked quantum mechanics as well as general relativity in their analyses of time travel.

Quantum Mechanics and Time Travel

One early science fiction technique for allowing backward time travel and a changeable past while still avoiding paradoxes is that of alternate Universes. According to this idea, if a time traveler journeys into the past and introduces a change (indeed, his very journey may be the change), then, as Gardner stated, reality splits into two versions, with one fork representing the result of the change and the other fork the original reality before the change. (To a fifth-dimensional observer, of course, all conceivable forks, all possible four-dimensional space-times, have always existed.) Indeed, with this view the entire Universe is splitting, every microinstant along every alternative decision path for every particle. This is often called the *theory of alternate realities with parallel time tracks*.

This fantastic view seems actually to have some scientific plausibility to it too because of the so-called many-worlds interpretation of quantum mechanics pioneered by Hugh Everett III in his 1957 Princeton doctoral dissertation. For this book, however, the underlying scientific theory of time travel is classical (i.e., nonquantum) general relativity, and this theory has nothing to say about alternate time tracks. For most time-travel theoreticians, there is *one* time track and the past is unique and inviolate. I agree with the great quantum physicist J. S. Bell, who (in "Quantum Mechanics for Cosmologists" in [Bell, 1987]) wrote of the Everett theory that, "if such a theory were taken seriously it would hardly be possible to take anything else seriously."[14]

Although most time-travel analysts base their work on general relativity, there are many who think quantum mechanics has much to contribute as well. One analyst who believes this is David Deutsch at the Oxford University Mathematical Institute. Deutsch feels [Deutsch, 1991] that general relativity is not the proper theory with which to study the physical effects of closed timelike lines. He believes that the traditional mathematical machinery of general relativity actually obscures, not clarifies, the difficult task of separating the merely counterintuitive from the truly unphysical. Indeed, Deutsch calls the conventional spacetime methods based on general relativity and differential geometry "perverse." He also does not like the technical and conceptual problems of general relativity's wormholes and singularities. Any nonquantum-mechanical discussion, he says, of what he calls the "pathologies" of backward time travel, is simply not adequate. In particular, Deutsch classifies these pathologies into two classes: (1) paradoxical constraints, e.g., the free-will problem in the grandfather paradox; (2) causal loops that create information, e.g., a mathematician who is visited in his youth by a time traveler from the future who gives him the proof of a theorem for which the mathematician is (will be) famous in the future; so *where* did the proof come from?

Deutsch claims his quantum analyses show the first class of pathologies simply does not occur. This is because the past the time traveler enters is, according to Deutsch, the past of a parallel world (see Note 14 again) and not that of the world the time traveler left. He also has arrived at certain preliminary results that lead him to believe that pathologies of the second class may be "avoidable." This is not the orthodox view among time-travel students, however (which does not mean Deutsch is wrong!), and general relativity *is* the standard tool used by most time-travel theoreticians. When quantum mechanics does enter the calculations of most analysts, it is generally on an ad hoc basis. Deutsch's position, of course, raises the question of what in fact motivates studying closed timelike curves in the first place, as they come from general relativity, not from quantum mechanics. Deutsch's response is that while that may be historically true, the still incomplete theory of quantum gravity (see Chapter One), in several of the approaches presently being developed *does* predict closed timelike lines, just as classical Einsteinian general relativity does. This is, in fact, an exciting observation because, as Deutsch writes, the results of his quantum study of closed timelike lines show that "contrary to what has usually been assumed, there is no reason in what we know of fundamental physics why closed timelike lines should not exist."

To address his concern about how to distinguish between the merely counter-intuitive effects of time travel and the "downright unphysical ones," Deutsch's interesting approach is that of studying various elementary computational circuits with negative time delays. (All ordinary physical systems, of course, have positive time delays.) Such circuits have information-processing loops not only in space, as with ordinary networks, but in time, too. Deutsch calls such a temporal loop a *chronology-violating link*. His reason for this approach is that it allows the study of a well-known physical system—basic computer gates, implementing the exclusive-OR Boolean logic function—under the unfamiliar situation of chronology violation, i.e., time travel. With such simple computer gates, Deutsch is able to construct computational analogs to the classical time-travel paradoxes, such as a time traveler going into the past to interact with an earlier version of himself. His general conclusion is that if classical physics is assumed for the operation of the gates, then certain logical yet what Deutsch calls paradoxical constraints are required (i.e., the principle of self-consistency); but if the gates are quantum devices, then there are no constraints. And, of course, the world is, at the fundamental level, quantum, not classical. Deutsch does leave unanswered one interesting question—how does one actually make a negative time delay, which is simply another name for a time machine?

Hans Moravec, a computer scientist at Carnegie Mellon, has similarly used negative time-delays and quantum mechanics to conceptually build systems with time travel logic, i.e., *chronocomputers* [Moravec, 1991]. With such computers,

Moravec shows how some famous computational problems, such as the traveling salesman puzzle, and chess, could be solved in zero time.

A very different quantum mechanical approach to time travel, as compared to Deutsch's and Moravec's has been reported by another physicist in [Vaidman, 1991]. Professor Vaidman describes a quantum time machine that "is not for time travel," but rather for modifying the *rate of time flow* for an isolated system. In this way the machine resembles the entropy time-cabinet [Farley, 1950] discussed in Chapter Three more than it does Wells' time machine. Vaidman's machine can alter the time flow by either a positive or a negative factor, and it is the second possibility that allows his machine to return to a previous quantum mechanical state (the "past"), which is what Vaidman means by time travel. There are at least three problems with this device. I have already mentioned the need to isolate Vaidman's machine from the rest of the world, a difficult (perhaps even impossible) requirement. If it is not isolated, then the machine returns to a *counterfactual* past; i.e., not to its actual past, but to the past it would have experienced if it had been isolated. Second, it works by surrounding a quantum mechanical system (e.g., an atom in an elevated energy state) with a massive spherical shell with variable radius; building such a machine would be an engineering nightmare. But worst of all is the random nature of its operation—the machine works only *some* of the time! In fact, the bigger it is, the less likely it is that it will work. This is not a feature of a practical time machine, and quantum mechanics does not (at least at present) seem likely to offer much promise to the hopeful time traveler.

Fiction, however, has enthusiastically embraced quantum mechanics and its possible connection with time travel. The first such tale in science fiction was probably "The Branches of Time" [Daniels, 1935], which also contained the observation that while alternate time tracks may allow changing the past for the better (something that can't be done with just one track), in the end any such change may still be futile.[15] As Daniels' time traveler puts it sadly: "I did have an idea to ... go back to make past ages more liveable. Terrible things have happened in history, you know. But it isn't any use. Think, for instance of the martyrs and the things they suffered. I could go back and save them those wrongs. And yet all the time ... they would still have known their unhappiness and their agony, because in this world-line those things have happened. At the end, it's all unchangeable; it merely unrolls before us." Many years later a philosopher/physicist, in a critique of the many-worlds idea, echoed Daniels [Shimony, QCST]: "[In the world] that I (subjectively) experience I may blunder, but [in another world], with equal actuality, I triumph gloriously. The Everett interpretation can be used this way to mitigate sorrows, but this use is two-edged, for it equally well implies the speciousness of happiness."

The theme in Daniels' story is what is called in [Lem, 1974] the *ergodic theory of history*; i.e., almost all possible histories have the same general characteristics, differing only in details. Another example of Lem's ergodic theory is "Ounce of Prevention" [Carter, 1950]. As the last man alive (*on Mars*) watches Earth burn in the Final Atomic War, he is offered a deal by scientifically advanced Martians.

They will send him back to Earth, back in time (a billion years back), along with a gadget to eliminate all fissionable elements. Thus—no Final Atomic War. Once back, however, he is confronted by himself, sent back by the Martians from the new reality he will create, to prevent the Final Biological War. That war will be caused by poverty and economic unrest because for some reason all fissionable materials had disappeared from Earth in the ancient past! In this (illogical) story, the details of history change, but not the big picture.

Perhaps one of the most imaginative alternate time track stories is "Sail On! Sail On!" [Farmer, 1986], which appeared in a 1952 issue of the science fiction magazine *Startling Stories*. In this story we read of an alternate world where radio was discovered rather earlier than in our world; one of Columbus' crew is a Friar Sparks, who sends morse code in Latin! And [Zebrowski, BT], which describes "The Cliometricon," a gadget (named after Clio, the Muse of history) that displays the alternate worlds of quantum mechanics, actually opens with a quote from a 1970 article in *Physics Today* on the quantum splitting of Universes!

Splitting Universes have been used in literary works outside the field of science fiction, too; e.g., "The Garden of Forking Paths" [Borges, 1964] and *Dangerous Corner* [Priestley, 1948], the first play J. B. Priestley wrote (1932). Typical of the fictional fantasies on splitting Universes is "Lost" [Dunsany, 1948], the tale of a man who goes back in time to correct "two or three mistakes he had made in his life." This he successfully does, but the result is a new, subtly different subsequent history. But not infinitely subtle; after the changes his home, his wife, all the details of his life, have vanished. As he relates to a visitor at the lunatic asylum he is confined to as the result of his dispair, "I tell you I'm lost. Can't you realize that I'm lost in time? I tell you that you can find your way traveling the length of Orion, sooner than you shall find it among the years. ... Don't go back down the years trying to alter anything ... Don't even wish to ... the whole length of the Milky Way is more easily traveled than time, amongst whose terrible ages I am lost."

In writings for the masses (rather than the more limited science fiction and fantasy audiences), perhaps the best known such work of alternate history is the novel by Ward Moore, *Bring the Jubilee* [Moore, 1953], in which Lee wins the Battle of Gettysburg (and the South wins the Civil War). Moore explores the implications of this, with the ending describing the invention of the HX–1, a time machine. By using the time machine, a historian travels from 1952 into the past of 1863 to study the battle, and he inadvertently disrupts events to the point that the North wins; i.e., reality splits, with the new fork in time representing the time track of *our* world. The historian is trapped on this new fork, cut off forever from his original track's future. Indeed, the entire novel is in the form of a discovered manuscript, written in 1877 and found in 1953, and the pathos of what must be the ultimate isolation gives great emotional impact to the story. Lem [1974] incorrectly associates this story with a grandfather-type of paradox, using a single time track, even though it is quite clear Moore had multiple tracks in mind.

More recently, the idea of an alternate time track being created by the disturbance of a time traveler has been treated in an interesting way in *The Trinity*

Paradox [Anderson and Beason, 1991]. In this novel a nuclear-weapons protestor causes an explosion while destroying a test site, and that explosion blasts her back in time to the Los Alamos of 1943. There she inserts herself into the Manhattan Project that is trying to build the first atomic bomb and thus finds herself in the perfect position to disrupt the history of her original time track. Before she is through, her efforts result in the radioactive destruction of New York City, the deaths of Edward Teller, General Groves, and Robert Oppenheimer, and the atomic bombing of the Nazi rocket base at Peenemunde. Somewhat more fortunate is Richard Feynman, who merely ends up as a wheelchair cripple. Whether all this tragedy has resulted in a better future is, of course, open for debate, in agreement with Lem's ergodic theory of history.

Filmmakers seem to have overlooked the dramatic plot device of alternate time tracks; the only attempt I know of is the 1971 British movie *Quest for Love* (based on the short story "Random Quest" [Wyndham, 1961]).

Causal Loops

Professor Dwyer, in offering a possible explanation [Dwyer,1978] for why his time traveler journeys back to 3000 B.C., introduces a paradox of far more mystery than the grandfather one: "In our time travel story it just may be that the traveler's interest in going back to ancient Egypt is stimulated by recently discovered documents, found near Cairo, containing the diary of a person claiming to be a time traveler; whereupon our hero, realizing it is himself, immediately begins ... construction of a rocket in order to 'fulfill his destiny'." In other words, (a) he builds a Gödelian rocket and goes back to the past because of the discovered diary, and (b) the diary is discovered because he goes back to the past. Both (a) and (b) alone have logical clarity, but together they form a *closed time loop* of enormous mystery.

The discovery of an anachronistic artifact (such as the diary), even without explicit mention of the closed-loop aspect, is certainly an intriguing idea. In "The Marathon Photograph" [Simak, 1974a], for example, it is the discovery of a holographic photograph of the Battle of Marathon, 490 B.C., that opens the discussion of time travel. And it is the later finding of another such three-dimensional image, a shocking view of the Crucifixion, that sends a time traveler back into the past. But it is the closing of the time loop that adds the real mystery. Simak clearly liked the idea of a closed time loop. In "The Birch Clump Cylinder" [Simak, S1] a private college, endowed decades before by a generous but mysterious benefactor, experiments with a time machine. Suddenly, one of the college's graduates is accidently sent a hundred years into the past—where she becomes the benefactor. The college comes into existence, therefore, because it will exist. In my own story "Old Friends Across Time" [Nahin, 1979a], for yet another example, I use an old photograph to convince the time-traveler-to-be that a trip to the past is in his future—it shows him in a group picture with men who died before he was born; I liked this theme enough to repeat it in "The Invitation" [Nahin, 1985].

The general plot device of a closed-loop artifact has a long tradition. In the early story "Via the Time Accelerator" [Bridge, 1931] we find one of the first sophisticated treatments of causal loops in science fiction. A time traveler in 1930, about to start his journey into the future in an airplane/time machine, wonders at the last moment if he should really go—then he sees himself returning and thus knows he will successfully make the trip. As he later tells a friend, "That decided me ... Paradoxical? I should say so! I had seen myself return from my time-trip *before* I had started it; had I *not* seen that return, I would *not* have commenced that strange journey, and so could *not* have returned in order to induce me to decide that I *would* make the journey!" And later, when he finds himself in a dangerous situation in the future, he draws hope from that startling experience: "I *would* escape ... It was so decreed. Had I not, with my own eyes, seen myself appear out of the fourth dimension back there in the Twentieth Century, and glide down to my landing-field? Surely, then, I *was* destined to return to my own age safe and sound."

Even more dramatic is the second, internal loop that ends the story. When the time traveler arrives in a ruined city in the year A.D. 1,001,930, he is greeted, *by name*, by an old man who says he is the Last Man alive. He knew the time traveler was coming because an ancient history book had said the Last Man had, in fact, appeared from the future in A.D. 502,101 in the very time machine out of which the time traveler had just stepped. The time traveler is so startled by all this that he decides to mull it over until the next day. As he wakes up in the morning, he is just in time to watch the Last Man depart for 502,101. Stranded in the future, the time traveler wanders the city in dispair until he chances upon a museum. And in the museum, sealed in a glass case, is his time machine(!)—it has been there for half a million years, since the end of the Last Man's journey. And so the time traveler is saved; he merely adds some oil to the still functional engine (if you can accept time travel, I suppose this is no more difficult to believe) and returns to 1930—just as he saw himself do when he began his trip.

Since Bridge, the idea of a causal loop has been used many times in science fiction stories. In "Weapon Out of Time" [Blish, 1941], for example, we find armed time travelers returning to the Triassic age to uncover the secret of a mysterious artifact; at the end we learn that it is the remains of their own automatic rifle. In "The Tides of Time" [Chandler, 1948] a time traveler journeys backward 500 years, suffers an accident that results in his being "agelessly stuck" in his time-traveling gadget until he is freed—by himself 500 years later. He then gets into the gadget to journey backward 500 years ... And in "A Two-Timer" [Masson, 1968] a time traveler from 1964 is secretly observed by one of the "locals" when he arrives in 1683. The oddness of the sudden appearance of the time traveler and his time machine ("It were a kind of Dazzle") makes the local think it might be that the stranger is the man who stole some items from his home the previous night, the same night he had an "ill Dream." Stealing the time machine after the time traveler has gone exploring, the local travels to 1964, where he learns how valuable antiques are—so back he goes to 1683, to the night before the time machine first arrived, to get some "antiques" from his house. And so he realizes who the thief was *really*. Before leaving he enters his own bedroom to see himself first asleep in bed and then awaken. And so he learns the cause of what he called his "ill Dream."

Such causal loops have continued to form the basis for some of the most puzzling science fiction stories. For example, in *The Technicolor Time Machine* [Harrison, 1967] we read of a movie production crew that goes into the past to make a film. At the end of the story it becomes clear that their presence in the past was not an insignificant event as one character realizes after seeing the evidence of how they affected (*not* changed!) the past: "If this is true, then the only reason that the Vikings settled in Vinland is because we decided to make a motion picture showing how the Vikings settled in Vinland." And in " 'Willie's Blues' " [Tilley, 1973] we have the moving story of a time traveler from 2078 who journeys back a century and a half to learn the details of the short career of a famous jazz musician and of his early death. On his trip the time traveler brings with him a recording of the musician's most brilliant performance, made the very night of his death. First arriving eighteen months before that night, he finds the musician a dispirited man. But then the time traveler plays the recording—and the musician finds his inspiration. That is, the man's talent is awakened, to florish until it *will* result in making the recording that is its own cause.

In [Fulmer, 1980] we find a philosopher telling a tale that puts the grandfather paradox to shame: "If James cannot decide whether to marry Alice or Jane, he simply travels to the future and learns that he is to choose Alice; he then chooses her for this reason. One wants to object that the decision to marry Alice was never really made at all! But this is not true; the decision was made—as a result of the knowledge that this was the decision ... It is not the case that the prospective bridegroom could visit the future and compare the results of marrying Alice with those of marrying Jane in order to decide between the alternatives. For if he visits the future he will learn only that in fact he chose Alice, for better or for worse!" Similiarly, when the time travelers in "The Time Cheaters" [Binder, 1940] arrive in the forty-sixth century, they find they are expected. Their host tells them why: "I have been awaiting your arrival, from the past. I have a written record of your coming. You see, I have a time machine myself ... With my time machine, I recently went a year into the future, and read the written account I had made, or will make after you leave. Then I came back, awaiting your arrival."

Professor Fulmer elaborated on this astonishing use of causal loops in time travel in a subsequent paper [Fulmer, 1981]. He asked, "What if time travel becomes commonplace, so that we must deal with a constant stress of time travelers returning from the future to reveal what they have seen?" Professor Fulmer answers, "I think it is clear that the ... causal loop we have been discussing would become very common, and would play a prominent role in human affairs." Fulmer denied such causal loops would mean a loss of free will, however. As he explained his position, knowledge of a rigged roulette wheel would not prevent you from putting your money on the table *if you want to*, but perhaps that knowledge will influence your *freely* made decision-making. Whether you learn by traditional means that the roulette wheel is rigged (e.g., you see magnets being installed under the table!) or by means of time travel is irrelevant—even with this knowledge you act freely.

Other philosophers, however, are so puzzled by causal loops (recall from Chapter Three that Murray MacBeath thinks they have a "queer smell") that they think such loops show the impossibility of time travel. (Fulmer and MacBeath, however, are not among this group.) For example, [Capek, VOT] rejects time travel because causal loops necessarily have spacetime diagrams that bend back on themselves. Declaring any idea of "time travelers visiting their own past or the past of their own ancestors" as nothing but "Wellsian fantasies," Professor Capek continues with "there would be some events which, beside being simultaneous with themselves would also be simultaneous with other instants of time! In other words, a certain event corresponding to a single point in which the corresponding world line recrosses itself would be simultaneous with a remote future instant. In such a case we would be clearly on the brink of magic."

When he asserted that 3000 B.C. happens twice, once without a time traveler and once again when the time traveler arrives, Hospers makes the same kind of error as Capek. In fact, 3000 B.C. (or any point in spacetime where a world line comes arbitrarily close to itself) happens *once*. In the case of a time traveler who goes back to talk with his younger self; there are of course two sets of memories in a single brain; one set as the younger and one set as the older, time traveler.[17] (This powerful idea has been used often in science fiction; e.g., "Who Else Could I Count On?" [Wellman, MT], " ... And It Comes Out Here" [del Rey, VIT], "By His Bootstraps" [Heinlein, AHT], and *The Man Who Folded Himself* [Gerrold, 1973]). With the four-dimensional block-Universe concept, all world lines lie tenseless in spacetime and so the encounter happens just once in spacetime—the older version speaks the same words he heard (even if he has forgotten them) when his older set of memories formed. He has to or else the past would be changed!

A story that makes the mistake of representing a time loop as a continual, cyclical process, with events repeating with every passage around the loop (with a consequent duplication of the time traveler "each time around"), is "The Trouble with the Past" [Eisentein, 1971]. This error is coupled with another—each time around the loop, the past changes. This continues in the story until the duplicated time traveler(s) figure it out and put a stop to it after the ninth passage. It's a nice story, but illogical. Similiar presentations, equally flawed in their logic, are in "Me, Myself, and I" [Tenn, 1955], "Of Time and Cats" [Fast, 1959], and "A Little Something for Us Tempunauts" [Dick, 1977].

Another interesting science fiction tale that makes the error of a closed time loop going around and around, endlessly repeating, is "Find the Sculptor" [Mines, 1946]. Here the inventor of the first time machine travels five hundred years into the future, where he finds a bronze statue of himself that honors his discovery of time travel. Suddenly injured, fatally, he returns to the present with the statue and then dies. As a memorial, the statue is placed in the very spot where the inventor found (will find) it. Like the watch in *Somewhere in Time* (see Note 11 for Chapter Three), we are left with the puzzle of who made the statue. As the tale ends, the late inventor's lab assistant wonders to himself about what has (will) happen five hundred years later: "Suddenly a strange machine will come out of the past and [the inventor] will be here again—though he is dead and has been dead five hundred years. [He will take the statue] and go back to the past ... to die ... And once again that maddening cycle will begin, to go on and on forever as long as time spins its threads." "MUgwump 4" [Silverberg, TIT] makes the same error.

Even philosophers with more understanding of time travel and causal loops can make the same error. For example, in [Reichenbach, 1956] we find that "there is nothing contradictory in imagining causal chains that are closed, though the existence of such chains would lead to rather unfamiliar experiences. For instance, it might then happen that a person would meet his own former self and have a conversation with him, thus closing a causal line by the use of sound waves. When this occurs the first time he would be the younger ego, and when the same occurrence takes place a second time he would be the older ego. Perhaps the older ego would find it difficult to convince the younger one of their identity; but the older ego would recall that an identical experience once happened to him long ago. And when the younger ego has become old and experiences such an encounter a second time, he is on the other side and tries to convince some 'third' ego of their physical identity. Such a situation appears paradoxical to us; but there is nothing illogical in it." What Reichenbach has erroneously described is the beginning of an endless succession of encounters around a closed causal loop.

Some physicists are so concerned about multiple trips around closed timelike curves (CTC's), (because they think that would allow the past to be changed) that they have felt it necessary specifically to forbid such a possibility. As [Friedman *et al.*, 1990] explains: "That the principle of self-consistency is not totally tautological becomes clear when one considers the following alternative: The laws of physics might permit CTC's; and when CTC's occur, they might trigger new kinds of local physics which we have not previously met. For example, a quantum-mechanical system, propagating around CTC's, might return to where it started with values for its wave function that are inconsistent with the initial values; and it might then continue propagating and return once again with a third set of values, then a fourth, then a fifth ... The principle of self-consistency by fiat forbids changing the past." This last statement is, of course, in agreement with the position of this book (accepted by most philosophers for nearly thirty years) that the past cannot be changed, but the authors of the principle of self-consistency seem to have been driven to it by a fear of the past "happening again" over and over. David Deutsch at Oxford, on the other hand, flatly rejects the need for the principle, calling it simply redundant [Deutsch, 1991].

Princeton University philosopher David Lewis has written with particular insight on causal loops, particularly on ones that involve just information transfer; e.g., a time traveler going back in time to tell his younger self how to build a time machine so that once it is constructed he can go back and tell himself how to do it. (This idea is found in the 1931 Nicholson letter quoted at the beginning of this chapter and as the second of David Deutsch's backward time travel "pathology classes.")[18] As Lewis explains the puzzle [Lewis, 1976]: "But where did the information come from in the first place? Why did the whole affair happen? *There is simply no answer* [my emphasis]. The parts of the loop are explicable, the whole of it is not. Strange! But not impossible, and not too different from inexplicabilities we are already inured to. Almost everyone agrees that God, or the Big Bang, or the entire infinite past of the Universe, or the decay of a tritium atom, is uncaused and inexplicable. Then if these are possible, why not also the inexplicable causal loops that arise in time travel?"

A few years later, Levin, another philosopher, gave a similiar response [Levin, 1980] to a paradox involving a causal loop similiar to Lewis'. Levin's tale is of a book containing instructions on how to make a time machine, a book that travels into the past on the machine so that it can be read (in order to make the machine). In answer to the question "Who wrote the book about building a time machine?" Levin says that this question is "no different from questions about where *anything* originally came from. We can ask about the origin of the atoms ... their time line is not neatly presented to us. The atoms either go back endlessly, or if the Universe is finite, they just start. In either case the question of ultimate origin is as unanswerable as the question of the book's origin. What makes us think that when such questions are asked about the loop they are different and *ought* to be answerable is that the entire loop is open to inspection. *Sub specie aeternitatis* this difference disappears."

An analyst who takes strong exception to Lewis' and Levin's views on causal loops is David Deutsch, who it will be recalled (from the previous section) illustrated his second class of time travel pathologies with a causal loop. Deutsch writes [Deutsch, 1991] that "the real problem with closed timelike lines under classical physics is that they could be used to generate knowledge in a way that conflicts with the principles of the philosophy of science, specifically with the evolutionary principle." What Deutsch is referring to is the metaphysical claim (attributed to the philosopher Karl Popper) that *knowledge comes into existence only by evolutionary, rational processes*, and that solutions to problems do not spring fully formed into the Universe. Deutsch uses the principle, for example, to reject creationism, the antievolution theory that "explains away" fossils millions of years old with the assertion that they were created, fully formed (by God, presumably) just a few thousand years ago. Deutsch's position, of course, is considered by nearly all scientists to be correct for the specific case of creationism, but the evolutionary principle does not tell us much about causal loops (other than to declare them impossible because they are not possible). (Two Russian analysts, Lossev and Novikov, have recently given a dramatic example of how an information-creating loop might be constructed, using a wormhole time machine, and that example is described in detail at the end of Tech Note 9.)

I believe Lewis and Levin have the causal-loop issue correct, but one can actually find similar ideas in science fiction considerably before Lewis' and Levin's papers. For example, "Absolutely Inflexible" [Silverberg, VIT] describes the world of A.D. 2784 as one which has eradicated all disease; as a consequence humanity had lost its immunity to even the most ordinary of illness. Thus, when time travelers from the past show up, they are immediately sealed into bulky space suits, screened by an administrator called "Absolutely Inflexible" Mahler, and then quarantined on the Moon. (Mahler has earned his nickname by being so hardened he has never let a time traveler go free.) Time travelers cannot be sent back home to the past because (so we are told) two-way time travel is impossible. At least it *was*, until one day a time traveler arrives with what he claims is a two-way time machine. Mahler doesn't believe him (and oddly enough, the time traveler understands immediately that to argue is useless) and promptly sends him off to the Moon. Then, curious, Mahler tries the gadget and, indeed, he goes into the past. Upon his return, however, he is seized and processed—by himself! As the story ends, "Suddenly Mahler saw the insane circle complete ... But how did the cycle start? Where did the two-way rig come from in the first place? He had gone to the past to bring it to the present to take it to the past to ... " Knowing it is useless to argue, Mahler goes off to the Moon without resistance.

Mahler's puzzle, of course, is precisely the same question about the origin of knowledge in a time loop that Professor Lewis asks. At least two science fiction writers have attempted answers to the origin question. In *The Technicolor Time Machine* [Harrison, 1967] one character is perplexed over a piece of paper with a diagram on it: "Then no one ever *drew* this diagram. It just travels around in this wallet and I hand it to myself. Explain that." His friend replies,

> "There is no need to, it explains itself. The piece of paper consists of a self-sufficient loop in time. No one ever drew it. It exists because it is, which is adequate explanation. If you wish to understand it, I will give you an example. You know that all pieces of paper have two sides—but if you give one end of a strip of paper a 180-degree twist, then join the ends together, the paper becomes a Möbius strip that has only one side. It exists. Saying it doesn't cannot alter the fact. The same thing is true of your diagram, it exists."
>
> "But—where did it come from?"
>
> "If you must have a source, you may say that it came from the same place that the missing side of the Möbius strip has gone to."

In "The Man Who Met Himself" [Farley, 1950], we find much the same explanation. As tribute to the mystery of causal loops, Farley has a Cambodian Buddhist monk explain matters to the hero (and to us):

"But you haven't yet told me where the time-machine came from!"

"You yourself brought it here out of 1935."

"But where did it come from *originally*?"

"There never was any 'originally'. You flew the time machine backward through time from 1935 to 1925. And this is why I now have the machine."

"To fly back again to 1925?"

"No. Nothing of the sort. There is no round-and-round circle of events; no repetition. Merely *one* closed cycle. *One* overlapping of events for only ten years ... One time-machine, found in 1935 and brought back to 1925—found in 1935 *because* brought back to 1925. That is all."

"But who made it in the first place?—Oh, skip the 'in the first place'. Just plain: who made it?"

"No one. It was never made ... It is here because it is here."

This is, of course, the issue young Mr. Nicholson raised as Item (1) in his 1931 letter to Hugo Gernsback, quoted in the second section of this chapter.

The causal loops discussed by philosophers are usually of the type that loop from the present into the past and back to the present, as do Farley's and Harrison's. This need not be so. One science fiction treatment that describes how a loop might extend into the future, for example, is "Dominoes" [Kornbluth, VIT]. A wealthy stock-market wheeler-dealer travels two years into the future to get an edge. While there, he quickly learns from newspaper archives that a stupendous economic crash occurred just hours after the start of his trip. He then returns to the present and unloads all of his holdings—and thus precipates the very crash he read (will read) about. The inventor of the time machine, who has lost all his wealth in the market plunge, strangles his greedy patron, thereby showing that there can at least be ordinary justice even in the strange world of time travel and causal loops.

When a loop involves just information, it is already certainly quite strange. But if there is a physical artifact in the loop, there is an additional puzzle that nearly all writers seem to have missed; I have found this puzzle mentioned in the philosophical literature only by [Nerlich, 1981] and [MacBeath, 1982]. Consider, for example, the watch in the causal loop of the film *Somewhere in Time* (see Note 11 for Chapter Three). Assume the watch received by the man in the present is bright and shiny. He then takes it back into the past and gives it to his love. It remains with her after his return to the present until, decades later, she gives it to him—bright and shiny. Why didn't it tarnish? Is there some peculiar property to the watch? Well, probably not—perhaps she polished it just before giving it to him. For a watch, this seems an acceptable (if smelling a bit of deus ex machina) explanation, but now replace the watch with a crisp, new book. He receives it, takes it back, leaves it with her, gets it back years later—crisp and new. Why haven't the pages turned yellow and brittle and dark with decades of fingerprints? Or, if they are yellow and brittle, then the unalterability of the loop is lost (as they were crisp and new the first time around). This is all much harder to explain than is the shiny watch, and it is one of the reasons given by MacBeath for why, although he believes in the logical possibility of time travel, he views causal loops with much suspicion.

Professor Nerlich is of the same persuasion as Professor MacBeath. In [Nerlich, 1981] he notes that "despite [strong] arguments for the consistency of time travel stories, the impression is apt to remain that something is wrong with them. I think this impression is correct." He then tells us a tale (that he attributes to one of his students) that he claims proves his point. The tale is remarkably similiar to the central puzzle in the well-known "As Never Was" [Miller, FSFS] (which Nerlich and his student were apparently unaware of, as no citation is given). In Miller's story a knife brought from a museum of the future arrives in the present with a flawless blade; but soon after gets a nick in it. So how, wonders the narrator, can the loop be completed again? I do not find this quite the puzzle Miller and Nerlich do. It is simply a variation of the grandfather paradox. If the knife is found flawless in the future, then it was not (will not) be nicked in the past.

Still, there is no question about it—to say causal loops are counterintuitive is to barely hint at their mystery. But they are *not* an argument against time travel. Rather, *if* time travel is possible, then it would seem we would have to accept causal loops, too; and *if* it is somehow shown that time travel is not possible, then for that same reason (whatever it might be), so too would causal loops thus be shown to be impossible. One time traveler in *Great Work of Time* [Crowley, 1991], a novel that is one gigantic causal loop from start to finish, certainly has matters right when he says "It *is* mighty odd. The paradox is acute: it is. Completely contrary to the usual cause-and-effect thinking we all do, can't stop doing really, no matter how hard we try ... Strictly speaking it is unthinkable. And yet there it is."

There is, I should add, one possible way to explain causal loops—by using the parallel-Universe concept mentioned earlier. The best way to illustrate this technique, I think, is with the example of the extremely clever story "Other Tracks" [Sell, SFAD], published in 1938. To improve the performance of his time machine, the inventor in this tale needs batteries with tremendous energy density, a density far in advance of the batteries in the present. Unable to travel far into the future (if he could obtain them there, of course, then a causal loop would be created upon his bringing them back to the present), his assistant first travels back to 1851. There he leaves a note on the desk of a well-known experimenter with a plea for him to devote his life to battery research; a copy of the 1937 Electrical Handbook is left with the note as proof there really has been a visit from the future. Before returning to the present, the assistant takes a sheet of (new) 1847 five-cent stamps from the experimenter's desk. Returning to the present, which is now different (a new time track), powerful batteries are readily available (because the experimenter believed the note). Buying several, using money obtained from selling the pristine stamps to a collector, the assistant returns to a slightly earlier 1851 than before, watches himself appear to leave the note and the Handbook, and then removes the both of them. Then, upon returning once more to the present, he finds all is as before—

except now he has the powerful batteries! As before, one might ask, Where did the batteries come from?—but unlike the previous mystery of causal loops, the answer is clear and nonmysterious—from the experimenter on a *different time track*.

This shuttling back and forth between time tracks is the signature of what is called a *cross-time* story, which attempts to avoid paradoxes while still allowing for changing the past. The first example of this time-travel subgenre was "Sidewise in Time" [Leinster, BGA2], published in 1934. Such stories reached a peak with "The Other Inaguration" [Boucher, 1953], in which two professors "rotate" themselves out of our world into an alternative one after the wrong (i.e., not their) candidate wins the Presidential election. Written as a response to McCarthyism in the early 1950s, it is an eerie tale of how alternatives aren't always improvements. A similiar thesis is advanced in "Minor Alteration" [Richards, 1965], in which an alteration in the activities of Booth on the night of April 14, 1865, leads to a world far more awful than with Lincoln's assassination. (In this tale, unlike Boucher's, the damage is undone.) *Vestiges of Time* [Meredith, 1978] has the interesting idea of the hero traveling cross-time from parallel world to endless parallel worlds in search of one in which a *true* time machine has been invented; i.e., a machine that travels forward and backward along *one* time line.

Interesting stories on the alternate-world theme have also been written with the twist that, given an infinity of such worlds, it may be awfully hard to find your way back to your original world (e.g., "One Way Street" [Bixby, 1954], "Rumfuddle" [Vance, 1973], "Trips" [Silverberg, 1986], and "Worlds Enough" [Thompson, BT]). Jack Finney's "The Coin Collector" [Finney, 1986], however, takes just the opposite position—a man enjoys two wives, each in a parallel Universe, and he flips back and forth between them with ease. *The Number of the Beast* [Heinlein, 1980] has a finite number of alternatives too, but the difficulty twist still applies, as the number is six raised to the sixth power, all raised to the sixth power, or, more precisely, the number of Universes is 10,314,424,798,490,535,546,171,949,056 (ten million sextillion!). In the paratime stories of H. Beam Piper the number of alternative Universes is even larger; $10^{100,000}$ [Piper, 1981].

Sexual Paradoxes

There are causal loops even stranger than the ones we have already discussed, hard as that may be to believe. These are the sexual paradoxes, first mentioned in 1931 in the Nicholson letter to Hugo Gernsback. As a character in *Up the Line* [Silverberg, 1969] declares with interesting enthusiasm, "You haven't lived until you've laid one of your own ancestors." Philosophers have found these particular paradoxes full of dramatic appeal, too. For example, as a challenge problem to the readers of *Analysis*, British philosopher Jonathan Harrison posed the following astonishing situation [Harrison, 1979]. A young lady, one Jocasta Jones, one day finds an ancient deep freezer containing a solidly frozen young man. She thaws him out and learns that his name is Dum and that he possesses a book that

describes how to make both a deep freezer and a time machine. They marry. Soon they have a baby boy and name him Dee. Years later, after reading his father's book, Dee makes a time machine. Dee and Dum, taking the book with them, get into the machine, and begin a trip into the past. Running out of food during the lengthy journey Dee kills his father and eats him. (In this story time-travel machines are like the reverse-entropy machine in "The Very Slow Time Machine" [Watson, 1979] described in Chapter Three.) Arriving in the past, Dee destroys the time machine, builds a deep freezer (again using the book), gets into it, and-
... wakes up to find a young lady, one Jocasta Jones, has thawed him out. When asked his name, he replies Dum, shows Jocasta his book, they marry, and ...

Professor Harrison concluded this tale with a challenge question for his readers: "Did Jocasta commit a logically possible crime?" This issue is just the surface of an ocean of puzzles found in this story! Jocasta's crime, of course, is that she has seemingly (if unwittingly) committed incest; readers who remember their Greek mythology, and the story of Oedipus and who his mother/wife was, will now see why Harrison named his heroine as he did. But what of Dee's crime?—he has, after all, eaten his father. But perhaps it isn't a crime after all since Dee and Dum are one-in-the-same, and is it a crime to eat yourself? According to [MacBeath, 1982], Harrison's tale is "a story so extravagant in its implications that it will be regarded by many as an effective *reductio ad absurdum* of the one dubious assumption on which the story rests: the possibility of time travel."[19]

Harrison's challenge provoked nearly a dozen replies [Harrison, 1980]. Oddly, [Denruyter, 1980] in particular attracted Harrison's favorable attention by presenting an absurd version of the story, an exercise that contributed nothing new to the question except the silly touch of a woman turning into a dog(!). More thoughtful was [Levin, 1980] (quoted earlier on causal loops), which also makes the interesting observation that not only has Jocasta committed incest, but she has done so with a single act of intercourse. As explained previously, the events in a causal loop do not happen endlessly, but rather only once, and Jocasta thaws Dum (Dee) out just once, marries him just once, and the two consummate their marriage just once. Ordinarily we think it takes two sexual acts to commit incest, with the first resulting in the birth of a child, and the second being union with the child, but this is not so in a causal loop. Time travel *is* an odd business.

And finally, in the only other printed solution to Harrison's challenge, [Godfrey-Smith, 1980] makes the telling point that irrespective of physics, the story is biologically flawed, and fatally so. As he writes: "The biological problem is the following. Dee is the son of Dum and Jocasta. So Dee obtained half his genes from Dum and half from Jocasta. But Dum is diachronically identical with Dee, and is therefore genotypically identical with him (i.e. himself). That is, Dee is both genotypically identical with and distinct from Dum, which is absurd." Professor Harrison seems amazingly unperturbed by this objection, dismissing it as a mere "law of nature, not of logic." If one is airily going to ignore laws of nature, then why bother debating time travel (or anything) in physics? Conservation of momentum is not a law of logic either; should we overlook it too when it suits us? It is interesting to note that Godfrey-Smith's biological objection had actually been raised some years earlier by a physicist [Schulman, 1971a] and by a science fiction writer in the 1955 story "Time Patrol" [Anderson, 1981].

While certainly instructive, the sexual-paradox stories by Harrison and Mac-Beath (see Note 19 again) are faulty on at least one other point—the authors do not indicate that the concepts they are writing about have long been a staple of science fiction, and that the sexual paradoxes had received much critical analysis in that genre long before philosophers discovered them. The philosophers' stories are, in fact, clever but derivative. From science fiction, for example, "The Pound-stone Paradox" [Dee, 1954] is the story of a young man who travels back 1250 years, from A.D. 3207 to 1957, to become his own grandfather fifty generations removed. But even this is tame compared to the sexual paradoxes other science fiction writers conjured up before philosophers discussed the idea.

In "Child by Chronos" [Harness, BFSF3], for example, we have the tale (written decades before Harrison's and MacBeath's) of a young lady caught up in a mind-twisting affair in which the mystery of a causal loop is the least of her troubles. In 1957 a girl is born, and after twenty years of intense competition with her mother (who has an uncanny ability to predict the future), she travels back from 1977 to a few months before her own birth. She becomes pregnant by a man, who she later discovers is her father, and gives birth to a girl. The new mother has, of course, knowledge of all that will happen during the next twenty years, including the fact that she will have an intense competition with her rebellious daughter ... .

In 1959 Robert Heinlein extended the sexual paradox with his recognized classic "All You Zombies—" [Heinlein, MI], generally thought to be the best sexual-paradox tale ever written. We are given only a hint of what is to come when a character listens to a song called "I'm My Own Grandpaw!" In 1945 a newborn girl, Jane, is found on the steps of an orphanage. At age 18, in 1963, she has a one-night affair with a mysterious stranger that leaves her pregnant. Some months later, during the birth of a daughter, it is discovered that Jane actually has a double set of sexual organs, and as the female set has been ruined by the pregnancy, the doctors restore her as a man. Soon after, the baby girl is kidnapped from the hospital ward. Years later, in 1970 Jane, now a man, meets another stranger who uses a time machine to transport both of them back to April 3, 1963. By April 24 male-Jane meets female-Jane and impregnates her. Meanwhile, the stranger with the time machine travels forward to March 10, 1964, a little after female-Jane has given birth, kidnaps the baby from the hospital, takes her back to September 20, 1945, and leaves her on the steps of an orphange. And so we see Jane is her own mother *and* father, thus outdoing Harness in the self-parenting game.

This is pretty impressive, but Heinlein still has one more twist left. After leaving baby-Jane in 1945, the time-machine stranger returns to April 24, 1963, retrieves male-Jane (who has just kissed female-Jane good-night after fathering her-himself in herself), and takes him to 1985 when he recruits him into the Temporal Service — and finally, the stranger jumps forward to 1999 to his "real time." At the end we at last learn the stranger is, in fact, an even older version of male-Jane—all the characters in the entire story are the same individual at various points along a single, highly twisted world line. The lone character in Heinlein's tale is truly a self-made man/woman in every sense of the phrase! This ultimate act of *creatio ex nihilo* has been called by Lem "smaller than the minimal loop" [Lem, 1974]. (In December 1958 in a letter to his literary agent Heinlein wrote of this story: "I *hope* that I have written in that story the Farthest South in time paradoxes."[20])

The sexual paradox has continued to fascinate science fiction writers to the present day. Consider, for example, Gregory Benford's beautifully written story "Down the River Road" [Benford, 1991], of a young man hunting the father who years before had abandoned him in a burning house. The death of the young man's mother in the flames has sent him on a ten-year chase up and down what is literally a river of time, where to travel one way ("up time") is to move into the past, while "down time" leads to the future (and to the legendary waterfall at the end of eternity). Eventually he corners his father and, despite the man's pleading, kills him. It is only later after examining papers he finds in his father's pocket that the boy realizes he has killed his future-self. Professor Benford's tale is reminiscent of Huck Finn on the Mississippi as well as of the 1954 Czechoslovakian film *Journey to the Beginning of Time*, in which four boys raft down the river of time into the prehistoric past. In Benford's story time is monstrously convoluted, and the ending hints at an explanation for an earlier, mysterious encounter the boy has with an older-self in a futile attempt to avert his (then) future murder/suicide. By having the young man kill his future-self, this tale has introduced the clever twist of inverting the grandfather paradox.

The biological objection raised by Godfrey-Smith to Harrison's story is, of course, equally valid for those of Harness, Heinlein, and Benford, too. David Gerrold avoided Godfrey-Smith's objection in his classic novel *The Man Who Folded Himself* [Gerrold, 1973] by having the protagonist become involved in a homosexual affair with himself; indeed with multiple, duplicate copies of himself ("The night when six of us, naked and giggling, discovered what an orgy *really* was")! Other than this curious story device, however, Gerrold's work holds little additional interest for us as its underlying logic is that the past can be changed at will. Stepping around this error, as well as avoiding the genetic objection, is *The Janus Equation* [Spruill, 1980]. Here, a brilliant mathematician attempting to unravel the theory of time travel undergoes a sexual identity crisis, and then he meets a beautiful woman who breaks him out of his slump and straightens him out; or at least she does until he learns she is himself, time traveling to the past after a sex-change operation and other sorts of plastic surgery! The story title refers to the two-faced Roman god Janus, who faced both the past and the future, but undoubtedly the author had this curious sexual time-travel coupling in mind, too.

Maxwell's Equations and Advanced Effects

Every physicist and electrical engineer knows that the mathematical description of the electromagnetic field is given by Maxwell's equations. In particular, radio engineers know that the waves of energy their antennas launch into space follow the predictions of the equations with astonishing accuracy. Indeed, when Einstein's relativity theory was complete, it was found that Maxwell's equations automatically satisfy relativity because since magnetic effects are relativistic effects, relativity is literally built into Maxwell's equations. While Newton's laws of dynamics had to be patched up, Maxwell's equations were untouched by the discovery of special relativity.

Thus it was a puzzle when physicists discovered that a careful study of the seemingly perfect Maxwell equations, when applied to radio antennas, apparently results in the prediction of causality violation. It is found, in fact, that the equations admit two solutions. One, as expected, contains the feature of time delay; i.e., creating an electromagnetic disturbance at the antenna now causes a detectable effect at a distant point in space later. This is the so-called retarded solution, and its common-sense physical interpretation is that of energy waves traveling away from the antenna. The shock was that Maxwell's equations also accept an *advanced* solution; i.e., energy waves arriving at the antenna from infinite space.

Paul Renno Heyl wrote perhaps the earliest scientific work discussing advanced effects in his 1897 University of Pennsylvania doctoral dissertation with the provocative title "The Theory of Light on the Hypothesis of a Fourth Dimension." Heyl cited the guru of the fourth dimension, C. H. Hinton (see Chapter Two), as his inspiration. The situation described by Heyl is something like two boys standing at the edge of a pond. One boy throws a rock into the middle of the pond and then watches ripples spread out and away from the splash. The other boy does nothing, but suddenly sees ripples appear all around the edge of the pond which then travel inward toward the center where they then all converge at once. A spout of water erupts at the meeting of the ripples, which then ejects a rock which lands in the astounded boy's hand! How absurd, you murmur, and who could blame you? This astonishing imagery of advanced effects is due to the philosopher Karl Popper [Popper, 1956], and it has come to be called the 'Popperian pond'.

Pursuing the mathematics of wave motion in the fourth dimension, Heyl wrote [Beichler, 1988]: "We are led to the curious conclusion that in Hinton's aether the nature of the central disturbance *after* a given instant can influence the form of the aether *before* that instant. In other words, the aether seems to be endowed with an uncanny faculty of foreknowledge." We can avoid such a counterintuitive implication of advanced effects, but only at a price that many physicists and philosophers consider equally unacceptable—information traveling from the future into the past. We can still think of the advanced solution as representing electromagnetic waves traveling away from a transmitting antenna (as being broadcast, just like the retarded solution, rather than being received) *if* we also think of the waves as traveling backward in time. That is, the advanced solution to Maxwell's equations holds out the suggestion of sending messages to the past, a sort of poor man's time travel. It may seem that we have simply traded one problem for another, however, because just sending *information* into the past can cause many of the same paradoxical, causality-busting situations that physical time travel is claimed to cause. Even before the turn of the century the self-described enfant terrible of Victorian literature and science, Samuel Butler (1835–1902), had a sense of the turmoil such transmissions through time might cause. In the "Imaginary Worlds" entry in *The Notebooks of Samuel Butler* he wrote, "Communication with a world exactly, to the minutest detail, a duplicate of our own [but] twenty thousand years ahead of us might ruin the human race as effectively as if we had fallen into the Sun."

The well-known cosmologists Fred Hoyle and J. V. Narlikar share Butler's opinion that communication backward in time could cause trouble. Concerning Maxwell's equations, they wrote in their book *Action at a Distance in Physics and Cosmology* [Hoyle and Narlikar, 1974] that "the equations supply us with both advanced and retarded solutions (and, because of their linearity, with any linear combination of them) ... With so many solutions theoretically possible, why does nature always select the retarded one? That this question cannot be answered within the framework of Maxwell's theory must be regarded as one of its intrinsic weaknesses."

Hoyle and Narlikar's branding of Maxwell's theory as having an "intrinsic weakness" because of its prediction of an advanced solution was unwarranted. Indeed, [Stephenson, 1978] has shown how the advanced solution can have a perfectly reasonable physical interpretation in the context of Maxwell's equations. Professor Stephenson imagines a transmitting antenna sending electromagnetic waves to an identical receiving antenna. At any point in space between the antennas there are electric and magnetic fields. Maxwell's equations allow us to calculate the fields produced by alternating currents in the two antennas. When we do an analysis of the relationship between the transmitting antenna's current and the fields, we use the retarded solution because the current is the cause and the fields are the effect. But in the analysis of the relationship between the fields and the receiving antenna's current, the fields are the cause and the current is the effect; i.e., the *advanced* solution is simply the mathematics relating the current in the receiving antenna *now* to the fields in the *past*. More recently, Hoyle had indicated he has had a change in his opinion of advanced effects [Hoyle, 1983].

It may still be tempting, however, just to dismiss the advanced solution as a mere anomaly of the mathematics; that is, to discard it on physical grounds. This is the traditional approach taken by physicists when confronted by noncausal solutions, and indeed that was what the Swiss physicist Walter Ritz (1878–1909) did with the advanced solution to Maxwell's equations. This approach involved him in the last year of his short life in a dispute with Einstein [Zeh, 1989]. For Ritz, the reversal of cause and effect was simply too violent to his intuition to be taken seriously. Ritz's approach *is* tempting; that is, using his approach we might just *impose* causality on Maxwell's equations, a condition they clearly do not inherently contain, by *a priori* rejecting all advanced solutions. Electrical engineers make similiar kinds of judgments all the time, of course, as when for example the solution of a quadratic equation for a passive (energy-dissipating) resistor gives both a positive value, which makes sense, and a negative one that doesn't and so is simply ignored.[21] A half century ago, however, the eminent MIT physicist Julius Adams Stratton warned against this temptation. He wrote of the disturbing advanced solution: "The familiar chain of cause and effect is thus reversed and this alternative solution might be discarded as logically inconceivable. However the application of 'logical' causality principles offers very insecure footing in matters such as these and we shall do better to restrict the theory to retarded action solely on the grounds that this solution alone conforms to the present physical data."[22] And, in their famous paper [Wheeler and Feynman, 1949] which will be discussed later in this chapter, physicists Wheeler and Feynman declared: "We conclude advanced and retarded interactions give a description of nature logically as acceptable and physically as completely deterministic as the Newtonian scheme of mechanics. In both forms of dynamics the distinction between cause and effect is pointless. With deterministic equations to describe the event, one can say: the stone hits the ground because it was dropped from a height; equally well: the stone fell from a height because it was going to hit the ground." For Wheeler and Feynman, apparently, the reversal of cause and effect inherent to backward time travel offered no conceptual difficulties! The elimination of an appeal to casuality, or to advanced waves, in arguing for the naturalness of the retarded solution to Maxwell's equation was first done in [Aichelburg and Beig, 1976]. The only auxiliary condition applied to the equations was simply that of requiring the initial field energy to be finite (see also [Anderson, 1992]).

Today there is still no experimental evidence for the reality of the advanced solution. Now and then one runs across speculations that the advanced waves of something might explain the so-called ESP talent of precognition (through waves sent backward to us from the future), but that is all it is—speculation [Hesse, 1961]. Yet, even before Wheeler and Feynman, advanced waves were hinted at in science-fiction writings. For example, it would probably take something like advanced waves to explain the funny doings in "Anachronistic Optics" [Schere, 1938], the story of a man caught in a time-machine accident. Nearly all of his body ends up four years in the future—nearly, because his eyes remain in the present! As one of the puzzled observers of this odd business wonders, "Strange, that his eyes, now, can convey a message to his brain, four years hence, and his brain tells the eye muscles to move the eyeballs which are four years behind them—" Strange, indeed.

Communication with the Past

Some of the most intriguing paradoxes of time travel involve no traveler (at least no living one)—only information. Of course, any information flow at all, independent of time travel, involves the flow of energy, and as Einstein showed, energy and mass are different aspects of the same thing, and so information time travel involves the transfer of mass. Thus, a man in the twenty-fifth century sending a backward-in-time "temporal radio" message to a twentieth-century woman stating that he loves (will love?) her is sending much more than mere emotion.[23] One point should be clearly understood—the paradoxes of information time travel, as with all time travel, arise only when backward time travel is involved.[24] Indeed, all forms of present-day communication are transmissions only to the future. If you speak to someone or send a radio message, there are delays depending on the distance of separation and the speed of transmission of sound and of light, respectively. If you want to send a message to the 125th century, you can; just write a letter and seal it in a pressurized bottle of helium (a version of this idea is in *Time Bomb* [Dixon, 1992]). This is all quite ordinary, but not so in the reverse direction.

What, for example, could be a more exciting message than the one received from the future by the young genius Cullen Foster, inventor of the first time machine in "How Much to Thursday?" [Stapleton, 1942]? After his initial experiment of sending the machine unmanned into the future, it returns with an envelope inside. Eagerly tearing it open, he finds the note is from the National Academy of Sciences: "We know from old records and museum models that this is the Cullen Foster experimental machine. Fifty years looks down on you and says 'Good work'."

Heady stuff, that, certainly, but as it turns out there are lots of other possible messages capable of competing with young Foster's in excitement. For example, suppose you had a gadget superficially similiar to a telephone, but such that it calls telephones in the distant future. You can hear the person (in the future) on the other end, but they cannot hear you (in their past). That is, information can flow only from future to past.[25] It is easy to create situations that at least seem paradoxical using this device. For example, suppose you call your own private number one month ahead. You hear your future-self first answer the phone and then recite the winning lottery number for the previous day, a month in your present-self's future. (Your future-self does this because a month from now you will remember when your private phone rings who is calling!) So now the present-you can make a fortune winning the lottery a month later. So far, of course, there is nothing paradoxical (or even illegal) in this—but what if when the phone rings in the future the day after you won the lottery, you then decide *not* to read the winning number? This particular paradox has already been treated earlier with the aid of the block-Universe view of spacetime. (It has been treated in fiction as well; e.g., "The Other End of the Line" [Tevis, 1961].) That is, if future-you spoke the lottery number, then present-you *must*, inevitably, read it.

Now suppose that instead of calling your future-self, you call the weather service and listen to the recorded message telling you the daily weather thirty days hence. You do this day after day, and after a while you get a reputation for being able to predict perfectly the weather for every day to come, up to a month into the future. Your reputation spreads far and wide, and after a bit the weather service hears about you. They check and find you're *never* wrong. Their computer models are only 80% accurate out to three days, and for a week's prediction and beyond, the general public might as well flip a coin on just whether it will rain or not rain. But you are 100% correct out to ten times their range and so they hire you— indeed, you get a second job, that of making the recordings for the daily weather.

(The voice on the other end of the gadget *has* sounded sort of familiar for the last month!) So here's the puzzle, a nice little information causal loop—just *where* is the information in the flawless weather predictions coming from?

One easy answer is that this question is meaningless because such a future-to-the-past information flow must be impossible. Indeed, if I am to avoid telling a "philosopher's fairy tale," such as those I criticized in Chapters Two and Three, I must admit that one consistent, nonparadoxical answer is found in recognizing that I have *assumed* those thirty day weather reports are correct, but maybe, in fact, they are no better than anybody else's predictions. And so you *don't* become famous, and so you *don't* get hired—and so there *isn't* any paradox. Is this the way to avoid paradoxes involving information flowing backward in time?

Perhaps not. As long ago as 1917 it was realized that special relativity does not preclude such an apparent backward flow. That is, if information could be transmitted faster than light, then messages could travel backward in time. It was then that Richard Tolman, a professor of physical chemistry at the University of Illinois and later at the California Institute of Technology, wrote [Tolman, 1917]: "The question naturally arises whether velocities which are greater than that of light could ever possibly be obtained." He then answered this question with his general conclusion being that if such velocities are possible, then a faster-than-light (FTL) observer could see the time order of two causally related events reverse. And thus the observer would see the result *before* the cause. Alternatively, a *sub*luminal (slower-than-light) observer could see the two events, which are connected via an FTL causal interaction, reversed in time order from what a stationary observer would see. This has come to be called Tolman's paradox (see Tech Note 7), but Professor Tolman himself was careful with his words: "Such a condition of affairs might not be a logical impossibility; nevertheless its extraordinary nature might incline us to believe that no causal impulse can travel with a velocity greater than that of light."

This was an astonishing statement to write, as Einstein himself had specifically stated in his original 1905 paper on special relativity that such a thing could not occur. Tolman's paradox *is* an extraordinary result, but it has in fact been extended even further. Tech Note 4 shows that the time order of two events can appear reversed even for a subluminal observer—but only if they are not causally related. Faster-than-light motion extends this reversal to causally connected events; that is, FTL motion and time travel to the past go hand in hand.

This rather technical connection between FTL speed and backward time travel made the transition from theoretical physics to popular culture very quickly. It was in the British humor weekly *Punch*, for example, that the famous (but almost always incorrectly quoted) limerick by Professor A. H. R. Buller (1874–1944) first appeared:

> There was a young lady named Bright
> Whose speed was far faster than light;
> > She set out one day
> > In a relative way
> And returned on the previous night.[26]

Where *Punch* dared to go, Hollywood could not, you'd think, be far behind. Indeed, in this case it was actually there first, with the 1922 one-reel silent comedy movie *The Sky Splitter*. (This was, however, just a short film since feature pictures generally had at least four reels, so it is not clear just how widely distributed and viewed it may have been.) The story is that of a scientist testing a new spaceship; when it exceeds the speed of light, he begins to relive his life.

The linkage between time travel and FTL motion continues to fascinate science fiction writers. In "Throwback in Time" [Long, 1953], for example, a time-machine experimenter in the twenty-seventh century wonders "Was the speed of light the core of the mystery? At the speed of light did the past and the future become a shining, merging road down which men could walk—in their ears the thunder of time's passing ... ?" Not everybody is pleased with the idea of such things, however; for example, one writer [Eddington, 1929] declared that "the limit to the velocity of signals is our bulwark against the topsy-turvydom of past and future."

One can reverse (conceptually) the sequence, too, and achieve FTL speed via time travel. To go from *A* to *B* at FTL speed, just follow this procedure: Put yourself in hibernation at *A*; cruise as slowly as you'd like to *B*; wake up, get into your time machine and travel backward in time by the temporal duration of your cruise (as measured by your wristwatch). This lets you actually achieve *infinite* speed. (Going back a little further means, of course, that you arrive at *B* before you leave *A*!).[27] This idea has also been used in science fiction; e.g., "Minimum Sentence" [Cogswell, GRSF2].

The obvious question at this point, of course, is to ask ourselves if it is even conceptually possible to build a gadget to send FTL messages backward in time? Einstein himself thought not, saying [Einstein, 1922] "We cannot send wire messages into the past." But was he right? One hint at the possibility of achieving FTL speeds is in Dirac's paper, discussed in Chapter Three [Dirac, 1938]. There in his remarks about pre-acceleration, Dirac wrote: "Suppose we have a pulse sent out from place *A* and a receiving apparatus for electromagnetic waves at a place *B*, and suppose there is an electron on the straight line joining *A* to *B*. Then the electron will be radiating appreciably [because accelerated charges radiate] before the pulse has reached its centre and this emitted radiation will be detectable at *B* at a time ... earlier than when the pulse, which travels from *A* to *B* with the velocity of light, arrives. *In this way a signal can be sent from A to B faster than light* [my emphasis]."

This conclusion is very exciting, a step beyond the usual examples of things that go faster than light.[28] Dirac had an equally exciting reaction to this. He wrote (and the emphasis is his): "This is a fundamental departure from the ordinary ideas of relativity and is to be interpreted by saying that *it is possible for a signal to be transmitted faster than light through the interior of an electron. The finite size of the electron now reappears in a new sense, the interior of the electron being a region of failure, not of the field equations of electromagnetic theory, but of some of the elementary properties of space-time.*" This last line sounds very much like the same sorts of things people say today about the singularity inside a black hole horizon, and yet Dirac was careful to point out that as weird as FTL speed may appear, special relativity is not violated because "in spite of this departure from ordinary relativistic ideas, our whole theory is Lorentz invariant."[29] Of course, as with any scientific theory, Dirac's theory is not necessarily the last word, and we have to admit the possibility that at least some of its implications (in particular, the possibility of FTL speeds) just aren't so. One also has to admit that it is one thing to talk of science fiction "Dirac radios," as mentioned in Chapter Three, and another to see how physics may actually enable one to talk to the past.[30]

Wheeler and Feynman and Their Bilking Paradox

In 1941, at a meeting of the American Physical Society, Princeton University physicist John Wheeler and his student Richard Feynman discussed a seemingly outrageous idea that provided a possible clue for how a Dirac radio might function. The idea was that the advanced wave solutions to Maxwell's equations are not mere mathematical curiosities, but rather have profound physical significance. Their talk received only a small abstract notice in *Physical Review* at the time, but after the war they wrote it all up in a beautiful paper [Wheeler and Feynman, 1945]. Their primary motivation was to explain the origin of the force of radiative reaction discussed by Lorentz earlier in the century. This reaction force is the cause of the energy loss suffered by an accelerated charged particle. Lorentz, who thought of charged particles as having finite size, attributed this reaction force to the retarded (by the time required for light to cross the width of the charged particle) coulomb repulsion force of one side of the particle's charge on the opposite side. Unfortunately, this leads to various conceptual and mathematical problems including an arbitrary assumption of how the charge is distributed over/through the finite volume, infinite self-interactions, and the issue as to what keeps the charge from blowing itself apart by internal coulomb repulsion.

Wheeler and Feynman's theory, on the other hand, avoided these problems by postulating point charges, since a point charge cannot repel itself. But then whence the reaction force if there is no repulsion? Their revolutionary explanation was first to imagine the accelerated point charge radiating outward; this *retarded* radiation is then eventually absorbed by distant matter. This distant matter, which itself consists of point charges that are accelerated by the received radiation, then radiates backward in time, back toward the original charge that started this chain of events. This backward-in-time, or *advanced*, radiation arrives back in the past of the original charge and is the cause of the observed reaction force. Indeed,

Wheeler and Feynman proposed that an accelerated charge will not radiate unless there is to be absorption at some other distant place and future time. The *future* behavior of a distant absorber determines the *past* event of radiation; there is simply no such thing as just radiating into empty space.

Astonishingly, this noncausal view had been around for at least twenty years; Wheeler and Feynman developed their views independently, but after their 1941 talk, Einstein (who perhaps recalled his 1909 debate about advanced effects with Ritz) brought a 1922 paper by Hugo Tetrode to their attention.[31] In that paper Tetrode had written that "the Sun would not radiate if it were alone in space and no other bodies could absorb its radiation ... If for example I observed through my telescope yesterday evening that star which let us say is 100 light years away, then not only did I know that the light which it allowed to reach my eye was emitted 100 years ago, but also the star or individual atoms of it knew already 100 years ago that I, who then did not even exist, would view it yesterday evening at such and such a time."

None of the preceding, of course, is obvious. As one writer put it in a tutorial appearing just two years after Wheeler and Feynman's 1945 paper [Berenda, 1947], "Any physical theory which seriously proposes that events in the future may be the efficient cause of events in the past certainly may be regarded—at least at first glance—as rather revolutionary doctrine." Indeed. To be sure the doctrine is clear, let me restate what Tetrode and later Wheeler and Feynman had in mind. Imagine we have an electric charge that we mechanically shake (i.e., accelerate). This allows us to assign a definite *cause* to the charge's acceleration, which of course creates radiation. This radiation travels outward into space as an observed retarded field and is eventually absorbed by distant matter. The charges in this distant matter are thus accelerated, and they in turn radiate. This induced radiation again consists, according to Wheeler and Feynman, of both retarded and advanced fields. The advanced fields radiate outward but backward in time toward the original charge, collapsing upon it at the precise instant we first shook it, thereby producing the radiative reaction force. At any instant of time, at any point in space, the observed field is the sum of the retarded field traveling away from the source into the future, and the advanced field traveling to the source into the past.

But, argued Wheeler and Feynman, there is one last point that has been left out—there is also another advanced field due to the original, mechanical shaking of the source charge. That field is traveling into the past and away from the charge. That is, somehow a field traveling *forward* in time will *converge onto* the source because we *will* shake it. Wheeler and Feynman showed that prior to the mechanical-shaking cause that starts this whole process, the advanced radiation field of the source and the advanced radiation fields of the absorbers exactly cancel each other at every point in space and time (if there is total absorption in the future), thus accounting for the experimental fact that we observe a zero total field before the shaking occurs.

Wheeler and Feynman showed that if we accept these ideas, then everything we actually observe is predictable: radiative reaction, the direction of the electromagnetic arrow from past to future (retarded-only effects), and the absence of infinite self-interactions.[32] That is, we gain these rewards if we accept backward time travel, a step too big for many in 1945 and for nearly as many today. This formulation of particle interactions is difficult for many physicists to swallow because it leads to apparent paradoxes. For the same reason Tetrode's earlier work also went virtually unnoticed during the two decades before Wheeler and Feynman.

Tetrode published in a German journal, but even in America Wheeler and Feynman's ideas were anticipated. Back in 1926 G. Lewis had stated that "I am going to make the ... assumption that an atom never emits light except to another atom, and to claim that it is as absurd to think of light emitted by one atom regardless of the existence of a receiving atom as it would be to think of an atom absorbing light without the existence of light to be absorbed." Wheeler and Feynman were by 1945 aware of Lewis. (There is no evidence that Lewis was aware of Tetrode.) Certainly they must have been intrigued by Lewis' paradox: "I shall not attempt to conceal the conflict between these views and common sense. The light coming from a distant star is absorbed, let us say, by a molecule of chlorophyl which has recently been produced in a living plant. We say that the light from the star was on its way toward us a thousand years ago. What rapport can there be between the emitting source and this newly made molecule of chlorophyll?" That is, if at some intermediate time and place the star's light is blocked, thus preventing the absorption, it would mean that we could alter the course of past events. Could, asked Lewis, refusing to look at a star *now* affect the emission of the star's light in the *past*? Lewis was making a clear statement of backward causation when posing this bilking paradox. Lewis' very next words show that he understood the likely reaction of his readers to all this: "Such an idea is repugnant to all our notions of causality and temporal sequence." As with Tetrode's work, Lewis' ideas were ahead of the times.

These astonishing puzzles of Tetrode and Lewis were, however, not repugnant at all, but rather were an inspiration to Wheeler and Feynman and almost certainly were the motivation for them to create their famous bilking paradox, which was presented in a sequel paper [Wheeler and Feynman, 1949]. Wheeler and Feynman opened their paradox as follows: "If the present motion of a is affected by the future motion of b, then the observation of a attributes a certain inevitability to the motion of b. Is not this conclusion in direct conflict with our recognized ability to influence the future motion of b?" Here, once again, the conflict between free will and determinism arises (see [Newton, CPT]), and to sidestep this human concern Wheeler and Feynman constructed a paradox machine, one that operates totally automatically and which in subsequent literature has come to be called [Fitzgerald, 1970] the "logically pernicious self-inhibitor." In their description of this paradox machine, Wheeler and Feynman ask us to imagine two charged particles a and b positioned five light-hours apart. As shown in Figure 17, a is attached to the arm of a pivoted shutter, toward which a pellet is moving from a great distance away. Normally the way we think of things happening involves just retarded fields. The

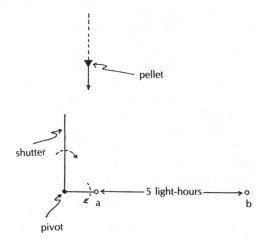

FIGURE 17. Wheeler and Feynman's paradox machine.

pellet hits the arm, knocking it downward, and thereby accelerating charge *a*; this acceleration of charge *a* creates a radiation field that arrives at charge *b* five hours later, thus accelerating charge *b*; this acceleration of charge *b* creates a radiation field that arrives back at charge *a* five hours later (ten hours after the pellet hit the arm).

The Wheeler and Feynman view, however, as stated earlier, claims that this description has left out half the picture—the *advanced* fields. Specifically, suppose the pellet will hit the arm and accelerate *a* at 6 P.M. Then, not only will *b* be affected five hours later at 11 P.M., but also five hours *earlier* at 1 P.M. This advanced acceleration of *b*, in turn, sends out an advanced field that arrives at *a* at 8 A.M. The paradox is now easy to see. As Wheeler and Feynman described events, we see *a* suffer a premonitory movement at 8 A.M. Seeing this motion in the morning, we conclude that the pellet will hit the arm in the evening. We return to the scene a few seconds before 6 P.M. and block the pellet from acting on *a*, a task automatically accomplished by the shutter in Wheeler and Feynman's machine. But then we are faced with the puzzle of explaining why *a* moved in the morning? Wheeler and Feynman claimed they had resolved this bilking paradox by using an argument based on the observation that discontinuous forces (more generally, *signals*) are never observed in nature. Wheeler and Feynman concluded that the shutter does not completely block the pellet, but rather the shutter suffers a "glancing blow." That is, a very weak advanced signal is received by charge *a*, moving the shutter just enough to induce the "glancing blow," and it is this partial interaction that results in the weakened signal.

Absorber Theory and Signaling to the Past

Wheeler and Feynman's argument *is* logically and physically sensible, as it is simply an early statement of the principle of self-consistency. However, I think it is amazing that few physicists challenged Wheeler and Feynman on it.[33] A philosopher did, however, and I think her analysis [Hesse, 1961] is correct as is her conclusion that "there is no solution in terms of classical physics," (although Hesse does talk about a quantum mechanical explanation). Many years later Feynman wrote (in his autobiographical *Surely You're Joking, Mr. Feynman!*) that at one time Wheeler and Feynman thought it would not be too hard to work out the quantum version of their theory. First Wheeler failed in the task, though, and then Feynman tried his hand at it, but as he stated: "I never solved it, either—a quantum theory of half-advanced, half-retarded potentials—and I worked on it for years." This paradox (if it is a paradox—after all, if advanced fields do not exist, then there is no problem) remains unresolved.

Wheeler himself summed matters up nicely years later [Wheeler, 1979]: "Interconnections run forward and backward in time in such numbers as to make an unbelievable maze. That weaving together of past and future seems to contradict every normal idea of causality. However, when the number of particles is great enough to absorb completely the signal starting out from any source, then this myriad of couplings adds up to a simple result: the familiar retarded actions of everyday experience, plus the familiar force of radiative reaction with its familiar sign." Is this view of nature correct?

Some physicists have simply assumed that the advanced field does exist and have explored where that assumption might go. In [Schild, 1963], for example, the relativistic motion of two point charges (in concentric circular orbits in the same plane) interacting through time-symmetric fields is shown to be consistent with stationary (i.e., periodic) solutions. And in [Driver, 1979] the one-dimensional motion (along the infinite x axis) of two point charges interacting through time-symmetric fields is shown to be unique provided that they are initially far enough apart (which does not have to be very far—4600 electron radii will do). As Driver observes, however, such few-body, time-symmetric interactions have received little attention.

Could we use advanced waves to signal to the past? Wright [1979] argues rather strongly (if not always coherently) that we could. Or if this requires some yet-to-be-developed technological breakthrough in transmitters (and if receivers were easier to construct), could we at least listen to the future (and could it send us the details of the transmitter breakthrough!)? Professor John Cramer at the University of Washington has advanced a clever suggestion on how to use such signals in principle, although he maintains a conservative skepticism about such fields in the absence of any experimental evidence. [34] Cramer, observing that there is about a 2.5 second roundtrip delay in transmitting a radar signal to the Moon and receiving the echo for retarded waves, extends this observation to advanced waves; the echo for the advanced-wave case would be received 2.5 seconds *before* transmission. By using multiple reflections of the advanced wave, one could then extend the echo as far back into the past as desired. Whether or not this would be "good" is more problematical for Cramer, who wrote (contrary to the arguments presented earlier in this chapter) that "if advanced waves [could be so used] then our grip on reality would become more tenuous. The past could never be considered over and done with, because anyone with the proper hardware could send messages back in time and alter what had already happened."

The suggestion of conducting an experimental test of the absorber theory was made as early as 1926 [Lewis, 1926], with a quick (but sympathetic) rebuttal in [Tolman and Smith, 1926]. The first experimental search for advanced waves seems to be the effort described in [Partridge, 1973]. Flaws in that search process prompted [Herron and Pegg, 1974], which discusses an experiment designed to detect advanced waves (if they exist); as these authors wrote, the exciting possibility of a positive result "would have such far-reaching consequences on our ideas of the unidirectionality of time and causality that ... the experiment justifies a large amount of effort, even if no conclusive result is obtained for years." A more recent attempt to detect advanced waves is described in [Schmidt and Newman, 1980]. All these searches gave negative results, however, and the world still waits for the first Dirac radio. Still, attempts have been made to support Wheeler and Feynman's bilking explanation theoretically through analyses of the various paradoxes caused by sending messages to the past via hypothetical FTL particles called tachyons (see [Shulman, 1971a], [Peres and Schulman, 1972]) or through the study of self-colliding billiard balls time-traveling through wormhole time machines (see Tech Note 9) and [Friedman et al., 1990], [Echeverria, Klinkhammer, and Thorne, 1991]). Novikov, [1992] has replaced the billiard balls with exploding bombs, a twist that gives the ultimate in "time bombs!"

Over the years the Wheeler and Feynman view has also been the object of many theoretical objections. Hogarth [1962], for example, rightfully complained that Wheeler and Feynman had assumed a static, time-symmetric spacetime for the Universe, in which the properties of all past and future absorbers are identical. This is obviously not so in an expanding (or contracting) Universe, and as Hogarth wrote, "No serious modern cosmological theory is framed in a static Universe."

Another puzzle for Hogarth is that Wheeler and Feynman took a time-symmetric theory in a time-symmetric Universe—and arrived at a *non* time-symmetric solution! As [Price, 1991b] aptly puts it, Wheeler and Feynman "plucked an asymmetric rabbit from a symmetric hat." Wheeler and Feynman performed this trick by supposing that while the Universe is static, it was created with asymmetrical initial conditions of low entropy. Thus, for Wheeler and Feynman the one-way thermodynamic arrow of time is the primary arrow, with the electromagnetic arrow its consequence. (The *how* of the low-entropy initial cosmological boundary condition was left unexplained.) This was the position adopted by Einstein in his 1909 debate with Ritz and by Stephen Hawking more recently [Hawking, 1985].

Many years later, [Wheeler, 1979] explained again Wheeler and Feynman's 1945 viewpoint: "The particles of the absorber are either at rest or in random motion before the acceleration of the source. They are correlated with it in velocity after that acceleration. Thus radiation and radiative reaction are understood in terms, not of pure electrodynamics, but of statistical mechanics." Hogarth objected to this explanation, which he felt was unnecessary, believing instead that the expansion of our actually nonstatic Universe would provide the required asymmetry. In Hogarth's view it is the cosmological arrow that is the primary one, and the electromagnetic arrow is its consequence.

Wheeler and Feynman had shown that both the advanced and the retarded solutions are self-consistent in a static Universe; Hogarth's interest was in whether the observed retarded solution alone would be self-consistent in an expanding Universe. His conclusion—it depends (on the details of the expansion)! Hoyle and Narlikar in 1964 expanded on Hogarth's study and claimed to have shown that the retarded solution *alone* is self-consistent *if* the expansion is steady-state through the continuous creation of matter. This would be the case because if only retarded effects are to occur, then each emitter of radiation needs a large number of absorbers (e.g., ionized intergalactic gas) in its future light cone to provide for complete absorption. This, in turn, requires that the density of matter not decline "too fast" with the expansion. That is, the future Universe must not be "too transparent."

This conclusion was embraced with enthusiasm by Hoyle, a British cosmologist whose name has long been identified with the idea of continuous creation of matter. Since then, however, continuous-creation cosmologies have fallen into disfavor, as it was in 1965, just a year after Hoyle and Narlikar wrote, that the cosmic microwave background radiation was discovered. This is now taken to be very strong evidence for the existence of the primordial fireball that was the Big Bang and equally strong evidence for rejecting a steady-state Universe (though not by Hoyle, who has an almost fanatical devotion to non-Big-Bang cosmologies; see [Hoyle, 1975] for Hoyle's explanation of the microwave background).

A real puzzle with the Big Bang Universe is that it expands from a dense, opaque past into a less dense, ever more transparent future, with each emitter having a large number of absorbers in its past light cone. That should result (according to Hoyle and Narlikar) in an observed advanced solution, and thus in a reversed electromagnetic arrow that should allow communication with the past. The fact that we have not yet discovered how to perform such communication might be taken to mean that the advanced waves of Wheeler and Feynman are, in fact, just a bit of pretty mathematics devoid of any physical reality.

One interesting rebuttal to this is that the analyses of Hogarth and of Hoyle and Narlikar were simply wrong [Davies, 1972a]! But Professor Davies' analysis has its puzzles, too, as he showed that all of the standard expanding relativistic cosmological models of the Universe are too transparent in the future to explain the observed retarded-only waves in terms of the Wheeler and Feynman absorber theory.

There is yet another problem with the Wheeler and Feynman absorber theory—the puzzle of neutrino absorption. Neutrinos are particles that interact so weakly with matter that a beam of them would have to travel through many hundreds of light-years of lead for there to be a significant attenuation of the beam intensity. How can such particles find enough future absorbers to make possible their observed journeys into the future of our expanding Universe? Narlikar [1962a] admitted that a continuous-creation Universe "only 'just' manages" to explain retarded neutrinos, but at least it manages—but again the 1965 discovery of the cosmic microwave background, the signature of a Big Bang origin of the Universe, fatally wounded that analysis.

For such an exciting idea as communicating with the past, I have been able to find only a few uses of advanced radio in science fiction. In the 1951 story "Earthman, Beware!" [Anderson, 1991], first published in the magazine *Super Science Stories*, Poul Anderson hinted at advanced waves with something called the "ultrawave effect": "While gravitational effects were produced by the presence of matter, ultrawave effects ... did not appear unless there was a properly tuned receiver somewhere. They seemed somehow 'aware' of a listener even before they came into existence [i.e., of a future absorber in Wheeler and Feynman's terminology]." And the evil scientific genius Lex Luthor, Superman's arch enemy, invented such a radio while in prison in 1961. Made from ordinary AM radio parts, he used it to call for rescue by (and to listen to messages from) the Legion of Super-Villains from the thirtieth century!

The most interesting science fictional use of backward-in-time signaling is in "Beep" [Blish, 1976]. Here the "Dirac radio" for instantaneous transmissions is described, and we learn that at the beginning of each received message there is always an irritating audio beep (hence the title) that is seemingly a useless artifact of the mysterious workings of the Dirac radio. Its only obvious characteristic is a continuous frequency spectrum from 30 hertz to well above 18,000 hertz. It is only at the end of the story that the main character learns that this spectrum is the "simultaneous reception of every one of the Dirac messages which have ever been sent, or ever will be sent."[35] There is no mention of advanced waves, but clearly Blish knew that instantaneous (infinite-velocity) signals would travel into the past. The story does a masterful job at presenting the mystery of listening to the future. At one point characters in the twenty-first century hear the commander of a time-traveling "worldline cruiser" transmit a poignant call for help from 11,000,000 light-years away, and from 65 centuries in the future. Most interesting of all, however, is Blish's statement of a technical issue that I have not seen raised before (although "Cambridge, 1:58 A.M." [Benford, E], the precursor story to the novel *Timescape* [Benford, 1980], hints at it in passing). Blish asks, If signals arrive at a receiver simultaneously from all future times, how can they be separated? Blish resorts to some scientifiction babble-talk to answer this question, but it remains a puzzle.

Tachyonic Signals, Spooky Actions, and the Bell Antitelephone

Science fiction writers have often used FTL motion to reverse time. For example, in "The Worlds of If" [Weinbaum, 1949] there is this throwaway line in a lecture on time travel from a curmudgeonly (but lovable) old physics professor,

Haskel van Manderpootz: "And as for the past—in the first place, you'd have to exceed light-speed, which immediately entails the use of more than an infinite number of horsepowers." This is a second reason, beyond the reversal of cause and effect, for why many physicists reject backward time travel (irrespective of the logical paradoxes); FTL motion implies travel to the past, but such FTL motion is impossible precisely because of the infinite energy required by special relativity to penetrate the "light barrier," and so time travel to the past must be impossible, too. The Professor's point is a good one (it comes straight from Professor Einstein, as seen in the opening quote in Tech Note 7), but maybe there is a way around his argument. The key to a possible rebuttal depends on the existence of FTL particles, the now well-known *tachyons*. (This name was coined by the American physicist Gerald Feinberg [Feinberg, 1967] from the Greek word *tachys* for "swift.")[36]

The idea of the tachyon is a very old one and can be found hinted at in the work of the Greek poet and philosopher Lucretius (who died twenty years before the birth of Christ). In his discussion of visual images in Book 4 of his giant (well over 7400 lines) science poem *De Rerum Natura,* we find the following words about particles of matter originating from deep inside the Sun:[37] "Do you see how much faster and farther they must travel, how they must run through an extent of space many times vaster in the time it takes the light of the Sun to spread throughout the sky?"

The first attempt at a relativistic treatment of such particles in the physics literature did not occur until two thousand years later in [Tanaka, 1960] and in [Bilaniuk *et al.*, 1962], which observed that special relativity is not violated by FTL motion.[38] Relativity theory precludes the acceleration of a massive particle to the speed of light but does allow a massless particle, the photon, to exist just at the speed of light. Photons are emitted during various physical processes, and they move from the instant of their creation at the speed of light;[39] the only way to slow down a photon is to destroy it by absorbing it. Advocates of the possibility of the existence of tachyons make a similiar argument when asking if there might not be particles emitted during various physical processes (yet unknown) which move from the instant of their creation at speeds greater than that of light. Such an argument neatly avoids the "acceleration through the light-barrier" problem, but then there are other concerns. For example, such FTL particles would have to have an imaginary mass (see Tech Note 7) if they are to carry real energy and momentum, and what can *imaginary mass* mean? This is convincingly answered by the proponents of tachyons, who say that the rest mass of a superluminal particle would be an unobservable because there is no subluminal frame in which the particle could be at rest. That is, there is no frame of reference in which the mysterious imaginary mass could be measured, and it is only observable changes in the real energy and momentum that characterize particle interactions.

A more serious problem for tachyons, according to those who dislike the ideas of backward causation and time travel, is the observation that in some frames of reference a FTL particle would appear to have *negative* energy. explaining why this is a problem, [Feinberg, 1967] states: "By the principle of relativity, any state

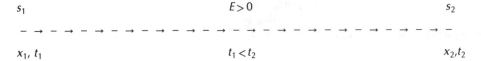

FIGURE 18. The emission of a positive energy particle, followed by absorbtion.

which is possible for one observer must be possible for all observers, and hence FTL particles can exist in negative-energy states for all observers ... The occurrence of negative-energy states for particles has always been objected to on the grounds that no other system could be stable against the emission of these negative-energy particles, an entirely unphysical behavior."

This kind of objection to FTL particles was raised early in the history of tachyons (even before they received their name!), and it was answered in [Bilaniuk et al., 1962], which proposed, the so-called *reinterpretation principle* (RP).

To see how the RP works, consider the illustration in Figure 18: a source S_1 at x_1 emits a FTL particle at time t_1. This particle then travels to an absorber S_2 at x_2, arriving there at the later time t_2. S_1 and S_2 are in the same reference frame, and for an observer in that frame the particle energy E is positive. However, it is always possible to find another observer in a relatively moving frame for whom this process would look as if t_2 is less than t_1 with $E < 0$. In other words, for the moving observer the particle would appear as a negative energy particle moving backward in time. (See Tech Note 7 where it is shown that the particle speed must be not just superluminal, but the even faster *ultraluminal*.) Note that for the moving observer the emission by S_1 of negative energy *increases* the energy of S_1, and the absorption of negative energy by S_2 decreases the energy of S_2. The decrease of S_2 occurs (for this moving observer) before the increase in energy by S_1 because, as noted above, $t_2 < t_1$. The moving observer naturally interprets this process as the emission of positive energy by S_2, followed by absorption by S_1. This reinterpretation thus preserves, so it would seem, our common-sense idea of causality and it avoids any mention of the problems of backward time travel.[40] The RP appears to have slipped around these problems merely by redefining which source is transmitting and which source is receiving the tachyon. Indeed, [Feinberg, 1967] claimed that the RP avoids the creation of causal loops and their associated paradoxes, a claim repeated in [Italiano, 1986] which used the RP to eliminate paradoxes from Gödel's time-travel Universe.

Despite Feinberg's paper, however, [Newton, 1970] argued that the effectiveness of the RP in avoiding causal loops is "illusory" and "irrelevant,"while [Thouless, 1969] and [Rolnick, 1969] concluded that the causal paradoxes would actually preclude the possibility of tachyons interacting with ordinary matter, which is a polite way of saying that tachyons have no more reality than do unicorns! (In Tech Note 7 I show what Thouless, Rolnick, and Newton meant by their criticisms of the RP, by giving an example of how such a paradoxical loop could be created by the exchange of FTL signals from which the RP cannot escape; indeed, the RP plays a crucial role in creating the paradox! This does not mean that the loop couldn't logically happen; it's just that backward causation and time travel to the past *are* such an odd business!)

The RP's effect of flipping the roles of transmitter and receiver also attracted criticism. Some analysts have pointed out that if one can modulate a superluminal signal to send a message into the past, then certainly one can *sign* the message. Since the RP cannot alter a signature, the origin of the message is consequently completely unambiguous. To quote the delightful example from [Benford, Book, and Newcomb, 1970]: "If Shakespeare types out *Hamlet* on his tachyon transmitter, Bacon receives the transmission at some earlier time. But no amount of reinterpretation will make Bacon the author of *Hamlet*. It is Shakespeare, not Bacon, who exercises control over the content of the message." This last line is of central importance. The authors emphasize its point by immediately observing that a signature is a relativistic *invariant*, and that, indeed, it establishes a causal ordering quite independent of any temporal ordering. As [Fitzgerald, 1974] and [Craig, 1988] put it, respectively, in such cases the RP "is laughed to scorn" and the RP "sounds merely like the endorsement of what can only be characterized as a fantastic delusion."

Even more sophisticated scenarios than the one by Benford *et al.* have been devised to show how backward causation can result from FTL signals irrespective of one's view of the RP. One such example involves a chain of signal transmissions between four observers, where the chain finally works its way back to the original observer who started the process. Bryce DeWitt, who created this example (called the "DeWitt Gambit" in [Fitzgerald, 1970]), showed how to arrange the spacetime geometry of the participants in the chain so that at each stage there is no dispute over who is sending and who is receiving, thus avoiding *a priori* the RP. And yet, when the chain reaches the last (first) observer, it is *before* he started(s) the chain! It is the time-travel version of Escher's famous visual paradoxes *Ascending and Descending* and *Waterfall*. For a theory of tachyons in which such causal loops cannot occur, see [Everett and Antippa, CPT].

Today, most physicists reject the possibility of backward-in-time messages, not because of flaws in the RP, but because such messages could create bilking paradoxes (as in the DeWitt Gambit and in the last example in Tech Note 7). Sudarshan, one of the original advocates of tachyons, had actually admitted the possibility of such paradoxes when he wrote in [Sudarshan, 1969] that "if FTL exist, we are provided with an *almost* [my emphasis] instantaneous communication channel. While distant observers can communicate by tachyons there is a physical limitation to the speeds that can be employed: two observers in relative motion with velocity $v < c$, can employ only [nonultraluminal] tachyons." This speed limitation is, of course, precisely what is required to forbid the sending of messages to the past and to prevent the consequent possibility of creating a bilking paradox.

More recently, [Arntzenius, 1990] has observed that although relativistically invariant, instantaneous action-at-a-distance theories exist, that all such theories impose on tachyons equations of motion that are exactly what is needed so that any procedure that could imaginably lead to a paradox (such as a bilking paradox), is not allowed *by the physics*. That is, we will never be in the position of having to make a metaphysical argument about free will to avoid the backward-causation problems of time travel.

The old Wheeler and Feynman idea for explaining bilking paradoxes, that no signal is really discontinuous, was reexamined by [Schulman, 1971a] in the context of tachyons. Schulman's paper asks us to consider the following situation: A human (call him *A*) has a lamp on a table before him. The lamp is controlled by a tachyon receiver—the lamp is illuminated only when a tachyon signal (a pulse) is detected. At three o'clock *A* will send a tachyon signal to *B* if the lamp does not glow at one o'clock. (*B* is an echo transmitter, rebroadcasting any signal it receives.) Now, the spacetime geometry of *A* and *B* is such that a signal sent by either travels one hour backward in time when sent to the other. Thus, if *A* sends at three o'clock, *B* will receive at two (and immediately echo), and the echo will arrive back at *A* at one o'clock. The paradox, of course, is that *A* sends a signal only if the lamp does *not* glow; that is, only if he does *not* send the signal!

Schulman next reminds us of the Wheeler and Feynman claim that every pulsed signal is actually continuous; this argument would include the illumination of the lamp. Therefore, the lamp is not just on or off, but is potentially at any level of illumination in between. So, there sits *A*, and at one o'clock the lamp seems to glow dimly; so, says Schulman, "*A* thinks it over, vacillating, finally sending a slightly late signal which isn't full-strength." So, of course, the echo isn't full-strength either, which nicely accounts for the original dim glow. This conclusion *is* consistent, but does seem to ask for a lot of supposing. Schulman himself is not so sure about the validity of Universal continuity, writing at the end that "it is not clear that the Wheeler-Feynman assumption ... ought to be made," but [Kowalczynski, 1984] disagreed wijth the assumption of Universal continuity and specifically declared that Schulman was wrong!) A generalization of Schulman's argument to cover all signals from simple pulse signals to arbitarily complex signals was presented in Donald [1978]. (The assumption of Universal continuity remains central in this work.) Donald believes that his generalization resolves *all* potential paradoxes that one could imagine resulting from the existence of a closed timelike curve. More recently, Kip Thorne at the California Institute of Technology has tried to avoid bilking paradoxes and backward causation in wormhole time machines (see Tech Note 9) by using Schulman's approach (see [Redmount, 1990], and [Friedman *et al.*, 1990]). Schulman's argument has even appeared in science fiction; for example, *Timescape* [Benford, 1980] tells a story in which the future tries to change the past by sending tachyon messages warning of impending disaster.

Not surprisingly, the supposed ability of a modulated beam of tachyons to send a message into the past raised concerns about free will and determinism. Suppose, went such arguments, you received a tachyon message from yourself from tomorrow informing you that a man you plan to kill tonight is still alive (tomorrow). Does that mean it is then beyond your power to kill him tonight? According to [Fitzgerald, 1970], the answer is no; you *could* kill—but if you did, then the message from tomorrow would not have arrived. And since ignorance is not a precondition to free will, your newly acquired knowledge does not, by itself, suddenly limit your ability to kill the man. But, Fitzgerald went on to write, if you do not attempt to kill the man because you believe the message from your future self, then in fact the time message *has* limited your free will.

Fitzgerald's position was rebutted in [Craig, 1988], which argues that it is not your ability to kill that is altered, but rather your motivation. Craig points out that such motivational changes can occur without invoking anything as radical as a message from the future. Suppose, Craig says, that just before you fire the fatal shot into your victim you learn from him that he is, in fact, your beloved, long-lost uncle. Clearly your motivation for killing him will be changed, but equally clearly your ability to kill him is unchanged. The mechanism for obtaining genealogical information, whether via time travel or as a last-minute appeal from your intended victim himself, is (says Craig) simply irrelevant.

One analyst who is not so sure of Craig's argument is Professor Schulman. In [Schulman, 1971a] he writes that "history is a set of world lines essentially frozen into spacetime. While subjectively we may feel strongly that our actions are determined only by our backward light cone, this may not always be the case ... ." That is, Schulman appears open to the possibility that influences originating in the future might indeed have impact on the present.

More recently, the romance of communication with the past via superluminal speeds has passed from tachyons to quantum mechanics because of a mathematical result called Bell's theorem. John Bell, a physicist at CERN, published his work "On the Einstein-Podolsky-Rosen Paradox" [Bell, 1987] as an unimposing little article in an obscure, now defunct journal. Since then it has certainly become one of the most cited physics papers of that decade. The paradox cited in Bell's title refers to a famous paper by Einstein [1935b], in which Einstein challenged the conventional view of quantum mechanics; that there is no objective reality to anything until it is observed. ([de Beauregard, 1980] says Einstein, alone, made the same challenge in different terms as early as 1927.)

The conventional view of quantum mechanics formulates physics in terms of probability wave functions that collapse into specific realities only when measurements are made of states of systems, which may be as elementary as a single particle (see Note 14 again.) Until such measurements are made, says quantum mechanics, a system has *no* specific state; instead it has a probability distribution over a set of possible states. Einstein and co-authors Boris Podolsky and Nathan Rosen (the same Rosen of the Einstein-Rosen bridge wormhole) rejected this probabilistic interpretation of nature (recall Einstein's famous dicitation "God does not play dice with the cosmos"). Einstein and his colleagues asserted that quantum mechanics may be valid as far as it goes, but that it leaves something (as yet unknown) out in describing reality; i.e., they suggest that quantum mechanics is "incomplete" and that it incorporates so-called "hidden variables." They posed this view in the form of a paradox, traditionally called the "EPR paradox." The paradox was posed as a thought experiment in which quantum mechanics declares that the properties of a spatially distributed system, when measured at point *A*, are forced to assume specific values at point *B* (without there being a measurement at *B*).

Thus, said Einstein, there are just two possibilities. Either the system properties at *B* must have been what they are from the very start (even if the measurement at *A* had not been done), the view he accepted, *or* there must have been a linkage between the system at *A* and the system at *B* so that the wave function collapse at *A* is instantly transmitted to *B* so that the wave function can collapse there, too. Because *A* and *B* may be arbitrarily far apart, this latter explanation obviously requires a FTL transmission mechanism, something Einstein called a "spooky action-at-a-distance"; the term expresses very well his opinion of the idea. (Some translations replace Einstein's word "spooky" with "ghostly," but the sentiment is clearly the same.) For nearly thirty years the debate between proponents of these two alternatives remained at a metaphysical, nonquantitative level. Then came Bell's paper in 1964.

Bell's theorem mathematically poses the choice between Einstein's and the conventional views of quantum mechanics through the use of an inequality involving certain measurable properties of a system. (The details are unimportant here, but Bell himself has written a nice exposition of it all for the layperson in "Bertlmann's Socks and the Nature of Reality" [Bell, 1987].) If these measurements are such that the inequality is satisfied, then Einstein's position would be vindicated. If, however, the measurements are such that the inequality is violated, then the conventional interpretation of quantum mechanics would be vindicated. That would mean that Einstein's FTL spooky action-at-a-distance" effect would exist.

Bell's great contribution, therefore, was to remove the debate about quantum mechanics from metaphysics and to place it in the realm of experimental physics. All that needed to be done was to make the necessary measurements. These technically quite difficult experiments were eventually performed by the French physicist Alain Aspect and his colleagues at the Institute of Applied Optics of the University of Paris a decade and a half after Bell showed what had to be done [Aspect *et al.*, 1981, 1982a,b]. The results unequivocally supported the conventional view of quantum mechanics. (Earlier experiments had been done, also showing quantum mechanics' predictions to agree with observation, but various technical details of these experiments still left some uncertainties about how to interpret the results; the Aspect experiments, however, are considered definitive.) Einstein was simply wrong, and his spooky action does in fact seem to exist. So, do we have, at last, experimental evidence of the possibility of information transfer at FTL speeds?

Well, it seems not. A paper that rejects the possibility of an FTL mechanism in quantum mechanics [Ghirardi, Rimini and Weber, 1980] identifies subtle loopholes in the arguments of those who thought they had found a way around special relativity. Indeed, the authors concluded their paper with the hope that their analysis would "stop useless debates on this subject." But alas! The majority of physicists today are actually more confused over Bell's theorem than they were with Einstein's original EPR paradox. In those early days one could agree with Einstein, who argued that quantum mechanics was valid *as far as it went* but that even though all our measurements are stochastic in result, a deeper theory would show the existence of hidden variables that would explain the reality of a system's specific properties. Because of the work by Bell and Aspect, however, it was shown that quantum mechanics as it stands leads to correct predictions. In other words, quantum mechanics is correct *without* invoking any so-called hidden variables (see [Wigner, 1970] for more on this point) and in addition one seems to have to accept FTL transmission to explain the experimental results. Just what this means is still the center of great controversy.[41] The consensus (among those who dare venture an opinion!) seems to be that there is no FTL-information-transfer mechanism involved in quantum mechanics. In a play on the hard-to-miss coincidence in names, the tachyonic antitelephone cannot, according to present thought, be made into a "Bell antitelephone."[42]

However, it isn't obvious to everyone that this is a correct conclusion. For example, Cornell physics professor N. David Mermin has reported that some years ago he received the text of a letter written by a senior person at an unspecified California think tank to the Under Secretary of Defense for Research and Engineering in the Pentagon;[43] there he read: "If in fact we can control the FTL nonlocal effect, it would be possible ... to make an untappable and unjammable command-control-communication system at very high bit rates for use in the submarine fleet. The important point is that since there is no ordinary electromagnetic signal linking the encoder with the decoder in such a hypothetical system, there is nothing for the enemy to tap or jam. The enemy would have to have actual possession of the 'black box' decoder to intercept the message, whose reliability would not depend on separation from the encoder nor on ocean or weather conditions ... ." One wonders what might have been the Under Secretary's response to this letter, and of what sorts of top secret experiments may have been conducted. It is almost certain that, whatever they may have been, they failed. As [Cramer, 1988b] put it, "Up to now nature has covered her tracks pretty well, blocking all possibilities for using the EPR effect for FTL communication."[44] Of course, the think-tank letter actually represents a *failure* of imagination, since the backward-causation effect of EPR's FTL effect is certainly a "quantum jump" beyond mere instantaneous communication.[45]

Most recently, [Price, 1991a,b] has reintroduced an idea first put forth in [Sciama, 1958], with the suggestion that it may again be time to think about a modified interpretation of Einstein's hidden-variables view of quantum mechanics. This altered interpretation, which avoids the constraints imposed by Bell's inequality, says hidden-variable values depend not only on previous states but also on future states of the system in question. Because the future states are unknown, any quantum theory developed will necessarily have an apparent indeterminate nature; and that, says this idea, is why quantum mechanics is statistical in nature. Professor Price then observes that "the fact that the instantaneous influence approach is nevertheless regarded as less implausible is an indication of how strongly counterintuitive we find the idea of influencing the past. But what is the basis of this intuition?'' Price believes it is simply ''prejudice, grounded ... in our own asymmetric nature and condition.''

All of this chapter, indeed this entire book, is concerned about controversal issues. What should readers think about all the debates over FTL speeds, quantum mechanics, backward causation, and time travel? By 1974 the outpouring of papers on tachyons, for example, and the arguments about the causal-loop paradoxes that tachyons seem to create had reached the flood stage. Some of the exchanges were becoming a bit heated, too, with opposing authors hinting (not always subtly) at the incredible obtuseness of the other side. For example, [Fox, Kuper, and Lipson, 1970] is relatively gentle in its evaluation: ''The quantum theory of free tachyons ... is an elegant but empty formalism,'' while [Kowalczynski, 1984] put it more bluntly: ''The [tachyonic] literature is infested with a large number of childish works.'' Indeed, with the publication in 1974 of a bibliography on FTL particle papers in the *American Journal of Physics*,[46] the Journal's editor felt compelled to write: ''Until tachyons are verified to exist by experiment, the prudent scholar will treat statements made in these references as hypotheses rather than statements of fact. Moreover, since these authors disagree among themselves, it is a logical certainty that at least some of them are wrong. Readers beware!''

Good advice, indeed, concerning tachyons—as well as of the spooky actions of quantum mechanics, and of time machines, too!

Epilogue

We all from time to time indulge in dreams about traveling back into time. Every time we recall something that happened in the past we make a mental journey back in time. But wouldn't it be grand if we could actually return physically to the most delightful moments of our memories? Wouldn't we all like to reexperience the bliss of childhood, the heydays of youth, or return to make that big decision which we failed to make then, for the lack of courage?

—A philosopher daydreams [Faye, 1987]

Who needs to know the time? It's always either too late, or too early.

—*Chekhov's Journey* [Watson, 1989]

I have been here before,
But when or how I cannot tell:
I know the grass beyond the door,
The sweet keen smell,
The sighing sound, the lights around the shore.
. . . .
Has this been thus before?

—Dante Rossetti, "Sudden Light"

What can be said in closing a book like this one? As the opening quote indicates, we seem to have come full circle. We are, of course, as we were in the beginning, still faced with an obvious question. Is time travel to the past possible? I have tried hard not to proselytize blindly for such a possibility and equally hard to present an even and balanced account of both sides of the matter. The main arguments against backward time travel, causality violation, and the logical paradoxes, are of course the major reasons for exactly what makes the question so interesting in the first place. Many, of course, find these arguments highly persuasive. In particular, many like to cite versions of the grandfather paradox, along with the claim that the only way out is to give-up free-will; a position that Chapter Four suggests has no logical or physical basis. It is astonishing, indeed, that the power of this philosophical red-herring has hardly abated since the days it appeared in the science fiction magazines more than a half-century ago. In a recent essay in *Science* on Gott's cosmic string time machine, for example, the grandfather paradox is called an "obvious problem" for time travel [Travis, 1992]. Because of that particular 'paradox,' many subscribe to the skeptical position that has been clearly stated by science fiction writer and critic Kingsley Amis, who wrote in *New Maps of Hell* [Amis, 1960] that "time travel is inconceivable."

In his introduction to [Lafferty, 1991], Isaac Asimov echoed Amis when he flatly stated, "I think scientists who think up methods of time travel are probably all wrong." Are Amis and Asimov right? Whether the answer is yes or no, the analyses since Gödel's pioneering time travel paper of 1949 have taken a long time to spread among even those who would surely find them high drama. Indeed, Gödel himself seems to be unknown outside of a limited mathematics and physics community. In 1952, for example, the anthologist Groff Conklin wrote in his introduction to "The Middle of the Week After Next" [Leinster, SFAD]: "In this tale we meet our first Mad Scientist. Just as in reality the thoroughly cracked pots used to be found inventing perpetual-motion machines, so in science fiction we find the lunatic fringe more often than not trying to perfect time-travel mechanisms." That same year H. L. Gold, the founding editor of *Galaxy Science Fiction Magazine,* declared [Gold, GRSF1] "Time travel requires a suspension of disbelief that is almost unbelievable ... scientifically, time travel can't stand inspection."

Taking a somewhat less rigid position than that of Conklin and Gold was the nonfiction essay "The Science of Man" in Chad Oliver's 1952 novel *Mists of Dawn* [Oliver, 1952], the story of a teenager who travels in a "space-time machine" back to 50,000 B.C., to the start of Cro-Magnon time: "It would be untrue ... to present the idea of a time machine as anything but what it is, an intriguing literary device, part of the bag of tricks of the science fiction writer ... there is no such thing as a 'science' of time travel." Since Conklin, Gold, and Oliver all wrote just three years after Gödel, perhaps it was simply too soon for his work to be widely known outside of the physics community.

More recent writers, however, are apparently just as unaware of Gödel's time travel analyses (or the later ones of Frank Tipler) as were those early commentators. For example, David Lowenthal repeatedly refers to time travel in his marvelous book *The Past is a Foreign Country* [Lowenthal, 1985] as "fantasy," and to science fiction stories about time travel as "unbridled by common sense." The well-known science fiction writer and critic Alexei Panshin, for yet another example, agrees with Lowenthal; in his Forward to Robert Heinlein's classic time-travel story "All You Zombies—" [Heinlein, MI], Panshin wrote "Time travel is a philosophical concept, not a scientific one. It is, in fact, as has often been pointed out, scientific nonsense ... That s-f writers ... kept returning ... to the scientifically unsensible theme of time travel indicates that their viscera knew something that their minds did not." Mr. Panshin, obviously, had not appreciated either Mr. Gödel or Mr. Tipler.

Professor Paul A. Carter, in his excellent analysis (*The Creation of Tomorrow* [Carter, 1977]) of the first half-century of the science fiction magazines was aware that time travel has a physical rationality to it—but even at that late date he apparently had not appreciated either Gödel's time-travel analyses or the ones that followed. After remarking on how the conventional view has been that backward time travel is simply impossible and then citing the work of Frank Tipler, Carter writes "Only as recently as 1974, in the sober pages of the *Physical Review,* has a physicist been more bold [than the conventional view] ... For seventy years in the meantime, however, without waiting for Professor Tipler to solve his equations ... writers had happily helped themselves to Mr. Wells' invention and sent their characters through time in every direction, forward, backward, and sideways.'' As *The Time Machine* was published in 1895, it is not clear how Carter arrived at the value of seventy, but in fact it was only fifty-four years between Wells' time-travel fiction and Gödel's time-travel physics.

And finally, consider the case of James Gunn, professor of English at the University of Kansas, past president of both the Science Fiction Writers of America and the Science Fiction Research Association, author of the novel *The Immortal* (inspiration for the 1970-71 TV series of the same name), and eminent scholar (*Alternate Worlds* [Gunn, 1975]). His literary credentials are impeccable and his critical influence profound. And yet, thirty years after Gödel and five after Tipler, Professor Gunn wrote in *The Road to Science Fiction* [Gunn, 1979]: "Time travel has been an anomaly in science fiction. Clearly fantastic—there is no evidence that anyone has ever traveled in time and *no theoretical basis for believing that anyone ever will* [my emphasis]."[1] If you've read this far, in particular of the modern analyses by Thorne, Gott, and Novikov, you now know that these last words are simply not so.

The eminent American physicist Freeman Dyson of the Institute for Advanced Study has commented [Dyson, 1979] on this sort of narrow mind-set, with words quoted from Steven Weinberg (who shared the 1979 Nobel Prize in physics), words reminding us that rigidity is not limited to science fiction writers: "This is often the way it is in physics—our mistake is not that we take our theories too seriously, but that we do not take them seriously enough. It is always hard to realize that these numbers and equations we play with at our desks have something to do with the real world. Even worse, there often seems to be a general agreement that certain phenomena are just not fit subjects for respectable theoretical and experimental effort."

Time travel, with its double burden of very difficult mathematics and nonintuitive philosophical implications, is an example of the phenomena that Dyson surely had in mind. This burden is not an easy one, even for those more open to the possibility of time travel. In an April 1991 letter to me, for example, Kip Thorne mentioned a recent visit of his with Stephen Hawking in Cambridge. They had met to review the current status of their work on closed timelike curves, and their joint conclusion concerning time travel was a sobering one: "We now think that we understand these issues less well than either he or I believed a few weeks ago." For example, in [Thorne, 1991] Professor Thorne lists at least three concerns he has about the physical possibility of wormhole time machines: (1) Spacetime may, in fact, be simply connected, so wormholes simply do not exist; (2) Even if wormholes do exist, quantum mechanics may enforce the average energy condition and thereby not allow wormhole throats to remain open; (3) The Cauchy horizon may be unstable and it may collapse into a singularity. Despite these concerns, Thorne thinks the definitive case against time travel is yet to be made. Hawking disagrees.

The split between Hawking's and Thorne's views about the plausibility of time travel is centered on the proper way to handle the quantum-gravitational details of wormholes and the stability of the Cauchy horizon. Hawking, in fact, takes the position [Hawking, 1992] that his analysis shows any mechanism for time travel, wormhole or otherwise, is forbidden (his *Chronology Protection Conjecture*). As he writes, "if you try to create a wormhole to use as a time machine, you have to warp the light cone structure of spacetime so much, that closed time like curves appear anyway," and so the specific details of a wormhole in particular are irrelevant. It is the creation of closed timelike curves by *any* means that Hawking denies. (This therefore also allows Hawking to dismiss the cosmic string time machine described in [Gott, 1991]—see Note 2 for Tech Note 9.)

On the other hand, Kim and Thorne [1991] disagree with some of the details of how Hawking does *his* quantum gravity! More recently, Kim [1992] has argued that the Cauchy horizon *is* stable at the quantum level, but Professor Matt Visser at Washington University in St. Louis has generalized (and endorsed) Hawking's conclusion forbidding time machines [Visser, 1993]—but he doesn't entirely agree with the details of Hawking's analysis, either! Still, Professor Visser does agree with Hawking's general result of the Chronology Protection Conjecture, and that it "makes the Universe safe for historians." Professor Igor Novikov, however, takes the position that with the principle of self-consistency the Universe will remain "safe" with time travel. Novikov also is not quite so ready to put his faith in quantum theory's ability, as we presently know it, to forbid time travel. As he and a colleague recently wrote [Lossev and Novikov, 1992], "our understanding of the fundamental structure of the vacuum and the effects of quantum fluctuations is so inadequate that from existing quantum theory only we should definitely exclude the possibility of the very existing of the Universe ... but experimentally it exists."

So, what can one conclude from all this controversy? Not much, I think, except that time travel is an open question, and will remain the subject of ongoing study. As I write, nobody knows the answers to Thorne's list of concerns, or the truth of Hawking's Conjecture, or whether Visser or Novikov is right or wrong, and the time travel debates among physicists continue. In a personal communication to me (12 August 1992) Tipler wrote that he tends to side with Novikov, but also that the present quantum arguments are all "order of magnitude handwaving."

As the writing of this book drew near to its end, I wrote to the great American physicist, John A. Wheeler, at Princeton University, whose work has been discussed all through this book, and put the question to him. I received a delightful letter in response, which opened as follows:

> The idea of going backward in time? Of it let me say what Thomas Brown said of the dean of his Cambridge college in 1680 when he threatened to expel Brown:
> "I do not like thee, Dr. Fell.
> The reason why, I cannot tell;
> But this I know, and know full well,
> I do not like thee, Dr. Fell."

The spectacular (and that seems the only proper word to use) time-travel analyses of Kip Thorne's theoretical astrophysics group at Caltech creates at least a *little* doubt about that assessment. (Thorne was Wheeler's doctoral student at Princeton in the early 1960s.)[2] Hawking's and Visser's theoretical doubts that I discussed earlier shouldn't be forgotten, of course, and Thorne would certainly be the first to admit that even if no flaws appear in the theory of time travel, the engineering limitations on the actual construction of a time machine are light years beyond the merely staggering. Thorne admits that Hawking's analysis is "a very powerful result" [Travis, 1992], and in a personal communication to me (4 August 1992) he wrote "the central issue in time machine research, now, it seems to me, is the issue of whether vacuum fluctuations of quantum fields ALWAYS destroy a time machine at the moment one tries to activate it. I suspect the answer is yes, but I also suspect we will not know for sure until we understand the laws of quantum gravity." Thorne has, in fact, been careful to state that the driving force behind his work is to discover what the laws of physics allow, and not actually to build a time machine.[3]

So, to get right to it, I don't know if it is possible or not to visit the past, and I fear the odds greatly favor that I'll learn the truth about Heaven (or Hell) in the next world before I learn the truth about time travel in this one. I am fairly certain that if time travel is ever achieved, it will be by means that we cannot today even begin to guess. I very much doubt that things will be quite so elementary as "Heritage" [Abernathy, OSF] tells us Nickolus Doody's time machine was: "If it were taken apart or put together before you, your wife, or the man across the street, you would wonder why you didn't think of it yourselves." Not only that, its power source was just two dry cells! The time machine in "In the Scarlet Star" [Williamson, 1933] is almost as simple, requiring only (besides a strange piece of crystal) a "little stack of dry cells, a Ford coil, a small brass switch, a radio 'B' battery, an electron tube, and a rheostat."

I am reminded by this of a passage from "The Twentieth Voyage of Ijon Tichy" [Lem, 1976]: "There have been mountains of nonsense written about traveling in time, just as previously there were about astronautics—you know, how some scientist, with the backing of a wealthy businessman, goes off in a corner and slaps together a rocket, which the two of them—and in the company of their lady friends, yet—then take to the far end of the Galaxy. Chronomotion, no less than Astronautics, is a colossal enterprise, requiring tremendous investments, expenditures, planning ... ." It is no wonder Lem so readily dismisses such stories that reduce space (and time) travel to weekend adventures in a home laboratory. As he wrote in another essay [Lem, 1977], time travel and its close relation faster-than-light space travel have reduced much of science fiction to "a bastard of myths gone to the dogs."

I don't know if time travel can be done, but I do know that once incredible speculations, ones that were classed with finding the philosophers' stone for turning base elements into gold, *have* eventually been realized (and come to think of it, with modern nuclear physics we have learned how to turn lead into gold, too, if only a few atoms at a time). Television, nuclear power, VCRs, and supercomputers that simulate the formation of black holes and galaxies would all be pure magic to nineteenth-century science. The ghosts of not a few Victorian scientists have watched their reputations eat some posthumous crow during the last one hundred years. My personal position is described by the rejoinder to the skeptic in "By His Bootstraps" [Heinlein, AHT] who after doing some time traveling still argues against time travel by invoking paradoxes and who is sharply rebuked with "Oh, for heaven's sake, shut up, will you? You remind me of the mathematician who proved that airplanes couldn't fly."[4] I subscribe to the optomistic philosophy of British writer Eden Phillpotts who wrote, in his 1934 novel *A Shadow Passes*, "The Universe is full of magical things, patiently waiting for our wits to grow sharper."

I believe that present-day philosophers and science fiction writers are going to have to become knowledgeable about the new work by physicists on time travel. It simply won't do any longer for Philosophy Professor X to invoke the grandfather paradox during a discussion of causality and free will and airily to declare them to be "obviously" incompatible with time travel to the past. And it simply won't do any longer for Famous S-F Writer Y to send his hero into the past to kill Hitler as a baby, and thereby change recorded history. (One might as well keep watching a videotape of the Challenger disaster in the vain hope that on the next viewing maybe the Shuttle won't blow up.) The principle of self-consistency around closed timelike curves is going to have to become as much a part of the science fiction writer's craft (or else he will be a writer of fantasy) as it will have to become part of the fundamental philosophical axioms.[5] The "time police" (such as science fiction writer Andre Norton's "operatives of the Bureau of Time Exploration and Manipulation") will have to be put out to pasture with the unicorns and telepathic dragons of fantasy fiction. Just as the recent physics literature on time travel has displayed a growing awareness of what science fiction writers and philosophers have had to say on the subject, writers and philosophers are going to have to learn some more physics. Lovers both of fiction and of the philosophical literature should view this development as exciting; there should be some *very* interesting reading in their futures!

Time travel to the past is a beautiful, romantic idea, and some words written by two physicists in a recent technical paper,[6] words embedded in the midst of swirls of tensor equations, show that even hard-nosed physicists can share this dream: "In truth, it is difficult to resist the appealing idea of traveling into one's own past ... ." The appeal of this dream is explained in Ray Bradbury's Foreward to a beautiful little book by Charles Champlin (*Back There Where the Past Was* [Champlin, 1989]). Bradbury, I think, has clearly illuminated why we want to go back to the past. It is for the same reason that we go, time and again, to see *Hamlet*, *Othello*, and *Richard III*: "We don't give a hoot in hell who poisoned the King of Denmark's semicircular canal. We already know where Desdemona lies smothered in bedclothes and that Richard goes headless at his finale. We attend them to toss pebbles in ponds, not to see the stones strike, but the ripples spread."

That's why a visit to the past is so mysteriously and marvelously fascinating. It would let us watch ripples spread through time. Our own visit, in fact, might even be the pebble in the pond that starts an interesting ripple or two that will one day sweep over—us! Who would want to miss that? Indeed, if modern philosophers are right, if the analyses of Chapter Four are correct, you *can't* (didn't/won't) miss it. I think time travel appeals, irresistibly, to the romantic in the soul of anyone who is human. For a time traveler passing back and forth through the ages, history would be the ultimate puzzle, a chronicle described in John Crowley's brilliant *Great Work of Time* [Crowley, 1991] as beginning "not in one time or place, but everywhere at once ... . It might be begun at any point along the infinite, infinitely broken coastline of time." A time traveler does not exist at either *here* or *then*, but rather *everywhen*. (Being romantic doesn't preclude a dark side to a return to the past, of course, as the time traveler from 1989 in *A Bridge of Years* [Wilson, 1991] realizes when he takes up residence in 1962. Falling asleep on a hot summer night in that long-ago year, he thinks "JFK slept. Lee Harvey Oswald slept. Martin Luther King slept. [I sleep and dream] of Chernobyl ... *I am a cold wind from the land of your children*.")

The eminent philosopher Sir Karl Popper opens his autobiography with a wonderful story about his apprenticeship as a young man in 1920s Vienna to a master cabinetmaker.[7] After winning the old man's confidence, the student learned his mentor's great secret: for years the master had been looking for the solution to perpetual motion. He knew what is the physicist's judgment about those sorts of machines (recall Groff Conklin's accurate assessment!), but nonetheless he had never given up his dream: "They say you can't make it; but once it's been made they'll talk differently!" The theoretical basis for time travel is very different from that of perpetual motion, of course, and so maybe some day, *just perhaps*, there might be a toast such as in the story "Time's Arrow" [McDevitt, FCW], when the inventor of the first time machine and his no longer skeptical friend successfully arrive in the Civil War past:

> "To you, Mac," I said.
> McHugh loosened his tie. "To the Creator," he said, "who has given us a Universe with such marvelous possibilities."[8]

NOTES AND REFERENCES

Prologue

1. An example of the sort of tale that gave an aroma of the sophomoric to early time travel science fiction is "The Brontosaurus" [Thompson, 1941]. This is the story of a young man of the far future, with access to a time machine, who wants to see a dinosaur before he dies. So back he travels, back, back, until he at last finds himself in a "subterranean cave, dark and foul-smelling." At first he is puzzled (did dinosaurs live underground?) but then suddenly he hears a thundering roar and sees a huge black shape in the gloom. There can be no doubt now, it *is* a dinosaur and he can see its red, gleaming eyes as it crushes him into a pancake. But that's okay; he saw a dinosaur before he died. Then comes the denouement. He hadn't really gone back quite as far as the Jurassic period, but only to the twentieth century where has been run down by the local express in a subway tunnel!

Chapter One

1. Many readers, I know, will fondly recall Mr. Peabody, that nice but slightly stuffy, professorial white beagle (don't all dogs wear glasses and a bow tie?) who, with his brainy adopted son Sherman, routinely traveled into the past in his "Way-Bac" machine to see what really happened.
2. It is not just radio tapes of long-ago broadcasts that sell well. One can now buy authentic reproductions (with modern electronics) of the old-time radios, too. As one manufacturer declares on its shipping boxes, "We Sell Yesterdays." Nostalgia, itself, is a subject that has received serious study; see F. Davis, *Yearning for Yesterday: a sociology of nostalgia* (New York: The Free Press, 1979) which never mentions time travel, even in passing.
3. Lucifer doesn't always win, of course, and the stories "The Brazen Locked Room" [Asimov, DD] and "Time Trammel" [deFord, DD] are examples of how Mr. Scratch sometimes loses. Both involve time travel but, I am sorry to say, in not very innovative ways. Much more interesting is [Beerbohm, DD], which may well result in many of its readers being in the Reading Room of the British Museum on 3 June 1997 to see if the doomed Enoch Soames really will appear. Also excellent is T. R. Cogswell, who wrote two devilish stories about time travel (found in the same anthology, DD). In particular, his "Threesie" shows just how careful one has to be in reading the fine print in a contract with Beelzebub. Joseph Cruthers advertises his soul for sale in the local newspaper, Satan replies, and the standard deal is struck: Joe's soul for three wishes. The first two are for the usual wealth and immortality, but the third is for three more wishes! And Joe gets them, too. He is sent back in time to the moment he places his advertisement, and so he gets wishes forever, the same three, in an endless, looping temporal treadmill that becomes Joe's own personal hell. For more on this idea, see "The Time-Wise Guy" [Farley, 1950] and also *The Third Policeman* [O'Brien, 1976], which tells us that "Hell goes round and round. In shape [in time] it is circular and by nature it is interminable, repetitive and very nearly unbearable."
4. Perhaps the definitive analysis of Jack's identity can be found in A. G. Kelly's *Jack the*

Ripper: a bibliography and review of the literature (London: Association of Assistant Librarians, S. E. D., 1972). Kelly specifically recommends Bloch's story, which has the Ripper brought into the future to serve as a sexual playmate for a spoiled woman, who has the tables turned on her in a most gruesome manner. Ellison's effort, which tells about Jack's ultimate fate in the year 3077, is a sequel to Bloch's. Neither story is for the faint-of-heart or the weak-of-stomach.

5. N. P. Davis, *Lawrence and Oppenheimer* (New York: Simon and Schuster, 1968), 95.

6. For more on the possibility of sound recordings from the ancient past, see D. E. H. Jones, *The Inventions of Daedalus* (San Francisco: CA: W. H. Freeman, 1982), 26–27. A letter from Woodbridge, in which he reveals that his paper was initially "perfunctorily rejected as being 'too specialized' " by *Nature*, is reprinted in Jones' book.

7. N. Berdyaev, *The Bourgeois Mind and Other Essays* (Freeport, N.Y.: Books for Libraries Press, 1966 [originally published in 1934], 50. Even philosophers are human, of course, and the story is told of Berdyaev once pleading with intensity and passion for the insignificance of time and who then, suddenly, stopped in mid-sentence, first to look at his watch and immediately after that to rush from the room crying, "I'm late, I'm late, I should have taken my medicine two minutes ago!" When Pierce wrote his story on the vaqueness of the past, he almost certainly had in mind a paper written by Einstein and two colleagues, some years earlier, on just this point [Einstein, 1931].

8. Reversing the idea in Anderson's tale is *The Way Back* [Chandler, 1978] which has its characters return from the past to their proper time by traveling even further backward, right through the Big Bang and into the previous (identical) cycle of time. Larry Niven argues [Niven,1971] that this is a conceptually valid way to travel into the past, but he does raise one cautionary note: "Removing your time machine from the reaction of the Big Bang could change the final configuration of matter, giving an entirely different ... history." In *Nature* 66 (3 July 1902): 223, there is a curious letter that bears on Niven's point written by Hiram S. Maxim, the American-born British inventor of the first fully automatic machine gun. In one place it reads: "The grandest words ever uttered by any man on this planet were spoken by Lord Kelvin when he said that if all the matter in the Universe were reduced to its ultimate atoms and equally divided through all space, the disturbance caused by the beating of the wing of one mosquito would bring about everything that we find in the material Universe today ." Presumably Maxim and Niven believe that any deviations in such a disturbance would result in different Universes. This idea has become popularly known today in mathematical chaos theory as the "Butterfly effect" (after Bradbury's use of it in his story "A Sound of Thunder"), but as the *Nature* letter shows, it should more correctly be called the "mosquito effect."

9. Originally published in 1748, *Enquiry* has been reprinted many times over the years. I used the work as published by The Open Court Publishing Company (La Salle, Ill., 1963).

10. P. Heath, "The Incredulous Hume," *American Philosophical Quarterly* 13 (April 1976): 159–163.

11. *New Scientist* 77 (26 Jan. 1978): 239.

12. Gödel's Universe is a rotating, infinite, static one. The observable Universe is nonrotating and expanding (that is, it has a red-shift), and so while Gödel's analysis satisfies the general relativity equations, its time-travel property does not hold in our Universe. (Gödel may have been inspired to study his model by a letter written three years before by George Gamow [Gamow, 1946]. See also [Narlikar, 1962b].) In [Birch, 1982]

astronomical data is presented that indicates the Universe is rotating no faster than once each 60,000 billion years, which is much slower than the minimum required by Gödel's solution (see Tech Note 8). The question asked by the title of Birch's paper has recently been answered, in the negative, by [Panov and Sbytov, 1992]. See also [Korotkii and Obukov, 1991] for more on the relationship between a shear-free rotation of the Universe, as in Gödel's analysis, and time travel. For technical analyses of Gödel's work see [Chandrasekhar and Wright, 1961], a faulty study cited as late as 1962 in [MacKinnon, 1962] in support of the view that Gödel had made an error, and [Stein, 1970], which shows how Chandrasekhar and Wright erred. (The critical point, elaborated on by Stein was actually mentioned some years earlier in [Earman, 1967a]). As far as I know, no one has written a time-travel story using the rotating-Universe idea, but if he had lived, perhaps the science fiction writer James Blish would have. In David Ketterer's biography of Blish, *Imprisoned in a Tesseract* (Kent, Ohio: Kent State Univ. Press, 1987), there is this comment by Blish from a 1970 letter: "I am especially intrigued by the spinning-Universe form of time travel, especially since ... nobody has touched it ... But I should really stop mentioning the spinning-Universe in public, or somebody will nobble onto it before I can get into it!" Gödel's time-travel idea still waits for its first fictional use. Dawson [1989] reports that a much longer version of Gödel's 1949a paper on time travel in rotating Universes remains unpublished in the archives of the Institute for Advanced Study.

13. In a footnote Gödel says that the time traveler would have to move at least as fast as nearly 71% of the speed of light, and that if his rocket ship could "transform matter completely into energy," then the weight of the fuel would be greater than that of the rocket by a factor of 10^{22} divided by the square of the duration of the trip (in years, in rocket time). A trip to the past in Gödel's Universe would require a time machine looking something like Dr. Who's telephone booth attached to a fuel tank the size of several hundred *trillion* ocean liners. Capek [BST] calls the whole business "fantastic." These *are* formidable numbers, (but see [Purcell, 1963] for an analysis of a fantastic rocket powered by matter/antimatter, a process that satisfies Gödel's vast energy requirement), but they require no violation of physical laws and that is what really counts if time travel is to be disproved. As pointed out in [Earman, 1972], Gödel's use of engineering limitations for explaining away backward time travel is worse than simply being wrong, since the puzzle is not in practicality but rather in showing how, assuming that general relativity is correct, correct mathematics and physics can lead to what seems to be a paradoxical conclusion. More recent analyses, [Chakrabarti *et al.*, 1983] and [Malament, 1985, 1987], have established that there must be a lower bound on the total integrated acceleration of a time traveler in order for him or her to move backward in time (see also [Pfarr, 1981]). As Malament put it, "Any 'time traveler' who would return to an 'earlier' point on his own world line must undergo some acceleration, sometime during the trip." That is, such a time traveler could not just fall freely through spacetime at a high speed (such a trajectory is called a *geodesic*), but rather must experience some force. It was on this point, in fact, that Chandrasekhar and Wright (see Note 12) went wrong; see also [Chandrasekhar, NT]. There are other Universes, however, in which free-fall geodesic time travel would be possible (see [Soares, 1980] and [Paiva, Reboucas, and Teixeira, 1987]).

14. This isn't to say that there aren't some problems with quantum mechanics, too. In particular, there is much confusion today over what seem to be FTL interactions in certain quantum systems, in direct violation of special relativity. Such interactions, if

they really exist, hold out the tantalizing possibility of being able to transfer information into the past (see Chapter Four and Tech Note 7). This is, of course, of special concern to physicists, who are either horrified or fascinated (or both) by such a prospect.

15. In actuality, the collapse may stop short of the singularity. (See, for example, [Israel, 1967] and [Donald, 1978], which suggest that a collapsing body will rebound after reaching a minimum nonzero volume, but even then it is also suggested that causality may still be violated!) The infinity of the singularity may just be the mathematics telling us that general relativity has finally failed. And yet, as Chapter Three explains, one modern view is that it is the occurrence of the singularities at the start (and perhaps at the end) of the Universe that force time to be linear rather than circular. What is meant by a singularity in relativistic gravitational field theory is given an excellent treatment in [Geroch, 1968], with the general conclusion being that it is not obvious what the term means. This essential difficulty with relativistic gravitational field theories does not occur in other field theories such as electrodynamics because such theories use space-time as a background; that is, a singularity in electrodynamics is simply a place where the electromagnetic field is undefined, with the "place" referenced to the background spacetime in which the field is embedded. In gravitational field theory, however, it is the very background spacetime itself that may be singular, and there seems to be nothing more fundamental to use as the reference; i.e., what could spacetime be embedded in?) For an explanation of the term *naked* singularity, see Note 22.

16. Curiously, Schwarzschild's result had been discovered earlier using Newton's theory of gravity, and the result was reported in a letter written in 1783(!) by the Reverend John Michell to the English scientist/recluse Henry Cavendish. Somewhat later, and independently, the great French scientist Pierre-Simon Laplace arrived at the same result, writing that "it is therefore possible that the greatest luminous bodies in the Universe are ... invisible" (see [Schaffer, 1979]). Pioneering analysis on the gravitational collapse of stars was done by the young Indian astrophysicist Subrahmanyan Chandrasekhar (see Note 12), who in 1931 combined special relativity and quantum mechanics to show that stars above a certain mass (the *Chandrasekhar limit*) will experience a different fate from less massive ones. Beyond this limit of about 1.4 solar masses, a star cannot simply evolve into a white dwarf, something that before Chandrasekhar had been believed to be the fate of all stars. For this work Chandrasekhar shared the 1983 Nobel prize in physics. Interestingly, even before Chandrasekhar's work, the classic science fiction tale "Sidewise in Time" [Leinster, BGA2] in the June 1934 *Astounding Stories* expressed similar ideas. This is primarily a parallel Universe story, about which more is said in Chapter Four, but near its conclusion in the obligatory genius-explains-it-all denouement, we read: "We know that gravity warps space ... We can calculate the mass necessary to warp space so that it will close in completely, making a closed Universe ... We know, for example, that if two gigantic star masses of certain mass were to combine ... they would simply vanish. But they would not cease to exist. They would merely cease to exist in our space and time." As another character sums it up, "Like crawling into a hole and pulling the hole in after you." The explicit use of the term *black hole* for a region of spacetime operating as a temporal and/or spatial portal can be found in science fiction before Wheeler's use of the term in the technical literature. (See, for example, "Typewriter From the Future" [Worth, 1950].)

17. A nonrotating black hole, which has a point singularity, cannot be used for time travel (but since angular momentum is conserved and since it is most unlikely that any

precollapsed star would have exactly zero spin, it is very unlikely that a black hole would not be rotating). A rotating Kerr hole, however, has a *ring* singularity through which a time traveler can theoretically pass (and still avoid the deadly infinity) to enter other Universes and/or to time travel in this one. The popular use of rotating black holes for interstellar and time travel, as discussed in science fiction (see, for example, "Singularities Make Me Nervous" [Niven, S1]), was at first flatly rejected by Caltech physicists Michael Morris and Kip Thorne [Morris and Thorne, 1988], with just one of their objections being the potential causality-violation paradox (i.e., the grandfather paradox). However, in a later analysis [Morris, Thorne, and Yurtsever, 1988], they along with their colleague Ulvi Yurtsever seem to be more willing to accept the possibility of backward time travel when they reported on their discovery that an advanced civilization might, indeed, be able to construct a machine for backward time travel. As they observed, "Some readers will wish to await a definitive answer from future research as to what the laws of physics prevent and what they permit." The idea that the interior of a black hole might "lead to other places" was originally seen as a way to avoid the singularity problem. That is, the collapse of a star into a black hole would not proceed all the way down to a point. Rather, the collapse would stop before reaching the singularity by gravitationally rebounding (see Note 15). This "bounce" would occur after the star was inside its Schwarzschild radius, and so an external observer, watching the initial collapse, would not see the later expansion. This expansion would be outward through the Schwarzschild radius into a *different region of the Universe*! The first paper I know of that developed this astonishing concept is [Novikov, 1966]. When Novikov's work was generalized in [De La Cruze and Israel, 1967], the authors clearly had a hard time believing this imagery despite their own mathematics, concluding with, "It then appears necessary to believe in the existence of other [regions of the Universe] similiar to but distinct from ours, which will accommodate the re-expansion. This seems at least as fantastic as the alternative of irreversible collapse to virtually point-like dimensions."

18. In 1974 Stephen Hawking announced [Hawking, 1974, 1975] an astonishing partial connection of quantum mechanics with general relativity's black holes. Hawking showed (contrary to the usual image of black holes as being one-way trap doors to ... ?), that black holes actually *must* radiate energy. His analysis, which stunned physicists by its beautifully simple arguments, invokes Werner Heisenberg's (1901–1976) uncertainty principle, one of the cornerstones of quantum mechanics. Hawking himself found the result "greatly surprising." The uncertainty principle states that there are certain pairs of variables associated with particles that cannot simultaneously be measured exactly. Time and energy are such a pair; i.e., a nonzero time interval is required to measure a particle's energy, and the product of the uncertainty in both the interval and the energy must be equal to or greater than a nonzero constant. This allows the process of *virtual particle creation*, the appearance of particle/antiparticle pairs just outside the surface of a black hole. The uncertainty in energy that is available to give the combined mass of the particles is the quantum fluctuation energy of the intense gravity field around the hole. The only constraint is that the energy be returned to the field (via mutual annihilation of the matter/antimatter pair) within the time uncertainty dictated by Heisenberg. But, as Hawking showed, this time interval, although incredibly short, is still long enough for the two virtual particles to separate before annihilation, with one falling into the hole and the other escaping. By this incredible quantum process, then, the black holes of general relativity slowly evaporate

as they glow with what is now called *Hawking radiation*. That is, black holes appear to be hot bodies. But hot is relative; as Hawking shows, a black hole with the mass of the sun acts as a body with a temperature just one *micro*degree Kelvin above absolute zero! And even more interesting for our purposes in this book, Hawking showed how the particle entering the hole could be thought of as an emission particle traveling backward in time (see [Hawking, 1977]). Later, this quantum process was found to be useful in stabilizing hyperspace wormholes (see Chapter Two), which can be used, in principle, to build time machines (see Tech Note 9).

19. See also [Starobinsky, 1980]. One paper, [Birrell and Davies, 1978], however, asserts that even without detailed knowledge of quantum gravity, quantum effects "would smash the idealized interior geometry" of a rotating, electrically charged black hole, thereby eliminating any possibility of using such a hole for time traveling, and [Morris and Thorne, 1988] supports this conclusion. But, more recently, [Mellor and Moss, 1990] disagreed. Details of the supposed time-traveling properties of black holes can be found in many of the books and papers on them (e.g., see [Weingard, 1979a], the excellent presentation in [Kaufmann, 1977], and [Parker, 1991]). However, since black holes are such bizarre objects, nearly as bizarre as time travel, it seems risky to try to understand the one in terms of the other. Whether or not black holes actually exist is now taken by theoreticians as a crucial test of general relativity under conditions of strong gravity. (All of the famous early tests of general relativity, such as the advance of the perihelion of Mercury's orbit, are for weak gravity, on the order of a million or more times weaker than one would find at the spacetime horizon of a black hole.) If general relativity fails this test, then of course all of its predictions under extreme conditions, including time travel, become suspect. To date, no black holes have been directly observed, but there are three excellent indirect candidates, each as one half of an x-ray binary system. The first, nearest, and best known is Cygnus X-1, discovered in 1971 at a distance of 10,000 light-years from Earth, with a suspected black-hole component of 16 solar masses. There is also speculation that any large number of closely spaced stars, such as occurs at all galactic cores, would almost certainly form a black hole with an average density of something like that of water. (The required average mass density of a black hole decreases with increasing hole size. Thus, if the radius is big enough, a black hole could have the density of air!) Galactic-core holes would be very massive black holes. The one at the center of the Milky Way, for example, may have the mass of five million Suns, while the core of Andromeda (two million light-years distant) may be home to a black hole with a mass of fifty million Suns. Dwarfing this is the suspected black hole at the center of the giant radio galaxy M87, with a mass of five billion Suns! John Wheeler calls such monsters *Nimmersatt*; German for glutton. The more matter they take in, the bigger they get; the bigger they get, the more matter they absorb. Such behemoths would literally "eat stars." Jonathan Swift caught the spirit of this image in his poem "On Time" in *Riddles* (circa 1724). Written as his view on the destructive nature of time, his words apply equally well to Wheeler's Nimmersatt: "Ever eating, never cloying,/ All-devouring, all-destroying,/ Never finding full repast,/ Till I eat the world at last."

20. A few years before Tipler, Brandon Carter used the term "time machine" in his analysis [Carter, 1968] of the Kerr solution. As mentioned in the text, Carter was not nearly so willing to entertain time machines as was Tipler, but he did write that under certain conditions the solution "has the properties of a time machine" and that "it is possible, starting from any point in the outer regions of space far away from a rotating mass, to

travel toward the mass and move backward in time as far as desired ." However, neither Carter nor Tipler was the first to describe the details of how to make a time machine if we count nontechnical publications. This was apparently done in 1899 by the notorious French novelist, poet, and artist Alfred Jarry (1873–1907) in the literary journal *Mercure de France*. See [Jarry, 1965] for a reprint and history of this interesting essay and [Henderson, 1983] for a discussion of Jarry's interest in time travel. Obviously tongue-in-cheek on the same topic is [Brunner, 1965]. A more recent time-machine proposal, which has a certain rugged charm to it, is in [Platt, 1974], printed the same year as Tipler's paper. Two years later, in 1976, Tipler's Ph.D. dissertation ([Tipler, 1976b]) was accepted, and in it he was even more direct about his interest in time machines than he was in his 1974 paper. This isn't to say that other physicists hadn't seriously talked about backward time travel before Tipler. Richard Feynman (1918–1988), for one, did in his Nobel prize lecture. "The Development of the Space-Time View of Quantum Electrodynamics," which was reproduced in *Science* 153 (12 Aug. 1966): 699–708. Feynman, who was John Wheeler's student, recalled how Wheeler called him up one day with his "proof" for why every electron in the Universe has exactly the same charge (using the argument that there is only *one* electron, weaving back and forth in time), with positrons being the backward-traveling electrons. Feynman then said, "I did not take the idea that all electrons were the same one ... as seriously as I took the observation that positrons could simply be represented as electrons going from the future to the past ... That, I stole!" Indeed, he wrote in [Feynman, 1948] that "this idea that positrons might be electrons with the proper time reversed was suggested to me by Professor J. A. Wheeler in 1941." In an astonishing coincidence, even as Feynman and Wheeler were talking, two science fiction writers also came up with the same idea. Writing as Will Stewart, Jack Williamson and John W. Campbell (the editor of *Astounding Science Fiction*) identified antimatter with backward time travel in "Minus Sign" [Williamson, 1942]. Later, Stanislaw Lem took this idea, combined it with the concept of energy fluctuation (see Note 18), and in "The Eighteenth Voyage" [Lem, 1982], came up with one of his typically outrageous ideas— shooting a single positron out of an accelerator back to the very beginning of time! He called this fantastic machine the "Chronocannon" and claimed that's what started the Universe! Soon after Lem, the philosopher Fulmer used a variant of this idea (in which the Big Bang creation of the Universe was caused by a time traveler from the future who saw a need—his own existence!—to generate the Big Bang) to speculate on the cosmological implications of God as a time traveler [Fulmer, 1983].

21. This restriction does prevent at least one particularly odd paradox from happening— that of a time traveler going backward to tell the inventor of the time machine (perhaps an earlier version of the time traveler himself) how to build the time machine. A story using this idea is "Package Deal" [Franson, MT]. This paradox belongs to a class called *causal loops*; such loops are very mysterious and still befuddle philosophers. (They are discussed in greater detail in Chapters Three and Four.) One could use a Tipler cylinder to travel forward in time, too; one would just orbit around it in the opposite sense. Again, one could not travel into the future beyond the time the cylinder ceases to exist. Science fiction writer Oliver Saari anticipated this point as long ago as 1937 in his story "The Time Bender" [Saari, 1937]; in an astonishing coincidence with Tipler's incredible cylinders, Saari uses a time machine that works by warping spacetime via a plate of superdense material. As the story explains, the time traveler "could not travel into the past, for the plate had to exist in all ages traveled, and it had not existed before he

had made it." Kip Thorne has rebutted Hawking's experimental evidence for his *Chronology Protection Conjecture* in [Thorne, 1991] by using Saari's kind of argument. Thorne indicates that (1) time machines, if possible, must have the property of not being able to travel back before their creation (as in the case of a Tipler cylinder), and (2) no time machine has yet been created. More on the Conjecture can be found in Note 2 of Tech Note 9.

22. A strange theoretical possibility is that at such incredible matter densities the propagation speed of low frequency sound waves (*density fluctuations*) might exceed the speed of light (see [Kirzhnits and Polyachenko, 1964], [Cutkosky, 1970], [Bludman and Ruderman, 1968, 1970]). An excellent book on the details of how matter crushes (i.e., on equations of state that relate the internal pressure response of matter to the compression of gravity) along with some fascinating history of the subject is [Harrison, *et al.*, 1965]. More on this can also be found in [Thorne, MWM], which presents the curious result that there cannot be a spacetime horizon around a gravitationally collapsed nonrotating infinite cylinder; in this physically implausible situation it seems that the threadlike singularity would be visible to a remote observer. (As mentioned in the text, such a singularity is said to be *naked*.) Many physicists believe this cannot actually happen, and declare its impossibility via a metaphysical law called *cosmic censorship*, put forth in 1969 by Roger Penrose (see [Wald, 1974] and [Kosso, 1988]). Thorne, however, conjectures that a naked singularity might form in a sufficiently aspherical collapse of a finite mass even if rotating, with the infinite nonrotating cylinder simply being one special limiting case [Apostolatos and Thorne, 1992]. Shapiro and Teukolsky [1991a,b], who describe computer simulations of the general relativistic collapse of prolate spheroids of gas, have seemingly confirmed Thorne's idea. See also [Christodoulou, 1984] and [Gott, 1991]. In the popular press, Robert Forward wrote with enthusiasm [Forward, 1980] about Tipler cylinders, for which he was politely but firmly rebuked in [Rothman, 1985] on the technical issue of self-gravitational collapse. Later, Forward again wrote on the subject [Forward, 1988], but he ignored the criticism, leaving the technical objection both unmentioned and unanswered.

23. It should be mentioned that Tipler was not the first to study rotating cylinders in the context of general relativity. Such cylinders had been around for decades (as Tipler himself notes), and a good reference is M. A. Mashkour, "An Exterior Solution of the Einstein Field Equations for a Rotating Infinite Cylinder," *International Journal of Theoretical Physics* 15 (Oct. 1976): 717–721. This paper contains citations to the earlier literature on rotating infinite cylinders dating back to 1932.

24. More recently Niven mentioned a Tipler cylinder in a very funny story entitled "The Return of William Proxmire" [Niven, WMHB], which tells about how Senator William Proxmire might use a time machine to undo the American space program.

25. To be absolutely sure I don't put my words in Tipler's mouth, I should mention a second paper of his [Tipler, 1976a] in which he somewhat more cautiously wrote: "There are many solutions to the Einstein equations which possess causal anomalies in the form of closed timelike lines (CTL). It is of interest to discover if our Universe could have such lines. In particular, if the Universe does not at present contain such lines, is it possible for human beings to manipulate matter so as to create them? I shall show in this paper that it is *not* [Tipler's emphasis] possible to manufacture a CTL-containing region without the formation of naked singularities, provided normal matter is used in the construction attempt." (For more on closed timelike loops see Tech Note 8.)

Chapter Two

1. [Dummett, 1969] has a very nice way of systematically generating this infinite regress of complex predicates: "Let us call 'past', 'present', and 'future' 'predicates of first level'. If, as McTaggart suggests, we render 'was future' as 'future in the past', and so forth, then we have the nine predicates of second level, where we join any of the three on the left with any of the three on the right:

past		past
present	in the	present
future		future

Similarly there are twenty-seven predicates of third level ... ." Indeed, this construction clearly shows that at the Nth level there are three to the Nth-power predicates, most of which are incompatible.

2. Quoted from B. Hoffmann, *Albert Einstein: creator & rebel* (New York: New American Library, 1972), 257–258.

3. An abridgement of Wells' thesis can be found in *Nature* 153 (1 April 1944): 395–397. The miserably brief duration of human history is nicely demonstrated in the well-known metaphor of the "cosmic year." If we imagine that the entire history of the Universe—about fifteen billion years—is compressed into just one year and that the Cosmic Clock has just struck midnight on December 31st to ring in the second Cosmic Year, then dinosaurs were walking the Earth until the middle of yesterday and Jesus died on the Cross four seconds ago.

4. See [Dyson, 1979] for fascinating analyses of how physics predicts the way the evolution of an open Universe would go. Such a Universe does not eventually collapse into a Big Crunch, and thus it would have an infinite future. As Dyson writes, "The main conclusion I wish to draw from my analysis is the following: So far as we can imagine into the future, things continue to happen. In an open cosmology, history has no end." Dyson, who assumes absolute stability for the proton, wrote his paper partly in response to a paper coauthored by time machine pioneer Frank Tipler [Barrow and Tipler, 1978]. In that paper Barrow and Tipler, who assume electrons and protons do eventually decay into radiation, are far less sanguine about the future than is Dyson.

5. J. Swift, *Gulliver's Travels* (New York: Heritage Press, 1940), 22–23.

6. An example of this attitude is in the excellent essay by N. J. A. Sloane, "The Packing of Spheres," *Scientific American*, Jan. 1984. This paper, which addresses such problems as how to pack spheres most tightly in spaces of dimensions up to 100,000 (a problem with enormous practical value in the design of electronic communications systems), says (correctly) that "there has been a great deal of nonsense written in science fiction and elsewhere about the mysteries of the fourth dimension." The author is a mathematician who takes a particularly skeptical view of assuming "as the physicist does, that the fourth dimension represents time."

7. The boring repetition of masculine heroes saving weeping women from ungodly horrors was not always appreciated by the male readers of the science fiction magazines. As one wrote in a Letter-to-the-Editor to *Astounding Stories* (June 1931): "Just why do you permit your Authors to inject messy love affairs into otherwise excellent imagina-

tive fiction? Just stop and think. Our young hero-scientist builds himself a space flyer, steps out into the great void, conquers a thousand and one perils on his voyage and amidst our silent cheers lands on some far distant planet. Then what does he do? He falls in love with a maiden—or it's usually a princess—of the planet to which the Reader has followed him, eagerly awaiting and hoping to share each new thrill attached to his gigantic flight. But after that it becomes merely a hopeless, doddering love affair ending by his returning to Earth with his fair one by his side. Can you grasp that—a one-armed driver of a space-flyer! ... We buy A.S. for the thrill of being changed in size, in time, in dimension ... not to read of love ... I wish ... for plain, cold scientific stories sans the fair sex.''

8. See "Like a Bird, Like a Fish" [Hickey, WT], for example, for what happens to time-traveling monsters from another dimension when they run afoul of a rural mechanical genius who fixes their machine after it breaks down. In my own attempt at this subgenre, "Twisters" [Nahin, 1988], I had a small-town doctor defeat (sort of) the insidious attack of other-world invaders who were using four-dimensional doughnuts as combination "bait and trap" devices to capture humans for their gourmet food shops back home. I am willing to admit that the only possible redeeming value in this story is that some young readers might find its description of a Klein bottle (a four-dimensional object of central importance to topologists) of sufficient interest that they look elsewhere for more information (see also Note 19).

9. G. F. Rodwell, "On Space of Four Dimensions" *Nature* 8 (1 May 1873): 8–9.

10. P. G. Tait, "Zollner's Scientific Papers," *Nature* 17 (28 March 1878): 420–422. Thus, Clifford Ashley's 1944 classic book on knots (advertised as "7,000 drawings for 3,900 knots") would be as meaningful to a four-dimensional being as would a book on unicorns. As for Zollner (1834–1882), he was a well-known (and somewhat unconventional) professor of physical astronomy at the University of Leipzig. After meeting William Crookes in 1875, he became intensely interested in Spiritualism, as well as being convinced that a fourth dimension to space would allow certain psychic phenomena a scientific explanation. As examples of such phenomena, Zollner used the claims [Zollner, 1878] of a then famous medium who was later convicted of fraud. (For more on this, see the amusing tale "The Church of the Fourth Dimension" [Gardner, 1969].) Because of this, Zollner's reputation fell, and for a while his name and the fourth dimension became identified with deceit. In 1893 Ambrose Bierce explicitly used the scientific idea of non-Euclidean space in his "Mysterious Disappearances" [Bierce, 1964], in a context that earlier times would have called supernatural.

11. I. M. Freeman, "Why is Space Three-Dimensional?" *American Journal of Physics*, 37 (Dec. 1969): 1222–1224, and L. Gurevich and V. Mostepanenko, "On the Existence of Atoms in n–Dimensional Space," *Physics Letters A* 35 (31 May 1971): 201–202. A more philosophical presentation is G. J. Whitrow, "Why Physical Space Has Three Dimensions," *The British Journal for the Philosophy of Science* 6 (May 1955): 13–31. See also [Abramenko, 1958], and [Good, 1965] for what the author himself describes as a "partly-baked idea" on how spacetime might be eight-dimensional. Less speculative arguments for a four-dimensional spacetime, based on field equations of equal mathematical strength, can be found in R. Penny, "On the Dimensionality of the Real World," *Journal of Mathematical Physics* 6 (Nov. 1965): 1607–1611. Penny admits that some may find the strength criterion (due to Einstein himself) to be "slightly metaphysical." A radically different argument is presented in [Rosen, 1968], where it is shown that only in a spacetime of even dimensions does the TCP theorem hold. This

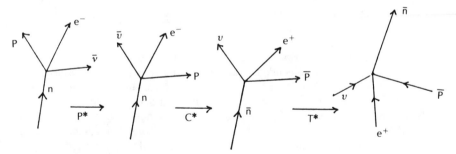

FIGURE 19. The TCP theorem predicts the antineutron.

theorem says that the "mirror-image" of a physical process is a legitimate process if the "mirror" reverses time (T), electric charge (C) (so that particle and antiparticle are interchanged), and parity (P) (the reversed of left and right that one observes when looking in a mirror); see E. P. Wigner, "Violations of Symmetry in Physics," *Scientific American* (Dec. 1965). If we let the symbol * denote *reversal*, then under successive P*, C*, and T* operations, the TCP theorem says that if the particle interaction on the left of Figure 19 is legitimate, then so is the interaction on the right: This example shows that the 1948 experimental observation of the beta decay of a free neutron into a proton and an antineutrino (i.e., decay by the ejection of an electron) immediately implied that the creation of an antineutron by a neutrino, a positron, and an antiproton must also be possible. There is strong reason to believe the TCP theorem because quantum field theory is compatible with special relativity only if the TCP theorem holds. A mathematical proof of the theorem is in the essay by W. Pauli, "Exclusion Principle, Lorentz Group and Reflection of Space-Time and Charge," *Niels Bohr and the Development of Physics* (New York: McGraw-Hill, 1955), 30–51. For a more recent philosophical discussion, including citations to the newer physical literature (including the possibility of a fractal dimensionality to spacetime), see F. Caruso and R. M. Xavier, "On the Physical Problem of Spatial Dimensions: An Alternative Procedure to Stability Arguments," *Fundamenta Scientiae* 8 (No. 1) (1987): 73–91.

12. K. Pearson, "Ether Squirts," *American Journal of Mathematics* 13 (1891): 309–362. The luminiferous ether was a mysterious substance thought to fill all space; its only role was to give light something through which to move. The response came from Arthur Schuster in *Nature* 58 (18 Aug. 1898): 367.

13. A very nice treatment of Hinton's life and work are in *Speculations on the Fourth Dimension: selected writings of Charles H. Hinton,* ed. R. Rucker (New York: Dover, 1980). All of Hinton's important 4-space essays are reprinted in it.

14. *Nature* 31 (12 March 1885): 431.

15. This story appeared in 1931, just a few years after the German physicist Theodor Kaluza had expanded four-dimensional spacetime to five dimensions. He did this in a successful attempt to unify gravity and electromagnetism. A brief, readable exposition of this theory is in H. T. Flint, *The Quantum Equation and the Theory of Fields* (New York: John Wiley, 1966). Perhaps Kaluza's work was Leinster's inspiration. The story was liked well enough to encourage the writing of a sequel, "The Fifth-Dimension Tube" [Leinster, 1933]. Kaluza's five-dimensional spacetime, in which gravity also

appears as electromagnetism in our apparent world of four dimensions, leaves open
the question of where is the extra dimension. For that reason, as [Dobbs, 1956]
observes, many physicists came to regard five-dimensional spacetime as "an artful
dodge having no physical significance." In 1926, five years after Kaluza, the Swedish
physicist Oscar Klein put forth an astonishing speculation of where Kaluza's fifth dimension might be. In a recent paper the eminent theoretical physicist Bryce S. DeWitt
has commented on this ("Quantum Gravity," *Scientific American*, Dec. 1983): "The
reason space *appears* to be three-dimensional is that one of its dimensions is cylindrical ... the circumference of the Universe in the cylindrical direction is only a few
(perhaps 10 or 100) Planck lengths. As a result an observer who attempts to penetrate
the fourth spatial dimension is almost instantly back where he started ... The fourth
spatial dimension is simply unobservable as such." That is, the fifth dimension is
periodic, and a particle moving along just this dimension would follow an incredibly
tiny circular path. More on this can be found in [Chyba, 1985]. Dobbs, however,
suggested that the fifth dimension is a second time dimension. (Multi-dimensional time
is discussed in detail in Chapter Three.) The idea of a unified field theory entered
science fiction quite soon. In "The Meteor Girl" [Williamson, 1975], published in
1931, the hero-genius is asked, "What's the good of Einstein, anyhow?," and before he
can reply, his interrogator goes on to say (as well as reminding us that those were the
early days of the Great Depression), "I know that space is curved, that there is really
no space or time, but only space-time, that electricity and gravitation and magnetism
are all the same. But how is that going to pay my grocery bill—or yours?"

16. The analogy involves a comparison with a prison in 2-space *flatland*, which would
merely be a circle around the captive. Knowledge of the third dimension would allow
escape by moving along that new direction, over the circle, and then back into the
plane. To a flatlander guard it would seem as if the prisoner suddenly vanished from
view inside the circle and then suddenly materialized again outside it. Similarly, to
escape from a 3-space prison one would merely move along the fourth dimension. In
the same way, one could remove the yolk from an Easter egg without damaging either
the shell or the white; indeed, one could remove the yolk directly from the chicken
without damaging the chicken. In fiction, this way of using the fourth dimension appears in "The Appendix and the Spectacles" [Breuer, MM], where it is used to perform
a wound-free appendectomy. (The concept was mentioned even earlier, in passing, in
the previous year's 1927 story "The Four-Dimensional Roller-Press" [Olsen, 1951];
see also the "Hyper-Forceps," which were invented in "Four Dimensional Surgery"
[Olsen, 1928c] and later used in "The Great Four Dimensional Robberies" [Olsen,
1928b] to rob locked safe deposit boxes.) Still later, in "The Four Dimensional Escape"
[Olsen, 1933], a man sentenced to die by hanging at San Quentin Prison is rescued
while standing on the gallows' trap by an inventor who pulls him through the fourth
dimension! Such ideas are far from new. The German mathematician and astronomer
August Möbius (1790–1868) discovered in 1827 that any three-dimensional object can
be converted into its mirror image by flipping it over through the fourth dimension;
e.g., a left-handed glove can thus be made by pure geometry (no scissors, thread and
needle required) into a precise copy of its right-handed mate. Later (but still in the
nineteenth century), in his Presidential Address to the American Mathematical Society,
Simon Newcomb made this very point (see Note 21). This idea has been used in
fiction; e.g., see "Left or Right?" [Gardner, MTMW], as well as "The Plattner Story"
[Wells, 1966]. Both of these stories, which involve flipping living organisms (i.e., hu-

mans) over through the fourth dimension, have a literally fatal flaw. Everything in the body would be reversed, including the optically active organic molecules which are involved in vital biological processes. These molecules, called *stereoisomers*, exist in two versions in nature (the left-handed and right-handed versions, if you will), but our bodies have developed the biological ability to use only one version. To be flipped through the fourth dimension would, for example, make some reversed stereoisomers unable to participate in the digesting of food and we would starve to death. This problem was first fictionally addressed in "Technical Error" [Clarke, SFF] (published in 1946), where the solution is to flip the victim through the fourth dimension a second time. (When *Thrilling Wonder Stories* reprinted this story in June 1950, the title was changed to the more appropriate "The Reversed Man," but for some reason the editorial lead-in spoke of the fifth dimension!) Later, "The Heart on the Other Side" [Gamow, ED] repeated the idea. There is more to worry about with dimensional flipping than eating, however. Indeed, since everything flips, matter should become antimatter, and Lewis Carroll was more correct than he could have imagined when he had Alice wonder in *Through the Looking-Glass*, "Perhaps Looking-glass milk isn't good to drink." Unless Alice is an anti-Alice, she and the anti-milk would mutually become pure energy via a spectacular 100% efficient explosion.

17. This surface, discovered in 1858 by Möbius (see Note 16), is easily made by taking a long strip of paper, giving it a half-twist, and taping the ends together. You can convince yourself that it is one-sided by coloring it with a crayon. During the coloring *do not lift the crayon from the paper.* You will find when you can color no more that every last bit of the paper is the same color. (You cannot do this with a flat piece of paper without lifting the crayon and turning the paper over because that paper is two-sided.) A hilarious story based on this property is "A. Botts and the Möbius Strip" [Upson, FM], published in 1945. A similiar idea appeared earlier in "The Geometrics of Johnny Day" [Bond, 1941a]. As these stories show, most people refuse to believe such an object actually exists until they see a demonstration, thus showing that even our ordinary three-dimensional space has some surprises left in it. Indeed, Sloane (see Note 6) makes this very point when he states that "all physicists know" what the maximally dense sphere packing in 3-space is, but nobody can prove it! This indicates that "the mathematical understanding of ordinary, three-dimensional Euclidean space is far from complete." I have heard of at least one practical use for the Möbius strip—as a conveyor belt in mines. Since the belt is one-sided, it lasts twice as long as a normal two-sided belt because every bit of its surface gets worn by the rocks, instead of just half. This idea has been used in fiction, too, e.g., in "Paul Bunyan versus the Conveyor Belt" [Upson, MM], but with, if I may use the word, a twist. This charming tale introduces the reader to one of many astonishing properties of the Möbius band. Cut the band lengthwise with a scissors. Most people believe you will get two strips, each the length of the original strip but each only half as wide. Actually, you get one strip with a full twist, (which means that the strip is a two-sided surface). And if you cut the new strip lengthwise once more, you will get two separate loops, linked together. Try it and see. But be careful. Science fiction writer Cyril Kornbluth warned of the possible danger of unlearned experimentation in such matters when he wrote:

> A burleycue dancer, a pip
> Named Virginia, could peel in a zip;
>   But she read science fiction

> And died of constriction
> Attempting a Möbius strip.

To get an idea of how Heinlein's four-dimensional house would look, see [Farley, 1939], which provides a fold-and-paste cut-out pattern to let you make your very own three-dimensional model of a tesseract. Since Heinlein's story appeared in 1940, Farley's article in *Scientific American* just the year before may well have been at least part of its inspiration. As the Bibliography indicates, Farley (the pen-name of Roger Sherman Hoar) was also a prolific writer of time-travel stories.

18. S., "Four-Dimensional Space," *Nature* 31 (26 March 1885): 481. In a 1931 edition of *The Time Machine* (New York: Random House), the Preface is by Wells himself. Of the idea for the novel, he says, "It was begotten in the writer's mind by students' discussions in the laboratories and debating society of the Royal College of Science in the eighties and already it had been tried over in various forms by him before he made this particular application of it." (See also Note 20.) In the biography by Geoffrey West (Wells' illegitimate son by Rebecca West), *H. G. Wells* (New York: W. W. Norton, 1930), it is stated that "the idea for a time machine story had come to him one day ... during the discussion following the reading of a paper—by another student in a debating society—on the fourth dimension." The date of S.'s letter would seem to be just about right to have S. be this mysterious other student. Or perhaps it was S.'s letter that inspired the other student who then inspired Wells.

19. The Klein bottle was discovered in 1882 by the German mathematician Felix Klein. It is closely related to the Möbius strip, but unlike the strip it cannot be made in 3-space. A 3-space bottle has an inside and an outside. This simply means that it has an *edge*; i.e., the mouth of the bottle, which separates the two surfaces just like the edge of a piece of paper separates its two sides. A Klein bottle has no such edge, and its inside flows smoothly into its outside. To make such a thing in 3-space requires an intersection in the side of the bottle, but in 4-space there would be no intersection. Yet, even though inside and outside are meaningless distinctions for the bottle, it could indeed hold water. And, paradoxical as it may seem, the Klein bottle can be made from two Möbius strips which *do* exist in 3-space. An anonymous wit put it thus:

> A mathematician named Klein
> Thought the Möbius band was divine.
>> Said he: "If you glue
>> The edges of two,
> You'll get a weird bottle like mine.

The trick is, unfortunately, that before you apply the glue you have to twist some edges through the fourth dimension. Never one to miss a chance to slip some mathematics into his children's stories, Lewis Carroll in *Sylvie and Bruno* describes a Klein bottle in everything but name in the guise of the "purse of Fortunatus." Stories involving a Klein bottle are not common, but two are "The Last Magician" [Elliott, FM] and "The Island of Five Colors" [Gardner, FM]. As a final comment on Klein, in 1896 (less than a year after *The Time Machine*) he gave a series of lectures at Princeton University. Published the following year as *The Mathematical Theory of the Top*, this book presents a four-dimensional non-Euclidean space with time as the fourth dimension.

20. The Time Traveler is never named. In an earlier (1888) attempt at a time-machine story

with the awful title *The Chronic Argonauts* (reprinted in [Wells, 1987]), which so embarrassed Wells that he later called it "imitative puerile stuff" and destroyed every copy of it he found, the hero is named: Dr. Moses Nebogipfel. There is one passage in *The Time Machine* that does tantalize; as the Time Traveler explores a museum of "ancient" artifacts in the Palace of Green Porcelain (they are, of course, artifacts of our *future*), he reveals that "yielding to an irrestible impulse, I wrote my name upon the nose of a steatite monster from South America that particularly took my fancy." Thus, the Traveler has given his name, but his signature exists in the future in a museum of the past that is yet to be built.

21. And so Newcomb was. Wells was a trained scientist (B.Sc. with first-class honors in zoology and second-class in geology in 1890 from the Royal College of Science) and he quite clearly kept up with technical developments. Certainly he read *Nature* and found Newcomb's address on 28 December 1893 to the New York Mathematical Society reprinted in full there [*Nature* 49 (1 Feb. 1894): 325–329]. The Time Traveler's dinner party must have taken place, therefore, in January or February of 1894. Several years later Newcomb expanded on his ideas in his Presidential Address to the American Mathematical Society [Newcomb, 1898]. He concluded his Address with the words "We must leave it to our posterity to determine whether ... the hypothesis of hyperspace can be used as an explanation of observed phenomena." It was less than two decades later that Einstein did precisely that, explaining gravity in terms of curved four-dimensional hyperspace (spacetime). Newcomb was no Johnny-come-lately to the fourth dimension, as he had published on the topic, including the concept of curved hyperspace, sixteen years before [Newcomb, 1877]. In his 1893 address he called four-dimensional space "the fairyland of geometry" (he repeated the phrase in his Presidential remarks, as well) and hinted at the modern idea of parallel Universes when he said, "Add a fourth dimension to space, and there is room for an indefinite number of Universes, all alongside of each other, as there is for an indefinite number of sheets of paper when we pile them upon each other." Newcomb's idea appealed to Wells' fancy enough so that he built two novels, *The Wonderful Visit* [Wells, 1895] and *Men Like Gods* [Wells, 1923], around it. In the first novel there is explicit mention of multiple worlds "lying somewhere close together, unsuspecting, as near as page to page in a book," and the second book talks of one parallel Universe being rotated into another. Other versions of the idea are in "The Invisible Bomber" [Farley, 1950], "The Magic Staircase" [Bond, 1946], and "Carbon Copy" [Simak, 1960]). Most recently, John Cramer (a University of Washington physicist) has repeated Newcomb's and Wells' parallel Universes/pages-of-a-book/rotation imagery almost word-for-word in his novel *Twistor* [Cramer, 1991c].

22. "Zoological Retrogression," *The Gentleman's Magazine*, 271 (7 Sept. 1891): 246–253.

23. "On Extinction," *Chamber's Journal* 10 (30 Sept. 1893): 623–624.

24. *Nature* 65 (6 Feb. 1902): 326–331.

25. *Nature* 52 (18 July 1895): 268.

26. An old but still very important historical analysis of Minkowski's spacetime is in [Holton, 1965]. For a more recent study that includes the original German text, careful English translations, and photographs of Minkowski's agonized corrections to his pre-address manuscript, see P. L. Galison, "Minkowski's Space-Time: From Visual Thinking to the Absolute World," *Historical Studies in the Physical Sciences* 10 (1979): 85–121. English texts can also be found in [Einstein, TPR] and [Minkowski, BST].

27. W. G., "Euclid, Newton, and Einstein," *Nature* 104 (12 Feb. 1920): 627–630. As is the

case with the mysterious "S." in Note 18, the editorial staff at *Nature* has informed me that there is no record of the identity of W. G. in the journal's archives. In "The Dimension Segregator" [Click, 1929] we have an early fantasy tale that shows the fascination Abbott's world of two dimensions had in the formative years of magazine science fiction—a scientist discovers how to project three-dimensional objects (including himself) onto a two-dimensional surface. There then follows a series of fantastic adventures until disaster falls. More recently, Abbott's satire inspired a nearly unbelieveably awful 1964 episode of television's "The Outer Limits." In "Behold, Eck!," a two-dimensional creature arrives on Earth through a time warp. Unfortunately, it has poor vision and loses its way. Eventually a helpful optometrist aids Eck in finding his way home, but only after the sharp-edged two-dimensional visitor accidently cuts a 37-story building in half!

28. *7th International Congress of Logic, Methodology and Philosophy of Science* Vol. 4 (Salzburg, Austria, 1983), 176. Popper describes his early discussions with Einstein on the reality of time and the four-dimensional Parmenidean block Universe in some detail in his autobiography; see Volume 1 of *The Philosophy of Karl Popper*, ed. P. A. Schilpp, The Library of Living Philosophers (La Salle, Ill., Open Court, 1974), 102–103. Einstein's final position on this matter may be that of the time traveler in "Throwback in Time" [Long, 1953]. After taking a little girl 25,000 years back into the past, where she sees an ancient ancestor of humanity, she asks if he is really alive. Replies the time traveler, "Every man who ever lived is still alive, child. In time there is no real death. When a man dies he's still alive ten minutes ago, ten years ago. He's always alive to those who travel back through time to meet him face to face." Did Einstein really believe this? Not everybody thinks so, and physicist-philosopher Milic Capek cites in [Capek, VOT, BST] an early Einstein comment to support his case. At the 1922 meeting of the French Philosophical Society, the philosopher of science Emile Meyerson asked Einstein if the spatialization of time (that is, the idea of time as a dimension on the same footing as the spatial ones; see [Christensen, 1981]) is a legitimate interpretation of Minkowski's spacetime [Meyerson, 1985]. To which came Einstein's terse answer [Einstein, 1922] that "it is certain that in the four-dimensional continuum all dimensions are *not* [my emphasis] equivalent." Of course, while this tells us Einstein's position in 1922, it may have nothing to do with his views thirty-three years later when he wrote to Besso's family. Certainly Einstein's later willingness to ponder Gödel's time-travel solution to the general relativity field equations shows his views had undergone some changes, and even Capek admits this [Capek, 1965, BST]. Even before the Besso letter, Einstein had said much the same thing; for example, in an appendix on Minkowski's spacetime in [Einstein, 1961] he wrote, "From a 'happening' in three-dimensional space, physics becomes, as it were, an 'existence' in the four-dimensional 'world'."

29. H. Weyl, *Philosophy of Mathematics and Natural Science* Princeton, N.J.: Princeton University Press, 1949), 116. Sir James Jeans had said the same, somewhat less elegantly, in his 1935 Sir Halley Stewart Lecture: "The tapestry of spacetime is already woven throughout its full extent, both in space and time, so that the whole picture exists, although we only become conscious of it bit by bit—like separate flies crawling over a tapestry ... A human life is reduced to a mere thread in the tapestry." Jeans then immediately *rejected* this fatalistic view. See *Scientific Progress* (New York: Macmillan, 1936), 20.

30. From a book review of [Whitrow, 1980] in *Scientific American* (April 1962), 179–185.

31. L. Silberstein, *The Theory of Relativity* (London: Macmillan, 1914), 134.

32. E. Cunningham, *The Principle of Relativity* (Cambridge: Cambridge University Press, 1914) 191.

33. Most recently, it has been shown that time travel does not imply any fatal violation of conservation of energy (see [Friedman *et al.*, 1990], [Deutsch, 1991]). Indeed, global energy-momentum conservation does not play the central role in general relativity that it does in classical physics. For example, nearly sixty years ago Richard Tolman showed how an oscillating Universe (alternating Big Bang and Big Crunches separated by "bounces") creates ever increasing total energy with each cycle of oscillation; i.e., in such a Universe energy is not conserved. For more information see Tolman's book *Relativity Thermodynamics and Cosmology* (Oxford: Oxford University Press, 1934 and [Trautman, GRAV]). More recently, the local and global conservation of energy and momentum in general relativity, in the context of FTL travel, has been discussed in [Bishop, 1984, 1988].

34. Hollis' story is, in fact, a very funny summary of all the previous storytelling, presented as a dialog between two men Box and Cox who discover they have been living in the same space (a bed-sitter at 2 Temporal Crescent, rented from a landlady named Mrs. Chronos!), but in different times. One of the most curious of philosophical tales concerning time can be found in [Schlesinger, 1982]. There we are asked to imagine that scientists have just discovered X, a solar-system "many billions of light years away ... We cannot interact with X except that we are able to communicate with them via some strange medium which transmits signals instantaneously." The author of this paper, who was attempting to explain the sense we all have of the passage of time, says nothing about the extraordinary conclusion concerning time travel that follows from this assumption (see Tech Note 7). Equally odd was the rebuttal from a fellow philosopher [MacBeath, 1986] that began by observing "To sidestep any relativistic explanation [we are asked] to accept that communication between us and the Xians is instantaneous." Rather than sidestep relativity this assumption of course throws the analyst *up to his neck* into relativity! MacBeath apparently did realize something was amiss, as he declared the assumption that "signals might travel billions of light years in no time at all" is absurd, but he said nothing of why he felt it was absurd.

35. Considerably predating both Putnam and Rietdijk with this argument was Philipp Frank, in a section of his book [Frank, 1957] called "Is the World 'Really Four-Dimensional'?" Frank attributes the argument to even earlier writers (see [Frank, BST], written in 1938, for specifics), and correctly concludes it has no merit.

36. Putnam's argument for a nonempty future was restated a few years later in [Sklar, 1974]. Sklar began by claiming that "the philosophers who maintain that past and future objects are not real existents, or that future events do not have determinate reality, are refuted out of hand by special relativity." Then he repeats Putnam's argument, but says nothing of the prior objections to it. He does, however, offer a little waffling on how convinced he is by it all: "But when we put the argument this baldly, the inability of the physical theory to resolve the philosophical dispute becomes obvious." The reason for the so-called failure is, of course, that special relativity is the wrong theory to use!

37. This is the issue of how we measure the speed of light. All the traditional techniques invariably measure the average speed over a two-way trip (with a reflection of the light beam at the far end of the path) back to the source. This allows a single clock at the source to make all the time measurements. A one-way measurement assumes two

distant clocks are synchronized, but how to achieve this presents unexpected problems. Einstein himself was well aware of this, and he commented on it in his 1905 paper [Einstein, TPR]. This is the starting point of the sporadic debate (mostly by philosophers) on the so-called "conventionality of simultaneity." For a treatment of the subtle points, see [Salmon, 1977] and [Petkov, 1989].

Chapter Three

1. The same argument appeared earlier in [Smart, 1954], and as [Webb, 1977] observes, one can find this particular objection to a flowing time as far back as Kant. Not every philosopher finds this a meaningful objection. For example, [Christensen, 1976] observes that the answer to how fast time is passing is just "one second per second" and makes it plain that not to understand this is to be dense. I don't think his position is that solid, and neither do others; [Morris, 1984] calls such a claim "as meaningful as defining the word *cat* by saying 'A cat is a cat'."
2. An extended discussion and analysis of Lewis's ideas on time is in R. W. Stuewer, "G. N. Lewis on Detailed Balancing, the Symmetry of Time, and the Nature of Light," *Historical Studies in the Physical Sciences*, Vol. 6 (Princeton: Princeton University Press, 1975). Lewis was not a physicist, but a chemist at the University of California at Berkeley (we owe the word *photon* to him), and his ideas on advanced waves predated those of the physicists Wheeler and Feynman by twenty years (which they acknowledged).
3. Quoted from *The Philosophy of Rudolp Carnap* (P. A. Schilpp, editor), The Library of Living Philosophers (La Salle, Ill.: Open Court, 1963), 37–38.
4. F. H. Bradley, *Appearance and Reality* (2nd ed.) (London: Oxford, University Press, 1897), 190.
5. J. N. Findlay, *Philosophy* 25 (1950): 346–347.
6. One submission that also argued against Findlay was easy for him to rebut. The analyst argued that a time-reversed world would be analogous to a world in which everything doubled in size, which would be undetectable. This erroneous reasoning was rejected by Findlay: "Surely the analogy is with a world in which size-relations are inverted, in which the least is largest and the largest least? And that, surely, *would* make a difference." The terror aspect of living backward in time is well captured in "Reversion" [Pease, 1949]. A scientist who is involved in an accident with radioactive materials has his sense of time flow reversed, and the story carefully and logically analyzes what his life would be like. For example, the scientist can talk (backward for others), but he is understandable only if his words are recorded and then played in reverse. He cannot eat, as for him that would involve the regurgitation of food. He cannot answer questions because "if he should answer any questions we put to him, it would mean he was giving the answer before he heard the question, on his time scale." And finally, he can't pick anything up because the normally stable position and velocity error-correction mechanism between hand and eye, which is a negative feedback system in normal time, becomes an unstable positive feedback system in reversed time. The horror of his existence is contained in the only words the man utters (deciphered after reversed playback): "Where am I? What's happened? Why are things so different? Why? Why?"
7. This idea can be found quite long ago in science fiction, as in "Minus Sign" [William-

son, 1942], which connects antimatter not only with physical time travel to the past, but also with telephone calls backward in time (see Note 20 for Chapter One). Not everybody likes the association of antimatter with backward time travel; for example, [Price, 1991a] refers to "Feynman's rather loose talk of particles 'travelling' backward ... in time," and in [Earman, 1967a] we read that "it is true that Feynman uses the slogan, 'Positrons are electrons running backward in time', but it is dangerous to draw conclusions from slogans." I am not sure what Professor Earman means by slogans; a reading of Feynman indicates that he took the matter quite seriously. In [Feynman, 1949a], for example, he wrote that "the idea that positrons can be represented as electrons with proper time reversed relative to true time has been discussed by the author and others," and also that "Previous results suggest waves propagating ... toward the past, and that such waves represent the propagation of a positron." Feynman declared the idea to be of value in understanding negative energy states in his famous book *Quantum Electrodynamics* (New York: W. A. Benjamin, 1961), 68. See also Note 20 for Chapter One for Feynman's Nobel Lecture comments on this topic. I see no slogans or "loose talk" in all this. The "others" Feynman had in mind included, in particular, the physicist Ernst C. G. Stueckelberg (1905–1984), who in a 1942 article in the Swiss journal *Helvetica Physica Acta* also wrote of waves scattering backward in time.

8. J. R. Lucas, *A Treatise on Time and Space* (London: Methuen, 1973), 43–47.

9. MacBeath spends some time in his paper discussing the nature of this window, which he shows is essential. Indeed, recalling the antimatter nature of Midge's world, it is vital to keep her and Jim apart. MacBeath observes that the window is actually double-paned, with a perfect vacuum in between. The exchange of light between the two worlds presents no problem (or does it?) because photons are their own antiparticles. In particular, there is no difference between the time sense of photons in either world because the flow of proper time for a photon (traveling at the speed of light) is zero (see Tech Note 5 and also see Note 13).

10. In a direct, vigorous attack on the possibility of time travel, Smart, a philosopher, cites this very problem of communication [Smart, 1963]. Professor Smart believes that travel back in time really means that one should be able to "have normal experiences," and of course this would not be so because one could not communicate. He mentions Norbert Weiner's position in *Cybernetics*, 2nd ed. (Cambridge: MIT Press, 1961), 34–35, in which Weiner calls the idea of a reversed-time being a "fantasy" and concludes that "within any world with which we can communicate, the direction of time is uniform." This is doubly irrelevant. First, as we have seen, communication is logically possible between reversed-time individuals, and second, once back in time (assuming one can actually get there), the time traveler's time direction would thereafter be that of the rest of the world (but see also Note 13).

11. Causal loops have been used in the movies with some effect. In the 1980 *Somewhere in Time*, for example, we see the following loop: The hero in the present is visited by a mysterious old woman who gives him an antique watch. Some time later he travels back to 1912 where he meets a girl to whom he gives the watch. He then returns to the present, and she lives out her life until she too reaches the present—where we discover she is the (now old) woman who gives the hero the watch. At every instant of its existence, the watch is in the possession of either the hero or the woman—so when was it made? A similiar loop is used in the 1983 film *Timerider*.

12. H. Putnam, *The Journal of Philosophy* 59 (12 April 1962): 213–216.

13. This point was elaborated on in [Swartz, 1973]. Here we read: "We have uncritically imagined someone looking in on ... two worlds having opposite time directions ... Part of the story we tell, of the process of seeing, involves the emission of photons from objects [e.g., computer screens] and the subsequent impinging of these photons on our retinas. But this process is obviously directed in time. In a world where time ran oppositely to ours, we could not see objects at all: objects would be photon-sinks, not photon-emitters." In true faustian fashion we would be unable to photograph such a Universe, and a being made of faustian matter would pass one of the tests for being a vampire—no reflection in a mirror—in our world.

14. Dick's first attempt at this idea can be found in the rather muddled short story "Your Appointment Will Be Yesterday" [Dick, 1966]. Its only bright spot is the wonderful line "The tasks of tomorrow become the worse tasks of today." Many of the problems of a backward-running world, poorly handled in this first try, are given better treatment in the novel. In his excellent Introduction to the novel Counter-Clock World [Dick, 1979], David Hartwell writes that Counter-Clock World is neither a tragedy nor a comedy. Rather, "It is a complex, ironic novel, continually mixing the colloquial and personal with the metaphysical." Hartwell is a far more astute science fiction critic than I could ever claim to be, and he might well take exception to my use of the term horror. I can only say I was horrified as I read the novel; the description of what it would be like for a dead body to come alive again in a buried coffin is the equal of anything Poe wrote. The most terrifying story about a reversal in the direction of time is, I think, Philip Jose Farmer's "Sketches Among the Ruins of My Mind" [Farmer, 1977]. This is the tale of how the world goes to bed each night and wakes up each morning with three more days of memories gone. People physically age, but mentally grow younger. What this does to families as parents watch their young children regress is pure and simple horror. A recent work that combines the reversal of cause and effect with horror is the novel Times's Arrow [Amiss, 1991], which is not actually a time-travel or a reversed-time tale; the narrator here tells us backward the story of his life as a former Nazi doctor at Auschwitz. Since the result of any action is related before its cause is presented, this novel has all the logical puzzles of Counter-Clock World without asking the reader to accept reversed time. The 1983 British film Betrayal did the same thing, with its unfolding of an adulterous affair backward in time. Again, this is not truly reversed time, but simply the visual equivalent of Amis' literary device reversing cause and effect. Still, when the picture was reviewed by the Monthly Film Bulletin (Oct. 1983), the critic could not resist a little fun: "The fact that Betrayal's narration advances backward rather than forward ... is neither there nor here."

15. Ignoring how such a thing might actually occur, one philosopher has argued it is at least logically possible [Woodhouse, 1976]. I must admit that this is one of those philosophical papers that has proven impossible for me to appreciate fully. More analytical is [Schmidt, 1966], which shows that under certain initial conditions at the Big Bang, one possible solution to the gravitational field equations is an oscillating Universe that temporally runs backward during the contraction phase; and [Walstad, 1980] further elaborates on this idea. Matthews argues in [Matthews, 1979] that the direction of time is local, not global, and that the arrow of time can point in opposite directions at different locations (at the same time?). In [Cocke, 1967] we find a physicist speculating on the possibility that if an observer in the expanding phase could survive into the contracting one ("perhaps by shutting himself in a vault, so that his own time sense remained unchanged"), then maybe he might disrupt things sufficiently to create large

regions of the Universe with different directions of time. This imagery is repeated in [Hawking, 1985]. John Wheeler is not at all happy with any of this, and certainly would be appalled at Dick's reversed-time world. As Professor Wheeler stated in the General Discussion at the end of [NT], "Most of us would probably agree that the Universe has not contained and will not contain any backward-looking observers. We do not expect to see caskets with corpses in them coming to life, nor do we expect to find bank vaults in which a gram of radium will integrate rather than disintegrate." The idea of time changing its direction after each bounce in an oscillating Universe (but pointing in the same direction during both the expansion and the contraction phases of a given cycle) is described in [Davies, 1972b]. Professor Davies shows how, with such a model, one can then derive the specific value of the observed Big Bang background radiation temperature. The following year [Albrow, 1973] showed how Davies' model also provides complete symmetry between matter and antimatter (if one assumes the TCP theorem always holds, even during bounces—see Note II for Chapter Two), even though during any one cycle one type of matter is dominant.

16. The same year that Dick published his work, Brian Aldiss published the nonmachine time-travel novel *An Age* [Aldiss, 1967], which finds its dramatic revelation in backward-running time. Aldiss is quite explicit in dealing with the human digestive track operating in reverse, but I find his technical presentation of reversed-time to be at least as flawed as Dick's. Aldiss has seen fit to fill his tale with mysterious, godlike beings who periodically arrive like cavalry to save the day, and scientific laws (such as the second law of thermodynamics) are brushed aside, when convenient, with no explanation.

17. For example, obtaining food from a grocery store was easily accomplished once Hull mastered the art of walking backward. As he put it, "A man walking backward from 12:00 to 11:55 looks like a man walking forward from 11:55 to 12:00." Thus, "A man moving in this way who enters a store empty-handed at 12:00 and leaves loaded with food at 11:50 looks like a normal man who comes in with a full shopping bag at 11:50 and leaves without it at 12:00—a peculiar procedure, but not one to raise a cry of 'Stop thief!'" For this to make sense Boucher did have to impose one extra condition of his own—as long as Hull grasped something, its time sense reversed, too.

18. One of the institutional villians in *Counter-Clock World*, for example, is The Library, which is controlled by a group called the Erads. This is a backward-running library that absorbs the written word, and its only goal is to eradicate knowledge. The Library, one of the groups desperate to censor the novel's resurrected prophet (indeed, the Erads finally murder him) is clearly a stand-in for the book burners of our world.

19. The *H*–theorem was a direct continuation of the pioneering work by the genius James Clerk Maxwell on the statistical properties of gas molecules (specifically, the calculation of the probability density function of the molecular speeds). In 1859 Maxwell found this function for a special case, and later, in 1866, he showed that his solution holds in the particular case of thermal equilibrium. In 1872 Boltzmann found the differential-integral equation the function satisfies in general, even out of equilibrium. From this Boltzmann was able to define a quantity *H* that he showed evolves in time such that the general solution always approaches Maxwell's equilibrium solution; i.e., the *H*–theorem says that *H* always decreases in systems not in equilibrium and is at a minimum in systems in equilibrium. Boltzmann's brilliant work can be found in his 1895 book *Lectures on Gas Theory*, which was translated into English by S. G. Brush (Berkeley, CA: University of California Press, 1964).

20. For more on Boltzmann's view on this matter, see the end of his letter "On Certain Questions of the Theory of Gases," *Nature* 51 (28 Feb. 1895): 413–415. He attributes this view, in an enigmatic aside, as "an idea of my old assistant, Dr. Schuetz." The philosopher Karl Popper called Boltzmann's willingness to consider the possibility that different regions of the Universe could have different directions of time "staggering in its boldness and beauty"; see Vol. 1 of *The Philosophy of Karl Popper* (P. A. Schilpp, editor), The Library of Living Philosophers La Salle, Ill: Open Court, 1974), 127–128. But Popper went on to assert that Boltzmann must be wrong because "it brands unidirectional change an illusion. This makes the catastrophe of Hiroshima an illusion." This is a metaphysical argument, of course, and while it has great emotional power for the human soul, I fail to see how it relates to physics. From time to time one can find in the modern physics literature on relativity serious speculations about reversed-time beings; e.g., [Belinfante, 1966], whose author tells us in a footnote that it took two years to get the paper published, as two referees could not understand it!

21. See [Haldane, 1928]. The googol is a gigantic number, far greater than the number of raindrops that have fallen on the entire Earth during its entire history. And the googolplex is light years beyond that. Using a wonderful bit of imagery that I have not seen repeated since, R. B. Braithwaite wrote in his critical analysis of [Eddington, 1929] entitled "Professor Eddington's Gifford Lectures," *Mind* 38 (Oct. 1929): 409–435: "If a man shuffled just a single pack of cards as rapidly as an individual molecule hits other molecules in air, and if a snail started to crawl around the Universe ... at the rate of one centimeter *during the life of the sidereal system* [my emphasis], the snail would have got round the Universe many millions of times before it would become at all likely that the man would have got the pack back to the original order." If this is what it takes to get a pack of cards back to its initial state, then try to conceive of the time required to restore the world to 7 December 1941. Stanley G. Weinbaum and Lyle D. Gunn were two authors who were not discouraged by such calculations, and they used the certainty of recurrence over infinite time in their fiction; see "The Circle of Zero" [Weinbaum, 1949] and "The Time Twin" [Gunn, 1939]. The notion of eternal recurrence considerably predates Poincaré, as shown in [Small, 1991], which traces its scientific (as opposed to astrological) study back to the fourteenth century.

22. Indeed, this connection provides a plausible link between the identity of our psychological direction of time to that of increasing entropy. Psychological time is in the direction of increasing memories (increasing information), and the direction of increasing information is in the direction of increasing entropy.

23. The fuzziness of the relationship between entropy and time was captured by one physicist who asked, "If it were found that the entropy of the Universe were decreasing, would one say that time was flowing backward, or would one say that it was a law of nature that entropy decreases with time?" For additional information see P. W. Bridgeman, *Reflections of a Physicist* (New York: Philosophical Library, 1955), 251. Even in a story in which we are told the physics of time travel "would have no meaning to you," the connection between time and entropy is made. When a character in *The Corridors of Time* [Anderson, 1966] asks how a time corridor works, he is told, "Think of it as a tube of force, whose length has been rotated onto the time axis. *Entropy still increases inside; there is temporal flow* [my emphasis]."

24. Bunge [1958] asserts that two-dimensional, complex time is old hat in the theories of spinning particles. There has also been some multidimensional time discussion in the physics literature concerning the superluminal Lorentz transformations associated with

FTL particles (issues discussed in Chapter Four and Tech Note 7), but advocates of this have been strongly rebutted by other physicists. For a short bibliography of the physical literature and a concise summary of the objections to multidimensional time, see [Kowalczynski, 1984].

25. A. S. Eddington, *The Mathematical Theory of Relativity*, 2nd ed. (Cambridge: Cambridge Univ. Press, 1924), 25.

26. Mirman [1973] asserts that this is the most fundamental property of time and argues that there can only be one-dimensional time.

27. Two other papers on two-dimensional time are [Nusenoff, 1976] and [Wilkerson, 1973], but neither treats the issue of changing the past. Coming at two-dimensional time from another angle are [Oaklander, 1983] and [Schlesinger, 1985], which discuss its applicability and use in the context of McTaggart's arguments about temporal becoming.

28. See [Dobbs, 1951a,b; 1956], which suggest that the specious present may be the physical manifestation of two-dimensional time, and [Broad, 1937] and [Broad and Price, 1937], which discuss two-dimensional time as an explanation for precognition. Dobbs' theory was rejected by [Mundle, 1954], but that didn't discourage Dobbs, who later advocated two-dimensional time as a rational mechanism for ESP [Dobbs, 1965]. An indirect experimental test, claims [Yndurain, 1991], can (and has) been done for compact multiple-time dimensions. This paper discusses the implications of extra timelike dimensions that are "curled-up," much like the spatial dimensions mentioned in Note 15 for Chapter Two. The author's conclusion is that such a situation would lead to the decay of quarks and protons at an experimentally detectable rate; since such decays are not observed, these compact additional time dimensions do not exist. Yndurian also includes this additional remark, however: "If there are extra time dimensions we get violations of causality, because one could sneak to yesterday through the extra dimensions, and ... if you had sneaked to yesterday, you would have disappeared from today." As Professor Meiland's analyses show, however, there is nothing at all illogical about such things with two-dimensional time.

Chapter Four

1. This experiment does motivate a curious question, however—does the cube travel through time or is its journey "instantaneous," so to speak? Sometimes this distinction is made by calling the first *sliding* and the second *jumping*. That is, does the cube travel around time? If through time, then the cube is present at every instant after the start of its trip, and so it should not vanish. The cube just gets to each instant before the observers do, but why this should produce the visual effect of disappearing is unclear. Brown's description implies that the cube traveled five minutes into the future without existing at any of the in-between instants. Wells tried to have it both ways in *The Time Machine* by invoking "diluted presentation," which is the reason why we cannot see "the spoke of a wheel spinning, or a bullet flying through the air." If the cube "is traveling through time fifty times or a hundred times faster than we are ... the impression it creates will of course be only one-fiftieth or one-hundreth." This explanation breaks down, of course, when one remembers that even if you cannot see the spoke or bullet, they are still there and you can get in their way—Wells, unfortunately, has one of his characters stick a hand into the space where the time machine was last seen.

2. Brown thought of everything in this tale. At this point in the story one of the colleagues, puzzled by how the inventor will be able to place the cube into the time machine at three if it has already vanished from his hand and appeared in the machine, asks "How can you you place it there, then?" Replies the inventor, "It will, as my hand approaches, vanish from the [machine] and appear in my hand to be placed there." Still, while I am an admirer of Brown's work, I certainly am not an uncritical one. For example, his time-reversed story "The End" [Brown, 1977] is a simplistic, nearly trivial presentation of a deep issue.

3. J. Hospers, *An Introduction to Philosophical Analysis*, 2nd ed. (Englewood Cliffs, NJ: Prentice-Hall, 1967), 175.

4. This work is in the form of a letter to his friend Desiderius (who later became Pope Victor III), in which Damian rebutted Desiderius' defense of St. Jerome's claim that "while God can do all things, he cannot cause a virgin to be restored after she has fallen." Desiderius thought the reason God could not restore virgins is that he does not want to, to which Damian replied this meant God is unable to do whatever he does not want to do, but this meant that God would then be less powerful than men, who are able to do things they don't want to do (e.g., go without food for a month). This is a good example of the danger in getting involved in debates with theologians.

5. Borges was so inspired by Damian's view that the past could be changed that he wrote a short story based on it ("The Other Death" [Borges, 1970]) and put a character named after Damian in it.

6. Two eminent physicists after Gödel have also taken this position in their very influential book; see S. W. Hawking and G. F. R. Ellis, *The Large Scale Structure of Space-Time* (London: Cambridge University Press, 1973), 189. See also Note 11. This same view was earlier endorsed by Whitrow as "logically irrefutable" in the 1961 edition of his impressive book [Whitrow, 1980]. The 1980 edition has curiously (but correctly) dropped this endorsement. In an equally curious footnote to this (found on page 306 in 1980 and on page 260 in 1961) Professor Whitrow writes, "It is interesting to note that in Wells' novel the Time Traveller returns from his trip into the future but not from his trip into the past!" It is amusing that Whitrow, who rejects time travel, finds Wells of all people a source of comfort. In any case, a careful reading of the novel's Epilogue shows that the direction of the last trip is an open question.

7. Lewis makes it clear that he believes it is a sin to pray for something known not to have occurred; e.g., to pray for the safety of someone known to have been killed yesterday. As he writes, "The known event states God's will. It is psychologically impossible to pray for what we know to be unobtainable; and if it were possible, the prayer would sin against the duty of submission to God's known will." This is a position of faith, of course, about which mathematical physics has nothing to say.

8. Dummett is fond of making up fairy tales to illustrate his belief in backward causation. Ten years later, for example, he was at it again [Dummett, 1964], this time with one that has become famous in philosophical circles—a tale about a tribal chief who finds that he can make young warriors to *have been* brave on lion hunts if he dances during their entire absence from home. The details of this story are simply unimportant for us, but other philosophers have responded; e.g., [Gorovitz, 1964] and the curious [Zetterberg, 1979], which attempts to use relativistic reasoning (but which seems to miss the distinction between affecting and changing the past). My view is that it is all so beside the point. There is no evidence for Dummett's alarm clocks, magicians, and dancing tribal chiefs. They are all made up—and we can make up anything we'd like!

What *is* of importance is the theoretical prediction of backward causation and time travel by the equations of physics. I think Dummett was correct in his conclusions, but consider his method of analysis as a distraction; indeed, as irrelevant.

9. J. R. Lucas, *A Treatise on Time and Space* (London: Methuen, 1973), 50. Many of Dwyer's arguments can also be found in [Dwyer, 1975].

10. "Of Warps and Wormholes," *Archaeology* (March/April 1989), 80.

11. See, for example, pages 238–240 in [Kaufmann, 1977]. Here we read that "the idea that time machines could exist is extremely troublesome to the scientist. Truly disturbing things could happen. ... time machines violate *causality* ... The idea that effects could occur before their causes is denied by the rational human mind." Kaufmann is also worried, I presume, by the possibility of changing the past in the way described in "Delvers in Destiny" [Kummer, 1945]. There, when a time traveler from the twenty-first century journeys back five centuries, he cuts down an oak sapling to make a club and uses it to kill a lamb for food. Because that sapling will (no longer?) grow to make future acorns and the lamb will have no descendents, certain alterations are induced. According to the story, for example, homes in the future vanish (no acorns in the past means no trees in the future and thus no lumber), and since a lot of wool isn't there anymore, trousers disappear off of men in mid-stride!

12. In opposition to this assertion, the final scene in *Time and Again* [Finney, 1970] has the hero return to the past and prevent the parents of another character from meeting. Fredric Brown directly tackled the grandfather paradox in "First Time Machine" [Brown, 1958], also with the idea that the past can be changed. This is, as argued in this chapter, not logical. More logical is "Don't Live in the Past" [Knight, GRSF1], in which a time traveler voyages back four centuries in a misguided attempt to prevent a "temporal accident" in the present from changing the past—once in the past, he discovers he is actually a historically important personage, and so his presence does not change the past (but certainly does affect it).

13. Playing change-the-past with the Civil War by using a splitting Universe is one of the more powerful time-travel subthemes (see the anthology FCW). Many writers in addition to authors of science fiction have amused themselves with this sort of speculation. See, for example, *IF: or History Rewritten* (J. C. Squire, editor), (New York: Viking, 1931). One of the included essays, by Winston S. Churchill, is a double twist, written as an analysis of future events if Lee had not won the Battle of Gettysburg!

14. See [DeWitt, 1973] for the details of Everett's work, and [Wolf, 1990] for an interesting treatment of it. Healey [1984] calls Everett's theory "highly controversial" and declares that "few working physicists take it seriously." Stein [1984] calls the theory "a bizarre notion." DeWitt himself writes "the idea of 10^{100} + slightly imperfect copies of [the Universe] all constantly splitting into further copies ... is not easy to reconcile with commonsense. Here is schizophrenia with a vengeance." Even the defense (sort of) of Everett in [Geroch, 1984] admits the theory is at best "incomplete." An indirect argument that has been used to support the many-worlds idea is the anthropic one. Smith [1986b] outlines this puzzle of why many of the physical constants of nature (e.g., the weak fine structure and the strong coupling constants) have just the values required to produce a Universe that supports life. Some have argued that all possible Universes exist, with all possible variations in the constants, and so there must be Universes (like ours) with life. Everett's theory is then invoked to explain all these Universes, but Smith argues that in fact Everett's theory offers no such explanation. For the theological aspects of the many-worlds idea, see [Craig, 1990], which calls the

concept "ontologically bloated" and "outlandish." John Wheeler, Everett's dissertation advisor, has changed his own mind about the concept [Wheeler, 1979]: "I once
subscribed to it. In retrospect, however, it looks like the wrong track ... its infinitely
many unobservable worlds make a heavy load of metaphysical baggage." Tipler
[QCST] disagrees, claiming that the enlarged ontology is a plus, not a minus! See also
[Tipler, 1986]. A rebuttal to Tipler is [Shimony, QCST]. Everett's theory is the antithesis
of what is commonly called the collapse of the wave function, the idea that all potential
possibilities have a nonzero reality until a consciousness actually decides or observes
which one will be. This quantum-mechanical concept gets its name from the probability wave equation due to the physicist Irwin Schrödinger. Before the observation, all
possible futures have various values of probability; after the observation (which collapses the wave function), however, one of the futures (*the* future) has probability one
and all the others have probability zero. The earliest stories I know of that treat the
collapsing-wave-function concept are *The Legion of Time* [Williamson, 1985] and
"Tryst in Time" [Moore, 1975], both published nearly twenty years before Everett's
dissertation (in 1938 and 1939, respectively). In Everett's many-worlds interpretation,
the wave function of the Universe does not collapse. (Indeed, it *couldn't*, as there is no
observer external to the entire Universe to observe the Universe); Instead the wave
function "splits" at every decision point in spacetime. Although this leads to a multi-
tude of realities beyond comprehension, cosmologists like it because it avoids the
puzzle of an observer outside the Universe. Writer L. Sprague de Camp was an early
pioneer of this idea in science fiction; e.g., in *Lest Darkness Fall* [de Camp, 1941] he
uses the analogy of a tree (the "main time line") that is always sprouting new branches.
The parallel Universe idea is different yet again in that *all* the possibilities *always* exist,
independent and parallel in time. Most recently, this approach has been used in *The
Hemingway Hoax* [Haldeman, 1990], which stated that "there is not just one Universe, but actually uncountable zillions of them," and in *Time and Chance* [Brennert,
1990] in which a man and his counterpart in a parallel world briefly exchange places.

15. The editorial introduction to this pioneering tale is interesting; the opening line is "To
say that this short story contains some revolutionary time-travel theories would be
putting it exceedingly mild." The editor then goes on to tell us enthusiastically that
"when the author ... submitted this story to us, his accompanying letter stated that in
it he had settled the time-travel question once and for all. We must admit that a broad,
unbelieving grin spread over our countenances when the author dared make this
assertion. BUT—the smile soon left our faces ... to our chagrin, Mr. Daniels had really
propounded so many brand new ideas about time and time-travel, and such logical
ones—*that he has not left one loophole in his argument!*" John W. Campbell, the first
(and only) editor of *Astounding Science Fiction* (today's *Analog*), called alternate-time-
track stories "mutant" because they represented the first new innovation (or mutation)
in the time-travel concept since H. G. Wells. Campbell claimed that *The Legion of
Time* [Williamson, 1985] originally published by *Astounding Science Fiction* in 1938,
was the first such tale (see Cambell's editorial in the May 1938 issue), and that "Other
Tracks" [Sell, SFAD] (which appeared in the magazine in October 1938) was the
second, but in fact it was Daniels who used the idea first.

16. But not always. For example, in both *The End of Eternity* [Asimov, 1986b] and "Time
Enough" [Knight, 1961] these forces (be they of human origin or just "fate") are the
central point of the story; they generate the tension and conflict that is vital to good
fiction.

17. Such self-encounters can even be misses and still have great impact. For example, in "Minus Sign" [Williamson, 1942] a spaceship fights a battle with itself as it self-interacts while traveling backward in time. And in "Let the Ants Try" [Pohl, 1956], a time traveler journeys back forty million years. Upon stepping out of his time machine, he hears a "raucous animal cry" from somewhere in the nearby jungle. Later, after other adventures in time, he returns to near the same point in spacetime. Indeed, after stepping out of his time machine he sees himself in the distance—the version of himself during the first trip. Then, suddenly, the time traveler meets a violent death; "As his panicky lungs filled with air for the last time, he knew what animal had screamed in the depths of the Coal Measure forest." And the time traveler in "The Uncertainty Principle" [Bilenkin, 1978] happens across his own grave while on a visit to the Middle Ages; he will die after another trip even further back in the past.

18. Lucas (see Note 9) had this particular puzzle in mind when he wrote of a loop that avoids direct human self-interaction: "It is very important, not only for reasons of modesty, that I should not be able to use a Time Machine to go into a public library and read my own biography." The protagonist in *Time and Again* [Simak, 1951] follows this advice when he discovers and refuses to read a book brought from the future by a time traveler, a book that he *will* write. On the other hand, Robert Heinlein did not agree with this view; in *The Door Into Summer* [Heinlein, 1986], the protagonist, an inventor, travels thirty years into the future where he reads some patent disclosures for inventions he does not remember—but which are under his own name. So, he returns to his own time and promptly files the patents! And in the earlier "By His Bootstraps" [Heinlein, AHT], the whole point of the story is the inexorable repetition of events as a time traveler doubles, triples, and more back on his own world line. In "Sam, This is You" [Leinster, BML] we get a very funny story (available today on audio tape as an "X–Minus One" radio drama) about a telephone lineman who starts getting telephone calls from himself from ten days in the future. The first call tells Sam how to make the gadget to transmit such calls. This idea appeared earlier in "Forever Is Not So Long" [Reeds, 1942]. In the suspenseful "Party Line" [Klein, BRW] a man receives telephone calls from *two* versions of himself, one ten years in the future saying he absolutely must accept an invitation to fly to the Bahamas that very day and another version calling from tomorrow that insists the plane will crash. What should he do? The time traveler in "A Thief in Time" [Sheckley, 1955] is constantly running into people who tell him what he will do (because for them he has already done them). A time machine experiment gone wrong allows thirteenth-century Roger Bacon to meet twentieth-century scientists in "Lost in the Dimensions" [Schachner, 1937], thus explaining the amazing forecasts in his *Opus Maius*. In "Fool's Errand" [Del Rey, 1951a] we discover how Nostradamus came to make *his* predictions—a time-traveling historian on a visit to A.D. 1528 from A.D. 2211 accidentally gives a copy of the predictions to the prophet while he is still a wild young student. In the film *Bill & Ted's Excellent Adventure* (where we learn that even the not-very-bright can be time travelers), a set of missing keys is necessary for the successful completion of a task. The two time travelers decide that after the task is done, they will go back in time, steal the keys (that's why they're missing!), and hide them so they can use them *now*. Where should they hide them? Why, "over there," says one of the boys, pointing at a hiding place—and, by gosh, when they go over and look, the keys are there. (They agree that once they have finished with the keys it will be *most* important that they really do put the keys in the hiding place!) Isaac Asimov made a similar causal loop the centerpiece of his major

time-travel novel *The End of Eternity* [Asimov, 1986b]. In it a time traveler journeys back to teach the "inventor" of time travel how to do it because ancient documents show that this is what happened (will happen). Asimov takes the position in his work that the past can be changed, that new and better realities can be engineered by wise men who guard the centuries, and that it is possible to "change yesterday today for a better tomorrow," a position that this entire chapter argues is illogical.

19. This isn't to say that MacBeath asserts time travel is impossible. Indeed, he boldly declares that he believes in the logical possibility of time travel, and his paper is devoted to discovering what he thinks is incorrect in Harrison's story. Professor Mac-Beath does this by retelling the story with what he believes are crucial modifications to make it sufficiently less outrageous so as to be taken seriously. Our new hero, thawed out from a deep freezer, is Arthur. Arthur is, unfortunately, suffering from total amnesia (this is MacBeath's way of avoiding the problem of Dee remembering he ate Dum, and of even worse yet to come), and so when asked his full name, he is himself sufficiently puzzled to reply, "Arthur who?"; he is finally called (what else?) Arthur Who. And as you can now no doubt guess, his son becomes Dr. Who! We are told of the son's genius (a 1999 Ph.D. at age 14, with a dissertation on the principles of time travel, is followed by a trip back into the past with his father, by the eating of the father by the son, by the entering of the deep freezer by Dr. Who, etc., etc.) The whole business is quite entertaining and *at least* as complex as Harrison's story. Just how complex is summed up in MacBeath's last, wonderful line: "The Who who was Dr. Who's father was not Dr. Who—that is, not the Dr. Who whose father he was." See [Gordon, 1987] for a pop-psychology analysis of the "incest urge" as the supposed reason for the fascination of time travel to the past. More recently, Karen B. Mann has written on the supposed linkage between sex and time travel to the past in "Narrative Entanglements: *The Terminator*," *Film Quarterly* 43 (Winter 1989–90): 17–27. Mann sees, I think, far more sexual imagery in time-travel movies than is warranted, and in at least one case completely misses the central point of the movie. Specifically, she calls the sexual paradox at the heart of *The Terminator* an "unnecessarily bizarre twist on time travel," and offers instead the banal theory that it is simply an excuse to send "as violent a creature as Arnold Schwarzenegger after a woman." In fact, the movie would be utterly pointless without the sexual paradox. For a very funny spoof of the coupling of time travel and incest, see "Klein's Machine" [Weiner, TT].

20. I agree with the assessment that Heinlein's is the best short time-travel story, but certainly the most complicated time-travel short story has to be one by Pierre Boulle (best known as the author of the book that inspired the time-travel film *Planet of the Apes*). This story, "Time Out of Mind" [Boulle, 1966], describes how two time travelers manage to murder each other—even though one was born 6000 years before Christ and the other 18,000 years later. Boulle takes the position, for which I have argued here, that the past is unalterable (and his tale also has some interesting discussion on free will and determinism). The world lines of each of the men is, as you might imagine, horribly twisted. As one of them accurately declares, "Our lives are so intertwined, my past with his future, my future with his past, that the gods themselves can't make head or tail of it any longer!" Certainly *I* couldn't! As a final twist, the story is told by a narrator who at the end gets caught (along with the reader) in a causal loop.

21. A similiar example is given in [Horwich, 1975]. To the claim that we can "rule out Gödel's solutions in the way that we often reject unacceptable mathematical solutions to mathematical problems," Professor Horwich replies in a footnote: "Suppose we

have to solve a quadratic equation in order to solve a problem about how many men would be required to dig a ditch, etc. If one of the roots is the square root of minus two it is instantly rejected." This is a poor example, however, because a fundamental result from algebra tells us that if we have a quadratic with real coefficients, then if one root is imaginary, so is the other. The proper conclusion in Horwich's example would be either that the original data is inconsistent or that we have made a mistake in constructing the quadratic equation itself. It is significant, I think, that when Horwich rewrote his essay for inclusion in his excellent book [Horwich, 1987], he deleted this footnote.

22. J. A. Stratton, *Electromagnetic Theory* (New York: McGraw-Hill, 1941), 428. Like all the other laws of physics (except for the rare *K* mesons mentioned in Chapter Three), Maxwell's equations are indifferent to the sign of time. However, as the late Stanford physicist Leonard Schiff has so nicely demonstrated [Schiff, NT], the Maxwell equations lose this indifference if there is such a thing as a magnetic monopole (either a north or south pole *alone* without the other kind attached). Monopoles have, as I write, not been observed, even by those who have looked very hard for them.

23. See "The Love Letter" [Finney, TOT] for a masterful demonstration of the emotional impact that such backward-in-time communications might have for lovers irrevocably separated in time. "When You Hear the Tone" [Scortia, 1981] does the same with telephone calls to the ever more distant past, with a clever twist at the end that lets the lovers finally meet. "Line to Tomorrow" [Padgett, WT], on the other hand, uses a similiar plot device for a grim conclusion leading to insanity and suicide.

24. Suppose a time traveler goes into the future and, before returning to his normal time, finds himself. Suppose further that the two quarrel and the time traveler kills his future self. This is not paradoxical, but rather a delayed form of a sort of suicide. But suppose it is the time traveler who is killed. This is then just a variant of the grandfather paradox, and all the previous arguments against it apply here, too. It is crucial to note that the assumption that the time traveler does in fact find an older-self in the future implies that a backward journey will take place. If a time traveler journeys forward and stays in the future, he will not find another version of himself there.

25. My example is somewhat flawed, of course. For the gadget to call ahead in time means that some sort of signal, as yet unspecified, has traveled into the future (because something made the future-phone ring). For the present discussion I have ignored this issue for the sake of the dramatic impact of the example. Soon, however, I will describe in some detail how one might, in principle, actually build this gadget, called an "antitelephone" in the physics literature. (Such a device is an *anti*telephone, because for it the receiver is in the sender's *past*, the opposite of the case for an ordinary telephone.) This sort of signal transmission was used in "You Want It *When?*" [Dalkey, 1991]. In that story a character who discovers how to send messages backwards in time soon after receives a congratulatory note from herself, from ten years in the future. In [Forward, 1980] we are told that we can send messages into the past by compressing a 15-billion-ton asteriod into a volume of an atomic nucleus(!), spinning it, and then aiming frequency-coded gamma ray bursts through the nearby region of "unhinged time." This is, of course, an artificial Kerr-black hole telegraph. Dr. Forward, evidently an optimist of the first-rank, thinks we will be able to this before the end of the twenty-first century. It would seem, then, that what should be done now is to build gamma ray receivers (well within present-day technology) and listen for such messages from the future. The technical details of such receivers would not matter, of

course, as long as they are put into the public domain. That way the future will know what they are (were?) merely by reading about them from a musty library book and it would build its transmitters to be perfectly compatible!

26. *Punch* 165 (19 Dec. 1923): 591.

27. Oddly enough, Isaac Asimov dismisses FTL motion in [Asimov, 1984a] without once mentioning the time-travel connection, which he had totally rejected just a few months before in [Asimov, 1984b]. Some discussion on a non-time-travel method for achieving FTL motion has appeared in the philosophical literature. Resurrecting the matter-transmitter idea of [Weingard, 1972a], the suggestion in [Elliot, 1981] is that "one's biochemical details are recorded and one's body is then disintegrated. The recorded biochemical blueprint is electro-magnetically transmitted to the arrival center at the desired destination." (Seeming to be unaware of this philosophical analysis, many later writers on this idea refer instead to the beam transporter in television's "Star Trek"). Elliot's idea has all sorts of obvious problems (not counting that "disintegration" business!), such as how the "arrival center" got there in the first place, the failure of distant simultaneity, and personal identity (the arrival center will reconstruct you from its element bank). For more on the brief debate Elliot's suggestion sparked, see [Brennan, 1982], [Ray, 1982], and [Elliot, 1982]. Some years later, an analysis of personal identity crises via time travel appeared [Ehring, 1987], which showed how our normal ideas of what constitutes distinct persons (different bodies, causal independence of those bodies, and the lack of a shared consciousness) fails in the case of a time traveler who journeys backward to talk to himself. To an observer this may look like two people talking, but in the spacetime view it is just one bent-back world line; i.e., *one* person.

28. See [Rothman, 1960] for the usual "things;" e.g., the intersection point of two very long, closing scissor blades. The explanation for such things is that they are massless, do not participate in a causal chain, and carry no information, and so special relativity is not violated. Much more perplexing, at first glance, are the FTL phenomena astronomers have observed in space; e.g., Supernova 1987A in the Large Magellanic Cloud displays apparent expansion speeds of up to twenty times the speed of light. The explanation for such events is that they are most likely light echo optical illusions. For more on this and other proposed explanations, all within the bounds of relativity, see [Blandford, McKee, and Rees, 1977] and [Sheldon, 1990].

29. That is, even though "faster than light" means "backward in time," which means "causality failure," special relativity still holds true and nothing awful happens to physics (only to our intuitions). The reason for this is simply that causality, contrary to common belief even among many physicists, is not a premise or starting point of special relativity. See [Nerlich, 1982] for an extended discussion on just this point: Even earlier than this [Kirzhnits and Polyachenko, 1964] had vigorously made this point before studying the possibility of superluminal sound in superdense matter.

30. The possibility of FTL "cosmic communication" was discussed by Herbert Dingle (see Tech Note 5) in a letter to *The Observatory* 85 (Dec. 1965): 262–264. Dingle rejected special relativity (he called it "no longer tenable") and claimed that "the Doppler effect affords a means of instantaneous communication over any distance at all." Dingle was rebutted by R. F. Griffin in a reply immediately following, and Dingle countered in the same journal [*The Observatory* 86 (Aug. 1966): 165–167]. Dingle had earlier (in 1960) written in much more detail on this in *The British Journal for the Philosophy of Science* 11 (May 1960): 11–31 and (Aug. 1960): 113–129. I know of no one who thinks Dingle

was onto anything, and in any case he said nothing about communication with the past, a concept that given his conservative, classical approach to physics would surely have rendered him unconscious on the spot. Poul Anderson, trained as a physicist and usually careful with the science in his science fiction, ignores the backward-time-travel effect in an instantaneous communication system in his story "Dialogue" [Anderson, FTL]. So does "Lightship, Ho!" [Bond, 1939b], a story of a man on Pluto who invents a way to send messages to Earth at twice the speed of light. (A would-be dictator is on his way to Earth in a light-speed rocketship, and only a FTL message can warn Earth in time.) Explaining the flaw in this signaling scheme (which Bond describes in some detail) would make a good question on a Ph.D. qualifying examination in physics or electrical engineering.

31. H. Tetrode, "Uber den Wirkungszusammenhang der Welt. Eine Erweiterung der Klassischen Dynamik," *Zeitschrift Fuer Physik* 10 (1922): 317–328. Tetrode's imagery was, curiously, captured decades before in the words of the nineteenth-century English poet Francis Thompson in his "The Mistress of Vision":

> All things ... near and far,
> Hiddenly to each other linked are,
> That thou canst not stir a flower
> Without troubling of a star.

32. Yet, as pointed out in [Gold, 1962] and [Cramer, 1980], it is not clear that Wheeler and Feynman's claim to have avoided the self-interaction problems by referring to advanced fields is a step forward. Indeed, the self-interaction of the electron is needed to explain the 1947 experiment by Lamb that measured the deviation (the "Lamb shift") of the spectrum of hydrogen from what Dirac's theory of the electron predicted. Ironically, it was this experiment that helped inspire the renormalization of quantum electrodynamics to get rid of the infinities then plaguing it, which led to Feynman's share of the Nobel prize in 1965. In fact, just four years after Wheeler and Feynman's first joint paper, Feynman [Feynman, 1949b] expressed his revised view that self-interaction could not be avoided. See [Teitelboim, 1970] for an explanation of how to get the radiative reaction without invoking advanced fields.

33. In a footnote, [Earman, 1969] cites a French source that he says does contain negative reactions by physicists to Wheeler and Feynman's "solution" to their bilking paradox. Earman himself calls their solution "brazen" [Earman, 1972].

34. This isn't to say that Professor Cramer dismisses advanced waves as a logical impossibility. Indeed, he has written on the Wheeler and Feynman absorber theory and has advanced an ingenious idea explaining why we see only the retarded solutions to Maxwell's equations and not the advanced ones [Cramer, 1983]. Visualizing the singularity of the Big Bang as a reflector of advanced waves back to the future (after all, you cannot go back in time further than the Big Bang), then advanced waves cancel themselves, leaving only the retarded ones. As Cramer has noted, this idea has an immediate cosmological implication—the Universe must not be fated to suffer a collapse in the distant future into the Big Crunch because then that singularity would be a reflector of the retarded waves (and thus cancel them out too). In such a case Cramer's theory says that we would observe *no* solutions to Maxwell's equations. Of course, in that case, we would not be here to "not observe" anything. Professor Cramer has also put forth an ingenious idea that explains how the thermodynamic arrow of time is a

consequence of the electromagnetic arrow [Cramer, 1988a]. Observing that Boltzmann assumed in his proof of the H–theorem (see Note 19 for Chapter Three) that the motions of molecules of gas are correlated *after* they collide, Cramer says that Boltzmann's assumption is consistent with a retarded electromagnetic arrow, i.e., with delayed electromagnetic interactions between molecules. If, on the other hand, we lived in a Universe with advanced waves, then molecular motions would be correlated before collisions, which would result in entropy decreasing with time. Thus, for Cramer, the expansion of the Universe (cosmological arrow), via its lack of a Big Crunch, allows for the (retarded) electromagnetic arrow, which in turn results in the observed thermodynamic arrow of increasing entropy. And, finally, it is this thermodynamic arrow that gives rise to the one-way chemical reactions in our brains that result in our sense of the subjective arrow of time (the "moving now").

35. Blish is actually pretty close to the mark here. A composite signal with a continuous spectrum (with the energy distributed uniformly in frequency), such as one might expect the overlay of many independent signals to be, does indeed have a narrow time structure. Such a signal would, if applied to a loudspeaker, sound like a sharp pulse or click—or even a *beep*. In the limit of an infinitely wide sprectrum, the time signal becomes one of infinite amplitude and zero duration, a singular impulse function called (by theoretical physicists and radio engineers, alike) the "Dirac delta function."

36. In fiction, Edward Page Mitchell, the Victorian pioneer in the time-travel-paradox story genre, who was mentioned in Chapter One, described a gadget (called, in anticipation of Feinberg, the *tachypomp*—literally "quick sender") for reaching any speed, no matter how great [Mitchell, FM]. This story originally appeared in the March issue of *Scribner's Monthly*—for 1874! The usual massive particles of physics, moving at less than the speed of light, are often called by the obvious (if vulgar) name *tardyons*. Disliking this and observing the classical origin of the word *tachyon*, [Fox, Kuper, and Lipson, 1970] and [Bers *et al.*, RAG] suggest that normal particles be called *ittyons*, from the Hebrew for "slow." This suggestion has, to my knowledge, not had much success. The tachyon, also called the *psitron* [Dobbs,1965] by psychical researchers, is well-known on paper but it has yet to be observed experimentally, although there have been extensive searches for it. See, for example, [Alvager and Kreisler, 1968], which describes an unsuccessful attempt to create electrically charged tachyon-pairs by bombarding a lead target with gamma rays and then looking for Cerenkov radiation (electromagnetic radiation emitted by an electrical charge exceeding the speed of light in the local medium). The theory behind this experiment was declared to be faulty in [Jones, 1972]. (The idea of looking for Cerenkov radiation as a signature for tachyons has already appeared in time-travel science fiction, e.g., *Time of the Fox* [Costello, 1990].) Lapedes and Jacobs [1972] suggests that the same effect should exist for gravitational radiation, but at a much reduced rate; a tachyonic electron would electromagnetically lose all its energy in a tenth of a nano-nanosecond, while a tachyonic neutron would take two million years to gravitationally radiate its energy. How to detect this faint gravitational radiation is an open question. There have been analysts who have questioned the perhaps too quick assumption that tachyons would be small. For example, [Schulman, 1971b] concludes that macroscopically sized tachyons with nuclear densities should produce gravitational shock waves detectable "across the entire solar system." Several years later, [Clay and Crouch, 1974], following the lead of [Murthy, 1971], reported the possible detection of tachyons via their precursor indication of subsequently measured Earth-surface air showers induced by cosmic rays

in the upper atmosphere. That is, FTL tachyons produced high above the surface reached the ground before the main burst of subluminal particles. Later researchers, however, have been unable to repeat this work. There have been various explanations put forth for these failures in addition to the direct one that tachyons simply do not exist. To explain *why* this would be so, [Bers *et al.*, RAG] argues that tachyons are *unstable* solutions to the Klein-Gordon wave equation that describes the motion of particles with the tachyonic properties of superluminality, imaginary mass, and zero spin. In contrast, [Peres, 1969] asserts that the quantum wave function of a tachyon is such that tachyons cannot be localized in space and so are simply unobservable. (See, for example, the infinite-velocity tachyons in Tech Note 7, which are "everywhere at once.") Making the same conclusion from a different angle is [Kirch, 1975], which asserts that the mass of a tachyon is so low as to be virtually zero, while [Wimmel, 1972] and later [Corben, 1976] assert that the failure to observe Cerenkov radiation is of no significance because a charged tachyon would not be a Cerenkov emitter, either electromagnetically or (even if uncharged) gravitationally. Parker [1969] suggests the scattering of photons by photons could be used to indirectly test for tachyons. Because of the very low cross-section of photons, however (on the order of 10^{-65} cm^2), the probability of a photon scattering off another photon is very small, and so very intense photon beams would be required to produce observable results. See [Csonka, 1967] for several imaginative suggestions on how sufficiently brilliant beams might be generated. In any case, if tachyons are one day discovered, then as an old joke puts it, the day before that momentous occasion a notice from the discoverers should appear in newspapers announcing "Tachyons have been discovered tomorrow."

37. My source for Lucretius' words is the translation of Book 4 by John Godwin (Wiltshire: Aris and Phillips, 1986), 23.

38. The British electrical engineer Oliver Heaviside theoretically studied FTL charged particles as long ago as 1888, using nonrelativistic classical physics; see my book *Oliver Heaviside: Sage in Solitude* (New York: IEEE Press, 1988), 124–126. Tanaka's work was discovered later not to be relativistically invariant. The question of invariance was first raised in [Broido and Taylor, 1968] and later in [Jones, 1972], which pointed out that the original quantum theory of tachyons (due to Feinberg) is not relativistically invariant. Attempts by tachyon advocates to address this failure can be found in [Arons and Sudarshan, 1968] and [Dhar and Sudarshan, 1968].

39. Some recent theoretical work hints at the possibility of FTL photons! The effect is very small, however, well below any present or near future experimental means of detection; the increase in speed is predicted to be at best one part in 10^{36}. See K. Scharnhorst, "On Propagation of Light in the Vacuum Between Plates," *Physics Letters B* 236 (22 Feb. 1990): 354–359. Even more provocative are the calculations in [Band, 1988a,b] showing how to achieve an electromagnetic (i.e., photonic) wave packet with a FTL group velocity. Electrical engineers and physicists almost intuitively associate the group velocity with the speed at which information is transferred, but Band reminds his readers that this speed is really the signal speed (the speed at which a "well-defined shape" propagates). The group velocity in an absorption band in a dispersive medium, can indeed be faster than light, but in this case the signal speed is still subluminal. (These points are discussed in Leon Brillouin's beautiful little book *Wave Propagation and Group Velocity* (New York: Academic Press, 1960). See also [Fox, Kuper, and Lipson, 1969, 1970], which explains why group velocity has no physical significance for tachyons.) Band's analysis, however, is interesting because he

arrives at his result using a non-dispersive medium, and so the signal speed does appear to be truly FTL! But then he pulls the rabbit out of the hat—his entire analysis depends on a geometry that has cylindrical symmetry (such as a coaxial cable or a transmission line), so if such an FTL cable connects A to B, then the addition of a return cable from B to A would ruin the symmetry; it is only through the presence of a *closed* communication path that paradoxes could occur. Band states that "there is a fascinating similiarity" between his superoptic wave packet and a tachyon, but he is not ready to go so far as to claim the wave packet is a realization of the tachyon.

40. There is a curious implication in this process. Even if we grant that the reinterpretation principle may avoid causal paradoxes (but see Tech Note 7 for reasons why most physicists in fact think it doesn't), the fact is that physics isn't fooled as easily as a human observer. That is, the receiver does actually lose energy upon the arrival of the tachyon, which is the opposite of what normally happens in a radio receiver when it receives a photon. Thus, the receiver must be in an elevated energy state prior to that arrival; it must be prepared beforehand to receive a message. If the receiver is passively sitting in its lowest energy state, it could not accept (or *eject*, according to the RP) the tachyon.

41. An excellent summary of the controversy in quantum mechanics in general and of the work by Bell and Aspect in particular (including interviews with both men) is *The Ghost in the Atom* edited by P. C. W. Davies and J. R. Brown (New York: Cambridge University Press, 1986). The EPR paradox has not been the only source of quantum-mechanical speculations about nonlocal effects. The Aharonov-Bohm effect, a quantum-mechanical phenomenon that allows the motion of a charged particle to be influenced by electromagnetic fields existing where the particle never goes, has also sparked a decades-long controversy. The history of this effect, from its 1959 prediction to its experimental verification in 1986, can be found in M. Peshkin and A. Tonomura, *The Aharonov-Bohm Effect* (New York: Springer-Verlag, 1989).

42. Polchinski [1991] uses the somewhat inconsistent name of EPR phone for the Bell antitelephone. Unlike the tachyonic antitelephone, the EPR version is a quantum antitelephone and, as Polchinski has shown, if quantum mechanics is actually slightly nonlinear (as are many other phenomena in physics at sufficiently high energy levels) and if one supposes the collapsing-wave-function interpretation of quantum mechanics (recall Note 14), then the EPR antitelephone will work. Polchinski has even suggested a far more radical quantum antitelephone called the Everett-Wheeler [anti]phone. Again, if one supposes that quantum mechanics is actually nonlinear and if one accepts Everett's many-worlds interpretation of quantum mechanics, then Polchinski has shown that one could communicate with not just the past, but with the infinitude of the many-pasts in the ever-splitting branches of the many-worlds! There is a very funny illustration in [Cramer, 1991a] that shows what that might be like. Professor Polchinski is well-aware of the spectacular nature of his results. As he writes, "Do the results imply that nonlinear quantum mechanics is inconsistent, and thus 'explain' the linearity of the theory? Communication between branches of the wave function ... seems even more bizarre than FTL communication ... but it is not clear that it represents an actual inconsistency." (See *The Quicksilver Screen* [De Brandt, 1992] for a science fiction use of this idea.) The possibility of communication between splitting branches is taken seriously by others besides Polchinski. For example, the Oxford theoretician David Deutsch [Deutsch, 1991] writes that "closed timelike lines would provide 'gateways' between Everett Universes." Deutsch has believed this for some years, in fact, as in

[Deutsch, 1985] he describes how to design super-fast quantum computers that solve different parts of a problem in different Everett worlds, and that which then collect the partial results from the different worlds by effectively photographing the other worlds [Albert, 1986]! For information on how some physicists are using quantum mechanics in time-machine analyses in somewhat less (but not much less!) exotic ways, see [Klinkhammer, 1991], which makes an attempt at applying quantum field theory to the averaged energy conditions that play an essential role in wormhole time machines, [Echeverria, Klinkhammer, and Thorne, 1991], which redefines the Cauchy problem in terms of quantum mechanics (so that well-defined is given a stochastic interpretation) and which thereby shows that a simplified form of the grandfather paradox is *always* self-consistent, and [Kim and Thorne, 1991] and [Frolov, 1991], which examine the possibility that fluctuations in quantum fields might destroy the Cauchy horizon that such time machines require. For more discussion on these points, see Tech Note 9.

43. N. D. Mermin, "Is the Moon There When Nobody Looks? Reality and Quantum The-ory," *Physics Today* (April 1985): 38–47. For more on the enigmatic letter on FTL effects, see Jack Sarfatti's letter to *Physics Today* (Sept. 1987): 118, 120.

44. Professor Cramer was specifically discussing a suggestion in [Datta, Home, and Ray-chaudhuri, 1987] for an EPR/FTL communication system. That paper received several highly critical replies pointing out crucial errors, all of which appeared in the December 1987 issue of the same journal. Earlier was the paper [Herbert, 1982] describing FLASH which referred to the "First Laser-Amplified Superluminal Hookup." Years later, in [Herbert, 1988], the author admitted "The FLASH scheme ... simply doesn't work" as a FTL communication system. But all is perhaps not lost concerning the military usefulness of quantum communication, as shown in [Ekert, 1991]. This paper gives a theory for how the experimental set-up used by Alain Aspect and his co-workers to test Bell's theorem might be used to send cryptographically unbreakable coded messages.

45. A discussion specifically addressing the possibility of explaining the "spooky actions" of quantum mechanics by backward causation, and certain causality paradoxes, is in [Sutherland, 1983].

46. L. M. Feldman, "Short Bibliography on Faster-Than-Light Particles (Tachyons)," *American Journal of Physics* 42 (March 1974): 179–181.

Epilogue

1. There is, *perhaps*, one possible exception to this statement; the case of two English academics from St. Hugh's College at Oxford. The Misses C. A. Moberly and E. F. Jourdain, while on holiday at Versailles in 1901, inadvertently made (or so they came to believe) a trip back to the year 1789. Moberly wrote the book *An Adventure*, (London: Macmillian, 1911), (first published under the pseudonyms of "Elizabeth Morison" and "Frances Lamont") describing their experience and an enthusiastic summary and evaluation of the affair can be found in [Phillips, FSFS].

2. Professor Thorne has, of course, become the leading American researcher on time machines, but Professor Wheeler's letter shows that there is a certain irony in this. In the early 1970s Thorne collaborated with Wheeler (and with Professor Charles Misner of the University of Maryland) on their gigantic *Gravitation* (W. H. Freeman, 1973). A desk-thumping 1279 pages literally stuffed with mathematics, this book has the heft of

the New York City telephone directory and speaks to every aspect of the general theory—except one. As Wheeler wrote me, one day he took Thorne around to meet Gödel at the Institute for Advanced Study, and they found that Gödel wanted to talk only of the rotating-Universe idea. Nearly a quarter of a century after the fact, his discovery of a time-travel Universe ("populated," wrote Wheeler, who had heard Gödel's original 1948 lecture at the Institute "by entities of a strange new character, closed timelike lines") still fascinated the old master. To their chagrin, however, Gödel's visitors "had to confess that we had not discussed the subject in our book; had not even considered it part of our task to look into any astrophysical evidence on the point." When he meet Gödel, Thorne would not have believed what his own research would be less than twenty years later.

3. See the cover story on Professor Thorne's time-travel research in *California Magazine* (October 1989). Thorne has been careful to state clearly the motivation behind his research in order to avoid the fate of the time traveler in "Forever Is Not So Long" [Reeds, 1942], who laments the fact that many people associate time machines with crackpots. As Reeds writes, "For time machines ... were things to be left to H. G. Wells ... It was no doings for a man of action and, above all, for a man of science." Even more direct on this point is the character in "Advice from Tomorrow" [Reynolds, 1953] who describes another character, a physicist, as "a crackpot. He used to have quite a reputation, but the last couple of years he's been working on time ... You know, time travel, that sort of rot. An A-1 crackpot." A nonfictional example of such a negative reaction can be found in William D. Gray's recent book *Thinking Critically About New Age Ideas* (Belmont, CA: Wadsworth, 1991). Gray is a philosopher who seems surprisingly unfamiliar with the time-travel literature in both physics and philosophy. For example, to support his claim that time travel is *a priori* illogical nonsense (and so anybody who studies time travel is a fool), he cites the grandfather paradox as if it actually proves something. ("If I went back to a point in time before I was born ... I could arrange it so my parents would never meet!") Gray declares that he finds time travel to be unintelligible (and his earlier statements have convinced me that he is indeed confused about time travel), and he ends with the chilling words "If a concept is unintelligible, scientific efforts to validate it are a waste of valuable resources." But who will decide what is "intelligible"?

4. Heinlein was referring to Simon Newcomb (1835–1909), who it will be recalled from Chapter Two was specifically named by H. G. Wells in *The Time Machine* as the expert who had lectured "to the New York Mathematical Society only a month or so ago" on the fourth dimension. At the turn-of-the-century Newcomb published "proofs" that it would be impossible with known science to build a "practicable machine by which men shall fly long distances through the air." See, for example, Newcomb's essays "Is the Airship Coming?" *McClure's Magazine* 17 (Sept. 1901): 432–435, and "The Outlook for the Flying Machine," *The Independent* 55 (22 Oct. 1903): 2508–2512. Frank Tipler could not resist concluding his pioneering doctoral dissertation [Tipler, 1976b] on time travel around rotating cylinders with an amusing reference to Newcomb's proofs.

5. In a recent work Bud Foote [1991], a professor of English at Georgia Tech, has stated that consistency is simply a well-used plot device, writing "the attempt of the time traveler to prevent something or take advantage of it [and so causing] the event in question, is so popular and so ubiquitous that it seems to be about worn out." Worn out or not, I believe that plot device to be correct science. A few years ago the novella

Hawk Among the Sparrows [McLaughlin, 1976] was considered science fiction. This story is of a nuclear bomb test that tosses a Mach 4 jet armed with atomic missiles back in time, from 1985 to 1918, to the days of aerial combat with the Lafayette Escadrille. The story is oblivious to the paradoxes of changing the past and the hero never displays the slightest concern about how he rewrites the past. Today this work would be labeled as fantasy. I think it interesting that a recent change-the-past novel, *Lord Kelvin's Machine* [Blaylock, 1992] is, in fact, being promoted as fantasy, not as science fiction. Fiction for young readers has already begun to reflect an understanding of this point as well. For example, the time traveling professor of history in *The Trolley to Yesterday* [Bellairs, 1989], who tries (and fails) to prevent a slaughter of innocents during the 1453 storming of Constantinople, shows he has learned the past cannot be altered when he declares: "I was just trying to change the course of history, but it seems that there is some evil genie in the Universe that won't allow you to do things like that." Even the recent mainstream novel *Crossover* [Fubank, 1992], in which mind transference is the explanation for time travel, has its discussion of the paradoxes of changing the past right.

6. A. J. Accioly and G. E. A. Matsas, "Are There Causal Vacuum Solutions with the Symmetries of the Gödel Universe in Higher-Derivative Gravity?" *Physical Review D* 38 (15 Aug. 1988): 1083–1086.

7. In Volume 1 of *The Philosophy of Karl Popper*, ed. P. A. Schilpp, The Library of Living Philosophers (La Salle, Ill.: Open Court, 1974), 3.

8. The alternate point of view is expressed by Allen and Simon [1992]. They conclude a discussion of time travel via strings (see Tech Note 9) with this assessment: "While there is still hope that one day a sufficiently clever design may make building a time machine possible, it is beginning to seem more and more improbable. Like the perpetual motion machines of the nineteenth century, the designs have an elegant simplicity (as well as enormous commercial potential), but it seems that Nature may abhor them just as much." Of course, at one time it was thought Nature abhorred a vacuum. Actually, Nature must love a vacuum, else why did she make so much of it? The big question, of course, is in which category did Nature place time travel; the one with perpetual motion, or the one with the vacuum?

TECH NOTE 1
WHAT TIME IS *NOW?*

If I can't make six clocks tick together, how in the world can I hope to make six nations tick together?

> —Charles the Fifth, Holy Roman Emperor, in a perhaps apocryphal story of his despair at achieving consensus ("political simultaneity")

The idea behind the above quote is to make explicit the first revolutionary insight into the nature of time (as opposed to mere metaphysical speculation) since the invention of the idea of time itself—the discovery that one clock's tick has nothing necessarily to do with another's tock; the discovery that one's present is not everybody else's present. It was an idea that could have been discovered long before it actually was. The discarding of the intuitively "obvious" concept of universal time was the first (but not the last) of the repercussions of Einstein's ponderings on the natures of space and time.

It is interesting to note that some poets understood this at the intuitive level before most physicists. In an 1817 letter [Mendilow, 1952], for example, the British writer Charles Lamb wrote: "Your 'now' is not my 'now'; and again, your 'then' is not my 'then'; but my 'now' may be your 'then', and vice versa. Whose head is competent to these things?" This last line still has meaning for students of time travel today!

The *present* is that instant in time that separates the future from the past.[1] To be just a little poetic perhaps, it is always the present for us, but as soon as the instant we call now arrives (from the future), it leaves us and recedes into the past. As Leonardo da Vinci wrote in one of his notebooks:[2] "The water you touch in a river is the last of that which has passed, and the first of that which is coming. Thus it is with time present." Or, finally, as one enthusiastic writer (whose name I cannot recall) said, "The present is the knife edge upon which the past and the future balance." We exist, or at least our conscious selves exist, only in the now and we use it both to anticipate the future and to remember the past.

Until Einstein it was universally believed that the present was a common experience so one could sensibly ask a question such as "I wonder what's happening right now on the largest inhabited planet (if any) in the Andromeda galaxy, two million light years away?" We subconsciously extrapolate our earthly belief that there is a planetwide now (a belief made easy to accept superficially by "instantaneous" satellite communication links) to a belief that there is a cosmic now. When two people talk across a continent on the telephone, they seem to be sharing a common now. So why couldn't two creatures, each in a different galaxy, do the same?

No less a thinker than Isaac Newton codified this belief. In 1687 in the

Scholium to the *Definitions* of his *Principia* he wrote:[3] "Absolute true and math-ematical time, of itself, and from its own nature, flows equally without relation to anything external, and by another name is called *duration*."

A cosmic clock, eternal in its tick and perfectly uniform in its tock, and every-where at once in its presence, was how Newton imagined God's absolute time-piece. For more than two centuries after Newton, this image was accepted by all as being beyond question. It was, after all, simply obvious and what more could you say? In 1905 Einstein showed that one definitely could say more; indeed, he showed that it just isn't true!

Einstein demonstrated the "relativity of the present," the fact that two observers can watch the same physical process and yet disagree on the times when various events in that process occur. He thereby stopped forever the pendulum of New-ton's clock—and perhaps equally astonishing is the fact that what Einstein did, so Newton could have. No new physical discoveries or fantastic mathematical the-orems were required. Einstein arrived at his result by the simplest imaginable arguments, using mathematics no more advanced than arithmetic.[4]

Here is how he did it.

To begin, we have to ask ourselves (as did Einstein) what we mean when we say that two events are simultaneous. We mean, of course, that they happen at the same time and, of course, this really begs the question. More precisely, we mean that we see the two events happen together in time. The word *see* is crucial. We see via light waves that travel from events to our eyes. However, it is clear that where we happen to position ourselves with respect to the two events will influ-ence how long it takes the light waves from each event to reach our eyes. If the two events occur at the same location in space, there is no problem about which event is first. We can, however, imagine two events being simultaneous (such as the explosion of two widely separated sticks of dynamite connected by equal lengths of wire to a common electrical detonator box) but not appearing to be simultaneous because our eyes are closer to one explosion than to the other. We ordinarily do not notice these time delays in light propagation because different places on Earth are not very far apart compared to the enormous speed of light.

We can eliminate the effects of these time delays due to the large but finite speed of light by arranging to observe two events from the position midway between them. Then, so it would seem, the two delays are equal, and so if we see the two events happen at different times, then they really are not simultaneous—or so it would seem.

Now, imagine a train on a straight stretch of track. Part of the train is a boxcar with an experimenter in it. He is standing precisely in the middle of the boxcar, with a laser equipped with focusing lenses under his control via a switch. When he closes the switch, the laser will fire and two tightly focused light beams will be transmitted, one forward and the other rearward. On the front and rear walls of the boxcar are photocells that, when hit by a light beam, generate an electrical current that triggers the illumination of an associated lamp. (Let us suppose that the forward lamp is red and that the rearward lamp is green.)

What could be more obviously true than the claim that if the experimenter closes the laser switch, then a very short time later he will see the red and green lamps glow simultaneously? After all, if the boxcar has length L, then the laser is exactly $L/2$ distant from each photocell, and the two laser beams (each traveling at the speed of light—call it c) will take the same time to reach each photocell. Indeed, the red and green lamps will both turn on $L/2c$ seconds after the laser switch is closed. Since it takes the red and green light an additional $L/2c$ seconds to travel back to the center of the boxcar, the experimenter will see both lamps glow, at the same time, L/c seconds after he closes the switch.

Now imagine a second experimenter standing outside the boxcar on the edge of the track. Also imagine that the train is moving from left to right at a constant speed past this second experimenter.[5] Matters are arranged so that at the instant the moving experimenter passes by his colleague on the ground, the laser switch is closed. Thus, at the start of the process that eventually results in the red and green lamps turning on, both experimenters are exactly midway between the two lamps. We have already decided what the experimenter inside the boxcar sees, but if the boxcar has transparent walls, what does the outside experimenter see?

He sees one laser beam shoot forward and another rearward, with the forward-traveling beam chasing after the red lamp's receding photocell and the rearward traveling beam on a head-on collision course with the green lamp's approaching photocell. To the outside experimenter, the rearward-moving beam gets to its photocell first because it has to travel less distance than does the forward-moving beam, which has to catch up with its target photocell. On top of this, the rear photocell will be closer to the outside experimenter than will be the forward photocell, and so the light from the green lamp has less distance to travel to arrive back to the outside experimenter's eyes than does the red light. The end result is that the outside experimenter sees the green lamp glow *before* he sees the red lamp—in stark disagreement with what the inside experimenter sees. The relative motion between the two observers has altered their perception of simultaneity!

So revolutionary was this idea that Kurt Gödel declared [Herbert,1987]: "The very starting point of relativity theory consists in the discovery of a new and very astonishing property of time, namely the relativity of simultaneity." But not everybody shared this belief. The Irish mathematical physicist Alfred A. Robb (1873–1936) was so scandalized by it all that he wrote:[6] "From the first I felt that Einstein's standpoint and method of treatment were unsatisfactory ... In particular I felt strongly repelled by the idea that events could be simultaneous to one person and not simultaneous to another ... This seemed to destroy all sense of the reality of the external world and to leave the physical Universe no better than a dream, or rather, a nightmare." And a year later, in 1922, the venerable Oliver Lodge wrote:[7] "A theory which renders it uncertain whether the Fire of London preceded or succeeded the outburst of Nova Persei [a spectacular stellar explosion, first observed in 1901] ... and whether a much-travelled man's death preceded his birth, should not be too positive when it leaves its own realm and enters the region of fact and reality. ... There is room not only for Einstein ... but also for Newton and Maxwell."

It is always hard to give up old ideas. We love these old ideas because they are so obvious, so intuitive, so *common sense*, but to echo Einstein himself,[8] "Common sense is that layer of prejudices laid down in the mind prior to the age of eighteen."

NOTES

1. The *now* is a mathematical instant, the temporal equivalent of a dimensionless point. Physiologically, however, for living creatures it is an interval, one that for humans extends perhaps a few tens of milliseconds into the past [Efron, NYAS]. Sometimes it is even longer; as Oscar Wilde put it in *De Profundis*, "Suffering is a long moment." In his essay "Explorations in the World of Dreams" in the issue of the *New York Times Magazine* of 10 July 1927, H. G. Wells wrote of the now, stating, "Our mind can be considered as existing in the past and in the future, as extending, so to speak, both ways beyond what we consider to be the actual moment. I hope that does not strike the reader as too crazy a proposition. Most of us have given very little thought to what we mean by the actual moment. What do we mean by 'now'? How much time is it? Behind 'now' stretches the past, ahead is the future, but is it itself an infinitesimal instant?" For a fictional treatment of the possible result of this interval of nowness extending even just a bit into the future, see the story "The Golden Man" [Dick, 1980]. For tales of people stuck in the present, see "All the Time in the World" [Clarke, PSF] and "In Frozen Time" [Rucker, 1986].

2. Quoted from *The Artist By Himself: self-portraits from youth to old age*, ed. J. Kinneir (New York: St Martin's Press, 1980), 205.

3. Quoted from A. Koyre, *Newtonian Studies* (London: Champman Hall, 1965), 103. We remember Newton's words because he was, of course, *Newton*, but as Newton himself said, he stood on the shoulders of giants and the origins of his views about absolute time are no exception. Capek [1987] traces the so-called *absolutist* view of time backward from Newton, and he convincingly documents the cases of several analysts who held similar, earlier ideas. For example, Isaac Barrow, Newton's influential contemporary and immediate predecessor as occupant of the Lucasian chair at Cambridge, wrote in his *Lectiones Geometricae* (1670) that "whether things run or stand still, whether we sleep or wake, time flows in its even tenor." When Barrow wrote this, Newton was his student. We find the same kinds of ideas even earlier in the French philosopher and scientist Pierre Gassendi's posthumous *Syntagma Philosophicum* (1658): "Even before there were things time flowed ... Even now, while they exist- ... time flows in the same tenor as it flowed before ... if God would wish to recreate the Universe, time would flow in the interval between its destruction and recreation." The alternative view that time is inseparately related to changes in the configurations of matter, which is the *relational* view, has even more ancient roots. We find, for example, in the First Book of Lucretius' *On the Nature of Things*: "Time itself does not exist, but from things themselves there results a sense of what has already taken place, what is now going on, and what is to ensue. It must not be claimed that anyone can sense time by itself apart from the movement of things." And in his *Physics* Aristotle declared

that "time cannot be disconnected from change; for when we experience no changes in consciousness, or if we are not aware of them, no time seems to have passed ... we are not aware of time when we do not distinguish any change."

4. While pretty close to the truth, some might argue that perhaps I have slightly warped the facts to make a better story. Indeed, Einstein himself said that he was led to his ideas on special relativity by his boyhood ponderings about what a light beam would look like if he could race along with it. Knowing of Maxwell's description of light as electromagnetic waves (moving at the speed of light, of course!) Einstein wondered how such waves would appear? Would they be frozen in shape? Could they then still be light? Newton, who thought of light as being composed of particles, just did not have such visual imagery to jump-start his curiosity and of course there was no reason for Newton not to believe that light moved infinitely fast, which *would* result in a Universal now. Curiously, there are those who write on time, *these* days, who are still in Newton's time. In [Wild, 1954], for example, we have a philosopher who wrote (incorrectly) "Everything in the world seems to be engulfed in an irreversible flux of time which cannot be quickened or retarded, but flows everywhere at a constant rate."

5. No mention of motion was made in the first analysis for the simple reason that there is no way for the experimenter inside the boxcar to sense any such motion! (I am assuming, of course, that there are no windows in the boxcar and that the train wheels are silent.) We can sense motion only through changes in speed, i.e, via accelerations or decelerations. This is, in fact, one of the fundamental postulates of dynamics, even before Einstein and relativity. Einstein's great insight was to extend the idea to all of physics including, for example, electromagnetics and gravity. The laws of physics and the results of experiments are the same for all experimenters who are in relative, uniform motion with respect to each other. Physics on a merry-go-round is very different from our boxcar physics, yes, but that is because the merry-go-round is an *accelerated* system even if the rotation rate is constant. Thus, what the experimenter inside the boxcar sees is independent of whether the train is sitting motionless on the tracks or is hurtling along at 150 miles per hour. Similarly, pouring coffee on the Concorde at twice the speed of sound is indistinguishable (as long as there is no turbulence, which is another name for accelerated motion) from pouring it at home at the kitchen table. Indeed, in Galileo's writings (which, of course, predate even those of Newton) we find the example of dropping a stone from a ship's mast. (This experiment was actually performed by Galileo's contemporary, the Frenchman Pierre Gassendi.) Whether the ship is tied up in port or is underway at sea at a constant speed, the rock hits the deck at the same spot at the base of the mast. Uniform, unaccelerated motion has no effect on what sailor observers on the ship would see.

6. Quoted from the Preface of Robb's book *The Absolute Relations of Time and Space* (Cambridge: Cambridge University Press, 1921). Robb was no fool. A Fellow of the Royal Society, he held three(!) doctorates and the esteem of many British scientific luminaries. A man of independent means, he never held an official academic position, but was allowed to reside at Cambridge and occasionally was even invited to offer lectures on mathematics. When he died, his obituary in *Nature* was written by no less a follower of Einstein than the English scientific superstar Arthur Stanley Eddington.

7. "Relativity and the Aether," *Nature* 110 (30 Sept. 1922): 446.

8. R. Skinner, *Relativity for Scientists and Engineers* (New York: Dover, 1982), 27.

TECH NOTE 2

TIME DILATION VIA THE PHOTON CLOCK

Time as we know it is not universally absolute. The rate of its passage depends to a great extent upon the velocity of its observer with regard to some certain reference system. A moving clock will run slower with respect to a selected coordinate system than a stationary one.

> —a time traveler explains how his time machine works in "Via the Time Accelerator" [Bridge, 1931]

Imagine two horizontal, parallel mirrors, one positioned over the other and separated by distance d. The two mirrors are in the same frame of reference with an observer; i.e., the observer is looking at two stationary mirrors. Between the two mirrors we further imagine that a particle of light, a photon, is bouncing endlessly back and forth, up and down, in relentless reflection. We define the time required for the photon to travel from one mirror to the other as a tick and the return trip defines the tock. This simple system is called a *photon clock* (or the Einstein-Langevin clock, after the French physicist Paul Langevin [1872–1946]), and it has been part of physics for decades. The rate of timekeeping, the time interval separating consecutive ticks, is obviously

$$t' = 2\,\frac{d}{c} \quad,$$

where c is the speed of light.

Suppose we imagine now that the observer and the mirrors and the bouncing photon are moving at constant speed v, to the right across our line of sight. The mirror/photon system is then in a different frame of reference from ours, and we will not see the photon bouncing up and down vertically. Rather, we see the photon tracing out a triangular path, as shown in Figure 20. One roundtrip of the photon evidently requires more time than before because the distance in the stationary (i.e., our) frame is now greater than in the moving observer's frame. In fact, if t is the time between consecutive ticks as seen by a stationary observer (us), then the total path length is

$$2\sqrt{d^2 + \left(\frac{vt}{2}\right)^2} \quad,$$

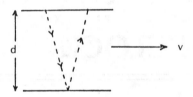

Figure 20. The photon clock.

and so

$$t = \frac{2\sqrt{d^2 + (vt/2)^2}}{c}.$$

This can be quickly manipulated algebraically and combined with the expression for t', the tick interval for an observer in the same frame as the clock, to give the tick interval for a moving clock as measured by a stationary observer (i.e., us):

$$t = \frac{t'}{\sqrt{1 - (v/c)^2}}.$$

Notice that this reduces to $t = t'$ when $v = 0$, i.e., when the clock is stationary.

This is the famous Einstein time dilation formula, which shows $t \geqslant t'$, and indeed $t = \infty$ when $v = c$. That is, the photon clock appears to run *slow* compared to clocks in our stationary frame of reference, and at the speed of light time *stands still*. This is what one writer was referring to when he wrote that "according to the theory of relativity, if the observer is moving with the velocity of light, time remains unchanged. This must have been the case with the Mad Hatter. With him it was always six o'clock, and always tea-time."[1] A curious anticipation of this association between light and timelessness can be found in a poem by the seventeenth century English writer Henry Vaughan. The opening words to his "The World," which appeared in 1650 as part of *Silex Scintillans* ("sparkling flint"), are

> I saw Eternity the other night
> Like a great *Ring* of pure and endless light,
> All calm, as it was bright,
> And round beneath it, Time in hours, days, years
> Driven by the spheres
> Like a vast shadow moved, in which the world
> And all her train were hurled.

For $v > c$, the equation says that time becomes imaginary, and this is one reason

TABLE 1. The Lorentz-FitzGerald time-slowing factor.

$\left(\dfrac{v}{c}\right)$	$1\Big/\sqrt{1-\left(\dfrac{v}{c}\right)^{2}}$
.1	1.005
.2	1.021
.5	1.155
.7	1.4
.9	2.294
.999	22.366
.9999	70.712

for claiming $v > c$ is not possible. Notice that this simple derivation could have been done centuries before Einstein—the mathematics is quite elementary, as is the physical model. However, not everyone believes that this simple model is valid (although only crackpots dispute the conclusion), and a good discussion of the objections is in [Schlegel, 1980].

A similar modification in length (measured in the direction of motion) occurs when $v > 0$. While an observer moving with an object will measure its length to be l', a stationary observer will report it contracted to the length

$$l = l'\sqrt{1-\left(\frac{v}{c}\right)^{2}}.$$

This effect is called the Lorentz-FitzGerald contraction.[2]

The time-slowing (or size shrinking) factor becomes pronounced only at values of v close to c; Table 1 shows this effect. For example, the last entry shows that a clock traveling at 99.99% the speed of light will register the passage of one year while nearly seventy-one years pass on Earth.

One possible objection to this analysis is that it has been done for a particular clock. How do we know that another clock, one using wheels and pendulums, for example, wouldn't be affected differently by motion? The answer comes from relativity itself, which says that there is no way to detect uniform motion. If two clocks did behave differently, then this difference could be used as a motion detector. This is not possible, however, and so all clocks, no matter what their internal mechanisms (including the complex biological clocks of our own bodies), must all respond to uniform motion in precisely the same way.[3]

NOTES

1. *Nature* 104 (12 February 1920): 627–630.
2. In the early days of science fiction this concept was fascinating to readers, but authors

often got it wrong. For example, in "Faster Than Light" [Haggard, 1930], the story of a runaway spaceship falling into the Sun, we find: "When our racing [ship] was drawn from the Earth's gravity and fell at ever increasing speed toward the Sun it soon approached the speed of light. As we fell faster and faster our length in the direction of the Sun progressed into nothingness. Then—it reached the speed of light—passed it. Now—mind you this—when the [ship] attained the speed of light it was of a *minus* length." This author managed to make four errors in three sentences! For the rather curious history of the Lorentz-FitzGerald contraction (dating from 1889) see [Bork, 1966] and [Brush, 1967].

3. Resistance to this conclusion continued for years. For example, see the letter "Relativity and Radio-activity" in *Nature* 104 (8 January 1920): 468. The author wondered if a clock based on radioactive decay might not somehow beat the "conspiracy" of moving clocks running slow compared to stationary ones.

TECH NOTE 3
THE LORENTZ TRANSFORMATION

If only he'd paid more attention to mathematics in school.

—Albert Eustace Rossi, the first time traveler ("Extempore" [Knight, 1961])

We begin by imagining two distinct frames of reference. One we take to be stationary, and the other as moving at a uniform speed v with respect to the first. We can always orient these two coordinate systems so that the motion occurs along just one axis (e.g., the x direction, as shown in Figure 21). We use primed variables for the moving frame. Thus the two frames have coincident x axes and parallel y and z axes that are moving apart at constant speed v. Let us also imagine that there is a clock at the origin of each frame, and that at the instant the origins match we synchronize the clocks; i.e., $t=t'=0$ is the instant the two coordinate systems coincide.

We next imagine that there is an observer at the origin in each frame. At some arbitrary instant of time, each observer records the coordinates of the arbitrary point P in space, as measured in his system. The observers could, for example, agree to record the coordinates of P when their respective system clocks each read five seconds. It seems immediately obvious (as it was for Newton—see Tech Note 1) that $t=t'$; i.e., time runs at the same rate in each frame and thus it makes sense to talk about the "same instant." (If you have already read Tech Note 2, you know this is *not true*, but temporarily forget that!) So at this "same instant" the stationary observer records (x, y, z) and the moving observer records (x', y', z'). What, we now wonder, are the relationships between the primed and unprimed coordinates: that is, what mathematical transformation converts from one frame to the other? The answer seems obvious:

$$y' = y,$$

$$z' = z,$$

$$x' = x - vt.$$

This transformation, called the *Galilean transformation* after the Italian Galileo Galilei (1564–1642), satisfies the relativity principle, which says that uniform motion leaves the laws of physics unchanged; e.g., in the stationary system the famous second law of Newton for a fixed mass m,

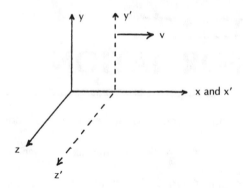

FIGURE 21. Two spatial reference frames in relative motion.

$$F = m \frac{d^2x}{dt^2},$$

becomes the identical appearing form

$$F' = m \frac{d^2x'}{dt'^2}.$$

More precisely, the laws of mechanics are unchanged. When the mathematical laws of electrodynamics were discovered by Maxwell in the nineteenth century, however, it was found that the Galilean transformation did not leave Maxwell's equations unchanged; i.e., the transformed equations predict electromagnetic effects for the moving system that are not predicted to occur in the stationary system. This means that there was theoretical support for the possibility that electromagnetic experiments might be devised to detect uniform motion, and this eventually led to the famous Michelson-Morley experiment of 1887.[1] This experiment, theoretically sensitive enough to detect the motion of the Earth itself through space, failed to detect any such uniform motion. The conclusion is clear— the extra electromagnetic effects predicted by the Galilean transformation do not exist, and so the transformation is wrong even though it works with the laws of mechanics. So what is going on?

The answer is inspired, and again returns us to the cornerstone of relativity: the idea that the laws of physics, all the laws, should look the same to observers in uniform relative motion. Evidence from an extremely broad variety of sensitive experiments had, by the end of the nineteenth century, convinced people that Maxwell's equations are correct. Thus, a new transformation was needed that leaves both the laws of mechanics and the laws of electrodynamics unchanged with motion. A single transformation that works on Maxwell's equations and on the mechanical laws would therefore mean that Newton's mechanical laws cannot be correct! This was a breathtaking conclusion, as Newton had been unchallenged for two centuries.

However, it turns out that Newton's laws were almost right. The only correction required is the idea that the mass of a moving body is not independent of speed, but rather varies as

$$m = \frac{m_0}{\sqrt{1-(v/c)^2}},$$

where m_0 is the rest mass when $v=0$. The variation of mass with speed was experimentally observed in 1901 by the German Walter Kaufmann (1871–1947). This effect shows that m is infinite at $v=c$ unless $m_0=0$, as it is for a photon), which is one reason for the belief that accelerating a mass (e.g., a spaceship) up to the speed of light is impossible, as that would require infinite energy. With this modification, the transformation that leaves all the laws unaltered in form by uniform motion is

$$y' = y,$$

$$z' = z,$$

$$x' = \frac{x-vt}{\sqrt{1-(v/c)^2}},$$

$$t' = \frac{t-vx/c^2}{\sqrt{1-(v/c)^2}}.$$

These equations are called the *Lorentz transformation* after the Dutchman Hendrik Antoon Lorentz (1853–1928), who discovered them in 1904 by direct mathematical manipulation of Maxwell's equations [Lorentz, TPR]. (Some historians give the Irish physicist Joseph Larmor (1857–1942) priority for his study of the Maxwell equations since his work was published in 1900.[2]) It was Einstein who in 1905 showed how to derive the transformation equations from a fundamental reexamination of space and time without concerning oneself about the details of specific laws.

The Lorentz transformation contains two results we have obtained in previous Tech Notes by using specialized arguments. For example, in Tech Note 1 we found that simultaneity is a relative concept in reference frames in relative motion. Therefore, now consider two events that occur specifically on the x axis. They are simultaneous in the stationary system (at, say, time $t=T$) but are at different places (at, say $x=X$ and $x=X+\Delta X$). Their occurrences in time for the moving observer are

$$t_1'=\frac{T-vX/c^2}{\sqrt{1-(v/c)^2}} \quad \text{and} \quad t_2'=\frac{T-v(X+\Delta X)/c^2}{\sqrt{1-(v/c)^2}}.$$

For the moving observer, therefore, the two events are not simultaneous, being separated in time by

$$t_1'-t_2'=\frac{v\Delta X/c^2}{\sqrt{1-(v/c)^2}}.$$

Only if $\Delta X=0$ (the two events occur at the same place) will $t_1'=t_2'$, i.e., only if $\Delta X=0$ are simultaneous events in one frame also simultaneous in another frame in relative motion.

In Tech Note 2 we found that time runs slow in one frame as observed from another frame in relative motion. This result is easy to obtain formally by using the t' equation in the Lorentz transformation. Thus, if we differentiate with respect to t, we get

$$\frac{dt'}{dt}=\frac{1-(v/c^2)dx/dt}{\sqrt{1-(v/c)^2}}.$$

But $\frac{dx}{dt}=v$, the speed of the moving frame as measured by the observer in the stationary frame. This gives

$$dt'=\sqrt{1-\left(\frac{v}{c}\right)^2}\,dt,$$

which is the same result we obtained by analyzing the photon clock.

The Lorentz transformation contains many other implications not explicitly stated in earlier Tech Notes. For example, we have often made special reference to the relativity principle, which says that uniform motion has no effect on the form of the physical laws—but how do we know who is moving and who is stationary? After all, a system moving to the right at speed v past a stationary system could just as well be viewed as a stationary system where the other system is moving to the *left* at speed $-v$. In fact, it is possible to invert the Lorentz transformation and solve for the unprimed variables in terms of the primed ones, and this is exactly what we get—the Lorentz transformation back again, with v replaced with $-v$. That is, the Lorentz transformation is symmetrical so that two observers in different frames of reference each say that the other's clock is running slow! The inverse transformation is

$$y=y',$$

$$z=z',$$

$$x=\frac{x'+vt'}{\sqrt{1-(v/c)^2}},$$

$$t=\frac{t'+vx'/c^2}{\sqrt{1-(v/c)^2}}.$$

As a final example of what the Lorentz transformation tells us, consider the so-called addition-of-velocities problem. Suppose you are in a high-speed spaceship traveling away from Earth at speed v. The Earth is our stationary system, and the spaceship is the moving system. (Assume that the x and x' axes are along the direction of motion.) Imagine next that you fire a gun toward the nose of your spaceship, with the bullet exiting the muzzle at speed w. How fast is the bullet moving away from the Earth? The common-sense Galilean transformation says $v+w$, but we now know that this transformation is wrong. Therefore, what does the Lorentz transformation say? Inside the spaceship the position of the bullet at time t' after the gun is fired (assuming that the gun is fired just as the rocket ship passes the Earth) is

$$x'=wt'.$$

From the inverse Lorentz transformation, the location of the bullet in the Earth's frame is

$$x=\frac{x'+vt'}{\sqrt{1-(v/c)^2}}=\frac{w+v}{\sqrt{1-(v/c)^2}}t'.$$

The transformation also tells us that

$$t=\frac{t'+vx'/c^2}{\sqrt{1-(v/c)^2}}=\frac{1+wv/c^2}{\sqrt{1-(v/c)^2}}t'.$$

The speed of the bullet in the Earth's frame is therefore

$$\frac{x}{t}=\frac{w+v}{1+wv/c^2}.$$

Notice that for a low-speed bullet ($w \ll c$) this result is close to $w+v$, but at high speeds it is very much different.[3] Indeed, suppose we do not fire a gun at all, but instead replace it with a flashlight. Now, instead of a bullet, we shoot photons at $w=c$. The Galilean transformation would say that a stationary observer on Earth would see the photons moving at speed $v+c$, which is a superluminal speed. The Lorentz transformation says that the Earth observer would see a speed of

$$\frac{c+v}{1+cv/c^2}=\frac{c^2(c+v)}{c^2+cv}=\frac{c^2(c+v)}{c(c+v)}=c.$$

That is, no matter what the speed of the moving observer is, he sees the light from his flashlight traveling at the same speed as does the stationary observer. This peculiar effect is unique to the speed of light ($w=c$). We have derived this effect as a consequence of the Lorentz transformation, but in fact Einstein actually did things in the reverse order. He began by postulating the invariance of the speed of light for all observers in uniform relative motion, combined this idea with the principle of relativity, which says that all physical laws look the same to these observers, and then derived the Lorentz transformation using no mathematics beyond algebra.

A question of great interest to historians of science is what led Einstein to take the nonobvious invariance of the speed of light as a given. As best as anyone can reconstruct Einstein's early thoughts, it appears as though it is the prediction by Maxwell's equations of a precise numerical value for the speed of light in empty space, independent of the speed of the observer's frame, that was the crucial stimulus.[4] This was known, of course, to many others but only Einstein had the nerve to use what Maxwell's equations said and to pursue the prediction to the logical conclusion. The experimental verification of the invariance of the speed of light was finally achieved in 1932.[5]

NOTES

1. An old but still authoritative paper is R. S. Shankland, "Michelson-Morley Experiment," *American Journal of Physics* 32 (Jan. 1964): 16–35. As Shankland points out, it was after reading a letter written by Maxwell in 1879 (the year of Maxwell's death) that Michelson first became interested in the problem that resulted in the 1887 experiment, and at least to some extent in his winning the 1907 Nobel Prize in physics. Maxwell's letter was reprinted in *Nature* 21 (29 Jan. 1880): 314–315. See also "Clerk Maxwell and the Michelson Experiment," *Nature* 125 (12 April 1930): 566–567.

2. The case for Larmor is not strong. A better one might be made for Woldemar Voigt (1850–1919), a German physicist who in 1887 arrived at the Lorentz transformation

while studying the Doppler effect. See M. N. Macrossan, "A Note on Relativity Before Einstein," *British Journal for the Philosophy of Science* 37 (June 1986): 232–234.

3. This result was first found by the great French theoretician Henri Poincaré (1854–1912) in June 1905, three months before the publication of Einstein's famous paper on special relativity which also derives the addition-of-velocities equation [Einstein, TPR]. It was Poincaré who gave the Lorentz transformation its name and he was also the first to state specifically the principle of relativity as covering all the laws, the electromagnetic as well as the mechanical ones. In an address to the International Congress of Arts and Science in St. Louis, on September 24, 1904, Poincaré specifically stated that in the mechanics of special relativity "no velocity could surpass that of light, any more than any temperature could fall below the zero absolute." For Poincaré's address, see "The Principles of Mathematical Physics," *The Monist* 15 (January 1905): 1–24. The addition formula can be derived without knowledge of the Lorentz transformation; see N. D. Mermin, "Relativistic Addition of Velocities Directly from the Constancy of the Velocity of Light," *American Journal of Physics* 51 (Dec. 1983): 1130–1131.

4. As mentioned in Note 4 of Tech Note 1, the traditional tale of Einstein's early start on relativity was his curiosity about what a light beam would look like if one could race alongside it. This *is* pretty precocious for a teenager, even an Einstein. What could have put such a thought in his head? I am only speculating now (and I have not seen this elsewhere), but in 1895 the French astronomer Camille Flammarion published a novel [Flammerion, 1897] that is entirely devoted to a discussion of the properties of light, including what might be seen if one could race along beside a light beam. Flammarion's ideas are mostly wrong, but could Einstein have gotten hold of a copy of this best-selling book? In 1895 Einstein was sixteen, the age at which he stated he began to think on these matters.

5. R. J. Kennedy and E. M. Thorndike, "Experimental Establishment of the Relativity of Time," *Physical Review* 42 (1 Nov. 1932): 400–418.

TECH NOTE 4
SPACETIME DIAGRAMS, LIGHT CONES, METRICS, AND INVARIANT INTERVALS

There is one metaphor in the physicist's account of space-time which one would expect *anyone* to recognize as such, for metaphor is here strained far beyond breaking point, i.e., when it is said that time is "at right angles to each of the other three dimensions." Can anyone really attach any meaning to this— except as a recipe for drawing diagrams?

—[Mundle, 1967]

It is helpful in discussions about spacetime to use what are called *spacetime diagrams*. These are plots of the spacetime coordinates of a particle; the resulting curve is called the *world line* of the particle. Such diagrams are four-dimensional (three space axes and one time axis) and thus hard to visualize (much less draw)! The convention is to make do whenever possible with a simplified spacetime that has just one space axis (horizontal) and one time axis (vertical). So for a particle at rest in some observer's frame of reference, its spacetime diagram for that observer is a vertical world line. If the particle moves, its world line tilts away from the vertical, and for an accelerating particle the world line curves away from the vertical. Straight (uncurved) world lines represent unaccelerated particles (i.e., particles experiencing no forces that are thus in free fall). I show in Figure 22 the world lines for these various cases on the same axes. (It is assumed in the figure that all three particles are at $x = x_0$ when $t = 0$).

Free-fall world lines are called spacetime *geodesics*. In ordinary use, a path that joins two points on a surface with the minimum length is called a geodesic of that surface. It is shown in Tech Note 5 that spacetime geodesics do indeed possess an extremal property, but rather than it being a minimum, it is a *maximum* property. Spacetime diagrams can be misleading on this matter, so it is important to be alert to the fact that such diagrams are not a perfect representation of all the properties of spacetime.

It has become convention to draw these diagrams with the speed of light as unity ($c = 1$). That is, a distance of 300,000 Km on the x axis is represented by the same extension as is one second on the t axis. This means that the world line of a photon is tilted away from the vertical time axis by 45°. Since photons can travel in both space directions in our simplified spacetime, and as the speed of light is the limiting speed (or so it is generally believed), we can represent the collection of all

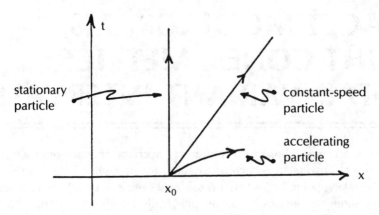

FIGURE 22. World lines of three particles.

possible world lines as those paths that never tilt more than 45° away from the vertical, as in Figure 23.

In Figure 24 I have taken $x=0$ at $t=0$ for all of the possible world lines involving speeds below the speed of light. Let us agree to call this point in spacetime the Here-Now. Then, points in the upward region are in the future of Here-Now; similarly, all points in the downward region are in the past of Here-Now. These regions are called *light cones* because if we include a second space dimension, say y, directed vertical to the page, then the upward and downward regions would be cones. We can draw a straight world line from Here-Now to any point in the Future cone with a tilt of less than 45° away from the vertical, which means that

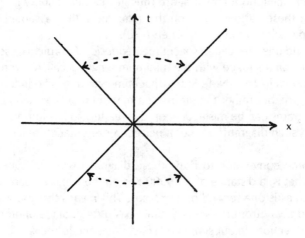

FIGURE 23. World lines of photons.

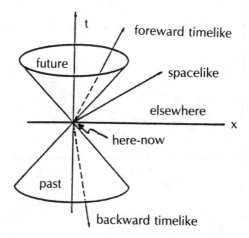

FIGURE 24. A light cone with spacelike and timelike world lines.

a particle could travel from Here-Now to that point at less than the speed of light. Similarly, a particle starting at any point in the Past cone could have reached Here-Now by traveling at less than the speed of light. Such world lines are called *timelike* (because their projection on the time axis is greater than their projection on the space axis), and they are the world lines of spacetime points that are at least potentially causally linked. That is, a cause at a spacetime point in the Past cone could have had an affect on the event at Here-Now even though its influence propagated at less than the speed of light. Also, a cause at Here-Now could affect the event at any point in the Future cone.

Any points in the regions of spacetime outside the Future and Past cones *cannot* be reached from Here-Now except by world lines tilted more than 45° away from the vertical. Such world lines, which represent travel at a speed in excess of that of light, are called *spacelike* (because their projection on the space axis is greater than their projection on the time axis). It is impossible for these world lines to connect causally linked events, and collectively they form the Elsewhere of Here-Now. It is very important to realize that every point in spacetime has its own light cone. Thus, if B is in the Future cone of A, then A is in the Past cone of B.

A spacetime diagram does not always have to have future-directed world lines. If a particle moves backward through time, assuming such a thing is possible, then the diagram can show this by having the world line double back on itself, as in Figure 25. In this example the world line curves back and comes arbitrarily close to itself. This is the world line of a particle that visits itself in the past. Notice that the world line does not actually touch or cross itself, as that would represent more than just a visit—that would be a particle occupying the same spatial location, at the same time, as its earlier self. That would be catastrophic (and, as discussed in Chapter Four, since it *did not* happen, then it *cannot* happen). The direction of the

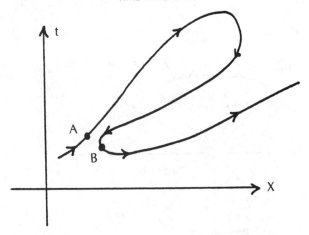

FIGURE 25. World line of a particle traveling backward in time from A to B.

arrows on the world line is always in the direction of the local future of the particle; e.g., if the particle is a human, then memories are formed in the direction of the arrows. The time traveler at B has more memories than he does at A even though A and B are nearly identical locations in spacetime.

There is a problem here that the alert reader may have caught—it is impossible to draw such a double-backed world line such that *at all places* it never tilts more than 45° from the vertical, i.e., at least some portion of such a bent world line will have

$$\left| \frac{dx}{dt} \right| > 1,$$

which represents superluminal motion. (We will return to this in more detail in Tech Note 7). One way to keep a bent-back world line always subluminal is to arrange for the light cones along the world line to be tilted relative to each other, as shown in Figure 26, which is possible only in a *curved* spacetime.This is the mechanism, for example, for backward time travel around a rotating Tipler cylinder,[1] which will be discussed in Tech Note 8.

It should now be clear that the only way a world line can bend back on itself for a close encounter visit is for both x and t to change, i.e., the world line of a particle that remains fixed in space and reverses just its time direction *runs into itself*. This is why the classic time machine of H. G. Wells could not possibly work. Any real time machine must move in space as well as time (e.g., a Gödel rocket or the DeLorean time car in the *Back To The Future* films).

Using the Lorentz transformation equations from Tech Note 3, we can establish quite general relationships between events in the Future, Past, and Elsewhere regions of spacetime. For example, (1) All events in the Future/Past for the Here-Now observer are in the Future/Past for any other nearby, relatively moving

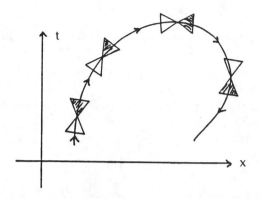

FIGURE 26. Tilted light cones. The future halves are shaded.

observer; (2) Any event in Elsewhere can appear to be simultaneous with the Here-Now for some observer and not simultaneous for other observers; (3) The temporal ordering (the relations of *before* and *after*) of causally related events is the same for all observers.

These statements are easy to prove. Consider statement 1, for example. From Tech Note 3 we have (with $c=1$, as before)

$$t'=\frac{t-vx}{\sqrt{1-v^2}} \quad \text{and} \quad x'=\frac{x-vt}{\sqrt{1-v^2}},$$

where t and x are the coordinates of some event A as measured by the observer in the stationary reference frame, and t' is the time measured by the observer in the reference frame moving at speed v. Thus,

$$x'^2-t'^2=\frac{(x-vt)^2-(t-vx)^2}{1-v^2}=\text{(after a little algebra)}, \ x^2-t^2.$$

For the stationary observer the criterion for an event to be in the Future cone is $t>|x|$, i.e., $t^2>x^2$. Thus, $x^2-t^2<0$ for all Future events. But the above result then says $x'^2-t'^2<0$, too, which is also the moving observer's criterion for the event being in his Future. The same sort of argument shows that the observers also agree on Past events.

Suppose next that two events A and B occur such that the stationary observer measures them to be $\Delta T=t_B-t_A$ apart in time. Then, we can establish statement 2 by writing

$$t'_A=\frac{t_A-vx_A}{\sqrt{1-v^2}} \quad \text{and} \quad t'_B=\frac{(t_A+\Delta T)-vx_B}{\sqrt{1-v^2}},$$

and so

$$\Delta T' = t'_B - t'_A = \frac{\Delta T + v(x_A - x_B)}{\sqrt{1 - v^2}}.$$

From this we have $\Delta T' = 0$ (that is, simultaneity) for the two events for the special observer moving at the speed

$$v = \frac{\Delta T}{x_B - x_A},$$

and this speed is less than the speed of light for the condition $x_B - x_A > \Delta T$. This, of course, is the condition for B to be in the Elsewhere of A.

Similarly, for event B to be in the causal Future of event A, we have the condition $x_B - x_A < \Delta T$. Then,

$$\Delta T' = \frac{\Delta T - v(x_B - x_A)}{\sqrt{1 - v^2}} > \frac{\Delta T - v\Delta T}{\sqrt{1 - v^2}} = \Delta T \frac{1 - v}{\sqrt{1 - v^2}}.$$

Thus, $\Delta T > 0$ says $\Delta T' > 0$ for $v < 1$, and this establishes statement 3.

If we were drawing diagrams with both axes representing space (e.g., a y versus x plot), we would normally define a *distance metric* for the diagram using our everyday ideas about distance. That is, we could say that if we make differential movements along the two coordinate axes of dx and dy, then the differential distance ds is given by

$$(ds)^2 = (dx)^2 + (dy)^2.$$

This is, of course, just the Pythagorean theorem. A distance function has several interesting properties,[2] but the one we are particularly interested in here is its invariance with respect to the coordinate system. For example, if we draw a line segment on a flat sheet of paper, the distance between its ends does not depend on how we happen to select the x and y axes, a fact illustrated in Figure 27. The coordinates for the endpoints A and B are obviously different in the two systems, but we still find that $(dx)^2 + (dy)^2 = (dx')^2 + (dy')^2$. We say that the Pythagorean distance function is *invariant*, the same for all coordinate systems.

We know that different observers if in relative motion in the same spacetime will see different space and time coordinates for the same event. So, a natural question is, what is the distance metric for flat spacetime? Is there some metric that gives the same distance between two events for all observers? We might try to generalize in the obvious way from the Pythagorean theorem:

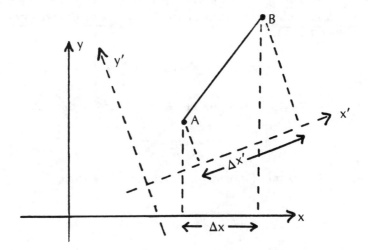

FIGURE 27. Rotated coordinated systems.

$$(ds)^2 = (dt)^2 + (dx)^2 + (dy)^2 + (dz)^2,$$

where now all four dimensions are included. We would then ask ourselves if it is true that

$$(ds)^2 = (ds')^2 = (dt')^2 + (dx')^2 + (dy')^2 + (dz')^2?$$

For our simple two dimensional spacetime, this question reduces to asking if

$$(dt)^2 + (dx)^2 = (dt')^2 + (dx')^2?$$

Using the Lorentz transformation equations from Tech Note 3, it is easy to discover that the answer is no. The "natural" generalization of Pythagorean distance for flat, two-dimensional spacetime fails when four dimensions are included. What do we do now? Recalling the quote that opened this Tech Note, we might wonder if the problem could result from the fact that there is no fourth direction along which the time axis can point at right angles to the three space directions. At least there is no real direction—but perhaps there is an imaginary one. So, with $i = \sqrt{-1}$, let's try:

$$(ds)^2 = (i\,dt)^2 + (dx)^2 + (dy)^2 + (dz)^2 = -(dt)^2 + (dx)^2 + (dy)^2 + (dz)^2.$$

Using imaginary time, something that seems to be in the realm of science fiction, has resulted in a change in the sign of $(dt)^2$. This is a crucial change, however, because this new metric is invariant. For a reason explained in Tech Note 5, we will use the negative of this metric (a choice that obviously has no impact on the invariance property). Thus,

$$(ds)^2 = (dt)^2 - (dx)^2 - (dy)^2 - (dz)^2.$$

For our simplified spacetime with just one space dimension this reduces to

$$(ds)^2 = (dt)^2 - (dx)^2.$$

As before, the Lorentz transformation equations (with $c=1$) are

$$x' = \frac{x-vt}{\sqrt{1-v^2}} \quad \text{and} \quad t' = \frac{t-vx}{\sqrt{1-v^2}}.$$

If we calculate dx' and dt' from these equations, using

$$dx' = \frac{\partial x'}{\partial x} dx + \frac{\partial x'}{\partial t} dt,$$

$$dt' = \frac{\partial t'}{\partial x} dx + \frac{\partial t'}{\partial t} dt,$$

which are the fundamental relations for the total differential of a function of two variables, and insert the results into $(dt')^2 - (dx')^2$, we quickly discover the invariance of this quantity (a result we actually found earlier in a different way when we showed that observers in relative motion agree about what events are in the Future and in the Past). Thus,

$$(dt')^2 - (dx')^2 = (dt)^2 - (dx)^2.$$

This quantity (on either side of the equality) is called the spacetime *interval* between the two events separated in flat spacetime by either dt, dx, dy, and dz, or dt', dx', dy' and dz'; that is, $(ds)^2 = (ds')^2$. The observers in the unprimed and primed systems see different individual space and time separations for two events, but they see the same interval.[3]

The spacetime discussed in this Tech Note is said to be *flat* since for every straight-line geodesic there are infinitely many others parallel to it. This is a feature of a flat sheet of paper, but one must be careful not to carry the analogy too far. The geometry of our spacetime is not the Euclidean geometry of a flat sheet of paper since the spacetime metric has both plus and minus signs.[4] The geometry of the spacetime discussed here is called *Minkowskian* (or complex-Euclidean or pseudo-Euclidean) because it is Euclidean geometry with an imaginary coordinate axis for the time axis. Flat Minkowskian geometry, in turn, is a special case of curved Riemannian geometry. The curvature explains gravity, as developed in Einstein's general theory of relativity;[5] our flat spacetime, by virtue of being un-curved, *has no gravity*. These geometries are not easy concepts to understand, and the metrics of curved spacetimes are even more complicated than that of the elementary spacetime developed here. (See Note 2 of Tech Note 8 for an example of a curved spacetime metric.) As one paper puts it:[6] "Experience has taught us that the space in which we live has a geometry that is three-dimensional and Euclidean ... We are very much at home with [that] geometry ... But the geomet-ric properties of a Minkowskian space are so alien to us that we may well despair of visualizing them, and a Riemannian space ... seems totally beyond comprehen-sion."

There is one special case of particular interest which will conclude this Tech Note. Imagine these two events in spacetime: Event 1 is the emission of a photon at one point in spacetime, and Event 2 is the absorption of that photon at some other point in spacetime. What is the interval between these two events? It might seem that we need to know more about the precise spatial and temporal coordi-nates of these two events, but in fact the interval is always zero for any two events connected by light! For our simple Minkowski spacetime, this is easy to see—just rewrite the metric as

$$\left(\frac{ds}{dt}\right)^2 = 1 - \left(\frac{dx}{dt}\right)^2,$$

and then since $(dx/dt)^2 = 1$ (because the photon travels at the speed of light), we have $(ds)^2 = 0$. The world line of any photon is said to have a *null* interval. Indeed, null interval world lines are always on the surface of light cones, while timelike world lines [in the interior of light cones, with $(dx/dt)^2 < 1$] have positive intervals, $(ds)^2 > 0$. Spacelike world lines (in the exterior of light cones, in Elsewhere) have negative intervals [since $(dx/dt)^2 > 1$], i.e., $(ds)^2 < 0$. This is one of the significant differences between distances in space and intervals in spacetime—in space, the distance is always non-negative.

A strange implication of this is that in spacetime we can have the interval between A and B as zero and the interval between B and C as zero, but the interval between A and C may not be zero! For example, plot the Minkowski spacetime coordinates of A, B, and C as (1,3), (2,2) and (1,1), respectively. Null-interval world lines have an interesting interpretation. As an early writer poetically put it:[7] "Any pair of points [in spacetime] which are separated by zero distance [our *interval*] are in *virtual contact*. In other words, I may say that my eye touches a star, not in the same sense as when I say that my hand touches a pen, but in an equally physical sense."

NOTES

1. The mere presence of mass tips light cones, but the effect is unnoticeable in everyday life on Earth. A truly enormous mass density is required to tip nearby light cones over so that their Future noticeably opens up toward the massive body. If the massive body is then set to rotating then a further consequence that results from Einstein's general theory is that the local light cones are tilted additionally in the direction of rotation; i.e., the Future cones in spacetime open up both toward the body and in the direction of the rotation. (See Tech Note 8 for how light-cone tipping affects time travel.)
2. This is the usual distance function (sometimes called the "as the crow flies" distance), but it is not the only one possible. Mathematicians have defined the general properties of distance as follows: If A and B are any two points and if $d(A,B)$ is the distance between A and B, then (1) $d(A,B)=d(B,A)$; (2) $d(A,B)=0$ if and only if $A=B$; and (3) if C is any third point, then $d(A,B) \leqslant d(A,C)+d(C,B)$. The Pythagorean distance function possesses these three properties, but so do many other functions. See, for example, E. F. Krause, *Taxicab Geometry* (New York: Dover, 1986) where the city-block distance function $ds=|dx|+|dy|$ is explored. In general relativity the metric of any four-dimensional spacetime is of the symmetric quadratic form

$$(ds)^2 = \sum_{i=1}^{4} \sum_{j=1}^{4} g_{ij}(dx_i)(dx_j), \quad g_{ij}=g_{ji},$$

where $x_1=t$, $x_2=x$, $x_3=y$, and $x_4=z$, and the 16 g's are all functions of these four variables. (Because of the symmetry condition, only 10 of the g's are independent.) In this notation flat spacetime is characterized by $g_{11}=1$, $g_{22}=g_{33}=g_{44}=-1$, $g_{ij}=0$ for $i \neq j$. For a given spacetime, one can arbitrarily choose an infinity of coordinate systems. If just one of this infinity of systems is such that the above g's occur, then that spacetime is flat. If no such coordinate system exists, then that spacetime is necessarily curved. The g functions are the components of the so-called metric tensor of the second rank of that spacetime. The g's at each point in spacetime are related to the curvature of spacetime at that point, which in turn is dependent on the g's and on the energy density at that point. In fact, the equations for the g's, which are the Einstein gravitational field equations, are both nonlinear and coupled; i.e., g_{ij} is, in general a nonlinear function of g_{lk}, which accounts for the notorious difficulty in finding analytic solutions except in certain highly special cases, such as around spinning spheres and rotating infinite cylinders.
3. The single time and the three space coordinates are said to form a four-vector that is invariant under Lorentz transformation. There are other four-vectors that are also invariant under Lorentz transformation, such as the energy-momentum, the velocity, and the force four-vectors. All have invariants that are formed the same way, by taking the difference of the square of the time and the sum of the squares of the space components. I will not pursue any of this here, but the interested reader will find a wonderfully readable exposition at the advanced undergraduate level in I. R. Kenyon, *General Relativity* (New York: Oxford, 1990).
4. A more intuitive formulation of flatness can be visualized in terms of the parallel

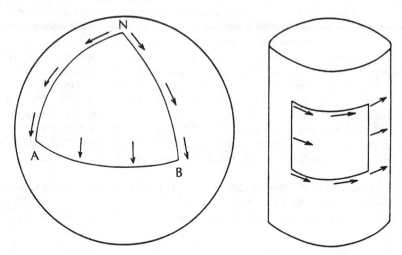

FIGURE 28. The curvature of a space can be revealed by the process of parallel transport. For example, this figure shows the parallel transport of a vector around a closed path over two, two-dimensional surfaces. Transport over a curved (e.g., spherical) surface results in a nonzero rotation of the vector, while transport over a flat (e.g., cylindrical) surface produces zero rotation.

transport of a vector around a closed path. In a curved space the vector will experience a rotation, which will not occur in a flat space. Two examples of parallel transport in two-dimensional spaces are shown in Figure 28. The spherical surface is curved. (In your mind, slide the vector from N to A to B to N, all the while keeping it parallel to its previous orientation. When it gets back to N, the vector will point toward B, not toward A, as it originally did.) A similar trip on the cylindrical surface, however, will result in zero rotation of the vector. Thus, a cylindrical surface is, despite superficial appearances, *not* curved.

5. The idea of linking the curvature of a four-dimensional space to physical phenomena predates Einstein. It can be seen in the work of the British mathematician William Kingdon Clifford [Clifford, BST] in the 1870s. Indeed, one can find it mentioned even earlier, a full decade before Einstein's birth; i.e., in a footnote from [Sylvester, 1869] we read: "It is well known ... we live in a flat or level space, our existence therein being assimilable to the life of the bookworm in a flat page: but what if the page should be undergoing a process of gradual bending into a curved form? Mr. W. K. Clifford has indulged in some remarkable speculations [supporting the idea that] our level space of three dimensions [is] in the act of undergoing in space of four dimensions ... a distortion analogous to the rumpling of the page." Remember, this is in 1869! Clifford, in turn, found inspiration in the even earlier work of the German mathematician Bernhard Riemann (1826–1866). See, for example, Clifford's translation of Riemann's 1854 lecture "On the Hypotheses which Lie At the Bases of Geometry," *Nature* 8 (1 May 1873): 14–17, and continued in the next issue of (8 May 1873): 36–37. Typical of the contemporary reaction to such a radical idea was that of the great Clerk Maxwell, who dismissed this part of Clifford's work as the speculations of a "space crumpler." Such

ideas continued to be the subject of debate for many years after Clifford. For example, [Kerszberg, 1987] reports a 1917 exchange between the two British astronomers Sir James Jeans and Sir Arthur Stanley Eddington. When Jeans declared "Einstein's crumpling up of his four-dimensional space may, for the present, be considered to be ... fictitious," Eddington quickly replied that what is crumpled is "the ordinary space which we are persuaded to discard." The prescient genius of Riemann is almost impossible to believe. In his 1854 lecture there is a throw away line about spaces with a metric (recall Note 2) given by the positive fourth root of a quartic differential form. Such spaces are known today as *Finsler spaces* (after the German mathematician Paul Finsler who developed Riemann's idea in his 1918 Göttingen doctoral dissertation "On Curves and Surfaces in General Spaces"), and their use in the theory of FTL speeds (see Tech Note 7) can be found in the recent series of papers [Shenglin, 1992a,b, 1990, 1988.]

6. R. W. Brehme and W. E. Moore, "Gravitation and Two-Dimensional Curved Surfaces," *American Journal of Physics* 37 (July 1969): 683–692.

7. G. N. Lewis, "Light Waves and Light Corpuscles," *Nature* 117 (13 Feb. 1926): 236–238.

TECH NOTE 5

PROPER TIME, CURVED WORLD-LINES, AND THE TWIN PARADOX

Before I realized the untenability of the special theory of relativity I was engaged in a vigorous controversy on the question whether relativity theory entailed the possibility of "asymmetrical ageing," e.g., of postponing the date of one's death, almost without limit, by high speed travel. It was, and still is, generally believed that relativity demands this possibility ... If I am right, [this belief in] asymmetrical aging ... shows that relativity theory is generally misunderstood.

> —1963 note to *Nature* by Herbert Dingle (former President of the Royal Astronomical Society) who rejected special relativity and engaged in a years-long effort to convince the world that there was a conspiracy to suppress him

What if Dingle is pulling the leg of the world? It is to me the most reasonable hypothesis to explain what is otherwise inexplicable to me. Knowing you as well as I do ... I cannot bring myself to believe that you are as stupid as you make yourself out to be. If my hypothesis is correct, I salute your sense of humor. No harm has been done. Printers have had good employment. My humiliation in having been taken in is swallowed up in my admiration at the way you have put the thing across.

> —1968 letter to Dingle, from the mathematical physicist J. L. Synge of the Dublin Institute of Advanced Studies

The spacetime interval introduced in Tech Note 4 has an important interpretation that will lead us to one of the more dazzling results of relativity—time travel into the future. First, recall the flat spacetime metric

$$(ds)^2 = (dt)^2 - (dx)^2 - (dy)^2 - (dz)^2,$$

in which the use of unprimed variables indicates that the measurements on the space and time coordinates of a moving particle are made with respect to a stationary observer's frame of reference. Now, suppose instead that the space and time coordinates of a moving particle are made with respect to the particle. Then, using primed variables for measurements made in this new frame of reference, we have $dx' = dy' = dz' = 0$ because the particle is always at the origin of its own coordinate system. Recalling the invariance of the spacetime interval for all observers, we then conclude that

$$(ds')^2 = (ds)^2 = (dt')^2.$$

That is, the spacetime interval between two events is the time lapse measured by a clock attached to a particle that moves from one event to the other. This time is called *proper time*, which gets its name from the idea that it belongs to, or is the *property* of, the moving particle.[1]

To establish one more preliminary result, we will next adopt what has come to be called the *clock hypothesis*, which states that an accelerated clock runs at the same instantaneous rate as does an unaccelerated clock that is moving alongside at the instantaneously same speed. As shown in Tech Note 2, if the accelerated clock's instantaneous speed is v, then its rate of timekeeping (dt') is related to that of a stationary clock (dt) as

$$dt' = \sqrt{1 - \left(\frac{v}{c}\right)^2}\, dt.$$

The clock hypothesis is generally assumed to be true. Einstein, himself, in his 1905 paper specifically took the rate of a clock's timekeeping to be velocity dependent only. However, one can still find those who object. In this book we side with Einstein.[2] Thus, the total elapsed time between two events A and B, as measured by the proper time of the accelerated clock making the journey, is

$$t' = \int dt' = \int_{t_A}^{t_B} \sqrt{1 - \left(\frac{v}{c}\right)^2}\, dt < t_B - t_A \quad \text{if } v \neq 0,$$

where $t_B - t_A$ is the elapsed time between A and B as measured by the stationary clock. This inequality results because for $v \neq 0$ the integrand is always less than one.[3]

We know that in a spacetime diagram the world line of the unaccelerated clock is a straight line, while the world line of the accelerated clock is a curved line. Thus, using Figure 29 combined with the inequality $t' < t_B - t_A$ gives the following central result: The world line of *maximum* proper time is the one that *looks the shortest*; i.e., the straight world line! On the spacetime diagram the curved world-line looks longer, but in fact any curved world line will have a smaller proper time than does the straight world line. This is a dramatic example of how Minkowskian spacetime geometry differs from Euclidean geometry; in the latter geometry there is no longest path between two points.

With these preliminary results established, we can now understand the famous paradox of the twins. Suppose we have twins Bob and Bill. Bill remains on Earth,

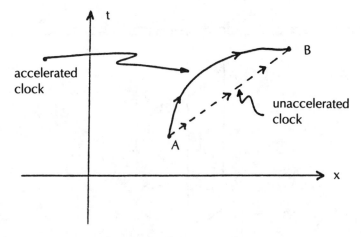

FIGURE 29. World lines of two clocks.

but Bob gets into a rocket ship and goes on a trip out into space, turns around by firing his motors, and comes home. The world lines of Bob and Bill are together, then diverge, and then come together again at the end of Bob's trip, as in Figure 30. The details of Bob's trip are not important for a general statement of the paradox (although in Tech Note 6 details are presented for one possible trip). All we need observe here is that Bill's world line from A to B is straight, while Bob's is curved. Bill's body (that is, his local clock) will therefore measure a greater proper time than will Bob's; i.e., Bob will be younger than his stay-at-home twin! Equivalently, upon his return Bob will hear his Earthbound brother declare the date to be further in the future than Bob's trip lasted (according to Bob). Bob will

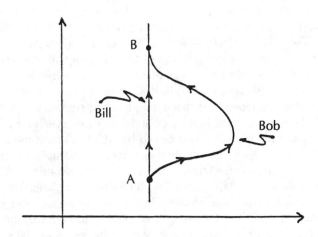

FIGURE 30. World lines of unaccelerated and accelerated twins.

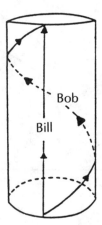

FIGURE 31. Unaccelerated twin paradox in a cylindrical spacetime.

conclude that he has traveled into the future. The difference in what each twin believes to be the date can, in fact, be truly astonishing (as Tech Note 6 shows). Oddly, this wonderful plot device seems not to have caught the attention of science fiction writers. As far as I know, the twin paradox has been used explicitly just as stated by just one author, Robert Heinlein, in his 1956 novel *Time for the Stars*.

The reason this situation is called a paradox is not because of the time travel aspect (there are no logical paradoxes with travel into the future), but rather because it seems to violate the very spirit of relativity.[4] That is, from Bill's point of view, Bob at first travels away and then returns. But one might argue that from Bob's point of view it is Bill who first recedes and then returns. So why is it Bob who is the younger? The classic answer is that the two points of view are actually not identical and that there is a definite asymmetry between Bill and Bob. After all, it is Bob who feels the acceleration from the rocket's engines, who feels forces, while Bill feels nothing unusual back on Earth. The more fundamental answer, however, is that Bob's world line in spacetime is curved, while Bill's is straight.

In an open flat spacetime, curved is indeed synonymous with accelerated, but this need not be so in a closed flat spacetime. In an open flat spacetime the only way two world lines can diverge in the past and then meet again in the future is for at least one of them to curve, but in a closed but still flat spacetime it is possible for two straight world lines to meet more than once. For example, in Figure 31 our simplified two-dimensional spacetime is the surface of a cylinder (which Note 4 for Tech Note 4 showed is flat), rather than an infinite flat plane. The two world lines are both straight. (To visualize this imagine cutting the cylinder open along the time dimension and then flattening it out.) Yet, Bob's looks longer on the spacetime diagram, so Bob's proper time will still be less than Bill's when they again meet even though now neither of them has experienced any acceleration.[5]

NOTES

1. This is the technical reason for why we took $(ds)^2 = (dt)^2 - (dx)^2$ rather than $(ds)^2 = (dx)^2 - (dt)^2$. Our choice avoids the somewhat awkward result of an imaginary proper time.

2. When asked during a 1952 interview if it is permissible to use special relativity in problems involving acceleration, Einstein replied, "Oh, yes, that is all right as long as gravity does not enter; in all other cases, special relativity is applicable. Although, perhaps the general relativity approach might be better, it is not necessary." See R. S. Shankland, "Conversations with Albert Einstein," *American Journal of Physics* 31 (Jan. 1963): 47–57.

3. For a more mathematical presentation of this result see Mary L. Boas, "The Clock Paradox," *Science* 130 (27 Nov. 1959): 1471–1472.

4. The paradox of the twins has generated a vast literature; e.g., see [Marder, 1971] for an excellent discussion and extensive bibliography up to 1968. The twin paradox is hinted at in Einstein's 1905 paper, but it is in a 1911 address to the International Congress of Philosophy, in Bologna, by the French physicist Paul Langevin, that a space traveler is first introduced. (The French writer Pierre Boulle was careful to mention this fact in his astonishing time-travel story "Time Out of Mind" [Boulle, 1966].) Fascination with the twin paradox continues to this day; e.g., [Prokhovnik, 1986] and [Cramer, 1990b]. Not everybody accepts the results we have claimed here, however. Herbert Dingle, for example, strenuously objected to them. Dingle was not a crackpot; the late Professor of History and Philosophy of Science at the University of London was generally well-regarded in scientific circles, but he went to his grave believing Einstein had got his sums wrong. The French philosopher Henri Bergson vigorously attacked Langevin's analysis of the clock paradox in a 1922 book, for which Dingle wrote a very interesting introduction [Bergson, 1965]. Dingle's position is examined in Marder's book, and Dingle tries to make his case in *Science at the Crossroads* (London: Martin Brian & O'Keeffe, 1972) (from which the quotes that open this Tech Note come). An interesting review of his book and a summary of where Dingle went wrong is by G. J. Whitrow, *British Journal for the Philosophy of Science* 26 (March 1975): 358–362. While Dingle is now gone from the scene, his cause still has followers. For example, in the same year that Marder's book was published Mendel Sachs, a professor of physics at the State University of New York at Buffalo, wrote a "Dingle-like" article entitled "A Resolution of the Clock Paradox," *Physics Today*, Sept. 1971. This article provoked a reaction so strong that the editors devoted essentially the entire Letters column in the January 1972 issue to the replies, which all rejected Sach's position.

5. C. H. Brans and D. R. Stewart, "Unaccelerated-Returning-Twin Paradox in Flat Space-Time," *Physical Review D* 8 (15 Sept. 1973): 1662–1666.

TECH NOTE 6

A HIGH-SPEED ROCKET IS A ONE-WAY TIME MACHINE TO THE FUTURE

A good many physicists believe that this paradox can only be resolved by the general theory of relativity. They find great comfort in this, because they don't know any general relativity and feel that they don't have to worry about this problem until they decide to learn general relativity. However, they are quite wrong. The twin effect ... is one of the special theory of relativity.

—[Schild, 1959]

The following analysis is essentially that of the German astronomer Sebastian von Hoerner, who published the basic ideas in *Science* in 1962 under the title "The General Limits of Space Travel." The following year it was reprinted in the classic anthology *Interstellar Communication* [von Hoerner, 1963]. Later, von Hoerner's somewhat muddy mathematics was cleaned up by Marder,[1] a British applied mathematician, who incorporated it into his brilliant, definitive book on the twin paradox of special relativity [Marder, 1971].

This analysis describes an accelerated rocket and assumes that the formulas of special relativity hold at every instant. This is a view that von Hoerner described as "generally assumed but not yet accepted."[2] To begin, our time traveler gets into his rocket ship at time $t=t'=0$ (t is time measured on Earth, and t' is time measured on the rocket). The Earth and rocket clocks are synchronized at the instant of departure. We assume that the rocket trip is to be made in comfort, so we let the rocket accelerate at a constant rate. (In the numerical calculations I will, in fact, let this constant be one gee, which is equivalent to the Earth's gravity, an acceleration we all live with through our entire lives.)[3] The traveler travels this way for a time interval of T (as measured on Earth) and T' (as measured on the rocket). Then he turns off the rearward engine and turns on a forward-mounted engine so as to experience a constant deceleration. Floor and ceiling interchange, but our traveler always weighs the same. If he does this for the same time interval (T in Earth time, T' in rocket time) as for the acceleration interval, then the rocket will be brought to rest with respect to the Earth. The time traveler then returns to the Earth using the same acceleration/deceleration process. The time traveler thus arrives back home gently with a final speed of zero with respect to the Earth (ignoring, of course, all the navigational problems due to the motion of the Earth during the trip).

The total duration of the trip has been $4T$ in Earth time, and $4T'$ in rocket time.

The claim is that $4T' < 4T$ (as is shown in Tech Note 5), and in fact the inequality can be absolutely astonishing in its unbalance. To show this, we define the rocket speed in the Earth's frame to be v. We can imagine that at any given instant there is a second reference frame moving at some fixed speed V (in the Earth's frame) in a direction parallel to the rocket's motion. The location of the origin of this moving system is arbitrary; it is not necessarily at the instantaneous location of the rocket. The distance of the rocket from the Earth is x, and the distance of the rocket from the origin of the second system is x'. The rocket's speed in the second system is v', and by the addition of velocities formula (see Tech Note 3) we have

$$v = \frac{v' + V}{1 + Vv'/c^2}.$$

The times in the Earth and moving systems (t and t') are related via the Lorentz transformation as

$$t = \frac{1}{\beta}\left(t' + \frac{Vx'}{c^2}\right), \quad \beta = (1 - V^2/c^2)^{1/2}.$$

Differentiating the first expression with respect to v', we easily find that

$$dv = \frac{\beta^2}{(1 + Vv'/c^2)^2}\, dv'.$$

Using the chain-rule for functions of multiple variables to find the total differential dt, we have

$$dt = \frac{\partial t}{\partial t'}\, dt' + \frac{\partial t}{\partial x'}\, dx' = \frac{1}{\beta}\, dt'\left(1 + \frac{V}{c^2}\frac{dx'}{dt'}\right).$$

Observing that dx'/dt' is the velocity of the rocket in the second system (i.e., v'), we have

$$dt = \frac{1}{\beta}\, dt'\left(1 + \frac{V}{c^2}v'\right).$$

We can now write the rocket's acceleration as seen from the Earth as the ratio of the dv and dt differentials:

$$\frac{dv}{dt} = \frac{\beta^3}{(1 + Vv'/c^2)^3}\frac{dv'}{dt'},$$

where dv'/dt' is the acceleration *according to the time traveler*. We have thus established the fact that the accelerations in the two frames are not equal.

We now explicitly set $V=v$, i.e., we set V equal to the speed of the rocket at some (any) given instant. At this instant, then, the second system is at rest with respect to the rocket, and so $v'=0$. The second system is called the co-moving system of the rocket; and the so-called hypothesis of locality, which is generally invoked in relativity analyses, asserts the instantaneous equivalence of the accelerated time traveler with an observer in the co-moving system. Thus, with this choice for V, we have

$$\frac{dv}{dt}=\beta^3\frac{dv'}{dt'} .$$

Since the experienced acceleration dv'/dt', is assumed to be a constant (call it a) this is a particularly easy equation to solve. Thus, as $V=v$, we have

$$\frac{dv}{dt}=\beta^3 a=\left(1-\frac{v^2}{c^2}\right)^{3/2}a$$

or

$$\frac{dv}{(1-v^2/c^2)^{3/2}}=a\ dt.$$

With $v=0$ at $t=0$ this integrates to give

$$v=\frac{at}{[1+(at/c)^2]^{1/2}} .$$

To find the relationship between T and T', we recall (see Tech Notes 2 and 3) that

$$dt'=\left(1-\frac{v^2}{c^2}\right)^{1/2}dt$$

and integrate to get

$$T'=\int_0^T\left(1-\frac{v^2}{c^2}\right)^{1/2}dt.$$

Inserting the expression for v as a function of t, this gives

TABLE 2. Time travel to the future on a rocketship accelerating at one Earth gravity.

EXPERIENCED ACCELERATION=ONE GEE	
Years for 4T' (rocket time)	Years for 4T (Earth time)
1	1.01
2	2.09
5	6.5
7	11.5
10	25.5
20	339
30	4 478
40	59 223

$$T' = \frac{c}{a}\ \sinh^{-1}\left(\frac{a}{c}\ T\right)$$

or equivalently

$$T = \frac{c}{a}\ \sinh\left(\frac{a}{c}\ T'\right).$$

Recall that the total round-trip time is $4T$ in Earth time, and $4T'$ in rocket time. Table 2 shows how $4T'$ compares to $4T$ for an experienced acceleration of a constant one gee. If humans can stand a two gee acceleration for indefinite periods of time, then significantly further penetration into the future would be possible during a single lifetime, as seen in Table 3.

TABLE 3. Time travel to the future on a rocketship accelerating at two Earth gravities.

EXPERIENCED ACCELERATION=TWO GEE	
Years for 4T' (rocket time)	Years for 4T (Earth time)
1	1.04
2	2.4
5	12.7
7	35.9
10	169.3
20	29 612
30	5 180 000
40	906 million (!)

Is it likely that such trips as these will someday be made in and into the future? Most probably, no.[4] Such trips result in speeds that are large fractions of or even nearly equal to the speed of light. To zip through space (which is not a perfect vacuum) at such speeds would result in a very high rate of collisions with stray hydrogen atoms (about one each cubic centimeter). The result of these energetic interactions would be the intense irradiation of the entire ship with a lethal dose of gamma rays long before the trip had even really begun. And, as von Hoerner showed in his paper, the energetics of such trips is mind-boggling. Still, the romantic idea of a relativistic space ship is a hard one to give up, and some good stories have been written using the concept; see, for example, Doris Pitkin Buck's "Story of a Curse" [Buck, SS], a tale about such a ship whose crew stays far too long away from home and of what they find has happened to the Earth during their absence. Another poignant tale based on time-dilation by high speed space flight is "Semley's Necklace" [LeGuin, 1975].

NOTES

1. The analysis done by von Hoerner is at best obscure. He does indeed arrive at correct analytical expressions, but even with correct formulas many of his numerical evaluations are incorrect. My presentation follows Marder's, and my numbers agree with his.
2. Consider, for example, this remark by Nobel laureate Julian Schwinger about the twin paradox in his book *Einstein's Legacy* (New York: Scientific American Library, 1986): "The observer on the spaceship, however, is *not* in uniform, unaccelerated motion, because he must be accelerated to *reverse direction* after having reached the objective. The special theory of relativity does not apply to such an accelerated observer." In a footnote [Horwich, 1975] makes the same assertion. However, this Tech Note takes the opposite view, which was put forth by C. W. Misner, K. S. Thorne, and J. A. Wheeler in their enormous book *Gravitation* (San Francisco: W. H. Freeman, 1973). See, in particular, their Chapter 6.
3. This is of practical importance, of course, because we do not want the experienced acceleration to be incompatible with the physical survival of the time traveler. All things considered, it is probably better to arrive in the future alive rather than dead from compression! Also we must be careful in this analysis with how terms are translated from one reference frame into another (that is, the Earth's and the rocket's). In particular, what is meant by a *constant acceleration*? The acceleration of the rocket will not appear to be the same to observers on the Earth and to the time traveler on the rocket. It is the time traveler who will experience the acceleration of the rocket and we can physically arrange for this acceleration to be a constant if in the rocket we keep fixed the extension of a spring that has a mass attached to one end that is free to move and bolt the other end to a wall. From the point of view of an observer on Earth, of course, the acceleration continually decreases toward zero as the rocket's speed approaches the limiting speed of light.
4. In response to von Hoerner's analysis, L. O. Pilgeram of the Arteriosclerosis Research Laboratory in Minneapolis wrote a letter [*Science* 138 (7 Dec. 1962): 1180] that objected to applying the laws of physics to biological systems (see Note 3 in Tech Note 2). Incorrectly asserting that time dilation "has never been proved or disproved exper-

imentally,'' Pilgeram further declared that ''there is no known causal means by which greatly increased velocity could alter, without destroying the very biochemical basis of the life process, those metabolic changes which are responsible for the aging process.'' Von Hoerner gave a reasoned reply that can be found immediately after Pilgeram's letter.

TECH NOTE 7
SUPERLUMINAL SPEEDS AND BACKWARD TIME TRAVEL

... velocities greater than that of light ... have no possibility of existence.

—Albert Einstein, 1905

So far we have limited our technical interpretation of relativity theory to speeds below the speed of light; that is, to the condition $v < c$, where v is the relative velocity of two reference frames. There was nothing, however, in the derivation of the Lorentz transformation equations that used this self-imposed constraint. What, in fact, happens for $v > c$? The answer is causality violation. If a material object goes faster than light (FTL), the mathematics seems to say that it could physically travel into the past, and if a signal bearing information goes faster than light, then the mathematics seems to say that a message could travel into the past. Such a signal might be, for example, a modulated beam of tachyons—if tachyons exist.

Several objections to the existence of tachyons have been put forth.[1] The relativistic expressions for the energy and momentum of a particle with rest mass m_0 moving with speed v, for example, are

$$E = \frac{m_0 c^2}{\sqrt{1 - (v/c)^2}} \quad \text{and} \quad p = \frac{m_0 v}{\sqrt{1 - (v/c)^2}}.$$

For $v > c$, the radicals in these expressions become imaginary, whereas E and p must always be real-valued (because they can be observed and even measured as a result of the interactions the particle has with other matter). The energy and momentum can regain the property of being real-valued if we write $m_0 = i\mu$ for a tachyon, where μ is the real-valued (but unobservable) meta-mass. Then (see [Parker, 1969]);

$$E = \frac{\mu c^2}{\sqrt{(v/c)^2 - 1}} \quad \text{and} \quad p = \frac{\mu v}{\sqrt{(v/c)^2 - 1}}.$$

An interesting consequence of this is that if tachyons lose energy, they speed up! This result, first stated by the German physicist Arnold Sommerfeld in 1904, means that if there is a mechanism for continuous energy loss (e.g., by Cerenkov radiation, either electromagnetic or gravitational), then tachyons will spontaneously accelerate without limit and enter what is called a transcendent state of

infinite speed. Curiously, the above equations show that such infinitely fast particles, while possessing zero energy, would carry a finite momentum of μc.

To see how the backward time travel and faster than light issues are related, it
is useful to establish a geometrical interpretation of the Lorentz transformation. As
shown in Tech Note 3, if the x',t' system is moving with speed v in the x (or x')
direction relative to the x,t system, then

$$x'=\frac{x-vt}{\sqrt{1-(v/c)^2}} \quad \text{and} \quad t'=\frac{t-vx/c^2}{\sqrt{1-(v/c)^2}}.$$

These equations make sense for $v<c$, and in fact we will retain this condition for
our two relatively moving frames of reference, and will in all that follows use the
symbol w to denote the speed of an FTL particle. Our human observers will always
be subluminal.

Now, recall what we mean by any line parallel to the x axis; it is a line with a
fixed time coordinate. Such a line is a cosmic moment line, with the equation
$t=$constant. Similarly, for the moving system we would write the equation of a
cosmic moment line as $t'=$constant, which after using the Lorentz transformation,
we see is equivalent to

$$t-\frac{vx}{c^2}=\text{constant.}$$

In particular, the x' axis (the $t'=0$ cosmic moment line), which passes through the
point $x=0$ at $t=0$, has the equation

$$t=\frac{vx}{c^2}=vx$$

(with our usual convention of $c=1$) .

In a similar way, recall now what we mean by any line parallel to the t axis; it
is a line with a fixed space coordinate. Such a line is the world line of a stationary
particle in the x,t frame, with the equation $x=$constant. Similarly, for the moving
system we would write $x'=$constant as the equation of the world line of a particle
stationary in that system. From the Lorentz transformation we see that this is
equivalent to

$$x-vt=\text{constant.}$$

In particular, the t' axis (which is the $x'=0$ world line of a particle stationary at the
origin of the moving system) passes through the $x=0$, $t=0$ point, and it has the
equation

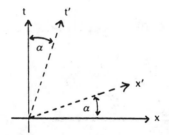

FIGURE 32. Spacetime coordinate rotation by relative motion.

$$x = vt.$$

Thus, superimposed spacetime coordinate axes for the two frames look like those in Figure 32. That is, the relative motion of the two frames results in a rotation of the spacetime axes; but it is a strange sort of rotation, with opposite senses for the space and time axes. The x' and t' axes make equal angles α with the x and t axes, respectively, where

$$\alpha = \tan^{-1}(v).$$

If we limit the moving frame to subluminal speeds (i.e., $0 \leqslant v < 1$), then

$$0 \leqslant \alpha < 45°.$$

At the speed of light ($v=1$) we have $\alpha = 45°$, and the x' and t' axes coincide—time and space have become indistinguishable!

It is important to realize that observers in either system would measure the same speed for a photon; i.e., each would see the world line of a photon as a line with slope 1.[2] The truth of this statement for the x,y system is obvious using the spacetime diagram. It is, perhaps, not so obvious with the x',t' system because of the nontraditional, nonperpendicular axes (as drawn on paper) in that system. In Figure 33 the world line of a photon is shown in both systems. In the figure we emit the photon at $x'=0$, $t'=0$, and later measure its coordinates at point A to be $x'=x'_A$ at time $t'=t'_A$. Notice carefully how this is done. We draw lines from point A parallel to the x' and t' axes until they intersect the t' and x' axes, respectively. This is similar to the way we would get the spacetime coordinates of A in the more familiar x,t system, where we would draw lines parallel to the x,t axes.

It should be obvious now that x'_A and t'_A have the same extension, just as they do in the unprimed system, and so

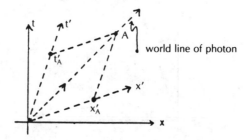

FIGURE 33. Invariance of the world line of a photon.

$$\frac{x'_A}{t'_A}=1, \text{ the speed of light.}$$

The speed of light is the *only* invariant speed under Lorentz transformation. Indeed, the modern approach to special relativity emphasizes this invariance, rather than the idea of being a limiting speed, as the central property of the speed of light (see [Jones, 1963]).

This geometrical interpretation of the Lorentz transformation lets us quickly make another interesting (and, I think, not very obvious) observation: If a particle is faster than light in the x,t system, then there exists a subluminal x',t' frame for which a particle is infinitely fast! Figure 34 shows the world line of an FTL particle in the x,t system. (It is, of course, below the world line of a photon.) Suppose the FTL particle has speed $w>c$, and its world line makes angle β with the x-axis: If we now pick v, the speed of the moving x',t' frame, to be such that $\alpha=\beta$, then the x' axis will coincide with the world line of the particle and the particle will appear to an observer in the x',t' frame to be *everywhere at once*, i.e., to be infinitely fast. We have, then,

$$\beta=\tan^{-1}(v)=\tan^{-1}\left(\frac{1}{w}\right),$$

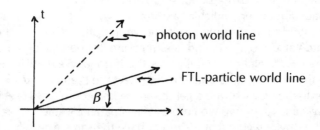

FIGURE 34. World line of a FTL particle.

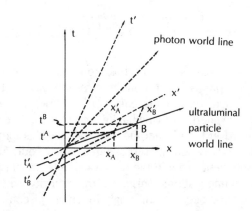

FIGURE 35. World line of an ultraluminal particle.

or $v=1/w$ which seems to be dimensionally wrong. Recall, however, that with our convention of $c=1$, the v in this result is a normalized speed. To return to the units of everyday use, we merely replace v with v/c and w with w/c; this makes our result

$$\frac{v}{c}=\frac{c}{w} \quad \text{or} \quad v=\frac{c^2}{w}.$$

We can, of course, turn this result around. If an FTL particle moves with speed w in the x,t frame, then to an observer in the x',t' frame moving with subluminal speed v, the particle will appear to be infinitely fast if $w=c^2/v$. A particle with $w \geqslant c^2/v$ is said to be not just superluminal (FTL) but *ultra*luminal.

If a particle has infinite velocity with $w=c^2/v$, then what happens if w is actually greater than c^2/v? The answer is easy to see from a spacetime diagram, as in Figure 35, where the x' and t' axes have been extended back to negative values: In this figure I have labeled two arbitrary events A and B on the world line of an ultraluminal particle (which thus lies below the x' axis) and have plotted their spacetime coordinates in both the x,t and x',t' frames. For the x,t frame we see that A is related to B by the relations $x_A < x_B$ and $t_A < t_B$, i.e., the particle is moving forward in time from A to B and is moving in space along the increasing x axis. In the x',t' system, however, A is related to B by the relations $x'_A < x'_B$ and $t'_B < t'_A$, i.e., the time order of A and B is reversed for an observer in the x',t' frame. To this observer the particle appears to be traveling backward in time!

But this isn't quite the end of the story. Following the approach used in [Bilaniuk and Sudarshan, 1969b], we note that if the energy of the particle in the stationary system is E, then the energy in the moving system is[3]

$$E' = \frac{1}{\sqrt{1-(v/c)^2}} \frac{\mu(c^2 - wv)}{\sqrt{(w/c)^2 - 1}} \; .$$

We see, then, that the sign of E' switches from positive to negative when w exceeds c^2/v, which is precisely the condition for the particle to go ultraluminal and to begin to appear to be moving backward in time, as seen in the primed system. That is, negative energy moving backward in time in one system is positive energy moving forward in time in another. Historically this idea led to the rein-terpretation principle (RP), which is discussed in Chapter Four. At one time the RP was claimed to be sufficient to avoid the backward-time-travel issue and all of the associated paradoxical implications. This is not the majority view today, however, and many physicists have been astonishingly inventive in constructing scenarios with causal paradoxes that the RP clearly fails to abolish.[4]

Consider, for example, the situation described by Shoichi Yoshikawa of Prince-ton University, in one of the replies received by *Physics Today* to Bilaniuk and Sudarshan's 1969 article (see Note 1). Yoshikawa's example even *uses* the RP to arrive at the causal paradox! As shown in Figure 36, Yoshikawa's example has an ultraluminal particle emitted by an observer P at A at time $t=0$ in the stationary system. For P this particle is moving forward in time and along the x axis in the positive direction. A relatively moving observer (call him Q) receives this particle at B. Now, as we have already established, what Q actually sees is a negative energy particle absorbed at B, but because of the RP, he interprets as if it were a positive energy particle emitted at B and traveling back down the x' axis in the negative direction. Now let us say that at the instant Q observes this emission, he emits a second tachyon that goes even faster down the negative x' axis. (This tachyon is more ultraluminal than the one originally emitted at A.) This tachyon is then absorbed at C, an event observed by a past version of P, since C occurs earlier on the t axis than does A! P sees this second tachyon as a negative energy particle, of course, and (again because of the RP) he interprets it as the emission of a positive energy particle. Thus, the emission of this tachyon at $t<0$ has been caused by the emission of the original tachyon at $t=0$. Thus, we have backward causation *because* of the RP, with P seeing something happen at $t<0$ because of something he *will* do at $t=0$. (Bilaniuk and Sudarshan admitted the strength of this example in undermining the RP, and could give only a weak reply that involved "cosmological boundary conditions.")

Of course, the problem now is the threat of a bilking paradox. After P sees the $t<0$ event, suppose that he then does *not* emit the original tachyon? In fact, [Benford et al., 1970] uses this puzzle as the concluding argument of its well-known "antitelephone" analysis of two people who each possess tachyonic trans-mitters that send messages one hour back in time: "Suppose A and B enter into the following agreement: A will send a message at three o'clock if and only if he does *not* receive one at one o'clock. B sends a message to reach A at one o'clock immediately on receiving one from A at two o'clock. Then the exchange of mes-

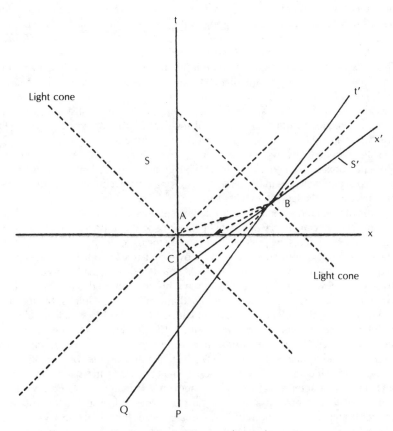

FIGURE 36. A FTL causal paradox.

sages will take place if and only if it does not take place.''[5] An analysis inspired by this, [Gatlin, 1980], makes a more extensive study of such backward-in-time agreements (or contracts, as Gatlin calls them), and she concludes with a provocative statement: "Although it will never be possible to design a communications system which transmits messages from the future [to the past] upon request-... messages from the future may sometimes reach [the past]." Perhaps a passive listening station for messages from the future (see Note 25 for Chapter Four) isn't so crazy after all!

NOTES

1. Tachyons became a popular topic in the physics literature with the publication of [Bilaniuk, Deshpande and Sudarshan, 1962]. After the appearance of this 1962 paper, Bilaniuk and Sudarshan published essentially the same ideas again in somewhat ex-

panded form in *Physics Today* [Bilaniuk and Sudarshan, 1969a]. This provoked a series of letters taking exception on a variety of interesting technical issues not addressed here, but which can be found (along with Bilaniuk and Sudarshan's replies) in the December 1969 issue of the magazine ["More About Tachyons," *Physics Today* (Dec. 1969): 47–52]. See also Note 36 for Chapter Four.

2. This view of the world line of a photon is literally built into the Lorentz transformation since one of Einstein's fundamental postulates for special relativity is the invariance of the speed of light.

3. This expression for E' is the result of applying the Lorentz transformation to E. The interested reader can find the details of the procedure worked out in A. P. French, *Special Relativity* (New York: W. W. Norton, 1968), 208–210.

4. The literature on tachyon paradoxes, pro and con, is enormous. A long summary of all these paradoxes, together with a large bibliography and rebuttal analyses, is given by an *advocate* of tachyons in [Recami, 1987]. For a strong rebuttal to the reinterpretation principle, in particular, see [Savitt, 1982].

5. A historically earlier, essentially equivalent superluminal analysis can be found in David Bohm's *The Special Theory of Relativity* (New York: W. A. Benjamin, 1965), 155–160. As Bohm (who rejects the possibility of sending messages to the past) writes at the end: "In effect, S could communicate with his own past at M, and tell his past self what his future is going to be. But on learning this M could decide to change his actions, so that his future at S would be different from what his later self said it was going to be. For example, the past self could do something that would make it impossible for the future one to send the signal. Thus, there would arise a logical self-contradiction." The error in Bohm's type of argument was discussed in Chapter Four (in "Communication with the Past"). Since Gregory Benford's novel *Timescape* [Benford, 1980], tachyons have often appeared in fiction, but not always faithfully. In *A Matter of Time* [Cook, 1985], for example, which at first has a tachyon generator sending messages into the past, we later find a character trying to build a tachyon communicator to transmit to the far future! For that, a note in a bottle is all that is needed. And this same story has a physicist utter the following muddled explanation of the RP: "A few years ago there was a flap over a hypothetical particle called a tachyon. At first it was supposed to move faster than light and have negative mass. Then it was supposed to have positive mass and a velocity below that of light, but was supposed to be moving backward in time." Oh, my.

Note added in proof: Just before his death in April 1992, Columbia University physics professor Gerald Feinberg co-authored (with philosophers David Albert and Shaughan Levine) a paper in which he seems to have abondoned his support (see Chapter Four) for tachyons as possible carriers of information backward in time. In that paper, which never mentions tachyons, the conclusion is that knowledge of both past and future is *necessarily* limited. See "Knowledge of the Past and Future," *Journal of Philosophy* 89 (December 1992): 607–642.

TECH NOTE 8
BACKWARD TIME TRAVEL ACCORDING TO GÖDEL AND TIPLER

... within forty-eight hours we had invented, designed, and assembled a chronomobile. I won't weary you with the details, save to remark that it operated by transposing the seventh and eleventh dimensions in a hole in space, thus creating an inverse ether-vortex and standing the space-time continuum on its head.

—probably *not* the way to build a time machine [de Camp, 1981]

In this Tech Note my intention is to demonstrate how you can visualize time travel to the past without the need for writing even a single line of mathematics. I will start with Gödel's example, which describes a rigid, uniformly rotating Universe. The one result from general relativity that we will use (without proof) is that the rotation of matter causes a distortion in spacetime that results in the tipping over of light cones, with the future half tilted in the direction of rotation. If we imagine a point in the Universe about which the rotation takes place, then this tipping effect increases with the radial distance from that point.[1] At a certain critical distance, in fact, the future half of the light cone for a given point in spacetime will tilt into the past half of similarly tilted light cones for nearby points. This is illustrated in Figure 37 (which was taken from [Herbert, 1988]). (A similar but somewhat more general picture can be found in [Malament, 1984].)

The figure shows a family of light cones in a rotating Universe. Because light cones are tilted by a rotation-induced twist in spacetime, a traveler can move around a circular path on a trip into his local future and end up in his own global past without ever going faster than light. This kind of roundtrip, whose trajectory winds back into the past without ever becoming spacelike, is an example of a closed timelike curve. From this illustration it should be clear how a time traveler beginning at A can weave his way along a circular path that brings him back into the past half of the light cone at A. (The path needs to have a radius at least as great as the critical value.) The traveler's world line is always inside the local light cone; i.e., he never exceeds the speed of light.[2]

As pointed out in Note 12 for Chapter One, the Gödel Universe is infinite in size and nonexpanding, so it must rotate fast enough to counter the gravitational tendency to collapse. The more matter in the Universe, the faster the minimum necessary rotation speed. If our Universe were Gödelian, it would have to rotate once each 70 billion years, and the critical radius would be 16 billion light-years.

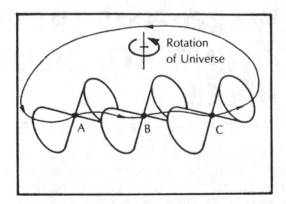

FIGURE 37. Tilted light cones in a rotating Universe.

(The circular orbit in Figure 37 would be at least 100 billion light-years around!) To send a human on such a trip in a reasonable lapse of proper time would require a rocket ship that was moving at near light speed, but of course a radio signal traveling at light speed could be used to send messages into the past—in a Gödelian Universe.

But our Universe is not Gödelian, and we do not have any such natural paths available for time travel and/or time telegraphy.[3] Tipler's rotating, infinite cylinder is a mechanism for artificially producing the tipped-over light cone effect, thus creating closed timelike curves. Figure 38 (taken from Tipler's dissertation [Tipler, 1976b]) shows how his cylinder works. The cylinder is represented by the central vertical axis. Far away from the cylinder the light cones in spacetime are upright, but as we move inward they tip over with the future halves opening up into the direction of rotation. (Only the future halves of the light cones are shown.) This direction, which is the direction that far away from the cylinder measures *space*, near the cylinder measures *time* (just as in the Gödelian Universe). To travel back in time, therefore, all the time traveler need do is leave the Earth and approach the cylinder until he is near enough to be in the tipped-over region of spacetime. Then he would follow a helical path around the cylinder and would spiral down in the *negative* time direction as far back as desired (but no further back than to the moment of the cylinder's creation). This motion is such that the time traveler is always moving into his local future, via the tipped-over light cones. Finally, he would withdraw from the cylinder and return to the Earth—in the past. The time traveler had better be a good space navigator, of course, as the Earth won't be where he left it!

NOTES

1. For a picture of this, see S. W. Hawking and G. F. R. Ellis, *The Large Scale Structure of Spacetime* (London: Cambridge University Press, 1973): 169. See also [Donald,

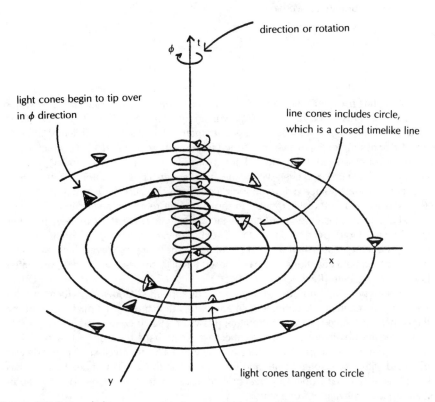

FIGURE 38. Future light cones point almost entirely in $+t$ direction far from rotating matter; they begin to tip over as the matter is approached. Note that there is a helical timelike path that moves locally into the *future* in the $-t$ direction: that is, it goes into the past as seen by an observer far from the rotating matter. (The world lines of rotating matter are helixes in the $+t$ direction.)

1978], especially its Figure 9, for more on light cone tipping.

2. The world line of the time traveler is always timelike. We can see how this works mathematically by taking the spacetime metric for Gödel's Universe (with, as usual, the speed of light $c=1$):

$$(ds)^2=(dt)^2-(dr)^2-(dy)^2+\sinh^2 r(\sinh^2 r-1)(d\phi)^2+2\sqrt{2}\ \sinh^2 r(d\phi)(dt),$$

where t, r, y, and ϕ are cylindrical coordinates in four-dimensional spacetime and by imagining our adventurer's world line as the helical curve $r=$constant, $y=0$, and $t=-\alpha\phi$. If as usual we take the time axis as vertical, then the time traveler's world line is a vertical helix in spacetime. For this curve, $dr=dy=0$, and $dt=-\alpha d\phi$. This last differential means, in particular, that whatever the sign of the constant α, we can choose that one of the two senses of movement in the spatial ϕ dimension that gives

$dt < 0$. Now, continuing, we have

$$(ds)^2 = [\alpha - 2\sqrt{2}\alpha \, \sinh^2 r + \sinh^2 r(\sinh^2 r - 1)](d\phi)^2,$$

or upon letting $u = \sinh r$ we have $(ds)^2 = [\alpha - 2\sqrt{2}\alpha u^2 + u^2(u^2 - 1)](d\phi)^2$. Now, for $\alpha = 0$ we have $(ds)^2 = u^2(u^2 - 1)(d\phi)^2$, which is greater than 0 if $u > 1$. This condition holds if $\sinh (r) > 1$, i.e., if $r = $ constant greater than $\ln(1 + \sqrt{2})$. For r sufficiently large (so that it reaches the critical value mentioned in the text) we have $(ds)^2 > 0$, which is the condition discussed in Tech Note 4 for a timelike interval. By continuity, we will continue to have $(ds)^2 > 0$ even with some (perhaps small positive or negative) value of α unequal to zero. Since ϕ is a periodic coordinate because we identify $\phi = 0$ with $\phi = 2\pi$), then as the traveler moves on the curve, he returns repeatedly to the same spatial points, but his time coordinate is increasingly negative. That is, he is traveling into the past. Note, once again, that in Gödel's Universe this property holds only for orbits with radii greater than a certain minimum. There are, however, other solutions of the Einstein field equations that have closed timelike curves at any radius, no matter how small (e.g., see [Reboucas, 1979]).

3. This conclusion would no doubt have greatly disappointed Gödel, who long after his 1949 papers retained a keen interest in any observational data that might support the thesis that our Universe could be rotating [Dawson, 1989]. Despite his admitted concern over the possibility of changing the past, or perhaps because of it, Gödel was obviously utterly fascinated by the idea of time travel. It is now well-known that he was obsessed with his personal health and was terrified at the thought of death, and it has been speculated that Gödel's interest in time travel sprang from some idea he had of it allowing a "reliving" of one's life.

TECH NOTE 9
THE WORMHOLE TIME MACHINE

This fact reinforces the author's feeling that [closed time loops] are not so nasty as people generally have assumed.

> —from [Friedman *et al.*, 1990], after a mathematical demonstration that time travel by wormhole does not conflict with the conservation of energy

Unless some really advanced beings have already made one of these things, we're not going back to visit the dinosaurs.

> —Frank J. Tipler, commenting on the wormhole time machine in *Discover*, June 1989

The wormhole is the latest addition to the approaches that have been advanced for building a time machine. Gödel rotated the entire Universe in 1949, while Tipler reduced the problem in 1974 merely to spinning an infinite cylinder. In 1988 Kip Thorne scaled things down even more, this time to the other extreme. His idea calls for pulling a wormhole on the scale of the Planck length out of the quantum foam that spacetime is, then enlarging it somehow to human scale, all the while stabilizing it against self-collapse, and finally using the time dilation effect of special relativity to alter time at one mouth of the wormhole as compared to the other mouth. The rest of this note will try to explain what all this means.

Wormholes, themselves, have been around in physics for decades, but they have always been thought to be so unstable as to exist only on paper, in the mathematics of general relativity. In an analysis [Fuller and Wheeler, 1962] published thirty years ago, for example, wormhole instability was shown to be so severe that not only would a human have no chance of getting through one, but also not even a single speedy photon could do so. Even at the speed of light, the photon could not zip through a wormhole before being trapped inside ("pinched off") in a region of infinite spacetime curvature. Wormholes would simply collapse too quickly after formation for even the so-called ultimate speed to save something inside. Indeed, the presence of matter-energy inside a wormhole accelerates its collapse! The dynamics of wormholes, it would seem, makes them simply untraversable.

And anyway, how would one get access to a wormhole in the first place? As suggested in [Morris and Thorne, 1988] one might perhaps imagine finding someday a rotating (Kerr) black hole that mathematically possesses in its interior so-called hyperspace tunnels to 'other places'—either in our Universe or in other

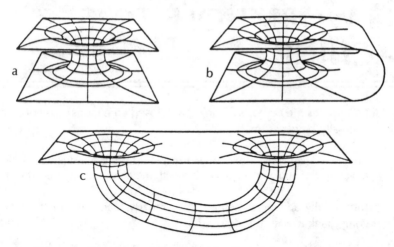

FIGURE 39. These sketches are unavoidably misleading, being two-dimensional renditions of wormholes connecting two places in a three-dimensional space. Time machine wormholes, on the other hand, connect two places in four-dimensional spacetime. In particular, the mouths of the wormholes will not appear to be depressions into which the time traveler's rocket ship dives, but rather as three-dimensional spheres. The wormhole in (a) connects to two disjoint Universes, while those in (b) and (c) are connections in the same Universe. As shown in these last two cases, the wormhole "handle" can either be long or short compared to the distance in external space between the wormhole mouths.

Universes (see Figure 39). In the case of a wormhole connecting two places in the same Universe, the external distance between the places may be very large (mega-light years) and the distance through the wormhole very small. This same paper, however, presents powerful arguments for why such Kerr wormholes probably do not exist and for why if they do exist, they would be untraversable. But all is not lost. Morris and Thorne go on to state that there are other exact solutions to the Einstein field equations that describe hyperspace wormholes with none of the Kerr wormhole problems.[1]

So how do we get our hands on one of these traversable wormholes? The authors are honest—they don't know! Their best suggestion, proposed in [Morris, Thorne, and Yurtsever, 1988], is that "one can imagine an advanced civilization pulling [such] a wormhole out of the quantum foam and enlarging it to classical size."[2] If so, then once inflated, the authors suggest, the wormhole could be stabilized against collapse by threading it with either matter or fields of stupendous negative (outward) tension—and by *stupendous* they mean STUPENDOUS. As the authors show, if b_0 denotes the minimum radius of the wormhole (the size of the so-called *throat* of the wormhole), then the tension (outward radial pressure) at that location must be at least

$$\tau_0 = \frac{3.8}{b_0^2} \times 10^{36} \, \frac{\text{tons}}{\text{in}^2} \, ,$$

where b_0 is expressed in feet.[3] For a wormhole with a throat radius of just several thousand feet, the value of τ_0 is of the same magnitude as the pressure at the center of the most massive neutron star. To stabilize a common sort of everyday wormhole (such as a subway tunnel), we can obtain the required tension/pressure by lining the tunnel with iron plates, but how for a hyperspace wormhole do we obtain "iron plates" that can achieve the required enormous tensions? As Morris, Thorne, and Yurtsever point out, such stuff could only be called "exotic." One possible strategy does not use matter at all. If we make b_0 *very* large, then non-material fields will do the job. Indeed, suppose b_0 equals one light-year (a large wormhole by anybody's standards). Then τ_0 is "only" 4000 tons/in², and that is achievable by threading the wormhole throat with a magnetic field of "only" 2,700,000 gauss![4]

As if all this isn't enough of a complication, Morris, Thorne, and Yurtsever then go on to show that there is another, even more curious problem. The geometrical requirement that the wormhole interior smoothly connect to the external, asymptotically flat spacetime demands that the wormhole throat flare outward, as shown in Figure 39. It turns out that this condition is mathematically equivalent to a requirement that τ_0 exceed the energy density of the throat material; and special relativity, in turn, says that for some observers the energy density will then actually be *negative*! (The condition of τ_0 exceeding the energy density of the wormhole throat is, in fact, the technical definition of *exotic*.[5])

At one time it was almost a law of nature that no observer should ever be able to measure a negative energy density (the so-called weak energy condition), but that is now known to be false. Indeed, the first hint that the possibility of a negative energy density is not crazy can be traced back as far as 1948, to a theoretical prediction by Dutch physicist Hendrick Casimir.

As pointed out in Note 18 for Chapter 1, the Heisenberg uncertainty principle allows a temporary violation of conservation of energy to occur, with the magnitude of the allowed violation increasing with decreasing time duration. Even in a vacuum, then, with particle/antiparticle creation and annihilation taking place, the average energy density being zero does not preclude fluctuations away from zero. What Casimir showed was that if one positioned two conductive plates parallel to each other, then the normal quantum fluctuations in this "vacuum sandwich" would be altered in such a way as to result in their mutual attraction—and this tiny effect was later actually observed.[6]

What does it mean to "alter the normal quantum fluctuations?" Consider, for example, the creation of a photon and its antiparticle, which is another photon (see Note 9 for Chapter Three). From the wave interpretation of particles, the parallel plates restrict the photons that appear in the vacuum layer to those that have wavelengths that "fit" because they have wavelengths that are submultiples of the plate separation. Photons with longer wavelengths than the plate separation cannot fit and thus do not appear. The absence of these photons lowers the average energy density between the plates, and since the average without the plates is zero, then the altered average energy density must be negative. Indeed, as the maximum allowed photon wavelength decreases with decreasing plate separation, the more negative the average energy density becomes in the enclosed Casimir vacuum.

Morris, Thorne, and Yurtsever [1988] use the Casimir effect to achieve the "exotic condition" *without* matter. They propose placing identical conducting, spherical plates carrying equal electrical charges at each end of the wormhole. (Remember that the wormhole mouths are spherically symmetric.) The two identical charges repel each other, of course, but the charge value is adjusted so that the gravitational attraction of the plates precisely cancels the repulsion. The authors then calculate that the Casimir effect results in a negative energy density sufficient to provide the required throat tension to prevent wormhole collapse.[7]

Now that I have sketched some of the difficulties wormholes have in simply existing, let's ignore all that and suppose we actually have one with both mouths in the same Universe. How can we imagine turning it into a time machine? Interestingly, while it is general relativity that gives us the wormhole, it is special relativity that adds the final touch of backward time travel. We begin by imagining that, somehow, one mouth of the wormhole can be moved with respect to the other mouth. For example, [Friedman, 1988] suggests using the gravitational attraction of a large asteroid to "drag" one end of the wormhole to induce a time-dilation effect.

Noting that, as shown in Tech Note 2, a moving clock runs slow with respect to a stationary clock, we next suppose that we have two clocks A and B, one in each mouth of the wormhole. These two clocks , and other clocks in the flat space outside the wormhole, are all initially running at the same rate and indicating the same time.[8] Now, recalling the twin paradox (see Tech Note 5), let each mouth-clock play the role of one of the twins. Imagine that A and B are now separated because mouth B is placed on board a rocket ship. The rocket ship takes a long, high speed trip out into space along the straight line path joining A and B in external space, and then returns, just as described in Tech Note 6. We unload mouth B from the rocket ship and reposition it at its original location.

What is the situation now? We can summarize matters as follows: (1) Clock A, in the nonmoving mouth, remains in-step with the local clocks in the space outside the mouth. (2) Clocks A and B, both inside the wormhole, have *not* moved with respect to each other because we are assuming a very short wormhole handle (as in part a of Figure 38). We can arrange for the motion of mouth B to be such that the handle is *always* short, and so the distance between clocks A and B changes by an arbitrarily small amount. Thus, clocks A and B remain in step with each other. (3) Clock B, because it has been moving with respect to its external space, arrives back at its starting position reading *behind* (i.e., earlier than) the clocks in the space outside mouth B.

For the sake of argument, then, suppose the journey of B is such that there is a two hour time-slip between clock B and its local, external clocks. Thus, if clock B reads 9 a.m., the clocks outside of mouth B will read 11 a.m. But since clocks A and B are in step, clock A reads 9 a.m., as do the clocks outside of mouth A. That is, the wormhole connecting mouth A to mouth B is a connection between two parts of the same Universe that are two hours apart in time. (See Note 8 again for an explanation of what this means.) Now, suppose the journey from mouth A to mouth B can be made through external space in one hour. Then, one could leave mouth A at 10 a.m., rocket to mouth B by 11 a.m., enter mouth B, and travel back to mouth A via the wormhole to the starting point—where it is 9 a.m., one hour *before* the trip began! One could imagine repeating this cyclic process, going back one additional hour for each new loop through the wormhole. One clear restriction, however, is that one could not go back in time to *before* the creation of the wormhole time machine (which is what Tipler meant by his quote at the start of this Tech Note). The wormhole works in the other direction, too. To see this, suppose the space traveler leaves mouth B at 8 a.m. and rockets to mouth A, arriving at 9 a.m. Entering mouth A, he exits from mouth B (where he started) at 11 a.m., two hours in the future.

Not everybody is convinced by all this, of course. Visser [1990] raises the possibility that if one mouth of a wormhole is accelerated, then this will induce a time-dilation canceling acceleration in the other mouth.[9] Another concern that has long bothered theoreticians is the possible instability of what is called the *Cauchy horizon*, the hyperspace surface in spacetime that separates the region where closed timelike loops can exist from the region where they cannot exist.[10] Particles that propagate in closed timelike loops and that thread through the wormhole on "straight lines" build up unbounded energy density levels at the horizon, and this destroys the horizon. In the wormhole time machine just described, for example, the horizon is thought to be unstable by some, but [Morris and Thorne, 1988] disagrees. Novikov's more recent analysis [Novikov, 1989] examines a wormhole time machine that has a circular motion for mouth B; that is, mouth B orbits around mouth A. The result here is that the Cauchy horizon does seem to be stable because now there are no fixed, straight line closed timelike loops threading the wormhole from A to B; i.e., B is a "moving target" and there is no point on the Cauchy horizon where the energy density becomes unbounded.

Most recently, in an attempt to study the grandfather paradox, self-interacting billiard balls traveling backward in time through wormholes have been studied [Echeverria, Klinkhammer, and Thorne, 1991]. The authors use billiard balls rather than human time travelers for the same reason Wheeler and Feynman used their pellet and shutter mechanism in their study of advanced waves (see Chapter Four)—to avoid any questions about free will. The central issue for these authors was to determine the multiplicity of trajectories for a single, self-interacting time traveling ball, where the Cauchy condition (see Note 10 again) for a well-defined trajectory is *unique* self-consistency.[11] That is, for the trajectory to be well-defined in the Cauchy sense, the authors expected a multiplicity of consistent trajectories of *one* for a self-interacting ball. A multiplicity of zero, of course, would be the physics declaring backward time travel to be nonsense (and the authors thought this a distinct possibility). Their actual results were startling—the authors found that under very general assumptions about the wormhole parameters, (1) there are *no* trajectories with zero multiplicity and (2) the multiplicity is also *not* one, but rather is always infinity! Thus, the billiard ball form of the grandfather paradox was found to be *not* well-defined, but not for the expected reason that there was no self-consistent solution, but instead because there were too many solutions.

However, this astonishing result, while completely unexpected, may in fact be just what is needed to support a continued study of time machines, i.e., it may allow a definition of "well-defined" in the Cauchy sense and still permit an answer to the free will question. The initial conditions of a time traveling ball give rise to an infinity of self-consistent trajectories, each occurring in the same way that a random variable takes on different values with each new performance of the experiment that the random variable is defined on. And yet, there are still unique probability density functions for all sets of measurements that one might make anywhere along these trajectories. Thus, the Cauchy problem is stochastically well-defined; at the start of any trajectory we do not know in detail what will happen (in a sense, this restores free will except that whatever does happen will be self-consistent). In this probabilistic sense then, wormhole time travel makes sense.

But how do we get a wormhole in the first place? As [Visser, 1989b] sums it up, "The big open question, naturally, is whether exotic matter is in fact obtainable in the laboratory. The theoretical problems are daunting, and the technological problems seem completely beyond our reach." Morris, Thorne, and Yurtsever have carefully acknowledged these problems, writing that it will take the skill of an "arbitrarily advanced civilization" to overcome them.[12]

Any such wormhole could, of course, be a very long way from Earth. It might be in another galaxy. So, even if it exists, what good would the wormhole do anybody? In a remarkable analysis [Lossev and Novikov, 1992] it is suggested such a wormhole might be very useful, even if its location is completely unknown! All that Lossev and Novikov assume is that the wormhole has existed for a sufficiently long time (what this means will be made explicit by the end of this Tech Note). With this assumption, they show how to make an information-creating time loop, the very sort of thing that David Deutsch argues against in Chapter Four (and which so many science fiction writers have used to good effect for decades, as also discussed in that chapter).

Lossev and Novikov begin their analysis by assuming that people have no knowledge of how to build a spacecraft that can make the interstellar voyage to the distant wormhole, even if they knew in which direction to go to reach the mouth that leads backward in time (mouth *B*). So, instead, they build an automatic spacecraft construction plant that can follow any detailed sequence of instructions provided to it, and they stockpile it with a supply of raw materials (energy, steel, plastic, computers, etc.) When the spacecraft construction is done, the last step before launching the spacecraft toward mouth B will be to load its on-board computer with the following three pieces of information:

a. the detailed sequence of instructions used for the construction of the spacecraft;

b. the direction from Earth to mouth B;

c. the direction from mouth A (the wormhole exit mouth into the past) back to Earth.

So, people build the automatic plant, load it up with raw materials, *and then withdraw.* This last step is crucial, as it eliminates human free will from further consideration, i.e., it removes any temptation to create a bilking paradox. So what happens next?

Lossev and Novikov suggest that what happens next is that a very old spacecraft suddenly appears in the sky and lands next to the automatic plant! In its on-board computer are items *a*, *b*, and *c*. Using item *a*, the automatic plant makes a new spacecraft, loads its new on-board computer with items *a*, *b*, and *c* from the very old spacecraft's computer, and then the new spacecraft is launched toward mouth B (using the information of item *b*). The very old spacecraft is given an honored place in a museum.

The new spacecraft arrives at the distant mouth B in the far future by when it is, of course, an old spacecraft (but not yet a very old one). It then plunges into mouth B and almost immediately emerges from mouth A, into the past. Indeed, it repeats this process as many times as required until it is in the far distant past, at a time even before it left the Earth.[13] Specifically, the spacecraft repeatedly uses the wormhole time machine until it is far enough in the past so that it can cruise back to Earth at normal speed (it knows the way back because of item *c*) and arrive as a very old spacecraft, just in time to be placed in the museum!

As Lossev and Novikov point out, this remarkable closed sequence of events has increased knowledge from what it was at the time just before the automatic plant was built.[14] People now know both how to build an interstellar spacecraft and the locations of both mouths of the wormhole. They also now possess a very old, used spacecraft. It is curious to note that while the information in the spacecraft's computer memory has traveled on a closed time loop, the spacecraft itself has not. This is because the spacecraft left Earth when new but arrived back (before it left) as very old, whereupon it promptly entered a museum. There is, therefore, no question about the origin of the very old spacecraft; but where did the information of items *a*, *b*, and *c* come from? Lossev and Novikov say it came from the energy gained by the spacecraft as it interacted (will interact?) with the rest of the Universe while on its journey.

As Lossev and Novikov also point out, however, all quantum mechanical considerations have been ignored in their analysis. As this book goes to press, they have promised a sequel analysis that will introduce the effects of quantum mechanics. Stay tuned!

NOTES

1. Such problems include the presence of a one-way event horizon, which precludes two-way travel (we assume that time and space travelers might wish to return), and enormous gravitational gradients (that is, tidal forces) that dismember (and worse) anything approaching and/or entering the hole. In fiction, of course, such problems are often ignored. For example, the time machine in *A Bridge of Years* [Wilson,1991] is in the form of a wormhole tunnel that time travelers can simply walk through!

2. "Quantum foam" refers to the idea that the topology of spacetime is always changing: the changes are topological fluctuations whose size is on the scale of the Planck length. Like the ocean surface at-large, large-scale spacetime is simply connected. But just as one sees all sorts of transient structure as one looks at the water more closely (beginning with waves and then the foam on the waves), spacetime too displays a fluctuating connectivity in-the-small. However, see [Anderson and DeWitt, 1986] for a rebuttal to the idea of changes in the topology of spacetime. (Also see [Gibbons and Hawking, 1992].) All is not lost for time travelers, however, as [Gott, 1991] gives a way to achieve closed timelike loops without either wormholes or topology changes. Gott gives exact solutions to Einstein's equations that (1) (unlike wormholes) do not violate the weak energy condition, (2) have no singularities or event horizons, and (3) are not topologically multiply connected. To achieve this, however, Gott requires either that two fast moving, parallel "cosmic strings" pass each other on a near collision course or that there be a closed-loop, elliptical string that collapses in a slightly nonplanar manner so that the opposite, nearly straight sides "just miss." (Cosmic strings are fantastically thin structures that are speculated to have formed at Big Bang time; according to current theories, they stretch the width of the Universe and have a linear mass-energy density on the order of a million billion tons per inch.) Gott showed that as the two strings pass, closed timelike loops encircle the strings. Later, [Ori, 1991a] pursued Gott's analysis in an attempt to see if these "time-travel paths" are created as the strings approach each other or if instead the paths exist at other times as well. This is an important question, as it gets to the idea of whether such paths can be used to create a time machine by a dynamical process or whether all such paths have existed since the formation of the Universe. Also, as Ori observes, this issue involves Hawking's so-called Chronology Protection Conjecture, which asserts that the laws of physics will always prevent the creation of a time machine. As discussed in Chapter One, one reason Hawking believes this assertion is because of the apparent absence of time travelers from the future among us now (in their past). The only possible exception allowed by the conjecture is closed-timelike-loop creation at the moment the Universe was created since at that unique moment there *was no past*. Ori proves that the closed timelike loops around Gott's cosmic strings are *always* present; i.e., a time machine is *not* created by the near-collision, and so Hawking's Conjecture is not refuted. (Cutler [1992] shows, however, that closed timelike-loops are not present everywhere in Gott's spacetime, i.e., that there are regions in Gott's spacetime that can be visited only once and where time travel would therefore be impossible.) Ori points out, however, that it is still an open question as to whether one can create closed timelike loops where none existed before by accelerating the two strings up to speed on their near-collision course. Another paper, [Carroll *et al.*, 1992], shows that Gott's "time machine" cannot be built in an open Universe that has a timelike total momentum (that is, in a Universe with subluminal net momentum). The authors show this by demon-

strating that Gott's cosmic strings as a pair have total tachyonic momentum (even though each string, individually, is subluminal), which they call "an insurmountable obstacle to building a time machine." A similar conclusion is reached in [Deser et al., 1992]. The question of what happens in a closed Universe is addressed in ['t Hooft, 1992], which shows that such a Universe would collapse in a Big Crunch before closed timelike loops could form. For a non-mathematical exposition on time travel via strings, see [Allen and Simon, 1992].

3. The equation for τ_0 given in [Morris and Thorne, 1988] is in units of dynes/cm^2, with b_0 expressed in meters. I have converted these units to the more familiar units of tons per square inch (with b_0 in units of feet) for dramatic purposes. The pressure (tension) unit of a dyne/cm^2 is so small that it relates to nothing of everyday significance.

4. To put this number in perspective, it is five million times greater than the Earth's magnetic field. To generate such a field artificially is not impossible, but it is presently strictly a laboratory exercise (e.g., electromagnetic railguns used as hypervelocity, armor-piercing antitank weapons use transient magnetic fields in the megagauss range). To understand how the calculation of a magnetic field is done from a pressure requirement, notice that pressure is dimensionally equivalent to field energy per unit volume, which in turn is given by a well-known result in electromagnetic theory.

5. Under everyday conditions, the exotic condition is never even remotely approached. For example, the maximum tension necessary to pull a piece of steel apart (the so-called tensile strength, of about 100,000 lbs/in^2) is a trillion times less than the mass-energy density of steel.

6. A complete presentation of Casimir's analysis (with citations to the original literature) can be found in L. E. Ballentine, Quantum Mechanics (Englewood Cliffs, NJ: Prentice-Hall 1990), 399–403. Robert Forward, an imaginative physicist who is an enthusiastic supporter of time travel (see Note 25 for Chapter Four), has described how the Casimir force might be used to extract energy literally from a vacuum! The theory of Forward's "vacuum-fluctuation battery" is given in his paper "Extracting Electrical Energy from the Vacuum by Cohesion of Charged Foliated Conductors," Physical Review B 30 (15 August 1984):1700–1702.

7. There are all sorts of weird aspects to this analysis, as one might suspect. For example, the authors assumed that the wormhole length is small compared to its radius, e.g. 10^{-10} cm long and 200 million miles wide! The short length is required, of course, as it represents the separation of the wormhole plates, and the smaller the separation the more negative the average energy density. (The functional dependence is as the inverse fourth power of the separation). Another problem is the balancing of the electrical repulsion and the gravitational attraction of the wormhole mouth plates. Such a balance is clearly an unstable one. Finally, since the two spherical plates completely fill the wormhole mouths, how would a traveler actually get through the wormhole? The "answer" is to drill a hole through the plates—and hope that doesn't perturb the Casimir vacuum too much! More recently, [Visser, 1989a,b] has shown how to build non-spherically symmetric wormholes that avoid this problem.

8. This may seem to be arguing for a Universe-wide now, a concept that Tech Note 1 argues has no meaning. All I mean here, however, is that if we take into account the various light-speed transit times between any pair of clocks and correct for these delays, then the clocks all agree. That is, an observer would be able to determine that the clocks were synchronized in the past. He would, of course, not be able to say they

are all synchronized *now* (until sometime later in the future, when *now* will have become a past *then*).

9. Frolov and Novikov [1990] actually show how to convert a wormhole to a time machine without moving either mouth—just place one mouth in an intense gravitational field (e.g., next to a neutron star) since this also leads to a time dilation effect (see [Dreitlein and Frazzini, 1975]). (For science fiction uses of this effect see "Neutron Star" [Niven, 1968] and "Kyrie" [Anderson, 1979].) As the authors put it, almost any interaction with surrounding matter and gravity fields almost inevitably turns a wormhole into a time machine. Visser, however, has recently argued that it is not the method of achieving time dilation that will cause trouble with wormhole time machines, but rather the positioning of the two mouths. His analysis [Visser, 1992] leads him to believe that the wormhole will inevitably be destroyed before the two mouths can be brought close enough together to create a time machine; i.e., sufficiently close that the trip in external space between the mouths is less than the time penetration into the past with each passage through the wormhole.

10. This name comes from the "Cauchy problem" (named after the nineteenth century French mathematician Augustin Cauchy) in the theory of partial differential equations. In this theory a Cauchy initial value problem is said to be well-defined if the initial conditions determine a unique solution *and* if a continuous variation in the initial conditions gives a continuous variation in the solution. In that part of spacetime where closed timelike loops are not allowed, backward causation does not occur (by definition), and the laws of physics (all expressed as differential equations) satisfy the Cauchy condition. Outside of this region (i.e., beyond the Cauchy horizon), however, the possibility of backward causation raises the possibility of violating the Cauchy condition. These ideas are central to Hawking's Chronology Protection Conjecture [Hawking, 1992]. His analysis leads him to conclude that a physical entity (the energy-momentum tensor) becomes unphysical on the Cauchy horizon. That is, because of time traveling quantum field fluctuations of the vacuum, that tensor diverges to infinity at the horizon. This results either in a failure of the horizon to form in the first place or, if it does form, in the creation of a singularity that "seals-off" the horizon to any would-be time travelers attempting to gain access to the closed timelike loops beyond the horizon. In a personal communication to me (12 August 1992) time machine pioneer Frank Tipler wrote "I think Hawking has taken too semi-classical a picture, and if you picture the Universe in a many-worlds way (like Deutsch ...) ... there will be no problem with the persistence of a Cauchy horizon in at least some of the worlds. "(See [Deutsch, 1991] and Note 14 of Chapter Four for Deutsch's and Tipler's favorable views of the many-worlds interpretation of quantum mechanics.) Tipler wrote this to me in response to my query about his recent paper [Tipler, 1992] in which he argues for the possibility that life could survive for an infinite (proper) time in a collapsing Universe, even when the radius has fallen below the Planck length. Tipler argues against the claim that quantum fluctuations would "preclude the existence of classical spacetime." My query to Tipler was if there might be a connection between the quantum fluctuations of time travel and of life in end-stage Universes. His reply: "I tend to agree with your opinion that there is a connection between whether quantum fluctuations wipe out a Cauchy horizon and whether they wipe out life near the final c-boundary [i.e., the end of future time]." A classic work on the mathematics of Cauchy problems is J. Hadamard, *Lectures on Cauchy's Problem in Linear Partial Differential Equations* (New York: Dover, 1952). There is a curious bit of irony in this.

In a section of his book, Hadamard uses spacetime to illustrate one possible four-dimensional space, and in passing he casually writes, "This conception was beautifully illustrated a good many years ago by the novelist Wells in his *Time Machine*." Hadamard wrote his book in 1923, and he would almost certainly have been astonished to have been informed that less than seventy years later his work would play a central role in the nonfictional theory of time machines. A more modern tutorial on the Cauchy problem is [Bruhat, GRAV].

11. The authors credit physicist/science fiction writer Robert Forward, who uses these ideas in his new novel *Timemaster* [Forward, 1992], for motivating part of their research. Most recently, [Lossev and Novikov, 1992] and [Mikheeva and Novikov, 1993] have continued this study of self-interacting billiard balls, with the additional complexity of nonelastic collisions and other forms of energy loss. This lets the authors study the thermodynamics of backward time travel.

12. The phrase "arbitrarily advanced civilization" was given some definition years ago by astrophysicists interested in the topic of extraterrestrial life. Very roughly, Type I, II, and III civilizations are those, respectively, of a contemporary terrestrial technology that could control a maximum of 10^{13} watts for interstellar radio broadcasts, a technology that could control the energy output of its parent star (10^{27} watts), and a technology that could control the energy output of its home galaxy (10^{38} watts). We are, today, clearly a long way short of being a Type II civilization, and it would probably take a Type III to build a wormhole. But, perhaps, there is no need for such a civilization, as a recent paper [Hochberg and Kephart, 1991] suggests wormholes may form naturally at any time. Using a quantum-mechanical process called vacuum squeezing (see [Cramer, 1992] for a nontechnical exposition on this), such wormholes require none of the exotic matter that was the main concern of Morris, Thorne, and Yurtsever. Indeed, vacuum squeezing automatically leads to negative energy densities and to an unavoidable violation of the weak energy condition. And so, recalling Tipler's quote at the start of this Tech Note, perhaps the dinosaurs *are* accessible!

13. To do this it might seem the spacecraft's computer memory needs a fourth piece of information; the direction from mouth A back to mouth B. But, in fact, items b and c are sufficient for the spacecraft to find its way from A to B. It is also now clear how long the wormhole must have been in existence.

14. Not surprisingly, not everybody finds such a tale convincing. One unimpressed analyst is research professor of physics Matt Visser at Washington University in St. Louis, whose support for Hawking's chronology protection conjecture is discussed in the Epilogue. When I asked Professor Visser what he thinks of time travel, he replied (personal communication, 24 August 1992), "If one insists permitting time travel in one's theories of the Universe, then Novikov's 'consistency conjecture' is probably the minimal modification of our current understanding of causality. I personally have a lot of trouble swallowing the "consistency conjecture" since it seems to me to be rather *ad hoc*. The "consistency conjecture" seems to me to essentially be equivalent to the statement: "the Universe IS consistent, no matter what, since it MUST be consistent, come hell or high water." I view this as begging the issue ... once one has opened Pandora's box by permitting time travel, I see no particular reason to believe that the only damage done to our notions of reality would be something as facile as the "consistency conjecture." Visser may well be right about time travel, of course, but I do think demanding consistency in the Universe is the *very heart* of physics. Without

consistency, physicists could not even have understandable debates about their disagreements!

Note added in proof: The latest word (as this book passes from my hands) on quantum mechanics and time travel is in a group of papers appearing in the 15 November 1992 issue of *Physical Review D* (volume 46). Showing the robust nature of the Cauchy horizon in Gott's cosmic string spacetime discussed in Note 2 is D. G. Boulware, "Quantum Field Theory in Spaces with Closed Timelike Curves," 4421–4441 ("there is no singularity in the stress energy [tensor] and, therefore, no mechanism for [Hawking's conjecture of] chronology protection"— recall Note 10). Another approach to the quantum mechanics of time travel involves the exploration of the property of unitarity in curved spacetimes; the scattering of interacting quantum fields is described by the so-called *S-matrix*, which is unitary in flat (uncurved) spacetimes. (A matrix is unitary if it is equal to the inverse of the complex conjugate of its transpose.) The physical problems associated with the failure of the S-matrix to be unitary in spacetimes with closed timelike curves (such as the apparent absence of self-consistent dynamics) are discussed in two papers; J. L. Friedman, N. J. Papastamatiou, and J. Z. Simon, "Failure of Unitarity for Interacting Fields on Spacetimes with Closed Timelike Curves," 4456–4469, and H. D. Politzer, "Simple Quantum Systems in Spacetimes with Closed Timelike Curves," 4470–4476. These papers, however, conclude that the inconsistency concerns can be answered via Feynman's famous "sum-over-histories" technique.

BIBLIOGRAPHY

Anthology codes:

AHT: *The Arbor House Treasury of Great Science Fiction Short Novels.* New York: Arbor House, 1980.

AO: *Alpha One.* Edited by R. Silverberg. New York: Ballantine, 1970.

BGA1: *Before the Golden Age.* Edited by I. Asimov. Vol. 1. New York: Doubleday, 1974.

BGA2: *Before the Golden Age.* Edited by I. Asimov. Vol. 2. New York: Doubleday, 1974.

BGA3: *Before the Golden Age.* Edited by I. Asimov. Vol. 3. New York: Doubleday, 1974.

BIPT: *Basic Issues in the Philosophy of Time.* Edited by E. Freeman and W. Sellars. LaSalle, IL: Open Court, 1971.

BSBSF: *The Bank Street Book of Science Fiction.* New York: Pocket, 1989.

BSFS2: *The Best from Fantasy and Science Fiction.* Vol. 2. Boston: Little, Brown, 1953.

BFSF3: *The Best from Fantasy and Science Fiction.* Vol. 3. Garden City, NY: Doubleday, 1954.

BML: *The Best of Murray Leinster.* Edited by B. Davis. London: Corgi, 1976.

BO: *The Best from Orbit.* Edited by D. Knight. New York: Berkley, 1975.

BRW: *The Best from the Rest of the World.* Edited by D. A. Wollheim. Garden City, NY: Doubleday, 1976.

BSF: *The Best of Science Fiction.* Edited by G. Conklin. New York: Crown, 1946.

BST: *Boston Studies in the Philosophy of Science.* Vol. 22. Boston: D. Reidel, 1976.

BT: *Beyond Time.* Edited by S. Ley. New York: Pocket, 1976.

BTS: *Beyond Time and Space.* Edited by A. Derleth. New York: Pellegrini and Cudahy, 1950.

CA: *Coming Attractions.* Edited by M. Greenberg. New York: Gnome, 1957.

CJSF: *Criminal Justice Through Science Fiction.* Edited by J. D. Olander and M. H. Greenberg. New York: New Viewpoints, 1977.

CPP: *Cosmology, Physics and Philosophy,* by B. Gal-Or. New York: Springer-Verlag, 1981.

CPT: *Causality and Physical Theories.* Edited by W. B. Rolnick. New York: American Institute of Physics, 1974.

D: *Dinosaurs!* Edited by J. Dann and G. Dozois. New York: Ace, 1990.

DD: *Deals with the Devil.* Edited by B. Davenport. New York: Dodd, Mead & Co., 1958.

DV: *Dangerous Visions.* Edited by H. Ellison. New York: Doubleday, 1967.

E: *Epoch.* Edited by R. Silverberg and R. Elwood. New York: Berkley, 1975.

ED: *The Expert Dreamers.* Edited by F. Pohl. Garden City, NY: Doubleday, 1962.

ET: *The Enigma of Time.* Edited by P. T. Landsberg. Bristol: Adam Hilger, 1982.

FCW: *The Fantastic Civil War.* Edited by F. McSherry, Jr. New York: Baen, 1991.

FM: *Fantasia Mathematica.* Edited by C. Fadiman. New York: Simon and Schuster, 1958.

FSFS: *Famous Science-Fiction Stories.* Edited by R. J. Healy and J. F. McComas. New York: Random House, 1957.

FST: *The Far Side of Time.* Edited by R. Elwood. New York: Dodd, Mead, 1974.

FTL: *Faster Than Light.* Edited by J. Dann and G. Zebrowski. New York: Harper & Row, 1976.

GG: *Grumbles from the Grave.* Edited by V. Heinlein. New York: Del Rey, 1990.

GRAV: *Gravitation: an introduction to current research.* Edited by L. Witten. New York: John Wiley, 1962.

GRSF7:   *The Seventh Galaxy Reader of Science Fiction.* Edited by F. Pohl. Garden City, NY: Doubleday, 1964.

GRSF2:   *The Second Galaxy Reader of Science Fiction.* Edited by H. L. Gold. New York: Crown, 1954.

GRSF1:   *The Galaxy Reader of Science Fiction.* Edited by H. L. Gold. New York: Crown, 1952.

GSF: *Great Science Fiction Stories by the World's Great Scientists.* Edited by I. Asimov, M. H. Greenberg, and C. G. Waugh. New York: Donald I. Fine, 1985.

GSFS: *Great Science Fiction by Scientists.* Edited by G. Conklin. New York: Collier, 1962.

GSSF: *Great Stories of Science Fiction.* Edited by M. Leinster. New York: Random House, 1951.

HJ: *Hibbert Journal.* Vol. 37. 1938–39.

HV: *Hitler Victorious.* Edited by G. Benford and M. H. Greenberg. New York: Berkley, 1987.

LDA: *Last Door to Aiya.* Edited by M. Ginsburg. New York: S. G. Phillips, 1968.

LME: *The Last Man on Earth.* Edited by I. Asimov, M. Greenberg, and C. Waugh. New York: Ballantine, 1982.

MBSFS: *My Best Science Fiction Story.* Edited by L. Margulies and O. J. Friend. New York: Merlin, 1949.

MDT: *Modern Developments in Thermodynamics.* Edited by B. Gal-Or. New York: John Wiley, 1974.

MI: *The Mirror of Infinity.* Edited by R. Silverberg. San Francisco: Canfield, 1970.

MM: *The Mathematical Magpie.* Edited by C. Fadiman. New York: Simon and Schuster, 1962.

MT: *Microcosmic Tales.* Edited by I. Asimov, M. Greenberg, and J. Olander. New York: Taplinger, 1980.

MTMW: *MATHENAUTS, Tales of Mathematical Wonder.* Edited by R. Rucker. New York: Arbor, 1987.

MWM: *Magic Without Magic: John Archibald Wheeler.* Edited by J. R. Klauder. San Francisco: W. H. Freeman, 1972.

NOT: *The Nature of Time.* Edited by R. Flood and M. Lockwood. Oxford: Basil Blackwell, 1986.

NT: *The Nature of Time.* Edited by T. Gold. Ithaca, NY: Cornell University Press, 1966.

NWF: *New Worlds of Fantasy.* Edited by T. Carr. New York: Ace, 1967.

NYAS: *Annals of the New York Academy of Science 138.* 6 Feb. 1967.

OSF: *Omnibus of Science Fiction.* Edited by G. Conklin. New York: Crown, 1952.

OW: *The Other Worlds.* Edited by P. Stong. Garden City, NY: Garden City Publishing, 1941.

PSF: *Prize Science Fiction.* Edited by D. A. Wollheim. New York: McBride, 1953.

PWO: *The Penguin World Onmibus of Science Fiction.* Edited by B. Aldiss and S. J. Lundwall. Middlesex: Penguin, 1986.

QCST: *Quantum Concepts in Space and Time.* Edited by R. Penrose and C. J. Isham. New York: Oxford University Press, 1986.

RAG: *Relativity and Gravitation.* Edited by C. G. Kuper and A. Peres. New York: Gordon and Breach Science Publishers, 1971.

RRSF: *Pre-Revolutionary Russian Science Fiction.* Edited by L. Fetzer. Ann Arbor, MI: Ardis, 1982.

S1:   *Stellar 1.* Edited by J.-L. del Rey. New York: Ballantine, 1974.

SFAD: *Science-Fiction Adventures in Dimension.* Edited by G. Conklin. New York: Vanguard, 1953.

SFD: *The Science Fictional Dinosaur.* Edited by R. Silverberg, C. Waugh, and M. Greenberg. New York: Avon, 1982.

SFF: *Science Fiction of the 40's.* Edited by F. Pohl. New York: Avon, 1978.

SFS: *101 Science Fiction Stories.* Edited by M. Greenberg and C. Waugh. New York: Avenel, 1986.

SFSSS: *100 Great Science Fiction Short Short Stories.* Edited by I. Asimov, M. Greenberg, and J. Olander. New York: Avon, 1978.

SFT: *Science Fiction of the 30's.* Edited by D. Knight. New York: Avon, 1975.

SS: *Starships.* Edited by I. Asimov, M. H. Greenberg, and C. G. Waugh. New York: Ballantine, 1983.

SSFT: *50 Short Science Fiction Tales.* Edited by I. Asimov and G. Conklin. New York: Macmillan, 1976.

TC: *The Time Curve.* Edited by S. Moskowitz and R. Elwood. New York:

Tower, 1968.

T3:   *The Time Travelers.* Edited by R. Silverberg and M. H. Greenberg. New York: Primus, 1985.

TOT: *Tales Out of Time.* Edited by B. Ireson. New York: Philomel, 1981.

TPR: *The Principle of Relativity.* Notes by A. Sommerfeld. New York: Dover, 1952.

TIT: *Trips in Time.* Edited by R. Silverberg. New York: Thomas Nelson, 1977.

TSF: *Treasury of Science Fiction.* Edited by G. Conklin. New York: Bonanza, 1980.

TT: *Time Travelers.* Edited by G. Dozois. New York: Ace, 1989.

TTT: *The Traps of Time.* Edited by M. Moorcock. Middlesex: Penguin, 1970.

TW: *Time Wars.* Edited by C. Waugh and M. H. Greenberg. New York: Tor, 1986.

TZ: *The Twilight Zone Companion,* by M. S. Zicree. New York: Bantam, 1982.

VIT: *Voyagers in Time.* Edited by R. Silverberg. New York: Meredith Press, 1967.

VOT: *The Voices of Time.* Edited by J. T. Fraser. New York: George Braziller, 1966.

WMHB: *What Might Have Been.* Edited by G. Benford and M. H. Greenberg. New York: Bantam, 1989.

WT: *Worlds of Tomorrow.* Edited by A. Derleth. New York: Pellegrini & Cudahy, 1953.

Authors:

Abbott, E. A. (1986). *Flatland.* New York: Penguin.

Abernathy, R. (OSF). "Heritage."

Abramenko, B. (1958). "On Dimensionality and Continuity of Physical Space and Time." *British Journal for the Philosophy of Science* 9 (August):89–109.

Abramowicz, M. A., and J. P. Lasota (1986). "On Traveling Round Without Feeling It and Uncurving Curves." *American Journal of Physics* 54 (October):936–939.

Aharonov, Y., J. Anandan, S. Popescu, and L. Vaidman (1990). "Superpositions of Time Evolutions of a Quantum System and a Quantum Time-Translation Machine." *Physical Review Letters* 64 (18 June):2965–2968.

Ahern, D. M. (1979). "Foreknowledge: Nelson Pike and Newcomb's Problem." *Religious Studies* 15 (December):475–490.

——— (1977). "Miracles and Physical Impossibility." *Canadian Journal of Philosophy* 7 (March):71–79.

Aichelburg, P. C., and R. Beig (1976). "Radiation Damping as an Initial Value Problem." *Annals of Physics* 98 (May):264–283.

Albert, D. (1986). "How To Take a Photograph of Another Everett World." *Annals of the New York Academy of Sciences* 480 (30 December):498–502.

Albrow, M. G. (1973). "CPT Conservation in the Oscillating Model of the Universe." *Nature Physical Science* 241 (15 January):56–57.

Aldiss, B. W. (1991). *Dracula Unbound*. New York: Harper Collins.

———— (SFD). "Poor Little Warrior!"

———— (1973). *Frankenstein Unbound*. New York: Random House.

———— (TTT). "Man in His Time."

———— (1967). *An Age*. London: Faber and Faber.

———— (1966). "T." In *First Flight*. Edited by D. Knight. New York: Lancer.

Alexander, L. (1963). *Time Cat*. New York: Holt, Rinehart, and Winston.

Alkon, P.K. (1987). *Origins of Futuristic Fiction*. Athens, GA: University of Georgia.

Allen, B., and J. Simon (1992). "Time Travel on a String." *Nature* 357 (7 May):19–21.

Allen, G. (BTS). "Pausodyne."

———— (1895). *British Barbarians*. London: John Lane.

Alvager, T., and M. N. Kreisler (1968). "Quest for Faster-Than-Light Particles." *Physical Review* 171 (25 July):1357–1361.

Amis, K. (1960). *New Maps of Hell*. New York: Harcourt Brace Jovanovitch.

Amiss, M. (1991). *Time's Arrow*. New York: Crown.

Anglin, W. S. (1981). "Backwards Causation." *Analysis* 41 (March):86–91.

Anderson, A., and B. DeWitt (1986). "Does the Topology of Space Fluctuate?" *Foundations of Physics* 16 (February):91–105.

Anderson, J. L. (1992). "Why We Use Retarded Potentials." *American Journal of Physics* 60 (May):465–467.

Anderson, K. J., and D. Beason (1991). *The Trinity Paradox*. New York: Bantam.

Anderson, M. (1937). *The Star-Wagon*. Washington, DC: Anderson House.

Anderson, P. (1991). "Earthman, Beware!" In *Alight in the Void*. New York: Tor.

———— (1988a). "The Man Who Came Early." In *The Great Science Fiction Stories*. Vol. 18. New York: DAW.

———— (1988b). "Delenda Est." In *The Great Science Fiction Stories*. Vol. 17. New York: DAW.

———— (SFS). "My Object All Sublime."

———— (SFD). "Wildcat."

———— (LME). "Flight to Forever."

———— (1981). "Time Patrol." In *The Guardians of Time*. New York: Pinnacle.

———— (1979). "Kyrie." In *The Road to Science Fiction*. Edited by J. Gunn. Vol. 3. New York: New American Library.

———— (1978). *The Avatar*. New York: Berkley.

———— (TIT). "The Long Remembering."

———— (FTL). "Dialogue."

———— (1973). "The Little Monster." In *Science Fiction Adventure from WAY OUT*. Edited by R. Elwood. Racine, WI: Whitman.

———— (1970). *Tau Zero*. Garden City, NY: Doubleday.

———— (1966). *The Corridors of Time*. New York: Lancer.

———— (1949). "Time Heals." *Astounding Science Fiction*, October.

Anonymous (1951). "Missing One's Coach: An Anachronism." In *Far Boundaries*. New York: Pellegrini & Cudahy.

Anonymous (1856). "January First, A.D. 3000." In *Harper's New Monthly Magazine* 12 (January):145–157.

Anscombe, G. E. M. (1971). "The Reality of the Past." In *Philosophical Analysis*. Edited by M. Black. Freeport, NY: Books for Libraries Press.

Anstey, F. (1891). *Tourmalin's Time Cheques*. New York: D. Appleton.

Apostolatos, T. A., and K. S. Thorne (1992). "Rotation Halts Cylindrical, Relativistic Gravitational Collapse." *Physical Review D* 46 (15 September):2435–2444.

Arntzenius, F. (1990). "Causal Paradoxes in Special Relativity." *British Journal for the Philosophy of Science* 41 (June):223–243.

Arons, M. E., and E. C. G. Sudarshan (1968). "Lorentz Invariance, Local Field Theory, and Faster-Than-Light Particles." *Physical Review* 173 (25 September):1622–1628.

Arthur, R. (1959). "The Hero Equation." *Fantasy and Science Fiction*, June.

_____ (1942). "Time Dredge." *Astounding Science Fiction*, June.

Ash, P. (SFD). "The Wings of a Bat."

Asimov, I. (SFSSS). "A Loint of Paw."

_____ (1988). "The Last Question." In *The Great Science Fiction Stories*. Vol. 18, New York: DAW.

_____ (SFS). "The Immortal Bard."

_____ (1986a). "When It Comes to Time Travel, There's No Time Like the Present." *New York Times*, 5 October, Sect. 2, pp. 1, 32.

_____ (1986b). *The End of Eternity*. New York: Del Rey/Ballantine.

_____ (T3). "The Ugly Little Boy."

_____ (1984a). "Faster Than Light." *Asimov's Science Fiction Magazine*, November.

_____ (1984b). "Time-Travel." *Asimov's Science Fiction Magazine*, April.

_____ (1984c). "The Winds of Change." In *The Winds of Change*. New York: Del Rey/Ballantine.

_____ (SFD). "A Statue for Father" and "Day of the Hunters."

_____ (AHT). "The Dead Past."

_____ (1975). "Button, Button" and "Blank!" In *Buy Jupiter and Other Stories*. Garden City, NY: Doubleday.

_____ (BGA3). "Big Game."

_____ (1972). "The Red Queen's Race," "Time Pussy," and "The Endochronic Properties of Resublimated Thiotimoline." In *The Early Asimov*. Vol. 2. Greenwich, CT: Fawcett Crest.

_____ (1968). "Impossible, That's All" In *Science, Numbers, and I*. New York: Doubleday.

_____ (SFAD). "What If ... ."

_____ (DD). "The Brazen Locked Room."

Aspect, A., *et al.* (1982a). "Experimental Test of Bell's Inequalities Using Time-Varying Analyzers." *Physical Review Letters* 49 (20 Dec.):1804–1807.

_____ (1982b). "Experimental Realization of Einstein-Podolsky-Rosen-Bohm *Gedankenexperiment*: A New Violation of Bell's Inequalities." *Physical Review Letters* 49 (12 July):91–94.

_____ (1981). "Experimental Tests of Realistic Local Theories via Bell's Theorem." *Physical Review Letters* 47 (17 August):460–467.

Augustynek, Z. (1976). "Past, Present and Future in Relativity." *Studia Logica* 35:45–53.

Baierlein, R. F., D. H. Sharp, and J. A. Wheeler (1962). "Three-Dimensional Geometry as Carrier of Information about Time." *Physical Review* 126 (1 June):1864–1865.

Bailey, J. O. (1972). *Pilgrims Through Space and Time*. Westport, CT: Greenwood Press.

Baker, A. (1970). "Time Reversal." In *Modern Physics and Antiphysics*. Reading, MA: Addison-Wesley.

Baker, G. L. (1986). "A Simple Model of Irreversibility." *American Journal of Physics* 54 (August):704–708.

Baker, J. R. (1972). "Omniscience and Divine Synchronization." *Process Studies* 2 (Fall):201–208.

Baker, L. R. (1975). "Temporal Becoming: The Argument from Physics." *Philosophical Forum* 6 (Spring):218–236.

Balderston, J. L. (1941). *Berkeley Square*. New York: Macmillan.

Ball, W. W. R. (1891). "A Hypothesis Relating to the Nature of the Ether and Gravity." *Messenger of Mathematics* 21:20–24.

Ballard, J. G. (1978). "Time of Passage." In *Time of Passage*. New York: Taplinger.

———— (1971). "The Sound-Sweep" and "Chronopolis." In *Chronopolis*. New York: G. P. Putnam's Sons.

———— (TTT). "Mr F is Mr F."

———— (NWF). "The Lost Leonardo."

Band, W. (1988a). "Can Information Be Transferred Faster Than Light? II. The Relativistic Doppler Effect on Electromagnetic Wave Packets with Suboptic and Superoptic Group Velocities." *Foundations of Physics* 18 (June):625–638.

———— (1988b). "Can Information Be Transferred Faster Than Light? A *Gedanken* Device for Generating Electromagnetic Wave Packets with Superoptic Group Velocity." *Foundations of Physics* 18 (May):549–562.

Banerjee, A., and S. Banerji (1968). "Stationary Distributions of Dust and Electromagnetic Fields in General Relativity." *Journal of Physics A* (*Proceedings of the Physical Society*) 1:188–193.

Banks, R. A. (1961). "This Side Up." In *The Fifth Galaxy Reader*. Edited by H. L. Gold. Garden City, NY: Doubleday.

Barr, R. (1989). "The Hour Glass." In *The Strong Arm*. New York: Frederick A. Stokes.

Barron, N. (1987). *Anatomy of Wonder: A Critical Guide to Science Fiction*. 3d ed. New York: R. R. Bowker.

Barrow, J. D., and F. J. Tipler (1978). "Eternity is Unstable." *Nature* 276 (30 November):453–459.

Bartlett, A. A. (1974). "A Simple Problem from the Real World That Can be Solved through Time Reversal." *American Journal of Physics* 42 (May):416–417.

Bass, R. W., and L. Witten (1957). "Remark on Cosmological Models." *Reviews of Modern Physics* 29 (July):452–453.

Bates, H. (SFT). "Alas, All Thinking"

Bayley, B. J. (1974). *The Fall of Chronopolis*. New York: DAW.

Bear, G. (MTMW). "Tangents."

Beason, D. (1990). "Ben Franklin's Laser." *Analog*, Mid-December.

Beerbohm, M. (DD). "Enoch Soames."

Beichler, J. E. (1988). "Ether/Or: Hyperspace Models of the Ether in America." In *The Michelson Era in American Science 1870–1930*. Edited by S. Goldberg and R. H. Stuewer. New York: American Institute of Physics.

Belinfante, F. J. (1966). "Kruskal Space Without Wormholes." *Physics Letters* 20 (15 January):25–26.

Bell, E. T. (1934). *Before the Dawn*. Baltimore: Williams & Wilkins.

———— (1931). *The Time Stream*. Providence, RI: Buffalo Book Co.

Bell, J. (1979). "The Infinite Past Regained: a reply to Whitrow." *British Journal for the Philosophy of Science* 30 (June):161–165.

Bell, J. S. (1987). "Quantum Mechanics for Cosmologists," "On the Einstein-Podolsky-Rosen Paradox" and "Bertlmann's Socks and the Nature of Reality." In *Speakable and*

Unspeakable in Quantum Mechanics. New York: Cambridge University Press.

Bellairs, J. (1989). *The Trolley to Yesterday*. New York: Dial.

Bellamy, E. (1983). *Looking Backward, 2000–1887*. New York: Bantam.

Benford, G. (1991). "Down the River Road." In *After the King*. Edited by C. Tolkien and M. Greenberg. New York: Tor.

———— (HV). "Valhalla."

———— (1986). "Time Shards." In *In Alien Flesh*. New York: Tor.

———— (1980). *Timescape*. New York: Simon and Schuster.

———— (E). "Cambridge, 1:58 A.M."

———— (1970). "3:02 P.M., Oxford." *If*, September.

Benford, G. A., D. L. Book, and W. A. Newcomb (1970). "The Tachyonic Antitelephone." *Physical Review D* 2 (15 July):263–265.

Bennett, J. G., *et al.* (1949). "Unified Field Theory in a Curvature-Free Five-Dimensional Manifold." *Proceedings of the Royal Society of London* 198A (July):39–61.

Berenda, C. W. (1947). "The Determination of Past by Future Events: A Discussion of the Wheeler-Feynman Absorbtion-Radiation Theory." *Philosophy of Science* 14:13–19.

Berger, G. (1971). "Earman on Temporal Anisotropy." *Journal of Philosophy* 68 (11 March):132–137.

———— (1968). "The Conceptual Possibility of Time Travel." *British Journal for the Philosophy of Science* 19:152–155.

Berger, T. (1989). *Changing the Past*. Boston: Little, Brown.

Bergonzi, B. (1960). "*The Time Machine*: An Ironic Myth." *Critical Quarterly* 2 (Winter):293–305.

Bergson, H. (1965). *Duration and Simultaneity*. New York: Bobbs-Merrill.

———— (1910). *Time and Free Will*. New York: Macmillan.

Bernal, A. W. (1940). "Paul Revere and the Time Machine." *Amazing Stories*, March.

Bers, A., *et al.* (RAG). "The Impossibility of Free Tachyons."

Bester, A. (1986). "Hobson's Choice." *The Great Science Fiction Stories*, Vol. 14. New York: DAW.

———— (1983). "Of Time and Third Avenue." In *Magic for Sale*. Edited by A. Davidson. New York: Ace.

———— (VIT). "The Men Who Murdered Mohammed."

Besterman, T. (1933). "Report of an Inquiry into Precognitive Dreams." *Proceedings of the Society for Psychical Research* 41:186–204.

Bierce, A. (1964). "An Occurrence at Owl Creek Bridge," "The Damned Thing," and "Mysterious Disappearances." In *Ghost and Horror Stories of Ambrose Bierce*. New York: Dover.

Biggle, L. Jr. (1967). "D.F.C." In *The Rule of the Door*. New York: Doubleday.

———— (1965). *The Fury Out of Time*. Garden City, NY: Doubleday.

Bilaniuk, O. M., and E. C. G. Sudarshan (1969a). "Particles Beyond the Light Barrier." *Physics Today*, 22 (May):43–51 [and the discussion that resulted in *Physics Today*, 22 (December):47–52].

———— (1969b). "Causality and Space-like Signals." *Nature* 223 (26 July):386–387.

Bilaniuk, O. M. P., V. K. Deshpande, and E. C. G. Sudarshan (1962). " 'Meta' Relativity." *American Journal of Physics* 30 (October):718–723.

Bilenkin, D. (1978). "The Uncertainty Principle," "Time Bank" and "The Inexorable Finger of Fate." In *The Uncertainty Principle*. New York: Macmillan.

Binder, E. (1953). "The Time Cylinder." *Science Fiction Plus*, March.

_____ (1940). "The Time Cheaters." *Thrilling Wonder Stories*, March.

_____ (1939). "The Man Who Saw Too Late." *Fantastic Adventures*, September.

_____ (1938). "Eye of the Past." *Astounding Science Fiction*, March.

Birch, P. (1982). "Is the Universe Rotating?" *Nature* 298 (29 July):451–454.

Birrell, N. D., and P. C. W. Davies (1978). "On Falling Through a Black Hole Into Another Universe." *Nature* 272 (2 March):35–37.

Bishop, N. T. (1988). "Is Superluminal Travel a Theoretical Possibility? II." *Foundations of Physics* 18 (May):571–574.

_____ (1984). "Is Superluminal Travel a Theoretical Possibility?" *Foundations of Physics* 14 (April):333–340.

Bixby, J. (1954). "One Way Street." *Amazing Stories*, January.

Black, M. (1959a). "Linguistic Relativity: The Views of Benjamin Lee Whorf." *Philosophical Review* 68:228–238.

_____ (1959b). "The 'Direction' of Time." *Analysis* 19 (January):54–63.

Blackford, R. (1985). "Physics and Fantasy: Scientific Mysticism, Kurt Vonnegut, and *Gravity's Rainbow*." *Journal of Popular Culture* 19 (Winter):35–44.

Blackwood, A. (1949). "Entrance and Exit" and "The Pikestaffe Case." In *Tales of the Uncanny and Supernatural*. London: Peter Nevill.

Blatt, J. M. (1956). "Time Reversal." *Scientific American*, August.

Blandford, R. D., C. F. McKee, and M. J. Rees (1977). "Super-luminal Expansion in Extragalactic Radio Sources." *Nature* 267 (19 May):211–216.

Blaylock, J. P. (1992). *Lord Kelvin's Machine*. New York: Ace.

Bleiler, E. F. (1990). *Science-Fiction: the early years*. Kent, OH: Kent State University Press.

Bloch, R. (DV). "A Toy for Juliette."

_____ (GRSF7). "Crime Machine."

Blish, J. (1976). "Beep." In *Galactic Empires*. Edited by B. W. Aldiss. Vol. 2. New York: St. Martin's Press.

_____ (MI). "Common Time."

_____ (1956). "A Matter of Energy." In *The Best from Fantasy and Science Fiction*. Edited by A. Boucher. Garden City, NY: Doubleday.

_____ (1942). "The Solar Comedy." *Future Fiction*, June.

_____ (1941). "Weapon Out of Time." *Science Fiction Quarterly*, Spring.

Bludman, S. A., and M. A. Ruderman (1970). "Noncausality and Instability in Ultradense Matter." *Physical Review D* 1 (15 June):3243–3246.

_____ (1968). "Possibility of the Speed of Sound Exceeding the Speed of Light in Ultradense Matter." *Physical Review* 170 (25 June):1176–1184.

Blumenthal, H. J., *et al.* (1988). *The Complete Time Traveler*. Berkeley, CA: Ten Speed Press.

Bohm, D. (BST). "Inadequacy of Laplacean Determinism and Irreversibility of Time."

Bond, N. (1946). "The Magic Staircase," "Johnny Cartwright's Camera," "The Einstein Inshoot," "Dr. Fuddle's Fingers," and "The Bacular Clock." In *Mr. Mergenthwirker's Lobblies and Other Fantastic Tales*. New York: Coward-McCann.

_____ (1942). "Horsesense Hank in the Parallel Worlds." *Amazing Stories*, August.

_____ (1941a). "The Geometrics of Johnny Day." *Astounding Science Fiction*, July.

_____ (1941b). "The Fountain." *Unknown*, June.

_____ (1939a). "The Monster From Nowhere." *Fantastic Adventures*, July.

_____ (1939b). "Lightship, Ho!" *Astounding Science Fiction*, July.

Borges, J. L. (1972). *Doctor Brodie's Report*. New York: E. P. Dutton.

———— (1970). "The Other Death." In *The Aleph and Other Stories 1933–1969*. New York: E. P. Dutton.

———— (1964). "The Garden of Forking Paths." In *Labyrinths*. New York: New Directions.

———— (1962). "The Secret Miracle." In *Ficciones*. New York: Grove.

Bork, A. M. (1966). "The 'Fitzgerald' Contraction." *Isis* 57:199–207.

———— (1964). "The Fourth Dimension in Nineteenth-Century Physics." *Isis* 55 (October):326–338.

Boucher, A. (1980a). "Barrier." In *The Great Science Fiction Stories*. Vol. 4. New York: DAW.

———— (1980b). "Snulbug." In *The Great Science Fiction Stories*. Vol. 3. New York: DAW.

———— (1953). "Elsewhen" and "The Other Inauguration." In *Far and Away*. New York: Ballantine.

———— (GSSF). "The Chronokinesis of Jonathan Hull."

Boulle, P. (1966). "Time Out of Mind." In *Time Out of Mind*. New York: Vanguard Press.

Boussenard, L. (1898). *10,000 Years in a Block of Ice*. New York: F. T. Neely.

Bradbury, R. (1988). "The Toynbee Convector." In *The Toynbee Convector*. New York: Knopf.

———— (TOT). "The Shape of Things."

———— (1981). "Forever and the Earth." In *Sinister, Strange and the Supernatural*. Edited by H. Hoke. New York: Elsevier/Nelson.

———— (1980). "A Sound of Thunder," "The Fox and the Forest," "Tomorrow's Child," and "A Scent of Sarsaparilla." In *The Stories of Ray Bradbury*. New York: Alfred A. Knopf.

———— (1966). "Time in Thy Flight." In *S is for Space*. Garden City, NY: Doubleday & Co.

———— (1950). *The Martian Chronicles*. New York: Doubleday.

Bradley, R. D. (1959). "Must the Future Be What It is Going to Be?" *Mind* 68 (April):193–208.

Brams, S. J. (1983). "Omniscience and Partial Omniscience." In *Superior Beings*. New York: Springer-Verlag.

Brennan, A. (1982). "Personal Identity and Personal Survival." *Analysis* 42 (January):44–50.

Brennert, A. (1990). *Time and Chance*. New York: Tor.

Bretnor, R. (1956). "The Past and Its Dead People." *Fantasy and Science Fiction*, September.

Breuer, M. J. (MM). "The Appendix and the Spectacles."

———— (GSFS). "The Gostak and the Doshes."

———— (FM). "The Captured Cross-Section."

———— (1932a). "The Finger of the Past." *Amazing Stories*, November.

———— (1932b). "The Einstein See-Saw." *Astounding Stories*, April.

———— (1930a). "The Time Valve." *Wonder Stories*, July.

———— (1930b). "The FitzGerald Contraction." *Science Wonder Stories*, January.

Bridge, F. J. (1931). "Via the Time Accelerator." *Amazing Stories*, January.

Brier, B. (1973). "Magicians, Alarm Clocks, and Backward Causation." *Southern Journal of Philosophy* 11:359–364 (and the reply by A. Flew, 11:365–366).

Brill, D. (MWM). "Thoughts on Topology Change."

Broad, C. D. (1937). "The Philosophical Implications of Foreknowledge." *Aristotelian Society Supplement* 16:177–209.

———— (1935). "Mr. Dunne's Theory of Time in *An Experiment With Time*." *Philosophy* 10:168–185.

Broad, C. D., and H. H. Price (1937). "The Philosophical Implications of Precognition." *Aristotelian Society Supplement* 16:211–228.

Broido, M. M., and J. G. Taylor (1968). "Does Lorentz-Invariance Imply Causality?" *Physical Review* 174 (25 October):1606–1610.

Brotman, H. (1952). "Could Space Be Four Dimensional?" *Mind* 61 (July):317–327.

Brown, F. (1986). "Hall of Mirrors." *The Great Science Fiction Stories*. Vol. 15. New York: DAW.

———— (MT). "Nightmare in Time."

———— (1977). "The Short Happy Lives of Eustace Weaver I, II, and III" and "The End." In *The Best of Fredric Brown*, New York: Ballantine.

———— (1958). "First Time Machine," "Blood," and "Experiment." In *Honeymoon in Hell*. New York: Bantam.

———— (1953). "Paradox Lost." In *Science Fiction Carnival*. Chicago: Shasta.

Brown, G. (1985). "Praying About the Past." *Philosophical Quarterly* 35 (January):83–86.

Bruhat, Y. (GRAV). "The Cauchy Problem."

Brumbaugh, R. S. (1980). "Time Passes: Platonic Variations." *Review of Metaphysics* 33 (June):711–726.

Brunner, J. (FST). "Lostling."

———— (1965). "Galactic Consumer Reports No. 1 -- Inexpensive Time Machines." *Galaxy Science Fiction*, December.

Brush, S. G. (1967). "Note on the History of the FitzGerald-Lorentz Contraction." *Isis* 58:230–232.

Bryant, E. (MT). "Paths."

Buchan, J. (1932). *The Gap in the Curtain*. London: Hodder and Stoughton.

Buck, D. P. (SS). "Story of a Curse."

Bulgarin, F. (RRSF). "Plausible Fantasies or a Journey in the 29th Century."

Bunge, M. (1958). "On Multi-dimensional Time." *British Journal for the Philosophy of Science* 9 (May):39.

Burger, D. (1983). *Sphereland*. New York: Harper & Row.

Busby, F. M. (1987). "A Gun for Grandfather" and "Proof." In *Getting Home*. New York: Ace.

Byram, G. (FCW). "The Chronicle of the 656th."

Cabot, J. Y. (1941). "Murder in the Past." *Amazing Stories*, March.

Cahn, S. M. (1967). *Fate, Logic, and Time*. New Haven, CT: Yale University Press.

Calinon, A. (BST). "Geometrical Spaces."

Callahan, J. F. (1948). *Four Views of Time in Ancient Philosophy*. Cambridge: Harvard University Press.

Campbell, J. W., Jr. (1948). "Twilight," "Night," and "Elimination." In *Who Goes There?* Chicago: Shasta.

Capek, M. (1987). "The Conflict Between the Absolutist and the Relational Theory of Time Before Newton." *Journal of the History of Ideas* 48 (October–December):595–608.

———— (1983). "Time-Space Rather Than Space-Time." *Diogenes* 123 (Fall):30–49.

———— (BST). "The Inclusion of Becoming in the Physical World."

_____ (1975). "Relativity and the Status of Becoming." *Foundations of Physics* 5 (December):607–617.

_____ (VOT). "Time in Relativity Theory: Arguments for a Philosophy of Becoming."

_____ (1965). "The Myth of Frozen Passage: The Status of Becoming in the Physical World." In *Boston Studies in the Philosophy of Science*. Vol. 2. New York: Humanities Press.

Carpentier, A. (1967). "Journey to the Seed." In *Latin American Writing Today*. Edited by J. M. Cohen. Baltimore, MD: Penguin.

Carr, J. D. (1951). *The Devil in Velvet*. New York: Harper & Brothers.

Carroll, J. A. (1959). "An Absolute Scale of Time." *Nature* 184 (25 July):260–261.

Carroll, S. M., et al. (1992). "An Obstacle to Building a Time Machine." *Physical Review Letters* 68 (20 January):263–266.

Carter, B. (1968). "Global Structure of the Kerr Family of Gravitational Fields." *Physical Review* 174 (25 October):1559–1571.

Carter, P. (1950). "Ounce of Prevention." *Fantasy and Science Fiction*, Summer.

Carter, P. A. (1977). *The Creation of Tomorrow*. New York: Columbia University Press.

Cartur, P. (SSFT). "The Mist."

Casella, R. C. (1969). "Time Reversal and the K° Meson Decays. II." *Physical Review Letters* 22 (17 March):554–556.

_____ (1968). "Time Reversal and the K° Meson Decays." *Physical Review Letters* 21 (7 October):1128–1131.

Causey, J. (SSFT). "Teething Ring."

Chakrabarti, S. K., et al. (1983). "Timelike Curves of Limited Acceleration in General Relativity." *Journal of Mathematical Physics* 24 (March):597–598.

Champlin, C. (1989). *Back There Where the Past Was*. Syracuse, NY: Syracuse University Press.

Chandler, A. B. (1978). *The Way Back*. New York: DAW.

_____ (1948). "The Tides of Time." *Fantastic Adventures*, June.

Chandrasekhar, S. (NT). "Geodesics in Gödel's Universe."

Chandrasekhar, S., and J. P. Wright (1961). "The Geodesics in Gödel's Universe." *Proceedings of the National Academy of Sciences* 47 (March):341–347.

Chari, C. T. K. (1960). "Time Reversal, Information Theory, and 'World-Geometry'." *Journal of Philosophy* 60 (26 September):579–583.

_____ (1957). "A Note on Multi-dimensional Time." *British Journal for the Philosophy of Science* 8 (August):155–158.

_____ (1949). "On Representations of Time as 'The Fourth Dimension' and Their Metaphysical Inadequacy." *Mind* 58 (April):218–221.

Christensen, F. (1981). "Special Relativity and Space-like Time." *British Journal for the Philosophy of Science* 32 (March):37–53.

_____ (1976). "The Source of the River of Time." *Ratio* 18 (December):131–144.

_____ (1974). "McTaggart's Paradox and the Nature of Time." *Philosophical Quarterly* 24 (October):289–299.

Christenson, J. H., et al. (1964). "Evidence for the 2π Decay of the K°_2 Meson." *Physical Review Letters* 13 (27 July):138–140.

Christodoulou, D. (1984). "Violation of Cosmic Censorship in the Gravitational Collapse of a Dust Cloud." *Communications in Mathematical Physics*, 93:171–195.

Chyba, C. F. (1985). "Kaluza-Klein Unified Field Theory and Apparent Four-Dimensional Space-Time." *American Journal of Physics* 53 (September):863–872.

Clarke, A. C. (1985). "About Time." In *Profiles of the Future*. New York: Warner.

———— (SFF). "Technical Error."

———— (FTL). "Possible, That's All!."

———— (1972). "Things That Can Never Be Done" and "Technology and the Future." In *Report on Planet Three and Other Speculations*, New York: Harper & Row.

———— (1959a). "Time's Arrow." In *Across the Sea of Stars*. New York: Harcourt, Brace & World.

———— (1959b). "The Wall of Darkness." In *The Other Side of the Sky*. New York: New American Library.

———— (PSF). "All the Time in the World."

Clarke, C. J. S. (1990). "Opening a Can of Wormholes." *Nature* 348 (22 November):287–288.

Clay, R. W., and P. C. Crouch (1974). "Possible Observation of Tachyons Associated with Extensive Air Showers." *Nature* 248 (1 March):28–30.

Cleugh, M. F. (1937). *Time and Its Importance in Modern Thought*. London: Methuen.

Click, J. H. (1929). "The Dimension Segregator." *Amazing Stories*, August.

Clifford, W. K. (BST). "On the Bending of Space" and "On the Space-Theory of Matter."

Clifton, M. (MM). "Star, Bright."

Clingerman, M. (SSFT). "Stair Trick."

———— (1958). "The Day of the Green Velvet Cloak." *Fantasy and Science Fiction*, July.

Coates, P. (1987). "Chris Marker and the Cinema as Time Machine." *Science-Fiction Studies* 14 (November):307–315.

Cobb, J. B. (1965). *A Christian Natural Theology*. Philadelphia: Westminster Press.

Coblentz, S. A. (1938). "Through the Time-Radio." *Marvel Science Stories*, August.

Cocke, W. J. (1967). "Statistical Time Symmetry and Two-Time Boundary Conditions in Physics and Cosmology." *Physical Review* 160 (25 August):1165–1170.

Coe, L. (1969). "The Nature of Time." *American Journal of Physics* 37 (August):810–815.

Cogswell, T. R. (DD). "Threesie" and "Impact with the Devil."

———— (GRSF2). "Minimum Sentence."

Cohen, J. M. (RAG). "The Rotating Einstein-Rosen Bridge."

Collins, L. (1959). "Triple-Time Try." *Amazing Stories*, October.

Compton, D. G. (1971). *Hot Wireless Sets, Aspirin Tablets, the Sandpaper Sides of Used Matchboxes, and Something that Might Have Been Castor Oil*. London: Michael Joseph.

Conrad, P. (1990). *Stonewords*. New York: Harper & Row.

Contento, W. (1978). *Index to Science Fiction Anthologies and Collections*. Boston, MA: G. K. Hall & Co.

Cook, G. (1985). *A Matter of Time*. New York: Ace.

Cook, M. (1982). "Tips for Time Travel." In *Philosophers Look at Science Fiction*. Edited by N. D. Smith. Chicago: Nelson-Hall.

Cooper, J. C. (1979). "Have Faster-Than-Light Particles Already Been Detected?" *Foundations of Physics* 9 (June):461–466.

Corben, H. C. (1976). "Thought Experiments at Superluminal Relative Velocities." *International Journal of Theoretical Physics* 15 (September):703–712.

Costello, M. J. (1990). *Time of the Fox*. New York: Penguin.

Cottle, T. J. (1976). "Fantasies of Temporal Recovery and Knowledge of the Future." In *Perceiving Time*. New York: John Wiley.

Cowper, R. (1977). "The Hertford Manuscript." In *The Best From Fantasy and Science*

Fiction. Edited by E. L. Ferman. Vol. 22. Garden City, NY: Doubleday.

Cox, A. J. (1950). "Linguistics and Time." *Astounding Science Fiction,* August.

Craig, W. L. (1990). " 'What Place, Then, for a Creator?': Hawking on God and Creation." *British Journal for the Philosophy of Science* 41 (December):473–491.

———— (1988). "Tachyons, Time Travel, and Divine Omniscience." *Journal of Philosophy* 85 (March):135–150.

———— (1986). "God, Creation and Mr. Davies." *British Journal for the Philosophy of Science* 37 (June):163–175.

———— (1985). "Was Thomas Aquinas a B-Theorist of Time?" *New Scholasticism* 59 (Autumn):475–483.

———— (1981). "The Finitude of the Past." *Aletheia* 2, 235–242.

———— (1980). "Julian Wolfe and Infinite Time." *International Journal for Philosophy of Religion* 11, 133–135.

———— (1979). "Whitrow and Popper on the Impossibility of an Infinite Past." *British Journal for the Philosophy of Science* 29 (June):165–170.

———— (1978). "God, Time, and Eternity." *Religious Studies* 14 (December): 497–503.

Cramer, J. G. (1992). "Natural Wormholes: Squeezing the Vacuum." *Analog,* July.

———— (1991a). "Quantum Telephones to Other Universes, to Times Past." *Analog,* October.

———— (1991b). "Quantum Time Travel." *Analog,* April.

———— (1991c). *Twistor.* New York: Avon.

———— (1990a). "More About Wormholes—To the Stars in No Time." *Analog,* May.

———— (1990b). "The Twin Paradox Revisited." *Analog,* March.

———— (1989). "Wormholes and Time Machines." *Analog,* June.

———— (1988a). "Velocity Reversal and the Arrows of Time." *Foundations of Physics* 18 (December):1205–1212.

———— (1988b). "Paradoxes and FTL Communication." *Analog,* September.

———— (1985a). "Light in Reverse Gear." *Analog,* August.

———— (1985b). "The Other Forty Dimensions." *Analog,* April.

———— (1983). "The Arrow of Electromagnetic Time and the Generalized Absorber Theory." *Foundations of Physics* 13 (September):887–902.

———— (1980). "Generalized Absorber Theory and the Einstein-Podolsky-Rosen Paradox." *Physical Review D* 22 (15 July):362–376.

Crawford, F. S. (1973). "Simple Demonstration of Time-Reversal Invariance in Classical Mechanics." *American Journal of Physics* 41 (April):574–577.

Crowley, J. (1991). *Great Work of Time.* New York: Bantam.

Csonka, P. L. (1970). "Causality and Faster-Than-Light Particles." *Nuclear Physics B* 21 (15 August):436–444.

———— (1969). "Advanced Effects in Particle Physics." *Physical Review* 180 (25 April):1266–1281.

———— (1967). "Are Photon-Photon Scattering Experiments Feasible? "*Physics Letters B* 24 (12 June):625–628.

Cummings, R. (1946). *The Shadow Girl.* London: Gerald G. Swan.

———— (1929). *The Man Who Mastered Time.* Chicago: A. C. McClurg.

———— (1921). "The Time Professor." *Argosy-All-Story,* 1 January.

Currie, G. (1992). "McTaggart at the Movies." *Philosophy* 67 (July):343–355.

Curry, T. (1931). "Hell's Dimension." *Astounding Stories,* April.

Cutkosky, R. E. (1970). "Macroscopic Properties of Dense Noncausal Matter." *Physical*

Review D 2 (15 October):1386–1389.

Cutler, C. (1992). "Global Structure in Gott's Two-String Spacetime." *Physical Review D* 45 (15 January):487–494.

Dales, R. C. (1988). "Time and Eternity in the Thirteenth Century." *Journal of the History of Ideas* 49 (January–March):27–45.

Dalkey, K. (1991). "You Want It *When?*" In *2041*. Edited by J. Yolen. New York: Delacorte.

Daniels, D. R. (1935). "The Branches of Time." *Wonder Stories*, August.

Datta, A., D. Home, and A. Raychaudhuri (1987). "A Curious Gedanken Example of the Einstein-Podolsky-Rosen Paradox Using CP Nonconservation." *Physics Letters A* 123 (13 July):4–8.

Davies, P. C. W. (1983). *God and the New Physics*. New York: Simon & Schuster.

———— (ET). "Black Hole Thermodynamics and Time Asymmetry."

———— (1981). *The Edge of Infinity*. New York: Simon & Schuster.

———— (1977). *The Physics of Time Asymmetry*. Los Angeles: University of California Press.

———— (1972a). "Is the Universe Transparent or Opaque?" *Journal of Physics A* 5 (December):1722–1737.

———— (1972b). "Closed Time as an Explanation of the Black Body Background Radiation." *Nature Physical Science* 240 (November):3–5.

Dawson, J. H. (1989). "Kurt Gödel in Sharper Focus." In *Gödel's Theorem in Focus*. Edited by S. G. Shanker. London: Routledge.

Day, D. B. (1952). *Index to the Science-Fiction Magazines 1926–1950*. Portland, OR: Perri Press.

De, U. K. (1969). "Paths in Universes Having Closed Time-Like Lines." *Journal of Physics A*, 2:427–432.

de Beauregard, O. Costa (1987). *Time, the Physical Magnitude*. Boston: D. Reidel.

———— (1980). "A Burning Question: Einstein's Paradox of Correlations." *Diogenes* No. 110 (Summer):83–97.

———— (1977). "Two Lectures on the Direction of Time." *Synthese* 35 (June):129–154.

———— (NYAS). "Two Principles of the Science of Time."

De Brandt, D. H. (1992). *The Quicksilver Screen*. New York: Del Rey.

de Camp, L. Sprague (1981). "Some Curious Effects of Time Travel." In *Analog Readers' Choice*, New York: Dial.

———— (1979). "Balsamo's Mirror." In *The Purple Pterodactyls*. Huntington Woods, MI: Phantasia Press.

———— (1978). "Language for Time Travelers" and "A Gun for Dinosaur." In *The Best of L. Sprague de Camp*. New York: Ballantine.

———— (1972). "Aristotle and the Gun." In *Alpha Three*. Edited by R. Silverberg. New York: Ballantine.

———— (1970). "The Best-Laid Scheme." In *The Wheels of IF*. New York: Berkley.

———— (1957). "How to Talk Futurian." *Fantasy and Science Fiction*, October.

———— (1941). *Lest Darkness Fall*, New York: Henry Holt.

Dee, R. (1954). "The Poundstone Paradox." *Fantasy and Science Fiction*, May.

Deeping, W. (1940). *The Man Who Went Back*. New York: A. A. Knopf.

deFord, M. A. (1960). "All In Good Time." *Fantasy and Science Fiction*, July.

———— (1958). "Timequake." *Fantasy and Science Fiction*, December.

———— (DD). "Time Trammel."

De La Cruze, V., and W. Israel (1967). "Gravitational Bounce." *Nuovo Cimento* 51A (1 October): 744–760.

del Rey, L. (SFF). "My Name is Legion."

———— (TC). "Unto Him That Hath."

———— (VIT). " ... And It Comes Out Here."

———— (1951a). "Fool's Errand." *Science Fiction Quarterly*, November.

———— (1951b). "Absolutely No Paradox." *Science Fiction Quarterly*, May.

de Maupassant, G. (1955). "The Horla." In *The Complete Short Stories of Guy de Maupassant*. Garden City, NY: Hanover House.

Denbigh, K. G. (1989). "The Many Faces of Irreversibility." *British Journal for the Philosophy of Science* 40 (December):501–518.

———— (1953). "Thermodynamics and the Subjective Sense of Time." *British Journal for the Philosophy of Science* 4 (November):183–191.

Denman, H. H. (1968). "Time-Translation Invariance for Certain Dissipative Classical Systems." *American Journal of Physics* 36 (June):516–519.

Denruyter, C. (1980). "Jocasta's Crime: A Science-Fiction Reply." *Analysis* 40 (March):71.

Dentinger, S. (1969). "The Future is Ours." In *Crime Prevention in the 30th Century*. Edited by H. S. Santesson. New York: Walker.

Deser, S., *et al.* (1992). "Physical Cosmic Strings Do Not Generate Closed Timelike Curves." *Physical Review Letters* 68 (20 January):267–269.

Deutsch, D. (1991). "Quantum Mechanics Near Closed Timelike Lines." *Physical Review D* 44 (15 November):3197–3217.

———— (1985). "Quantum Theory, the Church-Turing Principle and the Universal Quantum Computer." *Proceedings of the Royal Society* 400A (July):97–117.

Deutsch, A. J. (OSF). "A Subway Named Moebius."

DeWitt, B. S. (1973). "Quantum Mechanics and Reality." In *The Many-Worlds Interpretation of Quantum Mechanics*. Edited by B. S. DeWitt and N. Graham. Princeton, NJ: Princeton University Press.

Dhar, J., and E. C. G. Sudarshan (1968). "Quantum Field Theory of Interacting Tachyons." *Physical Review* 174 (25 October):1808–1815.

Dick, P. K. (1980). "The Golden Man" and "Meddler." In *The Golden Man*. New York: Berkley.

———— (1979). *Counter-Clock World*. Boston, MA: Gregg Press.

———— (1977). "A Little Something for Us Tempunauts." In *The Best of Philip K. Dick*. New York: Del Rey.

———— (1966). "Your Appointment Will Be Yesterday." *Amazing*, August.

Dieks, D. (1988). "Special Relativity and the Flow of Time." *Philosophy of Science* 55 (September):456–460.

Dirac, P. A. M. (1949). "Forms of Relativistic Dynamics." *Reviews of Modern Physics* 21 (July):392–399.

———— (1938). "Classical Theory of Radiating Electrons." *Proceedings of the Royal Society A* 167 (August):148–168.

Dixon, F. W. (1992). *Time Bomb*. New York: Pocket.

Dobbs, H. A. C. (1969). "The 'Present' in Physics." *British Journal for the Philosophy of Science* 19:317–324.

———— (1965). "Time and ESP." *Proceedings of the Society for Psychical Research* 54 (August):249–361.

———— (1956). "The Time of Physics and Psychology." *British Journal for the Philosophy of Science* 7 (August):156–160.

—————— (1951a). "The Relation Between the Time of Psychology and the Time of Physics. Part II." *British Journal for the Philosophy of Science* 2 (November):177–192.

—————— (1951b). "The Relation Between the Time of Psychology and the Time of Physics. Part I." *British Journal for the Philosophy of Science* 2 (August):122–137.

Donald, J. A. (1978). "Assumptions of the Singularity Theorems and the Rejuvenation of Universes." *Annals of Physics* 110 (February):251–273.

Dorling, J. (1970). "The Dimensionality of Time." *American Journal of Physics* 38 (April):539–540.

Dreitlein, J., and J. Frazzini (1975). "Aging in Gravitational Fields." *American Journal of Physics* 43 (July):596–598.

Driver, R. D. (1979). "Can the Future Influence the Present?" *Physical Review D* 19 (15 February):1098–1107.

Duclos, M. (1939). "Into Another Dimension." *Fantastic Adventures*, November.

du Maurier, D. (1969). *The House on the Strand*. Garden City, NY: Doubleday.

Dummett, M. (NOT). "Causal Loops."

—————— (1969). "A Defense of McTaggart's Proof of the Unreality of Time." *Philosophical Review* 69 (October):497–504.

—————— (1964). "Bringing About the Past." *Philosophical Review* 73 (July):338–359.

Dummett, M. E., and A. Flew (1954). "Can An Effect Precede Its Cause?" *Aristotelian Society Supplement* 28:27–62.

Dunne, J. W. (1958). *An Experiment With Time*. London: Faber and Faber.

Dunsany, Lord (1948). "Lost." In *The Fourth Book of Jorkens*. Sauk City, WI: Arkham House.

Dwyer, L. (1978). "Time Travel and Some Alleged Logical Asymmetries Between Past and Future." *Canadian Journal of Philosophy* 8 (March):15–38.

—————— (1977). "How to Affect, But Not Change, The Past." *Southern Journal of Philosophy* 15:383–385.

—————— (1975). "Time Travel and Changing the Past." *Philosophical Studies* 27 (May):341–350.

Dye, C. (1953). "Time Goes to Now." *Science Fiction Quarterly*, May.

Dyson, F. J. (1979). "Time Without End: Physics and Biology in an Open Universe." *Reviews of Modern Physics* 51 (July):447–460.

Earman, J. (1976). "Causation: A Matter of Life and Death." *Journal of Philosophy* 73 (15 January):5–25.

—————— (1974). "An Attempt to Add a Little Direction to 'The Problem of the Direction of Time'." *Philosophy of Science* 41 (March):15–47.

—————— (1972). "Implications of Causal Propagation Outside the Null Cone." *Australasian Journal of Philosophy* 50 (December):222–237.

—————— (1971). "Kant, Incongruous Counterparts, and the Nature of Space and Space-Time." *Ratio* 13 (June):1–18.

—————— (1970a). "The Closed Universe." *Nous* 4 (September):261–269.

—————— (1970b). "Space-Time or How to Solve Philosophical Problems and Dissolve Philosophical Muddles Without Really Trying." *Journal of Philosophy* 67 (May):259–276.

—————— (1969). "The Anisotropy of Time." *Australasian Journal of Philosophy* 47 (December):273–295.

_____ (1967a). "On Going Backward in Time." *Philosophy of Science* 34 (September):211–222.

_____ (1967b). "Irreversibility and Temporal Asymmetry." *Journal of Philosophy* 64 (September):543–549.

Earman, J., and M. Friedman (1973). "The Meaning and Status of Newton's Laws of Inertia and the Nature of Gravitational Forces." *Philosophy of Science* 40 (September):329–359.

Echeverria, F., G. Klinkhammer, and K. S. Thorne (1991). "Billiard Balls in Wormhole Spacetimes with Closed Timelike Curves: I. Classical Theory." *Physical Review D* 44 (15 August):1077–1099.

Eddington, A. S. (1935). "The End of the World." In *New Pathways in Science*, New York: Macmillan.

_____ (1929). *The Nature of the Physical World*. New York: Macmillan.

Edmondson, G. C. (1965a). "The Misfit." In *Stranger Than You Think* . New York: Ace.

_____ (1965b). *The Ship That Sailed the Time Stream*. New York: Ace.

Eells, E. (1988). "Quentin Smith on Infinity and the Past." *Philosophy of Science* 55 (March):453–455.

Effinger, G. A. (WMHB). "Everything But Honor."

_____ (1986). *The Bird of Time*. Garden City, NY: Doubleday.

_____ (1985). *The Nick of Time*. Garden City, NY: Doubleday.

Efron, R. (NYAS). "The Duration of the Present."

Eggleston, G. C. (1875a). "The True Story of Bernard Poland's Prophecy." *American Homes* (June):80–84.

_____ (1875b). "Who Is Russell?" *American Homes* (March):276–281.

Ehring, D. (1987). "Personal Identity and Time Travel." *Philosophical Studies* 52 (November):427–433.

Einstein, A. (1961). *Relativity: the special and the general theory*. New York: Crown.

_____ (TPR). "On the Electrodynamics of Moving Bodies" and "The Foundation of the General Theory of Relativity."

_____ (1949). "Reply to Criticisms." In *Albert Einstein*, Vol. 7 of *The Library of Living Philosophers*. Edited by P. A. Schilpp. Evanston, IL: Open Court, pp. 687–688.

_____ (1935a). "The Particle Problem in the General Theory of Relativity." *Physical Review* 48 (1 July):73–77.

_____ (1935b). "Can Quantum-Mechanical Description of Physical Reality Be Considered Complete?" *Physical Review* 47 (15 May):777–780.

_____ (1931). "Knowledge of Past and Future in Quantum Mechanics." *Physical Review* 37 (15 March):780–781.

_____ (1922). "La Theorie de la Relativite." *Bulletin de la Societe Francaise de Philosophie* 17:91–113.

Eisenberg, L. (AO). "The Time of His Life."

Eisentein, A., and P. Eisentein (1971). "The Trouble with the Past." In *New Dimensions 1*. Edited by R. Silverberg. Garden City, NY: Doubleday.

Ekert, A.K. (1991). "Quantum Cryptography Based on Bell's Theorem." *Physical Review Letters* 67 (5 August):661–663.

Eklund, G. (FST). "The Ambiguities of Yesterday."

Elliot, R. (1982). "Going Nowhere Fast?" *Analysis* 42 (October):213–215.

_____ (1981). "How to Travel Faster Than Light?" *Analysis* 41 (January):4–6.

Elliott, B. (FM). "The Last Magician."

Ellis, H. G. (1974). "Time, the Grand Illusion." *Foundations of Physics* 4 (June):311–319.

Ellison, H. (1989). "Soldier." In *The Great Science Fiction Stories*. Vol. 19. New York: DAW.

———— (DV). "The Prowler in the City at the Edge of the World."

England, G. A. (1905). "The Time Reflector." *The Monthly Story Magazine*, September.

Ernst, P. (BSF). "The 32nd of May."

Eshbach, L. A. (1938). "Out of the Past." *Tales of Wonder*, Autumn.

Everett, A. E., and A.F. Antippa (CPT). "Tachyons, Causality, and Rotational Invariance."

Everett III, H. (1957). " 'Relative State' Formulation of Quantum Mechanics." *Reviews of Modern Physics* 29 (July):454–462.

Fallon, S. M. (1988). " 'To Act Or Not': Milton's Conception of Divine Freedom." *Journal of the History of Ideas* 49 (July–September):425–449.

Farley, R. M. (1950). "The Man Who Met Himself," "I Killed Hitler," "Rescue into the Past," "The Immortality of Alan Whidden," "The Time-Wise Guy," "A Month a Minute," "The Invisible Bomber," and "Time for Sale." In *The Omnibus of Time*. Los Angeles: Fantasy Publishing.

———— (1939). "Visualizing Hyperspace." *Scientific American*, March.

Farmer, P. J. (1986). "Sail On! Sail On!" In *The Great Science Fiction Stories*. Vol. 14. New York: DAW.

———— (1975). *Time's Last Gift*. New York: Granada.

———— (1977). "Sketches Among the Ruins of My Mind." In *Strangeness*. Edited by T. M. Disch and C. Naylor. New York: Charles Scribner's Sons.

Fast, H. (1959). "Of Time and Cats." *Fantasy and Science Fiction*, March.

Faye, J. (1987). "The Past Revisited." *Danish Yearbook of Philosophy*. Vol. 24, 7–18. Copenhagen: Museum Tusculanum Press.

Fearn, J. R. (MBSFS). "Wanderer of Time."

Fehrenbach, T. R. (1963). "Remember the Alamo!" In *ANALOG I*. Edited by J. W. Campbell. New York: Doubleday.

Feinberg, G. (1967). "Possibility of Faster-Than-Light Particles." *Physical Review* 159 (25 July):1089–1105.

Feynman, R. P. (1965). "The Distinction of Past and Future." In *The Character of Physical Law*. Cambridge, MA: MIT Press.

———— (1963). "Relativity and the Philosophers." In *The Feynman Lectures on Physics*. Vol. 1. Reading, MA: Addison-Wesley.

———— (1949a). "The Theory of Positrons." *Physical Review* 76 (15 September):749–759.

———— (1949b). "Space-Time Approach to Quantum Electrodynamics." *Physical Review* 76 (15 September):769–789.

———— (1948). "A Relativistic Cut-Off for Classical Electrodynamics." *Physical Review* 74 (15 October):939–946.

Findlay, J. N. (1978). "Time and Eternity." *Review of Metaphysics* 32 (September):3–14.

Findlay, J. N., and J. E. McGechie (1956). "Does It Make Sense to Suppose That All Events, Including Personal Experiencies, Could Occur in Reverse?" *Analysis* 16 (June):121–123.

Finkelstein, D. (1958). "Past-Future Asymmetry of the Gravitational Field of a Point Particle." *Physical Review* 110 (15 May):965–967.

Finney, J. (FCW). "Quit Zoomin' Those Hands Through the Air."

———— (1986). "The Third Level," "I Love Galesburg in the Springtime," "Such Interesting Neighbors," "Of Missing Persons," "Where the Cluetts Are," "The Face in the Photo," "I'm Scared," "The Coin Collector," and "Second Chance." In *About Time.* New York: Simon and Schuster.

———— (TOT). "The Love Letter."

———— (1970). *Time and Again.* New York: Simon & Schuster.

———— (1966). "Double Take." In *The Playboy Book of Science Fiction and Fantasy.* Chicago: Playboy Press.

Fisk, M. (1963). "Cause and Time in Physical Theory." *Review of Metaphysics* 16 (March):522–549.

Fitzgerald, F. S. (1944). "The Curious Case of Benjamin Button." In *Pause to Wonder.* New York: J. Messner.

Fitzgerald, P. (1985). "Four Kinds of Temporal Becoming." *Philosophical Topics* 13 (Fall):145–177.

———— (1974). "On Retrocausality." *Philosophia* 4 (October):513–551.

———— (1972). "Relativity Physics and the God of Process Philosophy." *Process Studies* 2 (Winter):251–276.

———— (1970). "Tachyons, Backwards Causation, and Freedom." In *Boston Studies in the Philosophy of Science.* Vol. 8, 415–436.

———— (1969). "The Truth About Tomorrow's Sea Fight." *Journal of Philosophy* 66 (5 June):307–329.

Flagg, F. (1930). "An Adventure in Time." *Science Wonder Stories*, April.

———— (1927). "The Machine Man of Ardathia." *Amazing Stories*, November.

Flammarion, C. (1897). *Lumen.* New York: Dodd, Mead and Co.

Fleisher, M. L. (1978). *The Encyclopedia of Comic Book Heroes.* New York: Warner.

Foote, B. (1991). *The Connecticut Yankee in the Twentieth Century: travel to the past in science fiction.* Westport, CT: Greenwood Press.

Ford, J. M. (FCW). "Slowly By, Lorena."

Ford, L. S. (1968). "Is Process Theism Compatible with Relativity Theory?" *Journal of Religion* 48 (April):124–135.

Forward, R. (1992). *Timemaster.* New York: Tor.

———— (1988). "Time Magic." In *Future Magic.* New York: Avon.

———— (1980). "How to Build a Time Machine." *Omni*, May.

Fox, D. (1952). "The Tiniest Time Traveler." *Astounding Science Fiction*, December.

Fox, R., C. G. Kuper, and S. G. Lipson (1970). "Faster-Than-Light Group Velocities and Causality Violations." *Proceedings of the Royal Society of London* 316 A (May):515–524.

———————————————————— (1969). "Do Faster-than-Light Group Velocities Imply Violation of Causality?" *Nature* 223 (9 August):597.

Frank, E. (1948). "Time and Eternity." *Review of Metaphysics* 2 (September):39–52.

Frank, P. (BST). "Is the Future Already Here?"

———— (1957). *Philosophy of Science.* Englewood Cliffs, NJ: Prentice Hall.

Frankel, L. (1986). "Mutual Causation, Simultaneity, and Event Description." *Philosophical Studies* 49 (May):361–372.

Frankel, T. (1988). "Electric Currents in Multiply Connected Spaces." *International Journal of Theoretical Physics* 27 (August):995–999.

Franklin, H. B. (1966). *Future Perfect.* New York: Oxford University Press.

Frankowski, L. A. (1986). *The Cross-Time Engineer.* New York: Del Rey.

Franson, D. (MT). "Package Deal."

Fraser, J. T. (1978). *Time as Conflict*. Basel: Birkhauser Verlag.

_____ (VOT). "Note Relating to a Paradox of the Temporal Order."

Freedman, D. Z., and P. van Nieuweuhuizen (1985). "The Hidden Dimensions of Space-time." *Scientific American*, March.

Friedman, J., et al. (1990). "Cauchy Problem in Spacetimes with Closed Timelike Curves." *Physical Review D* 42 (15 September):1915–1930.

Friedman, J. L. (1988). "Back to the Future." *Nature* 336 (24 November):305–306.

Friedman, J. L., and M. S. Morris (1991). "The Cauchy Problem for the Scalar Wave Equation is Well Defined on a Class of Spacetimes with Closed Time Like Lines." *Physical Review Letters* 66 (28 January):401–404.

Friedman, M. (1983). *Foundations of Space-Time Theories*. Princeton, NJ: Princeton University Press.

Friend, B. (1982). "Time Travel as a Feminist Didactic in Works by Phyllis Eisenstein, Marlys Millhiser, and Octavia Butler." *Extrapolation* 23 (Spring):50–55.

Frolov, V. P. (1991). "Vacuum Polarization in a Locally Static Multiply Connected Space-time and a Time-Machine Problem." *Physical Review D* 43 (15 June):3878–3894.

Frolov, V. P., and I. D. Novikov (1990). "Physical Effects in Wormholes and Time Machines." *Physical Review D* 42 (15 August):1057–1065.

Fubank, J. (1992). *Crossover*. New York: Carroll & Graf.

Fuller, R. W., and J. A. Wheeler (1962). "Causality and Multiply Connected Space-Time." *Physical Review* 128 (15 October):919–929.

Fulmer, G. (1983). "Cosmological Implications of Time Travel." In *The Intersection of Science Fiction and Philosophy*. Edited by R. E. Meyers. Westport, CT: Greenwood Press.

_____ (1981). "Time Travel, Determinism, and Fatalism." *Philosophical Speculations in Science Fiction and Fantasy* 1 (Spring):41–48.

_____ (1980). "Understanding Time Travel." *Southwestern Journal of Philosophy* 11 (Spring):151–156.

Gale, R. (1966). "McTaggart's Analysis of Time." In *American Philosophical Quarterly* 3 (April):145–152.

_____ (1965). "Why a Cause Cannot Be Later Than Its Effect." *Review of Metaphysics* 19:209–234.

_____ (1964). "Is It Now Now?" *Mind* 73 (January): 97–105.

_____ (1963). "Some Metaphysical Statements About Time." *Journal of Philosophy* 60 (25 April):225–237.

Gal-Or, B. (MDT). "On a Paradox-Free Definition of Time and Irreversibility."

Gamow, G. (ED). "The Heart on the Other Side."

_____ (1946). "Rotating Universe?" *Nature* 158 (19 October):549.

Gardner, M. (MTMW). "Left or Right?"

_____ (1982). *aha! Gotcha*. New York: W. H. Freeman.

_____ (1979). "Mathematical Games." *Scientific American*, March.

_____ (1974). "Mathematical Games." *Scientific American*, May.

_____ (1969). "The Church of the Fourth Dimension." In *The Unexpected Hanging*. New York: Simon and Schuster.

_____ (FM). "No-Sided Professor" and "The Island of Five Colors."

Garrett, R. (TW). "Frost and Thunder."

Gatlin, L. L. (1980). "Time-Reversed Information Transmission." *International Journal of Theoretical Physics* 19 (January):25–29.

Geach, P. (1969). *God and the Soul*. London: Routledge & Kegan Paul.

———— (1968). "Some Problems About Time." In *Studies in the Philosophy of Thought and Action*. Edited by P. F. Strawson. New York: Oxford.

Geroch, R. (1984). "The Everett Interpretation." *Nous* 18 (November):617–633.

———— (1968). "What is a Singularity in General Relativity?" *Annals of Physics* 48 (July):526–540.

———— (1967). "Topology in General Relativity." *Journal of Mathematical Physics* 8 (April):782–786.

Gerrold, D. (1973). *The Man Who Folded Himself*. New York: Random House.

Ghirardi, G. C., A Rimini, and T. Weber (1980). "A General Argument Against Superluminal Transmission Through the Quantum Mechanical Measurement Process." *Lettere Al Nuovo Cimento* 27 (8 March): 293–298.

Gibbons, G. W., and S. W. Hawking (1992). "Kinks and Topology Change." *Physical Review Letters* 69 (21 September): 1719–1721.

Gibson, W. M. (1969). *Mark Twain's Mysterious Stranger Manuscripts*. Los Angeles, CA: University of California.

Gillespie, A. (NWF). "The Evil Eye."

Giuliano, C. R. (1981). "Applications of Optical Phase Conjugation." *Physics Today* 34 (April):27–35.

Godfrey-Smith, W. (1980). "Traveling in Time." *Analysis* 40 (March):72–73.

———— (1979). "Special Relativity and the Present." *Philosophical Studies* 36 (October):233–244.

Gödel, K. (BST). "Static Interpretation of Space-Time with Einstein's Comment on It."

———— (1952). "Rotating Universes in General Relativity Theory." *Proceedings of the International Congress of Mathematicians*, 1:175–181.

———— (1949a). "A Remark About the Relationship Between Relativity Theory and Idealistic Philosophy." In *Albert Einstein: Philosopher-Scientist*. Vol. 7 of *The Library of Living Philosophers*. Edited by P. A. Schilpp. Evanston, IL: Open Court.

———— (1949b). "An Example of a New Type of Cosmological Solutions of Einstein's Field Equations of Gravitation." *Reviews of Modern Physics* 21 (July):447–450.

Gold, H. L. (MT). "The Biography Project."

———— (SFAD). "Perfect Murder."

Gold, T. (MDT). "The World Map and the Apparent Flow of Time."

———— (1966). "Cosmic Processes and the Nature of Time." In *Mind and Cosmos*. Edited by R. G. Colodny. Pittsburgh, PA: University of Pittsburgh Press.

———— (1962). "The Arrow of Time." *American Journal of Physics* 30 (June):403–410.

Goldstone, C., and A. Davidson (1970). "Pebble in Time." *Fantasy and Science Fiction*, August.

Good, I. J. (1965). "Winding Space." In *The Scientist Speculates*. Edited by I. J. Good. New York: Capricorn.

Gor, G. (1969). "The Garden" and "The Minotaur." In *Russian Science Fiction*. Edited by R. Magidoff. New York: New York University Press.

Gordon, A. (1987). "*Back to the Future*: Oedipus as Time Traveller." *Science-Fiction Studies* 14 (November):372–385.

———— (1982). "Silverberg's Time Machine." *Extrapolation* 23 (Winter):345–361.

Gorovitz, S. (1964). "Leaving the Past Alone." *Philosophical Review* 73 (July):360–371.

Goswami, A. (1985). *The Cosmic Dancers: exploring the science of science fiction*. New York: McGraw-Hill, 1985.

Gott, J. R. (1991). "Closed Timelike Curves Produced by Pairs of Moving Cosmic Strings: Exact Solutions." *Physical Review Letters* 66 (4 March):1126–1129.

_____ (1974). "A Time-Symmetric, Matter, Antimatter, Tachyon Cosmology." *Astrophysical Journal* 187 (1 January):1–3.

Goulart, R. (1975). "Plumrose." In *Odd Job #101*. New York: Charles Scribner's Sons.

Graves, J. C., and J. E. Roper (1965). "Measuring Measuring Rods." *Philosophy of Science* 32 (January):39–56.

Grendon, E. (TSF). "The Figure."

Gribbin, J. (1983). *Spacewarps*. New York: Delacorte.

_____ (1979). *Time Warps*. New York: Delacorte.

Gribbin, J., and M. Rees (1989). *Cosmic Coincidences*. New York: Bantam.

Griffith, G. (1899). "The Conversion of the Professor." *Pearson's Magazine*, May.

Grigoriev, V. (LDA). "Vanya."

Grimwood, K. (1988). *Replay*. New York: Berkley.

_____ (1976). *Breakthrough*. Garden City, NY: Doubleday.

Gross, C. (1985). "Twelfth-Century Concepts of Time: Three Reinterpretations of Augustine's Doctrine of Creation *Simul*." *Journal of the History of Philosophy* 23 (July):325–338.

Gross, M. (SSFT). "The Good Provider."

Grünbaum, A. (1976). "Is Preacceleration of Particles in Dirac's Electrodynamics a Case of Backward Causation? The Myth of Retrocausation in Classical Electrodynamics." *Philosophy of Science* 43 (June):165–201.

_____ (1973). "Geometrodynamics and Ontology." *Journal of Philosophy* 70 (6 December):775–800.

_____ (BIPT). "The Meaning of Time."

_____ (1963). "Is There a 'Flow' of Time or Temporal Becoming?" In *Philosophical Problems of Space and Time*. New York: Knopf.

_____ (1955). "Time and Entropy." *American Scientist* 43 (October).

Grünbaum, A., and A. I. Janis (1978). "Can the Effect Precede Its Cause in Classical Electrodynamics?" *American Journal of Physics* 46 (April):337–341.

_____ (1977). "Is There Backward Causation in Classical Electrodynamics?" *Journal of Philosophy* 74 (August):475–482.

Gunn, J. (1979). *The Road to Science Fiction*. Vol. 3. New York: New American Library.

_____ (1975). *Alternate Worlds: the illustrated history of science fiction*. Englewood Cliffs, NJ: A&W Visual Library.

Gunn, L. D. (1939). "The Time Twin." *Thrilling Wonder Stories*, August.

Haggard, J. H. (1930). "Faster Than Light." *Wonder Stories*, October.

Haining, P. (1987). *Doctor Who: The Time-Travellers' Guide*. London: W. H. Allen.

Haldane, J. B. S. (1928). "The Universe and Irreversibility." *Nature* 122 (24 November):808–809.

Haldeman, J. (1990). *The Hemingway Hoax*. New York: William Morrow.

_____ (1984). *The Forever War*. New York: Del Rey.

Hale, E. E. (1986). "Hands Off." In *Alternative Histories*. Edited by C. G. Waugh and M. H. Greenberg. New York: Garland Publishing.

Hall, C. F. (1938). "The Man Who Lived Backwards." *Tales of Wonder*, Summer.

Hamilton, E. (LME). "In the World's Dusk."

_____ (1974). "The Man Who Evolved." In *Before the Golden Age*. Edited by I. Asimov. Vol. 1. Greenwich, CT: Fawcett.

_____ (MBSFS). "The Inn Outside the World."

_____ (1930). "The Man Who Saw the Future." *Amazing Stories*, October.

Harness, C. L. (FCW). "Quarks at Appomattox."

_____ (1988). *Krono*. New York: Franklin Watts.

_____ (TTT). "Time Trap."

_____ (BFSF3). "Child by Chronos."

Harris, C. W. (1947). "The Fifth Dimension." In *Away From the Here and Now*. Philadelphia: Dorrance.

Harris, E. E. (1968). "Simultaneity and the Future." *British Journal for the Philosophy of Science* 19:254–256.

Harrison, B. K., *et al*. (1965). *Gravitational Theory and Gravitational Collapse*. Chicago: University of Chicago Press.

Harrison, H. (1983). *A Rebel in Time*. New York: Tor.

_____ (1975). "The Secret of Stonehenge." In *The Ancient Mysteries Reader*. New York: Doubleday.

_____ (1974). "The Ever-Branching Tree." In *School and Society Through Science Fiction*. Edited by J. D. Olander, M. H. Greenberg, and P. Warrick. Chicago: Rand McNally.

_____ (1967). *The Technicolor Time Machine*. Garden City, NY: Doubleday.

Harrison, J. (1980). "Report on *Analysis* Problem No. 18." *Analysis* 40 (March):65–69.

_____ (1979). "Jocasta's Crime." *Analysis* 39 (March):65.

_____ (1971). "Dr. Who and the Philosophers, Or Time Travel for Beginners." *Aristotelian Society Supplement* 45:1–24.

Harrison, K. L. (1940). "The Blonde, the Time Machine and Johnny Bell." *Thrilling Wonder Stories*, December.

Hartland-Swann, J. (1955). "The Concept of Time." *Philosophical Quarterly* 5 (January):1–20.

Hartshorne, C. (HJ). "The Reality of the Past, the Unreality of the Future."

Hawking, S. W. (1992). "The Chronology Protection Conjecture." *Physical Review D* 46 (15 July):603–611.

_____ (1988). *A Brief History of Time*. New York: Bantam.

_____ (1985). "Arrow of Time in Cosmology." *Physical Review D* 32 (15 November):2489–2495.

_____ (1977). "The Quantum Mechanics of Black Holes." *Scientific American*, January.

_____ (1976). "Breakdown of Predictability in Gravitational Collapse." *Physical Review D* 14 (15 November):2460–2473.

_____ (1975). "Particle Creation by Black Holes." *Communications in Mathematical Physics* 43, 199–220.

_____ (1974). "Black Hole Explosions?" *Nature* 248 (1 March):30–31.

_____ (1968). "The Existence of Cosmic Time Functions." *Proceedings of the Royal Society* 308A (11 December):433–435.

Hawking, S. W., and G. F. R. Ellis (1973). *The Large Scale Structure of Space-Time*. Cambridge: Cambridge University Press.

Hawking, S. W., and R. Penrose (1970). "The Singularities of Gravitational Collapse and Cosmology." *Proceedings of the Royal Society* 314A (27 January):529–548.

Healey, R. A. (1984). "How Many Worlds?" *Nous* 18 (November):591–616.

Heffern, R. (1977). *Time Travel: myth or reality*. New York: Pyramid.

Heinlein, R. A. (1986). *The Door Into Summer*. New York: Del Rey.

_____ (AHT). "By His Bootstraps."

_____ (1980). *The Number of the Beast*. New York: Random House.

_____ (1979). "Life-Line." In *The Great Science Fiction Stories*. Vol. 1. New York: DAW.

_____ (MI). "All You Zombies—."

_____ (1964). *Farnham's Freehold*. New York: G. P. Putnam's Sons.

_____ (FM). "—And He Built a Crooked House."

_____ (1955). *Tunnel in the Sky*. New York: Scribner's.

_____ (1953). "Elsewhen." In *Assignment in Eternity*. Reading, PA: Fantasy Press.

Helliwell, T. M., and D. A. Konkowski (1983). "Causality Paradoxes and Nonparadoxes: Classical Superluminal Signals and Quantum Measurements." *American Journal of Physics* 51 (November):996–1003.

Henderson, L. D. (1983). *The Fourth Dimension and Non-Euclidean Geometry in Modern Art*. Princeton, NJ: Princeton University Press.

Hennelly, M. M., Jr. (1979). "*The Time Machine*: A Romance of 'The Human Heart'." *Extrapolation* 20 (Summer):154–167.

Herbert, N. (1988). *Faster Than Light: superluminal loopholes in physics*. New York: New American Library.

_____ (1987). *Quantum Reality*. Garden City, NY: Anchor.

_____ (1982). "FLASH -- A Superluminal Communicator Based Upon a New Kind of Quantum Measurement." *Foundations of Physics* 12 (December):1171–1179.

Herbert, R. T. (1987). "The Relativity of Simultaneity." *Philosophy* 62 (October):455–471.

Herron, M. L., and D. T. Pegg (1974). "A Proposed Experiment on Absorber Theory." *Journal of Physics A* 7 (October):1965–1969.

Hesse, M. B. (1961). *Forces and Fields*. New York: Philosophical Library.

Hickey, H. B. (WT). "Like a Bird, Like a Fish."

Hinckfuss, I. (1975). *The Existence of Space and Time*. London: Oxford University Press.

Hilton-Young, W. (SSFT). "The Choice."

Hinton, C. H. (1980). *Speculations on the Fourth Dimension*. Edited by R. Rucker. New York: Dover.

Hobana, I. (PWO). "Night Broadcast."

Hoch, E. D. (SFSSS). "The Last Paradox."

Hochberg, D., and T. W. Kephart (1991). "Lorentzian Wormholes from the Gravitationally Squeezed Vacuum." *Physics Letters B* 268 (October):377–383.

Hodgson, J. L. (1929). *The Time Journey of Dr. Barton*. Eggington: J. Hodgson.

Hogan, J. P. (1985). *The Proteus Operation*. New York: Bantam.

Hogarth, J. E. (1962). "Cosmological Considerations of the Absorber Theory of Radiation." *Proceedings of the Royal Society* 267A (22 May):365–383.

Hollinger, V. (1987). "Deconstructing the Time Machine." *Science Fiction Studies* 14 (July):201–221.

Hollis, M. (1967a). "Times and Spaces." *Mind* 76 (October):524–536.

_____ (1967b). "Box and Cox." *Philosophy* 42:75–78.

Holton, G. (1981). "Einstein's Search for the *Weltbild*." *Proceedings of the American Philosophical Society* 125 (February):1–15.

_____ (1965). "The Metaphor of Space-Time Events in Science." *Eranos-Jahrbuch* 34:33–78.

Horwich, P. (1987). *Asymmetries in Time*. Cambridge, MA: The MIT Press.

_____ (1975). "On Some Alleged Paradoxes of Time Travel." *Journal of Philosophy* 72 (14 August):432–444.

Horwitz, L. P., R. I. Arshansky, and A. C. Elitzur (1988). "On the Two Aspects of Time: The Distinction and Its Implications." *Foundations of Physics* 18 (December):1159–1193.

Hoyle, F. (1983). "Information from the Future" and "Loops in Time." In *The Intelligent Universe*. New York: Holt, Rinehart, and Winston.

_____ (1975). "On the Origin of the Microwave Background." *Astrophysical Journal* 196 (15 March):661–670.

_____ (1966). *October the First is Too Late*. London: Heinemann.

Hoyle, F., and J. V. Narlikar (1974). *Action at a Distance in Physics and Cosmology*. San Francisco, CA: W. H. Freeman.

_____ (1964). "Time Symmetric Electrodynamics and the Arrow of Time in Cosmology." *Proceedings of the Royal Society of London* 277A (January):1–23.

Hudec, G. (PWO). "The Ring."

Huggett, W. J. (1960). "Losing One's Way in Time." *Philosophical Quarterly* 10 (July):264–267.

Hughes, R. (MM). "The Vanishing Man."

Hunter, G. (1951). "Journey." *Fantasy and Science Fiction*, February.

Hunter, L. R. (1991). "Tests of Time-Reversal Invariance in Atoms, Molecules, and the Neutron." *Science* 252 (5 April):73–79.

Hunter, N. (1933). "The Professor Invents a Machine." In *The Incredible Adventures of Professor Branestawm*. London: The Bodley Head.

Hunting, G. (1926). *The Vicarion*. Kansas City, MO: Unity School of Christianity.

Hurley, J. (1986). "The Time-Asymmetry Paradox." *American Journal of Physics* 54 (January):25–28.

Inge, W. R. (1921). "Is the Time Series Reversible?" *Proceedings of the Aristotelian Society* 21:1–12.

Irwin, M. (BFSF2). "The Earlier Service."

Israel, W. (1967). "Gravitational Collapse and Causality." *Physical Review* 153 (25 January):1388–1393.

Italiano, A. (1986). "How to Recover Causality in General Relativity." *Hadronic Journal* 9 (January):9–12.

Jakiel, S. J., and R. E. Levinthal (1980). "The Laws of Time Travel." *Extrapolation* 21 (Summer):130–138.

James, H. (1917). *The Sense of the Past*. New York: Charles Scribner's Sons.

Jameson, M. (GSSF). "Blind Alley."

_____ (1941). "Dead End." *Thrilling Wonder Stories*, March.

Janifer, L. M. (1973). "A Few Minutes." In *Ten Tomorrows*. Edited by R. Elwood. Greenwich, CT: Fawcett.

Jarry, A. (1965). "How To Construct a Time Machine." Translated from the French and reprinted in *Selected Works of Alfred Jarry*. Edited by R. Shattuck and S. W. Taylor. New York: Grove Press.

Jeschke, W. (1982). *The Last Day of Creation*. New York: St. Martin's Press.

_____ (BRW). "The King and the Dollmaker."

Jespersen, J., and J. Fitz-Randolph (1982). *From Sundials to Atomic Clocks: understanding time and frequency*. New York: Dover.

Jobe, E. K. (1980). "Nature's Choice of Time." *Australasian Journal of Philosophy* 58 (December):347–359.

Jones, F. C. (1972). "Lorentz-Invariant Formulation of Cherenkov Radiation by Tachyons." *Physical Review D* 6 (15 November):2727–2735.

Jones, L. (BO). "The Time Machine."

_____ (TTT). "The Great Clock."

Jones, R. T. (1963). "Conformal Coordinates Associated With Space-Like Motions." *Journal of the Franklin Institute* 275 (January):1–12.

Karageorge, M. (1965). "The Life of Your Time." *Analog*, September.

Kaufmann, W. J. (1977). *The Cosmic Frontiers of General Relativity*. New York: Little, Brown.

Kendig, J., Jr. (1930). "Fourth-Dimensional Penetrator." *Amazing Stories*, January.

Kent, K. (OW). "The Comedy of Eras."

_____ (1939). "World's Pharaoh." *Thrilling Wonder Stories*, December.

Kerr, R. P. (1963). "Gravitational Field of a Spinning Mass as an Example of Algebraically Special Metrics." *Physical Review Letters* 11 (1 September):237–238.

Kerszberg, P. (1987). "The Relativity of Rotation in the Early Foundations of General Relativity." *Studies in History and Philosophy of Science* 18 (March):53–79.

Ketterer, D. (1984). *Science Fiction of Mark Twain*. Hamden, CT: Archon.

_____ (1982). "Oedipus as Time Traveller." *Science Fiction Studies* 9 (November):340–341.

Kilworth, G. (1985). "Let's Go to Golgotha!" In *The Songbirds of Pain*. London: Victor Gollancz.

Kim, S.-W. (1992). "Particle Creation for Time Travel Through a Wormhole." *Physical Review D* 46 (15 September):2428–2434.

Kim, S.-W., and K. S. Thorne (1991). "Do Vacuum Fluctuations Prevent the Creation of Closed Timelike Curves?" *Physical Review D* 43 (15 June):3929–3947.

Kimberly, G. (FST). "Minna in the Night Sky."

King, S. (1985). "Mrs. Todd's Shortcut." In *Skeleton Crew*. New York: G. P. Putnam's Sons.

Kirch, D. (1975). "Some Theoretical and Experimental Aspects of the Tachyon Problem." *International Journal of Theoretical Physics* 13 (June):153–173.

Kirkham, H. F. (1929). "The Time Oscillator." *Science Wonder Stories*, December.

Kirzhnitz, D. A., and V. L. Polyachenko (1964). "On the Possibility of Macroscopic Manifestations of Violation of Microscopic Causality." *Soviet Physics JETP* 19 (August):514–519.

Klass, P. (1974). "An Innocent in Time: Mark Twain in King Arthur's Court." *Extrapolation* 16 (December):17–32.

Klein, G. (BRW). "Party Line."

Klein, T. E. D. (MT). "Renaissance Man."

Klinkhammer, G. (1991). "Averaged Energy Conditions for Free Scalar Fields in Flat Spacetime." *Physical Review D* 43 (15 April):2542–2548.

Knight, D. (1990). "What Rough Beast." In *The Great Science Fiction Stories*. Vol. 21. New York: DAW.

_____ (1987). "Anachron." In *The Great Science Fiction Stories*. Vol. 16. New York: DAW.

_____ (1980). "I See You." In *The Best from Fantasy and Science Fiction*. Edited by E. L. Ferman. Vol. 23. New York: Doubleday.

_____ (1961). "The Last Word," "Thing of Beauty," "Extempore," and "Time Enough."

In *Far Out*. New York: Simon and Schuster.

———— (1956). "This Way To the Regress." *Galaxy Science Fiction*, August.

———— (OSF). "Catch That Martian."

———— (GRSF1). "Don't Live in the Past."

Knight, D. C. (1960). "The Amazing Mrs. Mimms." In *The Fantastic Universe Omnibus*. Edited by H. S. Santesson. Englewood Cliffs, NJ: Prentice-Hall.

Knight, N. L. (BSF). "Short-Circuited Probability."

———— (1940). "Bombardment in Reverse." *Astounding Science Fiction*, February.

Koestler, A. (1971). "The Boredom of Fantasy." In *Science Fiction: The Future*. Edited by D. Allen. New York: Harcourt Brace Jovanovich.

Kornbluth, C. M. (HV). "Two Dooms."

———— (1984). "The Little Black Bag." In *The Great Science Fiction Stories*. Vol. 12. New York: DAW.

———— (VIT). "Dominoes."

———— (CA). "Time Travel and the Law."

Korotkii, V. A., and Yu. N. Obukhov (1991). "Kinematic Analysis of Cosmological Models with Rotation." *Soviet Physics JETP* 72 (January):11–15.

Kosso, P. (1988). "Spacetime Horizons and Unobservability." *Studies in History and Philosophy of Science* 19 (June):161–173.

Kowalczynski, J. K. (1984). "Critical Comments on the Discussion about Tachyonic Causal Paradoxes and on the Concept of Superluminal Reference Frame." *International Journal of Theoretical Physics* 23 (January):27–60 [and the reply by E. Recami (1987) 26 (September):913–919].

Kreisler, M. N. (1973). "Are There Faster-than-Light Particles?" *American Scientist* 61 (March–April).

Kretzmann, N. (1966). "Omniscience and Immutability." *Journal of Philosophy* 63 (14 July):409–421.

Kriele, M. (1990a). "A Generalization of the Singularity Theorem of Hawking & Penrose to Space-Times with Causality Violations." *Proceedings of the Royal Society* 431A (8 December):451–464.

———— (1990b). "Causality Violations and Singularities." *General Relativity and Gravitation* 22 (June):619–623.

Kroes, P. (1985). "The Time Reversal Operator T*." In *Time: Its Structure and Role in Physical Theories*, 124–129. Dordrecht: D. Reidel.

———— (1984). "Objective Versus Mind-dependent Theories of Time Flow." *Synthese* 61 (December):423–446.

———— (1983). "Traces, Prediction, and Retrodiction." *Nature and System* 5 (September):131–146.

———— (1982). "Order and Irreversibility." *Nature and System* 4 (September):115–129.

Kubilius, W. (1951). "Turn Backward, O Time." *Science Fiction Quarterly*, May.

Kummer, F. A., Jr. (1945). "Delvers in Destiny." *Thrilling Wonder Stories*, Spring.

Kuttner, H., and C. L. Moore (T3). "Vintage Season."

———— (1980). "The Twonky." In *The Great Science Fiction Stories*. Vol. 4. New York: DAW.

Lafferty, R. A. (1991). "Rainbird." In *The Great Science Fiction Stories*, Vol. 23, New York: DAW.

———— (1971). "Through Other Eyes." In *Mind to Mind*. Edited by R. Silverberg. New York: Thomas Nelson.

_____ (1970). "The Six Fingers of Time." In *Nine Hundred Grandmothers*. New York: Ace.

_____ (AO). "Thus We Frustrate Charlemagne."

Lafleur, L. J. (1940). "Time As A Fourth Dimension." *Journal of Philosophy* 37 (28 March):169–178.

Landis, G. A. (D). "Dinosaurs."

Lapedes, A. S., and K. C. Jacobs (1972). "Tachyons and Gravitational Cerenkov Radiation." *Nature Physical Science* 235 (3 January):6–7.

Laski, M. (1954). *The Victorian Chaise Longue*. Boston: Houghton Mifflin.

Laumer, K. (1991). "The Propitiation of Brullamagoo." In *Alien Minds*. New York: Baen.

_____ (1971). *Dinosaur Beach*. New York: Charles Scribner's Sons.

_____ (1964). *The Great Time Machine Hoax*. New York: Simon and Schuster.

Laurence, L. (1939). "History In Reverse." *Amazing Stories*, October.

Laverty, D. (1948). "No Winter, No Summer." *Thrilling Wonder Stories*, October.

Leftow, D. (1991). "Why Didn't God Create the Universe Sooner?" *Religious Studies* 27 (June):157–172.

LeGuin, U. K. (1975). "April in Paris" and "Semley's Necklace." In *The Wind's Twelve Quarters*. New York: Harper and Row.

Leiber, F. (1987). "The Man Who Never Grew Old." In *Great Science Fiction of the 20th Century*. Edited by R. Silverberg and M. H. Greenberg. New York: Avenel.

_____ (SFS). "Try and Change the Past."

_____ (1976). *The Big Time*. Boston, MA: Gregg Press.

_____ (TC). "Nice Girl With 5 Husbands."

_____ (1961). "Damnation Morning," and "The Oldest Soldier." In *The Mind Spider and Other Stories*. New York: Ace.

_____ (1958). "Time in the Round." In *The Third Galaxy Reader*. Edited by H. L. Gold. Garden City, NY: Doubleday & Co.

Leiby, D. A. (1987). "The Tooth That Gnaws: Reflections on Time Travel." In *Intersections: Fantasy and Science Fiction*. Edited by G. E. Slusser and E. S. Rabkin. Carbondale, Illinois: Southern Illinois University Press.

Leinster, M. (BML). "Time to Die," "Interference," and "Sam, This is You."

_____ (SFT). "The Fifth-Dimension Catapult."

_____ (BGA2). "Sidewise in Time."

_____ (1967). "The Runaway Skyscraper." *The Best of Amazing*. Edited by J. Ross. Garden City, NY: Doubleday.

_____ (SFAD). "The Middle of the Week After Next."

_____ (GRSF1). "The Other Now."

_____ (1950). "The Life-Work of Professor Muntz." In *The Best Science Fiction Stories*. Edited by E. F. Bleiler and T. E. Dikty. New York: Frederick Fell.

_____ (1946). "Dead City." *Thrilling Wonder Stories*, Summer.

_____ (OW). "The Fourth-Dimensional Demonstrator."

_____ (1933). "The Fifth-Dimension Tube." *Astounding Stories*, January.

Lem, S. (1982). *Memoirs of a Space Traveler*. New York: Harcourt Brace Jovanovich.

_____ (1977). "Cosmology and Science Fiction." *Science-Fiction Studies* 4 (July):107–110.

_____ (1976). "The Seventh Voyage of Ijon Tichy" and "The Twentieth Voyage of Ijon Tichy." In *The Star Diaries*. New York: Seabury Press.

_____ (1974). "The Time-Travel Story and Related Matters of SF Structuring." *Science-

Fiction Studies 1 (Spring):143–154.

L'Engle, M. (1978). *A Swiftly Tilting Planet*. New York: Dell.

———— (1976). *A Wrinkle in Time*. New York: Dell.

Lenzen, V. (BST). "Geometrical Physics."

Le Poidevin, R. (1991). "Creation in a Closed Universe *Or,* Have Physicists Disproved the Existence of God?" *Religious Studies* 27 (March):39–48.

———— (1990). "Relationism and Temporal Topology: Physics or Metaphysics." *Philosophical Quarterly* 40 (October):419–432.

Leslie, J. (1976). "The Value of Time." *American Philosophical Quarterly* 13 (April):109–121.

Levin, M. R. (1980). "Swords' Points." *Analysis* 40 (March):69–70.

Lewis, C. S. (1986). *The Grand Miracle*. New York: Ballantine.

———— (1978). *Miracles*. New York: Macmillan.

———— (1977). *The Dark Tower and Other Stories*. New York: Harcourt Brace Jovanovich.

Lewis, D. (1976). "The Paradoxes of Time Travel." *American Philosophical Quarterly* 13 (April):145–152.

Lewis, G. N. (1930). "The Symmetry of Time in Physics." *Science* 71 (6 June):569–577.

———— (1926). "The Nature of Light." *Proceedings of the National Academy of Sciences* 12 (15 January):22–29.

Ley, W. (CA). "Geography for Time Travelers."

Lieb, I. C. (1972). "Individuals and the Past." *Review of Metaphysics* 25 (June supplement):117–130.

Lightman, A. (1986). "Time Travel and Papa Joe's Pipe." In *Time Travel and Papa Joe's Pipe*. New York: Penquin.

Lindsay, R. B., and Margenau, M. (BST). "Time: Continuous or Discrete."

Locke, R. D. (PSF). "Demotion."

Lodge, O. (1920). "The New World of Space and Time." *Living Age* 304 (24 January):240–244.

Long, A. R. (1934). "Scandal In the 4th Dimension." *Astounding Stories,* February.

Long, F. B. (1970). *Monster From Out of Time*. New York: Popular Library.

———— (1948). "A Guest in the House." In *Strange Ports of Call*. Edited by A. Derleth. New York: Pellegrini and Cudahy.

———— (1953). "Throwback in Time." *Science Fiction Plus,* April.

———— (1937). "Temporary Warp." *Astounding Stories,* August.

Lorentz, H. A. (TPR). "Electromagnetic Phenomena in a System Moving With Any Velocity Less Than That of Light."

Lossev, A., and I. D. Novikov (1992). "The Jinn of the Time Machine: Nontrivial Self-Consistent Solutions." *Classical and Quantum Gravity* 9 (October):2309–2321.

Lovecraft, H. P. (1982). "The Shadow Out of Time" and "The Dreams in the Witch-House." In *The Best of H. P. Lovecraft*. New York: Ballantine.

———— (1970). "The Silver Key" and "Through the Gates of the Silver Key." In *The Dream—Quest of Unknown Kadath*. New York: Ballantine.

Lovecraft, H. P., and A. Derleth (1957). "The Ancestor" and "The Lamp of Alhazred." In *The Survivor and Others*. Sauk City, WI: Arkham House.

Lowenthal, D. (1985). *The Past is a Foreign Country*. New York: Cambridge University Press.

Lundwall, S. J. (BRW). "Nobody Here But Us Shadows."

MacBeath, M. (1986). "Clipping Time's Wings." *Mind* 95 (April):233–237.

———— (1983). "Communication and Time Reversal." *Synthese* 56 (July):27–46.

———— (1982). "Who Was Dr. Who's Father?" *Synthese* 51 (June):397–430.

MacDonald, J. D. (SSFT). "Spectator Sport."

———— (1971). "Half-Past Eternity." In *The Human Equation*. Edited by W.F. Nolan. Los Angeles: Sherbourne Press.

———— (GRSF2). "A Game for Blondes."

Macey, S. L. (1980). *Clocks and the Cosmos: time in Western life and thought*. Hamden, CT: Archon.

Macfadyen, A., Jr. (SFT). "The Time Decelerator."

Mackie, J. L. (1966). "The Direction of Causation." *Philosophical Review* 75:441–466.

Mackie, P. (1992). "Causing, Delaying, and Hastening: Do Rains Cause Fires?" *Mind* 101 (July):483–500.

MacKinnon, E. (1962). "Time and Contemporary Physics." *International Philosophical Quarterly* 2 (September):428–457.

Malament, D. B. (1987). "A Note About Closed Timelike Curves in Gödel Space-Time." *Journal of Mathematical Physics* 28 (October):2427–2430.

———— (1985). "Minimal Acceleration Requirements for 'Time Travel' in Gödel Space-Time." *Journal of Mathematical Physics* 26 (April):774–777.

———— (1984). " 'Time Travel' in the Gödel Universe." *Proceedings of the Philosophy of Science Association* 2:91–100.

Malotki, E. (1983). *Hopi Time*. New York: Mouton.

Mandino, O. (1980). *The Christ Commission*. New York: Lippincott and Crowell.

Manley, E. A., and W. Thode (1930). "The Time Annihilator." *Wonder Stories*, November.

Manning, H. P. (1960). *The Fourth Dimension Simply Explained*. New York: Dover.

Manning, L. (BGA2). "The Man Who Awoke."

Marder, L. (1971). *Time and the Space-Traveller*. London: George Allen & Unwin.

Margenau, H. (1954). "Can Time Flow Backwards?" *Philosophy of Science* 21 (April):79–92.

Marlow, L. (1944). *The Devil in Crystal*. London: Faber and Faber.

Masson, D. I. (1968). "A Two-Timer." In *The Best SF Stories from 'New Worlds'*. Edited by M. Moorcock. New York: Berkley.

Martin, G. R. R. (SFSSS). "FTA."

Matheson, R. (1975). *Bid Time Return*. New York: Viking.

Matthews, G. (1979). "Time's Arrow and the Structure of Spacetime." *Philosophy of Science* 46 (March):82–97.

Maxwell, N. (1988). "Are Probabilism and Special Relativity Incompatible?" *Philosophy of Science* 55 (December):640–645.

———— (1985). "Are Probabilism and Special Relativity Incompatible?" *Philosophy of Science* 52 (March):23–43.

Mayo, B. (1955). "Professor Smart on Temporal Asymmetry." *Australasian Journal of Philosophy* 33:38–44.

McArthur, R. P., and M. P. Slattery (1974). "Peter Damian and Undoing the Past." *Philosophical Studies* 25:137–141.

McCall, S. (1976). "Objective Time Flow." *Philosophy of Science* 43 (September):337–362.

———— (1966). "Temporal Flux." *American Philosophical Quarterly* 3 (October):270–281.

McConnell, J. (1983). "Avoidance Situation." In *Starships*. Edited by I. Asimov, M. H. Greenberg, and C. G. Waugh. New York: Ballantine.

McDevitt, J. (FCW). "Time's Arrow."

McGivern, W. P. (1941). "Sidetrack in Time." *Amazing Stories*, July.

McKenna, R. (BO). "The Secret Place."

McKeon, D. G. C., and G. N. Ord (1992). "Time Reversal in Stochastic Processes and the Dirac Equation." *Physical Review Letters* 69 (6 July):3–4.

McLaughlin, D. (1976). *Hawk Among the Sparrows*. New York: Charles Scribner's Sons.

McTaggart, J. E. (1908). "The Unreality of Time." *Mind* 17 (October):457–474.

Mehlberg, H. (BIPT). "Philosophical Aspects of Physical Time."

———— (1961). "Physical Laws and Time's Arrow." In *Current Issues in the Philosophy of Science*. Edited by H. Feigl and G. Maxwell. New York: Holt, Rinehart, and Winston.

Meiland, J. W. (1974). "A Two-Dimensional Passage Model of Time for Time Travel." *Philosophical Studies* 26 (November):153–173.

———— (1965). "Can the Past Change?" In *Scepticism and Historical Knowledge*. New York: Random House.

Mellor, D. H. (1981). *Real Time*. New York: Cambridge University Press.

Mellor, F., and I. Moss (1990). "Stability of Black Holes in de Sitter Space." *Physical Review D* 41 (15 January):403–409.

Mendilow, A. A. (1952). *Time and the Novel*. New York: Peter Nevill.

Meredith, D. W. (1949). "Next Friday Morning." *Astounding Science Fiction*, February.

Meredith, R. C. (1978). *Vestiges of Time*. Garden City, New York: Doubleday.

———— (1976). *Run, Come See Jerusalem!* New York: Ballantine.

Merrill, A. A. (1922). "The t of Physics." *Journal of Philosophy* 19 (27 April):238–241.

Meyerson, E. (1985). *The Relativistic Deduction, Boston Studies in the Philosophy of Science*. Vol. 83. Dordrecht; Holland: D. Reidel.

Mikheeva, E. V., and I. D. Novikov (1993). "Inelastic Billiard Ball in a Spacetime with a Time Machine." *Physical Review D,* 47 (15 February): 1432-1436.

Miller, G. (1973). "The Inexactness of Time." *Foundations of Physics* 3 (September):389–398.

Miller, J. J. (1987). "Ouroboros." In *A Very Large Array*. Edited by M. M. Snodgrass. Albuquerque: University of New Mexico Press.

Miller, P. S. (FSFS). "As Never Was," and "The Sands of Time."

———— (1951). "Status Quondam." In *New Tales of Space and Time*. Edited by R. J. Healy. New York: Henry Holt and Co.

Miller, R. W., and G. B. Chamberlain (1982). "There Are Laws and Then There Are Laws." *Extrapolation* 23 Fall.

Mines, S. (1951). "A Taxable Dimension." *Startling Stories*, May.

———— (1946). "Find the Sculptor." *Thrilling Wonder Stories*, Spring.

Mink, L.O. (1960). "Time, McTaggart and Pickwickian Language." *Philosophical Quarterly* 10 (July):252–263.

Minkowski, H. (BST). "The Union of Space and Time."

Mirman, R. (1975). "The Direction of Time." *Foundations of Physics* 5 (September):491–511.

———— (1973). "Comments on the Dimensionality of Time." *Foundations of Physics* 3 (September):321–333.

Misner, C. W. (1969a). "Quantum Cosmology." *Physical Review* 186 (25 October):1319–1327.

_____ (1969b). "Absolute Zero of Time." *Physical Review* 186 (25 October):1328–1333.

Misner, C. W., and J. Wheeler (1957). "Gravitation, Electromagnetism, Unquantized Charge, and Mass as Properties of Curved Empty Space." *Annals of Physics* 2 (December):525–603.

Mitchell, E. P. (1973). "The Clock That Went Backward." In *The Crystal Man*. New York: Doubleday.

_____ (FM). "The Tachypomp: a mathematical demonstration."

Mitchell, M. (1936). *Traveller in Time*. New York: Sheed and Ward.

Moorcock, M. (1969). *Behold the Man*. London: Allison & Busby.

Moore, C. L. (1975). "Tryst in Time." In *The Best of C. L. Moore*. New York: Ballantine.

Moore, W. (1953). *Bring the Jubilee*. New York: Farrar, Straus, and Young.

Moravec, H. (1991). "Time Travel and Computing." Unpublished.

Morpurgo, G., B. F. Touschek, and L. A. Radicati (1954). "On Time Reversal." *Nuovo Cimento* 12 (November):677–698.

Morris, M. S., K. S. Thorne, and U. Yurtsever (1988). "Wormholes, Time Machines, and the Weak Energy Condition." *Physical Review Letters* 61 (26 September):1446–1449.

Morris, M. S., and K. S. Thorne (1988). "Wormholes in Spacetime and Their Use for Interstellar Travel: a tool for teaching general relativity." *American Journal of Physics* 56 (May):395–412.

Morris, R. (1990). *The Edges of Science*. Englewood Cliffs, NJ: Prentice-Hall.

_____ (1984). *Time's Arrows*. New York: Simon & Schuster.

Morrison, P. (ET). "Time's Arrow and External Perturbations."

Morrison, W. (1943). "Forgotten Past." *Startling Stories*, January.

Moskowitz, S. (TC). "Death of a Dinosaur."

Mundle, C. W. K. (1967). "The Space-Time World." *Mind* 76 (April):264–269.

_____ (1954). "Mr. Dobbs' Two-Dimensional Theory of Time." *British Journal for the Philosophy of Science* 4 (February):331–337.

Murphy, M. (1951). "Time Tourist." *Fantasy and Science Fiction*, February.

Murthy, P. V. R. (1971). "Search for Tachyons in the Cosmic Radiation." *Lettere al Nuovo Cimento* 1(2) (March):908–912.

Nahin, P. J. (1988). "Twisters." *Analog*, April.

_____ (1985). "The Invitation." In *The Fourth Omni Book of Science Fiction*. Edited by E. Datlow. New York: Zebra.

_____ (1979a). "Old Friends Across Time." *Analog*, May.

_____ (1979b). "Newton's Gift." *Omni*, January.

Narlikar, J. V. (1978). "Cosmic Tachyons: An Astrophysical Approach." *American Scientist* 66 (September–October).

_____ (1965). "The Direction of Time." *British Journal for the Philosophy of Science* 15 (February):281–285.

_____ (1962a). "Neutrinos and the Arrow of Time in Cosmology." *Proceedings of the Royal Society of London* 270 A (December):553–561.

_____ (1962b). "Rotating Universes." In *Evidences for Gravitational Theories*. Edited by C. Moller. Proceedings of the International School of Physics. Course 20, New York: Academic Press.

Nathan, R. (1968). "Encounter in the Past." In *The Best from Fantasy and Science Fiction*. Edited by E. L. Ferman. Vol. 17. Garden City, NY: Doubleday.

Nearing, H., Jr. (MM). "The Hermeneutical Doughnut."

_____ (BFSF3). "The Maladjusted Classroom."

_____ (BFSF2). "The Hyperspherical Basketball."

Nerlich, G. (1991). "How Euclidean Geometry Has Mislead Metaphysics." *Journal of Philosophy* 88 (April):169–189.

_____ (1982). "Special Relativity is Not Based on Causality." *British Journal for the Philosophy of Science* 33 (December):361–388.

_____ (1981). "Can Time Be Finite?" *Pacific Philosophical Quarterly* 62 (July):227–239.

_____ (1976). *The Shape of Space*. Cambridge: Cambridge University Press.

Neville, K. (1953). "Mission." *Fantasy and Science Fiction*, April.

New, C. (1992). "Time and Punishment." *Analysis* 52 (January):35–40.

Newcomb, S. (1898). "The Philosophy of Hyper-Space." *Science* 7 (7 January):1–7.

_____ (1877). "Elementary Theorems Relating to the Geometry of a Space of Three Dimensions and of Uniform Positive Curvature in the Fourth Dimension." *Journal fur die Reine and Ungewandte Mathematik* 83:293–299.

Newton, R. G. (CPT). "Relativity and the Order of Cause and Effect in Time."

_____ (1970). "Particles That Travel Faster Than Light?" *Science* 167 (20 March):1569–1574.

Newton-Smith, W. H. (1980). *The Structure of Time*. London: Routledge & Kegan Paul.

Nicholls, P. (1983). *The Science in Science Fiction*. New York: Alfred A. Knopf.

Nissim-Sabat, C. (1979). "On Grunbaum and Retrocausation in Classical Electrodynamics." *Philosophy of Science* 46 (March):118–135 [and the reply immediately following, 46 (March):136–160].

Niven, L. (WMHB). "The Return of William Proxmire."

_____ (1979). "Wrong-Way Street" and "Rotating Cylinders and the Possibility of Global Causality Violation." In *Convergent Series*. New York: Ballantine.

_____ (E). "ARM."

_____ (S1). "Singularities Make Me Nervous."

_____ (1973). "The Flight of the Horse," "Leviathan," "Bird in the Hand," "Death in a Cage," and "There is a Wolf in My Time Machine." In *The Flight of the Horse*. New York: Del Rey/Ballantine.

_____ (1971). "The Theory and Practice of Time Travel" and "All the Myriad Ways." In *All the Myriad Ways*. New York: Del Rey/Ballantine.

_____ (1968). "Neutron Star." In *Neutron Star*. New York: Del Rey.

Nolan, P. (1965). "The Time Jumpers." *Amazing Stories*, October.

Nolan, W. F. (SFSSS). "The Worlds of Monty Willson."

Nor, K. B. M. (1992). "A Topological Explanation for Three Properties of Time." *Il Nuovo Cimento* 107B (January):65–70.

Norden, E. (1977). "The Primal Solution." *Fantasy and Science Fiction*, July.

North, J. D. (1965). *The Measure of the Universe*. London: Oxford University Press.

Norton, A. (1970). *The Time Traders*. New York: Ace.

Norton, J. (1989). "Coordinates and Covariance: Einstein's View of Space-Time and the Modern View." *Foundations of Physics* 19 (October):1215–1263.

_____ (1986). "The Quest for the One Way Velocity of Light." *British Journal for the Philosophy of Science* 37 (March):118–120.

Nourse, A. E. (SSFT). "Tiger by the Tail."

_____ (1965). *The Universe Between*. New York: David McKay.

Novikov, I. D. (1993). "The Jinnee of the Time Machine." *International Journal of Modern Physics A*, in press.

———— (1992). "Time Machine and Self-Consistent Evolutions in Problems with Self-Interaction." *Physical Review D* 45 (15 March):1989–1994.

———— (1989). "An Analysis of the Operation of a Time Machine." *Soviet Physics JETP* 68 (March):439–443.

———— (1966). "Change of Relativistic Collapse Into Anticollapse and Kinematics of a Charged Sphere." *JETP Letters* 3 (1 March):142–144.

Nusenoff, R. E. (1976). "Two-Dimensional Time." *Philosophical Studies* 29 (May):337–341.

Oaklander, L. N. (1987). "McTaggart's Paradox and the Infinite Regress of Temporal Attributions: A Reply to Smith." *Southern Journal of Philosophy* 25 (Fall):425–431.

———— (1983). "McTaggart, Schlesinger, and the Two-Dimensional Time Hypothesis." *Philosophical Quarterly* 33 (October):391–397.

O'Brien, F. (1976). *The Third Policeman*. New York: New American Library.

O'Brien, F.-J. (1988). "What Was It? A Mystery." In *The Supernatural Tales of Fitz-James O'Brien*. Edited by J. A. Salmonson. Vol. 1. New York: Doubleday.

Odle, E. V. (1923). *The Clockwork Man*. Garden City, NY: Doubleday, Page.

Odoevski, V. F. (RRSF). "The Year 4338."

Ohanian, H. C. (1976). *Gravitation and Spacetime*. New York: W. W. Norton.

Oliver, C. (GSF). "Transfusion."

———— (1952). *Mists of Dawn*. New York: Holt, Rinehart, and Winston.

Olsen, B. (1951). "The Four-Dimensional Roller-Press." In *Every Boy's Book of Science Fiction*. Edited by D. A. Wollheim. New York: Frederick Fell.

———— (1934). "The Four Dimensional Auto-Parker." *Amazing Stories*, July.

———— (1933). "The Four Dimensional Escape." *Amazing Stories*, December.

———— (1928a). "Four Dimensional Transit." *Amazing Stories Quarterly*, Fall.

———— (1928b). "The Great Four Dimensional Robberies." *Amazing Stories*, May.

———— (1928c). "Four Dimensional Surgery." *Amazing Stories*, February.

Ori, A. (1991a). "Rapidly Moving Cosmic Strings and Chronology Protection." *Physical Review D* 44 (15 October):2214–2215.

———— (1991b). "Inner Structure of a Charged Black Hole: An Exact Mass-Inflation Solution." *Physical Review Letters* 67 (12 August):789–792.

Ouspensky, P. D. (1981). *Tertium Organum*. New York: Alfred A. Knopf.

———— (1948). *The Strange Life of Ivan Osokin*. London: Faber and Faber.

Overseth, O. E. (1969). "Experiments in Time Reversal." *Scientific American*, October.

Ozsvath, I., and E. L. Schucking (1969). "The Finite Rotating Universe." *Annals of Physics* 55 (15 October):166–204.

———— (1962). "Finite Rotating Universe." *Nature* 193 (24 March):1168–1169.

Padgett, A. G. (1989). "God and Time: Toward a New Doctrine of Divine Timeless Eternity." *Religious Studies* 25 (June):211–215.

Padgett, L. (1984). "Private Eye." In *The Great Science Fiction Stories*, Vol. 11, New York: DAW.

———— (1981). "Mimsy Were the Borogoves." *The Great Science Fiction Stories*. Vol. 5. New York: DAW.

———— (SFAD). "Endowment Policy."

———— (FSFS). "Time Locker."

———— (WT). "Line to Tomorrow."

———— (OSF). "What You Need."

———— (BTS). "When the Bough Breaks."

Paiva, F. M., M. J. Reboucas, and A. F. F. Teixeira (1987). "Time Travel in the Homogeneous Som-Raychaudhuri Universe." *Physics Letters A* 126 (28 December):168–170.

Palmer, R. A. (1938). "Matter Is Conserved." *Astounding Science Fiction*, April.

———— (1934). "The Time Tragedy." *Wonder Stories*, December.

———— (1930). "The Time Ray of Jandra." *Wonder Stories*, June.

Panov, V. F., and Y. G. Sbytov (1992). "Accounting for Birch's Observed Anisotropy of the Universe: cosmological rotation?" *Soviet Physics JETP* 74 (March):411–415.

Park, D. (1980). *The Image of Eternity*. Amherst, MA: The University of Massachusetts Press.

Parker, B. (1991). *Cosmic Time Travel*. New York: Plenum.

Parker, L. (1969). "Faster-Than-Light Inertial Frames and Tachyons." *Physical Review* 188 (25 December):2287–2292.

Parrinder, P. (1972). *H. G. Wells: the critical heritage*. London: Routledge & Kegan Paul.

Partridge, R. B. (1973). "Absorber Theory of Radiation and the Future of the Universe." *Nature* 244 (3 August):263–265.

Paul, T. (1983). "The Worm Ouroboros: Time Travel, Imagination, and Entropy." *Extrapolation* 24 (Fall):272–279.

Pease, M. C. (1949). "Reversion." *Astounding Science Fiction*, December.

Pei, M. A. (GSF). "The Bones of Charlemagne."

Penrose, R. (NOT). "Big Bangs, Black Holes, and 'Time's Arrow'."

———— (1978). "The Geometry of the Universe." In *Mathematics Today*. New York: Springer-Verlag.

Penrose, O., and I. C. Percival (1962). "The Direction of Time." *Proceedings of the Physical Society* (London) 79 (March):605–616.

Peres, A., and L. C. Schulman (1972). "Signals from the Future." *International Journal of Theoretical Physics* 6 (December):377–382.

Peres, A. (1969). "Where are Tachyons?" *Lettere Al Nuovo Cimento* 1:837–838.

Petkov, V. (1989). "Simultaneity, Conventionality and Existence." *British Journal for the Philosophy of Science* 40 (March):69–76.

Pfarr, J. (1981). "Time Travel in Gödel's Space." *General Relativity and Gravitation* 13 (November):1073–1091.

Phillips, A. M. (FSFS). "Time-Travel Happens!"

Philmus, R. M. (1969). "*The Time Machine*; Or, the Fourth Dimension as Prophecy." *Publications of the Modern Language Association* 84 (May):530–535.

Pierce, J. R. (GSFS). "John Sze's Future."

———— (1954). "Mr. Kinkaid's Pasts." In *Beyond the Barriers of Space and Time*. Edited by J. Merril. New York: Random House.

———— (1943). "Unthinking Cap." *Astounding Science Fiction*, July.

———— (1942). "About Quarrels, About the Past." *Astounding Science Fiction*, July.

Pike, N. (1965). "Divine Omniscience and Voluntary Action." *Philosophical Review* 74 (January):27–46.

Pinkerton, J. (1979). "Backward Time Travel, Alternate Universes, and Edward Everett Hale." *Extrapolation* 20 (Summer):168–175.

Piper, H. B. (1983). "Flight from Tomorrow," "Time and Time Again," and "Crossroads of Destiny." In *The Worlds of H. Beam Piper*. Edited by J. F. Carr. New York: Ace.

———— (1981). *Paratime*. New York: Ace.

Plachta, D. (SFSSS). "The Man from When."

Plass, G. N. (1961). "Classical Electrodynamic Equations of Motion with Radiative Reaction." *Reviews of Modern Physics* 33 (January):37–62.

Platt, C. (1974). "Time Machines for Domestic Use." *Harper's*, January.

Plimmer, D. (1941). "Man From the Wrong Time-Track." *Uncanny Stories*, April.

Podolny, R. (1970). "Invasion." In *The Ultimate Threshold*. Edited by M. Ginsburg. New York: Holt, Rinehart, and Winston.

Pohl, F. (SFSSS). "The Deadly Mission of Phineas Snodgrass."

———— (1975). "The Celebrated No-Hit Inning." In *Run to Starlight*. Edited by M. Greenberg, J. Olander, and P. Warrick. New York: Delacorte.

———— (1956). "Target One," "Let the Ants Try," and "The Mapmakers." In *Alternating Currents*. New York: Ballantine.

Polchinski, J. (1991). "Weinberg's Nonlinear Quantum Mechanics and the Einstein-Podolsky-Rosen Paradox." *Physical Review Letters* 66 (28 January):397–400.

Poleshchuk, A. (LDA). "Homer's Secret."

Popper, K. (1978). "On the Possiblity of an Infinite Past." *British Journal for the Philosophy of Science* 29 (March):47–48.

———— (1956). "The Arrow of Time." *Nature* 177 (17 March):538.

Porges, A. (SFS). "The Rescuer."

———— (CJSF). "Guilty As Charged."

Poynting, J. H. (1920). "Overtaking the Rays of Light." In Poynting's *Collected Scientific Papers*. Cambridge: Cambridge University Press.

Preuss, P. (1981). *Re-Entry*. New York: Bantam.

Price, H. (1991a). "The Asymmetry of Radiation: Reinterpreting the Wheeler-Feynman Argument." *Foundations of Physics* 21 (August):959–975.

———— (1991b). "Review Article." *British Journal for the Philosophy of Science* 42 (March):111–144.

———— (1984). "The Philosophy and Physics of Affecting the Past." *Synthese* 61 (December):299–323.

Priestley, J. B. (1964). *Man and Time*. New York: Doubleday.

———— (1953). "Look After the Strange Girl," "The Statues," and "Mr. Strenberry's Tale." In *The Other Place*. New York: Harper and Brothers.

———— (1939). *I Have Been Here Before*. London: Samuel French Limited.

———— (1948). *Dangerous Corner*. In *The Plays of J. B. Priestley*. Vol. 1. London: Heinemann.

———— (1937). *Time and the Conways*. London: William Heinemann.

Prokhovnik, S. J. (1986). "The Twin Paradoxes of Special Relativity: Their Resolution and Implications." *Foundations of Physics* 19 (May):541–552.

Purcell, E. (1963). "Radioastronomy and Communication Through Space." In *Interstellar Communication*. Edited by A. G. W. Cameron. New York: W. A. Benjamin.

Putnam, H. (1967). "Time and Physical Geometry." *Journal of Philosophy* 64 (April):240–247.

———— (1962). "It Ain't Necessarily So." *Journal of Philosophy* 59 (11 October):658–671.

Queenan, J. (1990). "Time Warp: Or, Investing in the Future Is a Bust." *Barron's* 70 (8 January):46.

Quinton, A. (1962). "Spaces and Times." *Philosophy* 37 (April):130–147.

Ramsaye, T. (1926). *A Million and One Nights*. Vol. 1. New York: Simon and Schuster.

Rao, B. S. (PWO). "Victims of Time."

Raphael, L. (1941). "The Man Who Saw Through Time." *Fantastic Adventures*, September.

Ray, C. (1991). "Time Travel." In *Time, Space and Philosophy*. New York: Routledge.

———— (1982). "Can We Travel Faster Than Light?" *Analysis* 42 (January):50–52.

Ray, R. (1934). "Today's Yesterday." *Wonder Stories*, January.

Reboucas, M. J. (1979). "A Rotating Universe with Violation of Causality." *Physics Letters* 70A (5 March):161–163.

Recami, E. (1987). "Tachyon Kinematics and Causality: A Systematic Thorough Analysis of the Tachyon Causal Paradoxes." *Foundations of Physics* 17 (March):239–296.

Redmount, I. (1990). "Wormholes, Time Travel and Quantum Gravity." *New Scientist*, 28 April.

Reeds, F. A. (1942). "Forever Is Not So Long." *Astounding Science Fiction*, May.

Reichenbach, H. (1958). *The Philosophy of Space and Time*. New York: Dover.

———— (1956). *The Direction of Time*. Los Angeles: University of California Press.

Reinganum, M. R. (1986). "Is Time Travel Impossible? A Financial Proof." *Journal of Portfolio Management* 13 (Fall):10–12.

Remnant, P. (1978). "Peter Damian: Could God Change the Past?" *Canadian Journal of Philosophy* 8 (June):259–268.

Reynolds, M. (1988). "Compounded Interest." *The Great Science Fiction Stories*. Vol. 18. New York: DAW.

———— (1986). "The Business, As Usual." In *The Great Science Fiction Stories*. Vol. 14. New York: DAW.

———— (1982). "Posted." In *Flying Saucers*. Edited by I. Asimor, M. H. Greenberg, and C. G. Waugh. New York: Ballantine.

———— (1959). "Unborn Tomorrow." *Astounding Science Fiction*, June.

———— (1953). "Advice from Tomorrow." *Science Fiction Quarterly*, August.

Reynolds, M., and F. Brown (GRSF1). "Dark Interlude."

Richards, J. (1984). "Deadtime." In *Universe 14*. New York: Doubleday.

Richards, J. T. (1965). "Minor Alteration." *Fantasy and Science Fiction*, December.

Richardson, C. A. (1944). *Happiness, Freedom and God*. London: George G. Harrap.

Rietdijk, C. W. (1987). "Retroactive Effects from Measurements." *Foundations of Physics* 17 (March):297–311.

———— (1981). "Another Proof that the Future Can Influence the Present." *Foundations of Physics* 11 (October):783–790.

———— (1978). "Proof of a Retroactive Influence." *Foundations of Physics* 8 (August):615–628.

———— (1976). "Special Relativity and Determinism." *Philosophy of Science* 43 (December):598–609.

———— (1966). "A Rigorous Proof of Determinism from the Special Theory of Relativity." *Philosophy of Science* 33 (December):341–344.

Rigaut, J. (1970). "Un Brilliant Sujet." In *Ecrits*, Paris: Gallimard.

Riggs, H. H. (HJ). "Immortality and the Fourth Dimension."

Rindler, W. (1977). *Essential Relativity*. New York: Springer-Verlag.

Robertson, H. P. (BST). "Geometry as a Branch of Physics."

Rocklynne, R. (1980). "Time Wants a Skeleton." In *The Great Science Fiction Stories*. Vol. 3. New York: DAW.

———— (1940). "The Reflection That Lived." *Fantastic Adventures*, June.

Rogers, J. T. (1953). "Moment Without Time." In *The Best from Startling Stories*. Edited by S. Mines. New York: Henry Holt.

Rolnick, W. B. (1972). "Tachyons and the Arrow of Causality." *Physical Review D* 6 (15 October):2300–2301.

_____ (1969). "Implications of Causality for Faster-Than-Light Matter." *Physical Review* 183 (25 July):1105–1108.

Rosborough, L. B. (1934). "Hastings -- 1066." *Amazing Stories*, June.

Rosen, R. (1985). *Anticipatory Systems*. New York: Pergamon Press.

Rosen, S. M. (1988). "A Neo-Intuitive Proposal for Kaluza-Klein Unification." *Foundations of Physics* 18 (November):1093–1139.

Rosen, S. P. (1968). "TCP Invariance and the Dimensionality of Space-Time." *Journal of Mathematical Physics* 9 (October):1593–1594.

Rosenbaum, J. (1957). "Now and Then." *Fantasy and Science Fiction*, November.

Ross, M. (1950). *The Man Who Lived Backward*. New York: Farrar, Straus and Company.

Rothman, M. A. (1988). *A Physicist's Guide to Skepticism: applying laws of physics to faster-than-light travel, psychic phenomena, telepathy, time travel, UFO's and other pseudoscientific claims*. New York: Prometheus.

_____ (1960). "Things That Go Faster Than Light." *Scientific American*, July.

Rothman, T. (1987). "The Seven Arrows of Time." *Discover*, February.

_____ (1985). "Grand Illusions: Further Conversations on the Edge of Spacetime." In *Frontiers of Modern Physics*. New York: Dover.

Rousseau, V. (1917). *The Messiah of the Cylinder*. Chicago: A.C. McClurg.

Rucker, R. (1986). "In Frozen Time." In *Afterlives*. Edited by P. Sargent and I. Watson. New York: Vintage.

_____ (1984). *The Fourth Dimension*. Boston: Houghton Mifflin.

_____ (1977). *Geometry, Relativity, and the Fourth Dimension*. New York: Dover.

Russell, E. F. (1980). "Mechanical Mice." In *The Great Science Fiction Stories*. Vol. 3. New York: DAW.

Russell, E. F., and L. T. Johnson (SFT). "Seeker of Tomorrow."

Saari, O. (1941). "The Door." *Astounding Science Fiction*, November.

_____ (1937). "The Time Bender." *Astounding Stories*, August.

Sachs, M. (1969). "Space, Time and Elementary Interactions in Relativity." *Physics Today* 22 (February):51–60.

Sachs, R. G. (1987). *The Physics of Time Reversal*. Chicago: University of Chicago Press.

_____ (1972). "Time Reversal." *Science* 176 (12 May):587–597.

_____ (1963). "Can the Direction of Flow of Time Be Determined?" *Science* 140 (21 June):1284–1290.

Sadler, M. (1986). *Alistair's Time Machine*. Englewood Cliffs, NJ: Prentice-Hall.

Saint Augustine (1961). *Confessions*. New York: Penguin.

Salecker, H., and E. P. Wigner (1958). "Quantum Limitations of the Measurement of Space-Time Distances." *Physical Review* 109 (15 January):571–577.

Salmon, W. C. (1977). "The Philosophical Significance of the One-Way Speed of Light." *Nous* 11 (September):253–292.

Savitt, S. F. (1982), "Tachyon Signals, Causal Paradoxes, and the Relativity of Simultaneity." *Proceedings of the 1982 Biennial Meeting of the Philosophy of Science Association*. Edited by P. Asquith and T. Nickles. East Lansing, MI. Vol. 1. 277–292.

Schachner, N. (BGA3). "Past, Present, and Future."

_____ (1937). "Lost In the Dimensions." *Astounding Stories*, November.

_____ (1934). "The Time Imposter." *Astounding Stories*, March.

_____ (1933). "Ancestral Voices." *Astounding Stories*, December.

_____ (1932). "The Time Express." *Wonder Stories*, December.

Schaffer, S. (1979). "John Michell and Black Holes." *Journal for the History of Astronomy* 10 (February):42–43.

Schere, M. (1938). "Anachronistic Optics." *Astounding Stories*, February.

Schiff, L. (NT). "Nuclear Moments and Time Symmetry."

Schild, A. (1963). "Electromagnetic Two-Body Problem." *Physical Review* 131 (15 September):2762–2766.

_____ (1959). "The Clock Paradox in Relativity Theory." *American Mathematical Monthly* 66:1–18.

Schlegel, R. (1980). "The Light Clock: Error and Implications." *Foundations of Physics* 10 (April):345–351.

_____ (VOT). "Time and Thermodynamics."

_____ (1961). *Time and the Physical World*. East Lansing, MI: Michigan State University Press.

Schlesinger, G. N. (1985). "How to Navigate the River of Time." *Philosophical Quarterly* 35 (January):91–94.

_____ (1982). "How Time Flies." *Mind* 91 (October):501–523.

Schmidt, H. (1978). "Can An Effect Precede Its Cause? A Model of a Noncausal World." *Foundations of Physics* 8 (June):463–480.

_____ (1966). "Model of an Oscillating Cosmos Which Rejuvenates During Contraction." *Journal of Mathematical Physics* 7 (March):494–509.

Schmidt, J., and R. Newman (1980). "Search for Advanced Fields in Electromagnetic Radiation (Abstract)." *Bulletin of the American Physical Society* 25 (April):581.

Schulman, L. S. (1973). "Correlating Arrows of Time." *Physical Review D* 7 (15 May): 2868–2874.

_____ (1971a). "Tachyon Paradoxes." *American Journal of Physics* 39 (May):481–484.

_____ (1971b). "Gravitational Shock Waves from Tachyons." *Il Nuovo Cimento* 2B (11 March):38–44.

Schuster, M. M. (1986). "Is the Flow of Time Subjective?" *Review of Metaphysics* 39 (June):695–714.

Schweber, S. S. (1986). "Feynman and the Visualization of Space-Time Processes." *Reviews of Modern Physics* 58 (April):449–508.

Sciama, D. W. (1958). "Determinism and the Cosmos." In *Determinism and Freedom in the Age of Modern Science*. Edited by S. Hook. New York: New York University Press.

Scortia, T. N. (1981). "When You Hear the Tone." In *The Best of Thomas N. Scortia*. Garden City, NY: Doubleday & Co.

Seabury, P. (1961). "The Histronaut." *Columbia University Forum* 4 (Summer):4–8.

Sears, F. W., and R. W. Brehme (1968). *Introduction to the Theory of Relativity*. Reading, MA: Addison-Wesley.

Sell, W. (SFAD). "Other Tracks."

Sellings, A. (1971). "The Last Time Around." In *World's Best Science Fiction*. Edited by D. A. Wollheim and T. Carr. New York: Ace.

Serling, R. E. (TZ). "Walking Distance," "Execution," "Back There," "The Odyssey of Flight 33," "A Hundred Yards Over the Rim," "Once Upon a Time," "No Time Like the Past," "A Kind of Stopwatch," "The 7th is Made Up of Phantoms," and "A Most Unusual Camera."

Shaara, M. (SFS). "Man of Distinction."

_____ (1954). "Time Payment." *Fantasy and Science Fiction*, June.

Shallis, M. (1982). *On Time*. London: Burnett.

Shapiro, S. (1986). *A Time To Remember*. New York: Random House.

Shapiro, S. L., and S. A. Teukolsky (1991a). "Formation of Naked Singularities: The Violation of Cosmic Censorship." *Physical Review Letters* 66 (25 February):994–997.

———— (1991b). "Black Holes, Naked Singularities and Cosmic Censorship." *American Scientist*, July–August.

Sharkey, J. (1965). "The Trouble with Hyperspace." *Fantastic*, April.

Sharp, D. D. (1939). "Faster Than Light." *Marvel Science Stories*, February.

Shaw, B. (TW). "Skirmish on a Summer Morning."

———— (TOT). "Light of Other Days."

Shay, H. J. (1953). "The Ambassador from the 21st Century." *Startling Stories*, March.

Sheckley, R. (1990). "The World of Heart's Desire." In *The Great Science Fiction Stories*. Vol. 21. New York: DAW.

———— (MTMW). "Miss Mouse and the Fourth Dimension."

———— (TIT). "The King's Wishes."

———— (1957). "The Deaths of Ben Baxter." *Galaxy Science Fiction*, July.

———— (1955). "A Thief in Time" and "Something for Nothing." In *Citizen in Space*. New York: Ballantine.

Sheldon, E. (1990). "Faster Than Light?" *Sky & Telescope* 79 (January):26–29.

Shenglin, C. (1992a). "The Theory of Relativity and Super-Luminal Speeds IV: The Catastrophy of the Schwarzschild Field and Superluminal Expansion of Extragalactic Radio Sources." *Astrophysics and Space Science* 193 (July):123–140.

———— (1992b). "The Theory of Relativity and Super-Luminal-Speeds III: The catastrophe of the space-time on the Finsler metric." *Astrophysics and Space Science* 190 (April):303–315.

———— (1990). "The Theory of Relativity and Super-Luminal Speeds II: Theory of relativity in the Finsler space-time." *Astrophysics and Space Science* 174 (December):165–171.

———— (1988). "The Theory of Relativity and Super-Luminal Speeds I: Kinematical part." *Astrophysics and Space Science* 145 (June):293–302.

Sherred, T. L. (1983). "E for Effort." In *The Great Science Fiction Stories*. Vol. 9. New York: DAW.

Shimony, A. (QCST). "Events and Processes in the Quantum World."

Shiner, L. (TT). "Twilight Time."

Shoemaker, S. (1969). "Time Without Change." *Journal of Philosophy* 66 (19 June):363–381.

Sigman, J. (1986). "Science and Parody in Kurt Vonnegut's *The Sirens of Titan*." *Mosaic* 19 (Winter):15–32.

Silverberg, R. (1991). "Hunters in the Forest." *Omni*, October.

———— (1990). *Letters from Atlantis*. New York: Antheneum.

———— (1987). *Project Pendulum*. New York: Walker.

———— (SFS). "The Assassin."

———— (1986). "In Entropy's Jaws," "Many Mansions," "Ms. Found in an Abandoned Time Machine," "When We Went to See the End of the World," "{Now+n, Now−n}," "Trips," and "What We Learned from this Morning's Newspaper." In *Beyond the Safe Zone*. New York: Warner.

———— (CJSF). "Hawksbill Station."

———— (TIT). "MUgwump 4."

_____ (1970). *Vornan-19*. London: Coronet.

_____ (1969). *Up the Line*. New York: Ballantine.

_____ (1967). *The Time Hoppers*. Garden City, NY: Doubleday.

_____ (VIT). "Absolutely Inflexible."

Simak, C. D. (1978). *Mastodonia*. New York: Ballantine.

_____ (BGA1). "The World of the Red Sun."

_____ (S1). "The Birch Clump Cylinder."

_____ (1974a). "The Marathon Photograph." In *Threads of Time*. Edited by R. Silverberg. New York: Thomas Nelson.

_____ (1974b). *Our Children's Children*. New York: G. P. Putnam's Sons.

_____ (TC). "Over the River & Through the Woods."

_____ (1962). "Project Mastodon." In *All the Traps of Earth*. Garden City, NY: Doubleday & Co.

_____ (1960). "Carbon Copy." In *The Worlds of Clifford Simak*. New York: Simon and Schuster.

_____ (1951). *Time and Again*. New York: Simon and Schuster.

_____ (1938). "Rule Eighteen." *Astounding Science Fiction*, July.

_____ (1932). "Hellhounds of the Cosmos." *Astounding Stories*, June.

Simak, C. D., and C. Jacobi (1975). "The Street That Wasn't There." In *Creatures from Beyond*. Edited by T. Carr. New York: Thomas Nelson.

Skillen, A. (1965). "The Myth of Temporal Division." *Analysis* 26 (December):44–47.

Sklar, L. (1974). *Space, Time and Spacetime*. Los Angeles: University of California Press.

Sladek, J. (1981). "The Singular Visitor from Not-Yet" and "1937 A.D.!" In *The Best of John Sladek*. New York: Pocket.

Sleator, W. (1990). *Strange Attractors*. New York: E. P. Dutton.

_____ (1986). *The Boy Who Reversed Himself*. New York: E. P. Dutton.

_____ (1981). *The Green Futures of Tycho*. New York: E. P. Dutton.

Small, R. (1991). "Incommensurability and Recurrence: From Oresme to Simmel." *Journal of the History of Ideas* 52 (January–March):121–137.

_____ (1986). "Tristram Shandy's Last Page." *British Journal for the Philosophy of Science* 37 (June):213–216.

Smart, J. J. C. (1981). "The Reality of the Future." *Philosophia* 10 (December):141–150.

_____ (1972). "Space-Time and Individuals." In *Logic and Art*. Edited by R. Rudner and I. Scheffler. Indianapolis: Bobbs-Merrill.

_____ (1967). "The Unity of Space-Time: Mathematics Versus Myth Making." *Australasian Journal of Philosophy* 25:214–217.

_____ (1963). "Is Time Travel Possible?" *Journal of Philosophy* 60 (April):237–241.

_____ (1958). "A Review of *The Direction of Time*." *Philosophical Quarterly* 8 (January):72–77.

_____ (1955a). "Mr. Mayo on Temporal Asymmetry." *Astralasian Journal of Philosophy* 33:124–127.

_____ (1955b). "Spatialising Time." *Mind* 64:239–241.

_____ (1954). "The Temporal Asymmetry of the World." *Analysis* 14 (March):79–83.

_____ (1949). "The River of Time." *Mind* 58 (October):483–494.

Smith, C. A. (1970). "An Adventure in Futurity." In *Other Dimensions*. Sauk City, WI: Arkham House.

_____ (1964). "Murder in the Fourth Dimension." In *Tales of Science and Sorcery*. Sauk City, WI: Arkham House.

_____ (1932). "Flight Through Super-Time." *Wonder Stories*, August.

Smith, G., and R. Weingard (1990). "Quantum Cosmology and the Beginning of the Universe." *Philosophy of Science* 57 (December):663–667.

Smith, G. H. (MT). "Take Me to Your Leader."

Smith, J. S. (1958). "Encountering Things Past." *Library Journal* 83 (15 November):3265–3268.

Smith, Q. (1991). "Atheism, Theism and Big Bang Cosmology." *Australasian Journal of Philosophy* 69 (March):48–66.

_____ (1988). "The Uncaused Beginning of the Universe." *Philosophy of Science* 55 (March):39–57.

_____ (1987). "Infinity and the Past." *Philosophy of Science* 54 (March):63–75.

_____ (1986a). "The Infinite Regress of Temporal Attributions." *Southern Journal of Philosophy* 24 (Fall):383–396.

_____ (1986b). "World Ensemble Explanations." *Pacific Philosophical Quarterly* 67 (January):73–86.

Soares, I. D. (1980). "Inhomogeneous Rotating Universes with Closed Timelike Geodesics of Matter." *Journal of Mathematical Physics* 21 (March):521–525.

Sokolowski, R. (1982). "Timing." *Review of Metaphysics* 35 (June):687–714.

Soleng, H. H. (1989). "Gödel-Type Cosmologies with Spin Density." *Physics Letters A* 137 (29 May):326–328.

Som, M. M., and A. K. Raychaudhuri (1968). "Cylindrically Symmetric Charged Dust Distributions in Rigid Rotation in General Relativity." *Proceedings of the Royal Society A* 304 (April):81–86.

Sorenson, R. A. (1987). "Time Travel, Parahistory and Hume." *Philosophy* 62 (April):227–236.

South, C. (1942). "The Time Mirror." *Amazing Stories*, December.

Spellman, L. (1982). "Causing Yesterday's Effects." *Canadian Journal of Philosophy* 12 (March):145–161.

Spinrad, N. (1980). "The Weed of Time." In *Alchemy & Academe*. Edited by A. McCaffrey. New York: Ballantine.

Sprague, C. (1951). "Time Track." *Startling Stories*, January.

Spruill, G. (1980). "The Janus Equation." In *Binary Star No. 4*. New York: Dell.

Stannard, F. R. (1966). "Symmetry of the Time Axis." *Nature* 211 (13 August):693–695.

Stapledon, O. (1953). *To the End of Time*. New York: Funk and Wagnalls.

Stapleton, D. (1942). "How Much To Thursday?" *Thrilling Wonder Stories*, December.

Starobinsky, A. A. (1980). "A New Type of Isotropic Cosmological Models Without Singularity." *Physics Letters* 91B (24 March):99–102.

Statten, V. (1953). *Zero Hour*. London: Scion.

Stearns, I. (1950). "Time and the Timeless." *Review of Metaphysics* 4 (December):187–200.

Stein, H. (1991). "On Relativity Theory and Openness of the Future." *Philosophy of Science* 58 (June):147–167.

_____ (1984). "The Everett Interpretation of Quantum Mechanics: Many Worlds or None?" *Nous* 18 (November):635–652.

_____ (1970). "On the Paradoxical Time-Structures of Gödel." *Philosophy of Science* 37 (December):589–601.

_____ (1968). "On Einstein-Minkowski Space-Time." *Journal of Philosophy* 65 (11 January):5–23.

_____ (1967). "Newtonian Space-Time." *Texas Quarterly* 10 (Autumn):174–200.

Stephenson, L. M. (1978). "Clarification of an Apparent Asymmetry in Electromagnetic Theory." *Foundations of Physics* 8 (December):921–926.

Stern, M. B. (1936). "Counterclockwise: Flux of Time in Literature." *Sewanee Review* 44 (July–September):338–365.

Stone, L. F. (1935). "The Man With the Four Dimensional Eyes." *Wonder Stories*, August.

Strauss, E. S. (undated). *The MIT Science Fiction Society's Index to the S-F Magazines, 1951–1965*.

Stromberg, G. (1961). "Space, Time, and Eternity." *Journal of the Franklin Institute* 272 (August):134–144.

Sturgeon, T. (SFAD). "Yesterday Was Monday."

Sudarshan, E. C. G. (1969). "The Nature of Faster-Than-Light Particles and Their Interactions." *Arkiv for Fysik* 39:585–591.

Sullivan, T. (D). "Dinosaur on a Bicycle."

_____ (TT). "The Comedian."

Sutherland, R. I. (1983). "Bell's Theorem and Backwards-in-Time Causality." *International Journal of Theoretical Physics* 22 (April):377–384.

Swartz, N. (1973). "Is There An Ozma-Problem for Time?" *Analysis* 33 (January):77–82.

Sweeney, L. (1974). "Bonaventure and Aquinas on the Divine Being as Infinite." *Southwestern Journal of Philosophy* 5 (Summer):71–91.

Swinburne, R. G. (1966). "Affecting the Past." *Philosophical Quarterly* 16 (October):341–347.

_____ (1965a). "Conditions for Bitemporality." *Analysis* 26 (December):47–50.

_____ (1965b). "Times." *Analysis* 25 (June):185–191.

Sycamore, H. M. (1959). "Success Story." *Fantasy and Science Fiction*, July.

Sylvester, J. J. (1869). "A Plea for the Mathematician." *Nature* 1 (30 December):237–239.

Szilard, L. (ED). "The Mark Gable Foundation."

Tanaka, S. (1960). "Theory of Matter with Super Light Velocity." *Progress of Theoretical Physics* 24 (July):171–200.

Taylor, R. (1987). "Time and Life's Meaning." *Review of Metaphysics* 40 (June):675–686.

_____ (1959). "Moving About in Time." *Philosophical Quarterly* 9 (October):289–301.

_____ (1955). "Spatial and Temporal Analogies and the Concept of Identity." *Journal of Philosophy* 52 (27 October):599–612.

Teitelboim, C. (1970). "Splitting of the Maxwell Tensor: Radiation Reaction without Advanced Fields." *Physical Review D* 1 (15 March):1572–1582.

Tenn, W. (1983). "Brooklyn Project." In *The Great Science Fiction Stories*. Vol. 10. New York: DAW.

_____ (TSF). "Child's Play."

_____ (1962). "Time Waits for Winthrop." In *Time Waits for Winthrop*. Edited by F. Pohl. Garden City, New York: Doubleday.

_____ (1955). "Me, Myself, and I." In *Of All Possible Worlds*. New York: Ballantine.

Tertletskii, Y. P. (1968). *Paradoxes in the Theory of Relativity*. New York: Plenum.

Tevis, W. (1961). "The Other End of the Line." *Fantasy and Science Fiction*, November.

Thom, R. (1975). "Time-Travel and Non-Fatal Suicide." *Philosophical Studies* 27 (March):211–216.

Thomas, T. (AO). "The Doctor."

Thompson, D. (BT). "Worlds Enough."

Thompson, R. G. (1941). "The Brontosaurus." *Stirring Science Fiction*, April.

Thomson, J. J. (1965). "Time, Space, and Objects." *Mind* 74 (January):1–27.

't Hooft, G. (1992). "Causality in (2+1)-Dimensional Gravity." *Classical and Quantum Gravity* 9 (May):1335–1348.

Thorne, K. S. (1991). "Do the Laws of Physics Permit Closed Timelike Curves?" *Annals of the New York Academy of Sciences* 631 (10 August):182–193.

———— (MWM). "Nonspherical Gravitational Collapse—A Short Review."

———— (1970). "Nonspherical Gravitational Collapse: Does It Produce Black Holes?" *Comments on Astrophysics and Space Physics* 2 (September–October):191–196.

———— (1965). "Gravitational Collapse and the Death of a Star." *Science* 150 (24 December):1671–1679.

Thouless, D. J. (1969). "Causality and Tachyons." *Nature* 224 (1 November):506.

Tilley, R. J. (1973). " 'Willie's Blues'." In *The 1973 Annual World's Best SF*. Edited by D. A. Wollheim and A. W. Saha. New York: DAW.

Tipler, F. J. (1992). "The Ultimate Fate of Life in Universes which Undergo Inflation." *Physics Letters B* 286 (23 July):36–43.

———— (1986). "Interpreting the Wave Function of the Universe." *Physics Reports* 137 (May):231–275.

———— (QCST). "The Many-Worlds Interpretation of Quantum Mechanics in Quantum Cosmology."

———— (1980). "General Relativity and the Eternal Return." In *Essays in General Relativity*. Edited by F. J. Tipler. New York: Academic Press.

———— (1979). "General Relativity, Thermodynamics, and the Poincaré Cycle." *Nature* 280 (19 July):203–205.

———— (1977). "Singularities and Causality Violation." *Annals of Physics* 108 (22 September):1–36.

———— (1976a). "Causality Violation in Asymptotically Flat Space-Times." *Physical Review Letters* 37 (4 October):879–882.

———— (1976b). *Causality Violation in General Relativity*. University of Maryland Ph.D. dissertation. Unpublished. Available as Dissertation 76-29,018 from Xerox University Microfilms, Ann Arbor, MI.

———— (1974). "Rotating Cylinders and the Possibility of Global Causality Violation." *Physical Review D* 9 (15 April):2203–2206.

Tiptree, J., Jr. (D). "The Night-Blooming Saurian."

———— (1988). "Backward, Turn Backward." In *Crown of Stars*. New York: Tor.

———— (1978). "Houston, Houston, Do You Read?" In *Nebula Winners Twelve*. Edited by G. R. Dickson. New York: Harper & Row.

———— (1975). "The Man Who Walked Home." In *Looking Ahead*. Edited by D. Allen and L. Allen. New York: Harcourt Brace Jovanovich.

Tolman, R. C. (1917). *The Theory of the Relativity of Motion*. Berkeley: University of California Press 54–55.

Tolman, R. C., and S. Smith, (1926). "On the Nature of Light." *Proceedings of the National Academy of Sciences* 12 (15 May):343–347.

Trautman, A. (GRAV). "Conservation Laws in General Relativity."

Travis, J. (1992). "Could a Pair of Cosmic Strings Open a Route Into the Past?" *Science* 256 (10 April):179–180.

Tucker, W. (1979). *The Year of the Quiet Sun*. Boston: Gregg.

———— (1958). *The Lincoln Hunters*. New York: Rinehart.

———— (1955). *Time Bomb*. New York: Rinehart.

Turtledove, H. (FCW). "The Long Drum Roll."

Tute, R. (1940). "Space-Time: A Link Between Religion and Science." *Hibbert Journal* 38:261–270.

Upson, W. H. (MM). "Paul Bunyan versus the Conveyor Belt."

―――――― (FM). "A. Botts and the Moebius Strip."

Uttley, A. (1964). A *Traveler in Time*. New York: Viking.

Vaidman, L. (1991). "A Quantum Time Machine." *Foundations of Physics* 21 (August):947–958.

Vance, J. (1973). "Rumfuddle." In *Three Trips in Time and Space*. Edited by R. Silverberg. New York: Hawthorn.

van Lorne, W. (BSF). "The Upper Level Road."

van Vogt, A. E. (1990). "Secret Unattainable." In *The Fantastic World War II*. Edited by F. McSherry, Jr. New York: Baen.

―――――― (SS). "Far Centaurus."

―――――― (1980). "The Seesaw." In *The Great Science Fiction Stories*. Vol. 3. New York: DAW.

―――――― (1954). *Weapons Shops of Isher*. New York: Ace.

―――――― (OSF). "Recruiting Station."

Varley, J. (1983). *Millennium*. New York: Berkley.

Verrill, A. H. (1927). "The Astounding Discoveries of Doctor Mentiroso." *Amazing Stories*, November.

Vidal, G. (1992). *Live from Golgotha*. New York: Random House.

Visser, M. (1993). "From Wormhole to Time Machine: comments on Hawking's Chronology Protection Conjecture." *Physical Review D* 47 (15 January): 554–565.

―――――― (1990). "Wormholes, Baby Universes, and Causality." *Physical Review D* 41 (15 February):1116–1124.

―――――― (1989a). "Traversable Wormholes from Surgically Modified Schwarzschild Spacetimes." *Nuclear Physics B* 328 (11 December):203–212.

―――――― (1989b). "Traversable Wormholes: Some Simple Examples." *Physical Review D* 39 (15 May):3182–3184.

Voinovich, V. (1987). *Moscow 2042*. New York: Harcourt Brace Jovanovich.

von Hoerner, S. (1963). "The General Limits of Space Travel." In *Interstellar Communication*. Edited by A. G. W. Cameron. New York: W. A. Benjamin.

Vonnegut, K., Jr. (1971). *Slaughterhouse-Five*. New York: Delacourte.

―――――― (1959). *The Sirens of Titan*. New York: Dell.

Wachhorst, W. (1984). "Time Travel Romance on Film." *Extrapolation* 25 (Winter):340–359.

Waelbroeck, H. (1991). "Do Universes with Parallel Cosmic Strings or Two-dimensional Wormholes have Closed Timelike Curves?" *General Relativity and Gravitation* 23 (February):219–233.

Wald, R. M. (1977). *Space, Time, and Gravity*. Chicago: University of Chicago Press.

―――――― (1974). "Gedanken Experiments to Destroy a Black Hole." *Annals of Physics* 83:548–556.

Walstad, A. (1980). "Time's Arrow in an Oscillating Universe." *Foundations of Physics* 10 (October):743–749.

Walton, H. (TSF). "Housing Shortage."

Ward, K. (1967). "The Unity of Space and Time." *Philosophy* 42:68–74.

Watson, I. (TT). "Ghost Lecturer."

_____ (1989). *Chekhov's Journey*. New York: Carroll & Graf.

_____ (1979). "The Very Slow Time Machine." In *The Best Science Fiction of the Year*. Edited by T. Carr. New York: Del Rey/Ballantine.

Watzlawick, P. (1976). *How Real Is Real?* New York: Random House.

Webb, C. W. (1977). "Could Space Be Time-Like?" *Journal of Philosophy* 73 (August):462–474.

_____ (1960). "Could Time Flow? If So, How Fast?" *Journal of Philosophy* 57 (26 May):357–365.

Weeks, J. R. (1985). *The Shape of Space*. New York: Marcel Dekker.

Weinbaum, S. G. (1949). "The Worlds of If" and "The Circle of Zero." In *A Martian Odyssey and Others*. Reading, PA: Fantasy Press.

Weiner, A. (TT). "Klein's Machine."

_____ (1983). "One More Time." In *Chrysalis 10*. Edited by R. Torgeson. Garden City, New York: Doubleday.

Weingard, R. (1979a). "Some Philosophical Aspects of Black Holes." *Synthese* 42 (September):191–219.

_____ (1979b). "General Relativity and the Conceivability of Time Travel." *Philosophy of Science* 46 (June):328–332.

_____ (1979c). "General Relativity and the Length of the Past." *British Journal for the Philosophy of Science* 29 (June):170–172.

_____ (1977). "Space-Time and the Direction of Time." *Nous* 11 (May):119–131.

_____ (1972a). "On Travelling Backward in Time." *Synthese*, 24:117–132.

_____ (1972b). "Relativity and the Reality of Past and Future Events." *British Journal for the Philosophy of Science* 23:119–121.

Weir, S. (1988). "Closed Time and Causal Loops: A Defense Against Mellor." *Analysis* 48 (October):203–209.

Weisinger, M. (1944). "Thompson's Time Traveling Theory." *Amazing Stories*, March.

_____ (1938). "Time On My Hands." *Thrilling Wonder Stories*, June.

Wellman, M.W. (1988). *Twice in Time*. New York: Baen.

_____ (MT). "Who Else Could I Count On?"

_____ (1949). " ... backward, O Time!" *Thrilling Wonder Stories*, October.

_____ (1939). "The Einstein Slugger." *Thrilling Wonder Stories*, December.

Wells, H. G. (1987). *The Time Machine*. In *The Definitive Time Machine*. Edited by H. M. Geduld. Bloomington: Indiana University Press.

_____ (1975). *H. G. Wells: Early Writings in Science and Science Fiction*. Edited by R. M. Philmus and D. Y. Hughes. Berkeley, CA: University of California Press.

_____ (1966). "The Plattner Story," "The New Accelerator," "The Invisible Man," and "The Story of Davidson's Eyes." In *Best Science Fiction Stories of H. G. Wells*. New York: Dover.

_____ (1924). *The Dream*. New York: Macmillan.

_____ (1923). *Men Like Gods*. New York: Macmillan.

_____ (1899). *When the Sleeper Wakes*. New York: Harper and Brothers.

_____ (1895). *The Wonderful Visit*. New York: Macmillan.

Westall, R. (1978). *The Devil On The Road*. New York: Greenwillow.

Weyl, H. (1952). *Space-Time-Matter*. Translated from the 1921 fourth edition in German. New York: Dover.

Wheeler, J. A. (1981). "The Lesson of the Black Hole." *Proceedings of the American Philosophical Society* 125 (February):25–37.

———— (1979). "Frontiers of Time." In *Problems in the Foundations of Physics*. Edited by G. T. diFrancia. Proceedings of the International School of Physics. Course 72. New York: North-Holland.

———— (NT). "Three-Dimensional Geometry as a Carrier of Information about Time."

———— (1962a). *Geometrodynamics*, New York: Academic Press.

———— (1962b). "Curved Empty Space-Time as the Building Material of the Physical World: An Assessment." In *Logic, Methodology and Philosophy of Science*. Stanford, CA: Stanford University Press.

———— (1961). "Geometrodynamics and the Problem of Motion." *Reviews of Modern Physics* 33 (January):63–78.

Wheeler, J. A., and R. P. Feynman (1949). "Classical Electrodynamics in Terms of Direct Interparticle Action." *Reviews of Modern Physics* 21 (July):425–433.

———— (1945). "Interaction with the Absorber as the Mechanism of Radiation." *Reviews of Modern Physics* 17 (April–July): 157–181.

Whiston, G. S. (1974). " 'Hyperspace' (The Cobordism Theory of Space-Time)." *International Journal of Theoretical Physics* 5 (December):285–288.

White, C. B. (1927). "The Lost Continent." *Amazing Stories*, July.

Whitehead, A. N., et al. (BST). Discussions on "The Paradox of the Twins."

———— (BST). "The Inapplicability of the Concept of Instant on the Quantum Level."

Whitrow, G. J. (1988). *Time in History*. New York: Oxford University Press.

———— (1980). *The Natural Philosophy of Time*. Oxford: Oxford University Press.

———— (1978). "On the Impossibility of an Infinite Past." *British Journal for the Philosophy of Science* 29 (March):39–45.

———— (BST). " Becoming' and the Nature of Time."

———— (NYAS). "Reflections on the Natural Philosophy of Time."

Whorf, B. L. (1956). *Language, Thought, and Reality*. Cambridge, MA: The MIT Press.

Wiener, N. (BST). "Spatio-Temporal Continuity, Quantum Theory and Music."

Wigner, E. P. (1970). "On Hidden Variables and Quantum Mechanical Probabilities." *American Journal of Physics* 38 (August):1005–1009.

Wilcox, J. T. (1961). "A Question from Physics for Certain Theists." *Journal of Religion* 41 (October):293–300.

Wild, J. (1954). "The New Empiricism and Human Time." *Review of Metaphysics* 7 (June):537–557.

Wildsmith, B. (1980). *Professor Noah's Spaceship*. New York: Oxford University Press.

Wilhelm, K. (1975). "The Time Piece." In *The Infinity Box*. New York: Harper & Row.

Wilkerson, T. E. (1973). "Time and Time Again." *Philosophy* 48:173–177.

Williams, D. C. (1951a). "The Myth of Passage." *Journal of Philosophy* 48 (July):457–472.

———— (1951b). "The Sea Fight Tomorrow." In *Structure, Method and Meaning*. New York: The Liberal Arts Press.

Williams, J. (TC). "Terror Out of Time."

Williams, J., and R. Abrashkin (1963). *Danny Dunn, Time Traveler*. New York: Whittlesey House.

Williams, R. M. (TSF). "Flight of the Dawn Star."

Williamson, J. (1985). "*The Legion of Time*." New York: Bluejay-Books.

———— (1979). "Hindsight." In *The Great Science Fiction Stories*. Vol. 2. New York: DAW.

———— (1975). "The Meteor Girl" and "Through the Purple Cloud." In *The Early Williamson*. Garden City, NY: Doubleday.

_____ (BGA1). "The Moon Era."

_____ (1942). "Minus Sign." *Astounding Science Fiction*, November.

_____ (1933). "In the Scarlet Star." *Amazing Stories*, March.

Willis, C. (1992). *Doomsday Book*. New York: Bantam.

_____ (1985). "Fire Watch." In *Fire Watch*. New York: Bluejay.

Wilson, R. C. (1991). *A Bridge of Years*. New York: Doubleday.

Wilson, R. H. (SFT). "Out Around Rigel."

_____ (1931). "A Flight Into Time." *Wonder Stories*, February.

Wimmel, H. K. (1972). "Tachyons and Cerenkov Radiation." *Nature Physical Science* 236 (3 April):79–80.

Windred, G. (1933–34). "The History of Mathematical Time. II." *Isis* 20:192–219.

_____ (1933). "The History of Mathematical Time. I." *Isis* 19:121–153.

Winterbotham, R. R. (1936). "The Fourth Dynasty." *Astounding Stories*, December.

Wolf, F. A. (1990). *Parallel Universes*. New York: Simon and Schuster.

Wolfe, G. (1974). "The Rubber Bend." In *Universe 5*. Edited by T. Carr. New York: Random House.

Wolfe, J. (1985). "The Impossibility of an Infinite Past: A Reply to Craig." *International Journal for Philosophy of Religion* 18, 91.

_____ (1971). "Infinite Regress and the Cosmological Argument." *International Journal for Philosophy of Religion* 2, 246–249.

Woodbridge, III, R. G. (1969). "Acoustic Recordings from Antiquity." *Proceedings of the IEEE* 57 (August):1465–1466.

Woodhouse, M. B. (1976). "The Reversibility of Absolute Time." *Philosophical Studies* 29 (June):465–468.

Woolfe, V. (1976). "A Sketch of the Past." In *Moments of Being*. Edited by J. Schulkind. Sussex: The University Press.

Worth, P. (1950). "Typewriter From the Future." *Amazing Stories*, February.

_____ (1949a). "Window To The Future." *Amazing Stories*, May.

_____ (1949b). "I Died Tomorrow." *Fantastic Adventures*, May.

Wright, P. B. (1979). "Immediate Interstellar Communications." *Speculations in Science and Technology* 2:211–213.

Wright, S. F. (1930). *The World Below*. New York: Longmans, Green and Co.

Wyndham, J. (T3). "Consider Her Ways."

_____ (TC). "Operation Peep."

_____ (1961). "Random Quest," "Odd," and "Stitch in Time." In *The Infinite Moment*. New York: Ballantine.

_____ (1956). "The Chronoclasm" and "Opposite Number" In *The Seeds of Time*. London: Michael Joseph.

_____ (1939). "Judson's Annihilator." *Amazing Stories*, October.

_____ (1933). "Wanderers of Time." *Wonder Stories*, March.

Xin, Y. (1992). "Does Einstein's G. R. Theory Predict Gravitational Radiation of PSR 1913+16?" *Astrophysics and Space Science* 194 (August):159–163.

Yarov, R. (1968). "The Founding of Civilization." In *Russian Science Fiction*. Edited by R. Magidoff. New York: New York University Press.

Yndurain, F. J. (1991). "Disappearance of Matter Due to Causality and Probability Violations in Theories with Extra Timelike Dimensions." *Physics Letters B* 256 (28 February):15–16.

York, J. W. (1972). "Role of Conformal Three—Geometry in the Dynamics of Gravitation."

Physical Review Letters 28 (17 April):1082–1085.

Young, R. F. (SFD). "When Time Was New."

Yurtsever, U. (1990). "Test Fields on Compact Space-Times." *Journal of Mathematical Physics* 31 (December):3064–3078.

Zacks, R. (1955). "Have Your Past Read, Mister?" *Startling Stories*, Winter.

Zahn, T. (1988). "Time Bomb." In *New Destinies* (Summer). Edited by J. Baen. New York: Baen Books.

Zebrowski, G. (BT). "The Cliometricon."

Zeh, H. D. (1989). *The Physical Basis of the Direction of Time.* Berlin: Springer-Verlag.

Zelazny, R. (TIT). "Divine Madness."

Zemach, E. M. (1979). "Time and Self." *Analysis* 39 (June):143–147.

Zetterberg, J. P. (1979). "Letting the Past Be Brought About." *Southern Journal of Philosophy* 17:413–421.

Zimmerman, E. J. (1962). "The Macroscopic Nature of Space–Time." *American Journal of Physics* 30 (January):97–105.

Zollner, J. C. F. (1878). "On Space of Four Dimensions." *Quarterly Journal of Science*, n.s. 8 (April):227–237.

Zwart, P. J. (1972). "The Flow of Time." *Synthese* 24 (1972):133–158.

Index

The fictional titles that appear in this index are, of course, only a small fraction of the entries in the Bibliography. The fictional works that are listed here are ones that I judged to be "known" to many people, or are ones that I want to particularly direct to your attention. The selection is naturally subjective and perhaps I've overlooked one or more works you think should be in the Index. For that I apologize, and can only hope that you will enjoy reading the book while you search for "your" title!